The End of French Predominance in Europe

The End of French Predominance in Europe

The Financial Crisis of 1924 and the Adoption of the Dawes Plan

by
Stephen A. Schuker

The University of
North Carolina Press
Chapel Hill

Manufactured in the United States of America
ISBN 0-8078-1253-6
Library of Congress Catalog Card Number 75-38799
First printing, November 1976
Second printing, March 1978

Library of Congress Cataloging in Publication Data

Schuker, Stephen A 1939–
The end of French predominance in Europe.

Bibliography: p.
Includes index.
1. Finance—France—History. 2. Money—France—History. 3. European War, 1914–1918—Reparations. I. Title.
HG186.F8S34 332'.0944 75-38799
ISBN 0-8078-1253-6

To my parents,
MILLICENT *and* LOUIS A. SCHUKER

Contents

Tables

Preface

A generation has passed since diplomatic historians pursued their craft simply by reporting and interpreting the cable traffic between foreign offices and embassies abroad. Nearly all recent diplomatic studies give appropriate emphasis also to the domestic political contingencies that influence and often decisively shape foreign policy. Recent archival developments in the countries of the North Atlantic community, by making available the papers of numerous business and banking leaders, permit the diplomatic historian to extend his range once more. The study presented here aims to blend diplomatic, economic, and business history. It draws on the records of American bankers and to a lesser extent on those of European bankers and businessmen. These records, used in conjunction with material from government archives, facilitate an exploration of a crucial turning point after the First World War—a point when, owing to a loss of financial independence, France found itself unable to maintain the political structure established in Europe by the Treaty of Versailles.

The present work forms part of a larger investigation dealing with European economic and financial reconstruction in the half-decade following the First World War. The creation of business and banking archives and the opening of government records for this period have progressed rapidly in the past few years. Limitations of space and focus allow me to display here only in part the extraordinary richness and diversity of sources now becoming available. Where I have been obliged to treat important issues summarily, I shall give them greater attention in a subsequent broader study now under way.

I wish to acknowledge my intellectual indebtedness to four remarkable scholars and teachers. Edward W. Fox, through the force of his magnetic personality, first awakened my interest in twentieth-century history more than fifteen years ago. William L. Langer trained me in diplomatic history and imbued me with standards of scholarship for which I will always be grateful. Frank Freidel taught me what I know about American history and provided a model of personal integrity and kindness that is so well known in the profession as to require no elaboration here. With unerring good judgment and unflagging encouragement, H. Stuart Hughes directed the doctoral dissertation out of which this book emerged. He and Judith M. Hughes offered close intellectual companionship for more than a decade. Mrs. Hughes, Charles S. Maier, and Samuel R. Williamson gave careful scrutiny to an original draft of the manuscript several years ago. Numerous other scholars have directed me to sources, offered comment on my views, or helped me overcome obstacles to research. I wish to express particular appreciation to Jacques Bariéty, Robert R. Bowie, Charles W. Brooks, Alfred D. Chandler, Jr., Marshall J. Cohen, Paul R. Duggan, J.-B. Duroselle, Gerald D. Feldman, Franklin L. Ford, François Goguel, James Joll, David S. Landes, Sally Marks, Ernest R. May, Arno J. Mayer, Charles Medalen, Pierre Miquel, Vincent Pitts, Pierre Renouvin, Susan C. Schneider, Ellen W. Schrecker, Theodore Schuker, A. J. P. Taylor, Thomas D. Walker, Dan S. White, and Leah Zell.

I am equally indebted to those who opened their homes and papers to me or facilitated my work in public archives. Jacques Millerand permitted me to use the Alexandre Millerand Papers still in his possession and shared his vivid reminiscences of the Third Republic. Claude François-Marsal gave me the run of his father's papers and generously allowed me to pass on my findings to other scholars. Mme. Bécourt-Foch authorized the use of Marshal Ferdinand Foch's diary notebooks at the Bibliothèque Nationale. Michel Soulié and Marcel Ruby arranged for me to consult the Edouard Herriot Papers when these still remained in private hands. Thomas D. Walker shared with me his copy of Emile Coste's unpublished memoirs as well as other material in his possession. Jacques Pinot opened the surviving Robert Pinot Papers for my perusal and recalled his own experiences as an aide to his father at the Comité des Forges. J. P. Ulrich of the Chambre Syndicale de la Sidérurgie Française and Arnaud de Villepin of the Compagnie de Saint-Gobain-Pont-à-Mousson broke tradition to facilitate my use of the Pont-à-Mousson archives at La Châtre. André François-Poncet, Minister Charles Reibel, President of the Council Paul Reynaud, Marcel Ribière (Raymond Poincaré's *chef de cabinet*), and Maurice Silhol (Rhineland High Commissioner Paul Tirard's *chef de cabinet*) sat patiently for interviews and recalled details of French political life two generations ago that were not available elsewhere. Numerous French government officials offered their cooperation in guiding me around the pitfalls of archival research in their country; my appreciation extends particularly to Minister Plenipotentiary Jean Laloy, Chief Archivist Maurice Degros, and Mme. Françoise Péquin of the Ministry of Foreign Affairs; to Mlle. Alice Guillemain of the Finance Ministry; to Bernard Mahieu of the Archives Nationales; and to Marcel Thomas of the Bibliothèque Nationale.

At the Bundesarchiv in Koblenz, West Germany, Oberarchivsrat Alfred Wagner and other officers of that splendid institution gave me every possible assistance during three extended visits. Archival director Bodo Herzog of the Gutehoffnungshütte in Oberhausen not only furthered my research at his own firm but offered invaluable guidance concerning other German industrial archives. Eric M. Warburg and Eduard Rosenbaum extended permission to use the Max M. Warburg Papers.

Viscount Scarsdale and Sir Philip Magnus kindly placed at my disposal the Curzon Papers at the India Office Library. P. A. S. Taylor, secretary of the Bank of England, and Denis H. N. Brookes, principal of the Archive Section, made available selections from Lord Norman's papers. Captain Stephen W. Roskill and the second Lord Hankey graciously gave permission to use the first Lord Hankey's papers. I thank the controller of Her Majesty's Stationery Office for permission to cite unpublished Crown copyright material in the Public Record Office.

I cannot hope to acknowledge fully my gratitude to the many people who have lightened the burden of my research in the United States. Laurence J. Kipp, librarian, and Robert W. Lovett, curator of manuscripts, at the Baker Library of the Harvard School of Business Administration, opened the Thomas W. Lamont Papers to me and offered unstinting help over a period of years. Agnes F. Peterson of the Hoover Institution made my work there a pleasure and gave me the benefit of her extraordinary expertise. Stephen V. O. Clarke of the Federal Reserve Bank of New York aided my research on the Benjamin Strong Papers; and Assistant Director Robert Wood went out of his way to assist me at the Herbert Hoover Presidential Library. Mr. and Mrs. S. Everett Case granted access to the Owen D. Young Papers and extended their gracious personal hospitality, and Amory Houghton, Sr., showed similar kind indulgence in permitting me to use the Alanson B. Houghton Papers at his home. Finally, I wish to record my gratitude to the members of the staff at Widener Library who have put up cheerfully with my importunities for many years, and especially to Chief Documents Librarian Michael G. Cotter, and to F. Nathaniel Bunker, Maria Grossmann, Fred Heryer, and David Silas of the Acquisitions Department, who have given unfailing support to my work in creating a collection of diplomatic archive microfilms at Widener.

While preparing this study, I received financial assistance from the National Endowment for the Humanities, and from the Center for European Studies and the Canaday Fund for Faculty Research Support at Harvard University. Alicia Campi and Nancy Cramer expertly typed the manuscript, and my student M. Devereux Chatillon volunteered her help with the bibliography.

I have reserved my compelling personal debts for last. I cannot sufficiently express my appreciation to three friends—Max Bluestone, J. Frederick Martin, and Nancy Lipton Rosenblum—who each gave a line-by-line review to earlier drafts of this study. Maria M. Tatar provided sustained and truly invaluable encouragement; she also took time out from her own scholarly work to give patient and expert criticism to the entire manuscript. And to Millicent and Louis A. Schuker, who offered practical assistance and support well beyond the call of parental duty, I owe special thanks.

Abbreviations

- BA — Bundesarchiv, Koblenz
- CAB — British Cabinet Office Records
- DWM — Dwight W. Morrow Papers
- F^{12} — Archives of the French Ministry of Commerce and Industry
- F^{30} — Archives of the French Finance Ministry
- F.O. — British Foreign Office Records
- G.F.M. — German Foreign Ministry Archives (U.S. National Archives Microfilms T–120)
- GHH — Historical Archive of the Gutehoffnungshütte, Oberhausen
- *J.O. Annexe* — *Journal Officiel, Annexe, Documents administratifs*
- *J.O.C. Déb.* — *Journal Officiel, Chambre des Députés, Débats parlementaires*
- *J.O.C. Doc.* — *Journal Officiel, Chambre des Députés, Documents parlementaires*
- *J.O.S. Déb.* — *Journal Officiel, Sénat, Débats parlementaires*
- *J.O.S. Doc.* — *Journal Officiel, Sénat, Documents parlementaires*
- PAM — Archives of Pont-à-Mousson (Compagnie de Saint-Gobain-Pont-à-Mousson), La Châtre
- P.R.O. — Public Record Office, London
- R 13 I — Records of the Association of German Iron and Steel Industrialists (Wirtschaftsgruppe Eisenschaffende Industrie, Verein Deutscher Eisen- und Stahl-industrieller)
- R 43 I — Records of the German Reich Chancellery (Alte Reichskanzlei)
- TWL — Thomas W. Lamont Papers
- U.S. — U.S. National Archives, Record Group 59, General Records of the Department of State, 1910–29

The End of French Predominance in Europe

Chapter 1

Introduction

The Legacy of the First World War

This study traces the decline of France as a world power in the years following the First World War. It analyzes the economic issues that necessarily underlie successful reconstruction of national strength. It focuses particularly on the financial crisis of 1924, which marked a major turning point in the history of Europe between the two world wars. This crisis led France—despite the transiently favorable outcome of its coercive occupation of the Ruhr—to give up any attempt at meaningful enforcement of the reparations clauses in the Treaty of Versailles. Henceforth, relative financial and economic weakness rendered the pursuit of a genuinely independent foreign policy by France impossible. In a larger sense, the juncture of financial and diplomatic events in the critical year of 1924 reflected the rapidity with which the real balance of power shifted in response to the industrial superiority and demographic preponderance retained by Germany notwithstanding its defeat on the battlefield in 1918.

Under any circumstances, France's geopolitical position would have been unenviable from the early years of the twentieth century onward. Germany, its neighbor and rival, developed so rapidly in the generation following unification in 1870–71 as virtually to foreordain eventual economic domination of the European subcontinent by the Reich. Moreover, in the decade preceding the First World War, a growing qualitative difference between the nationalist and imperialist foreign policies of Germany and those of the other major European powers emerged as the central issue in international relations. The absence of priorities, the want of moderation, and the unpredictability that characterized German foreign policy in those years can be traced in large measure to conflicts of internal politics. The Reich displaced domestic tensions outward in an effort to become a "world power" enjoying both primacy on the European continent and hegemony overseas. To achieve these ends it was willing to risk armed conflict in case diplomatic means proved unsuccessful. Through a mixture of intent and miscalculation, it bore primary responsibility for the outbreak of the world war. Through the inflexibility and seemingly limitless scope of its annexationist war aims it doomed the chance of any compromise peace. Significantly, Germany emerged from World War I despite military defeat less damaged in terms of human and economic resources than the other major European combatants and—the change in its form of government notwithstanding—undeterred from ultimate fulfillment of many of its prewar ambitions.[1]

There existed no small prospect that in the long run Germany might find a means to achieve a degree of continuity in its fundamental policy, since the war represented an economic and psychological crisis as great for the victors as for the vanquished. The war losses were everywhere so extensive as to rend the fabric of society, but because of the age composition of their population, the French suffered proportionally the greatest demographic holocaust. Moreover, the ten northern and eastern departments of France, along with parts of Belgium, had served as the main battleground of the war. Much of the industrial basis for French economic life disappeared as a result of devastation by the retreating Germans, purposefully calculated not merely to deny these resources to the Allied armies but also to accord a postwar advantage to German industry. And the expenses of four years of war had seriously eroded the French financial infrastructure.

In this situation, France required the support not only of Great Britain, but also of the United States, if it were to wring from military victory those arrangements in Europe capable of containing an inherently expansionist Germany. As is well known, the New World, which had come with evanescent enthusiasm to the rescue of the Old, was still too closely wedded to its isolationist heritage to assume any permanent responsibilities for preservation of the European security structure. And Great Britain, ostensibly France's principal ally, gradually reverted to a traditional policy of holding the ring evenhandedly between France and Germany, minimizing commitments on the Continent in order to channel its energies toward the Empire and extra-European affairs generally. The Anglo-American pact of guarantee that France had reluctantly accepted at Versailles in place of a permanent occupation of the Rhineland failed of ratification. Therefore, French security was unprovided for, even while France, alone among the major victors, retained a strong

1. The literature on all these subjects is enormous. See, e.g., Helmut Böhme, *Deutschlands Weg zur Grossmacht: Studien zum Verhältnis von Wirtschaft und Staat während der Reichsgründungszeit, 1848–1881* (Cologne, 1966); Gustav Stolper, *German Economy, 1870–1940* (New York, 1940); Luigi Albertini, *The Origins of the War of 1914*, 3 vols. (London, New York, and Toronto, 1952–57); Eckart Kehr, *Schlachtflottenbau und Parteipolitik, 1894–1901* (Berlin, 1930) and "Klassenkämpfe und Rüstungspolitik im kaiserlichen Deutschland," *Die Gesellschaft* 1 (1932): 391–414; Dirk Stegmann, *Die Erben Bismarcks: Parteien und Verbände in der Spätphase des Wilhelminischen Deutschlands. Sammlungspolitik, 1897–1918* (Cologne and Berlin, 1970); Jonathan Steinberg, *Yesterday's Deterrent: Tirpitz and the Birth of the German Battle Fleet* (New York, 1965); Gerhard Ritter, *Staatskunst und Kriegshandwerk: Das Problem des "Militarismus" in Deutschland*, vols. 2–4 (Munich, 1960–68); Hans W. Gatzke, *Germany's Drive to the West: A Study of Western War Aims during the First World War* (Baltimore, 1950); Fritz Fischer, *Griff nach der Weltmacht: Die Kriegszielpolitik des kaiserlichen Deutschland, 1914/18*, 3d ed. rev. (Düsseldorf, 1964); Fritz Fischer, *Krieg der Illusionen: Die deutsche Politik von 1911 bis 1914* (Düsseldorf, 1969); and the documentary collection, Jacques Grunewald and André Scherer, eds., *L'Allemagne et les problèmes de la paix pendant la première guerre mondiale*, 2 vols. (Paris, 1962).

sense of the wrongs inflicted by Germany in the past and the danger it represented for the future.[2]

The mood of France in the years after Versailles, often misinterpreted as bellicose in a world yearning for restoration of an effective peace, actually was nervous and defensive. No amount of self-reassuring rhetoric about the totality of victory could relieve the anxiety felt by the overwhelming majority of Frenchmen at the thought that the struggle might have to be resumed, whatever the reason, once the German colossus had reconstituted its military power. France's insecurity about the long-term prospects informed the whole direction of its postwar policy. This policy evidenced a certain measure of inconsistency. On the one hand, France tried to coerce Germany into compliance with the Treaty of Versailles, while attempting to conjure up some semblance of a security framework, however insubstantial in nature, through military arrangements with the "successor states" of eastern Europe. On the other hand, France attached the highest priority to maintaining the Entente with Great Britain, which French statesmen irrespective of party recognized as the sheet anchor of their military safety. Britain, however, became increasingly doubtful about the viability of the territorial settlement in eastern Europe and ultimately indifferent to it—certainly unwilling to risk British lives for its integral defense.[3]

Largely as a result of this inconclusive outcome of the peace settlement respecting military security, postwar economic and financial arrangements assumed added importance. The war-weary French population, reluctant to make further sacrifices in the financial sphere—even in the interests of indispensable reconstruction—and divided within itself concerning distribution of the fiscal burden, united in the conviction that Germany should be forced to pay the full costs of recovery. Frenchmen of all persuasions subscribed to the spirit given expression by the Allied and Associated powers at Versailles: "Somebody must suffer for the consequences of the war. Is it to be Germany or only the people she has wronged?"[4]

Although the peace conference adopted no formal war guilt clause, the reparations sections of the Versailles treaty did base Germany's obli-

2. On the basic dilemma of the 1919 settlement, see Bertrand de Jouvenel, *D'une guerre à l'autre*, 2 vols. (Paris, 1940); Alfred Fabre-Luce, *La Victoire* (Paris, 1924); William M. Jordan, *Great Britain, France, and the German Problem, 1918–1939* (London, 1943); Arnold Wolfers, *Britain and France between Two Wars: Conflicting Strategies of Peace since Versailles* (New York, 1940); Leopold Schwarzschild, *World in Trance: From Versailles to Pearl Harbor* (New York, 1942); Paul Birdsall, *Versailles Twenty Years After* (New York, 1941); Arno J. Mayer, *Politics and Diplomacy of Peacemaking: Containment and Counterrevolution at Versailles, 1918–1919* (New York, 1967); and A. J. P. Taylor, *The Origins of the Second World War* (London, 1961).

3. Jon Paul Selsam, *The Attempts to Form an Anglo-French Alliance, 1919–1924* (Philadelphia, 1936); Piotr S. Wandycz, *France and Her Eastern Allies, 1919–1925* (Minneapolis, 1962).

4. Reply of the Allied and Associated powers to the German delegation, 16 June 1919, cited in *A History of the Peace Conference of Paris*, ed. H. W. V. Temperley, 6 vols. (London, 1920), 2:262.

gation to repair the damage done by its armies and to pay the survivors' pensions squarely on its responsibility for and conduct of the war.[5] The vast majority of Germans, however, accepted neither the historical analysis nor the moral assumptions on which the whole idea of reparations was grounded. This rejection of responsibility, together with the magnitude of the economic stakes involved, made of reparations the pivotal issue in European diplomacy during the years after the war. France's inability to marshal its own economic and financial resources sufficiently to take an independent stand and in the last resort to compel payment led inexorably to its further relative decline, for the transfer of reparations meant the transfer of real wealth. In a period of world trade disruption, the country with cheap coal, coke, and capital could get a head start on economic revival, compete better in export markets, and more successfully acquire the political influence that accompanies economic ties. Such initial advantages were likely to prove enduring once stability returned.

Moreover, reparations took on a symbolic significance that magnified the importance of the actual economic and financial issues at stake. It became the vehicle for prolonging the Franco-German conflict. For the German government, and even at times for the French, it developed into nothing less than a continuation of the war by economic means. Thus, even when the nominal cause of dispute seemed petty enough—delivery of too few telephone poles or shipment of coal without quality control—the controversy grew into a test of wills. Just as virtually all Germans took exception to the moral judgment made in the Allied nations regarding war guilt, so they rejected the notion that the Treaty of Versailles was immutable. Once they succeeded in nullifying its reparations provisions, they could proceed to demonstrate that other elements of the Versailles edifice were, as a cabaret lyric of the period expressed it, "only paper." In this context it becomes evident why France's decline as a great power cannot be divorced from the outcome of the reparations controversy, and why the disappointing settlement finally reached with the adoption of the Dawes Plan in 1924 not only accurately reflected France's weakness at the time but also prepared the way for further erosion of the nation's diplomatic position on issues ranging from military security to Franco-German economic relations.

In retrospect it is apparent that the statesmen at the Paris Peace Conference made two serious errors concerning reparations—one bearing on its moral justification, the other of a broadly political character—which undermined subsequent efforts to make Germany pay.[6] The

5. Camille Bloch and Pierre Renouvin, "La Genèse et la signification de l'article 231 du traité de Versailles," *Revue d'histoire de la guerre mondiale* (January 1932): 1–24; Fritz Dickmann, *Die Kriegsschuldfrage auf der Friedenskonferenz von Paris, 1919* (Munich, 1964).

6. On reparations at the peace conference, see Philip Mason Burnett, *Reparation at the Paris Peace Conference from the Standpoint of the American Delegation*, 2 vols. (New York, 1940); Bernard M. Baruch, *The Making of the Reparation and Economic Sections of the Treaty* (New

moral issue was clouded from the start because the negotiators at Paris enlarged the German reparations liability to include pensions for disabled veterans as well as repair of the devastated areas. Since none of their territory had suffered physical destruction, Great Britain and the Dominions insisted on including pensions in order to justify the claim for a larger share of the indemnity. In theory this increased the total bill. In practice, because German payments were limited by economic capacity, adding pensions resulted in a mere redistribution of potential reparations receipts among the Allies.

Paradoxically, widening the basis on which the German liability was determined served to undermine the legitimacy of the assessment in the eyes of influential segments of educated British opinion. The later stages of the war had been fought under the banner of Wilsonian ideology. The treaty therefore invited moral judgment, not simply as a reasonable compromise consecrating a preponderance of power among the victors but rather as a "just peace" following a "just war." Those who experienced varying degrees of disillusionment because the treaty did not fully live up to its ideal aspirations were more numerous and better organized for molding public opinion in England than in other Allied countries.[7] No doubt British Treasury officials entrusted with day-to-day responsibility for reparations policy sought to formulate their recommendations on the basis of rational calculation of maximum national advantage. Still, over a period of time they could hardly remain immune to the influence of political currents in their society questioning how equitable it really was to fasten this large and undifferentiated burden of tribute on the German people. Not surprisingly British political leaders proved even

---

York and London, 1920); Thomas W. Lamont, "Reparations," in *What Really Happened at Paris: The Story of the Peace Conference by the American Delegates, 1918–1919*, ed. Edward M. House and Charles Seymour (New York, 1921); Louis-Lucien Klotz, *De la guerre à la paix* (Paris, 1924); André Tardieu, *La Paix* (Paris, 1921); David Lloyd George, *The Truth about Reparations and War Debts* (London, 1932), and *The Truth about the Peace Treaties*, 2 vols. (London, 1938); Paul Mantoux, ed., *Les Délibérations du conseil des quatre, 24 mars–28 juin 1919*, 2 vols. (Paris, 1955); Erich Wüest, *Der Vertrag von Versailles in Licht und Schatten der Kritik: Die Kontroverse um seine wirtschaftlichen Auswirkungen* (Zurich, 1962); and Peter Krüger, *Deutschland und die Reparationen, 1918/19: Die Genesis des Reparationsproblems in Deutschland zwischen Waffenstillstand und Versailler Friedensschluss* (Stuttgart, 1973).

The list of books on various aspects of the reparations problem is enormous. The most comprehensive study to date is Etienne Weill-Raynal's *Les Réparations allemandes et la France*, 3 vols. (Paris, 1947). John Maynard Keynes's tendentious but influential tracts, *The Economic Consequences of the Peace* (London, 1919) and *A Revision of the Treaty* (London, 1922), were ably refuted by Etienne Mantoux, *The Carthaginian Peace or the Economic Consequences of Mr. Keynes* (London, New York, and Toronto, 1946). Also useful are Carl Bergmann, *The History of Reparations* (Boston and New York, 1927); Richard Castillon, *Les Réparations allemandes: Deux expériences, 1919–1932, 1945–1952* (Paris, 1953); Gaston Calmette, *Recueil de documents sur l'histoire des réparations, 1919–5 mai 1921* (Paris, 1924); and Gaston A. Furst, *De Versailles aux experts* (Paris, 1927).

7. Arno J. Mayer, *Political Origins of the New Diplomacy, 1917–1918* (New Haven, 1959); T. E. Jessop, *The Treaty of Versailles: Was It Just?* (London and New York, 1942); R. B. McCallum, *Public Opinion and the Last Peace* (London and New York, 1944).

more sensitive to growing public doubts about the rights and wrongs of the matter; many members of the 1924 Labour government, as we shall see later in this narrative, came to view reparations as a hangover of wartime passions perpetuated by precisely those forces in British national life that they most abhorred.

Failure to determine the exact size of the German debt constituted the second major miscalculation made at the peace conference. Popular expectations of reparations payments in 1919 were so great in the Allied countries that the statesmen at Paris decided to postpone setting a total sum until calmer conditions permitted an objective assessment of the damages sustained. This seemed a sensible decision at the time. Yet its result was to contribute to postwar uncertainty and to foster suspicion among the Germans that the Allies wished to bleed them white for an indefinite period, as much to keep their nation prostrate as to maximize reparations revenue.

Moreover, the divergence in national interest between France and Great Britain, which of necessity had been muted while the exigencies of war remained paramount, reemerged to cause increasing and mutually reinforcing strains in the Entente over the Near East, eastern Europe, and most of all over policy toward Germany. Once France began heavy expenditures for reconstruction of the ten devastated departments to the north and east, the tangible signs of that effort sustained popular clamor for German payments to underwrite the enterprise. In Great Britain, on the contrary, the view gradually took hold that payments on the scale previously envisaged were not economically feasible. The British government and financial leaders in the City tended to overestimate the importance of German export competition resulting from reparations requirements as a factor in British industrial stagnation. High unemployment plagued Great Britain throughout the 1920s. It was actually caused by deflationary fiscal policy and by fundamental changes in the pattern of world trade that were reducing demand for Britain's major export products: ships, coal, and textiles.[8] These structural problems, however, went largely unrecognized. Moreover, British policy on reparations—as on other issues in the first postwar years—was frequently less dependent on sober assessment of the political and economic data by permanent officials in the ministries concerned than on the whims of Prime Minister David Lloyd George and his often superficially informed staff, lodged in the "Garden Suburb." The Foreign Office, which wished to maintain the Entente with France in Europe for the sake of British

8. Alfred E. Kahn, *Great Britain and the World Economy* (New York, 1946); A. J. Youngson, *The British Economy, 1920–1957* (Cambridge, Mass., 1957); Sidney Pollard, *The Development of the British Economy, 1914–1967*, 2d ed. rev. (Cambridge, Mass., 1969); Derek H. Aldcroft, *The Inter-War Economy: Britain, 1919–1939* (New York, 1970); G. A. Phillips and R. T. Maddock, *The Growth of the British Economy, 1918–1968* (London, 1972); Arthur Cecil Pigou, *Aspects of British Economic History, 1918–1925* (London, 1947); Arthur Lyon Bowley, *Some Economic Consequences of the Great War* (London, 1930).

interests in the Near East and overseas, found itself largely excluded by the prime minister from a determining role in the formation of German policy.[9]

German reparations represented only one part of the problem of international indebtedness resulting from the war. The United States had lent over $10.3 billion to the Allies. Some of these credits had been extended to finance the common struggle; others had been granted after the Armistice for relief and rehabilitation. The west European nations were both debtors and creditors. England, for example, had borrowed $6.5 billion but lent $10.4 billion, while France had borrowed $7.0 billion (from Great Britain and the United States) and lent $3.5 billion. However, the collectible value of these debts varied considerably. Roughly three-quarters of the American credits had been extended to the relatively solvent governments of Great Britain and France in return for precise pledges of repayment. Almost half of the English loans and a third of the French, on the contrary, had been made to the defunct Czarist regime in Russia and were now entirely worthless; many of the other intra-European credits had been given under ambiguous circumstances to nations in varying degrees of insolvency. It was virtually impossible to find a single formula according to which indebtedness of such diverse character could be equitably adjusted. Nevertheless, while war debts originated separately and rested on a moral basis different from reparations, as a practical matter it appeared difficult to the European nations to settle one issue without the other. The pressure from the United States for debt refunding, therefore, would largely determine the limits within which the European nations could afford to make concessions on German reparations while also settling debts among themselves.[10]

The United States could not escape exercising in some form the influence thrust upon it by its economic power. Europe looked to America not only for leadership on the debt issue, but also for the capital required

9. This emerges most clearly from Records of the Cabinet, CAB 23/14–39, Minutes of the War Cabinet, Conclusions of Cabinet Meetings, and Conferences of Ministers, 1918–22, Public Record Office, London (hereafter cited as P.R.O., CAB 23). On policy under Lloyd George, see also Lord Beaverbrook, *The Decline and Fall of Lloyd George* (London, 1963); Frank Owen, *Tempestuous Journey: Lloyd George, His Life and Times* (London, 1954); A. J. P. Taylor, ed., *Lloyd George: Twelve Essays* (London, 1971); Thomas Jones, *Whitehall Diary*, vol. 1, *1916–1925*, ed. Keith Middlemas (London, New York, and Toronto, 1969); Maurice Cowling, *The Impact of Labour, 1920–1924* (Cambridge, 1971); and the standard diplomatic account, F. S. Northedge, *The Troubled Giant: Britain among the Great Powers, 1916–1939* (London and New York, 1966).

10. Harvey E. Fisk, *The Inter-Ally Debts: An Analysis of War and Postwar Public Finance, 1914–1923* (New York and Paris, 1924); Harold G. Moulton and Leo Pasvolsky, *War Debts and World Prosperity* (New York, 1932). For the French debts, see Lucien Petit, *Histoire des finances extérieures de la France pendant la guerre, 1914–1919* (Paris, 1929), and *Histoire des finances extérieures de la France: Le Règlement des dettes interalliées, 1919–1929* (Paris, 1932), semiofficial studies based on discreet use of Finance Ministry files; and Germain Calmette, *Un des problèmes de la paix: Les Dettes interalliées* (Paris, 1926).

for economic reconstruction. In turn, the United States possessed a material interest in promoting Europe's return to financial stability. The need to expand export markets, for example, especially for products from the depressed agricultural sector of the economy, served as an important spur to American concern. It is true that the American people as a whole, in reaction against Wilsonian idealism, became as self-preoccupied as traditionally depicted. Nevertheless, a conscientious group of men in the State and Treasury departments sought to promote European economic recovery to the maximum degree that Congress and public opinion would permit.[11]

In certain areas the United States government was constrained from acting openly, and by default it fell to private bankers on Wall Street to exert financial leadership. In a time of great uncertainty in monetary relations, when neither government agencies nor supranational organizations had evolved to match the expanded need for cooperation across national boundaries, American private bankers wielded great power, not only in financial matters, but implicitly in the political sphere as well. In retrospect, the Wall Street bankers, chief among them J. P. Morgan & Co., stand out as a remarkably able and farsighted group. Nonetheless, as will become evident, the bankers found themselves faced with potential conflicts between their private and quasi-public responsibilities—conflicts which, in the absence of public accountability, they could only imperfectly resolve.

On the specific issue of war debts, the executive branch of the American government took a far more enlightened view than that for which it is usually given credit. However, Congress refused to allow the Treasury Department to handle the situation on its own, and early in 1922 created a World War Foreign Debt Commission including members of the legislative branch to keep watch over those representing the executive. Public opinion prevented either the administration or the debt commission from openly acknowledging any relation between war debts and reparations. Still, these authorities did show themselves willing to make relatively generous arrangements with the individual European debtor nations, based in each case on a fair appraisal of capacity to pay.[12]

11. On American policy and the national mood, see Selig Adler, *The Uncertain Giant, 1921–1941: American Foreign Policy between the Wars* (New York, 1965), and *The Isolationist Impulse: Its Twentieth Century Reaction* (New York, 1957); Jean Baptiste Duroselle, *From Wilson to Roosevelt: Foreign Policy of the United States, 1913–1945* (Cambridge, Mass., 1963); Merlo J. Pusey, *Charles Evans Hughes*, vol. 2 (New York, 1951); Benjamin H. Williams, *Economic Foreign Policy of the United States* (New York, 1929); James H. Shideler, *Farm Crisis, 1919–1923* (Berkeley, 1957); Herbert Feis, *The Diplomacy of the Dollar: First Era, 1919–1932* (Baltimore, 1950); Carl P. Parrini, *Heir to Empire: United States Economic Diplomacy, 1916–1923* (Pittsburgh, 1969); and Joan Hoff Wilson, *American Business and Foreign Policy, 1920–1933* (Lexington, Ky., 1971).

12. For the debate over war debts within the administration, see the State Department files on "financial affairs, general" and on the World War Foreign Debt Commission in Record Group 59, General Records of the Department of State, 1910–29, U.S. National

Great Britain nevertheless stoutly resisted negotiations for a reasonable scaling down of its debt until late in 1922. Unlike France or Italy, Britain could hardly plead inability to pay. As a center for world finance it was obliged to uphold what was commonly referred to—at least among creditors—as the "sanctity of international obligations." The British government calculated, however, that by delaying matters and blurring the distinction between its own financial solvency and the various degrees of insolvency of the other debtor powers it could embarrass the United States into outright cancellation.[13] The United States, justifiably suspicious of the European nations' intentions, refused to be drawn into economic conferences at which it might meet its debtors simultaneously or at which a discussion of international indebtedness as a whole might arise. This American refusal to contemplate a formal connection between reparations and war debts must be viewed against the background of repeated maneuvers by the British and the continental powers to throw the entire burden of adjustment on the American taxpayer. The tactics of the Europeans proved ultimately counterproductive. The British finally found it expedient to come to terms in early 1923; and while the other Allied nations procrastinated for a few more years, in the end they could not escape. As a legacy of the imbroglio over war debts, the reparations problem remained to be settled in the first instance between Germany and the Allied creditor nations without direct American government participation.

The reparations issue was inextricably woven into the fabric of domestic politics for every west European country, most of all for the two chief protagonists, France and Germany. World War I had been fought on an unprecedented scale; postwar economic and social problems were accordingly of such magnitude as to differ in kind from any previously faced by European statesmen and business leaders. France and Germany contrasted sharply in economic structure, social norms, and political ideology. Similarities in their respective responses to fiscal challenges are therefore all the more striking. In both nations disputes between capital and labor, conflict between bourgeois and socialist forces, and friction among the competing interests within each of these groups thwarted parliamentary consensus, precisely when adoption of consis-

---

Archives, Washington, D.C., U.S. 800.51/285–506; U.S. 800.51W89/1–110; U.S. 800.51W89 GB/49–164; U.S. 800.51W89 Fr/1–90 (hereafter cited as U.S.). The latest interpretive studies include Benjamin D. Rhodes, "The United States and the War Debt Question, 1917–1934" (Ph.D. diss., University of Colorado, 1965); William G. Pullen, "World War Debts and United States Foreign Policy" (Ph.D. diss., University of Georgia, 1972); and Ellen W. Schrecker, "The French Debt to the United States, 1917–1929" (Ph.D. diss., Harvard University, 1973).

13. P.R.O., CAB 23/25–30, Cabinet Conclusions: 37 (21), 10 May 1921; 93 (21), 16 December 1921; 35 (22), 16 June 1922; 36 (22), 30 June 1922; 38 (22), 7 July 1922; also Foreign Office, General Correspondence, Political, F.O. 371, vols. 4547–48, 5661–62, 7281–83, 8503–6 (hereafter cited as F.O. 371/volume number).

tent taxation policies appropriate to altered economic and monetary conditions required such consensus.

Even if the Germans had not intended to resist payment of reparations on foreign policy grounds, the stalemate over taxation would have made it difficult for them to raise the funds to meet their obligations. Because political compromise making adequate taxation possible could not be reached, German public finance became progressively more chaotic in the four years following the war. Government expenditures were met by printing paper money and discounting treasury bonds at the Reichsbank. According to a widely held (though erroneous) theory, improvement in public finance was impossible so long as the trade balance remained negative and reparations weighed adversely in the balance of payments. But once hyperinflation was in full swing, business and government leaders found a serious practical reason to justify their reluctance to stabilize the currency. Stabilization meant deflation, increased unemployment, and probable social unrest. The political balance was so precarious, threats to the Weimar system so serious, that until the final monetary collapse came in the autumn of 1923, fearful men in a weak position did not dare to take the risks inherent in decisive action.[14]

Similarly, the social and psychological strains left by the war were so great that France could not cope with a reconstruction effort entirely within a traditional framework. The French people viewed reparations as the deus ex machina that would enable them to finance the repair of the devastated areas, pay the pensions of the disabled, and carry through revival of national economic life. When reparations payments did not materialize to any appreciable extent, the French proved unable to reach a national consensus on taxation sufficient to meet their budgetary needs. They had recourse instead to an increase in the floating debt—that is, short-term obligations requiring frequent renewal—of such magnitude as to erode the value of the franc and endanger the whole structure of public finance. French financial weakness then hobbled the nation diplomatically at the very point when it appeared that German resistance to reparations payments had been vanquished at last.

French Difficulties in Context

This study examines the origins and consequences of these financial difficulties within France. It explains why the crisis which came to a head in 1924 rendered the French powerless to avert an outcome to the reparations controversy that would leave them to bear the remaining

14. Costantino Bresciani-Turroni, *The Economics of Inflation: A Study of Currency Depreciation in Post-War Germany* (London, 1937); Frank D. Graham, *Exchange, Prices, and Production in Hyper-Inflation: Germany, 1920–1923* (Princeton, 1930); Philip Cagan, "The Monetary Dynamics of Hyperinflation," in *Studies in the Quantity Theory of Money*, ed. Milton Friedman (Chicago, 1956); Karsten Laursen and Jørgen Pedersen, *The German Inflation, 1918–1923* (Amsterdam, 1964); Howard S. Ellis, *German Monetary Theory, 1905–1933* (Cam-

financial burdens of reconstruction largely with their own resources. It also indicates why the reparations settlement based on what became known as the Dawes Plan, and put into effect at the London Conference in the summer of 1924, foreshadowed the reemergence of Germany as the dominant economic power and *mutatis mutandis* as the leading military power on the European continent.

Unquestionably France's failure to receive substantial reparations and its inability to preserve the European political structure established at Versailles were of great importance. But France's decline as a great power, leading eventually to national catastrophe in 1940, must be attributed to other factors as well. The French financial problems considered here were troublesome, yet not impossible to solve. German reparations were highly desirable, but not an absolute prerequisite to modest economic recovery from the ravages of war. Proof of this lies in the fact that after a period of travail the French people did surmount their immediate financial difficulties—by the early 1930s the franc rated among the strongest of European currencies. The French also finally restored the devastated districts to full productivity without substantial German contributions. If France fell within two decades to the status of a second-rank power, it did so at least in part because other urgent problems—government modernization, technological innovation, improvement of industrial production and business marketing techniques, integration of the urban proletariat into the social order, population and family planning, above all reform of education for a modern, scientifically oriented society—were not faced in time. Failure to establish national goals and priorities in order to overcome the rigidity of the "stalemate society" frustrated the growth and change necessary to maintain the essential structure of that society against an external peril. In a sense, the way the French handled the financial crisis illustrates on a small scale the limitations which attended their approach to larger problems plaguing the nation throughout the interwar period.

Perhaps the psychological, demographic, and economic wounds of the First World War were too deep to heal within one generation. Possibly the form of government in the Third Republic was too inflexible to meet the challenges of a modern technological society. On the other hand, one might argue that internal adjustments were made as quickly as could be expected in view of the Gallic cultural heritage, and that the demands on France to uphold the political order created at Versailles were simply too great for a nation with its limited population and resources. Speculation on such a level of generalization is easy; it is more difficult to render definitive judgment. This study poses the more mod-

bridge, Mass., 1934); Paul Beusch, *Währungszerfall und Währungsstabilisierung*, ed. G. Briefs and C. A. Fischer (Berlin, 1928); Rudolf Stucken, *Deutsche Geld- und Kreditpolitik, 1914 bis 1963* (Tübingen, 1964).

est task of elucidating internal financial complications and ensuing diplomatic difficulties at a critical turning point of the postwar era. It will become clear that whatever the underlying weakness of their position, the French compounded the difficulties as a result of their own inadequate responses. As background, a brief narrative will trace the development of the reparations controversy up to the time when the financial structure of France faced serious danger of collapse, and when an international Committee of Experts under General Charles G. Dawes was appointed to devise a provisional solution for the reparations problem.

Reparations Diplomacy Reviewed

The Supreme Allied Council, after more than a dozen conferences interspersed through two years of wrangling, finally set Germany's total obligation to make reparation in May 1921 at 132 milliard gold marks ($33 billion).* This sum was supposed to represent a mathematical calculation by the Reparation Commission of the damage for which Germany stood legally responsible. In fact, the respective national claims for damages had proved none too reliable, as well as difficult to reconcile. The Reparation Commission actually reached its determination by revising downward the various estimates of loss submitted until it arrived at a figure that Allied statesmen meeting in conference considered an acceptable political compromise.[15] In any case, the 132 milliard figure was no more than theoretical. The negotiators divided the German debt into three series of bonds. The Weimar government was held liable to pay interest and amortization charges immediately only on the "A" and "B" bonds, which amounted to a total of 50 milliard marks. The London Schedule of Payments, as the plan set forth in May 1921 was called, specified that Germany should annually indemnify the Allies 2 milliard gold marks plus a sum equal to 26 percent of the value of its exports. The 82 milliards of "C" bonds bore no interest. They were not to be issued until the "A" and "B" bonds had been amortized—over a period of some thirty-six years—unless exceptional development of the German export trade justified their creation earlier.

The actual capital value of the London Schedule consequently depended on the future growth of the German economy. Even the most

*This book employs the term "milliard" to indicate a thousand millions when referring to European currencies. The more usual American word "billion" has an ambiguous meaning in European numeration.

15. Weill-Raynal, *Les Réparations allemandes*, 1:618–75; *Documents on British Foreign Policy, 1919–1939*, ed. Rohan Butler, J. P. T. Bury, and M. E. Lambert (London, 1967–68), Series I, 15:1–587, 16:439–595. For a more detailed account of these negotiations, see P.R.O., CAB 29/91–93, Cabinet Office, Allied and International Conferences on the Terms of Peace and Related Subjects, I. C. P. Series, January-May 1921 (hereafter cited as P.R.O., CAB 29).

optimistic Allied experts recognized at the time that issue of the "C" bonds was a remote prospect. They did not venture to estimate the capital value of the London Schedule at more than 64 milliard marks at a maximum. Realistic participants in the technical negotiations, in fact, conceded privately that Germany was hardly likely to shoulder any additional burden two generations hence, particularly if the Rhineland occupation—the principle means by which the Allies could enforce their demands—terminated on schedule within fifteen years. The "C" bonds, therefore, were from the start largely a convenient fiction. They served initially to mitigate the disappointment of Allied public opinion. Should the German economy expand with unexpected rapidity while the Rhineland occupation continued, they provided possible leverage to back an Allied demand to share in some of the benefits of German prosperity. Finally, if the United States government could be induced to forgive Allied debts in effect, the "C" bonds could be employed as ostensible payment to camouflage the operation from the American public. In short, the "C" bonds constituted a device to preserve flexibility in future settlement of international accounts more than a genuine claim on German resources.

In practice, therefore, the London Schedule signified a reduction of the German debt from the astronomical figures bandied about at the peace conference to a sum which, it could fairly be argued, was reasonably consonant with German capacity to pay. This schedule, if implemented, would have required Germany to transfer in cash and kind something on the order of 7 percent of its national income—a figure which, while requiring substantial sacrifice, did not represent an insuperable burden for a nation resolved to limit domestic consumption sufficiently to meet the levy.[16] However, Germany accepted the terms only under the threat of further occupation of its territory, and with barely concealed reservations. Thus nothing was solved. Reparations remained the stumbling block to all more general efforts at the coordination of European reconstruction.

Germany did make a first payment of 1 milliard marks ($250 million) in the summer of 1921. However, in order to effectuate a capital transfer representing real resources, a nation must first tax itself. Disposable income in the paying country is thus initially reduced by the same amount as disposable income rises in the recipient country after payment. The specific means chosen to raise funds in the donor country and to employ them in the recipient country may influence the symmetry of

16. Mantoux, *Carthaginian Peace*, pp. 115, 147. On the economic issues, see also Fritz Machlup, *International Payments, Debts, and Gold* (New York, 1964), pp. 367–464; R. W. Goldsmith, "Measuring the Economic Impact of Armament Expenditures," in *Studies in Income and Wealth*, comp. Conference on Research in Income and Wealth (New York, 1943), 6:47–93; Arthur Smithies, "National Income as a Determinant of International Policy," in *Studies in Income and Wealth* (New York, 1946), 8:49–72.

the operation. The important point, however, is that the citizens of the recipient country will be able to purchase the products that the citizens of the donor country can no longer afford, so that if artificial barriers are not interposed, income changes resulting from the money transfer will facilitate the real transfer of goods. But the Germans had no intention of making the tangible sacrifice in the form of higher taxes that was necessary to promote effective transfer. Instead, the German government collected the foreign currency required to complete the first payment by the simple expedient of selling paper marks on the open market. Naturally, this procedure resulted in an immediate and precipitous fall in the exchange value of the mark. Each time that the Allies demanded another payment the process could be repeated; thus the German government could appear to demonstrate that reparations "caused" the fall of their currency.

From the start, then, Berlin's posture of compliance was largely pretense. Chancellor Joseph Wirth, a moderate Center party politician, acquired a public reputation as a proponent of *Erfüllungspolitik*—the policy of fulfilling treaty obligations within reason. Actually, he cherished a burning resentment of the Allies, whose exigence he believed to be harming the prospects for democratic government within Germany. After the partition of Upper Silesia, a bitter blow on patriotic as well as economic grounds, he ordered preparation of what would be presented for tactical reasons as a "moratorium" plan, but which in reality constituted a demand for thoroughgoing revision of the London Schedule.[17]

In France, meanwhile, the Briand cabinet faced a swelling current of dissatisfaction in the fall of 1921. The unrest extended to many issues—the Washington naval conference, the Near East, domestic problems—but of these, reparations was the most important. It became increasingly evident that, barring a dramatic change, German payments would never bridge the growing deficit in the special budget for "recoverable expenses" used to defray the cost of reconstruction in the devastated areas.

The conference that met in January 1922 at Cannes to consider the German demand for a moratorium faced momentous decisions on several related issues. Lloyd George was bent on calling a subsequent world economic conference to arrange business consortiums linking the Allies with Germany in joint ventures to stimulate the reconstruction of Soviet Russia. His idea was politically premature as well as fanciful in economic terms, for the Allies had not the capital to spare nor could the Bolsheviks

17. The records of the German Reich Chancellery do not substantiate the generous interpretation of Wirth's intentions and those of his chief adviser, Walther Rathenau, found in the two most recent monographs on the subject: Ernst Laubach, *Die Politik der Kabinette Wirth, 1921/22* (Lübeck and Hamburg, 1968); and David Felix, *Walther Rathenau and the Weimar Republic: The Politics of Reparations* (Baltimore and London, 1971). Compare the original records: R 43 I, Alte Reichskanzlei, Auswärtige Angelegenheiten, Ausführung des Friedensvertrags, Bundesarchiv, Koblenz, esp. vols. 20–32 (hereafter cited as BA, R 43 I/volume number).

offer the necessary security for investment. But the British prime minister had visions—wholly unsupported by any trade statistics—of vast untapped markets for British exports in Russia. His febrile imagination was already sketching the possibilities for fruitful cooperation with Germany in promoting recovery in eastern Europe. By this time strongly inclined to favor revision of the reparations schedule, he saw the problem as one of cajoling the French into taking the broader view.

Thus when Briand proposed to revive the idea of the abortive 1919 Anglo-American treaty of guarantee—this time in the form of a bilateral arrangement with England that might later be widened into a nonaggression pact including Germany—Lloyd George and his cabinet colleagues perceived an opportunity to turn the request to their own advantage. The French premier calculated that even if he could not win British support for a pact with meaningful military provisions, formal signature of any treaty would mark progress toward "moral solidarity" with Great Britain. This in turn might augur hopefully for the future. British statesmen, worn down by years of bickering, had by this time quite lost the sense of comradeship that had bound them to France during the war. Few were inclined to favor a pact on the grounds of mutual sympathy. Foreign Secretary Curzon expressed their sentiments with typical flourish, recalling that ever since the days of the Bourbons, consistent cooperation between the two nations had been rendered difficult by the Gallic penchant for "relentless promotion of French prestige and the gratification of private, generally monetary and often sordid, interests or ambitions, only too frequently pursued with a disregard of ordinary rules of straightforward and loyal dealing which is repugnant and offensive to normal British instincts."[18] If the British nonetheless showed themselves ready to accommodate Briand, it was primarily because they believed that in return for a paper agreement involving few practical obligations, they could extract tangible and substantial concessions from France on reparations and numerous other matters of foreign policy from Tangier to Turkey. The analysis given in the privacy of the British cabinet room was a bit coldblooded but perfectly straightforward: "Germany is to us the most important country in Europe not only on account of our trade with her, but also because she is the key to the situation in Russia. By helping Germany we might under existing conditions expose ourselves to the charge of deserting France; but if France was our ally no such charge could be made."[19]

The negotiations at Cannes were interrupted by signals from the French cabinet, abetted by President Millerand, indicating lack of confidence in Briand. The anxiety in Paris was largely justified. Briand seemed

18. "Memorandum by the Marquess Curzon of Kedleston on the Question of an Anglo-French Alliance," 28 December 1922, *Documents on British Foreign Policy*, Series I, 16:867.

19. P.R.O., CAB 23/29, Cabinet Conclusions: 1(22), 10 January 1922.

so intent on chasing the will-o'-the-wisp of security that he might very well have been tempted to sacrifice vital French reparations interests in return for a paper pact. The premier probably retained enough support in the Chamber of Deputies to have surmounted this challenge by his colleagues. But, unable to carry through his most cherished diplomatic objective, Briand sensed the inevitable weakening of his position, and his shrewd political sense moved him to resign voluntarily.[20]

Raymond Poincaré became the "national man." The prestige he had garnered as wartime president of the Republic remained untarnished. Named to preside over the Reparation Commission, he had stepped down in 1920 in protest against its weakness; and his acerbic articles in the *Revue des deux mondes* over the following two years suggested that if anyone could make the Germans pay, it was he.[21] Millerand harbored a personal animosity born of disillusioned youthful friendship for Poincaré, but given the political circumstances he could designate no other successor to Briand.

Poincaré appealed to the broad center group in the *Chambre bleu horizon*—the legislature elected at the height of patriotic fervor after the war—and under the banner of a *union sacrée*, he offered a domestic program politically neutral, the better to face external difficulties. He retained many of Briand's cabinet colleagues and, in the realm of foreign policy too, modified style more than he changed fundamental direction. For Briand's charm, flair, and nonchalant ignorance of detail, Poincaré substituted a hard-driving legal mentality.[22] He reacted with the skepticism of the provincial bourgeois to grand schemes for recasting Europe economically so long as the German debt, with its psychological as well as its material significance, remained unpaid. He saw no logic in making concessions on reparations—the issue most vital for France's immediate future—in order to advance negotiations for the shadow of a security pact which, though not without a measure of spiritual import, bound Great Britain militarily no more than geography would have bound it in the absence of a pact.

Still, Poincaré's basic orientation did not differ strikingly from that of his predecessor. The German information services assiduously propagated the myth that he represented the Napoleonic tradition of French imperialism; the Communists at home contributed scurrilous attacks against *Poincaré-la-guerre*; and the new premier's abrasive temperament evoked the personal animosity of Lloyd George and Lord Curzon. In reality, while Poincaré was as suspicious of the hereditary enemy across

20. Georges Suarez, *Briand, sa vie, son oeuvre*, vol. 5, *L'Artisan de la paix* (Paris, 1941), pp. 352–417.

21. Jacques Chastenet, *Raymond Poincaré* (Paris, 1948); Pierre Miquel, *Poincaré* (Paris, 1961).

22. Emmanuel de Peretti de la Rocca, "Briand et Poincaré: Souvenirs," *Revue de Paris*, 15 December 1936, pp. 775–88.

the Rhine as most French politicians of his generation, his designs extended no further than what he considered the just enforcement of the treaty. Maintenance of the Entente with England, for him as much as for Briand, remained the cardinal aim of diplomacy, and if he insisted that it not be bought at the expense of the Versailles settlement, his sense of the high value of that Entente would always limit the extent of unilateral French action in defense of treaty rights.

A combination of circumstances rather than a change in French policy worked against an amicable resolution of the reparations dispute. Poincaré reluctantly acceded to Lloyd George's demand for holding a world economic conference at Genoa, though he robbed that gathering of its greatest significance by insisting that reparations be excluded from the agenda. After a desultory exchange of views, both sides tacitly agreed to shelve the project for an Anglo-French alliance. At Cannes, the Reparation Commission had granted temporary relief to Germany in return for a promise of vigorous action by the German government to balance the budget and levy adequate taxes. However, the Wirth government procrastinated: although the progress of inflation had already outdated its token tax reform program, it refused to consider substantial alterations on the ground that the painfully achieved fiscal compromise represented the maximum that was politically feasible.

The Germans were encouraged in their resistance by broad hints from Whitehall that revision of the London Schedule was inevitable. Foreign Minister Walther Rathenau, whom the English held in high esteem as an advocate of moderation, actually spearheaded sentiment within the confidential councils of the German government for setting the strictest limits to compliance with reparations demands. In this spirit Finance Minister Hermes, though personally inclined to be somewhat more flexible, deliberately dragged his feet when meeting with the Reparation Commission in May and June 1922. Thus, direct negotiations led nowhere.

Simultaneously, the prospect of assistance by an international banking consortium vanished. French officials in high places—even some specialists in the Finance Ministry who should have known better—maintained the hope that a way might yet be found to induce American private investors to purchase large amounts of reparations bonds, in effect furnishing the capital with which Germany could liquidate its debt to France and the other Allies. A bankers' committee headed by J. P. Morgan, called in to advise the Reparation Commission in June, dispelled the illusion that significant sums could be raised on private financial markets for such a risky enterprise. The bankers insisted, furthermore, on a long moratorium and downward revision of the London Schedule as prerequisites even to a loan of modest proportions for the carefully circumscribed purpose of stabilizing the German currency. These conditions Poincaré refused to contemplate. On the heels of the discouraging report from the bankers came another bad omen: Rathenau was gunned down by right-wing extremists, who were unaware of how tenaciously he had fought for many of their concerns.

In the second half of 1922 a showdown over reparations was postponed from month to month by a series of makeshifts. The German financial situation deteriorated at an accelerating rate. The most influential forces in German industry and banking, convinced that currency depreciation gave their nation an export advantage, deemed the deflationary consequences of stabilization still unacceptable. The Wirth government clearly commanded neither the respect nor the power to enforce an alternative view.

At an interallied conference in London in August, Poincaré called for "productive guarantees"—Allied control of German state forests and mines—as the price of a further moratorium. He declared that in the absence of British collaboration, France might find itself obliged to seize such guarantees forcibly in the Ruhr. Within the councils of the German government, powerful forces including Reichsbank President Havenstein argued that, whatever the consequences, the time now had come to put an end to the pretense even of token "fulfillment."

At the last minute the forces of temporization carried the day. France backed away from action. The Belgians, terrified at the prospect of having to declare their loyalties in the event of a break between France and England, offered to accept German treasury bonds in place of cash payments due them for the remainder of 1922, and this compromise was secretly underwritten by the Bank of England. Nothing constructive was accomplished, however, during the short reprieve purchased by this arrangement. In fact Anglo-French relations deteriorated further with a new eruption of the rivalry in the Near East that had been smoldering since 1919. In both nations, diplomats privately expressed the premonition that a showdown over reparations could not be indefinitely deferred.

Poincaré's ministry, which not many months before had enjoyed the support of the overwhelming majority in the Chamber of Deputies, appeared headed for stormy political weather. Critics charged that his firmness on reparations had been confined to rhetoric, that his harsh verbal pronouncements had contributed to a deterioration of the international climate while bringing no greater progress on substantive matters than Briand had achieved. War Minister Maginot, prompted by Marshal Foch and the military commander in the occupied Rhineland, strongly urged the occupation of the Ruhr. This had always been the ultimate weapon in the French arsenal, and contingency plans were ready. Arguing for rapid action, the military underscored the desirability of carrying through the Ruhr occupation before the scheduled reduction of the military service requirement to eighteen months crippled French capacity to undertake offensive operations.[23] Spokesmen for certain segments of the French steel industry, frustrated by failure to secure a satisfactory supply of Ruhr coke for their mills in any other way, also favored the occupation. Normally the steel industry, contrary to the accepted myth, enjoyed very little influence with the French government.[24] In this particular instance, however, President Millerand echoed their views, contending that a Ruhr occupation might serve not only as a means of pressure to compel reparations payments narrowly speaking, but could also provide the impetus for an agreement on favorable terms between French and German industry.

Poincaré initially offered a measure of resistance to these pressures from his government colleagues. As late as mid-November 1922 he violently denounced Millerand's proposal for a Ruhr occupation as fraught with military and financial perils, and he threatened to resign rather than carry it out.[25] Yet clearly something had to be done to break the deadlock. Not only had all efforts to extract cash payments from Germany proved fruitless; the Reich had also defaulted on promises to make deliveries in kind, after the French government had gone to considerable trouble to overcome opposition from protectionist-minded French businessmen who feared the competitive impact on their sales. German heavy industry, finally, had indicated in response to overtures from its French counterpart that mutually profitable business arrangements for exchange of coke against iron ore and metallurgical semiproducts would have to await resolution of the reparations question on terms tolerable to Germany—the implication being that the settlement should make the Germans the dominant partner in the business combination.[26]

The last months of 1922 witnessed the frantic preparation of plans on all sides. In the Allied camp, general agreement prevailed that German finances could not be reestablished on a sound basis without outside help, but no consensus emerged on the form intervention should take. English Treasury experts analyzed the problem as primarily economic. They believed that German financial officials lacked not simply the political power, but more importantly the technical ability to stem the

23. François-André Paoli, *L'Armée française de 1919 à 1939: La Phase de fermeté* (Paris, 1971), pp. 238–41; General Degoutte, *L'Occupation de la Ruhr* (Düsseldorf, 1924), pt. 1. (A copy of the latter book, printed for official use by the French Army of the Rhine, may be found at the Service Historique de l'Armée, Château de Vincennes, France.)

24. See notes by Camille Cavallier on meetings of the Comité des Forges in vols. 7245–46, Archives de Pont-à-Mousson, Compagnie de St.-Gobain-Pont-à-Mousson, La Châtre (Indre), France (hereafter cited as PAM/volume number).

25. Alexandre Millerand, "Mes souvenirs–Contribution à l'histoire de la Troisième République," pp. 113–14, describing the cabinet meeting of 13 November 1922 (MS in Alexandre Millerand Papers, in family possession, Paris).

26. See material in "Förderung internationaler Wirtschaftsbeziehungen: Industrielle Verständigung mit Frankreich, 1922–31," vol. 255, Wirtschaftsgruppe Eisenschaffende Industrie, Verein Deutscher Eisen- und Stahlindustrieller, R 13 I, Bundesarchiv, Koblenz (hereafter cited as BA, R 13 I/255).

runaway inflation without a long and complete moratorium on reparations payments. For the French, the essence of the problem lay in the political sphere. In their view the German government, under the influence of industrialists profiting from inflation, was deliberately failing to take the steps requisite to halt the financial debacle. Germany was heading for fraudulent bankruptcy, they thought, in order to avoid payment of the indemnity. In retrospect, it is clear that the British correctly perceived the nature of the political stalemate and the inadequate level of competence among German monetary managers. At the same time, ample documentary confirmation can be found to support the French contention that Germany was mounting a political revolt against reparations as a symbol of the Versailles treaty.[27]

Despite increasingly stern admonitions from the Reparation Commission, the German government made no serious efforts to cope with financial deterioration except to redouble the activity of the note presses. By contrast, high-level committees including government officials, bankers, and businessmen in Berlin busied themselves with alternative schemes to whittle down the reparations burden. The greatest of the industrialists, Hugo Stinnes, talked up his own plan to the Allied powers behind Chancellor Wirth's back, offering radically scaled-down payments as part of a comprehensive political agreement including evacuation of the Rhineland and return of the Saar, commercial advantages on world markets for the Reich, increased power for the industrialists within Germany, and reintroduction of the ten-hour working day.[28] Caught between the contempt of industry on one hand and the opposition of the Social Democrats on the other, the Wirth ministry fell in November 1922. It is often claimed that the successor cabinet, headed by Wilhelm Cuno of the Hamburg-America Line and composed largely of nonparty technical experts, marked a sharp shift to the right compared with Wirth's "fulfillment" government, and that it signified an abdication by the democratic parties which made up the Weimar coalition.[29] Actually, a striking continuity was manifest in foreign policy. The reparations plan finally drawn up at the end of December 1922 reflected a consensus reached after consultation with representatives of all significant political organizations and economic groups in German society.

27. BA, R 43 I/30–33, Ausführung des Friedensvertrags, August-December 1922; also the documentary collection, *Akten der Reichskanzlei, Weimarer Republik. Das Kabinett Cuno: 22. November 1922 bis 12. August 1923*, ed. Karl-Heinz Harbeck (Boppard am Rhein, 1968).

28. The fullest exposition of Stinnes's views is found in Stinnes to American Ambassador Alanson B. Houghton, 14 October 1922, Alanson B. Houghton Papers, in family possession, Corning, N.Y. Stinnes later urged a revised version on the Cuno government: "Zehn Punkte Stinnes," December 1922, filed with other business and banking proposals in BA, R 2/1369, Reichsfinanzministerium, Reparationsvorschläge.

29. Erich Eyck, *A History of the Weimar Republic*, trans. Harlan P. Hanson and Robert G. L. Waite, 2 vols. (Cambridge, Mass., 1967), 1:228; cf. Heinz Hellmut Kohlhaus, "Die Hapag, Cuno und das deutsche Reich, 1920–1933" (D. Phil. diss., University of Hamburg, 1952), pp. 109–85.

This proposal amounted in effect to a calculated decision by Germany to force a confrontation. It made an Allied promise to terminate the Rhineland occupation at an early date a precondition of a voluntarily accepted reparations settlement. It proposed a complete four-year moratorium without security. It offered a total sum designed to appear in form as large as possible, but amounting to a real "present value" (as of 1922) not exceeding 12 milliard gold marks—less than a quarter of the "A" and "B" bonds. It insisted on an end to interference by outside powers with the German economy. Finally, it suggested that though the Reich could not afford to deliver coal and coke on reparations account, German industrialists would be willing to sell these products to the French on a commercial basis (presumably at a price that left German industry in a position of advantage). Despite a certain amount of self-deceptive advertisement of the plan as a great step forward by Berlin, the urbane Carl Bergmann, German reparations adviser in Paris, entertained no illusions that it offered a real basis for discussion: he did not even bother to present it formally at the Quai d'Orsay.

The Allies, meanwhile, could no longer paper over their differences. Once the amiable Andrew Bonar Law replaced Lloyd George, the element of personal friction among the leaders no longer complicated Anglo-French relations. But substantive differences could still not be bridged. The English took pride in the fact that by dint of self-discipline they managed their public finances on a sounder basis than did the French, but, they insisted, Great Britain faced graver problems of unemployment and more stresses in the economy generally. They could neither afford to participate in territorial sanctions against Germany nor to countenance cheerfully the disruption of trade attendant upon further political disturbance in central Europe. Moreover, having decided after much tergiversation to settle their own war debt to Washington, they felt less able to make vital concessions with regard to the French debt to Great Britain. Without a write-off of war debts, Poincaré remained unwilling to accept any reduction in reparations that would leave France with less than the amount necessary to rebuild its devastated districts—a sum which, according to French calculations, at least equaled their full 52 percent share of the "A" and "B" bonds.

In preparation for the Paris conference of January 1923 the British Treasury readied a proposal for German economic rehabilitation so complicated that many key members of the British delegation did not fully understand it. Even German representative Bergmann quipped: "I would rather pay reparations than try to understand the Bonar Law Plan."[30] This scheme contained many meritorious elements, but its key feature provided a four-year moratorium for Germany without any

30. Jones, *Whitehall Diary*, 1:224–25; Jacques Seydoux, *De Versailles au plan Young* (Paris, 1932), p. 193.

tangible guarantees to ensure that reparations would resume afterward. The French regarded this as outside all bounds of political practicality. Poincaré, though willing to be flexible about the specific pledges to be physically taken over, refused to budge from the general formula, "no moratorium without guarantees." There appeared no alternative but to confirm the two Allies' disagreement, a *mésentente cordiale*, as it was called.

In the December days before the Paris conference various dramatic gestures were made to stave off the inevitable. For months Secretary of State Charles Evans Hughes had been urged by American diplomats in Europe to propose an independent committee of financial experts to develop a fair payments plan. He finally heard the same advice from "the voice of God"—or so he later told the story—and made a public appeal, offering the participation of American representatives in such an inquiry.[31] Chancellor Cuno, meanwhile, following the advice of American Ambassador Alanson B. Houghton, suggested a four-power nonaggression pact on the Rhine, according to which the signatory powers would agree not to declare war for a generation without a plebiscite.[32] Both these gestures were harbingers of future developments, the first of the Dawes Committee, the second of the Locarno pact. But neither proposal spoke to the burning issue of the hour, which concerned neither Germany's momentary capacity to pay in the absence of financial reform, nor the advisability of a paper security guarantee limited to the west and excluding eastern Europe from its purview. The basic problem was Germany's unwillingness to pay.

For France, assured of Belgian support and armed with legal justification by a Reparation Commission ruling that Germany stood in default, there now seemed no practicable alternative to proceeding with an occupation of the Ruhr. By nature, Poincaré feared decisive action. Through an ironic twist of fate, he was forced into a situation—as he had been during the months before the outbreak of war in 1914, and was to be again during another crisis in 1926—that precluded temporization. Not to act, he realized, would serve no purpose but to destroy his reputation as a strong man and bring to power someone committed to a more radical version of the occupation.[33]

Rejecting a number of proposals from the Ministry of War for an immediate full-scale envelopment of the Ruhr, Poincaré decided to place chief reliance initially on a corps of a few dozen engineers—the so-called *Mission interalliée de contrôle des usines et des mines* (M.I.C.U.M.)—

31. Merlo J. Pusey, *Charles Evans Hughes*, 2 vols. (New York, 1951), 2:581.

32. For proof that Houghton originated the idea which developed into Cuno's nonagression proposal and later into the Locarno pact, see Alanson B. Houghton Diary, 4–30 December 1922, Houghton Papers.

33. Chastenet, *Poincaré*, p. 245.

entrusted with the mission of supervising state mines, forests, and other facilities designated as "productive guarantees."[34] The premier was reluctant to discard the hope, despite his own forebodings, that he might yet succeed in confining the role of the military to protecting the engineers' mission. The German government, however, resolved at once to resist by every means within its power. Advised by General von Seeckt that active military measures stood no chance of success, it meticulously organized and coordinated what became known as "passive resistance." The ministries in Berlin determined every feature of this resistance, from noncooperation by the citizenry, railway workers and factory owners alike, to actual sabotage carried out by paramilitary bands. Characteristically, German government agencies were so thorough that they even developed an effective public relations campaign portraying the resistance as spontaneous.[35]

The French ministries responsible for planning the operation, on the other hand, had failed to coordinate their work—a situation equally typical of haphazard French methods of governmental administration. Poincaré envisioned the occupation primarily as a means of pressure on the German government and the industrialists who owned the mines and mills in the Ruhr to fulfill their reparations obligations under the London Schedule of Payments. At the time, he was accused of harboring vast designs for achieving security aims frustrated at Versailles, and it is true that once French forces became established in the Ruhr, many French officials who had advocated dismemberment of Germany at the peace conference—Marshal Foch chief among them—dusted off their plans and began to push for them once again. This does not negate the fact that Poincaré's objective when the occupation began was modest, namely, to create a situation sufficiently unpleasant for industry in the Ruhr that the Germans would decide to comply with the treaty to secure release from vexatious interference by French supervisory agencies there.[36]

The Franco-Belgian engineers' mission proved quite unprepared for the magnitude of the effort necessary to seize the "productive pledges" and, in the face of German noncooperation, to work them directly in a profitable way. Nevertheless, once committed to the operation, the French and their Belgian allies had no choice but to meet each German step of escalation with an answering turn of the vise. A full-scale test of strength ensued. Despite initial reverses, the Poincaré government calculated correctly that France could stand the strain longer than Germany. It cost the German government more to finance "passive resistance" by

34. Emile Coste, "La Préparation de l'occupation de la Ruhr, 1920–1923," MS in family possession, Paris.

35. BA, R 43 I/203–30, Akten betreffend Besetzung des Ruhrgebietes, 1923.

36. Ludwig Zimmermann, *Frankreichs Ruhrpolitik: Von Versailles bis zum Dawesplan*, ed. Walther Peter Fuchs (Göttingen, Zurich, and Frankfurt am Main, 1971).

the entire Ruhr population for nine months than it had paid in reparation in all the years since the war. Eventually this effort resulted in the complete collapse of the German currency. After attempting in vain to elicit mediation by the Anglo-Saxon powers, the Germans found themselves obliged to come to terms directly with the French.[37]

In August 1923 Gustav Stresemann forged a "great coalition" to end the active phase of the Ruhr struggle on the best terms obtainable, in order that domestic financial reconstruction might begin. Stresemann's stewardship of the Reich in his hundred days as chancellor was remarkable. Rejecting the counsels of the "bitter-enders," he demonstrated the ability so characteristic of his later statesmanship to make compromises in international politics, not because he favored "understanding," but rather on the ground that such compromises offered the greatest promise in the long run of restoring his country's power.[38] On 26 September the German government formally declared passive resistance at an end. This did not mean that the Germans had undergone any change of heart toward their reparations obligations. Their failure to resume deliveries in kind immediately, it is true, was attributable to financial penury, not to deliberate ill will, as Poincaré professed to believe. Yet despite the serious internal problems facing the Reich, Stresemann and his associates considered the decision to end resistance not as a defeat, but rather—as many Germans had regarded the Armistice of 1918—as a tactical retreat.

The limitations on French policy, in these circumstances, were greater than they appeared to some optimists in the first flush of victory. France could hardly expect to implement forcibly a reparations settlement inimical to British interests without permanently alienating its only significant potential military ally, nor could any program for European economic recovery hope to be ultimately successful without enlisting the active support of American capital. But the German Republic faced so many grave challenges during the autumn of 1923 that French officials assigned to duty in the Ruhr and occupied Rhineland were led to exaggerate the significance of the visible signs of social and political disintegration around them. Forgetting the long-term economic and military constraints, some of these officials and their supporters in Paris perceived an opportunity to restructure the entire European balance of power. The industrialists in the occupied areas, temporarily left to shift for themselves by Berlin and consequently obliged to seek the occupa-

37. On the history of the occupation see Paul Wentzcke, *Ruhrkampf: Einbruch und Abwehr im rheinisch-westfälischen Industriegebiet*, 2 vols. (Berlin, 1931); and Jean-Claude Favez, *Le Reich devant l'occupation franco-belge de la Ruhr en 1923* (Geneva, 1969).

38. Henry Ashby Turner, Jr., *Stresemann and the Politics of the Weimar Republic* (Princeton, 1963); Roland Thimme, *Stresemann und die deutsche Volkspartei, 1923–1925* (Lübeck and Hamburg, 1961).

tion authorities' cooperation in reviving production at their idle mines and mills, signed the so-called M.I.C.U.M. agreements, which stipulated that they would finance deliveries in kind out of their own pockets. Leading circles in Rhineland political life also flirted with the movement for provincial autonomy in order to cope with social disorganization, forestall the more extreme separatist bands, and enlist French support for a stable Rhineland currency.[39]

Yet important as these developments were, Poincaré and his principal professional advisers at the Quai d'Orsay recognized that they could not by themselves offer an alternative to a reparations agreement achieved within the wider interallied perspective of the Reparation Commission. The major opportunity missed by France in the autumn of 1923, it now appears evident, lay not in the failure to push decisively for an industrial entente with Germany or for a Rhineland state, but rather in the failure to develop an imaginative program for consideration by the Reparation Commission. The so-called Belgian studies of possible sources of reparation revenue had laid the technical groundwork for maneuver along these lines. But Poincaré let the initiative pass to others.

Great Britain then proposed to revive the suggestion made by the American secretary of state at the end of 1922 for an inquiry into the whole subject by a committee of business and financial experts free from official direction. Secretary Hughes, concerned by the danger of economic chaos in Europe, proved receptive even though, in order to protect himself from criticism by domestic isolationists, he characteristically set the condition that all parties to the dispute request America's participation as a kind of "impartial arbiter." Negotiations stalled for two months, first because the British failed to be entirely candid with the French regarding the exclusion of war debts from discussion, but mainly because the French sought to limit the inquiry's terms of reference. By restricting the scope of investigation to German capacity to pay up to 1930, Poincaré hoped to preserve the option of eventually reinstituting the London Schedule of Payments. Hughes, braving the censure of the internationalist press in Washington and New York (which wanted the United States to "do its part" as it had in wartime), refused to accept these limitations and broke off discussion. Without an alternative policy, Poincaré was then obliged to sue for a resumption of negotiations. He found no escape from vital concessions concerning the scope of the inquiry, since without American participation the proposed Expert Committees would not command the universal confidence requisite for success.

After arrangements were completed, members of two related Expert

39. Karl Dietrich Erdmann, *Adenauer in der Rheinlandpolitik nach dem Ersten Weltkrieg* (Stuttgart, 1966); Erwin Bischof, *Rheinischer Separatismus, 1918–1924: Hans Adam Dortens Rheinstaatbestrebungen* (Bern, 1969).

Committees converged on Paris to begin their investigation in January 1924. The more important of these committees, which became known after its chairman as the Dawes Committee, expected to go beyond its official mission, namely suggesting methods to balance the German budget and stabilize the German currency; it intended to propose a comprehensive plan for readjustment of the entire reparations burden. Selected by the respective Allied governments because of high standing in the business or financial world, the Experts served with the nominal status of mere private advisers to the Reparation Commission. In actual fact, once the Expert Committees began work, they quickly gathered such momentum that it would have proved difficult for any single nation to turn down their unanimous recommendations.

The French army still held the Ruhr securely, but the policy of sanctions had already achieved its maximum effect. The guarantees seized by the occupying forces, though profitable enough to underwrite the immediate military costs of the operation, were yielding no more than a modest amount of additional revenue for the French budget of recoverable expenses. The government in Paris would have to weigh seriously the advantages of a plan conceived by the Experts against the risks of continuing to go it alone in the Ruhr. The German cabinet would have to calculate with equal care what pecuniary sacrifices would be worthwhile in order to secure a larger measure of American and British participation in reparations diplomacy. On all sides there existed a presentiment that this might very well be the final opportunity to involve the United States, and in particular American private capital, in European financial reconstruction. In short, the Expert inquiry constituted a major historical event with which each protagonist would have to come to terms. At this point France was suddenly plunged into financial turmoil, which fatefully conditioned the pattern of its response to the judgment rendered by the Experts and ultimately shaped the European settlement that emerged.

Part I

The French Financial Crisis

Chapter 2

Origins of the French Financial Crisis

Financial Weakness and Diplomatic Consequences

On the very January day in 1924 that the Expert Committees convened with high hopes at the Hotel Astoria in Paris, just across town at the Bourse the bottom seemed to drop out of the franc. At a critical moment for French foreign policy, the financial storm which for several years had hung threateningly over France finally broke out. In the Chamber, the acknowledged expert on public finance compared the mood of the nation with its consternation at the bloodletting of Chemin-des-Dames, that most futile of wartime offensives: "The monetary armament of France appeared to be broken, and all her substance might have flowed out through the breach," he observed with as much genuine alarm as dramatic effect. "The anxiety reflected in conversations and on faces resembled the anguish caused in wartime by communiqués announcing bad news from our armies."[1]

In view of the government's fiscal policies, the real surprise is that the financial crisis had not begun earlier. Ever since the nineteenth century, the ordinary Frenchman had placed most of his savings in fixed-income government obligations; after the war, only the continued fidelity of the rentier to prewar habits of investment permitted postponement of fundamental fiscal reform for so long. Now, however, negotiations leading to the Dawes Plan had to be carried out in an atmosphere of panic at the exchange and chronic financial uncertainty on the domestic front. The nation's diplomatic weakness at this juncture stemmed directly from its inability to solve problems of public finance earlier. The French were to pay grievously for their failure to shoulder the burden of increased domestic taxation immediately once it became clear that the large German payments on which they had counted to finance reconstruction of the devastated areas would not soon materialize. Paradoxically, by postponing the painful readjustment in their thinking after German default,

1. Maurice Bokanowski, *rapporteur-général* of the Finance Commission, in *Journal Officiel, Chambre des Députés, Débats parlementaires*, 25 January 1924, p. 274 (hereafter cited as *J.O.C. Déb.*).

the French crippled their own power to compel Germany to help meet French needs. Furthermore, by responding in a confused and dilatory fashion at a point when the financial crisis was hard upon them, French legislators limited their government's freedom of maneuver in responding to the Dawes Plan and dealing with its subsequent implementation.

It was of course no new story that inadequate finance constituted the Achilles' heel of French foreign policy. Over the centuries the struggle for maintenance of individual liberties and class prerogatives against the exigencies of national power had found expression in France through resistance to taxation. From the reign of Philip the Fair to that of Louis XVI, major wars requiring expansion of central tax powers led time and again to internal crises, for which mysterious forces, unknown speculators, or foreign powers were made the scapegoats. So too after the First World War there existed a widespread disinclination to face financial realities. In 1919, after the end of exchange controls which had held the franc close to its prewar parity, that currency depreciated in irregular fashion. During the war the national debt had skyrocketed. Nevertheless, a rigorous overhaul of the tax system, return to a balanced budget, and consolidation of emergency wartime loans into permanent obligations would have provided the prerequisites for currency stabilization at some reasonable level. Instead, taxation remained relatively low. Government revenue amounted to no more than a fraction of expenditure. The French treasury continued to meet its needs by issuing short-term national defense bonds. The government's fiscal policy would ordinarily have led to rapid price inflation. To guard against this, the nation's monetary watchdogs imposed an unrealistically low and rigid *plafond*, or maximum figure for currency in circulation. If the short-term bonds were not renewed, the treasury would be unable to cope with its immediate responsibilities through other means. It would be placed in the position of a bank with large deposits but insufficient liquidity to meet its obligations in the event of a run.

In their imposing headquarters on the rue de Rivoli, treasury officials consequently found themselves engaged in a perpetual struggle to keep their financial heads above water. In political circles, however, the hope lingered that some kind of miracle—a "wave of a magic wand," as sometime finance minister Joseph Caillaux later put it[2]—would dispel all difficulties and restore the simpler world familiar to the rentier before the war. Gradually during 1921 and 1922, financial planners and even some of the more perspicacious among French politicians came to recognize that without the confidence of international financial markets, the problem of obtaining investment capital for European reconstruction could not be completely solved. The most diverse schemes for mobilizing the world's available resources for this purpose, whether through private

2. Raymond Philippe, *Le Drame financier de 1924–1928* (Paris, 1931), p. 79.

underwriting of reparations bonds, direct or indirect forgiveness of war debts, or ordinary commercial investment, rested on the common assumption of participation by private investors in London and particularly in New York. By 1923 even most partisans of the Ruhr occupation realized that whether or not coercion increased German willingness to pay, it did not by itself provide a total solution: international sanction and the lubrication of international loans were conditions precedent to a viable long-term reparations arrangement, conceived of as a stepping-stone to general European economic recovery.

Yet in the field of domestic finance, France had been able to limp along on its own until 1923. Whatever the difficulties in meeting the expenses of rebuilding the devastated areas, underwriting war pensions, and keeping up an imposing military establishment, the nation had faced them somehow without major dependence on Anglo-Saxon financial cooperation. If France remained in a position to pursue a relatively independent reparations policy through 1923, this independence was based on its capacity, in the absence of reparations receipts, to tap the savings of the French population through domestic bond issues. The exchange crisis of 1924 marked the beginning of a substantial change. Subsequently foreign bankers seemed at times to wield life and death power over French finance.

Neither private banking interests nor the American government took advantage of the situation to extract direct political concessions in this, the first of the "franc" crises. On the contrary, as will become evident, the New York bankers acted with considerable restraint during the emergency. With their support, the French met the bear raid on the franc successfully and routed the speculators. Yet the underlying weaknesses in the nation's financial structure remained. Little had been done to coordinate fundamental reform of the tax system and the budget with progress toward monetary stabilization. The French government had finally reached the limits of its long-term domestic borrowing capacity. Foreign exchange reserves available to meet new speculative threats against the franc were limited. Between 1924 and 1928 the guardians of French finance would have to appeal repeatedly to central bankers and the financial communities in New York and London. Under any conditions the difficulties of reorganizing public finances would be formidable. How much more arduous would they be for a nation intent on employing political methods that did not inspire confidence in American lenders of capital and their spokesmen!

The American private investor's priorities differed from those which had hitherto prevailed at the Quai d'Orsay. As an investor he was interested in promoting European "pacification" as rapidly as possible to develop a favorable business climate. For the same reason he favored an orthodox or "sound" approach to public finance, one that did not rely on substantial foreign payments to achieve a balanced budget. The mechanisms adopted to assure reparations transfers were of considerably less importance to him. In his private capacity as a citizen who had fought the Great War, he might still—despite the progress of "revisionism"—feel strongly that compensation should be paid for wartime injustices. But when making investment decisions, he did not really concern himself with the detailed terms of the European settlement that were of such vital interest to the French; he sought rather to avoid involvement in purely "political" quarrels, which were bad for business whatever the rights or wrongs of the matter.

Why did France fail to make financial adjustments early enough to avoid narrowing its options for diplomatic maneuver? Such adjustments were indeed onerous, but the rapid recovery of the French economy from the war brought them within the realm of possibility. The controversy of 1924 illuminates a concatenation of forces that continued to work in destructive combination throughout subsequent years. The highest levels of government and the Bank of France held to rigid preconceptions and exhibited an inability to master the changes necessary in monetary policymaking in the postwar world. They continued to chase the chimera of revaluation of the franc to its prewar standard instead of accepting its stabilization at a level that accurately reflected the productivity of the French economy. The population, ignorant of the consequences of the prolonged crisis and equally wedded to outdated economic views, modified its resistance to taxation reluctantly and incompletely. The inflexibility of French parliamentary practice played a crucial role. As so often happened in the "stalemate society"[3] of the later Third Republic, the political parties in the Chamber of Deputies and Senate—obsessed with doctrinal disputes and absorbed in fighting among themselves about distribution of the fiscal burden—found it impossible to reach a pragmatic consensus expeditiously. The French parliamentary system was by its very nature ill adapted for rapid response to complex economic problems. Yet disagreement regarding division of the fiscal burden also reflected fundamental fissures within the society. The parliamentary system may have continued to function as well as it did precisely because problems were not seriously confronted until an emergency arose. Financial issues were potentially so politically explosive that perhaps only the fear of real catastrophe (as later in 1925–26) could have provided enough impetus for their solution without splitting the country.

At any rate the painful process of coming to terms with the financial legacy of the war took several years and left behind deep social scars. This readjustment could not begin in earnest until the Ruhr occupation and the reparations issue had been disposed of as subjects of contro-

3. The phrase has been popularized by Stanley Hoffmann. See "The French Political Community," in his *In Search of France* (Cambridge, Mass., 1963), pp. 3–21.

versy. Only after the Dawes Plan was put into operation, setting strict limits to German obligations and ending lingering hopes that reparations might provide substantial relief for the French budget, could internal financial questions move to the center stage of political life. What is most noteworthy about the fiscal controversy of 1924 is that even when the outcome would affect the nation's diplomatic destiny, petty considerations of domestic politics should still play the dominant role in public and parliamentary dialogue.

The final result of French financial weakness was a subtle shifting of international power relationships in the spring and summer of 1924. Banking and financial considerations were given more weight, political considerations relatively less, than in previous years. International finance did not seek to dictate political solutions peremptorily or in a crude way. Rather the bankers spelled out conditions for their assistance and left it to French policymakers to reassess the relative merits and costs of an independent foreign policy and to draw the obvious conclusions. Whatever the form in which they were clothed, the constraints imposed by the bankers' attitudes were decisive in the whole process of jockeying over the Experts' Report, from its formulation in April through the final issue of the bonds that brought the plan to fruition in October 1924. The London Conference of July and August operated in a more businesslike climate than any since the world war. It foreshadowed the atmosphere that would increasingly pervade diplomacy in the later 1920s. Debts and loans, tariffs and trade, industrial cartels and arrangements, indeed the whole nexus of international economic relationships was to play an increasingly important role in reshaping—to France's disadvantage—the international political and military structure erected by the peace conference of 1919.

The Vagaries of Postwar Financial Experience

A retrospective look at French financial experience will illuminate the problems that reached crisis proportions in 1924. When Poincaré's cabinet took office in January 1922, the position of the French treasury seemed on its way to substantial improvement. This improvement resulted, paradoxically, from a business depression that began in the fall of 1920 and continued through the end of the following year. The economic downturn left a great deal of capital idle. Therefore, even though the budget remained badly in deficit, the government experienced no immediate difficulty in covering its needs by floating short-term treasury bonds. The depression also caused a fall in the wholesale price level. Following the classic pattern, exports increased. The abnormally large surge of imports that had distorted accounts soon after the war virtually disappeared. The franc had in any event depreciated in 1919–20 somewhat less than considerations of fundamental economics would have justified, because speculators betting on eventual reappreciation of the currency to the prewar gold parity buoyed the franc through their purchases. Now that the closing of the balance-of-payments deficit ended one important cause of depreciation, the drop in the exchange value of the franc gradually came to an end.[4]

Yet another consequence of the depression was to make possible a contraction of the currency. The money supply served a still more important function in regulating the French economy than it did in England or America. The average Frenchman, on principle and by habit (and with the further motive of keeping his affairs secret from the tax collector), preferred to deal in cash rather than to use checks. The French businessman, in contrast with his Anglo-Saxon counterpart, kept large cash reserve funds and where possible avoided recourse to bank credit for expansion. (As one indication of this difference, the 3:2 ratio of bank deposits to currency in circulation in France compared with a 20:1 ratio in America and a 16:1 ratio in England.) Therefore, the sevenfold increase of currency in circulation during the period December 1913 to December 1920, from 5.7 to 37.9 milliard francs, held particular significance. This increase, most of which took the form of "extraordinary" advances by the Bank of France to the state, far exceeded the country's normal business requirements. It served as a major means of war finance, and constituted the leading cause of inflation as well.[5]

Both the Bank of France and the treasury considered this rise in fiduciary circulation an unavoidable but temporary phenomenon. With considerable pride, both sides in April 1920 endorsed the so-called François-Marsal Convention, which obligated the government to reimburse the Bank two milliard francs at the end of every year.[6] The first reimbursement took place without trouble at the end of 1921; it was facilitated by a decline in demand for currency resulting from the business slump. At the same time, for reasons essentially unrelated to reimbursement, the franc appreciated between December 1920 and April 1922 from 17.04 to 10.82 to the dollar. Most of the nation's financial managers interpreted this coincidence as evidence corroborating the view that through monetary deflation it would be possible to restore the franc to its prewar gold parity.[7]

4. League of Nations, *International Currency Experience* (Princeton, 1944), p. 113; Robert Murray Haig, *The Public Finances of Post-War France* (New York, 1929), p. 449.

5. Martin Wolfe, *The French Franc between the Wars, 1919–1939* (New York, 1951), pp. 25–26; David B. Goldey, "The Disintegration of the Cartel des Gauches and the Politics of French Government Finance, 1924–1928" (D. Phil. diss., Oxford University, 1961), p. 18; Margaret Myers, *Paris as a Financial Center* (New York, 1936), p. 128; David S. Landes, "French Entrepreneurship and Industrial Growth in the Nineteenth Century," *Journal of Economic History* 9 (May 1949): 45–61.

6. Wolfe, *French Franc*, pp. 28–29; Georges Lachapelle, *Le Crédit public* (Paris, 1932), pp. 109–16.

7. Robert Wolff, *Economie et finances de la France* (New York, 1943), pp. 152–53.

During the months when the franc was appreciating, J. P. Morgan & Co., the American banking house which had long served as financial adviser to the French government, repeatedly and insistently recommended that the nation take advantage of the favorable circumstances to stabilize its currency. Dwight W. Morrow,* chief expert on the French economy at Morgan's, was most impressed by France's rate of economic recovery since the Armistice. Morrow stood convinced that, wartime inflation notwithstanding, French public finance had never gotten out of hand. He thought that France "could not if she would and should not if she could attempt to bring the franc back to gold parity." But like other Morgan partners, he remained confident that France possessed the resources to manage its public debt and approach stabilization at then current levels—even without significant help from reparations. Authorities in Paris, however, scouted the idea of immediate stabilization. They insisted that to fix a gold redemption value for their paper currency below the metallic value would constitute a repudiation of the domestic debt. The paper franc, they believed, would reach a "natural level" in world money markets, and then over a long period of years would gradually work its way back to its gold equivalent.[8]

In cold reality, a permanent deflationary movement of this amplitude was out of the question. Continued appreciation of the franc on the exchange and a concomitant fall of the internal price level would make the "real" value of the internal debt so heavy that enough tax revenue could not possibly be raised to pay interest on it. In other words, the franc would have to be stabilized at some level at which the claims of the French rentier for interest and amortization could be met by the proportion of earned income which the French taxpayer was willing to devote to that purpose.[9] What should this level have been? Considering the size of the debt and the extent of reconstruction yet to be completed, it can be

*Dwight W. Morrow (1873–1931), Wall Street lawyer, 1899–1914; partner, J. P. Morgan & Co., 1914–27; adviser to the Allied Maritime Transport Council, 1918; ambassador to Mexico, 1927–29; delegate to the London Naval Conference, 1930; senator from New Jersey, 1930–31. Extremely knowledgeable about international finance, Morrow claimed to be indifferent to wealth and was never entirely happy on Wall Street; he possessed a scholar's cast of mind and often made a show of regretting not being a college professor; "a completely civilized human creature . . . high-minded and right-minded" (Jean Monnet); the only man who had ever "voluntarily quitted a really first-class business like J. P. Morgan to associate himself with a second-class business such as the government of the United States" (Will Rogers).

8. Dwight W. Morrow to J. P. Morgan, 14 March 1921; N. Dean Jay to Morgan, Harjes et Cie, 25 February 1922; Morrow to Roland W. Boyden, 25 September 1922; Morrow with the assistance of Prof. Joseph S. Davis, "Memorandum on the Economic and Financial Condition of France," 15 April 1921 (Dwight W. Morrow Papers, Amherst College Library, Amherst, Mass. [hereafter cited as DWM]).

9. For an elegant contemporary formulation see John Maynard Keynes, *A Tract on Monetary Reform* (London, 1923), and "The French Franc," in his *Essays in Persuasion* (New York, 1931), pp. 105–13; also Goldey, "Disintegration of the Cartel des Gauches," pp. 21–22.

argued—in the light of modern economic theory—that a policy of moderate, carefully controlled deficit finance represented a reasonable method of apportioning the costs. In short, France was wise to accept a certain degree of further inflation before stabilization. The effect of the alternative policy of deflation, or even of balancing the budget strictly, would have been to depress general business and employment conditions below a socially tolerable level. John Maynard Keynes suggested in retrospect that France, by avoiding deflationary sacrifices, inadvertently handled postwar finance better than did England, where orthodox fiscal policy contributed to the sluggish performance of the British economy in the 1920s.[10]

At this time, however, the effects of fiscal policy on the economy were imperfectly understood. The French did not discuss the fiscal options in this way at all. Debate focused instead on management of the monetary system and the public debt. Confidence of financial markets at home and even abroad depended as much on the treasury's solvency as on an assessment of broader trends in the economy. Many, even in business circles, hailed the appreciation of the franc during 1920–22 without understanding how it contributed to the industrial slowdown. Forces all along the political spectrum agreed that the most important object of financial policy should be to avoid additional inflation which would exacerbate social maladjustments as well as undermine confidence in government securities.

While the franc was rising in value, the Finance Ministry succeeded in following contradictory policies. It carried out a policy of monetary deflation as stipulated by the François-Marsal Convention, reducing the state's debt to the Bank of France and consequently sustaining public hopes for a progressive revaluation of the currency and of *rentes* (long-term government bonds). At the same time it practiced fiscal inflation on a scale hitherto unknown. The war had so disrupted both the technical services of the Finance Ministry and the country's private financial apparatus that no one could tell precisely what government receipts and expenditures had been for any period since 1914.[11] It is clear, however, that budget deficits for the postwar years exceeded those for the war years.[12] Deficit financing of ordinary government operations and massive expenditures of borrowed funds for reconstruction of the devastated areas masked for a time the aggregate economic effects of monetary deflation.[13]

This double policy of fiscal inflation and monetary deflation appeared

10. Keynes, *Essays in Persuasion*, pp. 116–17.
11. Wolfe, *French Franc*, p. 24.
12. Haig estimates the deficit for 1919–22 at 130 milliard francs, compared with a deficit of 128 milliards for 1914–18 (*Public Finances*, p. 432).
13. Ibid., pp. 413–43.

feasible only because the French public expected large payments from Germany that would expedite early retirement of the huge debt incurred in the so-called recoverable budget. As illusions over the size of German payments diminished, French investors and especially foreign holders of francs began to take alarm. Continued government budget deficits, they recognized, would ineluctably lead to monetary depreciation sooner or later. The franc in fact began a slow depreciation on the exchange in May 1922. So long as the adjustment of the domestic price level lagged, moderate depreciation provided a welcome stimulus for the export sector of the economy, but in the long run, it signaled danger for the French treasury.

At the beginning of 1922 the industrial recession still made it easy for the treasury to borrow funds. As the economic upturn gathered momentum in the spring of that year, difficulties began to appear on the horizon for the treasury and the Crédit National. In order to attract investors, they found it necessary to raise the interest rate on the latest long-term bonds issued to finance reconstruction in the devastated areas. This reduced the attractiveness of short-term national defense bonds. With a view to saving money, the treasury traditionally kept interest rates on short-term bonds well below commercial rates and even below the Bank of France's discount rate. In the best of times this was a risky policy—one which foreign critics could explain only by hypothesizing that the treasury must be working under the assumption that "the laws of the dismal science, though well enough in their way, are inapplicable to *la belle France*."[14] In 1922, investors cashed in some of their short-term bonds in order to take advantage of the higher rate on the long-term flotation, and for the first time, the treasury failed to obtain the new resources it sought.[15]

Permanent treasury officials viewed this development with mounting concern. In the months before the Ruhr occupation, many of them acquired the conviction that drastic changes in treasury policy would become unavoidable should any further delay ensue in securing tangible reparations receipts. Whatever illusions politicians and the directing spirits of the Bank of France might harbor, the permanent officials of the French treasury generally exhibited a clear-sighted understanding of the

14. Russell C. Leffingwell of J. P. Morgan & Co., "Memorandum on French Public Debt," 19 May 1925, Box 95, Folder 9, Thomas W. Lamont Papers, Baker Library, Harvard Business School, Boston, Mass. (hereafter cited as TWL Box/Folder). Leffingwell and other foreign critics of French finance believed throughout the 1920s that the treasury would do better to "meet the market price for money."

15. Georges Lachapelle, *Le Crédit public*, pp. 136–40. Haig, *Public Finances*, pp. 229–37, notes the unreliability of Finance Ministry statistics regarding the amount of short-term debt outstanding. A large discrepancy that came to light in March 1922, though in the government's favor, undermined investor confidence in treasury accounting procedures.

financial choices facing the nation. Jean Parmentier,* director of the *Mouvement général des fonds* (a position equivalent to permanent under secretary) summarized the disquiet they felt on 14 November 1922 in a long memorandum to Finance Minister Charles de Lasteyrie.[16]

Germany had financed government operations since the Armistice by pure and simple inflation—the printing of bank notes without any real economic underpinning. In contrast, Parmentier noted, the French state had met expenses amounting to well over twice its revenue from taxation by legitimate borrowing from its own nationals. Monetary inflation, properly speaking, had been avoided. While currency in circulation increased from some 31.1 milliard francs to 37.7 milliards in the year 1919, it had actually decreased slightly since then, to 36.8 milliards. Parmentier pinpointed the main weakness in the government's financial strategy: the need to issue the major portion of its bonds not on a perpetual or long-term basis, but as short-term or "floating" debt. By late 1922 some 76.6 milliard francs worth of short-term paper, with maturity periods ranging from one month to one year, was outstanding. The sum was so large that it dwarfed the government's normal annual revenue. Parmentier conceded that economic and political uncertainty had affected the bond market in such a way that resort to this expedient was unavoidable. Nevertheless, until the short-term debt could be consolidated, it had to be continually renewed. This constituted the treasury's greatest problem and posed evident perils.

Parmentier argued against the view that these short-term obligations represented "disguised inflation." Holders of the bonds considered them not an instrument of payment (analogous to a demand deposit) but rather a means of saving or a temporary haven for industrial reserve funds. So long as confidence persisted, they would convert them under normal circumstances only into other forms of saving, securities, or real estate.[17] But since the national defense and treasury bonds figured as a

*Jean Victor Guislain Parmentier, born 1883, joined Inspectorate of Finance in 1908 and rose meteorically, becoming deputy director of finance for Morocco within five years; fought on the western front, twice wounded and cited for bravery, 1914–15; served as assistant private secretary to the finance minister, 1917; deputy director at the Central Administration, 1919–21; then director of the *Mouvement général des fonds* until he resigned in protest in March 1923. Universally held in high regard for his technical competence, Parmentier served on the Dawes Committee and later as French representative on the Transfer Committee to oversee operation of the Dawes Plan, but devoted most of his later life to amassing a large fortune in banking, insurance, steel, transport, and the electrical industry.

16. Parmentier to Lasteyrie, 14 November 1922, copy in Edouard Herriot Papers, Ministry of Foreign Affairs, Quai d'Orsay, Paris; first published in *L'Avenir*, 2 February 1928; quoted in part by Lachapelle, *Le Crédit public*, pp. 140–46.

17. The Bank of France was legally obliged to reimburse national defense bonds due within three months on demand at face value minus a discount equal to the prevailing bank rate. Holders of longer-term paper could secure a loan amounting to 80% of face value. Nevertheless, scholars have upheld Parmentier's view that the population at large did not regard these bonds as a means of payment. See the excellent discussion of the controversy in Eleanor Lansing Dulles, *The French Franc, 1914–1928* (New York, 1929), pp. 241–53.

potential form of liquid capital, the public authorities had in effect lost complete control over the money supply. As Parmentier realized, if the population's needs (measured by the volume of business and movement of prices) were to mount, investors would simply not renew the bonds. In this event, it would be impossible to avoid "an increase in the fiduciary circulation covered by advances from the Bank to the state." Furthermore, if confidence in the franc were shaken, the French people and foreign holders of franc balances alike would attempt to exchange francs for real values, and short-term treasury bonds would either be used directly as a means of payment or cashed promptly when they came due. The "potential monetary inflation" represented by the short-term bonds, Parmentier warned, would "suddenly become a real inflation, and the circulation would be carried at a stroke to more than 100 milliards." Depreciation of the franc would follow rapidly. Caught in the vicious cycle of inflation, the franc "would not take long to catch up with the mark in the plunge toward the abyss."

A fall in the franc's foreign exchange value, Parmentier observed, would be the first symptom of panic and at the same time a cause of it. The laws against export of capital afforded France some measure of protection against its own nationals beginning the movement. But the French government held no powers to stop foreign holders of francs from throwing them on the market if they lost confidence. A prolonged fall of the franc might end in panic, and a corresponding rise of the internal price level would certainly follow. And even if the nation were to escape a complete catastrophe, the treasury would have to raise interest rates on short-term bonds in order to induce investors to renew them. The costs of debt service to the treasury would increase far out of proportion to the benefits derived.

All this was unexceptionable economic analysis. Parmentier did not hesitate to draw the somber conclusion: "From now on, those who consider the situation coldly may take the view that if the French state continues to borrow, it will be manifestly incapable in the future of paying the arrears on its debt at the present value of the franc, unless it carries out a capital levy victimizing all holders of francs." Current activity on the exchanges indicated that many foreign holders of francs were acquiring the conviction that depreciation did lie ahead. Of course, the great mass of Frenchmen still hoped that reparations would soon make further borrowing unnecessary. But by November 1922, after months of fruitless negotiations and makeshift adjournments from one moratorium to another, Parmentier was realistic enough to understand that a practical solution to the reparations problem was too uncertain and lay too far in the future to figure importantly in the French treasury's immediate plans. The only way to avoid disastrous exchange depreciation and inflation on the German model, it seemed to him, was to cut back drastically on government expenditures and to move without delay toward a balanced budget. For the coming year, Parmentier proposed to reduce by half the projected borrowing program of 29 milliard francs.

This would require not merely limitations in military expenditures and rigorous pruning in other parts of the ordinary budget, but also suspension of compensation payments for material damages in the devastated areas, and revision of the military pensions law to strike everyone but disabled veterans off the rolls.

Parmentier continued to advocate retrenchment through early 1923, repeatedly appealing to his own chief, to Minister of Liberated Regions Charles Reibel, and to Poincaré himself. Finance Minister Charles de Lasteyrie* shared the bureaucrats' sense of urgency. But he was unable to convince his cabinet colleagues to make such a drastic and politically hazardous reduction in the budget. The members of the government, Poincaré not least among them, exhibited great sensitivity to charges voiced in the Chamber that their much vaunted firmness toward Germany had proved hollow and brought no financial relief. Divided over future reparations strategy and the advisability of a Ruhr occupation, the ministers did not wish to exacerbate the parliamentary rumblings by amputating popular government services at this delicate moment.

Moreover, Parmentier's principal target, the Ministry of Liberated Regions, would not agree that financial penury justified suspension of the war damages legislation, even when the assurance was given that some building construction might in practice continue.[18] It was no secret that the procedures governing evaluation and reimbursement of war damages, adopted when everyone thought Germany would foot the entire bill, were excessively generous. Indeed, one quite moderate member of the Chamber Finance Commission termed them "madly prodigal" and "a veritable scandal," though in retrospect it appears that the fault lay as much in administrative confusion as in outright fraud.[19] But

*Count Charles Ferdinand de Lasteyrie du Saillant (1877–1936), lineal descendant of Lafayette; graduate of the Ecole des Chartes, lawyer, inspector of finance, lecturer at the Ecole des Sciences Politiques; handled financial questions connected with the blockade at the Foreign Ministry, 1915–17; financial delegate on the Armistice Commission and secretary-general of the Reparation Commission at the peace conference. Elected to the Chamber as member of the *Entente républicaine*, 1919–24, 1928–36, he became *rapporteur* of the budget of recoverable expenses; first attracted national attention with articles denouncing fraudulent German bankruptcy after a tour there in 1921; served as finance minister, January 1922-March 1924; later identified himself with the principles of "order" and "authority" as an opponent of the Popular Front. With his long nose, prominent ears, and sharp chin protruding from a narrow-boned face set off by formal dress and exaggerated wing-tip collars, Lasteyrie cut a figure made to order for Paris press cartoonists.

18. Much of the following information derives from a second letter from Parmentier to Lasteyrie, 19 February 1923, Herriot Papers; published by *L'Avenir*, 2 February 1928, and quoted in part by Lachapelle, *Le Crédit public*, pp. 151–53.

19. Lucien Lamoureux, "Souvenirs politiques, 1919–1940," p. 626, microfilm of MS at Bibliothèque de Documentation Internationale Contemporaine, Nanterre. *Le Quotidien* cited some flagrant abuses in a series on "The Panama of the Devastated Regions" in the fall of 1923. But compare the scholarly assessments: Edmond Michel, *Les Dommages de guerre de la France et leur réparation* (Paris, 1932); Jacques Romanet du Caillaud, *L'Indemnité de dommages de guerre: Son évaluation, son remploi, son paiement* (Paris, 1923); and Alfred

officials at the Ministry of Liberated Regions felt that it was now too late to undertake a fundamental reassessment of reimbursement awards, especially when the issue was so emotionally charged. Immediately after the war, priority had been given to rebuilding the industrial infrastructure in the area devastated by the Germans. Little had been done with residential reconstruction up to the middle of 1922. Every week Charles Reibel and his top aides went out to visit the stricken departments, and they were "very moved" to find people still living in wooden barracks and often using makeshift plumbing and heating facilities. Reibel and his staff refused to evaluate the issues in terms of cold economic statistics when human suffering—which they had witnessed personally—was involved.[20] After examining various methods of stretching out the reconstruction program, for example by paying claims with thirty-year annuity bonds instead of in cash, ministry officials finally came out against such disguised postponement of payment. At most they agreed to shave projected expenditures for 1923 from 13 to 11 milliards—a reduction hardly of the magnitude necessary to relieve the anxiety of financial specialists at the rue de Rivoli.

Thus political circumstances made it impossible to follow Parmentier's advice to temper inflationary fiscal policy by reducing expenditures. Meanwhile, the exigencies of politics obliged the government to continue its deflationary monetary policy by reimbursing the Bank of France's "advances" as stipulated in the François-Marsal Convention. Given the size of the floating debt, this deflationary monetary policy exposed the treasury to continual embarrassment. Whenever investors failed to renew part of the short-term debt, the government had no way to meet its expenses except by additional borrowing from the Bank. As early as April 1922 the permanent staff at the rue de Rivoli—without challenging the principle of deflation *after* consolidation of the debt—urged termination of the François-Marsal Convention. They emphasized that a drop in the exchange rate could have a deleterious influence on the floating debt, and thus on the dependence of the treasury on the Bank. The burden of upward spiraling interest rates necessary to keep up bond subscriptions in a period of monetary depreciation was too heavy a price to pay for maintaining the agreement with the Bank. Parmentier and his deputy, Pierre de Mouÿ, conceded that a more flexible arrangement—one that did not require mandatory monetary deflation—might temporarily fracture foreign and domestic confidence. But, they argued, it was better to make the change at a time when the government could still employ counterbalancing fiscal measures to in-

Sauvy, *Histoire économique de la France entre les deux guerres*, 2 vols. (Paris, 1965–67), 1:183–212.

20. Personal interview with Charles Reibel, 2 March 1965.

crease public confidence than to let things drag along to an even less favorable juncture.[21]

Lasteyrie declined to follow this advice, and eventually Parmentier resigned. Because of the treasury's straitened circumstances, however, the Bank of France gave approval on 21 December 1922 to an "exceptional" arrangement, reducing the authorized maximum of advances by a mere 1 milliard francs—half the expected reimbursement. It gave consent reluctantly and only under extreme pressure. Leading officials of the Bank have been accused of focusing single-mindedly on two figures, the magnitude of the Bank's advances to the state and the corresponding increase in the total money supply, as the sole determinants of inflation.[22] Did they really believe that the process of monetary inflation could be reversed without much consideration of fiscal policy, the balance of payments, or the volume of the debt, foreign and domestic? Apparently certain Bank officials did entertain the rather simplistic notion that over a period of years, progressive reduction of the permissible upper limits or *plafonds*, governing the level of advances and the amount of currency in circulation would "restore" the currency, so that when the advances were entirely repaid, the franc would recover its "intrinsic" prewar value. Modern notions of flexible currency management being developed in other countries, such as the concept of legal reserve requirements, were held not to apply to the French case. The "intrinsic" value of the bank note depended on the amount of gold in the vaults of the Bank of France. This gold, according to the theory prevailing at the Bank, had to be kept intact at all costs as a guarantee of the franc's intrinsic value, and therefore could not be flexibly employed as might otherwise seem desirable to maintain the currency's exchange value.

The criticism directed against the Bank of France was undoubtedly warranted. However, its governor, Georges Robineau,* did offer a de-

*Georges Robineau (1860–1927) grew up in Bar-le-Duc with Poincaré and remained his close friend throughout life; trained in law rather than finance but spent his entire career beginning in 1887 at the Bank of France; rose through bureaucratic ranks to the position of director, Discount Department; served as governor from August 1920 until dismissed for resisting de facto stabilization in June 1926. With habitual dark suit, white walrus moustache, and grave expression, he looked typecast for the part, but he put allegiance to the Regents and stockholders of the Bank above his role as a modern central banker.

21. Mouÿ reviewed the circumstances of this démarche, which took place on 15 April 1922, in a later note for Minister of Finance Etienne Clémentel, 27 June 1924, Herriot Papers; see also Parmentier to Lasteyrie, 19 February 1923, ibid.

22. Many treatments of the monetary policy of the Bank of France leadership are tinged with passion. The usually sober banker Robert Wolff, *Economie et finances de la France* (New York, 1943), pp. 137–52, strikes a revealingly polemical tone. Goldey, who used some Bank of France records in his "Disintegration of the Cartel des Gauches," pp. 26–29, is also critical. The leading contemporary analyst, Georges Lachapelle, *Les Batailles du franc* (Paris, 1928), and *Le Crédit public*, pp. 147–49, showed more sympathy for the Bank. On the Bank of France's general policy, see also A. Dauphin-Meunier, *La Banque, 1919–1935* (Paris, 1937); A. Schneider, *La Banque de France depuis 1914* (Nancy, 1933); and two lectures

fense of the François-Marsal Convention on sophisticated pragmatic grounds. Robineau distinguished between money placed in circulation as a consequence of advances from the Bank to the state, and that resulting from "commercial" demand. The former, he stated, possessed a "rigid and artificial character" and often increased at an inopportune time in the business cycle. Commercial circulation, in contrast, could be expanded or contracted according to the needs of the economy. He desired, therefore, to liquidate the Bank's advances to the state as soon as possible, "though it be to make way for an equal commercial circulation, which would quite naturally follow the fluctuations in the general level of business and prices." Almost in the same breath, however, Robineau intimated that he was a deflationist after all. Insisting that France could maintain "relative stability" in the monetary sphere only by upholding confidence, he argued that the country should give first priority to managing its currency in such a way as to furnish no pretext for panic among foreign holders of franc balances. This seemed to him all the more imperative in view of the "precise proofs" obtained by the Bank of foreign designs against the franc's stability. Finally, Robineau wanted the state to repay the Bank so that in case of "dangerous unforeseen eventualities" it could come to the rescue again, as it had during the war, without risking monetary disaster.[23]

The Bank of France was not alone in believing that the slightest concession to monetary inflation might lead to catastrophe. This view was widely held—often almost with religious fervor—by the educated public, writers for the newspapers' financial pages, and by the overwhelming majority of the parliament. Most of the French elite at the time were abysmally ignorant even of the rudimentary principles of economics. A few specialists on the Paris law faculty—the one major educational institution stressing economics—were doubtless as sophisticated as any economists in the world. But the education of the Third Republic's governing class was oriented toward literature and the humanities. Economics simply did not figure as a standard part of the curriculum.[24]

---

by Jules Decamps, director of economic studies at the Bank, issued in pamphlet form as *Problèmes financiers d'après-guerre* (Paris, 1922), and *La Situation monétaire et l'avenir du franc* (Paris, 1925).

23. Georges Robineau to Louis Loucheur, 8 November 1922, Box 10G, Louis Loucheur Papers, Hoover Institution, Stanford University, Stanford, Calif.

24. This problem has received wide though not yet systematic attention. See "L'Enseignement économique en France et à l'étranger," in *Cinquantaire de la revue d'économie politique*, ed. C. Rist and G. Pirou (Paris, 1937), pp. 1–65; G. Vedel, "Le Rôle des croyances économiques dans la vie politique," *Revue française de science politique* 1 (January 1951): 40–50; D. W. Brogan, *France under the Republic: The Development of Modern France, 1870–1939* (New York and London, 1940), pp. 155–56; Marguerite Perrot, *La Monnaie et l'opinion publique en France et en Angleterre, 1924–1936* (Paris, 1955), esp. pp. 199–208. Numerous contemporaries touched on the issue, including André François-Poncet, *La Vie et l'oeuvre de Robert Pinot* (Paris, 1927), introduction; A. Siegfried, *Tableau des partis en France* (Paris, 1930), p. 40; F. Pietri, *Le Financier* (Paris, 1931), pp. 7, 39, 43.

What little economics middle-aged men in positions of responsibility remembered from their youth generally was irrelevant to monetary problems in the postwar world. A time-lag in the general diffusion of advances in economic knowledge is a well-known phenomenon: Keynes was to complain of it in his *General Theory.*[25] The problem was even more acute in France than in Anglo-Saxon countries.

Small wonder, then, that many, remembering the fate of the assignats in the French Revolution and contemplating the example of runaway inflation in Germany closer at hand, concluded that deflation remained the indispensable prerequisite for sound money. Even the partial departure from the François-Marsal Convention in December 1922 led to sharp criticism in parliament, where it was stigmatized as a moral lapse from a sacred obligation.[26] While opinion leaders were quick to take alarm at the slightest hint of monetary inflation, they remained at the same time apparently oblivious to the inflationary consequences of a lopsidedly unbalanced budget.

In this atmosphere Lasteyrie rejected his staff's advice to reduce government expenditure and to change monetary policy; both courses of action posed too many political risks. The finance minister reached the conclusion instead that only by means of higher taxes could he hope to reduce borrowing to manageable proportions. For Lasteyrie this represented a radical shift in position. Just a few months earlier, in October 1922, he had argued against raising taxes further before the ministry had increased its internal revenue staff and added to the sophistication of its tax collection procedures. He agreed—and indeed had long served as a leading spokesman for the view—that the 1920 tax increase had represented an "unprecedented" effort and that additional levies would compromise the chances for business recovery. He had not hesitated to pontificate upon the government's duty to employ "all means within its power" to force Germany to pay before demanding new sacrifices from the French people.[27] The failure of the London Conference in December 1922, however, put the quietus on such faint hopes as were still entertained at the rue de Rivoli that the French budget might profit from substantial German aid without further long delay.[28]

25. "In the field of economic and political philosophy there are not many who are influenced by new theories after they are 25 or 30 years of age, so that the ideas which civil servants and politicians and even agitators apply to current events are not likely to be the newest" (John Maynard Keynes, *The General Theory of Employment, Interest, and Money* [London, 1936], pp. 383–84).

26. See speeches by François-Marsal and Henry Bérenger in *Journal Officiel, Sénat, Débats parlementaires*, 30 December 1922, pp. 1659–62 (hereafter cited as *J.O.S. Déb.*). Cf. however the defense of a flexible reimbursement policy by Alexandre Ribot, who had been finance minister when the advances began in 1914.

27. *Journal Officiel, Chambre des Députés, Documents parlementaires*, 1922, no. 4220, pp. 99–118 (hereafter cited as *J.O.C. Doc.*); *J.O.C. Déb.*, 24 October 1922, p. 2803, 26 October 1922, pp. 2845–51, 13 November 1922, pp. 3077–82, 3091–94. See also the brief summary in Haig, *Public Finances*, pp. 78–83.

28. See Lasteyrie's account in *J.O.C. Déb.*, 14 February 1924, p. 723.

The Succession of Expedients in 1923

With evident discomfiture at the need to make a *volte-face*, Lasteyrie appeared in parliament on 11 January 1923—the very day the Ruhr was occupied—to ask for a *double décime*, a 20 percent across-the-board increase in almost all French taxes. This would cover the expected budget deficit for one year. The embarrassed minister tried to merchandise this request as a temporary sacrifice. He held out the prospect that within a short time the Ruhr occupation would bring a favorable outcome to the reparations dispute, and that this, with the help of improved methods of tax collection, would allow a return to previously existing tax rates.[29]

The *double décime* met with bitter criticism in the press and ran into headlong opposition in the Chamber and Senate Finance commissions. These commissions were wracked by internal political cleavages: they numbered among their members proponents of almost every conceivable financial alternative. They could reach agreement only in opposition to the tax increase proposed by the government.[30] And the cabinet soon made it clear that it did not intend to risk a vote of confidence on the matter. Poincaré, to be sure, had always privately regretted the parliament's failure in 1920 to adopt the heavy tax schedule worked out by the Senate Finance Commission under Paul Doumer, instead of the much smaller increase finally voted. But all parties had nurtured the hope that as business recovered, the consequent increase in revenue would progressively eliminate the deficit in the ordinary budget, and that the treasury's borrowing powers would suffice to meet the needs of the devastated districts until German reparations became available. Certainly by January 1923 it should have been perfectly clear that such calculations were illusory. Nonetheless, Poincaré believed that the exigencies of parliamentary politics made it inadvisable for him to push too hard. The essential issue for his ministry was the occupation of the Ruhr. A conflict with the Chamber over increased taxes could only obstruct efforts to rally the population behind the Ruhr policy.[31]

The *double décime* was sidetracked. Months dragged on while the Chamber Finance Commission disputed with the Ministry of Finance over a technical issue: the best administrative means to discourage tax evasion on bearer securities. Meanwhile, government operations were financed by provisional monthly appropriations known as *douzièmes*, an expedient to which the nation had resorted periodically since 1914 whenever financial confusion became greatest. Finally, the Senate Finance Commission suggested a new method of estimating tax revenue in anticipation of business improvement rather than on the basis of the

29. *J.O.C. Doc.*,1923, no. 5432, pp. 8–10.

30. Edouard Bonnefous, *Histoire politique de la Troisième République*, vol. 3, *L'Après-guerre, 1919–1924* (Paris, 1959), pp. 341–42, 359–64.

31. *J.O.S. Déb.*,10 April 1925, pp. 850–58.

previous year's return. This ingenious accounting innovation permitted adoption of a "balanced" regular budget on 30 June 1923—just six months behind schedule.[32] It was already time to begin discussion of the budget for 1924. If precedent provided any guide, consideration of the new budget would drag on inconveniently into the election campaign planned for the spring of 1924 and also retard work on other essential measures. So the legislators fastened on the happy expedient of applying the 1923 budget to the following fiscal year as well.[33]

This evasion meant that borrowing would have to continue as the source of funds for most of the "recoverable" budget and a large segment of other government operations, though because of the confusion in treasury accounts, no one knew precisely how much.[34] From the start of the Ruhr occupation the foreign exchange value of the franc began slowly to decline and the retail price level began to increase. The public, however, did not understand the reasons for these developments. The press attributed the price rise to "speculators" and to the policies followed by the Agriculture Ministry, whose hapless head, Henri Chéron, became known as "Chéron-la-vie-chère." Short-term fluctuations in the franc-dollar exchange rate, influenced by speculative demand, did show a marked correlation with political developments in the Ruhr, at the Lausanne Conference on Near Eastern problems, and elsewhere. This encouraged even the informed public to ignore the effect of fiscal policy on the long-term downtrend.[35]

In August 1923 *Le Temps*, reflecting typical establishment views, categorically denied that the state of French public finances was so precarious as to justify "serious anxiety." Pointing to the prediction of a bountiful harvest, the flourishing state of foreign trade, and the absence of monetary inflation as measured by advances to the treasury from the Bank of France, *Le Temps* concluded with characteristic optimism: "It is reasonable to expect that sooner or later the franc will adjust itself to this ensemble of favorable indicators, and that the machinations of international speculation will not succeed in maintaining our exchange rate below the value which these indicators justify. For it is clear that the latest rise of foreign currencies is due solely to speculation, that is, to factors of a psychological and political order."[36]

Few foreign observers were this sanguine. At the Reparation Commission, United States delegate James A. Logan drew up an evaluation of French financial prospects for Secretary Hughes in which he placed

32. See Bokanowski's final report, *J.O.C. Doc.*, 1923, no. 6244, pp. 1330 ff.

33. Lachapelle, *Le Crédit public*, pp. 154–55.

34. Haig, who analyzes problems in ascertaining government expenditures precisely for this period and compares various attempts to do so, estimates net borrowing for 1923 at between 15.8 and 18.1 milliard francs (*Public Finances*, pp. 88, 432).

35. See the excellent monthly reports on the franc-dollar exchange rates by Charles D. Westcott, U.S. economist consul in Paris, U.S. 851.5151/14–32.

36. "Notre change," *Le Temps*, 14 August 1923.

increased taxation in the forefront as the "essential factor" in ultimate financial rehabilitation. Even should one accept the French treasury's habitually optimistic interpretation of the data as accurate, Logan pointed out, the outlook remained grave. Direct reconstruction of public facilities in the devastated areas by the state (rebuilding railway lines, highways, and canals, filling in trenches and shell holes, clearing barbed wire and unexploded shells) was now reaching completion. But private reconstruction in the ravaged departments would stretch on at least through 1926, and by the time the government finished paying for it, the total domestic French debt would probably exceed 320 milliard francs—some ten to fifteen times annual government revenue.[37]

Was so great a debt manageable without further inflation? Logan thought that it might be, but only under certain conditions. The first requirement was monetary stabilization, which would facilitate consolidation and refunding of the entire debt over a period of several years at a sharply reduced interest rate. Ordinary tax revenue, meanwhile, should be increased by a quarter—from 20 to 25 milliards. A stringent economy drive would be necessary to reduce ordinary domestic expenditure from 7 to 6 milliards annually. Finally, international peace was essential if military expenditures were to be kept within the 5 milliard range, without recourse to the sort of supplemental credits that paid the French army's bills in the Ruhr and the Levant. Even should all this be achieved, the French budget could still not be balanced without "substantial reparations payments" from Germany, on the order of $250 million a year (an amount implying a total German payment exceeding 2 milliard gold marks annually). Furthermore, Logan reminded Washington, "no resources whatsoever" were available to meet indebtedness due the United States and Great Britain unless derived from German payments above $250 million a year.

Foreign bankers in Paris who made similar calculations looked on with admiration mixed with no little wonder as the French people continued to manifest confidence in the government's solvency by keeping up their purchases of treasury bond offerings.[38] The first Crédit National loan of 1923 proved a great success, though it was placed on the market as French troops were marching into the Ruhr and in the middle of Chamber debates showing the financial situation to be far from satisfactory. It was really too much to expect that such results would continue indefinitely, and later in 1923, as inflation increased, funds were withdrawn from short-term government securities. An upturn in the business cycle resulted in more favorable private investment oppor-

37. James A. Logan to Charles Evans Hughes, 2 March 1923, U.S. 851.51/385.

38. N. Dean Jay to Thomas Lamont, 8 February 1923 (enclosed in Lamont to Hughes, 12 March 1923), Box 30, Charles Evans Hughes Papers, Library of Congress, Washington, D.C.

tunities. Though the money managers increased interest rates, subscriptions to short-term treasury and national defense bonds lagged behind redemptions by over 4 milliards during the year. Consequently, the treasury was obliged to call on the Bank of France in August and October for advances right up to the legal limit. It avoided exceeding the stipulated maximum only by arranging secret temporary loans from private credit institutions, disguised as "advances" on the anticipated yield of future bond issues. In October also, a long-term Crédit National flotation, though marketed with a high rate of return, was subscribed almost entirely with funds withdrawn from short-term bonds, the total of which plunged accordingly. This provided a clear indication that the French treasury's capacity to borrow at reasonable interest rates had been fundamentally impaired.[39]

The permanent officials at the treasury became alarmed. Pierre de Mouÿ,* who had succeeded Parmentier as director of the *Mouvement général des fonds*, warned Lasteyrie in October and again, most insistently, in December 1923 that the situation was "desperate." Unless the government was prepared to change its fiscal strategy radically, by proposing a tax increase so massive as seemingly to lie outside the bounds of practical politics, Mouÿ saw no alternative to immediate termination of the François-Marsal Convention. This agreement, he stated plainly, was based on a "complete failure to understand" the financial techniques that had permitted development of the floating debt to its current proportions. Recourse to advances from the Bank of France within broad limits served as the unique safeguard of flexibility in the management of that debt. The treasury was even now grazing the upper limit of permissible borrowing from the Bank. Rather than reduce further the maximum of advances to the state which the Bank was authorized to extend, the treasury should insist that the maximum be raised back to the level prevailing before "reimbursements" began in 1920. If this were not done, Mouÿ asserted categorically, the treasury would have no alternative but to sue for a secret advance from the Bank of France. It would also have to resort to irregular borrowing from private credit institutions in order to disguise its plight. The latter expedient was all the more undesirable because the treasury, having scheduled a new Crédit National

*Louis Henri Pierre de Mouÿ, b. 1887, member of a family distinguished in diplomacy; entered general accounting office (*Cour des comptes*) at the Finance Ministry, 1911; served in uniform, 1914–19; became Parmentier's protégé and assistant director at the Central Administration, 1921; named director of the *Mouvement général des fonds*, March 1923; alienated political superiors by his forthright advice and was kicked upstairs to position of director of the customs, December 1924; retired from government service to become vice-president of Société Générale, 1930.

39. Lachapelle, *Le Crédit public*, pp. 155–61; also Robineau to Minister of Finance, 29 April 1925, Herriot Papers.

refunding operation for the beginning of 1924, counted on these same private banks to reserve their free resources so that they could serve as purchasers of last resort in the loan drive.[40]

This was an updated version of the advice given by Parmentier a year earlier; once again, and for similar reasons, Lasteyrie hesitated to follow it. In the public mind, to renounce the François-Marsal Convention was tantamount to opening the door to uncontrolled inflation. Governor Robineau and his staff at the Bank of France sought to foster such sentiments by calculated leaks to the financial press. The Bank's maneuver outraged Mouÿ and sophisticated legislators like Maurice Bokanowski of the Chamber Finance Commission, who understood how senseless it was to elevate constriction of the money supply into a sacrosanct dogma that took precedence over all other considerations in the management of public finance. Nevertheless, the Bank's tactics met with success. André Tardieu's *Echo national* published a series of alarmist articles warning of a two-sou franc, and other newspapers followed suit.[41]

Lasteyrie crumbled under the pressure and on 14 December 1923 struck another compromise with Robineau. The treasury made a public show of fulfilling part of its commitment under the François-Marsal Convention by reimbursing the Bank 800 million francs and thus reducing the legal maximum of advances to 23.2 milliards. In return the Bank promised informally to subscribe, as circumstances required, to an unspecified quantity of one-month treasury bills, in effect placing resources from its free reserves at the treasury's disposal. This bookkeeping arrangement gave the treasury the right to draw unpublicized indirect advances from the Bank of France on an ongoing basis, though the Bank made no accounting, and treasury officials had no more than an approximate idea of the amount of assistance received at any particular time.

The governor of the Bank considered the understanding, which was never formalized in writing, an unfortunate necessity required by the treasury's straitened circumstances; it possessed, in his eyes, the merit of providing some leverage to force liquidation of the secret advances as soon as this became feasible. Permanent officials at the rue de Rivoli were also uneasy about this irregular procedure and about the risks of its possible disclosure on confidence in investment markets. Still, they were

40. Mouÿ to Lasteyrie, 13 December 1923, and Mouÿ note for Clémentel, 27 June 1924, Herriot Papers. See also *J.O.C. Déb.*, 9 April 1925, pp. 2146–47, for abridged versions of Mouÿ's memorandum of 16 October and letter of 13 December 1923.

41. Mouÿ to Lasteyrie, 13 December 1923, Herriot Papers; Maurice Bokanowski, "La Bataille du franc," 1 March 1924, Millerand Papers; *L'Echo national*, 9–12 December 1923; also *L'Information*, *Le Quotidien*, and *Le Figaro*, 9–15 December 1923. For a survey of press opinion on monetary phenomena, 1924–26, that indirectly illuminates public attitudes in the preceding period, see Marguerite Perrot, *La Monnaie et l'opinion publique en France et en Angleterre*, pp. 114–90.

obliged to take recourse to it on a permanent basis from January 1924 onward, as well as to a whole arsenal of other unorthodox measures.[42] Between January and April 1924 unacknowledged treasury borrowings from the Bank of France and from various deposit and investment banks exceeded 2.5 milliard francs.[43] In the late spring of 1924 these borrowings were temporarily reduced in magnitude, but never entirely repaid. The subterfuges eventually used to dissemble the real level of advances and currency in circulation were several: direct purchase or discount of all sorts of government securities by the Bank of France; credits extended to the treasury on the "anticipated" yield of taxes, customs, or national defense bonds; credits supplied in return for the temporary deposit of foreign exchange holdings earmarked for settlement of international accounts; discount of the deposit banks' commercial paper to free their resources for purchase of treasury bonds; and subsequently some even riskier schemes.[44]

But since these operations remained hidden from view, might not the publicly announced continuation of the François-Marsal Convention have constituted another of those imperfect compromises, distressing to the handful of monetary specialists, discussed more or less inadequately for a few days in the financial press, but soon dismissed by the man in the street as an abstruse question bearing little on his own life? It soon became evident that this was not to be the case, for during December 1923 a fall in the external value of the franc and a noteworthy increase in the cost of living were transformed with startling suddenness into major public issues.

The franc's depreciation was all the more unexpected because politically motivated speculation against the currency had appeared to ebb just weeks before. During most of 1923, speculative activity on the franc-dollar exchange responded more to psychological factors than to considerations of fundamental economics. The franc drifted downward during the Anglo-French diplomatic duel over the Ruhr occupation during that summer, but then staged a remarkable recovery in September 1923 in anticipation of the end of German passive resistance. It slipped again slightly when the reparations controversy was not immediately "solved" by some bold initiative. Yet once the German industrialists signed agreements in November with the Franco-Belgian industrial mission in the

42. Mouÿ to Lasteyrie, 13 December 1923; Mouÿ notes for Clémentel, 17 and 27 June 1924; Governor Georges Robineau to Finance Minister Clémentel, 29 April 1925, all in Herriot Papers.

43. Finance Minister François-Marsal statement for Raphaël Milliès-Lacroix, president of the Senate Finance Commission, 19 April 1924; see inexact reproduction in *Le Quotidien*, 9 April 1925, and Herriot's corrections, *J.O.C. Déb.*, 9 April 1925, pp. 2148–49. The standard authority, Emile Moreau, *Souvenirs d'un gouverneur de la Banque de France: Histoire de la stabilisation du franc, 1926–1928* (Paris, 1954), p. 6, understates the difference between the official and the true figures during this period and later.

44. Robineau to Clémentel, 29 April 1925, Herriot Papers.

TABLE 1 / Average Monthly Franc-Dollar Exchange Rates

Francs per Dollar			January 1922–September 1924			
	Jan.	Feb.	Mar.	Apr.	May	June
1922	12.30	11.50	11.10	10.80	10.97	11.45
1923	14.98	16.30	15.94	15.02	15.06	15.87
1924	21.43	22.66	21.70	16.37	17.36	19.11
	July	Aug.	Sept.	Oct.	Nov.	Dec.
1922	12.13	12.58	13.05	13.57	14.62	13.85
1923	16.98	17.70	17.14	16.81	18.19	19.02
1924	19.57	18.36	18.85			

Source: U.S. 851.5151/27–34.

Ruhr, promising to resume deliveries of reparations in kind, foreign observers concluded that the political situation "ceased to be the controlling factor in exchange fluctuations."[45] Nevertheless, the franc continued to plummet—from 15.92 to the dollar at the end of passive resistance to a low of 19.61 to the dollar at the end of 1923.[46]

For the full year, the decline in the franc's external value, after considerable intermediate fluctuation, was 30.94 percent (see table 1). The political storm, however, resulted from the increase in the domestic price level. According to statistical indices the cost of living rose 15 percent for the full year, 5 percent in the fourth quarter. Even more ominous, the wholesale price index, which generally anticipates future movement of retail prices, rose almost 8 percent in December alone.[47]

Moreover, because price increases were disproportionately large on such visible items as meat, bread, fruits, and vegetables, they appeared greater to the average consumer than the bare statistics would suggest. Such inflation posed evident political dangers for the government on the eve of a national election campaign. On 26 October, an interministerial committee had been set up under Keeper of the Seals Maurice Colrat to study ways of holding down the cost of living. But this committee skirted basic issues of fiscal policy and concerned itself instead with matters directly affecting the man in the street, such as rent controls and

45. Economist Consul Charles D. Westcott, "Franc-Dollar Exchange Rates during 1923," 9 January 1924, U.S. 851.5151/27. See also the sensible analysis in the London *Economist* for the whole period under discussion.

46. Dulles has collected daily dollar exchange rates on the Paris Bourse, and other important economic indices, in easily available tabular form (*French Franc*, pp. 455–80).

47. Ibid., pp. 519–26; Lachapelle, *Le Crédit public*, p. 162.

wholesalers' markups. It did not get far. A Chamber Finance Commission subcommittee also conducted a perfunctory investigation. In urban centers, opposition newspapers grumbled that by imposing grain and meat duties, the Agriculture Ministry had protected rural interests at the consumers' expense. In the autumn months people living on fixed incomes—state functionaries, municipal workers, retired folk—held numerous meetings in Paris and the large provincial cities, and occasionally even staged demonstrations for higher wages. Still, it was only in the second half of December and then with a sudden fury that the theme of *la vie chère* became a universal preoccupation, discussed daily on the front pages of the newspapers, in the Chamber lobbies, and in cafés across the country.[48]

Lasteyrie evidently hoped that despite the mounting accumulation of financial difficulties, France would somehow squeak through again without a crisis. Speaking to the Senate on 26 December 1923, the finance minister struck a note of guarded but definite optimism, even of self-congratulation. After rehearsing the favorable economic indicators, he concluded that the franc was "undervalued" on the exchange purely for psychological reasons. "Certain foreign newspapers" had dared to assert that France did not have the courage to vote new taxes and would be forced into a policy of inflation, but these were "abominable calumnies." Germany's failure to carry out the Treaty of Versailles provided the sole remaining cause of difficulty, Lasteyrie declared, and even in this area—in view of the successful direct operation of productive pledges in the Ruhr and the imminent beginning of the Expert Committees' investigation—there were "certain possibilities shining on the horizon."[49]

Henry Bérenger, the cynical *rapporteur-général*, and his colleagues on the Senate Finance Commission accepted these assurances with an outward show of relief. But did Lasteyrie convince himself by repetition of a script whose main outlines were now only too familiar? More likely he was whistling in the dark to keep up his courage. For at the same time, the Finance Ministry quietly revised its projected schedule of 1924 short-term reconstruction bond offerings downward from 11 to 8 milliards, notwithstanding the wails of protest that would inevitably follow from the devastated areas.[50] Another disappointment followed shortly. Banking houses in London and New York, asked by the treasury to float loans for the Crédit National and the state railways, flatly ruled out such operations until the French government changed its financial policies.[51]

48. The rising public agitation over inflation is best followed in the press of the Cartel des Gauches, the left-wing electoral bloc. See particularly *L'Oeuvre* and *Le Quotidien*, October–December 1923. Both newspapers ran a series of articles on the issue.

49. *J.O.S. Déb.*, 26 December 1923, pp. 2104–8.

50. See Lasteyrie's subsequent statement, *J.O.C. Déb.*, 14 February 1924, p. 725.

51. Lachapelle, *Les Batailles du franc*, p. 115.

The lobbies of the Palais Bourbon—headquarters of the Chamber of Deputies—buzzed also with the well-founded rumor that Poincaré, pleading the press of business at the Quai d'Orsay, had twice refused Lasteyrie's appeal that he appear personally in parliament to defend the government's financial policies. Already thinking of the election that lay ahead, Poincaré sought to get through the parliamentary session without a full-dress interpellation on any domestic issue, and he was not above distancing himself from his ministerial colleagues to achieve this purpose. A financial debate would inevitably force him back on the support of President Millerand and the right, make the benevolent neutrality of Herriot and his left-center Radical-Socialists impossible, and thus narrow the potential base of support for the government's foreign policy. But the Radicals saw through the tactic and began to joke about *Poincaré-la-remise*. Clearly the first hint of trouble would expose the fractured nature of the premier's majority.[52]

The German Embassy took a realistic view, therefore, when it rated the cabinet's position as "not very satisfactory." As Leopold von Hoesch, the highly professional and sharp-eyed German chargé d'affaires assessed the situation, energetic tax measures were "hardly to be expected" from the outgoing parliament. The budget deficit, possible further inflation, and the fall of the franc constituted "grounds for serious anxiety" on the part of the French government. Although he did not yet discern tangible evidence of any substantive change in foreign policy, Hoesch already rated the financial situation as one of several factors obliging France to explore possibilities of a new modus vivendi with Germany.[53]

After the turn of the year, the franc continued to fall. For the first time, the newspapers quoted the exchange rate daily on their front pages. Lasteyrie consulted frenetically with bankers, businessmen, even with the special police of the Bourse. Finally, with a show of urgency, the cabinet voted on 8 January 1924 to undertake a number of technical measures against speculation. It strengthened the laws against propaganda discouraging the sale of public securities, slightly increased the discount rate to counteract the tendency of exporters not to repatriate foreign currency earnings, and barred "undesirable elements" from the neighborhood of the exchange market. With great fanfare, one minor employee of a Dutch bank was put over the border.[54]

But suddenly, Lasteyrie found that he had lost credibility. His an-

52. See the well-informed "Bonneteau politique" in *Le Progrès civique*, 29 December 1923, pp. 11–12; 5 January 1924, pp. 16–18. This column was written by Radical-Socialist Senator François-Albert under the pen name of Pierre du Clain.

53. Hoesch telegrams, 23 and 29 December 1923, 3 January 1924, German Foreign Ministry Archives, U.S. National Archives Microfilms T-120, Washington, D.C., 4478/2214/E088661–666, K936/4505/K239268–275, K239281–282 (hereafter cited as G.F.M. serial/reel/frame number).

54. *Le Temps*, 10 January 1924; *Le Matin*, 9 January 1924.

nouncement that those responsible for machinations against the franc were to be prosecuted met with derisive laughter. "Will our ministers therefore be arrested?" asked Robert de Jouvenel, a prominent columnist who was read appreciatively by all shades of political opinion.[55] The finance minister's attempt to rally the nation with the familiar tactic of blaming the Germans proved no more effective. Citing an alleged plan by German bankers to sell francs against dollars, Lasteyrie charged that the Germans, as "past masters at this kind of operation," were plotting to "bring pressure to bear on the foreign policy of France and to induce M. Poincaré's government to renounce its action in the Ruhr."[56] But whatever the accuracy of the charge, exhortation was now largely irrelevant. The time had passed when either technical tinkering or patriotic press releases from the rue de Rivoli could stem the tide of speculation.

55. *L'Oeuvre*, 7 January 1924.

56. *Le Temps*, 10 January 1924. Lasteyrie cited a decision allegedly made by bankers from the occupied regions of Germany, meeting under the chairmanship of a Reichsbank representative in Frankfurt on 6 November 1923, to convert all francs at their disposal into dollars. The previous week, an insiders' Paris financial journal, *Le Pour et le contre*, purported to give details of such a meeting (see Hoesch tel., 5 January 1924, G.F.M. 4478/2214/E099635). However, there were perfectly sound reasons having to do with local currency requirements for bankers in the occupied areas to purchase stable-value dollars; political objectives need not have motivated such a decision.

Chapter 3

Government Proposals and the Parliamentary Roadblock

Poincaré's Program and Its Political Ramifications

Only after the panic at the Bourse—*la grande peur*, it was called—on 14 January 1924, did the government fully realize the gravity of the crisis facing it.[1] At the ministries of Finance and Commerce, lights burned late into the night as bankers and specialists labored over the problems in a frantic round of conferences.[2] Poincaré was taken by surprise and overwhelmed as the many ramifications of the situation were borne home to him—not merely the exchange difficulties, but also the collapsing market for *rentes* and, worse yet, for short-term national defense obligations. Though Poincaré had served competently as finance minister during the early part of his political career, he was not really at home in the complicated world of postwar finance. Overburdened by his duties at the Quai d'Orsay and as president of the council, constitutionally unable to delegate burdens that fell within his sphere of direct responsibility, he had relied for financial advice almost entirely on Lasteyrie. The finance minister was surely no theoretician, but he had proved his mettle in the rigorous training ground of the Inspectorate of Finance. Technically he was fully up to the job; his colleagues rated him one of the most able of postwar finance ministers. By standing up for the unpopular *double décime* in 1923 he had also demonstrated a measure of courage. However, by temperament and habit he was overcautious and inclined to postpone decisive action. These traits had made him the ideal *chef de cabinet* to Denys Cochin at the Blockade Service during the war and also meshed well with the personality of his present chief. But he was not ideally suited to rise to a sudden emergency. Poincaré, after two years of almost complete absorption in foreign affairs, had to take charge himself. With characteristic confidence in his ability to master a previ-

1. The term was used by, among others, François-Albert in the "Bonneteau politique," *Le Progrès civique*, 26 January 1924, p. 17.

2. The Cartel press, especially *L'Oeuvre*, *Le Quotidien*, and *L'Ere nouvelle*, 15 January 1924 et seq., best capture the hectic atmosphere of those days. *Le Matin* and *Le Temps* provide more sober commentary.

ously neglected subject by studious and methodical application, he called for the dossiers.[3]

The difficulty was to devise a program that was economically sound but at the same time not politically disastrous. Poincaré considered a confrontation with parliament over finance a last resort. He, no less than Lasteyrie, was generally disposed to procrastinate rather than meet intractable problems head-on. Moreover, in the parliamentary lobbies he made no secret of his hope to execute a "quarter-turn to the left" before the general election scheduled for the spring of 1924. For many months, and especially since President Millerand's partisan summons to action at Evreux the previous October, he had skillfully avoided being pushed forward as the leader of the right-wing Bloc National in the election campaign. He believed that the best strategy to prevent creation of a cartel linking the parties on the left was to form a center coalition, stretching from the more progressive members of the *Entente rêpublicaine* through the "national" Radicals of the Franklin-Bouillon persuasion.

Poincaré considered himself a man of the *juste milieu*, and up to the end of 1923 his cultivation of the moderate left had paid high dividends. Since the march into the Ruhr, his personal position at the Palais Bourbon had remained virtually unassailable; parliamentary criticism had been deflected to his ministers and subordinate officials. Yet by pursuing this "center strategy" and attempting to sidestep potentially divisive questions of domestic policy, the premier sought something other than political advantage. In a country where domestic affairs constituted the essence of parliamentary life, Poincaré was exceptional in placing primacy on "national union," the better to carry out objectives of foreign policy.[4] The right could be counted upon to support a hard line on foreign policy in any event. A center strategy that neutralized the Radical-Socialists would provide the greatest breadth of backing for a continued firm stand in the Ruhr.

Despite the normal fluidity of French political alliances, however, no hope existed of forming a center coalition to pass tax measures that were bound to be unpopular with the electorate. For this, Poincaré had to fall back on the right. He found his reputation as a political thaumaturge precipitously shattered; and the familiar intrigues against the ministry soon got under way all across the political spectrum in the lobbies of the Palais Bourbon and the Luxembourg. Nonetheless, the premier's calcu-

3. The account of Poincaré's working habits is based on a personal interview with Marcel Ribière, his *chef de cabinet*, on 11 June 1965; and on Emmanuel de Peretti de la Rocca, "Briand et Poincaré: Souvenirs," *Revue de Paris*, 15 December 1936, pp. 775–88. For Poincaré's reaction to this particular crisis see the "Bonneteau politique," *Le Progrès civique*, 26 January–19 March 1924. Frédéric Françqis-Marsal provides a good appraisal of Lasteyrie as finance minister in "Souvenirs: La Crise présidentielle et l'éviction de Millerand, 1923–1924," p. 8, François-Marsal Papers, in family possession, Paris.

4. See the sensitive discussion of Poincaré's notion of service to the state in Pierre Miquel, *Poincaré* (Paris, 1961), pp. 609–17.

lation that the Bloc National would in the end have to swallow whatever financial plan he determined to push proved correct. Most members of the Bloc, with the exception of the Tardieu-Mandel faction, realized that to oppose the government was not politically realistic. They hoped by a show of reluctance mainly to sell their support for a price. To their intense displeasure, Maurice Maunoury, the middle-of-the-road minister of the interior, had directed the prefects to show strict neutrality in the election campaign. Right-wing parliamentary leaders demanded his replacement so that the prefects could follow the time-honored tradition of distributing patronage on the local level to influence the election outcome.

That price Poincaré was not willing to pay. Yet he did distribute a variety of promises in the Chamber, using both carrot and stick to firm up his majority. To win the support of the Finance Commission, he held out to Louis Loucheur and Maurice Bokanowski, its most influential members, the bait of eventual participation in a recast cabinet. He worked closely with Raoul Péret, president of the Chamber and a leader of the moderate wing of the *Gauche radicale*, to avoid a possibly embarrassing confrontation on the matter of pension legislation. He offered a postponement of the elections until May in order to give the *Entente républicaine*, the largest right-wing party, more time to develop support in the countryside. The government even threw a bone to the clerical group, abandoning its opposition to a diocesan reform bill. And to limit defections on the left flank of his majority, Poincaré played on the fear of a *ministère introuvable* of the extreme right, which would see the ruthless Georges Mandel, former henchman of Clemenceau, controlling the well-developed bureaucracy for domestic surveillance at the Place Beauvau.

In spite of this skillful maneuvering, a long parliamentary battle lay ahead, bound to exhaust the premier personally and politically. Almost inevitably larger questions peripheral to finance but central to the nature of the regime—electoral reform, administrative reorganization, republican ideology—would be brought into debate. A variety of particularist interests, successfully submerged earlier by Poincaré's strategy of moratorium on domestic disputes, would press for satisfaction. The atmosphere of partisanship would inevitably push the Radical-Socialists into more uncompromising opposition in foreign affairs. Even if he managed to pilot the government's financial proposals through the shoals of partisan politics, Poincaré could not hope to avoid ramifications on French foreign policy. For under the circumstances, would it not become more difficult for France to take an obstinate stand in the Ruhr if the Experts' Report turned out not to its liking?

The government found a greater challenge in devising an acceptable political strategy than in working out the specific details of its financial package. Virtually all the measures that Poincaré proposed to the Chamber on 17 January 1924 had been widely discussed in banking and financial circles for some time past.[5] The *double décime*—that familiar 20 percent across-the-board increase in most existing taxes—formed the centerpiece of the program. Poincaré held out the prospect that a considerable sum could also be saved on the expenditure side of the ledger by streamlining government operations, and he asked for exceptional authorization to carry through administrative reforms by decree for a period of six months. He served up a judicious mix of proposals reflecting the long-held views of Finance Ministry bureaucrats on the best methods of improving tax collection and added some politically inspired variants designed to make the whole palatable to the parliamentary majority. He suggested a system to keep track of dividend and interest payments to individuals;[6] stronger measures against evasion of income and inheritance taxes; creation of an independent pension fund with a fixed and constant treasury contribution; stricter control of foreign exchange operations, requiring authorization from local Chambers of Commerce for purchase of foreign currency; an increase in postal, telegraph, and telephone rates; finally, the sale of unprofitable state enterprises, notably the match monopoly, to the private sector. The revenue from all these measures, contrary to the claims made by government supporters, would not really balance the total consolidated expenditures of government. However, it would be sufficient to cover, for the first time since the war, what the Finance Commission called the "permanent expenses of the nation," including interest and amortization charges on the debt. Further borrowing would be necessary only to meet nonrecurring capital outlays for reconstruction.[7]

5. *J.O.C. Déb.*, 17 January 1924, pp. 121–24. The text of the draft legislation proposed by the government is found in *J.O.C. Doc.*, Annexe nos. 6972–73, January 1924, pp. 137–49.

6. Poincaré set forth the proposal recommended by the Finance Ministry for a *bordereau de coupons*, that is, a system requiring banks to keep a record of all dividends and bond coupons cashed by customers and to report these transactions to tax authorities. The Finance Commission substituted a plan providing for a *carnet de coupons*, namely, a booklet showing coupons cashed which the individual holder would submit to the district inspector of internal revenue along with his tax return. The measure as drafted by the Finance Commission served to allay taxpayer anxieties regarding the banks' surveillance of their financial affairs, but was for that very reason less effective.

7. This account is based primarily on a study of the parliamentary debates, *J.O.C. Déb.*, 17 January, 25 January–22 February, 11 March, 21 March 1924; and *J.O.S. Déb.*, 13–22 March 1924. The key documents supplementing the debates are Bokanowski's report on behalf of the Chamber Finance Commission, *J.O.C. Doc.*, Annexe no. 6980, 22 January 1924, pp. 151–76; Henry Bérenger's report for the Senate Finance Commission, *Journal Officiel, Sénat, Documents parlementaires*, Annexe no. 160, 13 March 1924, pp. 126–63 (hereafter cited as *J.O.S. Doc.*); and a report on speculation against the franc by Bokanowski, based on a study by A. S. Cahen and Robert Wolff, copy in Millerand Papers, abridged version in *J.O.C. Doc.*, Annexe no. 7353, 20 March 1924, pp. 639–44. No complete secondary account of the tax controversy of 1924 is available, but Robert Murray Haig, *The Public Finances of Post-War France* (New York, 1929), pp. 89–98, briefly reviews the economic issues, and Edouard Bonnefous, *Histoire politique de la Troisième République*, vol. 3, *L'Après-guerre, 1919–1924* (Paris, 1959), pp. 400–409, summarizes political aspects. Only the Senate side of the debate has received serious scholarly attention: François Goguel-Nyegaard, *Le Rôle financier du Sénat français* (Paris, 1937), pp. 158–81.

The Chamber Finance Commission obligingly hurried through preliminary consideration of these measures. Armed with its report, the full Chamber began a debate on 25 January that continued without interruption for five long weeks. Carried on day and night with the greatest passion, the discussions often left the deputies bleary-eyed at their seats in the hemicycle even after the gray dawn of the Paris winter morning had already broken. Inevitably, the participants found themselves perpetually exhausted and without time for reflection. Perhaps this accounts in part for the stale rhetoric that so greatly outweighed analysis in the debates. Although they were followed with rapt attention by the French public, the most striking characteristic of the debates was the extent of their irrelevance. Throughout these weeks international speculation continued to threaten the franc's stability. The stake for France's foreign policy position was exceptionally high. Yet the urgency of the crisis commanded attention only infrequently. If the financial debates hold our retrospective interest, it is because they illustrate concretely and with particular poignancy some problems of French political institutions that are often discussed in terms of general platitudes.[8]

Parliament proved unable to respond with the necessary promptness and effectiveness to an emergency in which the overriding urgency of war was absent. Undoubtedly part of the difficulty was institutional; those who argued throughout the interwar years for constitutional reform could point to numerous instances when a strong and relatively independent executive drawing on specialized talents in the ministries might have functioned more effectively as the leading branch of government than an unwieldy legislative body dependent for its smooth operation on tenuous political alliances. A major difficulty lay in the fact that most of the parliament was primarily responsive to local interests in the provinces, where international issues seemed of far less moment than philosophical doctrine and details of domestic policy. With a stagnant population and a slow rate of industrialization, France to a greater extent than any other major European nation retained the social habits and political patterns of an earlier age. Throughout the Third Republic, the small towns and the countryside remained insular, their inhabitants preoccupied with parochial concerns. In the years before the First World War, the French people had shifted their national energies to cope with the threat from abroad only belatedly and reluctantly.[9] Now that the war

8. For the best general treatment of French political institutions and society, see David Thomson, *Democracy in France* (London, 1958); François Goguel, *Histoire des institutions politiques de la France de 1870 à 1940* (Paris, 1951); André Siegfried, *De la Troisième à la Quatrième République* (Paris, 1957); A. Thibaudet, *La République des professeurs* (Paris, 1927).

9. See Eugen Weber, *Nationalist Revival in France, 1905–1914* (Berkeley, 1959), and Gilbert Ziebura, *Die deutsche Frage in der öffentlichen Meinung Frankreichs von 1911–1914* (Berlin, 1955), for evidence that the nationalist mood of prewar France was primarily a defensive response to German world policy rather than an outgrowth of domestic political developments.

was over, most Frenchmen felt an intense desire to return to their traditional focus of interest.

This was particularly true of the Radical-Socialists, whose position in the Chamber and especially in the Senate (where they went under the name of the *Gauche radicale*) was crucial. Before the war the Radicals had constituted the main governing party. They nurtured an ambition to recover that position in the scheduled spring elections. The Radicals, particularly those whose political experience extended back a generation, defined their position in terms of a fierce loyalty to republicanism and a commitment to defend the "little man" against the state, the ill-defined predatory interests, and the powers of clericalism. Though these doctrines had functioned as vital rallying calls at the time of the Dreyfus affair, they provided little relevant guidance to the complex social and economic questions troubling France between the wars.[10] The financial debates of 1924 indicate how the Radicals were impelled to adopt a vague anticapitalist rhetoric verging at times on a sentimental sympathy for socialism, though they did not accept the Socialists' positive orientation to economic problems and indeed did not develop any clearly defined, practical economic program of their own. Of course, this deficiency was not new in 1924. D. W. Brogan has observed, in the context of a general criticism of the governing class's education in this "Republic of Professors," that its finest products "had to fight a temptation to believe that the laws of economics, even of arithmetic, were inventions of reaction, to be safely ignored by the mandatories of universal suffrage, or to be refuted by eloquence."[11] The Radicals' ignorance merely exemplified in quintessential form a state of mind that obtained quite generally in both houses of parliament. If this specific crisis bears witness to the particular financial ineptitude of the left, the events of the next years were to show that similar disabilities were shared across the political spectrum. The differences between the parties were in any case so great that coalitions usually represented a form of negative agreement that could be maintained only by avoiding potentially divisive economic and social issues. The difficulty of pushing through broad financial legislation of any sort in such a situation is obvious.

Poincaré and those of his colleagues who formulated the tax legislation intuitively understood all this wisdom later to be elucidated by political scientists. The government consequently attempted to minimize the ideological confrontation by arguing for adoption of the tax package on the most narrow grounds of patriotism and necessity. Poincaré interpreted the aims of the offensive against the franc as "certainly at least as much political as financial," and as the rhetoric of debate escalated, he

10. The extensive literature on this subject is summarized by Peter J. Larmour, *The French Radical Party in the 1930's* (Stanford, 1964), especially pp. 6–37, 60–99.

11. D. W. Brogan, *France under the Republic: The Development of Modern France, 1870–1939* (New York and London, 1940), p. 156.

began to warn of national "catastrophe" if the tax measures were not adopted intact. He emphasized constantly that the nation's foreign policy hung in the balance: "If we wish to be able to follow a genuinely independent policy, it is necessary first, once again, to assure our financial position beyond challenge." The premier reiterated, as he had so often since the occupation of the Ruhr, that such independence was entirely compatible with a policy of conciliation and straightforward relations with the Allies. France's role in setting up the Expert Committees, he contended, served as proof of this. But the nation could not sacrifice its essential interests. Poincaré conceded that if, instead of facing underlying financial problems, the nation were to reverse course and withdraw from the Ruhr, and if the cabinet were to heed its critics and resign, an artificial and precarious respite on the exchanges might result. But France would remain "at the mercy of a new enterprise of intimidation." Poincaré also adduced moral reasons to stay the course, and his appeal on this ground carried with it the accent of his deepest convictions. "Who can seriously believe," he asked, ". . . that a backward movement of French policy, a more or less disguised abandonment of our national claims, a renunciation of our guarantees of payment or security, could fail to produce at home as an immediate repercussion, a moral depression, a disappointment, a malaise resulting in the greatest damage to our activity, our strength, and our credit?"[12]

For the specific financial measures proposed the premier made no exaggerated claims. He conceded that everyone shared a degree of responsibility for the many financial errors of commission and omission made since 1919. But recriminations, he argued, were senseless. New taxes could be postponed no longer, though deputies courageous enough to vote for them might be handicapped in the coming elections. It was essential to settle upon a form of tax legislation already given serious study by parliament, which could be applied without long administrative preparation by the Finance Ministry, and which would bring immediate revenue to the treasury. The *double décime* met these requirements. Poincaré admitted that any plan to increase taxes and crack down on tax evasion was open to criticism. Still, he reminded the deputies by quoting d'Alembert, "the best is the enemy of the good." The national interest required immediate stabilization of the currency—not for reasons of international policy alone, but also, implicitly, on grounds of social justice. Here Poincaré sought to stake out his political position as a man of the center, almost above party. "To defend the franc," he observed,

12. Poincaré's major speeches during the debates are found in *J.O.C. Déb.*, 17 January 1924, pp. 121–24; 26 January, pp. 312, 321–30; 5 February, pp. 504–12; 22 February 1924, pp. 1014–15. Cf. also his address to the Senate, *J.O.S. Déb.*, 13 March 1924, pp. 281–86; and his interventions in the final debate, *J.O.C. Déb.*, 21 March 1924, pp. 1481–1510. He explained the foreign policy implications more frankly in closed testimony to a Senate committee: Sénat, Commission des Finances, séance du 8 mars 1924, audition de M. le Président du Conseil et de M. le Ministre des Finances, copy in Herriot Papers.

"is above all to perform a service for the immense group of small investors, minor civil servants, humble pensioners, workers and employees, of all those living on fixed incomes. It is, above all, to come equally to the aid of all consumers, that is, of the entire nation."

The premier's attempt to soften the partisan impact of the request for decree powers to streamline government operations proved less successful. Wartime expansion of government services had been rapid and, it was generally recognized, of necessity somewhat improvised. In August 1922 Louis Marin, vice-president of the Chamber, had been named to head a committee charged with recommending ways to reduce the cost of government operations. The Marin Committee conveniently completed its work in November 1923, and the cabinet seized on its timely report as the basis for its own economy plan.[13] This plan emphasized administrative simplification. Advances in communication and transport now made it feasible for the *département* to take over some of the main responsibilities for dispensing financial, judicial, and other services at a local level, thereby phasing out superfluous rural schools, tribunals, and sinecures and limiting the role of the *arrondissement* (a smaller administrative unit). Poincaré recognized that if administrative reform were made a subject for parliamentary horsetrading, every interest group would seek to protect its own domain. Each deputy would find himself under irresistible pressure to demonstrate his "inventive and creative imagination" to voters in his constituency. Even after interminable discussion, it was unlikely that major cost-cutting could be effected. If, on the contrary, decisions were made as part of a comprehensive plan, even on a provisional basis, the "interests" might calm down and resign themselves to a fait accompli.

There was, however, one complication. Even a moderate reduction of prerogatives and services at the *arrondissement* level struck at the power of the *sous-préfecture*, one of the most important sources of patronage and organization for the Radical-Socialist party.[14] The resulting dilemma was altogether characteristic of the Third Republic: an issue clothed with one sort of national and international significance for the policymaker in the Paris ministries presented quite a different aspect to those intimately involved in provincial politics. The local effects of the proposed cost-cutting system were mentioned explicitly by no one in the debates, but they were never forgotten in private calculations.

Lasteyrie, stung by the heavy-handed sarcasm with which his earlier optimism was now recalled, deemed it the better part of discretion to play a relatively subordinate role in the debates. When he did speak, he often conveyed the impression of a bureaucrat overwhelmed by techni-

13. "Premier Rapport de la Commission des Réformes, instituée par le décret du 3 août 1922," pp. 885–953, in *Journal Officiel, Annexe, Documents administratifs*, 10 December 1923 (hereafter cited as *J.O. Annexe*).

14. Brian Chapman, *The Prefects and Provincial France* (London, 1955), pp. 97–100.

cal detail. Yet however petty the administrative problems confronting his ministry might seem when taken individually, the complicated nature of their interconnections did restrict the range of policy options. The Finance Ministry had barely recovered from its wartime disorganization. It was just building a staff of seasoned agents and working out effective methods of collecting existing taxes. Lasteyrie argued that it would be more profitable to channel all efforts toward further rationalization of the present system than to overwhelm the tax bureau with unfamiliar duties. The *double décime* was therefore the easiest reform to apply, not only for the central tax administration in Paris, but also in determining the complicated coefficients for subsidies to departmental and communal bodies.[15]

Moreover, a tax on capital constituted the only alternative sufficient to raise the amount of new revenue required. Even the opposition, Lasteyrie contended, could not deny that a capital levy might destroy the confidence of the business community and provoke a flight of capital precisely when the money market's support was most essential to keep up subscriptions to government bonds and to facilitate consolidation of the floating debt. Lasteyrie also demonstrated that many of the suggestions made by outsiders for increasing revenue and improving tax collection procedures betrayed inadequate comprehension of the intricacies involved. Some of these notions, such as recovery of excess profits from wartime contracts and of overpayments for reconstruction in the liberated areas, held great political appeal. But, as the minister pointed out, his department was proceeding as fast as practicable in promising areas, and even if all delinquent payments were recovered forthwith, they could make no more than a subsidiary contribution to covering the budget deficit.[16]

To the latter-day observer, Lasteyrie's defense of his ministry's opera-

15. Lasteyrie's main contributions to the debates are in *J.O.C. Déb.*, 14 February 1924, pp. 723–38, and 20 February 1924, pp. 884–88.

16. The nature of the difficulties with which the Finance Ministry had to contend can be illustrated by considering the wartime excess profits tax. The law establishing this tax, passed in July 1916, directed the creation of a collection system so complicated that the ministry did not even attempt to begin action until after the Armistice. It then required declarations of wartime profits and negotiated the payment due with each firm liable for tax. However, difficulties in finding trained personnel delayed the work of adjudication commissions set up to settle cases in which taxpayers contested government assessments. Meanwhile, many firms with large liabilities for wartime profits suffered reverses in the 1920 depression. The treasury could not collect without forcing them into bankruptcy. Solvent taxpayers, scrutinizing government policy closely, determined not to become the *poires* or suckers who paid the bill while others secured postponements. Those liable for tax realized that, because of exchange depreciation and the low interest rate on the final adjudicated settlement, it lay in their advantage to drag out litigation. Socialist critics charged that small merchants had been subjected to ruinous settlements, while larger businesses and banks succeeded in postponing payment. Since the larger firms employed the more experienced tax lawyers, there was probably a measure of truth in this accusation. Yet by February 1924, about two-thirds of the 16.4 milliard francs due had finally been collected. Those cases still in litigation mostly represented bad debts and would yield little more.

tions carries a ring of plausibility. Certainly France's wartime record on tax legislation and administration left much to be desired. But could a qualitatively better record be reasonably expected in a nation just beginning to develop a modern system of direct taxation and in which, up to a few years earlier, the major direct taxes had remained those tradition-encrusted levies assessed on external indications of wealth (the *quatre vieilles contributions*) that harked back to the Ancien Régime? At any rate, whatever the deficiencies of policy during the war and immediate postwar period, parliamentary critics could point to no important measures for reform of the tax collection administration that the Finance Ministry had not seriously considered by 1924.[17]

The thankless burden of day-to-day technical economic defense of the government's case was undertaken by Maurice Bokanowski,* the articulate *rapporteur-général* of the Chamber Finance Commission. As a result of connections with Paris investment banking circles and long study on his own, Bokanowski had become one of the few members of parliament who possessed a complete mastery of public finance and international economics. Partly with a view to educating the public as well as his fellow deputies, Bokanowski repeated his explanations of fundamental issues time and again. Drawing on the lessons of postwar monetary experience under flexible exchange rates in all European countries, he sought to convince the Chamber of two essential points. First, fiscal policy was the most important long-run determinant of the franc's exchange value, while other factors (reduction of the money supply, limitations on export of capital, direct efforts to control speculation) could have at most a subsidiary effect. Second, a direct connection existed between the foreign exchange value of the franc and the cost of living, so that if exchange depreciation took place, domestic prices would inevitably rise to a point corresponding to the world price level.

These statements seem elementary enough nowadays; they were nevertheless vehemently contested by the opposition in the debates. Bokanowski emphasized that if new taxes were not voted, massive inflation was unavoidable. The real alternatives, he kept insisting, lay

*Maurice Bokanowski (1879–1928), born into a family of Jewish textile merchants, showed remarkable academic promise at the Paris law faculty; practiced law in Paris and Marseille, won election to the Chamber, 1914; left to join the army, was torpedoed off Salonika and wounded on the western front but survived; reelected to the Chamber from Paris in 1919 on *Action républicaine et sociale* ticket. He soon became *rapporteur* of the Finance Commission and outstanding spokesman for moderates on economic problems; was rewarded with the Navy Ministry in the March 1924 cabinet reshuffle. Minister of commerce and aeronautics in the National Union Cabinet of 1926, he seemed destined for a major ministerial career but perished in an airplane accident in September 1928. His brother-in-law, Robert Wolff, headed the foreign department of A. S. Cahen et Cie, a prominent investment banking firm.

17. Alfred Georges Gressent, *Le Mystère de la rue de Rivoli: Grandeur et décadence du franc sous le ministère de M. de Lasteyrie* (Paris, 1924).

between consenting willingly to "known and limited sacrifices" and condemning the country through inaction to "unlimited and incalculable sacrifices, accompanied by irremediable economic crisis and profound social disturbances." Bokanowski freely conceded the opposition's point that the increase in the turnover tax (*l'impôt sur le chiffre d'affaires*) might directly cause a 2 to 4 percent increase in the cost of living. But this had to be measured against a potential price rise of 40 percent, which would correspond to the external depreciation of the franc in the previous three months alone. Only by first balancing the budget to restore confidence, Bokanowski reminded his colleagues finally, could one hope to escape from "intolerable pressure" on French foreign policy and "become more free to demand payment of the debt from Germany."

Bokanowski contended that by adopting the tax package without unreasonable delay and giving the impression to the rest of the world that henceforth public finance would be properly managed, the parliament could create excellent prospects for exchange recovery. After all, the fundamental economic position of the country was good. An examination of various economic indicators—the favorable balance of payments, the high level of employment—revealed no insuperable structural barriers to currency stabilization. Nor did the large supply of outstanding "floating francs" necessarily afford speculators against the franc an insurmountable advantage. The majority of foreign franc holdings had been acquired in 1919–20 with the hope that the currency would appreciate; those who held such franc balances did not wish to take a loss by liquidating their holdings at current levels and would do so only in case of panic.

Bokanowski offered no more than a measured endorsement of the *double décime*. When it was first proposed by Lasteyrie in 1923, he had fought against it in the Finance Commission and pressed the ministry to recast the tax structure instead. Now, however, he argued that even after the elections, it would take months to reach a consensus on a fundamental tax reform which would embody the new indications of the popular will. Meanwhile, the *double décime*, as a proportional surcharge on the tax system established in the last general financial debate of June 1920, was the levy that best reflected the sentiment of the present Chamber. Bokanowski compared the situation to an emergency in which a river overflowed its banks. The government was asking for a protective dike: "The time is short; we have no choice of materials. Let us use the earthen bags that we have at hand. When the torrents have been controlled, the architects will have the leisure to resume their work."[18]

18. For Bokanowski's main contributions to the debate, see *J.O.C. Doc.*, Annexe no. 6980, 22 January 1924, pp. 151–76; *J.O.C. Déb.*, 25 January 1924, pp. 274–79; and 13 February 1924, pp. 710–19.

The Nature of the Tax System

Together, Poincaré, Lasteyrie, and Bokanowski made what appears in retrospect a rather convincing case for passage of the government's proposals, at least on an emergency basis. Even brief consideration of the social obstacles to more fundamental tax reform at the time strengthens this impression. Contrary to a widespread belief, resistance by the upper classes to meaningful direct taxation no longer posed the only difficulty, or even the principal barrier to French tax reform. It is true that the bitterness engendered by the prewar struggle over adoption of an income tax still lingered. As late as 1920, shortly before his appointment as finance minister, Frédéric François-Marsal* insisted that the income tax and tax declarations, or "fiscal inquisition" as he called it, bore the stamp of German *Kultur* "most particularly odious to our French genius." Only the traditional indirect levies—taxes on expenditures or possessions—met his rigorous standards of compatibility with the principles of the French Revolution and the "mentality of our race."[19] During the following years, quite a number of writers in the *bien-pensant* press continued to embroider this theme with the suggestion that a return to the old haphazard system of the *quatre vieilles contributions* assessed on external signs of wealth remained a distinct possibility. Yet the significance of this literature should not be exaggerated. Poincaré himself had contributed a telling appraisal of it on the occasion of the tax debate in 1920. "The Frenchman is so formed by nature," he observed wryly, "that he bleeds and even dies with a smile, but never pays [his taxes] without grumbling. . . . Still . . . he pays all the same."[20]

The reforms that had passed in June 1920 after many months of tortuous discussion preserved and extended the progress made during the war toward development of a modern direct tax system. The balanced assortment of taxes then adopted proved acceptable to everyone except the Socialists. On the one hand, a turnover tax, the *impôt sur le chiffre*

*Frédéric François-Marsal (1874–1958) graduated first in his class at Saint-Cyr, the French military academy; joined Doumer's military staff in Indochina, 1900; resigned from the army to enter a prominent Protestant bank in Lyons, 1905. Impeccably connected, he rejoined the military, 1914, quickly rose to lieutenant colonel; served on the staff of Joffre and Castelnau, subsequently at G.H.Q.; then as head of the Service of Financial and Economic Studies on the staff of President of the Council Clemenceau. Closely identified with heavy industry, François-Marsal became general director of the Banque de l'Union Parisienne, 1919; advocated firm measures against Germany as columnist for the conservative *Echo de Paris* under the pseudonym Custos; was named finance minister under Millerand and Leygues in 1920 though elected to the Senate only in 1921 as a member of the right-wing *Union républicaine*; reappointed finance minister to succeed Lasteyrie, March 1924. He acted briefly as premier in June 1924, forfeiting his political future to support his friend Millerand in the controversy over the presidency of the Republic.

19. F. François-Marsal, "Impôts réels ou impôts personnels," *Revue politique et parlementaire*, 10 January 1920, pp. 13–26.

20. "Chronique de la quinzaine," *Revue des deux mondes*, 1 June 1920, p. 709.

d'affaires, was instituted as a simple, easy-to-administer indirect levy. On the other hand, a steeply progressive income surtax was adopted, with rates as high as 50 percent applying in addition to scheduled taxes on various forms of income.[21] Significantly, exemptions at the base were so generous that 70 percent of the citizenry, including virtually the entire agricultural population and all manual workers, still paid no direct taxes whatever. In 1924 only 1,487,828 Frenchmen found themselves subject to the income surtax.[22] These, however, paid heavily. In short, it appears that despite the continuing bias toward indirect taxation, the tax structure of France, taken as a whole, was—at least in theory—already fairly progressive by the standards of the day.[23]

In practice, of course, a tax system may operate differently than it does in theory. Professionals at the Finance Ministry believed that further revision of the balance between direct and indirect taxes should be given a lower priority than administrative measures to make the nominal rates effective. National psychology afforded them solid grounds for this belief. It is useful to reflect that, after half a century's experience with the income tax, there still remains a wide social tolerance of tax evasion in France. Only a small minority—a mere 12 percent of Frenchmen—oppose tax fraud on moral grounds.[24] A highly visible, progressive direct tax system must depend in large degree on voluntary compliance. The majority of French taxpayers in most occupational categories continue to prefer indirect, invisible taxes that minimize intrusion by the authorities

21. For a summary of political stands on the 1920 tax, see François Albert, "Chronique politique," *Revue politique et parlementaire*, July 1920, pp. 136–40; also the monthly articles by Professor Edgard Allix under the rubric "Revue économique et financière" in the same journal throughout 1920. Haig, *Public Finances*, pp. 56–69, provides a clear though brief account; Carl S. Shoup, *The Sales Tax in France* (New York, 1930), gives a comprehensive analysis of the origin of the turnover tax.

22. Haig, *Public Finances*, p. 82; Ministère de l'Economie Nationale, *Annuaire statistique de la France, résumé retrospectif, 1946* (Paris, 1946), p. 214; "Progression des impôts de 1913 à 1925 en France et en divers pays," *Bulletin de la statistique générale de la France et du service d'observation des prix*, July 1925, pp. 415–41.

23. Haig compares the system favorably with that of America at the time and concludes that in spite of its "high proportion of indirect taxes," the French tax system was "so devised as to spare, to a remarkable extent, the poorer elements in its population" (*Public Finances*, pp. 395–412).

The complicated structure of French taxation in the 1920s is discussed exhaustively in Camille Rosier, *Tous nos impôts* (Paris, 1926), and *Traité théorique et pratique de législation fiscale*, 2 vols. (Paris, 1926); Edgard Allix, *Traité élémentaire de science des finances et de législation financière française* (Paris, 1921 and 1927); Edgard Allix and Marcel Lecerclé, *L'Impôt sur le revenu*, 2 vols. (Paris, 1926).

24. A recent sociological sampling of French taxpayers found 42% ready to condemn tax fraud. But this group was composed for the most part of people from occupational groups in which tax evasion was difficult, and who felt penalized in comparison with others. Only 12% of the entire sample stigmatized tax evasion as morally reprehensible. Perhaps even more revealing, less than 4% of those engaged in large business enterprises and the liberal professions, and a statistically insignificant number of artisans and retail shopkeepers, held moral objections to tax evasion (see Jean Dubergé, *La Psychologie sociale de l'impôt dans la France d'aujourd'hui* [Paris, 1961], pp. 91–103).

into their personal affairs. The turnover tax remains the single most important levy in France. It is simple and inexpensive to collect; it minimizes the possibility of fraud; and, because it may be considered either as a tax on business or as one passed on to the consumer, its economic impact is difficult to evaluate. Even today the tax least objectionable to Frenchmen is the one designed so that no one but the statisticians can tell who actually pays it.[25]

The resistance to direct taxation was all the greater in the 1920s when the income tax appeared to be class legislation, with very steep rates bearing on only a small minority of the population, mostly in the urban business and professional classes. The feeling persisted that it was an *impôt des poires*—a "suckers' tax"[26]—to be paid only by those who could not escape it. In time the calculations of the Finance Ministry proved correct: as it bettered its collection methods and enforced the nominal existing rates, government revenue from direct taxation would rise dramatically.[27] A final argument may be added in favor of the *double décime* as a tactical measure in 1924. French taxpayers, as a matter of national psychology, tend to oppose innovations in tax matters; they view the status quo as a lesser evil than any readjustment of the system, whatever the nature of the change.[28] It is consequently likely that in 1924 any alternative to the *double décime* would have met with at least as much or more resistance.

The importance of these technical considerations, which weighed so heavily with internal revenue specialists at the rue de Rivoli, must not be underestimated. Yet they do not tell the whole story. In the long run, the most reliable indicator of a tax system's acceptability across the spectrum of parties and classes is likely to be its compatibility with perceived notions of social justice rather than its technical efficiency. Around the time of the First World War, deeply ingrained assumptions of the self-assured European bourgeoisie regarding the proper distribution of income and the tax burden suddenly appeared open to fundamental challenge. Almost every European nation experienced serious conflict over taxation during interims of social unrest and monetary instability in the 1920s. France, for several decades before the war, had been characterized by relative stability of incomes, prices, and class structure. Then, within the space of a few short years, radical changes took place in the distribution of income and capital assets, changes that had complex but

25. Ibid., pp. 127–46; Maurice Lauré, *Traité de politique fiscale* (Paris, 1956), pp. 361–82; Pierre Tabatoni, "France," in *Foreign Tax Policies and Economic Growth*, comp. National Bureau of Economic Research (New York, 1956), pp. 275–336.

26. The phrase was ascribed to Louis Loucheur (see *J.O.C. Déb.*, 19 June 1924, p. 2340).

27. See the table in Haig, *Public Finances*, p. 318. Government revenue from direct taxation took a particularly large jump in 1926 when, upon the recommendation of a committee of experts, the nominal rate of the general income tax was cut in half.

28. Dubergé, *La Psychologie sociale*, pp. 127–46.

ill-understood consequences. Inflation rather than the tax system played the major role in effecting this massive redistribution of wealth and in allotting the war's financial burdens among the various social classes. Nevertheless, class antagonisms inevitably found a focus in disputes over taxation.

During the 1924 tax debate, spokesmen for the left frequently contended that the costs of the war and reconstruction were shouldered disproportionately by the poor, the working classes, by the "little people" generally. The rough statistical data available do not, on the whole, bear out this contention. It is true that the distribution of income and wealth before 1914 was far more unequal than it is today. However, labor took advantage of serious personnel shortages during the war to increase its share of national income at the expense of capital. National income accounts, though still statistically rudimentary at this time, suggest that in the postwar period labor maintained much though not all of this gain (see table 2). The general adoption of the eight-hour working day in 1919 represented another victory for labor and facilitated the maintenance of full employment throughout the postwar decade. Wages more than kept pace with the cost of living between 1920 and 1924 and generally speaking continued to keep up thereafter, except for a period of months following de facto stabilization in 1926. Wage patterns did show considerable regional and occupational variation. Skilled craftsmen, artisans, and workers in industries suffering from chronic labor shortages such as coal mining and metallurgy did particularly well. Some groups at the bottom of the social scale, domestic servants and agricultural employees, experienced a slower growth of real wages. Lower level white-collar and sales personnel, on the other hand, actually lost ground, as did some government employees (though primarily those in the upper echelons). Retired people fared worst of all. In summary, however, it is clear that

TABLE 2 / National Income Accounts, 1913–28

Source of Income	Percentage of National Income							
	1913	1920	1921	1922	1923	1924	1926	1928
Income from capital (securities, real estate, other property)	26	17.5	20	21	22	22	22	21
Salaries and wages	43.5	51.5	50.5	48	46.5	46	44	44.5
Pensions	1.5	2.5	3	3	3	3	3	4.5
Mixed incomes (agriculture, industry, liberal professions)	29	28.5	26.5	28	28.5	29	31	30

Source: Michel Huber, *La Population de la France pendant la guerre* (Paris and New Haven, 1932), p. 959.

TABLE 3 / *Inheritance Patterns, 1913–25*

	1913	1925	1925 Real Worth as Percentage of 1913 Real Worth†
Total number of estates	360,539	385,943	
Value (millions of francs)	5,531.5	9,801.3	39.3
Number of large estates*	15,450	15,286	
Value (millions of francs)	3,861.6	5,696.3	32.9

Sources: Huber, *La Population de la France*, p. 964; "Successions selon l'importance de l'actif net," Ministère de l'Economie Nationale, *Annuaire statistique de la France, résumé retrospectif, 1946* (Paris, 1946), p. 207.

*Large estates are defined as those valued at 50,000 francs or more in 1913 (4.3% of total), and 100,000 francs or more in 1925 (4.0% of total).
†Adjusted for increase in cost of living (450% of 1913 level).

very little of the cost of the war was reflected in the wage structure or the material style of life of the lower classes in the population.[29]

By contrast, war and postwar developments inflicted tremendous losses on the capital-owning classes. The aggregate value of inheritances provides one good measure of the decline in bourgeois fortunes. Adjusted for the cost of living, aggregate inheritances totalled only 39.3 percent as much in 1925 as in 1913. The largest estates appeared to have suffered disproportionately, their real worth sinking to a mere 32.9 percent of the comparable 1913 figure (although this figure may be distorted by changing patterns of tax evasion in probate declarations). (See table 3.)

Considerable shifts of fortune within the ranks of the bourgeoisie

29. Michel Huber, director of French statistical services at the time, summarizes available data in "Les Revenus privés en France avant et après la guerre," appendix to *La Population de la France pendant la guerre* (Paris and New Haven, 1932), pp. 911–65. Inadequate statistical data, shifting age and occupational distribution of the population, and changing components in the cost of living complicate the task of estimating real wages. Huber therefore cautions that figures on personal or national income should be considered "a simple attempt to represent an order of magnitude" rather than a precise calculation.

See also the many studies published by the *Bulletin de la statistique générale de la France*, e.g., "Enquête sur les salaires en France," October 1924, pp. 168–92; "Salaires dans les industries métallurgiques dans la région parisienne," July 1926, pp. 420–22; "Salaires journaliers moyens des ouvriers dans les mines de houille," April 1925, p. 256, and subsequent issues. Alfred Sauvy summarizes work by private economists on salaries in *Histoire économique de la France entre les deux guerres*, 2 vols. (Paris, 1965–67), 1:344–62. Sauvy's earlier study with Pierre Dupoid, *Salaires et pouvoir d'achat des ouvriers et des fonctionnaires entre les deux guerres* (Paris, 1946), raises important theoretical issues but deals only fleetingly with the period before 1928. Relevant material for the wartime era may be found in William Oualid, *The Effect of the War upon Labor in France* (Oxford, 1923); William Oualid and Charles Picquenard, *Salaires et tarifs* (Paris and New Haven, 1928); John Bates Clark, *Effects of the World War on French Economic Life* (Oxford, 1923); and Charles Gide and William Oualid, *Le Bilan de la guerre pour la France* (Paris and New Haven, 1931).

accompanied this general decline in capital values. Entrepreneurs well situated to take advantage of war contracts and to participate in the postwar industrial and commercial reconstruction business profited enormously. So did those people with enough economic sophistication (or the requisite contacts) to place their portfolios in the hands of knowledgeable Paris stockbrokers and who made shrewd investments in selected foreign and colonial securities, the new consumer growth industries, or in such recovering sectors of the economy as textiles, construction materials, and coal mining. But sophisticated investors were a small minority. The typical provincial bourgeois, the well-to-do peasant, the civil servant or white-collar employee laying aside savings for his old age and his children continued to place his money almost exclusively in government and railway bonds. For generations before the war, such securities had remained gilt-edged investments, while frequent "busts" or scandals rocked the most highly touted private ventures. The French middle classes took the lesson to heart. Their wills and marriage contracts characteristically included provisions mandating the retention of government and railway bonds in the family portfolio. Such investments proved to be the worst possible in the postwar era. Indeed, even those who tried to keep up with the changing times by investing in domestic industrial stocks, still an uncommon practice in the middle class, found that the value of their holdings did not begin to keep pace with the cost of living (see table 4).

TABLE 4 | Capital Values, 1919–26

Index	1919	1920	1921	1922	1923	1924	1925	1926
Fixed revenue securities	83	74	72	77	75	67	58	60
Variable revenue securities	123	151	113	119	172	208	200	233
Foreign securities	118	158	127	142	226	298	444	663
Retail prices (Paris)*	260	371	337	301	332	380	425	554
Retail prices (average, other cities)*	291	386	374	317	349	406	450	571

Sources: "Cours et revenu des valeurs mobiliers," *Bulletin de la statistique générale de la France*, July 1927, pp. 390–406; *Annuaire statistique de la France, résumé retrospectif, 1946*, p. 199.

Note: 1913 = 100.

*1914 = 100.

The profound social transformations caused by these developments were not complete by 1924, but signs of them were everywhere. The moderate Socialist Joseph Paul-Boncour struck a sympathetic note across the whole Chamber as he movingly described the visible social injustice, taking place on a scale so great as to rival comparison with the Directory of the 1790s. There arose a class of the newly rich—conspicuous consumers, buyers of prized rural properties—whose fortunes dated from the misfortune of the country at large. At the same time others—employees, functionaries, and modest professionals—found that their salaries did not keep pace with rising prices and lost or were forced to spend the savings acquired over generations. Could not some imaginative way be found to recast the fiscal structure, many wondered, to counterbalance such inequities?[30]

Of course the average Frenchman had never heard of national income accounts, and among the deputies, few attempted to gather the sort of statistical information presented here. The members of parliament, whatever their political orientation, tended to stake out positions regarding tax legislation on the basis of ideological persuasion. Even their personal observations were often made in a restricted and relatively homogeneous class setting and were refracted through the prism of ideology. The deputies, nevertheless, did mirror fairly the feeling prevailing in many different segments of the population that the structure of society had already put them at a disadvantage. This widespread popular discontent, however unspecific in nature it might be, set in motion a strong current of resistance to the tax increase.

Parliamentary Resistance

The motives of the parliamentary opposition were so complex that no single explanation does full justice to their views. Certainly the deep and, it seemed at times, willful misunderstanding of the theoretical economic issues accounted for some foot-dragging among the legislators. Many saw political mileage to be gained through opposition, and they resented the fact that a government which had so long neglected to face up to its financial responsibilities should now attempt to maneuver parliament into sharing the odium of public reprobation. Not least important, some leaders of the emerging left-wing electoral coalition, the Cartel des Gauches, did not scruple to use the financial crisis as a vehicle for undermining the government's policy in the Ruhr. By no means all of those at the Palais Bourbon and the Luxembourg who fought the government's financial proposals shared this fundamental lack of sympathy for its foreign policy. Yet the final outcome of the long parliamentary stalemate that developed, as we shall see, was a diminution of France's diplomatic independence and severe constriction of its freedom to maneuver in the difficult reparations negotiations to come.

The Socialists, Radical-Socialists, and other parties in the electoral

30. *J.O.C. Déb.*, 4 February 1924, pp. 486–92. On the general subject of income changes within the ranks of the bourgeoisie, see André Bouton, *La Fin des rentiers* (Paris, 1930); Institut National de Statistiques et d'Etudes Economiques, *L'Intérêt du capital depuis 1857* (Paris, 1958); and also Miquel, *Poincaré*, pp. 496–509.

Cartel remained sharply divided among themselves in their positive prescriptions for French financial and foreign policy. The parliamentary debates, however, blending imperceptibly as they did into the election campaign proper, tended to submerge such differences. The cacophony of opposition gave the impression, to those among the general public who did not strain to catch fine distinctions, of a frontal assault on the Poincaré government and its management of public affairs.

Vincent Auriol, the ebullient former editor from Toulouse, led the Socialist attack on the government's tax proposals. Auriol passed as the Socialist party expert on financial matters, and he was a popular figure on the Finance Commission and in the Chamber as a whole. In his personal relations he already gave evidence of the remarkable ability to conciliate and work with all groups which was to make him a generation later such an effective president of the Fourth Republic. But at this time—before the maturing experiences of the interwar years, ministerial responsibility, and the Resistance—he remained a fiercely partisan politician. The Socialist party as a whole was still somewhat ambivalent in the 1920s about acknowledging its role as a parliamentary rather than a revolutionary party. Preoccupied with ideological formulations and with an analysis of society's ills in terms of class conflict, it self-consciously adopted the posture of defending the working class against exploitation by the bourgeoisie. To be sure, this was not logically incompatible with consideration of macroeconomic policy from a technical and administrative point of view. Yet rank and file party workers, the so-called militants, could be roused more effectively with the rhetoric of class struggle than through sober economic analysis. Auriol, like other Socialist leaders more sophisticated than their followers, often found it useful to expatiate on the financial oligarchies' alleged conspiracies and nefarious activities. Even a decade later, during his disastrous tenure as finance minister under the Popular Front, Auriol was wont to play to the gallery by insinuating that financial problems could be solved by closing the banks and putting the bankers into prison: "les banques, je les ferme; les banquiers, je les enferme."[31]

Expressing the Socialist position in the 1924 debates, Auriol denied that "any connection" existed between fiscal policy and the value of the franc. In fact, he claimed, a tax increase might even produce a deleterious effect on the exchange rate, because it would raise the cost of living and require an increase in the money supply; the ensuing inflation would

31. For general assessments of Auriol in his later years, see Adrien Dansette, *Histoire des présidents de la république* (Paris, 1953), pp. 262–71; Philip M. Williams, *Crisis and Compromise: Politics in the Fourth Republic* (Hamden, Conn., 1964), pp. 197–201; also Paul Reynaud, *Mémoires*, vol. 2, *Envers et contre tous* (Paris, 1963), p. 91. Georges Lefranc, *Histoire du front populaire* (Paris, 1965), pp. 365–82, gives a detailed account of Auriol's administration at the rue de Rivoli in 1936. Gilbert Ziebura, *Léon Blum: Theorie und Praxis einer sozialistischen Politik* (Berlin, 1963), pp. 246–71, makes the best possible case for Socialist financial policy in the 1920s.

also make renewal of treasury bonds more difficult. The Socialists did not oppose a balanced budget in principle, as witnessed by the taxation schemes they had offered in 1920, which Auriol recalled in great detail. But since he knew that these, notably the tax on capital, would be unpopular, Auriol carefully avoided proposing them anew. "I propose nothing," he stated explicitly.[32]

Instead he stuck to traditional socialist rhetoric, reminding the Chamber in the stirring manner that always made a hit at party conferences of "old people suffering destitution at the same time as they suffer in their mutilated bodies or their bereavement," watching "the infernal and macabre dance of billions in profits for others." The poor and the victims of the war, he asserted, would bear the "iniquitous taxes" now proposed, while the big banks, which with the state's "complicity" held tax-exempt treasury bonds in their portfolios, escaped entirely. Auriol favored cracking down on the "intolerable speculation" of the metallurgical industry and other exporters, and he appeared to include in his anathemas the most ordinary foreign trade transactions.[33] He argued too that banks should be subject to control by the League of Nations in deference to the "sufferings of all peoples." But much of this was electoral embellishment. Auriol's basic point was to urge postponement of any fundamental recasting of fiscal policy. For the moment, he advocated nothing more than steps to support the franc on the exchange directly, and he proposed for this purpose to requisition foreign currency from the major banks and heavy industry unless private firms placed their resources at the disposal of the treasury voluntarily.

His party, Auriol insisted further, was sure that only a drastic change in foreign policy could solve the problem of the depreciating franc. The French occupation of the Ruhr provided the basic reason for lack of confidence, the Socialists maintained, and French currency circulating in the Saar, Rhineland, and Ruhr furnished the francs which, transferred to Amsterdam, constituted the "mass of maneuver" employed by the speculators. According to Auriol, the need of the hour was to replace the "formalist conception" of international relations held by the diplomat and jurist with an "economic and humane conception." If France were to give up the Ruhr occupation and instead "seek and accept the collaboration of the world," then somehow the "mechanism of credits" could be enlisted to "stabilize currencies and at the same time assure the complete payment of reparations in the near future."

Naturally, Auriol did not go beyond this elusive rhetoric to spell out in

32. Auriol's major speeches are found in *J.O.C. Déb.*, 26 January 1924, pp. 306–21; 13 February 1924, pp. 702–9, 716.

33. Auriol considered the fact that the Wendel interests had negotiated steel export contracts providing for settlement in pounds sterling a particularly "grave" transgression from the moral and patriotic point of view. In reply, François de Wendel demonstrated clearly that his firm had followed standard business practices. *J.O.C. Déb.*, 13 February 1924, pp. 709–10.

detail how the "mechanism" would operate. It is probable that leading Socialists, who had never experienced the responsibilities of governing, had not yet developed the habits of considering policy alternatives in such down-to-earth bureaucratic fashion. Some years afterward, following his own sobering experience handling foreign affairs during the Popular Front, party leader Léon Blum would view things differently. "Only now," he would then lament, "do I understand the harm done our nation's best interests by the rebuff administered to Poincaré's policy in 1924."[34] But in 1924 Blum and his fellow Socialists were not yet ready to take the long view. Their aim was not to suggest a workable substitute policy, but rather to pin the badge of failure squarely on the government in the eyes of the electorate. Blum made this clear in his final peroration: "Your new taxes are the ransom of the Ruhr policy which for almost two years has prevented any amicable and productive settlement of the reparations problem. They mark . . . the bankruptcy of the Ruhr policy."[35]

The Radical-Socialists and other parties of the moderate left found themselves in a quandary over the tax issue. Under great pressure to demonstrate their solidarity with the Socialists, their electoral allies in the Cartel des Gauches, they did not really wish to cripple the government in an emergency. Radical votes, though not required to secure passage of the tax package in the Chamber, were essential in the Senate. Accordingly, Radical party leader Edouard Herriot took a somewhat confused line. He admitted that he found the controversy over the exchange rate somewhat abstruse. Nevertheless, he echoed Auriol in insisting that no proof existed to show that a tax increase would have any effect on the value of the franc. The government, he argued, had therefore made an error in submitting the fiscal projects so quickly. Personally he saw "no reason . . . to lose our sangfroid." If new taxes were unavoidable, said Herriot, at least they should be "good taxes." But aside from a deliberately vague call for a patriotic appeal to the moneyed classes, he declined to be drawn into a discussion of what specifically he had in mind, while André Renard, Herriot's rival for party leadership, could suggest nothing more original than the appointment of a study committee.[36]

The "good tax," as a member of the rightist *Entente républicaine* observed tartly, appeared to be the one that was "inscribed in the party platform and never applied."[37] Almost alone among major leaders of the Cartel des Gauches, Republican-Socialist Paul Painlevé endorsed the

34. Pertinax [André Géraud], *The Gravediggers of France* (Garden City, N.Y., 1944), p. 374.

35. *J.O.C. Déb.*, 22 February 1924, p. 1014. See also Blum's statement in *J.O.C. Déb.*, 15 January 1924, pp. 90–91.

36. Herriot's major speeches: *J.O.C. Déb.*, 26 January 1924, pp. 333–40; 5 February 1924, pp. 500–503; 7 February 1924, pp. 571–72; 13 February 1924, pp. 697–701.

37. Deputy Camille Blaisot, in *J.O.C. Déb.*, 13 February 1924, p. 699.

principle of a tax increase and, though critical of the *double décime*, called for straightforward discussion of the concrete form that new measures should take.[38] But there was no organized attempt to work out a serious alternative of this sort on the left; the numerous suggestions made on the Radical-Socialist backbenches ranged from the impractical to the frivolous.[39]

The Radicals focused their most passionate opposition on the government's request for powers to effect economies by decree. The Marin Committee's proposals for administrative reform posed a threat to Radical-Socialist party organization at the *arrondissement* level. Even more important, the "decree-laws," as they came to be called, represented an affront to the most cherished tenets of the party creed—suspicion of strong central government and belief in legislative supremacy as an indispensable guarantee of the rights of the "little man." The Radicals viewed this proposal as another scheme of the executive to encroach on parliament's prerogatives, analogous to the more general and much feared ideas of President Millerand for altering the balance of power among the branches of government. In point of fact there were ample precedents for giving the executive limited decree powers, both during the war and more immediately in the case of measures employed to reintegrate Alsace-Lorraine in the French polity. Nevertheless, academics in the service of the Cartel, such as Professor Alphonse Aulard, discoursed learnedly on the misuse of decree powers by Napoleon and Charles X.[40] The issue drew from Herriot a characteristically emotional profession of faith, replete with all the shibboleths of Radical-Socialist ideology and including the inevitable appeal to Montesquieu: "I am a Republican, doctrinaire, yes! Jacobin if you will. I believe that one must

38. See his subtle and suggestive article in *L'Oeuvre*, 21 January 1924.

39. The most interesting was Léon Castel's proposal to substitute a mildly progressive capital levy (1–2.5%) for increased income and inheritance taxes, on which the maximum nominal rates were already so high as to furnish an incentive for evasion. The proposal was abandoned when Lasteyrie pointed out that the time was not right to trouble capital markets. But the attention given Castel's suggestion indicated that a number of thoughtful moderates and conservatives—Bokanowski, Albert Sarraut, Emmanuel Brousse, even Jean Ybarnégaray of the *Entente républicaine*—were not so far caught in a doctrinal straightjacket as to reject a priori a moderate and fairly applied capital levy (*J.O.C. Déb.*, 15 February 1924, pp. 767–70).

The baroque suggestions of Louis-Lucien Klotz were more typical of Radical-Socialist thinking. Klotz proposed a compulsory lottery loan that would provide a "mass of maneuver" for use against the speculators. He glibly assured the Chamber that a fantastic sum from secret profits on international oil stocks could be tapped for this purpose. (The alleged machinations of international oil companies figured as one of the favorite subjects of muckraking magazines during this era.) Klotz's solution to the problem of rising living costs was to make it a penal offense for merchants to raise prices without approval by consultive commissions to be set up in each *département*! (*J.O.C. Déb.*, 12 February 1924, pp. 713–14). Evidently Klotz did not learn much about economics even after Clemenceau cast aspersions on his wartime competence as finance minister; in 1928 he was arrested for passing bad checks (Bonnefous, *Histoire politique de la Troisième République*, 4:308).

40. *Le Quotidien*, 16 February 1924.

hold stoutly to principles. . . . When I hear talk of decree-laws I see looming on the horizon the Consultative Senate of Floréal, year XII."[41]

What then were the practical proposals of the Radicals for solution of the financial crisis? Herriot took refuge in the gentlemanly banalities so effective on the hustings, solemnly affirming his conviction that there was "no monetary peace without a political peace and no political peace without monetary peace."[42] Some Radical-Socialist newspapers went considerably further, and *Le Quotidien*, which was rapidly assuming the status of main press organ for the Cartel, virtually adopted the Socialist point of view. *Le Quotidien* found the real reason for the fall of the franc in the government's general policy. It castigated the military occupation of the Ruhr and denounced Poincaré's actions in conveniently turning a blind eye to the favor shown Rhineland separatism by French generals, the limitations the premier sought to place on the Expert Committee's terms of reference, his squandering of hundreds of millions of francs to arm "vassal governments" in eastern Europe, his "dry and cutting speeches," and his general attitude of "lordly intransigeance." The resignation of the government and adoption of a different foreign policy seemed to *Le Quotidien* the only means of salvation.[43]

The more conservative Radicals in the Chamber, however, held themselves back from this pitch of excitement. They did not fail to recall that though the Socialists were their temporary allies in the electoral Cartel, ministerial responsibility in case of victory might be theirs alone. The Socialists opposed the Ruhr occupation in principle. In contrast, most of the Radicals were unhappy that the occupation had been necessary and were resolved to end it, but if possible not on unsatisfactory terms. The difference was fundamental. As the election campaign progressed, Herriot himself preferred to put stress on a "positive" alternative to productive guarantees in the Ruhr, namely an international loan of 10 milliard marks ($2.5 billion) to be used in part for stabilizing the mark but chiefly for payments to France.[44]

But where was such a gigantic sum to come from? On this issue Herriot and other Cartel spokesmen exhibited noteworthy circumspection, falling back on "precious hopes" for a successful outcome to the Expert Committee's endeavors, which alone gave promise in their eyes of an international loan to save French credit.[45] Probably some of the leaders of the left entertained private doubts whether the Dawes Committee could really serve as deus ex machina. But it is striking to note the perverse consistency between this new illusion about help from without and the one not yet fully abandoned on the other side of the political

41. *J.O.C. Déb.*, 26 January 1924, p. 339.
42. Ibid., p. 334.
43. *Le Quotidien*, 28 January 1924.
44. *L'Oeuvre*, 22 February 1924.
45. See, e.g., Robert de Jouvenel in *L'Oeuvre*, 24 February 1924.

spectrum, that direct seizure of pledges could yield reparations revenue on a scale adequate to satisfy French needs. One hope represented but the obverse of the other—that France could somehow find, even at this date, an alternative to further domestic taxation.

Yet for irrelevance and illogical thinking no one could match the Royalists and Communists, antiparliamentary extremists at each end of the political spectrum. Their views were generally frivolous, their numerical strength inconsequential. But they compensated for these deficiencies by the violence of their continual interruptions in the Chamber, and by scurrilous personal attacks in party journals. Their antics only foreshadowed the parliamentary difficulties that would arise a decade later when the extreme parties obtained a significant following. Still, both Royalists and Communists managed by their efforts to lower the level of debate and to gain attention out of all proportion to their real strength.

The financial specialists of the Royalist *Action française* felt sure that the laws governing the ebb and flow of the exchange rate were "as unknown as the laws governing the tides and tempests of the oceans." Léon Daudet assured the Chamber that the trouble originated with Jewish financiers who, gleefully "rubbing their hands together," had given self-serving advice. The tax increase was a scheme to discourage propagation of large families. His own solution was to hang Senator Ernest Billiet (president of the Union of Economic Interests, a conduit for electoral campaign contributions by business), to denounce and mete out punishment for corruption, to set up courts of proscription against war profiteers, and to take stern measures against the "bandits" and "thieves" at the head of various banks and industrial corporations.[46]

To this theme the Communists warmed in turn, and extreme right and left dilated in elaborate counterpoint on the immorality of insurance, banking, sugar and petroleum refining, and other industries in disfavor.[47] The Communists were particularly inventive in disrupting the proceedings. They read interminably from a list of industrial connections of members of parliament; they postured at length as defenders of Republican legality against the "fascist dreams" of the Quai d'Orsay and the Faubourg St.-Honoré; and they urged the abolition or reduction of diverse branches of the armed forces. Instead of new taxes they favored

46. *J.O.C. Déb.*, 25 January 1924, pp. 290–92; 13 February 1924, pp. 717–18. There is little evidence to support the common view, characteristically expressed by Eugen Weber, *Action Française: Royalism and Reaction in Twentieth-Century France* (Stanford, 1962), pp. 136–38, 149–50, that there existed a "striking" coincidence of views between the Royalists and the Poincaré government. Charles Maurras later stated explicitly that Poincaré was "ashamed" of support by *Action française* at the time of Briand's overthrow in 1922 and that accusations of intimacy with Léon Daudet got on his nerves. By the same token Maurras considered Poincaré a "faithful and disciplined partisan" of the left ("La Politique: Le 4 décembre 1923," in *Action française*, 6–7 December 1941).

47. *J.O.C. Déb.*, 18 February 1924, pp. 791–800.

the repeal of indirect taxes already in effect, adducing as justification that the national budget was really a "class budget," including enormous sums for museums, roads, and interest on the national debt, items that benefited only the bourgeoisie. Deputy Renaud Jean carried the Communist argument to its logical conclusion. The current crisis, he stated, proved that the hour approached for settling accounts between classes. The Communists would watch with joy the collapse of "your country—the country of the million and the billion, of high finance and the great employers' associations, the country of cheap profiteers."[48]

Faced with opposition of this tenor, many deputies in the government parties felt constrained on patriotic grounds from giving public expression to the full measure of their frustration. But privately their bitterness was extraordinary. Some indication of it appeared in the establishment press. The trade journal that faithfully reflected the views of finance and industry expressed regret that the government's fiscal proposals had been hastily improvised, and that they were unaccompanied by a plan for positive intervention on the exchange.[49] An unwonted passion overcame the semiofficial *Le Temps*, which, eliminating the customary circumlocutions, castigated those who "by their lack of foresight have conducted us to the edge of the abyss." For years there had been an unbroken line of rhetoric that the Germans would pay, complained *Le Temps*; now the bill was being presented to the French taxpayer. At least this was how it would appear to the voting public.[50]

André Lefèvre, the outspoken but unsophisticated former war minister, came as close as any government supporter to voicing openly in the Chamber the sentiments expressed by the deputies in the lobbies: "I ask you, gentlemen, did you win the war or did you lose it?"[51] The last thing he wanted to do, Lefèvre assured his colleagues, was to serve as the catspaw of a foreign maneuver to bring down the minister of foreign affairs, as Delcassé had been brought down in 1905. But by presenting the electorate with a burden of this magnitude, did one not ensure the fall not merely of the cabinet, but of the Chamber majority and its policy as well?[52]

In all the wearying weeks of debate, André Tardieu was virtually the only deputy who sought to transcend such temporal preoccupations of electoral politics and to address the fundamental difficulties of public administration in the Third Republic. As chief deputy to Clemenceau during the war, Tardieu had become intimately acquainted with the lack of ministerial coordination, the bureaucratic infighting of almost comic

48. Ibid., 28 January 1924, p. 356.

49. *Bulletin quotidien de la société d'études et d'informations économiques*, 12 February 1924. This daily, edited by André François-Poncet, had close ties to the Comité des Forges.

50. *Le Temps*, 21 January 1924.

51. *J.O.C. Déb.*, 4 February 1924, p. 493.

52. Ibid., pp. 492–94; 6 February 1924, pp. 544–46; 15 February 1924, p. 771.

proportions, and the failure to anticipate future problems that hindered the efficient functioning of government in France—no matter who took charge nominally of the affairs of state. He drew on this experience to frame a powerful indictment of the Poincaré government for its inertia in every facet of long-term economic planning. "The two *décimes* are isolated," Tardieu pointed out, "from an exchange policy, a credit policy, a consolidation policy, and a general policy which alone could make them effective." The government had developed no strategy to cope with the special monetary problems accompanying the Ruhr occupation. It had failed to control the exchange rate by direct intervention at crisis points as had been done during the war. It had not even attempted to minimize foreign exchange losses by coordinating coal purchases in England, nor had it seriously tried to control the expenditure of francs by the occupation army in the Ruhr. The two-year record on credit policy was no better. Lasteyrie had unfrozen the *rente* market directly upon taking office in January 1922, but had failed to follow through with the next step, namely reducing the interest rate on national defense bonds. The government's proposals for consolidating the floating debt had never passed beyond the stage of pious hope. It had devised no policy to keep down the prices of key agricultural commodities like wine, sugar, and wheat (admittedly there were great political difficulties in doing so). Finally, Tardieu underscored the crucial sin of omission in the government's foreign policy. He did not subscribe to the simplistic thesis of the left that the Ruhr occupation had caused the fall of the franc. But, he noted, the sharp decline dated from the time when it first became evident that France, despite its declaration of victory, possessed no coherent, comprehensive plan for using the occupation as a steppingstone toward solution of the general reparations problem.[53]

Of course, Tardieu could speak so freely because politically he had little to lose. For several years he had dissipated the magnificent force of his intelligence in acerbic criticism, for which the dominant motive seemed to be pique at his exclusion from power rather than pure conviction. He had thus created an unbridgeable gulf between himself and the government, and alienated the majority of deputies who sat on his own side of the Chamber. It was nevertheless evident that he had identified crucial issues. Maurice Bokanowski, who faultlessly played the part of defender of the government proposals in public, really agreed with much of Tardieu's analysis. In private, he frankly told Poincaré that the "absence on our part of any budgetary, monetary, or financial policy whatsoever" had played a major role in encouraging the speculators. Moreover, Bokanowski observed, even when the government rightly decided on new taxes, almost all of the other measures it undertook to accompany the new fiscal policy "bore the stamp of incoherence and in-

53. Ibid., 12 February 1924, pp. 672–80.

comprehension." The police measures adopted to combat speculation—export prohibitions, expulsion of foreigners, surveillance of telegrams, closure of the commodity exchange—bore witness in his view to "an incapacity and a lack of sangfroid" that constituted "in and of themselves the greatest encouragement to bear speculation against the franc."[54]

Jacques Seydoux,* chief specialist in economic affairs at the Quai d'Orsay and by far the most lucid mind among senior French bureaucrats in the 1920s, was no less scathing in the confidential report that he prepared on the government's economic policies for Poincaré (who had previously been too busy to take these problems personally in hand). Seydoux noted that in the absence of any mechanism for centralized decision making, the several bodies responsible for policy proceeded in completely uncoordinated fashion, finding themselves pushed first one way and then another by private pressure groups, often for trifling reasons. Seydoux's deputy, who sat on several of these committees, reported "ministers acting without the knowledge of their departments, departments repudiating their ministers, varying systems adopted and then rejected by turns, no clearly defined line of conduct; in short, absolute incoherence."[55]

It is a telling illustration of the way the French parliamentary system worked that the glaring inadequacy of general economic planning which so disturbed those on the "inside" should, aside from Tardieu's allusions to it, pass almost without parliamentary echo. Instead, in the Chamber, discussion of trivialities dragged on. The Finance Commission had made a tactical mistake, perhaps, in reporting the draft legislation with 109 individual articles. This provided a pretext for interminable discussion of matters ranging from the dangers of a resurrection of clerical influence in education to the cost of picture postcards, by deputies defending special interests or merely wishing to record statements

*Charles Louis Auguste Jacques Seydoux (1870–1929), member of a Protestant textile family distinguished for public service; spent most of his diplomatic career at the Quai d'Orsay rather than in the field; a self-effacing, nonpolitical, but independent-minded civil servant who put his expertise at the service of the most diverse political superiors and managed to win the admiration of them all; figured as the real organizer of the Blockade Department during the war; was appointed assistant director for commercial affairs, May 1919–October 1924; deputy director of political and commercial affairs, October 1924–December 1926. Despite constant pain from rheumatoid arthritis, which progressively crippled him, Seydoux wrote virtually every important position paper on economic questions at the Foreign Ministry for nearly eight years, and won recognition from his colleagues as the most creative thinker on political matters as well; he attended postwar conferences as the chief French reparations specialist; later served as the moving spirit of Franco-German industrial rapprochement.

54. Bokanowski to Poincaré, 1 March 1924, copy in Millerand Papers. The version published in *J.O.C. Doc.*, Annexe no. 7353, 20 March 1924, pp. 639–44, omits all passages even hinting at Bokanowski's real views.

55. Note Seydoux 24–55, "Défense du franc, mesures économiques," 7 March 1924; enclosing note by his deputy, Prosper Brugière de Barante, 6 March 1924, copy in Millerand Papers.

that would be advantageously reproduced in the newspapers of their home *arrondissements*. The proposal to turn over the state match monopoly to private enterprise generated an enormous amount of heat. The matter was financially insignificant: it made virtually no difference in terms of revenue whether the monopoly was retained or taxes collected from private manufacturers. But the question did provide the government with an opportunity to offer some ideological compensation to right-wing groups called upon to assume the electoral onus of voting higher taxes, and this led in turn to histrionic doctrinal confrontation about the proper role of the state in the economy.[56] Finally, after an all-night session on 22–23 February 1924, the Chamber passed the fiscal package by a vote of 312–205.

Procrastination in the Senate

But the difficulties of Poincaré's government were far from over, for passage of its tax package was by no means assured in the Senate. The balance in the upper house lay somewhat further to the left than in the Chamber. The senators belonging to the *Gauche radicale* stood generally on the more conservative wing of the Radical-Socialist party. They did not really wish to throw up unnecessary obstacles at a time of crisis. On the other hand, they felt a party obligation to make perfectly clear their disengagement from any responsibility, lest they provide an opportunity for opponents of the Radicals to point in the election campaign to embarrassing divergencies within the Cartel on financial matters. Moreover, many members of the *Gauche démocratique*—the large amorphous grouping of the center-left which set the tone in the Senate—who agreed to go along, however unenthusiastically, with the substance of the tax increase, drew the line at the "decree laws" and sale of the state match monopoly. Still, party considerations motivated the Senate's resistance only in part. Right across the political spectrum at the Luxembourg, a deep conviction reigned that the Senate had been slighted in its institutional role. Members of the Finance Commission were miffed at being forced to hurry their study, with the implication that the Senate was a less important body and should proceed with less profound deliberation than the Chamber.[57]

56. Historians have subsequently paid an inordinate amount of attention to this issue. François Goguel, *La Politique des partis sous la IIIe République* (Paris, 1957), p. 198, argues that abandonment of the match monopoly became a major focus of doctrinal confrontation between the "party of movement" and the "party of order." Emmanuel Beau de Loménie, *Les Responsabilités des dynasties bourgeoises*, 4 vols. (Paris, 1943–63), 3:344–45, repeats innuendos bruited about at the time that the government proposal was designed as a concession to Ivra Kreuger, a shady wheeler-dealer of Swedish extraction who was said to be behind France-Afrique, a company that hoped to dominate the free market in matches. For the extensive parliamentary discussion on the subject, see *J.O.C. Déb.*, 18–21 February 1924, pp. 876–914.

57. On the mood of the Senate, see particularly Bérenger's report, *J.O.S. Doc.*, Annexe

Within the confines of commission hearings, the senators could scarcely contain their outrage that the government, which had seemingly done nothing to anticipate the crisis, should now plant news stories in the semiofficial press insinuating that the Senate Finance Commission was at fault for holding up a solution to the country's financial problems. For at least two fiscal years the commission had looked with a jaundiced eye on continued budget deficits, while Lasteyrie had held the line against cuts in government services and suggested with a certain degree of flippancy that "budgets in deficit are sometimes the best." Commission members expressed their dissatisfaction with the absence of a broadly conceived and coordinated program for the settlement of war debts, renegotiation of tariffs, rationalization of domestic and colonial production—in short, for liquidation of the economic legacy of the war. Moreover, François-Marsal and certain other senators had gotten wind, possibly from Governor Robineau himself, of the irregular arrangements made by the treasury with the Bank of France in regard to repayment of the Bank's "advances." This fueled their irritation further. The government, they felt, should at least make a "gesture of courtesy" to show that it had taken the commission into its confidence, particularly since in the forthcoming general elections the majority would probably pay a heavy price for such cooperation. Instead of "sharing its anxieties" and seeking the genuine collaboration of the commission, they complained, the government had sought merely to pacify it with warmed-over variations on the optimistic statements routinely cooked up for public consumption.

At the same time, even the best informed senators—*rapporteur-général* Henry Bérenger,* for example, and former Finance Minister Paul Doumer—obstinately refused to yield a jot of their own illusions. They still maintained that the government could, if it wished, negotiate a large capital loan from the United States and Great Britain to spare the French

*Henry Bérenger (1867–1952), Radical-Socialist (*Gauche radicale*) senator from Guadaloupe, 1912–40; French gasoline and fuel commissioner, 1918–20; *rapporteur* of the Senate Finance Commission, 1922–26; ambassador to the United States, 1926–28, where he negotiated the war debt settlement; president of the Senate Foreign Affairs Commission, 1931–39; opposed full powers for Pétain, 1940. A man of inexhaustible energy, Bérenger labored indefatigably in committee meetings, all the while putting out a steady stream of serious and popular writing on a wide variety of subjects (biography, fiction, belles-lettres, foreign affairs, petroleum policy, even symbolist poetry).

no. 160, pp. 126–63, which reflects much of what went on in commission hearings from 28 February to 13 March 1924; the revealing transcript of the key hearing, Sénat, Commission des Finances, séance du 8 mars 1924, audition de M. le Président du Conseil et de M. le Ministre des Finances, copy in Herriot Papers; the debates themselves, particularly *J.O.S. Déb.*, 13 March 1924, pp. 276–81; François-Marsal, "Souvenirs: La Crise présidentielle et l'éviction de Millerand, 1923–1924," pp. 8–9; and *J.O.S. Déb.*, 10 April 1925, pp. 846–47, when Herriot read from a transcript of François-Marsal's statements in commission meetings in March 1924. Goguel-Nyegaard, *Le Rôle financier du Sénat français*, pp. 159–81, presents a straightforward and convenient summary.

taxpayer until Germany began to pay reparations. "This policy they ask us to adopt," fulminated Bérenger, "weighs down the French taxpayer with burdens which should not fall upon him. . . . He had been told that the German taxpayer would foot the bills. That absolutely must be achieved."[58]

Unhappily, Lasteyrie was not up to dealing with the senators in their angry mood. He was worn out and irritable after his experience with the Chamber. Instead of treating members of the Senate commission as professional colleagues and candidly explaining the considerations that had led to formulation of the particular measures proposed by the rue de Rivoli, he responded defensively to the questions put to him; in the senators' eyes he conducted himself like a guilty defendant before a hostile tribunal. His testimony only worsened matters. Poincaré followed with a personal appearance before the commission to plead for quick action: "There's a hole in the bottom of the boat. We've simply got to plug it up." The premier went as far as he could to propitiate the senators, holding out to them the prospect that the Dawes Committee would certainly arrange for the "relatively rapid" payment of reparations annuities, and (though undoubtedly he knew better) carefully avoiding any direct contradiction of the commission's hopes for capital payments. The senators, however, were not to be mollified. Several accused Poincaré to his face of having solicited the telegrams sent from French embassies abroad reporting that delay in approving the financial package was sustaining the campaign against the franc. When the premier departed, even the quite conservative François-Marsal declared himself sick at heart. "The government has not been candid and has shown no confidence in us," François-Marsal exhorted his colleagues; "it no longer has a right to our confidence."[59]

President Millerand put heavy pressure on his friend François-Marsal not to carry this opposition to the public forum. But the continued controversy, coming after the Chamber debate, compromised the authority of the cabinet without and led to inevitable strains within it. Poincaré apparently lost confidence in Lasteyrie. Charles Reibel, minister of liberated regions, caught in a crossfire between critics of waste and corruption and representatives of the devastated regions who thought their interests were being sacrificed, seemed to have compromised his usefulness. Poincaré also found himself under increasing pressure to take sides openly on the question of electoral reform and other delicate issues of domestic policy. How long could he escape by marshaling what were recognized as "elegant and academic equivocations"? Weeks of obstruction had so taxed the premier's energies that notwithstanding his usual resiliency, he came close several times to losing control of himself

58. Sénat, Commission des Finances, séance du 8 mars 1924, copy in Herriot Papers.

59. Ibid. See also François-Marsal's similar statements in Sénat, Commission des Finances, séance du 12 mars 1924, copy in Herriot Papers.

in parliament. His dejection extended even to foreign affairs: in informed parliamentary circles it was rumored that Poincaré had abandoned hope of using the Ruhr as more than a bargaining point with the Committee of Experts.[60]

Meanwhile, from January to March the position of the treasury deteriorated. Accelerated inflation resulted in further upward pressure on the amount of currency in circulation and advances from the Bank of France to the state. Although sophisticated private bankers knew that a modest increase in circulation was not in and of itself dangerous, the investing public as a whole had come to look on the level of advances as the chief index to the health of the treasury. If it were suddenly revealed that the legal *plafonds* had been exceeded, the public might panic, cease to renew the short-term treasury bonds, sell off its liquid franc holdings and send the franc plummeting beyond recovery. The treasury, therefore, cast about for every possible expedient that might help it to avoid nominally exceeding the *plafonds*. It first turned to the Bank of France to discount various securities, then on 21 February disposed of some of its sterling balances with a repurchase option, and finally on 6 March obtained a large disguised loan from the commercial banks and the Bank of Algeria.[61]

The treasury found itself unable to postpone a long-planned 3 milliard franc Crédit National bond issue. The private banks, after a certain amount of arm-twisting, gave their assistance even to the extent of violating sound business principles by discounting ninety-day commercial paper at the Bank of France and using the proceeds to augment their subscriptions to the long-term bonds. But the public remained wary—a campaign against the loan by *Le Quotidien* did not help—and the flotation was undersubscribed by almost a half. As an emergency measure, the Bank of France was obliged to take up the remainder directly.[62] Naturally, the financial authorities maintained the greatest possible secrecy about these departures from established banking practice. But it was impossible to disguise the embarrassment of the treasury entirely in the guarded weekly statements published by the Bank of France, and these balance sheets, however inadvertently, dampened what confidence remained and furnished additional ammunition for the speculators.

In summary, at the beginning of March 1924 the nation's financial

60. "Bonneteau politique," *Le Progrès civique*, 16 February, 23 February, 1 March, 8 March 1924.

61. These procedures were summarized in the confidential statement sent by François-Marsal (then finance minister) to Raphaël Milliès-Lacroix, president of the Senate Finance Commission, 19 April 1924, cited by Herriot in *J.O.C. Déb.*, 9 April 1925, pp. 2148–49, and inaccurately reproduced by *Le Quotidien* on the same date.

62. François-Marsal in *J.O.S. Déb.*, 10 April 1925, p. 838; Herriot in *J.O.C. Déb.*, 9 April 1925, p. 2149 (reporting data supplied by the Finance Ministry); Georges Lachapelle, *Le Crédit public* (Paris, 1932), pp. 163–64; *Le Quotidien*, especially 8 January–3 February 1924.

problems were still a long way from resolution. While the experts of the Dawes Committee pursued their investigation and the French government held with rapidly diminishing confidence to its position of control and direct exploitation in the Ruhr, the dispute over division of the fiscal burden unfolded along traditional lines, as if the international implications of delay were peripheral. In the highly charged preelection atmosphere, domestic politics—quarrels of party, doctrine, and parliamentary prerogative—took precedence. As the standard of living of the ordinary French family began to decline noticeably under the impact of inflation, the politicians grew ever more loath to impose yet another burden on it. Only a more explicit threat, in the form of a full-scale, organized international attack by speculators against the franc, was to give rise briefly to a sense of urgency.

Chapter 4

Saving the Franc: International Speculation and International Assistance

The Bear Raid on the Franc

While the Senate procrastinated, the franc entered a new cycle of depreciation. After the great drop in the first fortnight of January 1924, the exchange recovered somewhat upon mere introduction of the new fiscal proposals. It then held relatively steady for the better part of a month in spite of the interminable delay in adoption of the tax package. Suddenly, shortly before the Chamber finally passed the legislation, the franc resumed its downward movement. The pound sterling, worth 97.63 francs on 17 February, was quoted at 103.70 on 20 February, 104.15 on 28 February, and then on 4 March—a lugubrious Mardi Gras indeed for the Paris financial community—at 106.53. There were funereal headlines in the newspapers on that day; concierges and taxi drivers expatiated heatedly on the theory of forward exchange and other abstruse subjects. The eyes of all France, it seemed, were focused on the currency market in the Salle des Banquiers at the Bourse. Here, in a high narrow room where the windows never gave enough light, a distraught, gesticulating crowd of bankers' agents and currency brokers jostled each other in a scene approaching pandemonium.[1] The panic was on.

Although the general public remained frightened and confused, private banks in Paris were quickly able to establish what was afoot through discreet inquiries on the various European currency exchanges. Why, they sought to determine, did the franc fall so precipitously in late February and early March? What role did organized international speculation play in its collapse? The initial judgments of the Paris banks were borne out by events, and our narrative will follow their investigation closely. The French government, of course, was particularly concerned with finding out to what extent the new wave of speculation was politically motivated, and if its purpose was to force withdrawal from the Ruhr. We will examine here the price that the French government had to pay for foreign assistance to save the franc. We will consider finally

1. "La Foire aux devises," *Le Quotidien*, 12 March 1924.

whether, by misinterpreting the significance of the franc's temporary recovery on the exchange, the French again missed their opportunity to carry out more fundamental reform—thus remaining in a position of continued dependence on the international financial community.

Knowledgeable members of the banking fraternity found themselves in close agreement about the underlying reasons for the new exchange panic.[2] The franc had been potentially vulnerable to bear speculation on technical grounds ever since its recovery in 1921 to one-third the prewar par. At this level the currency undeniably appeared overvalued to many foreign exchange specialists. These experts correctly observed that the country had not yet restored its full productive capacity, that it labored under a chronic budget deficit linked to the repair of war damage, and that it met with growing difficulty in continuing domestic borrowing. Foreign holders of francs had reason to become increasingly skeptical on both economic and diplomatic grounds whether France would ever succeed in collecting reparations on a scale comparable to the expenses of reconstruction. The long parliamentary controversy in the first half of 1923, ending with rejection of the government's appeal for higher taxes, had shown the legislators prey to illusions and unwilling to cover reconstruction expenses through taxation. Even financial observers who thought the occupation of the Ruhr entirely justified by Germany's recalcitrance could not help but note the disproportion between the political and military risks taken and the actual economic results achieved. This disproportion became painfully evident when, after the long-awaited termination of German passive resistance in September 1923, the promise of tangible reparations payments appeared no closer to realization. Direct operation of the productive pledges, and even agreements for deliveries in kind negotiated by the Franco-Belgian engineers' mission (M.I.C.U.M.) with the German industrialists, left no more than a modest surplus for the French budget after payment of occupation costs. Nor

2. I have relied heavily on the analysis made by A. S. Cahen and Robert Wolff of A. S. Cahen et Cie, 29 February 1924; given by Bokanowski to Poincaré, 1 March 1924, copy in Millerand Papers, excerpted in the Chamber Finance Commission report, *J.O.C. Doc.*, Annexe no. 7353, 20 March 1924, pp. 640–42. Supplementary details are provided by Raymond Philippe, *Le Drame financier de 1924–1928* (Paris, 1931); Pierre Frayssinet, *La Politique monétaire de la France, 1924–1928* (Paris, 1928); Jean Casamajor, *Le Marché à terme des changes en France* (Paris, 1924); Robert Wolff, *Economie et finances de la France* (New York, 1943); Georges Lachapelle, *Les Batailles du franc: La Trésorerie, le change et la monnaie depuis 1914* (Paris, 1928), and *Le Crédit public* (Paris, 1932); James Harvey Rogers, *The Process of Inflation in France, 1914–1927* (New York, 1929). The best contemporary analysis is found in F. Maroni's weekly "Revue financière" in *Le Journal des débats*; in John Maynard Keynes's articles for the *Nation and the Athenaeum*; and in the *Economist* (particularly 2 February 1924). The American economist consul in Paris compiled a useful summary of banking and newspaper opinion in his reports, U.S. 851.5151/14–32. For the Bank of France view see "Banque de France, Assemblée générale ordinaire du 31 janvier 1924, Compte rendu des opérations de la banque . . . par M. Robineau, gouverneur," in *Les Assemblées générales, 1924. Premier semestre. Rapports des conseils d'administration et des commissaires des comptes*, pp. 117–24; and a similar report dated 29 January 1925, reviewing the fiscal year 1924, in *Les Assemblées générales, 1925* (summarized in U.S. 851.5151/43).

did the French victory in the Ruhr lead to a general political détente in Europe. The Paris government had no workable option but to refer the whole problem back to the Reparation Commission bureaucracy.

All these discouraging economic and political developments converged to create an atmosphere conducive to a foreign crisis of confidence in the franc. Under the system of flexible exchange rates in the 1920s, money market specialists all over the world sought to predict how basic economic considerations and trader psychology would intersect to determine future trends, in much the same way as stock market analysts make their forecasts today. The job of these foreign exchange specialists was to estimate the franc's value as a short-term trading vehicle as well as to evaluate its fundamental economic worth. Analysts abroad were generally less tolerant of financial mismanagement, less ready to extend their continued confidence, than French investors who through close exposure had gradually accustomed themselves to financial assumptions and practices that appeared alarming when judged by normative standards. It was all the more noteworthy, therefore, when renewed downward pressure on the franc originated in November 1923 from Paris itself. Large imports of cotton, wool, cereals, and other commodities customarily caused the French currency to depreciate in early autumn. But in September 1923 importers had deferred their commodity purchases in the hope that victory in the Ruhr would lead to additional improvement in the exchange rate and enable them to buy more cheaply. When the franc failed to rise further, they hastened to cover themselves en masse. The situation deteriorated because many firms were required to settle year-end foreign balances in December, just when the French government entered the currency market in order to secure dollars to meet interest payments on war matériel purchased from the United States. The widely remarked increase in the Bank of France's note circulation in December 1923, and the treasury's failure to reimburse the Bank by the full amount of "advances" expected, gave rise to attacks against the state's creditworthiness and focused public attention on the mounting menace of domestic inflation. The police measures taken at the Bourse in the first week of January 1924 served to convince the knowledgeable, at home as well as abroad, that the authorities misunderstood the root causes of the difficulty. After the Bourse panic on 14 January, the general public grew anxious for the first time and inundated the banks with orders for the sale of fixed-interest *rentes* and the corresponding purchase of foreign securities.

Only at this point, after a period of gradually mounting activity, did foreign speculators begin to play the primary role. Successive depreciation of the Austrian, Hungarian, and German currencies had created huge profits for a particular class of people in central Europe. Those engaged in banking, in the export-import business, and others working in financial markets found that speculation became of necessity a fact of everyday life. When the central European currencies were stabilized in the autumn of 1923, it was to be expected that many would continue to succumb to the lure of easy profit and would seek a new arena for their operations. Some of the more sober German bankers felt from the beginning that the risks were too great. Hamburg's Max Warburg, for example, judged the French government's international credit rating still sufficiently high so that a concerted effort on its part to squeeze the "bears" offered a good prospect for success.[3] But cautious voices were in the minority. By late February, bankers and speculators on German regional exchanges were heavily involved. Diplomatic observers reported them to be "elated over the continued depreciation" of the franc.[4]

The primary center of speculation, however, was located not within Germany but in Amsterdam. By remaining neutral in the world war, the Netherlands had secured a strategic and vastly profitable position as the trading intermediary between Germany and the rest of the world. After the war, the Amsterdam banking community managed to consolidate and even to enlarge its role by discreetly providing facilities for currency exchange to its German correspondents, who in this way found shelter for their operations from the rigors of the German banking laws. Dr. Fritz Mannheimer,* head of the Amsterdam branch of Mendelssohn & Co. and the leading banker of German nationality in the city, had earlier taken advantage of these facilities to funnel a major share of the business transactions arising from postwar speculation on the mark through his firm. At the beginning of 1924, Mannheimer began to talk up a large concerted maneuver against the franc as a "sure thing" and offered a guarantee of the credit facilities of his house to participating banks throughout central Europe. The antithesis of a careful, conservative banker, Mannheimer was a corpulent, full-blooded man of immense energy, ability, and imagination. Without a notable excess of scruples, to be sure, he seemed to have the golden touch. He had already made a fortune speculating on the wildly depreciating central and east European currencies. So where he led, other speculators—including some of the most respected banks in central Europe—followed, in hopes of a bonanza.[5]

*Fritz Mannheimer trained as a broker in Paris and then in Amsterdam before the war; used his considerable charm to build intimate connections to normally closed Dutch banking circles; served as Amsterdam representative of the Reichsbank and head of foreign wheat procurement for the German armed forces (through *Zentraleinkaufsgesellschaft*), 1914–18; made the Amsterdam branch of Mendelssohn & Co. so profitable that the parent firm in Berlin, long prominent in Reich banking councils, was able to maintain its importance in the postwar period despite loss of its former position as main international banker of the Russian state; grazed the thin edge of the law several times with his financial maneuvers; died in 1939, just before his bank failed owing to speculation on the Dutch florin.

3. Max M. Warburg, *Aus meinen Aufzeichnungen* (Glückstadt, 1952), pp. 124–25.

4. U.S. 862.00/1428, summarizing reports from American consular officials in late February and early March 1924.

5. The scope of the speculative movement can be gauged from the fact that when the

Operating with a considerable degree of coordination, the Amsterdam-based speculators began their maneuver by selling francs short against sterling or dollars on the Paris exchange. To cover themselves they were obliged to borrow from the supply of "floating francs," foreign-owned franc balances on account in French banks that derived from France's balance-of-payments deficits in previous years. Those who held such franc balances could be induced to lend them if the interest rate was high enough. The rate on borrowed francs soon rose to 25 percent on an annual basis, but this did not appear prohibitive to speculators who expected to make that much in a few days through depreciation of the currency. The floating-franc balances, therefore, constituted the speculators' "mass of maneuver."

The dramatically widening gap between the "spot" and "forward" quotations of the franc—that is, between the rates for present exchange of francs and for delivery in one to three months—served as the first public signal of the operation. In normal times the difference between the spot and forward rates simply reflects an arbitrage commission for those who handle such transactions. When this difference quadrupled within two weeks, it called attention to the existence of a large short position against the franc. The public notice helped the speculators because it inspired legitimate businesses to protect themselves by selling francs immediately too, in order to cover anticipated foreign exchange needs.

Luckily for the French authorities, the supply of floating francs proved more limited than was generally believed. But when, at the end of January, the French Finance Ministry adopted a rudimentary form of exchange control, restricting the loans of such franc balances to foreign establishments, the speculators were ready with a new and even more effective approach. From their experience on central European markets, they knew that as a currency depreciated, foreign or gold-value securities rose proportionately. They proceeded, therefore, to purchase calls (rights to future purchase) on stable-value securities like Suez quoted on the Paris Bourse, and also to buy cotton, coffee, and other commodity futures on the French exchange. This operation produced a double

French government finally brought the franc under control, the Allgemeine Industriebank of Vienna failed immediately; half a dozen other major establishments in that city, including the Austro-Polish and Austro-Orient banks, Kolmat & Co., Kettner, Brüder Nowak, and the Austrian postal savings bank, found themselves in severe difficulty. At the same time, Hungary's usually stable bank stocks lost up to a fifth of their value in a week, and the Berlin commodities market fluctuated dramatically (Frayssinet, *La Politique monétaire*, p. 27).

On Mendelssohn and the Amsterdam banking community, see Felix Pinner [Frank Fassland], *Deutsche Wirtschaftsführer* (Berlin-Charlottenburg, 1925), pp. 226–28; Henri Coston, *L'Europe des banquiers* (Paris, 1963), pp. 191–95; J. W. Beyen, *Money in a Maelstrom* (New York, 1949), pp. 23–24; Philippe, *Le Drame financier*, pp. 25–27; and *Berliner Tageblatt*, 28 March 1922.

effect. The sellers or commodity brokers were obliged to make additional purchases abroad in order to reconstitute their own inventory and converted francs for this purpose. At the same time, the rise in commodity prices and gold-value securities fostered a mood of panic among French industrialists and holders of capital.

The scheme appeared virtually foolproof. Inevitably a certain number of French capitalists would seek to protect their assets by joining the flight to gold-value securities. They would consequently sell fixed-income securities, principally government bonds, which would inevitably drop disastrously, further damaging the state's credit. The cost to the speculators would be minimal. They could borrow money from French banks to finance commodity purchases at the normal commercial rate for such transactions, which was no more than a fraction of the rate on floating francs. They could also pyramid their operations, by first purchasing commodities on current account when futures were not available and then using the commodity warehouse warrants as security to obtain new credits for additional commodity purchases or other maneuvers against the currency.

It took the cumbersome bureaucracies at the Finance and Commerce ministries six weeks to develop administrative rules which blocked these operations. During that period the speculators ran up high profits, multiplying the reserves with which they could protect themselves from countermeasures. Finally, in the last days of February, the resourceful speculators turned to yet another tactic, namely, direct manipulation of the exchange rate by skillful orchestration of the sale of francs on markets located in different time zones. Shortly before the late afternoon closing they dumped francs on smaller continental money markets; then they continued the movement on the New York exchange (open later because of the time difference). They thus nurtured a psychological climate in which the Paris market, at the opening the next morning, tended to follow and prolong the downward movement created on lower-volume, more easily influenced exchanges elsewhere.

The speculators' ultimate objective was to provoke the wider franc-holding public into panic selling, depressing the market to a point which enabled them to liquidate their own short positions at a large profit. If the depreciation of the franc were to continue long enough, the speculators could run their profits so high as to become invulnerable to counterattack. The French government would have to reckon with the prospect of a rise in the domestic price level, a second round of cost-push inflation, general discontent, and an attempt by French citizens to export capital—in short, a duplication of the lugubrious train of financial and social catastrophes that had ravaged the weak-currency nations of central and eastern Europe since the war.

The Speculative Movement and International Politics

The professional speculators based in Amsterdam and elsewhere carried out their operations against the backdrop of a routine volume of currency transactions made to finance international trade. In much the way that a gold discovery can provide an irresistible attraction for every would-be miner with a pick and shovel, the lure of easy money also drew thousands of amateur speculators all over the world into hazarding a portion of their savings on the currency exchanges. As the extensive speculative movement gathered force, the motives behind it became a burning political issue in France. Was this maneuver, like so many directed against vulnerable currencies in the era of flexible exchange rates, undertaken principally out of personal cupidity? Or did it mask a conscious attempt on the part of foreign governments to exploit French financial weakness for diplomatic ends? For German bankers and their allies, of course, there existed no conflict of interest between an appreciation of the business possibilities and political loyalty: hardly anyone in central Europe would consider refraining from profitable operations out of sympathy for French foreign policy. From the beginning of the Ruhr occupation, however, many French newspapers had voiced the suspicion that Germany, Great Britain, or even the United States was employing this means to exert political pressure on France.[6]

Such charges, harmonizing with the conspiratorial interpretation of events that has long exerted an appeal in France, were set forth with more assurance in the general political press than in specialized financial journals. Indeed during most of 1923 they found little acceptance in financial circles generally. But by early 1924 highly placed French government figures, echoed by virtually the entire press, believed that there was some political component in the currency speculation. Bokanowski made this assessment in guarded fashion at the time;[7] François-Marsal referred even in later years to the "foreign conspiracy against France, against her flag, against her political action."[8] Poincaré claimed repeatedly that the offensive "certainly aimed at least as much at political ends as financial."[9]

Nevertheless, publicly the premier could offer nothing more than fragmentary and circumstantial evidence to support this claim. He noted that from the middle of January on, the Reichsbank quoted the franc slightly below the free exchange "par" every day. Bavarian banks accepted francs unwillingly and only at a discount allowing for future

6. See the many examples cited by Jacques Fiérain, "La Presse française et l'occupation de la Ruhr" (Thèse d'études supérieures, Sorbonne, 1950). Marguerite Perrot, *La Monnaie et l'opinion publique en France et en Angleterre, 1924–1936* (Paris, 1955), pp. 155–62, provides a summary of 1924 newspaper views on the political component in the speculation.

7. *J.O.C. Doc.*, Annexe no. 7353, 20 March 1924, p. 639.

8. *J.O.S. Déb.*, 10 April 1925, p. 837.

9. Ibid., 13 March 1924, p. 281.

depreciation. Many German financial institutions advised their clients to sell franc holdings. The Reichsbank, Poincaré further charged, had "visibly inspired" a German press campaign against the stability of the French currency. German banks had propagandized actively against the franc throughout central Europe and in Holland. An obscure American banking house had put out a tract appealing to German-Americans to sell the franc short and thus to combine personal profit with assistance to the "heroic people of the Ruhr," who would benefit if France were forced to evacuate its armies because of financial distress. Finally, Poincaré asserted, the principal banking houses in Berlin had held a secret meeting on 4 March, at which a German Foreign Ministry representative read a message intimating that gloomy forecasts for French finance might contribute to the campaign for revision of the Versailles treaty, not only in regard to reparations and the Rhineland occupation but also with respect to the Polish frontier. Yet despite the pattern suggested by these developments, Poincaré was obliged to concede that the franc holdings in Germany proper which would determine the impact of such maneuvers were in all probability of "small importance."[10]

It is not possible to determine with complete assurance whether the German government in fact played an active role in speculation against the franc. It appears that officials in Berlin did examine the possibility of putting pressure on France in this way during 1923, but that nothing tangible materialized. The Wilhelmstrasse first gave serious consideration to an attack on the franc in March 1923, when it became clear that German passive resistance could not be maintained indefinitely. The American ambassador in Berlin, Alanson B. Houghton, who often reflected the views of the government to which he was accredited, advised Secretary Hughes that France had to be met by force and emphasized that the franc was "the obvious point of weakness." If the United States and Great Britain were to "overcome the artificial support now given the franc," Houghton suggested, then the "sane majority" in France could be brought to reason.[11] This proposal for active intervention, however, ran counter to Washington's European policy, and Houghton was ignored.

In June 1923 German Foreign Office bureaucrats explored the idea that the Reichsbank might use its influence to sustain a franc panic should one arise, but by this time Germany's own financial difficulties had grown so acute as to make direct action impracticable.[12] On 24 July Count Harry Kessler, the author and former diplomat often employed by the German government for delicate, unofficial missions, called on Secretary Hughes in Washington to inquire cautiously about the possibility

10. *J.O.C. Déb.*, 26 January 1924, pp. 321–30; *J.O.S. Déb.*, 13 March 1924, pp. 281–86.

11. Houghton to Hughes, 6 March 1923, Box 4B, Hughes Papers.

12. Austausch der deutschen und englischen Industrien, 25 June 1923, G.F.M. 3398/1736/D739823–824.

of "cooperation by America in case of economic pressure by England on France . . . for example, if England were to withdraw her support for the French franc and French securities." Hughes urbanely turned aside the suggestion with an explanation of the State Department's powerlessness to influence American banks, many of which, he pointed out frankly, favored the Ruhr occupation. A solution, he indicated, was "not to be found in this direction."[13]

Even this tentative feeler made through Kessler antedated the end of passive resistance in the Ruhr and the final collapse of the mark. The monetary chaos that engulfed Germany in the fall of 1923 hardly allowed scope for maneuvers against any foreign currency. The rentenmark, a new monetary unit created in November, remained on shaky ground for many months. The German government fully understood the precariousness of its financial situation. There was a dearth of capital throughout the country. The Reichsbank found its foreign currency reserves reduced to a minimum. It depended on the Bank of England's good will for underwriting the Gold Discount Bank (which financed what remained of German foreign trade), and on the entire international banking community for the capital resources required to revive the economy after the monetary debacle. "A definitive stabilization," the Wilhelmstrasse informed the German chargé in Paris at the beginning of February 1924, "is out of the question unless foreign countries provide financial assistance to establish a permanent gold currency."[14] Therefore, whatever private satisfaction German officials took in the franc's difficulties, they recognized that the Reich could exert no more than a marginal influence on exchange markets in early 1924. The Marx cabinet, by that time, had come to believe that the best chance for getting rid of the intrusive French presence in the Ruhr and Rhine provinces lay in cooperation with the Expert Committees. In the meantime it sought to find a modus vivendi with France in order to alleviate the rigors of the regime in the occupied areas. A unilateral challenge to the French seemed, for the moment, a less promising tactic. Thus it is not surprising that during the crucial months from January to April 1924, the depreciation of the franc never appeared on the formal agenda for German cabinet meetings.[15]

By contrast, some persons in America with German sympathies apparently did speculate against the franc during the decisive period. A suspect New York firm called Morgan, Harwood & Co. enjoyed a brief moment of notoriety by widely distributing a circular to the German-

13. Carl von Schubert to Reich Chancellor Gustav Stresemann, 17 August 1923, summarizing Kessler to Schubert, 25 July 1923, BA, R 43 I/39/77–78.

14. Instruktion für den deutschen Geschäftsträger in Paris, 1 February 1924, G.F.M. K936/4505/K239303–309.

15. Alte Reichskanzlei, Akten betreffend Kabinettsprotokolle, vol. 45–46, U.S. National Archives Microfilms T-120, Washington, D.C., 3491/1751–52 (January–April 1924).

American community urging short sales of francs through its facilities. A State Department investigation turned up a link between Morgan, Harwood and certain German-American congressmen, and also uncovered presumptive evidence that the firm had deliberately chosen its name to resemble that of Morgan, Harjes et Cie (the Paris branch of J. P. Morgan) with a view to confusing investors. Yet it would be a mistake to overestimate the impact of propaganda from such marginal sources, which would have had scant effect on money markets had fundamentals remained sound.[16]

England possessed a means of putting pressure on France, since the French war debt to Great Britain, amounting to £612 million, took the form of twelve-month treasury bills. Normally these bills were routinely renewed upon French government demand. Shortly before Prime Minister Stanley Baldwin met with Poincaré in September 1923, however, British officials indirectly conveyed to the French premier the intimation that if basic differences dividing the two countries could not be reconciled, the British government might find it difficult to continue to renew these obligations. Since Poincaré assured Baldwin that, once passive resistance ended, he would not object to further examination of the reparations problem by all the Allies, the British prime minister deferred action on the matter.[17] In any case, his warning could not be taken at face value. To be sure, if the British government had carried out its threat and the French had been forced to default, there would have been a serious repercussion on the foreign exchange value of the franc. But Sir Philip Lloyd-Greame, president of the Board of Trade, the "more responsible" leaders in the City, and even some officials at the Foreign Office concerned with economic affairs inclined to the view—so they told American diplomats—that such a bald attempt at coercion was too risky. It would give France a plausible excuse to default on its war debt, and Britain, by forcing repudiation, stood to lose more than would France.[18]

Still, the general idea remained in play. When in mid-November the French government attempted to impose restrictions on the scope of the Experts' inquiry into German capacity to pay, the Foreign Office asked the Treasury to consider what particular form of financial pressure would be most likely to bring the French to heel. Officials at Whitehall were already in high dudgeon at this time because they had learned that the French planned to extend military loans to Yugoslavia, Romania, and Poland, all the while maintaining that they could not afford to begin payment on their debt to Great Britain.[19] The permanent officials at the

16. Memorandum by the Economic Adviser, 14 April 1924, U.S. 851.51/452.

17. George Harvey to State Department, 28 September 1923, U.S. 851.51/403.

18. Post Wheeler to State Department, 20 November 1923, U.S. 851.51/411–412.

19. Foreign Office to Treasury, 14 November 1923, F.O. 371/9682: C 19472/1/18; Central Department memorandum, 28 January 1924, and Miles W. Lampson minute, 29 January 1924, F.O. 371/9682: C 1540/11/62.

Treasury had long been anti-French. They rather relished the idea of using the available financial levers to break French recalcitrance. Unaccountably, however, they did not present a concrete set of recommendations for seven weeks, by which time it was too late for the lame-duck Conservative government to take action.

When the controller of finance, Sir Otto E. Niemeyer, completed work on the Treasury plan in early January 1924, he did not mince his words. "The only thing likely to move the present French government towards a more reasonable reparations policy," he asserted, "apart from a slowly growing feeling of disquiet at French isolation amid the reprobation of a world horrified at starvation and ruin in Germany, is a fall in the French franc sufficiently serious to shake the confidence of the French peasant in his national securities." It most certainly lay in Great Britain's power to create a "lively fear" of this development in France. World opinion might consider it unsporting should Britain brusquely refuse to renew the French treasury bills as they came due. But, Niemeyer pointed out, it was quite unnecessary to resort to so drastic a measure. Whitehall could achieve its aim simply by inviting all European debtor nations to enter simultaneously into funding arrangements, privately notifying Italy and the minor allies—who would never pay much anyway—that they would be granted "very liberal terms" provided they agreed to abstain from coercive measures against ex-enemy countries not unanimously approved by all allied powers. If France declined to enter into negotiations under such conditions, Britain could then marshal any of several weapons in its arsenal.

The mere demand to fund, as the Treasury saw it, would constitute a recall to "realities" and "tend to put the now overvalued franc at its proper level." As the next turn of the screw, the British government might exercise its legal option to take over the gold that the Bank of France had deposited in England during the war as security for the debt and thereby compromise the stated gold reserve of the Bank of France. Alternatively, Britain might sell a portion of its holdings of French treasury bills on the private market, where they would fetch so low a price as to destroy French credit. An exchange of French bills for German bonds figured as a third possibility; the German government could then tender the French bills in reparations payment, and the French could hardly refuse to accept their own bills at par, no matter what their actual value. Finally, Britain could impose a selective tariff on imports from defaulting debtor countries. Since the French could not find substitute markets for the wine, silk, and fancy goods that comprised the bulk of their exports to England, they would be hit particularly hard. Niemeyer expressed confidence that the mere threat of such measures would so damage French credit that private firms and municipalities, unable to obtain financing abroad even for routine business operations, would soon generate sufficient pressure on the French government to change its foreign policy.[20]

Initially, the Foreign Office reacted enthusiastically to the Treasury recommendations. Miles W. Lampson, head of the Central Department, thought that the French had been "behaving in a peculiarly unpleasant manner" and saw no reason why the British government should refrain from using the "weapon of overwhelming power" available to it. Lord Curzon, the retiring foreign secretary, regretted that he did not have time to seek the cabinet's sanction for measures of relief from "an altogether intolerable situation, brought about by the purely selfish and exclusive policy of France."[21] Curzon may well have expected the successor Labour government to grasp every lever known to finance capitalism to bring the French into line. Labour party ultras such as E. D. Morel, chairman of the party's executive committee, had long called for flamboyant gestures to emphasize British opposition to French foreign policy.[22] H. N. Brailsford, publisher of the party's leading weekly, egged on the faithful with cartoons explaining "why France cannot pay her debts" by depicting Poincaré feeding money to snake-like vultures representing the armies of France, Romania, Czechoslovakia, and Poland.[23] And when French Socialist Albert Thomas, head of the International Labor Organization, came to London in early January 1924 to make informal contact with the incoming government on Poincaré's behalf, Prime Minister and Foreign Secretary-designate J. Ramsay MacDonald pointedly let fall the remark: "If the British government was not to renew the French treasury bills, the franc would go down to 250, would it not?" Mrs. Beatrice Webb and MacDonald's other inexperienced colleagues, tasting the heady nectar of power for the first time, relished the spectacle as Thomas visibly turned pale and threw up his hands in despair.[24]

Once MacDonald assumed his duties at the Foreign Office on 22 January, however, he paid no more attention than politeness required to the giddy extremists in his own party. The top civil servants at Downing Street and in the Foreign Office worked hard to overcome the barriers of social class and ideology that separated them from the Labour prime minister. MacDonald responded to their overtures with a warmth and alacrity that would have scandalized his former associates at the Union of Democratic Control. Almost immediately, he proved as adept in

20. Treasury to Foreign Office, 4 January 1924, F.O. 371/9682: C 203/11/62.

21. Lampson and Curzon minutes, 8 January 1924, F.O. 371/9682: C 203/11/62.

22. Robert C. Reinders, "Racialism on the Left: E. D. Morel and the 'Black Horror of the Rhine,'" *International Review of Social History* 13 (1968): 1–28; Henry R. Winkler, "The Emergence of a Labour Foreign Policy in Great Britain, 1918–1929," *Journal of Modern History* 28 (1956): 247–58.

23. *New Leader*, 11 January 1924, cover, cited in F.O. 371/9682: C 1008/11/62.

24. *Beatrice Webb's Diaries, 1924–1932*, ed. Margaret Cole (London, New York, and Toronto, 1956), p. 2 (8 January 1924). See also Albert Thomas to Poincaré, 25 January 1924, vol. 16017, pp. 476–77, Raymond Poincaré Papers, Bibliothèque Nationale, Paris.

assimilating the bureaucratic approach of his chief professional advisers at the Foreign Office as he showed himself at ease in the best London clubs.[25] Betraying no trace of the flippancy he had lately shown to Thomas, the new prime minister asked the Foreign Office staff for a sober judgment as to whether financial pressure on France would help or hinder acceptance of the recommendations of the Expert Committee already at work under General Dawes examining the reparations problem. Upon reflection, Miles Lampson of the Central Department reversed his stand and advised that "action before the issue of the Experts' report would tend to prejudice their prospects of success." Lampson also observed that premature pressure regarding the French debt might serve as a fillip to Poincaré's waning popularity. "Rather let him have more rope," he counseled, "and his obstinacy, left alone, will do the rest." Permanent Under Secretary Sir Eyre Crowe adduced yet another reason for temporization. MacDonald desired to coordinate any action taken with the United States. In Crowe's view, financial pressure had to be kept absolutely secret ahead of time, and in his experience, it was "quite impossible to keep anything secret which is known to the State Department." On the whole, therefore, he thought it best to keep the option of using the financial club in reserve.[26]

MacDonald declared himself convinced. He ordered the Treasury plan "pigeonholed" until the Expert Committee had reported.[27] He resolved to do nothing to bring fundamental Anglo-French divergencies into the open before the forthcoming French elections, and found encouragement in the counsels of French Socialists that this was the best tactic to maximize the Cartel des Gauches's prospects for victory at the polls.[28] Foreign Office officials privately explained to the Germans that their main objective was to "weaken the domestic political position of Poincaré." At the same time, MacDonald also felt that a certain public show of unity with France was the best way to encourage continued American participation in European affairs after the Dawes Committee had reported, and this American presence, he calculated, would give him more leverage over France in the long run.[29] The delay in exerting financial pressure cost him nothing, since he could always revive the plan to give "a hint on the subject of debts" should difficulties arise either within the Expert Committee, or later, after the Experts had set

25. Stephen Roskill, *Hankey: Man of Secrets*, vol. 2 (London, 1972), pp. 353–59.

26. MacDonald memorandum, 28 January 1924; Lampson minute, 29 January, Crowe minute, 30 January 1924, F.O. 371/9682: C 1540/11/62.

27. MacDonald minute, 2 February 1924, F.O. 371/9682: C 1540/11/62.

28. H. N. Brailsford to MacDonald [reporting the views of Léon Blum], 3 February 1924, F.O. 800/218/189–190, James Ramsay MacDonald Correspondence, Public Record Office, London.

29. Dufour-Feronce tel., 23 February 1924, reporting the explanation by Parliamentary Under Secretary Arthur Ponsonby, G.F.M. 4478/2214/E088429–434; also Dufour-Feronce tels., 28 February and 6 March 1924, G.F.M. 4478/2214/E088401–410, E088376–381.

forth their plan. Meanwhile, MacDonald ruled out premature action against the franc partially, as he told a deputation of visiting German businessmen, because "if we smash the franc to 150 or indeed 200 to the pound, we will get an increase in French competition and [domestic] unemployment."[30]

In summary, then, neither the German nor the English government seems to have taken part directly in a maneuver against the French currency. On the other hand, both Berlin and London welcomed the franc's fall and confidently expected this development to force the French to be more amenable to an "international" solution to the reparations problem. In Germany Chancellor Wilhelm Marx justified his policy of "watchful waiting" until the Experts rendered their judgment on the ground that their report would strengthen "economic rationality" and, by reestablishing a "world economic balance," help to bring about the "necessary political reaction" in the Entente states. "It is probably no accident of fate," he told Reichstag colleagues privately, "that exactly at the present moment, this most efficacious factor in the determination of policy has come so decisively to the foreground, with the sudden fall of the franc in the case of our pitiless enemy to the west."[31]

German diplomatic observers in Paris were quick to attribute any signs of increased French flexibility to financial developments. "The fall of the franc and the financial helplessness to which France now suddenly sees herself reduced have had a salutary effect," reported chargé d'affaires Leopold von Hoesch on 14 February. "Public opinion inclines toward peace and quiet, settlement and stable conditions." Hoesch believed it significant that the influential newspapers which habitually supported the government had begun to stress that France could not muster the strength to hold down Germany permanently and to oppose the other great powers at the same time. He also noted a growing disillusionment with the financial results of direct exploitation of the Ruhr through the M.I.C.U.M. agreements.[32]

The renewed fall of the franc, Hoesch advised later in February, fostered public expression of the view that "France must seek deliverance in an international solution to the reparations problem." Several highly placed Frenchmen had sought him out to report that Poincaré was now urgently seeking a settlement and stood ready to accept the Experts' recommendations as a basis of discussion. Minister of Justice Maurice Colrat, for example, who boasted long personal association with

30. Memorandum by German industrialist ten Bosch (associate of Hermann Röchling), 4 April 1924, G.F.M. L1491/5352/L436703–709.

31. Wilhelm Marx to Kommerzienrat Joseph Böhm, member of the Reichstag Foreign Affairs Committee, 26 January 1924, BA, R 43 I/40/160–62.

32. Hoesch tel., 14 February 1924, G.F.M. K936/4505/K239318–325, 4478/2214/E088497–503.

Poincaré, assured him that the premier would prove "very flexible."[33] Personally, the German diplomat placed greater stock in the evolving public mood than in second-hand accounts of the premier's change of heart. Press discussions, he cautioned his superiors at the Wilhelmstrasse, tended to exaggerate policy shifts in official quarters. Past experience led him to predict that Poincaré would follow rather than lead the change in public opinion and would alter his basic policy aims only under "the strong pressure of inescapable necessities." Germany's best bet, he counseled throughout the franc crisis, remained the "well-founded hope" for a strong swing to the left in the coming French elections—so that afterward Berlin could deal with a different man.[34]

In England, Labour ministers made a strikingly similar assessment of the political prospects. "The franc is our best ally," Chancellor of the Exchequer Philip Snowden told the German minister in London; it represented the best weapon "the English and ultimately also the Germans have against Poincaré."[35] Foreign Office officials, and also bankers in the City, consistently attributed indications that Poincaré might adopt a more flexible reparations policy to pressures generated by the fall of the franc and related problems of domestic politics.[36]

Certain influential London bankers were critical of the Foreign Office decision to refrain from bold action until after the Experts had reported and the French elections had taken place. Reginald McKenna, influential chairman of the Joint City and Midland Bank who also served as chairman of the second and less important Committee of Experts, objected to what he considered "excessively kind treatment" of the French by the British Foreign Office, which he feared might lead the French government to ask for an emergency loan. When McKenna saw Poincaré in Paris in mid-February on matters connected to the Experts' work, he made a point of informing him that the British financial world would not consider granting credit unless "a more reasonable settlement of the reparations question was brought about beforehand."[37] Within the Expert Committees sentiment varied widely. Even the other British delegates would probably have objected to the categorical tone of McKenna's warning, and the American Experts, had they known of it, would have declined to endorse its substance also. Nevertheless, the Experts and their supporting staff did not fail to realize how developments on the

33. Hoesch tel., 21 February 1924, G.F.M. 4478/2214/E088473–474; Hoesch tel., 28 February 1924, G.F.M. 4478/2214/E088418–423, K936/4505/K239331–337.

34. Ibid.; also Hoesch tel., 5 March 1924, G.F.M. 4478/2214/E088394–395.

35. Memorandum by Dufour-Feronce of conversation with Snowden, 17 February 1924, G.F.M. 4478/2214/E088462–470.

36. Dufour-Feronce tels., 21 and 28 February 1924, G.F.M. 4478/2214/E088451–458, E088401–410.

37. Memorandum by Dufour-Feronce of talk with McKenna, 16 February 1924, G.F.M. 4478/2214/E088488–493; Dufour-Feronce tel., 28 February 1924, G.F.M. 4478/2214/E088401–410.

exchange had strengthened their hand. Arthur N. Young, State Department economic adviser on temporary assignment in Paris to help out the American Experts, typified sentiment among the staff in his report to Washington: "The franc has fallen very opportunely and the result has been a great increase of reasonableness in this country."[38]

As of the beginning of March 1924, then, the financial crisis in its various manifestations had contributed to a preoccupation with domestic affairs in France and a growing doubt in the Paris ministries whether direct exploitation of the Ruhr and Rhineland could be indefinitely prolonged. This development was matched by increasing confidence in London, Berlin, and Washington that an international solution proposed unanimously by the Expert Committees might under the circumstances prove the most attractive reparations alternative for the French themselves. But none of this was as yet definitive, or imminent.

The Currency in Danger

The menace of a real catastrophe for France became more acute in the week following the sharp decline of 4 March. Alarmed Paris banking specialists reached the conclusion that it was now too late simply to pass the government's fiscal package and to wait for recognition of France's determination to curb the budget deficit to produce its eventual effect on the exchange. The French people were now too close to "the limits of elasticity of confidence . . . in their own currency," and as Bokanowski frankly added in his private report to Poincaré, their confidence in the "capacity of their leaders" was similarly approaching its limits. If there were any further delay, the speculators could repurchase the francs they had borrowed to start the currency's downward slide and sell foreign currencies on the Paris market to the panic-stricken public at a rate so high that they would become invulnerable to counterattack. The cost of bringing the exchange rate down, if that could be done at all, would then be borne by the French people themselves, with incalculable risk for foreign policy and domestic stability.[39]

The only solution was immediate, direct counterintervention on the exchange by the Bank of France. On 1 March, Bokanowski passed on to Poincaré and Lasteyrie a detailed memorandum by two bankers, Salomon Cahen and his own brother-in-law Robert Wolff, analyzing the causes of the speculation and recommending vigorous counteraction. Lazard Frères, considered by fellow bankers to be "the most capable exchange people on the continent," also urged this course on the govern-

38. Arthur N. Young to William R. Castle (chief of the West European Division, Department of State), 22 February 1924, Box 1, Arthur N. Young Papers, Hoover Institution, Stanford University, Stanford, Calif.

39. A. S. Cahen et Cie note, in Bokanowski to Poincaré, 1 March 1924, Millerand Papers; excerpted in *J.O.C. Doc.*, Annexe no. 7353, 20 March 1924, pp. 640–42.

ment.[40] Political and financial leaders favorable to immediate intervention sought each other out. On the evening of 4 March, Raymond Philippe of Lazard's presented the case to one of the more economically sophisticated regents of the Bank of France. The next day Philippe, accompanied by Michel Lazard, Bokanowski, Wolff, and M. Maroni, financial editor of the *Journal des débats*, called on Lasteyrie to press their arguments. They received little satisfaction. The finance minister put on a brave front, suggesting that "anxiety was localized purely in money market circles" and that reasons for optimism still existed.[41]

The Philippe group was close to despair. The main stumbling block, as they saw it, lay in the refusal of the Bank of France to pledge its gold reserve even temporarily in order to obtain the necessary dollars and pounds sterling, which would comprise the "mass of maneuver" to be employed against the speculators. The role of the Bank of France, they insisted, should be to protect the national monetary standard in the broadest sense. Under stable monetary conditions before the war this could be achieved by maintaining the gold supply intact as a guarantee of integral convertibility for the bank note. But under flexible exchange rates, was not the Bank of France justified in using the gold reserve to intervene directly on money markets when necessary in order to maintain an exchange value for the currency corresponding to the general economic situation, the price level, and the financial position of the treasury?[42] The Bank claimed that it could not enter the exchange market below the 1914 gold-franc rate because that would constitute a form of legal recognition of the depreciation which had already taken place. It could not lend its gold to the treasury for the purpose of intervention since that would amount to complicity in a potentially inflationary increase in the Bank's advances to the state. But in a time of crisis, the Philippe group believed, it was fatal to stick to such old-fashioned monetary dogma.[43]

Dismayed by the cabinet's continued passivity, Bokanowski carried the case for intervention to the informed public in a strongly worded article in *Le Matin*.[44] Meanwhile Philippe enlisted the assistance of Octave Homberg, wartime president of the Commission des Changes, a banker who in the course of a long career on the fringes of politics had gained some intimacy with Poincaré. The premier had never quite outgrown the visceral suspicion of the provincial bourgeois that bankers in general place their own welfare ahead of the public good. He often professed the view that it was improper for politicians of independent

40. The favorable assessment of Lazard's was made by N. Dean Jay of Morgan, Harjes et Cie, Jay to Lamont, 6 January 1926, TWL 113/5.

41. Philippe, *Le Drame financier*, pp. 31–32.

42. See Bokanowski's analysis in *J.O.C. Doc.*, Annexe no. 7353, 20 March 1924, pp. 643–44.

43. Wolff, *Economie et finances*, pp. 137–52, 154–57.

44. *Le Matin*, 6 March 1924.

spirit to cultivate close relations with private banking interests, and characteristically, he and Madame Poincaré kept their personal accounts at the Bank of France by special arrangement with their friend Robineau. Moreover, Poincaré harbored a specific distrust of Lazard's; and he had many times voiced his displeasure at private citizens' meddling with decision making by the properly designated and legally responsible authorities.[45] Homberg nevertheless boldly appealed to the premier to set aside his scruples and seize the psychological moment for counter-attack, even if it meant using the Bank of France's gold reserves. "Napoleon sacrificed his guard at the decisive moment in order to win the battle," Homberg argued dramatically (if not accurately).[46] "In financial matters also there are reserves which it would be absurd to treat as fetishes and which one must know how to use at the chosen moment."[47]

Still Poincaré remained hesitant to act. As his later political record would abundantly demonstrate, Poincaré moved uneasily in the complicated world of fluctuating exchanges and creative central banking, notwithstanding his diligent mastery of details and his eventual acquiescence in the recommendations of financial specialists. He instinctively felt that it was not the Bank of France's function to "fiddle around with the exchange rate," and with his usual scrupulous regard for the division of administrative responsibilities, he was particularly reluctant to lean on Robineau.[48] However, the circle of influential figures pressing for intervention continued to widen. Bokanowski succeeded in galvanizing President Millerand into action with a simple political equation: "The pound sterling at 105 for another week equals success for the left wing block. The pound sterling brought down to 85 within a week equals success for the present majority."[49] In his usual energetic manner, Millerand threw himself into the endeavor to round up conservative support for intervention. "I know my country well," he confided to Philippe. "It can stand anything, except a financial crisis."[50] François-Marsal, whose conversion was important because of his unimpeachable standing as a deflationist, lobbied hard in the Senate Finance Commission and with his friends at the Bank of France.

Even when subjected to this formidable array of pressures, the Bank of France remained loath to pledge its gold reserve directly or to make a gold remittance abroad in order to obtain the foreign currency necessary

45. Jacques Chastenet, *Raymond Poincaré* (Paris, 1948), pp. 271–72; Octave Homberg, *Les Coulisses de l'histoire: Souvenirs, 1898–1928* (Paris, 1938); also see Poincaré's correspondence with Robineau, vol. 16016, pp. 71–102, Poincaré Papers. I rely here in addition on a personal interview with Jacques Millerand, 15 March 1965.

46. In fact the sacrifice at Waterloo was made in vain.

47. Philippe, *Le Drame financier*, pp. 33–34.

48. Ibid., pp. 115–45; Frédéric François-Marsal, "Souvenirs: La Crise présidentielle et l'éviction de Millerand, 1923–1924," p. 8, François-Marsal Papers.

49. Bokanowski to Millerand, 2 March 1924, Millerand Papers.

50. Philippe, *Le Drame financier*, p. 19.

for intervention. The Bank insisted, moreover, that intervention would not work, and might even prove counterproductive, unless accompanied by a whole complex of other financial reforms going beyond adoption of the *double décime*. The Bank did express its willingness, provided that the government met its demands, to extend whatever assistance it could short of pledging its gold reserve. It volunteered to provide an indirect guarantee against exchange loss to private French banks or businesses should they contract a foreign loan.[51] But this offer found no takers.

The hard-pressed Lasteyrie cast about for help in every conceivable direction, only to find that the patriotism of many private interests found its limits where pecuniary risk began. Much to his chagrin, the banking and commercial leaders he approached offered the excuse that since wartime exchange controls theoretically remained in force, they had not accumulated enough foreign currency to assist the government substantially. The directors of the French railway networks, while not refusing outright Lasteyrie's appeal that they pledge their assets for a foreign loan, hedged their agreement round with so many stipulations regarding future rate relief and settlement of old claims against the government that the questions raised could not be satisfactorily disposed of in time for the railways to provide practical assistance.[52] Bankers in New York, London, and Amsterdam who were asked to examine the feasibility of extending a loan based on the credit of the railway networks, furthermore, all stated that they could not entertain the possibility until the French government had put its financial house in order.

Meanwhile the Senate Finance Commission still balked at accepting the government's proposals intact and on Thursday, 6 March, flatly refused Poincaré's ultimatum that it be ready to report after the weekend. Some members of the cabinet (seven by one account) wavered and were even prepared to withdraw the request for decree powers to achieve economies.[53] The Bank of France's balance sheet, also issued on 6 March, showed an increase of currency in circulation amounting to 921 million francs in one week; and on the very same day the treasury was obliged to dragoon the private banks into giving it a secret advance in order to mask the drop in subscriptions to treasury bonds. The pound sterling closed at 113.05 on 7 March. On 8 March, the situation deteriorated from hour to hour, the pound finally closing at 123 francs, up 10

51. Banque de France, "Compte rendu des opérations de la Banque," 29 January 1925; Lachapelle, *Le Crédit public*, pp. 167–68; Lachapelle, *Les Batailles du franc*, p. 125. See also François-Marsal to Raphaël Milliès-Lacroix, 7 April 1924, and Henry Bérenger's account, "Opérations faites par la Banque de France pour soutenir le change" (based on information supplied by the Bank of France), in Sénat, Commission des Finances, "Exposé sur les finances publiques fait par M. Henry Bérenger, rapporteur-général," 4 June 1924, pp. 69–74, copy in Herriot Papers.

52. Directors of French railways to Minister of Finance, [5?] March 1924, Millerand Papers.

53. *L'Oeuvre*, 7 March 1924; *Le Matin*, 7 March 1924.

percent in one day. "The franc is without buyers," telegraphed Lazard's New York branch after the close.[54]

The International Bankers Come to the Rescue

Only direct aid from the international bankers could now save the French currency. Just a few days earlier, the Philippe-Bokanowski group had entertained the hope that the French government could rout the speculators by the judicious expenditure of a relatively small amount of foreign exchange—no more than $10 million to start—which the Bank of France could obtain without making embarrassing political commitments.[55] Now it appeared that at least five to ten times this sum would be required. With some trepidation, the French government appealed for help to J. P. Morgan & Co., the leading Wall Street firm, which time and again had shown itself to be France's staunchest friend in the international banking community. Morgan's proved more than willing to help. It considered the $50 million requested by the French insufficient to impress the speculators and offered double that sum.[56] But it also imposed conditions. Herman Harjes,* head of Morgan's Paris branch, transmitted the decision of his partners in New York. They would make available a dollar credit if secured by the Bank of France gold reserve, but only on condition that the French government insist on immediate and integral passage of the tax package in the Senate and undertake to bring public expenditures strictly in line with revenue. They required also that, pending significant improvement in its financial position, the government make no new appeal to domestic credit markets except to consolidate the floating debt. Finally, they asked the French to make a permanent commitment not to market subsequent loans, even for the completion of reconstruction in the liberated regions, unless their service could be assured through normal income from taxation.[57]

It was suspected in certain quarters at the time that Morgan's insisted on the further requirement that France pledge to accept the Dawes Committee's recommendations for a reparations settlement, or even that the United States government laid down such a condition before it would authorize Morgan's to proceed with the loan. Through a rather

*Henry Herman Harjes (1875–1926), banker, sportsman, social figure; born in Paris of a family prominent in the American community there, privately educated; entered J. P. Morgan & Co., 1896; partner in Morgan, Harjes et Cie, 1898–1908, president, 1908–26; representative of the American Red Cross in France, 1914–17; lieutenant colonel, U.S. Army, 1917–19, served as chief liaison officer between the American Expeditionary Force and the French government; died playing polo when kicked in the head by a horse.

54. Philippe, *Le Drame financier*, p. 35.
55. Bokanowski to Poincaré, 1 March 1924, Millerand Papers.
56. Bérenger, "Opérations faites par la Banque de France pour soutenir le change."
57. J. P. Morgan & Co. to Secretary of State, 21 March 1924, U.S. 851.51/444.

strange process, the contemporary suspicion has entered the scholarly literature.[58] In fact, neither the American bankers nor the United States government sought to take advantage of France's weakness to make political demands. The bankers set conditions only of a financial nature, designed to jog the French out of their inertia and to strengthen the hand of the Bank of France in demanding comprehensive fiscal reform.[59] Far from stipulating that the French agree in advance to accept the Experts' plan then being formulated, the Morgan partners had not been consulted during the evolution of that plan and were themselves not committed to it. Sympathetic to the French predicament, they later sought to justify the conditions upon which they insisted as being in the interest of the French themselves:

> The businessmen of the world are not so blind as to suppose that the borrowing of a paltry $100,000,000 for three or six months could stem the flood of selling which was based upon the apprehension that the French government would continue to keep its budget out of balance and to increase the public debt of France year after year. It was the announced determination of the French government to balance its budget coupled with our credit, carrying banking confirmation of its ability and willingness to do so, that made possible the appreciation of the franc. Without that announcement our credit would have been useless and worse than useless for it would have inevitably resulted in frittering away the resources of the Bank of France.[60]

But whatever the explanation offered by Morgan's, its conditions caused an uproar when communicated to the Council of Ministers on the afternoon of 8 March.[61] Had not Poincaré reiterated throughout the reparations controversy that the rights of France were not subject to

58. When negotiations for the Morgan loan were concluded in March 1924, several French newspapers insinuated that the bankers had laid down hidden political conditions. But most of these journals, representing the two extremes of the political spectrum, were known to practice imaginative distortion of the news according to the dictates of ideology. Few observers took their charges seriously. Then, on 2 May 1924, the London *Daily Telegraph* reported that the Morgan firm had insisted on a personal engagement by Poincaré, committing France to accept the recommendations of the Experts and to restore German administrative unity and economic sovereignty in the occupied areas. Since Professor Gerothwohl, diplomatic correspondent of the *Daily Telegraph*, was well connected at the Foreign Office and enjoyed a deserved reputation for accuracy, there exist grounds for suspicion that someone in Whitehall leaked the story in order to compromise Poincaré shortly before the French elections. Despite a vehement denial by the Quai d'Orsay, the report was given a big play by the Cartel press (*L'Oeuvre*, 4 May, 13 May 1924) and proved deeply embarrassing to the French premier. The claim that Morgan's insisted on the Dawes Plan's acceptance has been given credence subsequently by most historians. See, e.g., Lachapelle, *Les Batailles du franc*, p. 125; Edouard Bonnefous, *Histoire politique de la Troisième République*, vol. 3, *L'Après-guerre, 1919–1924* (Paris, 1959), p. 407; E. Beau de Loménie, *Les Responsabilités des dynasties bourgeoises*, vol. 3 (Paris, 1954), p. 351; Pierre Miquel, *Poincaré* (Paris, 1961), p. 495. Etienne Weill-Raynal, attempting to be judicious in his standard account, *Les Réparations allemandes et la France*, 3 vols. (Paris, 1947), 2:600, concludes that Morgan's probably laid down its conditions "more discreetly."

59. Herman Harjes to J. P. Morgan & Co., 14 March 1924, TWL 83/17.

60. J. P. Morgan & Co. to Herman Harjes, 5 June 1924, TWL 95/12.

61. Lachapelle, *Le Crédit public*, p. 169.

arbitration by foreign financiers? Had he not said, on the day the Ruhr was occupied, that he would "never agree, even in financial matters, to confide the destinies of France to international bankers?"[62] According to sources close to Lasteyrie, Poincaré deemed it incompatible with national honor to accept the Morgan conditions.[63] That evening the premier, with Lasteyrie in tow, came to the Elysée and offered to resign. President Millerand, however, moved boldly; he saw acceptance of the Morgan loan as the only option left open, and he suspected also that Poincaré might be seeking an excuse for retirement in order to avoid leading the Bloc National in the elections. Millerand therefore stated that he would accept only the resignation of the full cabinet, whereupon he would deliver a dramatic message exposing "the situation in all its gravity and summoning the Chambers to adopt the measures . . . indispensable for public safety."[64] He left no doubt that he would not shrink, if necessary, from proroguing the Chamber and postponing the general elections for two years, at which time, in his view, the electorate was more likely to make a "thoughtful and serene response" than it would under the immediate impact of financial sacrifice. Poincaré was appalled by this proposal, which would have irremediably compromised his future acceptability to the moderate left. In the end the two men, adopting Lasteyrie's suggestion, decided to call an emergency meeting of key cabinet members with the Council of Regents of the Bank of France and to make one last attempt to resolve their differences.

This meeting took place under dramatic circumstances at the Elysée on Sunday morning, 9 March.[65] Poincaré, his hesitations overcome at last, now backed Lasteyrie to the hilt. He promised to undertake the full panoply of measures advocated by the bankers: pressure on the Senate to pass the fiscal legislation, temporary suspension of disbursements in the liberated areas, exemption of short-term treasury bonds from the income tax, development of a plan for consolidating the existing debt, and restriction of commercial credit to induce a mild deflation. Governor Robineau and his colleagues, skeptical whether even these measures would prove sufficient to stem the panic, fought to the end against pledging their gold. But Millerand and the ministers overcame their doubts through a strong patriotic appeal, to which Baron Edouard de Rothschild and several other leading regents were particularly susceptible, and apparently also by dealing tactfully with François de Wen-

62. *J.O.C. Déb.*, 11 January 1923, p. 17.

63. L. Marcellin, *Voyage autour de la Chambre du 11 mai* (Paris, 1925), p. 36.

64. Alexandre Millerand, "Mes souvenirs–Contribution à l'histoire de la Troisième République," pp. 116–17, Millerand Papers.

65. For details of this meeting, see Lachapelle, *Les Batailles du franc*, pp. 125–27, and *Le Crédit public*, pp. 170–73; Frayssinet, *La Politique monétaire*, pp. 28–29; Philippe, *Le Drame financier*, p. 36; Wolff, *Economie et finances*, pp. 156–57; also Harjes to J. P. Morgan & Co., 14 March 1924, TWL 83/17.

del, a regent involved in a business controversy with the government.[66] The Bank of France agreed to close the deal with J. P. Morgan & Co. for a six-month revolving credit. The governor of the Bank succeeded in saving the appearance of principle through a technicality: Morgan's professed itself satisfied with an undertaking by the Bank of France to make reimbursement in gold only if it did not have the necessary amount of dollars on hand when the loan fell due. This enabled Robineau to draw a fine distinction and later to maintain that the credit "did not require a gold remittance or pledge of any kind."[67] Even after making its decision, the Bank of France leadership evidently remained ambivalent about the operation. One source of continuing embarrassment lay in the necessity, owing to the absence of personnel skilled in foreign exchange operations at the Bank, to entrust the technical end of the operation to Lazard Frères—a delegation of responsibility that Bank officials preferred to avoid mentioning publicly once the franc had been saved.[68]

In New York the partners of J. P. Morgan & Co. were relieved to learn that the French would accept their assistance. "There has never been an operation that has given us more satisfaction," wrote Thomas W. Lamont,* the guiding spirit of the firm, who managed the credit at the American end.[69] Lamont immediately telephoned Secretary Hughes to

*Thomas W. Lamont (1870–1948), partner of J. P. Morgan & Co., 1911–43, chairman of the board, 1943–48; U.S. Treasury representative and reparations expert on the American Commission to Negotiate Peace, 1919; member of the Committee of Experts on German reparations that developed the Young Plan, 1929; a man of wide literary interests, one-time reporter, author of several books. *Current Biography*, assessing Lamont's impact on international finance and politics, noted in 1940 that he had "exercised more power for twenty years in the Western Hemisphere, . . . [and] put into effect more final decisions from which there has been no appeal, than any other person."

66. Poincaré normally opposed all attempts by private interests to seek special favor from the government. Consequently, his intervention in a dispute concerning Regent François de Wendel takes on particular significance. The Wendel firm owned a coal mine in the Rhineland with a checkered record of control. This mine, the Frédéric Henri, was taken over by the Rheinische Stahlwerke during the war, but was subsequently returned to its French proprietors. In 1923 it participated in passive resistance (its German director claiming that cooperation with the occupation forces would compromise the future of his enterprise). Later, however, it claimed exemption from the coal tax levied by the M.I.C.U.M. on the ground of French ownership. François de Wendel told Poincaré that he would rather let the mine be seized than pay the tax. Four days after the meeting at the Elysée, Poincaré ordered General Degoutte, commanding officer in the occupied territories, to desist from plans to take over the mine because such action would have a "deplorable effect . . . in present circumstances and a few days before deposition of the Experts' Report." Six months later Edouard Herriot, Poincaré's successor, reversed the decision, ruling that the coal tax constituted an interallied levy and that the French government could not exempt its own firms unilaterally. (See Poincaré-Degoutte and Herriot-Degoutte correspondence, February-October 1924, in Herriot Papers; also a report by Deputy Lucien Lamoureux, who carried out an investigation for the Herriot ministry in the occupied territories, *J.O.C. Doc.*, Annexe no. 537, October 1924, pp. 2143–44; Weill-Raynal, *Les Réparations allemandes*, 2:467–68; Michel Soulié, *La Vie politique d'Edouard Herriot* [Paris, 1962], p. 223.)

67. Banque de France, "Compte rendu des opérations de la banque," 29 January 1925.

68. Bérenger, "Opérations faites par la Banque de France pour soutenir le change."

69. Lamont to Harjes, 28 March 1924, TWL 83/17.

seek the State Department's approval, mandatory according to foreign loan procedures in effect at the time. Hughes must have been tempted by the opportunity to nail down a French commitment to the forthcoming Experts' report. The department's economic adviser was "a bit sorry . . . that we did not attach more conditions," and some other subordinate officials felt the same way.[70] But the secretary preferred to remain faithful to the policy he had consistently followed since the beginning of the Ruhr operation, namely, that the United States could not "assume the role of a dictator" in the reparations question, but could only "endeavor to get the question out of politics."[71]

True to this guideline, Washington (aside from excluding war debts from the agenda) had not given directives to the American members of the Expert Committees, even though the Experts representing the European nations consulted frequently with their respective governments. In the case of the Morgan loan, Hughes, without consulting his staff,[72] told Lamont that if the operation did not adversely affect the prospects for the Experts' recommendations, he would raise no objection to it. Characteristically, Hughes's one request was that the loan be called a "private banking credit" not subject to official government scrutiny, so that in case of inquiries from isolationist or pro-German congressmen, the State Department could disclaim knowledge of the transaction.[73] Following the procedure upon which Hughes and Lamont had agreed, Herman Harjes dropped in on 11 March to seek approval from the American Experts in Paris. Since Harjes and General Dawes were old friends who had served together in the American Expeditionary Force and continued to see each other socially, the matter could be settled informally. Dawes and Owen D. Young, the second American Expert, readily agreed that "no harm would be done" by allowing the loan to go through.[74]

Actually, by this time Dawes and Young felt reasonably confident that their committee would reach agreement on fundamental principles. The French had already made the concession that they deemed essential for a unanimous report. On 26 February the French Expert, Jean Parmentier,

70. Arthur N. Young Diary, 12 March 1924, Arthur N. Young Papers.

71. Hughes "Memorandum," 1 February 1923, explaining principles underlying the State Department's European policy, enclosed in Hughes to Senator Henry Cabot Lodge, 6 February 1923, Box 4B, Hughes Papers.

72. Under Secretary William Phillips did not learn details of the transaction until Lamont showed him the Morgan file a month later. "It was a revelation to me," Phillips then noted, "to see the frank words of advice and caution which Morgan's has been giving to the French government . . . and which must have had a powerful influence in bringing the French . . . to their senses" (Phillips Diary, 9 April 1924, William Phillips Papers, Houghton Library, Harvard University, Cambridge, Mass.).

73. J. P. Morgan & Co. to Secretary of State, 21 March 1924, U.S. 851.51/444. (When the loan was renewed in September 1924 the fiction of a "private banking credit" was dropped, and it was submitted for State Department review in the usual way [U.S. 851.51/485].)

74. Charles G. Dawes, *A Journal of Reparations* (London, 1939), pp. 159–61; see also Charles G. Dawes file in TWL 91/9.

had appealed to Dawes to provide in the report for continuation in skeleton form of French economic control of the Ruhr. Dawes, who of all the Anglo-Saxon delegates was the most sympathetic to France, agreed to sound out his colleagues but told Parmentier frankly that "opposition to any semblance of a remaining economic control in the Ruhr after settlement was very strong in the committee."[75] Meanwhile, Dawes learned from another of his wartime comrades, General Payot, that Marshal Foch had conceded that economic agencies of pressure were not essential to maintain military control of the Ruhr. Within the French bureaucracy, opinions divided on the feasibility of blocking restoration of Germany's complete economic sovereignty. Poincaré was disinclined to accept the recommendations of his chief professional adviser, Jacques Seydoux, that he acquiesce in restoration of German economic unity. On the other hand, he did not wish to give direct instructions to Parmentier, since he thought that this might prematurely commit him to whatever compromise the Experts reached. In the absence of a clear directive from the Quai d'Orsay, Parmentier made his own assessment of what was politically possible. On 29 February he submitted a formula, which became the basis for the guarantees section of the Dawes Report, providing that measures hampering economic activity in the Ruhr should terminate as soon as Germany put the proposed plan into effect and should not be reimposed except in the event of flagrant default.[76]

Thus, by the time Harjes sought Dawes's sanction for the Morgan loan, the latter's chief concern was not to put pressure on France, but rather to ensure that nation's solvency, which he thought depended in part on a successful outcome of his committee's deliberations. "The incident," Dawes noted, "shows the thinness of the ice upon which French finance is standing. One hundred million dollars will do no good in stabilizing the franc if public confidence is once seriously undermined. Unless our report is unanimous (as it will be) and is accepted, the franc will go far toward joining the mark. . . . If our plan succeeds, returning confidence may save the franc."[77]

Because it took time to clear various formalities, the Morgan credit did not become available until 12 March. In order to stem the panic, however, it was essential to begin the support operation when the exchange opened on Monday, 10 March. The Bank of France therefore arranged a temporary $5 million credit from Lazard's New York branch.[78] Not wishing to be "at the mercy of the United States," whatever the professions of goodwill by Morgan's, the Bank of France also sought to obtain

75. Charles G. Dawes, "A Journal of Reparations," Diary MS, Charles G. Dawes Papers, Northwestern University Library, Evanston, Ill. (The passage is omitted from the published *Journal*, p. 126.)

76. Dawes, *A Journal of Reparations*, pp. 130–35.

77. Ibid., p. 160.

78. Philippe, *Le Drame financier*, p. 40.

balancing help from England.[79] Sir Robert Kindersley, a British member of the Expert Committee and chairman of Lazard Brothers, London, worked out a £5 million sterling credit from a syndicate of four English banks. Would the British government and the Bank of England sanction the arrangement?

Montagu Norman, governor of the Bank of England, who coincidentally was in Paris to testify before the Dawes Committee, found himself torn. Norman despised the French so passionately that, despite his commitment to monetary stability in his capacity as a public official, he could scarcely contain his *Schadenfreude* at any evidence of their discomfiture.[80] On the other hand, he had come to Paris in order to fight against the recommendation contemplated by the Experts' banking subcommittee to establish the new German currency on the gold standard—in effect the dollar standard—from the outset.[81] Norman sought to line up the Bank of France's support for placing the new German mark instead on a sterling basis, which would provide an advantage for British trade and finance. "I am aware, of course, that sterling is depreciated in terms of gold," Norman had written earlier to a fellow central banker, "but it remains the main basis on which European exchanges are operated and I am most strongly of the opinion that as Europe obtains no financial assistance or cooperation from America, Europe should no further attach herself to the basis which for the present America controls."[82]

In the end Norman's jealousy of American financial preeminence prevailed over his Gallophobia. He did not choose this moment to reiterate the political demands made by his associate McKenna the previous month. Instead, he limited himself to a private gesture of disapproval for the Lazard credits, permitting them to go through.[83] The British Foreign Office arranged not to be officially consulted about the Lazard deal, enabling MacDonald to assure German industrialists subsequently that his government had had nothing to do with saving the franc and that he himself had learned of the support operation only through the newspapers.[84]

At any rate, with available funds Lazard's Paris headquarters set in

79. Bérenger, "Opérations faites par la Banque de France pour soutenir le change."

80. For proof of the mutual antipathy between Norman and French political and financial leaders, see Benjamin Strong memorandum regarding discussions at the Bank of France, 27 May 1928, Box 15, George Leslie Harrison Papers, Columbia University Library, New York, N.Y.; also Emile Moreau, *Souvenirs d'un gouverneur de la Banque de France* (Paris, 1954), pp. 24, 49; and Andrew Boyle, *Montagu Norman* (London, 1967), pp. 174, 221–38, 303.

81. E. W. Kemmerer to Hughes, 24 June 1924; Arthur N. Young memorandum, "The Question of the Gold Standard in Germany and the Experts' Report," 9 June 1924, U.S. 462.00R 296/380a, 380b, 386.

82. Montagu Norman to Dr. Gerard Vissering, president of the Netherlands Bank, 14 January 1924, Montagu Norman Papers, Bank of England, London.

83. Sir Henry Clay, *Lord Norman* (London, 1957), pp. 144–45.

84. G.F.M. L1491/5352/L436703–709.

motion a vast operation, offering hard currencies for francs on all the principal European exchanges. To oversee the operation a committee of bankers and treasury officials met every morning at the Bank of France under the deputy governor, Ernest-Picard.[85] The first two days proved difficult. The speculators continued to pour francs on the market. Only with great difficulty did Lazard's bring the pound sterling down from 123 to 116 francs. The Bank of France remained jittery lest the foreign exchange already committed be lost, while the opposition press warned darkly that these "maneuvers" might provide "the outward appearance of a provisional result," but in the absence of a fundamental change in foreign policy, only at the cost of frittering away the "national fortune."[86] However, on Wednesday, 12 March, the rout of the speculators began. On Thursday the Morgan loan was announced with suitable fanfare; on Friday night the Senate voted to accept the *double décime*. By 18 March the pound had been brought down to 84.45 francs, and the French syndicate began to recoup some of the $55 million of foreign exchange it had expended. It was now the speculators' turn to panic, and they rushed to cover their positions at any price. By 24 March the pound dropped to 78.10 francs—below purchasing power parity—and within a matter of days the hard currency credits that had been expended during the operation were entirely recouped. The immediate battle of the franc was won.

The Domestic Political Aftermath

Having accepted foreign assistance to save the French currency, Poincaré was hardly in a position to alienate world opinion by rejecting the forthcoming Experts' report in principle. But this had never been his intention. The political circumstances made the realization inescapable, in France as elsewhere, that the Experts' work would have to form the starting point for the next round of negotiations on reparations. With successful defense of the franc on the exchange and passage of the tax legislation, the option at least remained open for France, freed from the disabling fear of imminent financial catastrophe, to negotiate on specific matters within the general framework of the Experts' recommendations. Indirectly, however, financial difficulties continued to circumscribe France's capacity to salvage something from its occupation of the Ruhr. Most immediately, the tax increase could not fail to have an impact on

85. For a colorful history of the French counteroffensive see Mermeix [Gabriel Terrail], *Histoire du franc depuis le commencement de ses malheurs* (Paris, 1926), pp. 99–114; also the accounts by Philippe of Lazard's, *Le Drame financier*, pp. 40–46; by Lachapelle, who presents the Bank of France view, *Les Batailles du franc*, pp. 129–32, and *Le Crédit public*, pp. 173–75; and by Frayssinet, *La Politique monétaire*, pp. 31–39.

86. Robert de Jouvenel in *L'Oeuvre*, 10–11 March 1924; see also Georges Boris's similar assessment in *Le Quotidien*, 11 March 1924.

the election results. Then, because the French public at large and even many parliamentary leaders misunderstood the process that had led to the franc's recovery, the momentum for consolidation of fundamental financial reform was lost.

Despite the victory over the speculators, the most vulnerable ministers —Lasteyrie, Reibel (blamed for the cessation of funding for the devastated areas), Chéron, and Dior—continued to feel the lash of public criticism. For some time the cabinet had been kept in power mainly by what diplomatic observers described as Poincaré's own "high moral authority."[87] The lobbies at the Palais Bourbon buzzed with rumors representing the premier as awaiting a suitable occasion to recast his ministry and to drop those colleagues who, whatever their loyalty and past services, had become political liabilities.[88] His opportunity came on 26 March, when Lasteyrie posed the question of confidence on a minor pension bill in the Chamber and unexpectedly lost. It never became clear whether this defeat stemmed from a concerted plan to force a ministerial reorganization, or was simply an accident that occurred because the finance minister had neglected, before asking for the vote, to count the number of government supporters who had arrived early at the Chamber that morning.[89] In any case, it was common practice in the Third Republic for a ministry to be defeated on a technical rather than a substantive issue. This procedure had become in a sense a rule of the parliamentary game, ensuring that cabinet members would not lose face and would remain eligible for participation in another ministerial combination.[90]

President Millerand resolved to countenance no fundamental change in French policies at this delicate juncture. Arguing that the Chamber's vote had been irregular, he at once appealed to Poincaré to remain in office with the same cabinet.[91] Poincaré, however, preferred to consummate his long-delayed "quarter turn to the left" and insisted on forming an entirely new cabinet, perfectly balanced between right and left. He retained only the two men most responsible for occupation policy in the Ruhr, André Maginot at the War Ministry and Yves Le Trocquer at the Ministry of Public Works. These reappointments symbolized the continuity of French foreign policy. At the same time, the selection of Henry de Jouvenel, Daniel-Vincent, Louis Loucheur, and Justin de Selves for the key ministries dealing with education, labor and health, commerce, and internal policy betokened a desire to make a clear concession to the center-left on domestic issues. These choices represented a masterly

87. U.S. 851.00/495.
88. "Bonneteau politique," *Le Progrès civique*, 5 April 1924, pp. 12–13.
89. Ibid.; also Bonnefous, *Histoire politique de la Troisième République*, 3:420–21.
90. A. Soulier, *L'Instabilité ministérielle sous la Troisième République, 1870–1938* (Paris, 1939), pp. 107–249.
91. Millerand, "Mes souvenirs," p. 119; *Le Matin*, 27 March 1924.

stroke on the part of Poincaré, enabling him to stake out a position between the two electoral blocs and to promote dissension on the right flank of the Radical-Socialist group. Sharp attacks on this "most immoral gesture" in the Cartel press underlined its effectiveness.[92]

Privately, nevertheless, Poincaré was somewhat disheartened. The mutually reinforcing constraints of the foreign and domestic political situation weighed heavily on his mind. To François-Marsal, who fifteen months earlier had put pressure on him to embark upon the Ruhr occupation and now, for reasons of balance, was designated finance minister, the premier remarked wryly: "Well, I trust you are satisfied with *your* Ruhr policy."[93] Just as Poincaré had been obliged the previous year to take responsibility for the occupation because every viable alternative was exhausted, now by another capricious turn of the wheel of fortune he found himself—again reluctantly—chained by the financial crisis and the new tax legislation to the right-wing Bloc National.

With the elections only six weeks away, neither Poincaré, nor other French political leaders, nor the nation's monetary managers found it easy to take a dispassionate approach to the task of consolidating the franc's exchange position. This proved particularly unfortunate because, in the last week of March 1924, as the Amsterdam and central European operators hastened to cover themselves, a speculative movement in the opposite direction—betting on a rise of the franc—began in New York.[94] The French public at large considered further revaluation of the currency, no matter how far the movement went, as a national "victory" constituting additional progress toward the hoped-for restoration of the prewar gold standard. The Bank of France, where sentiment for revaluation ran deep, was reluctant to stop an autonomous appreciation of the currency. The Bank was also eager to drive up the franc as high as practicable, at least temporarily, in order to ruin the foreign speculators utterly.[95] Despite the political attractiveness of this course, the foreign exchange specialists representing Lazard Frères began to argue within the bankers' syndicate at the end of March in favor of defensive counter-intervention. They wished to prevent the franc from appreciating to a level which, however gratifying for considerations of prestige, was not economically desirable. Too rapid appreciation, Lazard's observed, would cheapen imports and reduce the competitiveness of exports to the point where French production and employment would suffer, exposing the nation to the risk of a trade deficit. It would also increase the real burden of France's domestic debt at a time when industrial stagnation

92. Jacques Dupont, "La Campagne de presse du Cartel des Gauches" (Thèse, Institut d'Etudes Politiques, 1950), pp. 87–95.

93. François-Marsal, "Souvenirs: La Crise présidentielle et l'éviction de Millerand, 1923–1924," p. 9.

94. Frayssinet, *La Politique monétaire*, p. 34.

95. Georges Robineau to Lazard Frères, 29 March 1926, copy in Herriot Papers.

might diminish tax resources. Lazard's therefore advocated selling francs in order to amass a hard currency reserve that could be used in the event of a new speculative attack.[96]

J. P. Morgan & Co. echoed Lazard's recommendations. The New York bankers were worried by the "apparent complacency" of most French monetary advisers in the face of what analysts at Morgan corner considered a mere "momentary triumph." The technical recovery on the exchange did not impress them as decisive. Nothing had actually happened since establishment of the Morgan credit, they felt, besides "an important shift in the psychological situation." The firm advised the French government to take advantage of the opportunity to improve monetary fundamentals: authorities in Paris should stabilize the franc, accumulate foreign currency reserves "while the going is good," and take other measures (such as refunding part of the floating debt) to increase confidence; finally, they should publish frequent and clear financial statements so as to prove that there existed "in fact—not merely in hope—a balanced budget." When the improvement on the exchange rested on something substantial—a "manifest determination to set and keep the house in perfect order"—there would be time enough to undertake further appreciation of the franc. No course of action, cabled New York, "could be better calculated in a political sense as well as financial to strengthen France's world position."[97]

But Morgan's counsel found little resonance among French monetary managers, let alone among politicians preoccupied by the election campaign. The time was hardly propitious for considering an ambitious and comprehensive program for further financial reform. The Bank of France belatedly and reluctantly gave Lazard's authorization to sell francs in order to build up a £10 million sterling reserve once the Morgan credit had been completely reconstituted. The French treasury also made some purchases of foreign currency. But the rate at which dollars and sterling were purchased proved insufficient to control the exchange, and on 23 April the pound fell to a low point of 63.50 francs.

François-Marsal, in his new position at the rue de Rivoli after the cabinet reshuffle, recognized that if the franc rose too rapidly, "a catastrophe for French industry" would result.[98] On the other hand, he continued to view the battle of the franc largely as a struggle between governments rather than one against private speculators alone. Convinced that the danger of renewed attack against the currency was not over, he was inclined to give credence to a report reaching him from business associates at the Bank of Luxembourg that the German govern-

96. Lazard Frères to Governor of the Bank of France, 26 March 1926, Herriot Papers; also Philippe, *Le Drame financier*, pp. 47–51.
97. J. P. Morgan & Co. to Herman Harjes, 29 March 1924, TWL 95/11.
98. See his retrospective statement in *J.O.S. Déb.*, 10 April 1925, p. 839.

ment continued to stand behind the speculators. The growing passion of the electoral campaign further strengthened François-Marsal's tendency to exaggerate the political component of the problem. To better coordinate the battle against the speculators, he directed that the text of all suspicious telegrams be communicated to his office and ordered a wiretap put on the Paris-Amsterdam telephone lines. Meanwhile, the Bank of France monitored suspect checks in order to trace hidden foreign political contributions. Initially these cloak-and-dagger activities did not yield much. The ministry was able to confirm that foreign subsidies to certain opposition journalists and newspapers increased as the pound was driven down and the election date drew nearer. The Amsterdam bankers who were being squeezed expressed the hope that François-Marsal, to whom they referred by the code name of "the gardener," would soon be driven from office. None of this was out of the ordinary.

Suddenly François-Marsal's *chef de cabinet* discovered that someone had placed a tap on the private wire connecting the finance minister with the president of the council. The alarmed François-Marsal, putting together the available evidence, now thought he discerned a pattern of German or English espionage and recommended a full-scale investigation. Poincaré, more familiar with the seamy side of international politics, calmed him down. The premier did not want to create an international incident that would irritate foreign statesmen with whom he might shortly be obliged to negotiate. "As minister of foreign affairs," he explained at an emergency cabinet meeting called to discuss the issue, "I do exactly what M. François-Marsal supposes that M. Ramsay MacDonald or M. Stresemann is doing. The secret funds at my disposal are used principally to subsidize newspapers in London, Prague, and Rome . . . to furnish support for the activities of friendly journalists and political figures, there and elsewhere. A scandal stirred up here, if after all there is a scandal, will inevitably boomerang on us."[99] There the matter rested. It is easy to see, nevertheless, why in this tense preelection atmosphere the Bank of France, working closely with François-Marsal and sharing his suspicions of foreign intrigue, was tempted to postpone establishing an economically appropriate level for the franc while seeking final "victory" over the speculators.

When on 23 April the franc came under renewed pressure on the exchange, Lazard's counseled that the downward movement be allowed to run its course until the pound reached 80 francs, roughly corresponding to purchasing power parity. But the Bank of France insisted on maintaining the rate at 68 for another fortnight, though it expended in this endeavor the entire $30 million foreign exchange profit it had accumulated earlier. The Bank's intelligence reports indicated that Mann-

99. François-Marsal, "Souvenirs: La Crise présidentielle et l'éviction de Millerand, 1923–1924," pp. 10–12.

heimer and other German and Austrian speculators would not be able to complete their disengagement until sometime in May. The Bank was resolved, as Governor Robineau later put it, not to permit before that date "a fall of the franc liable to mitigate the consequences for the foreign speculators of the position which they had taken against the franc."[100] Did the Bank of France also harbor a subsidiary motive, as Lazard's continued to suspect, namely to keep the exchange rate low for political purposes in view of the immediacy of the election date?[101] The evidence is not entirely clear. Robineau, claiming that the Bank had been influenced solely by calculations of public interest, indignantly denied the charge.[102] Nevertheless, the governor's further explanation that the Bank sought temporarily to keep the franc at an advantageous rate in order to provide French businessmen and merchants with an opportunity to cover their foreign exchange requirements rings hollow. Only a few weeks earlier, the Bank had affected such scrupulousness as to resist intervening on the exchange for purposes much more legitimately related to the state of the money market.[103] Banking considerations alone appeared to offer insufficient reason to fritter away in this manner the hard currency reserve arduously built up in the first stage of the franc rescue operation.

In any case, when Raymond Philippe of Lazard's appealed directly to François-Marsal on 5 May 1924, the finance minister was easily persuaded to end artificial support for the currency rather than dip into the Morgan credit again. Poincaré, too, despite his instinctive preference for revaluation, "finally let himself be convinced."[104] Eventually the Bank of France came around. When free market conditions were restored on 6 May, it developed that the speculators had already managed to clear themselves. The Bank of France immediately began to reconstitute its foreign currency reserves by purchases in the Far East, notwithstanding the fact that these transactions contributed to the fall of the franc from 68 to 74 to the pound in the two days just before the elections.[105] Temporarily, the franc shortly leveled off at an economically appropriate level. Unfortunately, official and public attention had focused so exclusively

100. Robineau to Lazard Frères, 29 March 1926, Herriot Papers.

101. Philippe, *Le Drame financier*, p. 52.

102. "Visite au gouverneur de la Banque de France" [by Bérenger and Milliès-Lacroix, 5 June 1924], in Bérenger, "Exposé sur les finances publiques," pp. 100–103, Herriot Papers.

103. Bérenger, "Opérations faites par la Banque de France pour soutenir le change."

104. Some years later, Poincaré sought to give the impression that, fully cognizant of the dangers of economic stagnation and unemployment, he had gladly taken the responsibility for allowing the franc to slip back from 68 to 76 to the pound sterling (*J.O.C. Déb.*, 3 February, 21 June 1928). Philippe, on the contrary, recalled that the premier had given his assent reluctantly (*Le Drame financier*, p. 53). In the absence of testimony by a neutral party, it is difficult to judge from this incident how clearly Poincaré understood the fundamental economic issues and to what extent he functioned simply by attempting to reconcile competing views among the government's economic advisers.

105. Robineau to Lazard Frères, 29 March 1926, Herriot Papers.

on the exchange rate itself and had been so mesmerized by a desire for "victory" over the foreign speculators as to dissipate whatever slender possibilities might otherwise have existed for structural improvements in French finance.

TABLE 5 | *French Elections of 1924*

Parties	Average Popular Vote	Deputies Elected	Result According to Proportional Representation
Conservatives (Action Française)	328,003	229	221
Republican Union and National Concord (Bloc National)	3,190,831		
Left Republicans, National Radicals	1,020,229	47	66
Total	4,539,063		
Cartel des Gauches	2,644,769	266*	219
Socialists (standing independently from Cartel)	749,647		
Total	3,394,416		
Communists	875,812	26	56
Others	89,235	0	6
Total average votes (on departmental basis)	8,898,526	568	568

Source: Georges Lachapelle, *Elections législatives du 11 mai 1924* (Paris, 1924), pp. 26–27.

*Since the middle formations were flexible, the number of deputies in the new Chamber who would support the "left" (excluding the Communists) varied. 328 voted against the François-Marsal ministry in June 1924; 313 voted to confirm the Herriot ministry; 287 (excluding the Left Republicans) made up the so-called little Cartel.

Meanwhile, on 11 May the Cartel des Gauches scored a victory in the French elections. Two days later the Poincaré cabinet offered its resignation. This has often been interpreted as a great political and diplomatic turning point: "the essential bifurcation," André Siegfried called it, in France's political history after the war.[106] During the period of postelection euphoria, Cartel press organs tried to create the impression that the left's success at the polls had been overwhelming. "The Republic has won, and its triumph is even more complete than we dared to hope," wrote *Le Progrès civique*, adding in a hyperbolic style that mirrored the

106. André Siegfried, *Tableau des partis en France* (Paris, 1930), p. 134.

mood of the moment: "Monarchists, sectarian clericals, and fascists have been swept away with a completeness and vigor of which there is no other example in electoral history."[107] Actually, the electoral shift to the left was moderate in extent, and its causes were largely specific repercussions of the financial crisis and the measures adopted to deal with it.[108]

It is true that a score of prominent right-wing deputies went down to defeat. Nevertheless, the total popular vote for the parliamentary groups which had consistently backed the Poincaré ministry and supported the occupation of the Ruhr exceeded that for the Cartel des Gauches and the Communists combined (see table 5). Initially, the left could count on a slender majority in the new Chamber. The complicated electoral system accorded a substantial advantage to coalition lists, and while in 1919 this system had worked to the advantage of the Bloc National, in 1924 it gave the Cartel forty-seven seats more than the latter would have obtained under a strict system of proportional representation. Moreover, the amorphous center-left groups (including the National Radicals and the Republicans of the Left), which supported a firm foreign policy and remained fundamentally conservative on most social and economic issues, identified sentimentally with the "left." In the national perspective generated by the financial crisis and the election campaign, these swing groups rallied to the Cartel. A left-wing majority was therefore available for symbolic gestures against the church, the army, upper-class elements in the civil service, and—of more substantive importance—for the affirmation of conciliatory intentions in foreign affairs.[109] But the new political lineup did not really indicate an explicit repudiation of French foreign policy of the preceding period. It represented rather a shifting inward of national concerns, a return to the traditional preoccupations of the prewar Radical-Socialist republic.

Five years after the end of the fighting, a reaction against the atmosphere of tension, sacrifice, and eternal vigilance in defense of the Versailles treaty was altogether natural. More than any other factor, the financial crisis catalyzed the longings for renewed emphasis on matters closer to home. American diplomatic observers confirmed that "it was no objection to Poincaré's foreign policy, but domestic grievances which brought the voters to the polls." They unhesitatingly ascribed the defeat of government forces to the fact that Poincaré's program had been "entirely concerned with foreign affairs, to which he gave his whole

107. *Le Progrès civique*, editorial, 17 May 1924.

108. No definitive scholarly study of the 1924 elections is available. See, however, Georges Lachapelle, *Elections législatives du 11 mai 1924* (Paris, 1924), pp. 5–55; Siegfried, *Tableau des partis*, pp. 125–34; Albert Thibaudet, *La République des professeurs* (Paris, 1927); Jean Prévost, *Histoire de la France depuis la guerre* (Paris, 1932), pp. 195–214; Marcellin, *Voyage autour de la Chambre du 11 mai*, pp. 11–93; J. Kessel and G. Suarez, *Le 11 mai* (Paris, 1924), and *Au camp des vainçus ou la critique du 11 mai* (Paris, 1924).

109. Siegfried, *Tableau des partis*, pp. 123–38.

attention, neglecting matters of domestic economy which affect more closely the daily life of the population."[110]

The continual rise in the cost of living coupled with the tax increase shortly before the elections had generated a wave of general discontent. The country south of the Loire returned almost entirely to its prewar Radical-Socialist allegiance; in the small towns there the threat that the subprefecture might be eliminated probably contributed even more than the *double décime* to the Cartel victory. Moreover, the extended parliamentary wrangle over taxation had shaped political divisions on seemingly unrelated matters. By making Poincaré's strategy of a union of the centers impossible, the financial dispute led to increased polarization on domestic issues such as educational reform and the alleged dangers of clericalism, which had constituted the meat of French politics before the war. Thus the whole basis for political alignments altered. The moderates of the center-left would vote with the Cartel on such issues, instead of joining in solidarity with the more conservative side of the Chamber as they had done earlier in support of Poincaré's foreign policy.

Did the new political configuration necessarily portend a fundamental reorientation of French foreign policy? MacDonald and Stresemann had both expected that this would be the eventual consequence of the financial crisis. Poincaré himself believed that any French government would be obliged to follow much the same course regarding both reparations and security following the Dawes Committee's report.[111] Most professional diplomats tended to discount Cartel press statements predicting the dramatic opening of an era of international conciliation and open diplomacy. The changes, they believed, would be mainly in "men and methods."[112] But this too was significant.

France faced a difficult series of negotiations to settle the terms for implementation of the Experts' report and the future of the Ruhr occupation. Others held the trumps, but skillful playing could still produce a few tricks for the French hand. In twenty-nine months in power, Poincaré had defended French interests with great thoroughness and competence, if with little imagination or boldness. He had explored the alternatives to the Ruhr occupation and determined to limit its scope when no other course of action appeared feasible. He had pursued the circumscribed objective set forth at the start, reluctantly rejecting the temptation to create artificial separatist states in the Rhineland or to conclude industrial agreements with Germany that would have exceeded the framework of the Versailles system and the tolerance of the British alliance. It remained to be seen if a less experienced successor could do as well, now that France's financial vulnerability had been exposed to the world.

110. Sheldon Whitehouse to State Department, 16 May 1924, U.S. 851.00/514.

111. So he told U.S. Ambassador Myron T. Herrick (Herrick to State Department, 2 June 1924, U.S. 851.00/518).

112. U.S. 851.00/516.

Chapter 5

Cartel Finance and French Diplomacy

The Chains of Dependence

By the beginning of June 1924, the immediate threat to the franc seemed to have dissipated. The speculators had been routed. The Bank of France had recouped the $100 million credit advanced by J. P. Morgan & Co. Throughout the summer the franc fluctuated within limits considered normal before the crisis, between seventeen and twenty to the dollar.[1] Diplomatic developments and the dramatic events of domestic politics that followed upon the Cartel election victory dominated newspaper headlines. Reports from the money markets were once again relegated to obscure positions on the business pages. A certain measure of peril and confusion in financial matters had been customary for so long in France that politicians and the public alike were inured to the professional money managers' perpetual cries of alarm. The casual observer would have thought that the nation's financial difficulties, though not solved, had diminished to a tolerable level. In fact, the opposite was true.

France continued to depend on potential foreign assistance to protect the franc. This dependence circumscribed French action during the whole period of negotiation over the Dawes Plan—before, during, and even after the London Conference of July and August 1924. The world's principal central bankers still consulted irregularly at this time, and they were not yet organized to oversee international credit operations. Direct governmental participation in foreign lending remained unusual. Only later in the decade, following restoration of the gold-exchange standard and organization of the Bank for International Settlements, did central bankers evolve regular procedures for mutual assistance and cooperation on monetary problems.[2] International credit operations remained for the most part within the province of private banking establishments

1. Daily quotations are provided by Eleanor Lansing Dulles, *The French Franc, 1914–1928* (New York, 1929), pp. 468–69.

2. Stephen V. O. Clarke, *Central Bank Cooperation, 1924–31* (New York, 1967), pp. 27–44; William Adams Brown, Jr., *The International Gold Standard Reinterpreted, 1914–1934*, 2 vols. (New York, 1940), 1:340–57; Lester V. Chandler, *Benjamin Strong, Central Banker* (Washington, D.C., 1958), pp. 247–90; J. W. Beyen, *Money in a Maelstrom* (New York, 1949), pp. 30–39.

in 1924. J. P. Morgan & Co., commonly acknowledged to be the dominant firm in the New York securities market, was therefore called upon to play a decisive role in assisting the French with their continuing problems of domestic finance as well as in floating the loan necessary to launch the Dawes Plan. Further loans to France also required approval by the American government. This provided Washington with additional leverage to achieve diplomatic objectives. The State Department sought to bring about a settlement of the reparations controversy on the basis of the Dawes Plan. It saw this development as an essential first step toward European stabilization and the creation of a business climate receptive to private investment. It hoped also that, once the Dawes Plan met with success, it could induce the continental allies to fund their overdue war debts to the United States.

In order to understand international power relationships as negotiations to implement the Dawes Plan proceeded, it is necessary to carry the account of French financial troubles further—into the autumn of 1924. The chains of financial dependence would have limited France's freedom of diplomatic maneuver in any event. Unquestionably, however, specific fiscal and monetary decisions that the new Herriot government made—or in many cases failed to make—magnified the extent of its dependence on the goodwill of Washington and Wall Street.

Admittedly financial exigency was not the sole determinant of the new government's foreign policy. Edouard Herriot and his colleagues were committed heart and soul to international conciliation, to a virtual mystique of peace, as venerable in inspiration as Michelet's, yet endowed with renewed urgency as a consequence of the terrible suffering caused by the war. During the election campaign influential Cartel publicists had drawn a sharp contrast between Poincaré, whom they represented as the embodiment of the Ruhr policy and intransigence, and the leaders of their own bloc, who were said to stand foursquare for peace. In lyrical terms they offered a bold endorsement of a new era of international collaboration between fraternal peoples—peoples divided by diplomats rather than by substantive differences. In the postelection period too, the vocal yearning for peace constituted the one theme upon which the otherwise divided groups making up the Cartel could enthusiastically agree. It provided the cement to maintain solidarity within the electoral alliance.[3] By temperament, ideology, and political commitment, therefore, Herriot was triply bound to accept in principle the evacuation of the Ruhr and an "international" solution for the reparations problem through the Dawes Plan.

But the concrete issues to be decided were those of the plan's imple-

3. On the French left's mystique of peace and its historical roots, see André Siegfried, *Tableau des partis en France* (Paris, 1930), pp. 105–20; Emmanuel Berl, *La Politique et les partis* (Paris, 1932), pp. 57–59, 81–87, 146–53; also the evocative essay by Albert Thibaudet, *La République des professeurs* (Paris, 1927).

mentation: the precise conditions for military and economic evacuation; procedures for applying sanctions in the event of future German default; and a possible connection between the reparations settlement and French desiderata in regard to security, war debts, and tariffs. In his first ministerial address, Herriot confirmed that he stood for a measure of continuity in policy respecting these practical concerns. He declared that it was not possible to evacuate the Ruhr "before the pledges provided for by the experts . . . had been constituted and vested in international bodies qualified to administer them, with equitable and effective guarantees of execution."[4] France's financial dependence became a major variable influencing its capacity to achieve the goals outlined by Herriot. Although that dependence was revealed in day-to-day diplomatic conversations at the London Conference only in part, it created an undercurrent affecting the entire atmosphere in which negotiations took place there.

Herriot's Outlook

In the month following the elections, a movement to compel Millerand's resignation as president of the republic raised political passions in France to an extraordinary pitch. Yet the foreordained accession of Herriot to the premiership provided some reassurance, even to determined enemies of the Cartel. During the election campaign, representatives of both sides had resorted to inflated and at times frenzied rhetoric. Despite his partisan role, Herriot had managed to maintain a degree of circumspection throughout. His extensive literary culture and his extraordinary forensic talent in evoking the verities of the republican faith and endowing them with profound spiritual significance exerted a wide appeal even outside his own party. Herriot's entire demeanor—his rumpled attire, his expansive girth (the result of almost legendary gourmandism), his ubiquitous pipe—somehow confirmed the sincerity that radiated from his countenance. His devotion to the national interest was evident from his obvious discomfort with the excesses of the election campaign and with the movement to eject Millerand from the Elysée.[5]

On the other hand, Herriot had but slight executive experience on a national level—and that experience had been an ignominious failure. When he was entrusted with responsibility for dispensing heating fuel as minister of supply in the Briand cabinet of 1916–17, the population of Paris shivered all winter; and Herriot himself was obliged to admit that

4. *J.O.C. Déb.*, 17 June 1924, p. 2307.

5. On Herriot, see his own revealing memoirs, *Jadis*, vol. 2, *D'une guerre à l'autre, 1914–1936* (Paris, 1952); Michel Soulié, *La Vie politique d'Edouard Herriot* (Paris, 1962); J.-L. Antériou and J.-J. Baron, *Edouard Herriot au service de la république* (Paris, 1957); and the shorter descriptions in Peter J. Larmour, *The French Radical Party in the 1930's* (Stanford, 1964), pp. 50–51; Joseph Paul-Boncour, *Entre deux guerres: Souvenirs sur la Troisième République*, 3 vols. (Paris, 1945), 2:87–88; Thibaudet, *La République des professeurs*, pp. 33–35, 101, 209–11.

he had "very imperfectly resolved" the problems of coal procurement and distribution.[6] In financial matters particularly, Herriot can only be described as incompetent. He did not hesitate to confess publicly that he had not studied the most important available documents relating to the financial crisis.[7] Perhaps this accounts for the fact that Herriot, like his fellow leaders on the left, continued to evince the grossest misunderstanding of the monetary debacle and the methods by which it had been arrested. Even after intervention on the exchange succeeded, spokesmen for the progressive parties still claimed—against all the evidence—that creation of a "mass of maneuver" had alone led to the fortunate outcome. Achievement of a nominally balanced budget, they maintained, contributed not at all to saving the franc. "It is not the taxes which produced this result," asserted Herriot, and Léon Blum trumpeted with equal assurance that depreciation of the currency had been halted "in spite of the taxes and not because of them."[8]

Events after the elections provided further evidence that Herriot's talents did not lie in the realm of finance. Poincaré sought to resign immediately following the balloting in order to avoid compromising his standing with the center-left. He eventually yielded to Millerand's appeal that he remain in office on a caretaker basis for a transition period, but insisted that the new leaders be asked to collaborate on the vital issues of finance and foreign affairs during the interregnum. The president of the republic arranged a meeting for Poincaré and François-Marsal with Herriot and Republican-Socialist party head Paul Painlevé on 21 May.[9] Painlevé followed the outgoing ministers' exposition of the financial situation with the closest attention, but Herriot became impatient with the complex graphs and charts, and his mind soon began to wander.[10] Of course, Herriot had just arrived in the capital to begin shaping his cabinet, and it is easy to understand why he appeared distracted at this moment. It can also be said in extenuation that both Cartel leaders suspected Millerand of staging the meeting as a political maneuver to legitimize himself with the new majority; they even thought he might have deliberately aimed to split the Cartel by not inviting a Socialist.[11] Yet Herriot's comportment at the meeting was no isolated incident. Gaston Bergery, Herriot's *chef de cabinet* in 1924, later recalled that when-

6. Soulié, *La Vie politique d'Edouard Herriot*, pp. 60–68; Herriot, *Jadis*, 2:60–72.

7. *J.O.C. Déb.*, 21 March 1924, p. 1482.

8. Ibid., p. 1485. Bokanowski and Poincaré demonstrated clearly in this debate that the new fiscal policy constituted a "formal and explicit condition" for obtaining foreign credits as well as an economic prerequisite for their successful use, but they failed to make the slightest impression on the opposition.

9. *L'Oeuvre*, 22 May 1924, *Le Quotidien*, 22 May 1924; Herrick to State Department, 22 May 1924, U.S. 851.51/459.

10. Frédéric François-Marsal, "Souvenirs: La Crise présidentielle et l'éviction de Millerand, 1923–1924," pp. 13–15, François-Marsal Papers.

11. Notation of 20 May 1924, Herriot Papers; Herriot article in *L'Information*, 22 May 1924; also *L'Oeuvre* and *Le Quotidien*, 22 May 1924.

ever he consulted his chief about economic matters, Herriot would simply hold his head in his hands and tell Bergery to take whatever course he thought proper.[12]

François-Marsal, who moved almost entirely within an ambience of business executives and members of the Paris administrative elite, was scandalized by this revelation of Herriot's lack of financial sophistication; and it did not serve to increase the cynical Bergery's respect for his patron. But Herriot, with his literary cast of mind, typified the intellectuals from the provinces who set the tone for the Cartel.[13] Their rhetoric was suffused with declarations of loyalty to an almost ineffable constellation of mystiques that together defined republican purity—the passion of the commitment and the elusiveness of the diction were quintessentially expressed in Alain's *Eléments d'une doctrine radicale*. Was it wise for the statesman to clutter up his mind with information on exchange rates, circulation levels, and the intricacies of monetary theory? Was it not rather the function of the democratic leader to set forth general principles and to ensure that the technicians at the Quai d'Orsay and the rue de Rivoli paid heed to the mandates of universal suffrage?

Herriot also faced a serious practical problem: aside from the inexperienced Bergery and a few academic economists who had written position papers for the Cartel, he knew no one to whom he could turn with confidence for reliable and sympathetic advice on economic problems. True, the new premier remained on cordial terms with the business community in Lyons. His long tenure as mayor there had not won him a reputation for financial stringency, but he had secured the Chamber of Commerce's approval through diligent efforts to promote the Lyons fair.[14] However, he did not possess the intimate social and political contacts with the interlocking world of finance and heavy industry at the highest level that might have given him the confidence to delegate financial decisions. As a result, Herriot shared the primitive fear of banks so common in his party and ascribed to bankers a mysterious power to exact retribution if displeased by public policy.[15] "It is sad but true," he later remarked, "that a conservative government can with impunity allow itself every imprudence. With a democratic government, nothing is overlooked."[16] Largely owing to this anxiety, Herriot felt himself obliged to follow the path of hidebound monetary orthodoxy charted by the Bank of France notwithstanding his continued verbal bravado on the hustings.

Undoubtedly Herriot was shaken by the outcome of a heated contro-

12. Larmour, *French Radical Party*, p. 71.

13. On the renovation of the political elite in 1924, see Thibaudet, *La République des professeurs*, pp. 11–35.

14. Herrick to State Department, 7 June 1924, U.S. 851.002/109.

15. Larmour, *French Radical Party*, p. 72.

16. *J.O.C. Déb.*, 9 April 1925, p. 2151.

versy over the so-called electoral franc that ignited in the supercharged postelection atmosphere. The known facts are simple. The foreign exchange value of the franc continued to rise until shortly before the elections. Suddenly on 7 May it began to fall again, dropping within forty-eight hours from 68 to 74 to the pound sterling. Following the Cartel victory on 11 May the franc declined further, within a month falling more than 20 percent from its post-speculation high. Finally, in the first half of June, it stabilized precariously between 80 and 85 to the pound, just above the exchange rate prevailing in December 1923. The reader will recall the explanation given in the previous chapter of the franc's variations up to the election date. After the banking syndicate's initial success in stemming the tide of bear speculation, an exchange movement in the opposite direction carried the franc up to heights that the relative productivity of the French economy did not justify. Though this appreciation gratified the French desire for prestige of their national monetary unit, it could not be indefinitely sustained. The Bank of France, apparently motivated by a mixture of financial and political considerations, artificially supported the franc at an unrealistically high level until 6 May. But several days before the elections, the Bank terminated this support and left the franc to seek an equilibrium dictated by forces of the marketplace.

Officials at the Bank of France and in the caretaker Poincaré administration were disturbed when the franc continued to depreciate steadily after the elections. Considering it politically unwise to dip into the Morgan funds again, the Bank of France discreetly threw the whole of the Lazard credit available to it—$22 million—on the exchange. The Bank was puzzled when the market absorbed these dollars as fast as they were offered, with no apparent effect in checking the decline of the franc.[17] Financial experts could not discover who was leading the new speculative wave. The French financial attaché in New York discerned some participation by the original speculative group which was seeking to liquidate its remaining short position. But he was inclined to believe that the general American public, "a bit worried by the inevitable lack of precision" in declarations by Cartel leaders concerning their future policies, was doing most of the selling.[18] Herman Harjes of Morgan's Paris branch, on the other hand, thought that French businessmen who had lost confidence in the country's financial managers were taking the lead in selling their own currency.[19] Whoever was actually responsible for the renewed decline of the franc, it is clear that this development caused

17. "Opérations faites par la Banque de France pour soutenir le change," in Sénat, Commission des Finances, Exposé sur les finances publiques fait par M. Henry Bérenger, rapporteur-général, séance du 4 juin 1924, pp. 71–74, copy in Herriot Papers.

18. Tel. no. 59 from Brouzet (New York), 23 May 1924, copy in Millerand Papers.

19. Myron T. Herrick to Parmely W. Herrick, 2 June 1924, Folder 4, Container 16, Myron T. Herrick Papers, Western Reserve Historical Society, Cleveland, Ohio.

dismay at the Bank of France. Officials of the Bank did their best to keep trading orderly, even though they were obliged to call off a second round of massive support operations because their intervention was not proving efficacious.[20]

Despite the absence of proof, the left began to charge almost immediately after the elections that the fall of the franc represented a "reactionary reprisal" for its victory at the polls.[21] Lazard Frères, the firm managing the bankers' syndicate, was concerned from the start lest fear or uncertainty over the new government's fiscal and economic policies add to downward pressures on the currency. Lazard partners sought out Léon Blum, always more moderate in private than when preaching to a Socialist party audience. Blum agreed to draw up a statement indicating that the new majority placed attainment of a "really balanced budget" at the forefront of its legislative program. The signatures of Herriot and Painlevé were also corralled for this reassuring document, and it was released to the press on 16 May.[22]

But by this time *Le Quotidien* had launched a full-scale attack on the financial integrity of the outgoing government. This newspaper had served so effectively as the Cartel's chief organ of propaganda that it had acquired independent influence. Its editors were eager for transformation of the electoral alliance into a parliamentary alliance. Radicals and Socialists, though deeply divided on substantive issues of domestic policy, could maintain a broad measure of agreement on replacing officials sympathetic to the Bloc National. Socialist deputy Pierre Renaudel coined an immodest definition of Cartel patronage demands: "*Toutes les places et tout de suite*"—an absolute version of "to the victors belong the spoils." *Le Quotidien* lost no time in getting down to specifics. It attached great symbolic value to supplanting Millerand as president of the republic and initiated a massive campaign to compel his resignation. The franc's new decline conveniently provided ammunition for this maneuver. Seconded by *L'Oeuvre*, *L'Ere nouvelle*, and other Cartel dailies, *Le Quotidien* accused both Millerand and the outgoing government of using public funds to manipulate the franc for electoral purposes, and thereby of ruining numerous individuals in order to gratify their spite. The charges by Georges Boris of *Le Quotidien*'s staff grew more outlandish as the series of articles progressed.[23]

Boris first identified the guilty parties simply as "certain ministers of the Poincaré government," but then zeroed in on Millerand and his "varlets," "accomplices," and "tools" François-Marsal and Robineau. These malefactors, as Boris told the story, had first driven up the franc

20. Bérenger, "Opérations faites par la Banque de France pour soutenir le change."
21. *L'Oeuvre*, 14 May 1924.
22. Raymond Philippe, *Le Drame financier de 1924–1928* (Paris, 1931), pp. 55–56; *Le Temps*, 18 May 1924; *L'Oeuvre* and *Le Quotidien*, 17 May 1924.
23. "The Scandal of the Electoral Franc," *Le Quotidien*, 14–19, 22, 24 May 1924.

without giving a thought to whether the rate could be maintained, merely for electoral advantage. They had desisted only when J. P. Morgan allegedly became irate, saying that he had "come to the aid of France and not that of a clique of politicians," and had threatened to withdraw his support unless the "mad policy" were ended at once. Even worse, Millerand had reputedly forbidden the Bank of France to support the franc in the wake of postelection selling, because he wanted to "throw public opinion into a panic and make it believe that the victory of the Bloc des Gauches meant ruin." He allowed the Bank to intervene on the exchange again in a limited way only because of a premonitory fear of prosecution by the High Court. Boris emphasized that this was of course only the "most abominable" in a long list of transgressions by the Bloc National. "How much longer," he asked, "will republicans tolerate at the Elysée the person guilty of this crime, this abuse of authority?"[24]

Even in these weeks of political delirium more sober heads set the hyperbole of the party press in its proper perspective. Nevertheless, the wide credence accorded the "electoral franc" charges served to underscore the financial gullibility of many in the new legislative majority. Cartel supporters displayed an ominous propensity to underrate the importance of fiscal and monetary policy and to overestimate the role of "market action" in determining the fate of the franc. The "electoral franc" controversy also focused political conflict on the Cartel's financial intentions, conjuring up expressions of anxiety on the right that matched those on the other side of the political spectrum in virulence. *Le Temps* sounded the tocsin for the bourgeoisie: "No matter how belated the cry of alarm may be, France must be informed that it runs a mortal danger. A majority spendthrift on principle, meddlesome in regard to private wealth, makes ready to throw confusion in every direction. . . . Already a financial crisis without precedent is to be foreseen."[25] *Le Temps* and other establishment newspapers painted a dismal picture of what might happen if Cartel campaign oratory became reality—an end to economy in government, billions squandered for unproductive purposes, and drastic new taxes on capital, profits, and property. These charges stung Herriot to the quick; he lashed out in turn against "defeatists of the franc" who, he proclaimed, were attempting to ruin the nation's credit in a "contemptible maneuver of domestic politics."[26]

24. *Le Quotidien*, 16 May 1924. Boris and his colleagues on other Cartel newspapers offered little hard information to support their allegations. They made much of one piece of circumstantial evidence, namely, that Marcel Hutin, a prominent right-wing editor supposedly familiar with the "thoughts and intentions" of highly placed persons, had urged the government in late March and April to continue the franc offensive in order to bring down the cost of living before the elections. (For Hutin's views, see *L'Echo de Paris*, 21–22 March, 8, 10 April 1924.)

25. *Le Temps*, 21 May 1924.

26. *L'Information*, 23 May 1924; see also Herriot, *Jadis*, 2:200; and Soulié, *La Vie politique d'Edouard Herriot*, pp. 145–46.

The right's forebodings about Herriot's intentions were excessive. Yet it was perfectly true that he could not hope to fulfill even a fraction of his electoral promises without considerably increasing government expenditure. He had committed himself to immediate revocation of the "decree-laws" (thus canceling government economies), salary raises for state employees, recognition of their right to unionize, higher pensions for veterans, and to rapid completion of restoration work in the devastated areas. Nevertheless, he was utterly sincere in advocating a balanced budget. In his maiden ministerial address, he stated unequivocally that to propose any new appropriations not covered by tax revenue would be "the most elementary and glaring blunder." At the same time, he opposed crippling new taxes liable to frighten the propertied classes. While reiterating a campaign pledge to institute a "really democratic tax system," he made it clear that this meant not a capital levy but simply rigorous enforcement of the income tax.[27] Moreover, he believed (though he put it on record only later) that the income tax schedule already was so high as to discourage initiative and the productive use of capital.[28]

It was obviously not possible to fulfill electoral promises, balance the budget, and avoid raising taxes without compromising somewhere. Herriot's public statements suggest that his economic views at this time were confused, if not logically contradictory. His clearest commitment was to proceed with a "vigorous inventory of the situation." Yet as a tactical expedient, a certain amount of imprecision was not necessarily an error. Overwhelming political constraints limited Herriot's ability to stake out a bold financial course on the eve of a major international conference. He felt obliged to try to please everyone by conveying the impression of financial responsibility and circumspection. "Be reassured," he said to the Chamber. "We are well-informed. We are prudent."[29]

Herriot confirmed his good intentions by selecting a finance minister acceptable to moderates. Actually, Herriot was one of the few Radical party leaders who, on political grounds, would have genuinely welcomed Socialist participation in his cabinet.[30] But the Socialists would have insisted on imposing Vincent Auriol as finance minister, and also on adoption of an impractical capital levy, inimical to confidence within France and abroad and exceeding the enforcement capabilities of the Finance Ministry bureaucracy.[31] Herriot declined to consider Socialist

27. This account of Herriot's fiscal intentions is based on his ministerial statement and the subsequent interpellations: *J.O.C. Déb.*, 17 June 1924, pp. 2305–7; ibid., 19 June 1924, pp. 2321–40.

28. *J.O.S. Déb.*, 10 April 1925, pp. 844–45.

29. *J.O.C. Déb.*, 19 June 1924, p. 2339.

30. Paul-Boncour, *Souvenirs*, 2:92–93; Soulié, *La Vie politique d'Edouard Herriot*, pp. 146–48.

31. This Socialist proposal for a 10–12.5% capital levy, linked to a scheme for reimbursement of the Bank of France's advances and for appreciation of the franc, was publicly

participation on these terms. Instead, he designated Senator Etienne Clémentel* for the rue de Rivoli. Though nominally on the left, Clémentel counted himself as a supporter of what he later termed the Poincaré ministry's "valiant" campaign against the franc's collapse. He did not intend to prepare a "budget of social revolution."[32] The business community might entertain doubts whether the courteous and obliging Clémentel possessed the toughness of character required to impose painful fiscal measures on a politically minded parliament, but no one could question his sobriety and level-headedness. Auriol was relegated to the post of president of the Chamber Finance Commission. Under his direction, the commission would draw up its own proposals to counter those of the ministry, greatly complicating Clémentel's task.[33] The real danger, however, proved to be not hasty action, but inaction.

Principles and Problems of Cartel Finance

Despite manifest good intentions, Herriot and Clémentel found themselves trapped between contradictory fiscal and monetary policies. Their electoral commitments imposed the necessity of periodic verbal genuflexion to the left and, notwithstanding their own wishes to achieve a balanced budget, made it difficult in practice to curb the deficit that

*Etienne Clémentel (1864–1936), of peasant origins, aspired to be a painter, but abandoned the fine arts under family pressure to become a notary and to embark on a career in municipal government; elected deputy from rural Puy-de-Dôme, 1900–19, senator, 1920–35. Aligned with the *Gauche radicale*, thrice a minister by 1914, he also acted as *rapporteur* of the budget. Minister of commerce and industry, 1915–19, he participated in interallied councils on transport and raw materials, made many contacts abroad; at home, he encouraged formation of the *Confédération générale de la production française*, forerunner of the modern *Patronat* organization, and won the confidence of business. Clémentel broke with Herriot on financial policy and resigned in April 1925; he subsequently served as president of the Senate Finance Commission, 1927–30.

unveiled in May 1925. See Georges Lachapelle, *Le Crédit public* (Paris, 1932), pp. 228–30. Gilbert Ziebura, *Léon Blum: Theorie und Praxis einer sozialistischen Politik* (Berlin, 1963), pp. 246–81, provides an ingenious defense of Socialist notions of finance under the Cartel.

32. See Clémentel's exposition of his fundamental views in *J.O.S. Déb.*, 2 April 1925, pp. 526–34.

33. In the summer and autumn of 1924, loose talk concerning the imposition of a drastic capital levy continued, quintessentially expressed in Pierre Renaudel's phrase: "Nous prendrons l'argent où il est" (*J.O.C. Déb.*, 7 November 1924, p. 3389). In practice the Chamber Finance Commission concentrated its attention on gift, inheritance, and income taxes, and on modification of the turnover tax. However, Auriol and his courageous but sectarian *rapporteur-général*, Maurice Viollette, relied for technical advice largely on lower-ranking bureaucrats who belonged to the socialist-oriented government employees' union (*Syndicat des fonctionnaires*). The latter were at daggers drawn with the Inspectorate of Finance and the *hauts fonctionnaires* at the rue de Rivoli. As a consequence, the Finance Ministry and the commission found it increasingly difficult to cooperate, and the tax system remained a political football. (See the superb analysis by Lucien Lamoureux, "Souvenirs politiques, 1919–1940," pp. 719–35, microfilm of MS at the Bibliothèque de Documentation Internationale Contemporaine, Nanterre.)

remained the fundamental fiscal cause of inflation. At the same time, both men were determined to prove their sense of responsibility by continuing the policy of monetary deflation; in this respect they were loath to depart in the slightest degree from the dogma propagated by the Bank of France.

Spokesmen for the previous government sought to demonstrate that the financial outlook was relatively auspicious when Herriot assumed office. Maurice Bokanowski contended that France's position, measured in terms of the budget, balance of payments, industrial production, and prospects for the franc's stability, was "the most favorable known since the end of the war."[34] In certain respects this argument appeared plausible. The Bank of France still had at its disposal most of the foreign credits—all of the Morgan funds, and most of the Lazard reserves (which it managed to reconstitute during June through a series of small purchases on obscure markets in the Far East).[35] The treasury had temporarily repaid the secret advances made to it by the deposit banks. Subscriptions to national defense bonds were picking up again, in part owing to a March 1924 law exempting these bonds from the income tax. An increase of foreign investment in French treasury obligations, and the fact that the public rather than the banks was doing most of the domestic buying, provided clear signs of restored confidence.[36]

However, most of these developments were easily reversible. Close scrutiny of the figures underlying the outgoing government's claims of budgetary improvement led the majority of the Senate Finance Commission to a rather less optimistic assessment. Back in March, Poincaré had promised to use the decree powers granted him to make "permanent savings" in the budget.[37] Now the senators discovered to their dismay that a considerable proportion of the much-touted reduction in government expenditure represented an accounting fiction—cancellation of unexpended appropriations and postponement of mandatory long-term outlays to the next fiscal year. Finance Commission *rapporteur* Henry Bérenger flayed the now-departed Poincaré government for having passed off a mere public relations stunt, "an illusory gesture devoid of substance," as a great achievement.[38] Could anyone familiar with administrative practice in the French government put aside the suspicion that additional irregularities would turn up in the event that its entire financial structure was subjected to rigorous analysis?

Permanent treasury officials, who were in the best position to judge,

34. *J.O.C. Déb.*, 19 June 1924, p. 2321.

35. Bérenger, "Opérations faites par la Banque de France pour soutenir le change."

36. See François-Marsal's review of the Finance Ministry's figures in *J.O.S. Déb.*, 2 April 1925, pp. 534–45; 10 April 1925, pp. 838–39.

37. Sénat, Commission des Finances, séance du 8 mars 1924, audition de M. le Président du Conseil, copy in Herriot Papers.

38. Sénat, Commission des Finances, "Exposé sur les finances publiques fait par M. Henry Bérenger, rapporteur-général," séance du 4 juin 1924, pp. 64–67, 97–99.

ranged themselves squarely on the side of the pessimists. Failure of the February 1924 loan had indicated to them that the days of unlimited borrowing in capital markets were over. Since maturity dates on long-term treasury bonds had not been scheduled with much foresight, an abnormally large volume—more than 30 milliard francs, a sum as large as the annual government budget—would come due for renewal in 1925. This refunding operation would have to be carried out while the treasury also sought to keep up subscriptions to the unconsolidated floating debt, now amounting to the imposing total of 58 milliard francs with a turnover rate averaging six months. Under the circumstances, continuation of a deflationary monetary policy entailed grave disadvantages. The basic problem did not differ appreciably from that which Pierre de Mouÿ and his predecessor as director of the *Mouvement général des fonds*, Jean Parmentier, had periodically outlined to their political superiors during the previous two years. But the conjuncture of an abnormally heavy refunding schedule with political circumstances in which the new government might not be able to avoid an inflationary fiscal policy made the danger for the treasury particularly acute. Mouÿ moved immediately to alert Clémentel and Herriot to the "risks inherent in the situation."[39]

Treasury officials realized that the budgetary deficit provided the fundamental impulse for long-term deterioration of the franc. Until deficit financing was brought to an end, gradual adaptation of the domestic price level to the exchange value of the currency would inevitably require a further increase in bank note circulation. Mouÿ pointed out that even if the *double décime* were kept in force—contrary to the Cartel's election pledge—a large budget deficit would remain. Above all, he counseled fighting inflation with fiscal policy and warned against "weakening" the movement toward budgetary stringency that he credited to the Poincaré regime. But in view of the size of the floating debt, he considered almost equally important the recognition that monetary deflation was no longer feasible. Once again, therefore, he called for revision of the François-Marsal Convention and termination of the government's obligation to reimburse the "advances" made by the Bank of France on a definite schedule. Mouÿ recommended asking parliament, or to avoid political complications the *Conseil d'Etat*, to sanction a higher limit both for note circulation and Bank of France advances to the state.

Since the issue is technical, its bearing on French foreign policy may not be apparent at first glance. But as Mouÿ pointed out, the levels of actual advances and of currency in circulation had not ceased to scrape against the authorized maximums, notwithstanding the "victory" of the

39. Mouÿ met with Clémentel and then sent him a note summarizing his oral arguments on 17 June 1924, the day the ministry was confirmed. He then prepared a second and more comprehensive "Note pour le ministre," 27 June 1924. Copies of both documents are found in the Herriot Papers. Herriot read excerpts to the Chamber, *J.O.C. Déb.*, 9 April 1925, p. 2150, and also reproduced certain parts in *Jadis*, 2:201–5.

franc. In preceding months, the real level of advances would indeed have consistently surpassed the legal limit without resort to secret help from the private banks as well as to a wide variety of unconventional treasury operations. Despite some improvement, an accurate accounting in mid-June would still have shown the treasury indebted to the Bank through various subterfuges for 581 million francs over what was publicly admitted. Mouÿ considered it highly dangerous to continue masking the true situation through irregular expedients that might come to light at an awkward movement. Moreover, a new downward fluctuation of the exchange rate was liable to affect renewal of the floating debt adversely and oblige the treasury to borrow even more from the Bank of France to cover its obligations. If an increase in advances from the Bank were ruled out, France would have to desist from any measure of foreign policy that might disturb confidence abroad and cause depreciation of the exchange.

Mouÿ conceded that because of the importance which domestic public opinion mistakenly attached to the François-Marsal Convention as a bulwark against inflation, its revision would represent a calculated risk. But he considered the risk eminently worth taking. If revision were postponed, it would later assume the appearance of a desperate measure. Presented in careful fashion forthwith, as part of a program for "financial reconstruction of the nation," it stood a good chance of acceptance with no more than a "trivial and momentary repercussion on public credit."

The financial community split in reaction to Mouÿ's proposal along now-familiar lines. Lazard Frères and other sophisticated banking houses hailed his suggestion as "clairvoyant and courageous." Lazard's thought it better to face readjustment of the circulation level at a time when foreign speculation had been put to rout than to hazard a political crisis the following year in the midst of an effort to refund the anticipated overstock of national defense bonds. It concurred also with Mouÿ's judgment that continued public anxiety about an eventual increase in circulation limits constituted a greater obstacle to renewal of the floating debt than prompt and decisive action. In any case, Lazard's did not attach exaggerated importance to limiting the amount of currency in circulation as a deterrent to inflation. As the firm's prescient Raymond Philippe observed, "one doesn't fight a sick man's fever by pushing down the column of mercury in the thermometer."[40]

The Bank of France took the opposite view. Governor Robineau was concerned lest inflationary pressures on the Cartel government become irresistible and ruin French credit abroad. From the day the new cabinet was confirmed, he repeatedly called on Clémentel, urging him to follow the double-barreled policy of rigorously collecting existing taxes and concomitantly pursuing monetary deflation. "The peril of inflation, in

40. Philippe, *Le Drame financier*, pp. 59–66.

whatever insidious form it may be presented," Robineau stated categorically, "is a deathly menace which must be averted at all costs."[41] Bank of France officials believed that accelerated collection of taxes, coupled with a tight money policy and technical measures to discourage hoarding of bank notes, might reduce demand for currency sufficiently to allow continued reduction of the money supply. This formula had in fact facilitated contraction of the circulation during the 1920–21 recession. To expect the same strategy to work under boom conditions in 1924 was "so mad a hope," as Lazard's stigmatized it, that only "incomprehension of monetary phenomena" at the Bank of France could account for it.[42]

Nevertheless, Herriot and Clémentel chose to follow the Bank's advice rather than that given by Mouÿ and the treasury. On 1 July the Council of Ministers voted to maintain the François-Marsal Convention in force. To meet the treasury's exceptional needs at the end of the first semester, they authorized another appeal to the private banks, for the largest secret loan extended up to that time.[43] When Mouÿ continued to object to government policy, he found himself eased out of his job and eventually kicked upstairs to the directorship of the customs.

In later years Herriot came to realize how grievously he had compromised France's freedom for maneuver abroad and at the same time undercut his own position by vetoing Mouÿ's plan to increase the legally permissible fiduciary circulation.[44] His subsequent attempt to shift responsibility indicates that he keenly regretted the error. When financial troubles stemming from this decision brought down Herriot's ministry ten months later, he and Clémentel advanced a number of explanations, not all of them fully consistent, for their rejection of the treasury's advice.[45] Herriot then lamented that he had not sufficiently appreciated Mouÿ's "intelligence, perspicacity, and devotion to the public interest." He offered the excuse that the demands of foreign policy had so preoccupied him as to leave no time for serious consideration of Mouÿ's recommendations.[46] In view of the gaps in Herriot's economic education, the problems must have struck him as technical and abstruse. The notations that he made in April 1925 on Mouÿ's formal memoranda

41. Robineau to Minister of Finance, 29 December 1924, 29 April 1925, Herriot Papers; also quoted in part by Lachapelle, *Le Crédit public*, pp. 203–4. See also Robineau's further justification of this position in Governor of the Bank of France to Minister of Finance, 8 June 1925, F^{30}/1432, Ministère des Finances, Administration centrale, Mission des Archives, Paris (hereafter cited as F^{30}/Box number).

42. Philippe, *Le Drame financier*, p. 63.

43. Soulié, *La Vie politique d'Edouard Herriot*, pp. 224–25.

44. Edouard Herriot, *Etudes françaises* (Geneva, 1950), pp. 227–28.

45. This analysis is based principally on the accounts given by Herriot and Clémentel at the time their government fell, Herriot in *J.O.C. Déb.*, 9 April 1925, pp. 2143–54, and in *J.O.S. Déb.*, 10 April 1925, pp. 842–50; Clémentel in *J.O.S. Déb.*, 2 April 1925, pp. 526–34. Herriot's memoirs provide a characteristically evasive recollection: *Jadis*, 2:199–226. M. Clémentel, *Inventaire de la situation financière au début de la treizième législature* (Paris, 1924), also casts light on the finance minister's thinking.

46. *J.O.C. Déb.*, 9 April 1925, pp. 2147, 2050–51.

betray a concern only for political consequences and evidence no comprehension of economic principles.[47] It is plain that in June 1924 Herriot simply did not understand how his resolve to maintain the money supply ceiling would increase his dependence on foreign banking opinion and limit his diplomatic options. And Clémentel was positively convinced that revelation of the treasury's real position would irredeemably shake foreign confidence in the franc. At any rate, he argued, the risk could not be taken on the eve of the London Reparations Conference.[48]

This view also drew support from stalwarts of the left majority in parliament. Henry Bérenger of the Senate Finance Commission adorned his admonitions to respect the double *plafonds* "at any price" with apocalyptic rhetoric—indistinguishable from that served up by the Bank of France—regarding the danger of inflation. Bérenger and his colleagues advised the cabinet to "do everything possible to inspire the most massive confidence at home and abroad." Monetary deflation and budgetary restriction to reassure holders of the floating debt, they believed, should be key ingredients of the program. According to the Finance Commission's elusive formation, these policies constituted logical domestic counterparts to an effort to reestablish cordial relations with the United States and Great Britain in order to "resolve the twin difficulties of German payments and settlement of interallied debts."[49]

The desirability of maintaining a national consensus on financial matters appeared self-evident to the cabinet. In his first experience as a major executive officeholder, moreover, Herriot wished to oblige his parliamentary associates. He was further influenced by the categorical tone in which the Bank of France rendered its advice. Easily intimidated by bankers holding positions of eminence, Herriot considered collaboration with the Bank of France the only prudent policy for a government of the left. A decision to endorse the treasury view, as Clémentel later put it, might have appeared to be "inspired by a party spirit" rather than national needs.[50] The Cartel leaders failed to realize that by sanctioning the system of secret advances and false public accounting, they put themselves in the position of petitioners to the Bank of France, pleading for time to reduce the actual money supply within legal limits and vulnerable to political blackmail.[51]

Unquestionably, however, Herriot and Clémentel acted as much from genuine conviction as out of a feeling of duress. Both were as committed

47. Herriot notations on Mouÿ's notes for Clémentel, 17 and 27 June 1924, Herriot Papers.

48. Clémentel's testimony quoted in Herriot, *Jadis*, 2:204–5.

49. Sénat, Commission des Finances, "Exposé sur les finances publiques fait par M. Henry Bérenger, rapporteur-général," séance du 4 juin 1924, especially pp. 97–99.

50. Cited by Herriot in *Jadis*, 2:204–5, and in *J.O.S. Déb.*, 10 April 1925, p. 843.

51. See especially Herriot to Robineau, 3 March 1925, Herriot Papers.

to deflation as was the Bank of France. Herriot, it will be recalled, believed that fiscal policy did not affect the price level. This inclined him to emphasize monetary policy all the more as the key tool for revaluation of the franc. Clémentel reiterated throughout his term in office that to raise the circulation limits would constitute "a crime against the nation."[52] In his view, the statutory limit on note issue and the stipulations of the François-Marsal Convention provided "precious guarantees" of eventual currency revaluation to those holding government bonds and therefore were essential to maintain French credit.[53] Arguing by analogy to combat, Clémentel proclaimed that "the best way to fight is to defend the first trench, to hold there to the end, and not to begin the action by a retreat, even a strategic one."[54]

Finally, in the back of his mind Herriot harbored a grand design for rehabilitation of French finance. He disdained any kind of "little operation" as a mere treasury "expedient." He preferred to "try to make Germany pay as much as possible" at the London Conference first, and then to follow with "a summons to the nation"—not simply to balance the budget, but to retire the national debt as well. The public, he argued nebulously, would "make sacrifices for the revaluation of its franc, of its *rente*, of its property, if it knows that the money will go into a fund separated from the normal government budget by a watertight bulkhead, for the purpose of monetary contraction."[55] But since Germany could no longer be expected to play deus ex machina, where could one find sufficient tax revenue to make this ambitious concept a reality? What effect would massive fiscal deflation have on the economy? And if radical fiscal deflation were to produce the desired reduction in demand for currency over a period of time, why not profit from flexible monetary policy in the interim? If Herriot even thought about such questions, much less formulated answers to them, it was not easily discernible through the fog of parliamentary oratory.

In short, economic ignorance, the exigencies of politics, and genuine conviction all played a part in determining the Cartel's financial strategy. Proceeding without deviation on the path marked out by conservative predecessors, a government of the left rejected an innovation which, at the cost of only slight monetary inflation, would have immeasurably increased the treasury's room for maneuver. A cabinet boasting of its intention to sweep away outdated institutions paradoxically embraced the most orthodox monetary policy possible, a policy doubly unrealistic in view of France's fiscal constraints and world position. The result exacerbated the precarious financial situation throughout the following

52. Clémentel, *Inventaire de la situation financière*, p. 254; same phrase in *J.O.S. Déb.*, 2 April 1925, p. 532.
53. Clémentel, *Inventaire de la situation financière*, pp. 51–52.
54. Quoted in Herriot, *Jadis*, 2:205.
55. *J.O.S. Déb.*, 10 April 1925, p. 848.

months. Just as Mouÿ had predicted, the treasury was obliged to operate so close to the margin that it could not count on meeting its obligations in the event of a decline, however temporary, in tax revenue or bond refunding income. Any diminution of foreign confidence would heighten fear at home lest the floating debt not be renewed and the treasury forced to violate the *plafonds*. The policy adopted thus rendered France more vulnerable to foreign pressures that could be exerted directly against the franc at a time of important diplomatic negotiations.

The Bankers' Conditions for Continued Assistance

In point of fact, Clémentel implicitly based his financial policy on the expectation of continued American support from the day he assumed office. Information reaching the Finance Ministry led him to believe that some speculators had not lost hope of "revenge" in a return battle on the exchange. The banking credit from J. P. Morgan & Co. to the Bank of France would expire on 12 September. The French hoped to renew it. But even if New York agreed to an extension of some months' duration, France might find itself forced to cover by shipping gold or purchasing dollars in the open market at the end of that period. The peril would remain live until a long-term foreign loan could be arranged. Clémentel also considered such a foreign loan a prerequisite for the operation that constituted the linchpin of his project for domestic financial reform, namely, the conversion of the short-term floating debt into a long-term obligation.[56]

At the London Conference and after it, consequently, the French would have to negotiate within circumscribed limits. These were the bounds of tolerance within which United States government officials, international bankers, and the wider investing public in America (and Great Britain) would vouchsafe continued support to the French credit structure. J. P. Morgan & Co., which had so often given advice that it considered in France's own interest, stood ready to help again. The implicit price for this assistance became manifest gradually: France could not diverge radically from a financial program—and therefore a political course—considered "sound" in America.

To be sure, the protagonists on the two sides did not fully recognize the nature of the emerging bargain, much less formulate it explicitly in this bald way. Early relations between the new-minted Cartel government and Morgan's provide evidence to illustrate the point. Herriot was rather inclined to criticize the prominent role played by the Morgan bankers in the March crisis. Gossiping with political cronies in the Chamber lobby on 1 June, he reproached his predecessors for making

56. For Clémentel's retrospective discussion of the consolidation loan, see *J.O.S. Déb.*, 21 November 1924, pp. 1471–72.

commitments of a general character in return for credit from "money lenders." "This method of treating France like Turkey is extraordinary," he fulminated with more passion than prudence. Never the most discreet of men, Herriot did not intend this ventilation of his private feelings to reach the press. When it did, he promptly labeled the report inaccurate and personally called at Morgan-Harjes offices in the Place Vendôme, where he dismissed the incident as mere parliamentary "intrigue."[57]

Nevertheless, the Morgan partners in New York bridled at the criticism. In general they were favorably disposed toward Herriot and not put off by his political orientation. Reassured by his repeated declarations in favor of a balanced budget, they took the view that the particular kinds of taxes adopted to attain that goal were "no concern" of theirs. They could not let pass the opportunity, however, to remind the Cartel leaders that in extending the $100 million credit they had been "moved not by ordinary commercial considerations but by [a] desire to serve a difficult situation." The bankers protested that they had sought neither to dictate French policy nor to exert political pressure:

> When approached by the French government and the Banque de France . . . we did indeed promptly point out the financial measures which must be taken if stabilization of the franc were to be accomplished. But our advice on these financial questions was accompanied by a very clear and explicit statement at the very outset of negotiations that "all of us here have a feeling of strongest sympathy for France in her perplexing problems and we do not for a moment venture a suggestion on the question whether France should or should not at this time subordinate political to financial objectives."[58]

The Morgan partners consistently adopted this position—at least in the realm of theory—even in private communications with each other. Conscious of the heavy responsibilities that the institutional structure of American capitalism thrust upon them as private citizens, they resolved not to use the extraordinary political power which was theirs by circumstance in an illegitimate way. J. P. Morgan preferred to think of himself as a sort of high-level bond salesman, "simply an expert . . . upon the marketability of securities"; and his reluctance to serve as chairman of the Bankers' Committee on reparations in 1922 bore witness to this attitude.[59] Other partners of the firm, notably Thomas Lamont, Dwight Morrow, and Russell Leffingwell, felt more comfortable with the pivotal role played by Morgan's in European public finance. But they too wished to exercise restraint in employing the firm's financial power to impose their personal political preferences on foreign nations.

Tradition ascribes to Wall Street bankers the position of dollar diplo-

57. Lamont to Hughes, 2 June 1924, enclosing copies of Morgan telegrams regarding the incident, Box 62, Hughes Papers; also U.S. 851.00/525.

58. J. P. Morgan & Co. to Herman Harjes, 5 June 1924, TWL 95/12.

59. See the extensive correspondence on this subject in TWL 108/13, 113/14.

macy advocates, while American "liberals" were supposed to favor less naked use of the country's financial muscle abroad during the 1920s. In reality, the roles were frequently reversed.[60] Herbert Croly of the *New Republic*, for example, argued that "the most effective way to discourage French imperialism is to deny the French access to American money markets until [France] makes some attempt to pay the war debt and until she allows Germany a chance to recover." Thomas Lamont, equally characteristically, opposed such "government blackmail" and questioned whether the United States could feel sure enough of its stand to justify imposing policies by means of a financial blockade. Lamont, echoed by other bankers, repeatedly insisted that "the way to lead France out of her problems is not by waving the big stick of American finance."[61]

In practice, however, the line between offering financial advice and exerting political pressure was exceedingly fine. Notwithstanding periodic incantations to the contrary, political overtones could not be kept out of the earnest discussions of French finance that took place in Morgan offices at Broad and Wall streets throughout the summer of 1924. Since the bankers believed that the French economy was fundamentally sound, and that the nation's troubles stemmed almost entirely from poor management of public finance and insufficient parliamentary courage in economic affairs, discussion of such matters could hardly be avoided.

Morgan-Harjes forwarded an analysis showing that after adoption of Poincaré's tax package, the presumably balanced budget still showed an actual deficit of over nine billion francs. Russell Leffingwell,* acknowledged to possess the sharpest analytic mind in the firm, deplored the "evident persistence in the policy of self-deception which has been pursued ever since Armistice Day by the French government." Almost immediately upon Clémentel's assumption of office, Leffingwell conveyed to him the firm's advice really to balance the budget, to raise the bank rate, and to seize the "golden opportunity" for accumulating dollars against a time of need. Leffingwell sought to dampen Clémentel's

*Russell C. Leffingwell (1878–1960), lawyer in the eminent Wall Street firm of Cravath, Henderson & de Gersdorff, 1902–17, 1920–23; assistant secretary of the treasury, 1917–20; architect of much of the Wilson administration's foreign economic policy, responsible for U.S. war loans to the European allies and for floating Liberty bonds; partner of J. P. Morgan & Co., 1923–48, chairman of the board, 1948–50; long-time chairman of the Council on Foreign Relations; author of many articles on international finance; described by *Business Week* (21 February 1948) as "a business intellectual, a man who gains his points by persuasive argument, not by table pounding."

60. See the perceptive article by Richard M. Abrams, "United States Intervention Abroad: The First Quarter Century," *American Historical Review* 79 (February 1974): 72–102.

61. Editorial, *New Republic*, 14 January 1925, pp. 186–87; Lamont to Herbert Croly, 23 January 1925, TWL 95/9. See also Lamont's long correspondence with Oswald Garrison Villard, editor of the *Nation*, which covers the same ground, in TWL 115/5.

optimism about revaluation of the franc, and he strongly advocated stabilization at the current rate against either appreciation or depreciation. Morgan's had counseled adoption of this general line of policy insistently since 1922. The bankers felt, however, that the time for implementation was now particularly propitious.[62]

Clémentel took care to respond in conciliatory fashion. He also assured Herman Harjes in Paris that he wished to arrive at "an early agreement upon the question of interallied debts." This made a good impression in New York. The Morgan partners believed that Great Britain's settlement of its debt in January 1923 had constituted a political "masterstroke"; they thought the time ripe for France to follow suit. Leffingwell noted that since the Dawes Plan pointed up the limits on German capacity to pay, France too could plausibly request remission of interest on its debt over a term of years, and thereafter a low interest rate and a remote date of maturity on the principal.[63] Lamont, who planned to confer with Clémentel during a forthcoming European trip, compiled a list of policies that would strengthen the case for generous treatment if French representatives approached the World War Foreign Debt Commission after the end of the London Conference. High on the list were monetary reform, including stabilization of the franc, and achievement of a truly balanced budget. Significantly, Lamont added two political desiderata, a "whole-souled acceptance" of the Dawes Plan and a reduction of the French military service requirement from eighteen to nine months.[64] Admittedly, Lamont's list represented no more than an indication of tentative thinking at Morgan corner in late June. The crucial issue was what conditions the firm would lay down as the sine qua non for further credit to the French treasury.

During the summer the partners in New York considered two separate but related questions. Should the credit to the Bank of France be renewed in September? And should France be granted alternatively, or in addition, a long-term loan, and if so, for what purposes? Under the right circumstances, the leading members of the firm favored a long-term loan as the most suitable remedy for the French treasury's financial embarrassment. Easing of money rates in the United States, they thought, made it feasible to market such a loan commercially if Clémentel would stabilize the franc and balance the budget "without relying too much upon deliveries from Germany."[65]

At the beginning of July, Dwight Morrow drew up the outline of a $50 million one- or two-year loan, for which Herriot could be given the

62. Morgan, Harjes et Cie to J. P. Morgan & Co., 14 April 1924; Russell C. Leffingwell to N. Dean Jay, 23 June 1924; both in TWL 95/11.

63. Russell C. Leffingwell memorandum, 27 June 1924, TWL 95/9.

64. Lamont to Harjes [not sent], 27 June 1924, TWL 95/9.

65. Morrow "Memorandum for T. W. L.," n.d. [circa 1 July 1924], T. W. Lamont file 1924–36, DWM.

public credit. Initially, Morrow conceived this loan as an inducement for France to forego reparations in kind during the first two years of the Dawes Plan, thus providing a margin of safety so that Germany would not be overburdened during the early stage of its financial recovery. Subsequently, Morrow reached the conclusion that, entirely apart from the reparations settlement, it would be "an excellent thing" for the French to contract a government loan. The French treasury could use the proceeds to pay off some of its debt to the Bank of France; the Bank in turn could use the funds for stabilization, that is, establishment of a dollar-exchange standard for the franc.[66] Concomitantly, Morgan partners weighed the advisability of a financial rehabilitation loan to Belgium. During the early part of the London Conference, however, Morgan representatives maintained for tactical reasons a discreet public silence about the chances of floating these loans. Preferring to await developments in London and then to gauge the progress made toward European pacification, they followed instructions to refrain from uttering "a single encouraging word" to anyone outside the firm.[67]

The future of the short-term credit to the Bank of France therefore became the immediate financial issue to be settled while the conference remained in session.[68] The bankers expected that Clémentel would press the matter. They were "strongly against renewal," and the course of events during the conference made them even less keen on it.[69] In July a spate of articles appeared in the New York financial press pointing out that the French bond market had never recovered after the March crisis and suggesting that the flight from fixed income securities reflected the market's pessimistic assessment of the franc's fundamental position.[70] This judgment greatly disturbed the Morgan partners. They were obliged to agree that the "profound distrust which Frenchmen themselves had shown for their own government's obligations . . . could only be regarded by the rest of the world as a danger signal flown within."[71]

They also viewed the technical position as bearish. The speculators' need to cover a large short position and autonomous purchases of French currency sparked by the approaching tourist season had facilitated the

66. Morrow to Lamont, 24 July 1924, Lamont file, DWM; Morrow to Leffingwell, 11 August 1924, J. P. Morgan & Co., Partners–Leffingwell file, DWM.

67. J. P. Morgan, E. C. Grenfell, T. W. Lamont to J. P. Morgan & Co., 9 August 1924, J. P. Morgan & Co., Partners–Leffingwell file, DWM.

68. Clémentel's retrospective analysis, in *J.O.S. Déb.*, 21 November 1924, pp. 1471–72.

69. Harjes to Lamont, 6 August 1924, TWL 176/22; J. P. Morgan & Co. to Lamont, 1 August 1924, TWL 95/12.

70. The *Journal of Commerce* observed on 18 July 1924 that "confidence in the franc has not returned, as the artificial character of its rise in April becomes more and more apparent. French exchange is again weak, constitutionally so, and political and technical influences do not come to its aid." The *Wall Street Journal* struck the same note in its leader on 31 July 1924: "Credit crisis seen in French issues. Investors chary of reconstruction issues owing to uncertainty of franc's action."

71. J. P. Morgan & Co. to Lamont, 1 August 1924, TWL 95/12.

operation to save the franc the previous March. These conditions would no longer obtain in the autumn. Indeed, exchange requirements for cotton and wheat imports would stack the deck against the franc at that time. If the credit were renewed, the Bank of France might well be forced to hand over the gold earmarked as security when it finally expired. This would make the American bankers "most unpopular" in France. And had not Herriot objected to Poincaré's arrangements with Morgan's for hypothecation of gold as well as to the former premier's pledges of budgetary reform? To be sure, Herriot had subsequently apologized profusely and denied any intention to disparage the bankers, but the latter could not overlook the fact that the Cartel chieftain had never specifically withdrawn his substantive criticism of Poincaré's commitments. Moreover, analysts at Morgan corner thought that to renew the credit would create a "bad impression" among their colleagues on Wall Street. French financial standing in America would benefit if the old credit were allowed to expire. This consideration assumed particular importance, they noted, if the French government anticipated that it might ultimately have to request assistance to defend the franc again.

Not least important, the course of diplomatic conversations at the London Conference itself reinforced the bankers' inclination to view renewal of the credit as an unattractive proposition. France's tentative efforts there to stake out a position at variance with J. P. Morgan & Co.'s preferences elicited from the latter the complaint that French policies had "not been such as to reassure banking institutions," but on the contrary had "given rise to the fear that France still prefers political to financial objectives." This did not mean that if the Bank of France insisted on renewal, the Morgan firm in the final analysis would refuse. The partners in New York made it clear in midsummer, however, that renewal was predicated not only upon a more concrete demonstration of the intention to balance the French budget, but also on approval by the State Department in Washington and on evidence that the outcome of the London Conference would be "on the whole reassuring to the financial community."[72]

Clémentel did not formally bring up the question of renewal of the credit with Morgan representatives in London until 9 August, just before he and Herriot made a flying trip to Paris to seek cabinet sanction for important concessions concerning the timetable for withdrawal from the Ruhr. After returning, the French finance minister met again with Thomas Lamont, chief Morgan negotiator at the conference. Clémentel assumed the posture of soliciting the bankers' technical advice. But although he was extremely conciliatory, the divergence between his own ideas and the Morgan conception of a French loan became immediately apparent.

Lamont, tempering the peremptory tone of the cables from New York,

72. Ibid.

offered his "personal view" that a new short-term credit to the Bank of France could probably be arranged some weeks after expiration of the old one, provided that the conference met with success. Lamont took care, however, to underscore the need for general coordination of French financial policy. He emphasized that a long-term loan for the purpose of currency stabilization should replace the credit as soon as possible, while simultaneously the French government took other measures to promote fiscal stability. Clémentel, on the other hand, sought a long-term loan not as a replacement for the Bank of France credit, but in addition to it; and he planned to employ the proceeds to cover his immediate foreign currency needs, estimated at no less than $125 to $140 million in the current fiscal year. Lamont did not betray any lack of sympathy, but he declined to commit himself, except to "keep in touch" after the conference ended.[73] Clémentel, by his own report, tried to draw the attention of Secretary of State Hughes, as well as that of Lamont and J. P. Morgan, to the parallels between French and German economic disabilities. Both nations suffered similar balance-of-payments problems occasioned by a flight of investment capital. But he failed to secure more than a vague assurance that America would "manifest its feeling" for France once the Dawes Plan was placed in operation and functioning smoothly.[74]

Consideration of the French request for financial aid was thus to remain suspended until the conference came to an end. The bankers set forth no concrete political demands as direct prerequisites for their continued advice and assistance; that sort of dramatic gesture was alien to their way of thinking. They insisted on "the very important distinction between the attempt to dictate French policies—and such an attempt we have never made—and the attempt to explain very frankly and clearly what seemed to us to be the conditions of a successful operation for the stabilization of the franc."[75] From the vantage point of New York, the French remained free to decide whether or not they wished to qualify for further assistance, just as the Germans were theoretically at liberty to accept or reject the Dawes Plan. Despite grave reservations, the German government acquiesced in the Dawes settlement because, after carefully weighing the alternatives, it judged other options even less palatable. The full ramifications of the constraints hedging France were less obvious. The continued French efforts to secure financial aid after the London Conference, however, make unmistakably clear why Herriot and Clémentel could not consider a course of action there that failed to furnish the basis for such assistance.

73. Lamont to J. P. Morgan & Co., 9 August 1924, TWL 176/23; J. P. Morgan & Co. to Lamont, Lamont to J. P. Morgan & Co., Lamont to Clémentel, all 11 August 1924, TWL 176/24.

74. *J.O.S. Déb.*, 21 November 1924, pp. 1471–72.

75. J. P. Morgan & Co. to Lamont, 1 August 1924, TWL 95/12.

The provisions of the Dawes Plan and the negotiations for a comprehensive reparations settlement at London will be treated in later chapters. Here it is sufficient to note that J. P. Morgan & Co. was not entirely satisfied either with the Dawes Plan itself or with the conditions agreed upon for its implementation. When the conference ended in mid-August, Lamont personally judged its accomplishments sufficient to warrant the firm taking the lead in a syndicate to float a loan for German financial rehabilitation, without which the Dawes Plan could not be put into operation. But not for another month was it certain that his partners, and their associates at the Bank of England, would finally decide to go ahead. Even then several obstacles of more than negligible importance remained. For many weeks, Lamont and other members of the firm fought to secure modifications of the London agreements, which they deemed necessary for the security of a German loan. In Paris, Lamont and Herman Harjes, occasionally joined by American Secretary of the Treasury Andrew Mellon, held a round of conferences with Herriot, Clémentel, Mouÿ, Robineau, and French private bankers. These discussions turned simultaneously on conditions for a German loan and for French participation in floating it, and on French demands for financial assistance from the United States. Meanwhile, Prime Minister Georges Theunis of Belgium pursued parallel negotiations for American financial help to his country.[76]

Russell Leffingwell, anchor man at Morgan's home office during the summer, had felt uneasy about the whole drift of the preliminary talks between Clémentel and Lamont in London. He wished to take a stiffer line toward France. "We seem to have allowed ourselves to slip back a long way from the constructive program which we started with in our

76. The Guaranty Trust Company, an affiliate of the Morgan group, had traditionally handled Belgian financing in the United States. In late July, Theunis approached J. P. Morgan in London and outlined what his country would require to "consolidate and clean up its position." Belgium had long been eager for the United States to participate actively in European affairs, and Theunis would probably have followed much the same course at the London Conference, even if he had not sought to prepare the ground for a Belgian loan in New York. However, as a former banker himself, he found it easier than many politicians to understand the American and British bankers' point of view. Since he intensely desired a successful outcome to the conference both on political and financial grounds, Theunis bent every effort there to mediate between the French and the bankers. J. P. Morgan, accordingly, assured him that he would do his best to meet legitimate Belgian requirements in due course. After the conference ended, Theunis explained his needs further in Brussels to Morgan partner George Whitney and to de Waele of the Guaranty Trust. In October the Belgian National Bank presented a precise plan for a $100 million flotation to Morgan and Lamont. Once the Dawes loan had been marketed, the American bankers accommodated Belgian wishes, issuing one loan in December 1924, and another—after a delay owing to State Department insistence on a war debt agreement—in June 1925. The French, who followed these negotiations closely, recognized that Belgium would inevitably place its own financial needs above loyalty to the French alliance. See de Waele to Lamont, 21 August 1924, TWL 177/3; Lamont memorandum on Belgian finance, 22 May 1925, TWL 84/4; and for a more general perspective, Henry L. Shepherd, *The Monetary Experience of Belgium, 1914–1936* (Princeton and London, 1936).

own minds," he complained as the conference came to an end. A large French loan, as New York had conceived it, would serve a constructive program in two ways. It would obviate the need to renew the Bank of France credit, and it would deflate the pressure for immediate payment of reparations in kind by Germany. A loan for general budgetary purposes, in contrast, would simply be "one more uninteresting operation in the perennial struggle of France to keep water from running downhill."

Leffingwell fretted that Clémentel had drawn the wrong conclusion from Lamont's cautious encouragement. The French finance minister appeared to assume blithely that renewal of the Bank credit would be more or less a matter of course if political circumstances remained favorable. In the Morgan view, the emergency credit extended the previous March represented "the very last dollar in the bottom of the box . . . adopted as a last resort in a great crisis when it seemed to all the world that the franc was about to fade off the horizon after the mark and the rouble." To renew the credit when everyone supposed the storm to be over would convey weakness and fear rather than reassurance. Technically, also, it would constitute "a blunder of the first magnitude." For if the Bank of France pledged its gold in return for renewal when no emergency existed, what would be left to pledge in case of another concerted attack on the franc? Unless Clémentel was prepared to carry through the financial recommendations made by the firm as elements of a coordinated policy, Leffingwell warned plainly, the franc was "bound in time to pursue its downward course until it correctly reflects the market's estimate of French credit."[77]

The tone of communications within the House of Morgan thus made it apparent that in the forthcoming negotiations for American assistance, Clémentel and Robineau would be the suitors, the bankers the ones to set the terms. Lamont took Leffingwell's jeremiad to heart.[78] In consultations that began on 21 August, he and Herman Harjes repeated the whole Morgan litany on fiscal integrity to French officials. The bankers and the French found themselves at cross-purposes in these discussions, which continued through the early fall of 1924. Clémentel eagerly sought to win agreement by Morgan's to renew the Bank of France credit forthwith and to float a long-term loan on the New York bond market without delay. Morgan's, however, preferred a different set of priorities. The firm now proposed to examine Europe's requirements for American capital as a whole.

Initially, J. P. Morgan & Co. had not considered a loan to Germany an absolute prerequisite for successful implementation of the principles

77. Leffingwell to Lamont, 15 August 1924, copies in TWL 176/27 and in J. P. Morgan & Co., Partners–Leffingwell file, DWM. See also the cables on French and Belgian financial matters from Morgan & Co. to Lamont and Whitney, 14 August 1924, TWL 176/26.

78. Lamont, Harjes, and N. Dean Jay to J. P. Morgan & Co., 11 September 1924, TWL 95/14.

underlying the Dawes Plan. As wartime bankers for the Allies, the partners did not relish the notion of raising money for Germany. As late as the final weeks of the London Conference, analysts at Morgan corner still toyed with the idea of offering the loan to France instead. In return, France would be required to give up its claim on reparations in kind during the moratorium period provided by the Dawes Plan. Germany would thus be accorded the relief necessary for financial recovery in an indirect manner. Publicity attendant upon the conference, however, convinced world opinion that a direct loan to Germany, as stipulated by the original Dawes Report, remained indispensable in order to restore normal economic conditions in Europe. The Morgan partners recognized that investment markets did not expect them to propose additional financing for France. They concluded that, under the circumstances, they would have to make the so-called Dawes loan to Germany the first order of business. Should they accord priority to French needs, it would create the impression of "some hitch in the German loan and the whole Dawes Plan," and imply that this "essential step toward restoration of European credit, including that of France, [had] gone wrong."[79]

Consequently, on 21 August Lamont could offer Clémentel and Robineau nothing more than a carefully hedged assurance that after the Bank of France credit expired, his firm would look favorably upon a request for temporary renewal. He consoled the disappointed Frenchmen with the hope that even a brief extension would buy time. If a German loan were floated successfully, Morgan's might then give consideration to a long-term French issue that would replace the Bank of France credit.[80] Clémentel and Robineau at once grasped the threat implicit in this delay, since the bankers declined to make a commitment to launch the German loan. Both J. P. Morgan & Co. and the Bank of England maintained that the political arrangements arrived at by the London Conference provided insufficient security for that loan. Lamont's willingness to prolong the Bank of France credit on an interim basis rested not only on his genuine sympathy for France, but also on his cautious optimism that a satisfactory accommodation would eventually be reached regarding the terms of a German loan. In this respect he was far more sanguine than some of his partners. J. P. Morgan, on vacation in Scotland, and particularly Russell Leffingwell, determining the home office's policy in New York, were apprehensive about the future of Europe and the security of any loan to Germany. Leffingwell, also, persisted in believing it inadvisable to extend the credit, for however short a period, in the absence of a crisis comparable to that of March 1924.[81]

79. J. P. Morgan & Co. to Lamont, Whitney, and Jay, 20 August 1924, TWL 177/2.

80. Lamont to Clémentel, 21 August 1924, TWL 95/12 and 177/3; Lamont to J. P. Morgan & Co., 22 August 1924, TWL 177/4.

81. Leffingwell to Lamont and Lamont to Leffingwell, 25 August 1924, TWL 177/6; Lamont to J. P. Morgan & Co., 26 August 1924, TWL 95/12.

The French could not claim that their current difficulties equaled in magnitude those obtaining the previous March. Nevertheless, Governor Robineau feared that removal of the credit's protective umbrella, even for a moment, might encourage speculators to "make another drive at the franc."[82] During the last fortnight before the credit expired on 12 September, Robineau pressed vigorously for renewal of the full amount for six months. Anything less, he felt, would affect public opinion in a "most detrimental" way and provoke pointed inquiries in parliament. These factors, in his mind, outweighed the disadvantage of an adverse reaction expected from American investment markets. If the credit were prolonged, Robineau argued with a touch of desperation, its use would probably not be necessary. So long as France maintained "this cushion to look at," he told Herman Harjes, "just so long we shall not have to lie down upon it." Harjes, his sympathies engaged, agreed to cable New York that termination would "create a decided feeling of anxiety and possible distrust amongst the people."[83] Robineau also managed to round up support from Secretary of the Treasury Mellon and Montagu Norman, governor of the Bank of England.[84] Meanwhile, Herriot sought to allay the resentment which still rankled as a result of his gratuitous remarks about the bankers the previous June, moving Lamont to reflect that, after all, one could not "ask these politicians to eat their words too much in public." Clémentel, not to be outdone, spoke of "drastic economies" and portrayed himself as so thoroughly determined to balance the budget that he would succeed where the preceding regime had proved wanting. Under this avalanche of appeals, Morgan's finally agreed to prolong the credit for $100 million, though New York cautioned once again that the extension constituted no more than a "gesture" to discourage undue manipulation on the exchange: in the long run the franc's fate would continue to depend on "the strength of the French government's fiscal policy."[85]

The French made the most of the bankers' reluctant acquiescence. They announced the renewal with great fanfare. "It is the sword of Damocles suspended over the head of any would-be speculator on the fall of the franc," a spokesman for the Bank of France trumpeted, while treasury representatives buttonholed *New York Times* correspondent Edwin L. James to emphasize their "complete accord" with J. P. Morgan & Co. Officials at both the Bank and the treasury took considerable satisfaction in thus retaining protection against speculative movements on the exchange. They held this protection to be no small advantage

82. Lamont to J. P. Morgan & Co., 26 August 1924, TWL 95/12.

83. Harjes to J. P. Morgan & Co., 2 and 4 September 1924; J. P. Morgan & Co. to Harjes, 4 September 1924, all in TWL 95/12.

84. Lamont to J. P. Morgan & Co., 8 September 1924, TWL 95/13.

85. Lamont, Harjes, and N. Dean Jay to J. P. Morgan & Co., 11 September 1924, TWL 95/14; J. P. Morgan & Co. to Lamont and Harjes, 9 September 1924, TWL 95/13.

during a period when the largest volume of long-term government obligations since the end of the war would fall due for refunding. Nevertheless, the ballyhoo fashioned to provide window dressing for the financial pages did not obscure to insiders that the understanding prerequisite to long-term financing still remained incomplete.[86]

The pressure of time was great. Clémentel had to organize plans for balancing the budget before parliament's return in early October 1924. At the rue de Rivoli, civil servants scrambled to prepare an "inventory" of the financial situation designed to serve political as well as economic purposes.[87] Lamont realized that the emergent national and parliamentary mood would inevitably complicate the finance minister's problems. In reports to New York, Lamont did not spare his sympathy: "Many of the French people—when the Dawes Plan goes into effect—are apt to say: 'Thank God, Germany at last is going to pay and we won't have to, nor will we, pay these nasty new taxes anymore.' "[88] Morgan's disposition to help France arrange long-term foreign financing would depend, nevertheless, on Clémentel's ability to balance the budget even in the face of unfavorable public sentiment.

Reflecting further on his requirements in the American market, Clémentel meanwhile concluded that he needed not only $100 million to replace the Bank of France credit, but also an additional $100 million during the following two years. This sum would obviate the necessity to meet foreign claims on France by direct purchases on the exchange before projected revenue from the Dawes Plan became large enough to cover the balance-of-payments gap.[89] Immediate monetary difficulties reinforced Clémentel's wish to arrange this relief speedily. Note circulation in September 1924 was on the rise again, grazing the legal limit which, against treasury advice, the government had decided to maintain inviolate. The Bank of France, caught in a classic squeeze, felt constrained from raising the discount rate as a countermeasure because that would also necessitate a higher interest rate on national defense bonds. Governor Robineau considered the best strategy to be postponement of the discount rate increase until after transformation of the $100 million Bank credit into a long-term loan on the New York bond market. Successful completion of that negotiation would raise France's international credit rating. The "psychological moment" would then arrive for the treasury to market a large domestic consolidation loan on advantageous

86. Lamont to Morrow, 12 September 1924, Lamont file, DWM; *New York Times*, 12 September 1924; U.S. 851.51/485, 495. For Clémentel's veiled account, see *J.O.S. Déb.*, 21 November 1924, pp. 1471–72.

87. M. Clémentel, *Inventaire de la situation financière de la France au début de la treizième législature* (Paris, 1924).

88. Lamont to Morrow, 23 September 1924, Lamont file, DWM.

89. Lamont and Harjes to J. P. Morgan & Co., 12 September 1924, TWL 177/3; Lamont and Harjes to J. P. Morgan & Co., 11 September 1924, TWL 95/14; J. P. Morgan & Co. to Morgan, Harjes et Cie, 20 September 1924, TWL 95/14.

terms.[90] Clémentel, too, came to view the long-term American loan as an indispensable prerequisite to the domestic consolidation issue. If the American loan failed to materialize, he despaired of carrying through the domestic operation, though such a collapse of his financial program might compel his own resignation or even lead to the fall of the Herriot government.[91]

The Morgan partners were not slow to recognize just how completely Clémentel based his plans on the promise of their help. "What worries me," Herman Harjes wrote to Dwight Morrow in the home office, "is that your friend M. Clémentel is reposing absolute confidence in the House of Morgan and really expects it to do wonders for him. I am afraid he will get quite a jolt if we do not come across."[92] Thomas Lamont filled in the picture for Morrow: "You know better than I the type Clémentel is, honest, straightforward, sincere, but not always very clear-thinking and in fact at times rather stupid. He is most terribly earnest in his desire to reform and rebuild French government finance. He has some good ideas but at times loses himself both politically and economically. . . . He is not quite shrewd enough to take the adroit political step; and also his education in economics is sufficiently lacking so as to threaten now and again false moves on that line."[93] Sincerely committed to helping stabilize French finance, Lamont nevertheless found that his negotiations in Paris reminded him of dealing with "the Mexican Ministry of Finance."[94] He and other Morgan partners in Europe were eager for Morrow to come over and "hold Clémentel's hand for a time," giving him "good counsel" in the difficult months ahead. Since Clémentel relied on Morgan's to "an almost pathetic degree" and invoked the claims of long friendship, members of the firm on both sides of the water felt under obligation to give him "especial consideration."[95] It is nevertheless clear from the bankers' patronizing tone that the French government had become the "client" of J. P. Morgan & Co. in more than the strict banking sense.

Considering the extent of French reliance upon them, the bankers used their power with relative restraint. They did not, in the end, persist in demanding further political safeguards of German territorial integrity and economic independence beyond those erected by the London Con-

90. Harjes to Lamont, 22 September 1924, and Lamont to Harjes, 23 September 1924, H. H. Harjes file, DWM. On Robineau's strategy, see also his letter to the Minister of Finance, 29 December 1924, Herriot Papers. For a technical discussion of discount policy as a means of credit control at this point, consult James Harvey Rogers, *The Process of Inflation in France, 1914–1927* (New York, 1929), pp. 173–81.

91. Under Secretary Joseph Grew, "Memorandum of Conversation with Lamont" [in which Lamont reported on discussions between Clémentel and Harjes], 18 November 1924, U.S. 851.51/500.

92. Harjes to Morrow, 25 September 1924, Harjes file, DWM.

93. Lamont to Morrow, 23 September 1924, Lamont file, DWM.

94. Lamont to Harjes, 10 October 1924, TWL 113/2.

95. Lamont to Morrow, 23 September 1924, Lamont file, DWM.

ference. They agreed to go ahead with the Dawes loan to Germany, after achieving what they considered only relative security against subsequent unilateral French action to enforce reparations claims. The bankers did exert their muscle, however, on a subsidiary question, that of French participation in the Dawes loan. The course of negotiations over this seemingly minor issue bears witness to the potential force that Morgan's could have applied had it remained fundamentally out of sympathy with the European political settlement arranged at London.

The American bankers considered some French participation in the German bond issue essential to reinforce the confidence of American investors called upon to subscribe the major portion of it. The French viewed the prospect of placing even a small amount of their own capital in German hands with repugnance. The idea of beginning a new reparations plan by transferring capital from France to Germany struck the French popular imagination as unjust. Furthermore, Germany's past record of default disinclined French investors to risk their own carefully husbanded funds, whatever the theoretical guarantees of repayment. When the French bankers held back despite repeated appeals, Lamont prepared a memorandum reminding Clémentel how greatly French credit was "enmeshed with this whole Dawes Plan operation." Lamont's formulation really left the French no choice:

> Unless the operation is successfully completed all hope must be abandoned of a French government operation this autumn. . . . Reluctance of spirit is going to have an immediate effect upon the American market, not only as to the subscription for this German loan itself but as to French government credit. . . . It is highly essential for the French bankers . . . to realize that the market value of the franc is going to be dependent to a considerable extent upon their own attitude in this present matter.[96]

The substance of this message, conveyed with a decorous fig leaf of subtlety through Jean Parmentier, French member of the Dawes Committee, produced the desired result. Herriot personally convened the major French bankers at the Quai d'Orsay and won their agreement to float a modest share of the Dawes loan.[97]

Once that loan had been successfully arranged, the Morgan group set aside its reservations and proceeded energetically to bail out the French. Examined purely from a business standpoint, after all, a French loan appeared to be a worthwhile investment. From his study of the postwar French economy, Dwight Morrow acquired the conviction that the underlying economic structure of the country was sound. Rehabilitation of French finances, consequently, presented no "insuperable difficulties." A return to financial solvency, Morrow pointed out, simply required "the prompt application of measures, the validity of which have been amply

96. Lamont to Clémentel, 6 October 1924 [not sent], TWL 177/25.

97. Harjes to Lamont, 7 October 1924, TWL 177/26; Harjes to Lamont, 9 October 1924, TWL 178/2.

tested in a wide variety of instances and conditions." Comparative experience suggested that taxes, particularly on the agricultural sector, could be raised substantially above the level established by the *double décime*. Since currency inflation up to 1924 had "unquestionably" played a part in French industrial recovery, Morrow considered it by no means an unmitigated disaster if it could be promptly brought under control.[98] The political strength and courage of the French government represented the main undetermined variable, and Morgan's was willing to give Clémentel and Herriot a chance to make good their promise of a "serious and energetic effort" to straighten out French public finance.

As the waves of wartime bitterness began to recede in the halcyon years of the mid-twenties, leaders of the American banking community took it as an article of faith that a return to financial stability would be a prelude to political reconciliation, which in turn would provide the basis for business expansion and a recovery of international trade. Many Wall Street bankers counted themselves as liberal internationalists. They remained profoundly influenced by Wilsonian ideals. Several Morgan partners had served the Wilson administration in a financial capacity. As practical men of affairs, they had managed on the whole to maintain their sobriety in an era characterized by passionate intensity of feeling. They had not fallen victim to wartime hysteria, and more realistic about the possibilities presented by peace than millenarian Wilsonian publicists, they had shown themselves immune to the excesses of postwar disillusionment.[99] They now found the idea of fulfilling the American "mission" by generously oiling the machinery of international politics with dollars particularly congenial. Dwight Morrow articulated the general view: with Germany back on the road to financial stability, the French loan, if it led France to balance its budget and stabilize the franc, might help the principal countries of Europe "go forward—not to the millennium, but to a gradual burying of their intense feeling against each other."[100]

For J. P. Morgan & Co., sentiment and business judgment converged. The firm undertook to float a $100 million twenty-five-year loan for France on the American market.[101] But what changes there had been in the balance sheet of international politics during that year of 1924! With the end of passive resistance in the Ruhr in September 1923, stunning

98. "Memorandum on the Economic and Financial Condition of France," 1925 draft, France–Economic and Financial Conditions file, DWM. (Morrow had completed a study on the same subject in 1921 with the assistance of Professor Joseph S. Davis, later of the Dawes Committee staff.)

99. For the Morgan partners' fundamental views on international relations see particularly the correspondence between Thomas and Florence Lamont and Morrow in T. W. Lamont file 1918–20, DWM.

100. Morrow to Gates W. McGarrah, 25 November 1924, Germany–miscellaneous file, DWM.

101. J. P. Morgan & Co. to Secretary of State, 12 November 1924, U.S. 851.51/495.

diplomatic success had seemed not far from France's grasp. A favorable outcome to the reparations dispute, a continental economic bloc formed with German industry, even a reshaping of the territorial settlement and security structure bequeathed by Versailles—nothing appeared totally beyond the realm of possibility.[102] To be sure, Frenchmen who hoped for a new organization of the European continent under their own hegemony, with common Franco-German economic interests forming the basis for durable rapprochement, incorrectly assessed the strength of France and the tenacity with which Germany would resist cooperation except on its own terms. Still, one would hardly have expected France to become itself so dependent on foreign assistance within a short period of time. The relations between the Morgan bankers and French leadership in the summer and fall of 1924 bear eloquent witness to a fundamental alteration in France's diplomatic stance, no less profound because it took place behind the scenes and on a level of financial complexity not readily capsulated in newspaper headlines. France's financial weakness, for which its own poor management was largely responsible, added another dimension—a harsh practical one—to the profound ideological commitment of the Herriot government to international conciliation.

The Morgan Loan, the French War Debt, and the Coolidge Administration

Would the United States government permit the bankers to proceed with the loan, or would the Coolidge administration seize upon the French request for financial aid as an opportunity to pursue wider political aims? The still unfunded French war debt provided the United States with a readily available means to exert pressure. The war debt issue thus set yet another limitation on French freedom of action.

A procedure established in 1921 required all international banking firms to keep the State Department informed of loans to foreign governments and, as a practical matter, not to issue such loans until the department had informally indicated that it made "no objection."[103] Before 1924, the State Department had not frequently employed the power thus conferred upon it as an instrument of foreign policy. But the option remained open, and in fact Secretary of Commerce Herbert Hoover periodically reminded the cabinet of the merits of bringing this convenient financial lever to bear.[104] Largely because of the continuing impasse over war debts, administration sentiment in 1924 was cool to

102. Jacques Chastenet, "Une Occasion manquée: L'Affaire de la Ruhr," *Revue de Paris*, July 1959, pp. 5–19.

103. Lamont to Frank B. Kellogg, 6 March 1925, U.S. 800.51/503, reviews the origins and history of this procedure. See also Herbert Feis, *The Diplomacy of the Dollar: First Era, 1919–1932* (Baltimore, 1950), pp. 7–14, 18–20.

104. In January 1922, toward the end of the Washington Disarmament Conference, the State Department discouraged one loan to the French department of the Seine, though it stopped just short of outright disapproval. American feeling against France ran high at the

further private loans to France. The United States did not attempt to take advantage of its creditor position directly at the London Conference. But the unspoken realities, illuminated by subsequent controversy over the new French loan, could not help but influence negotiations at London, though in a less obvious way.[105]

Settlement of the long-festering reparations controversy through adoption of the Dawes Plan was bound to shift the focus of diplomatic attention to the unresolved problem of continental allied war debts. The British had funded their debt to the United States in January 1923. The World War Foreign Debt Commission granted Great Britain an interest rate reduction equivalent to forgiveness of 30 percent of the amount due.[106] These were relatively generous terms in view of the fact, long admitted by British Treasury officials among themselves, that—considering economic capacity alone—their nation could well afford to pay the debt in full.[107] However, the French displayed no eagerness to follow suit.

Throughout the Ruhr occupation period, American Ambassador Myron T. Herrick sought to convince French government, parliamentary, and banking leaders that since cancellation was politically impossible, their nation would be well advised to make some funding proposal. He held out the prospect that the United States would demonstrate its customary "broadmindedness and altruism" once negotiations began. Secretary Hughes, in fact, authorized him to intimate to the French in the autumn of 1923 that the State Department would react favorably to a plan providing a complete moratorium over a number of years and stipu-

---

time because the French had declined to reduce their military establishment and had offered armaments credits to the new nations of eastern Europe (U.S. 851.51/218–49). When foreign borrowing surged upward in the spring of 1922, the State Department encouraged adoption of "buy American" clauses in foreign loans. Secretary of Commerce Hoover strongly defended this principle in a heated exchange with Benjamin Strong, governor of the Federal Reserve Bank of New York. In the end, the administration contented itself with moral suasion and did not impose its will categorically on the banks that marketed the loans. (U.S. 851.51/273, 277, 284, 295; U.S. 800.51/312, 316, 421, 425, 506. See also the Hoover–Strong correspondence, April–June 1922, in Correspondence file 013.1, Benjamin Strong Papers, Federal Reserve Bank of New York, New York, N.Y. For additional data on the Commerce Department position, see Box 375, Herbert Hoover Papers—Commerce Official files, Herbert Hoover Presidential Library, West Branch, Iowa.)

105. For the best general treatment of the French war debt problem to date, see Ellen W. Schrecker, "The French Debt to the United States, 1917–1929" (Ph.D. diss., Harvard University, 1973).

106. Harold G. Moulton and Leo Pasvolsky, *War Debts and World Prosperity* (New York, 1932), pp. 100–101.

107. See, for example, Controller of Finance Basil P. Blackett's memorandum, "British Government's Debt to the United States Government," C.P. 1259, 11 May 1920, in P.R.O., CAB 24/105. Blackett conceded that a payment schedule requiring $415 million for the first two years and $200 million thereafter "did not appear to be unduly burdensome." The January 1923 funding agreement called for payments approximating $160 million annually during the first ten years and rising subsequently to $180–185 million.

lating an interest rate when repayment began of only 2 to 2.5 percent, approximately one-half of that mandated by Congress.[108] Responsible French officials, including Jacques Seydoux of the Quai d'Orsay, chairman Raphaël Milliès-Lacroix of the Senate Finance Commission, and President Millerand took care to respond to Herrick's overtures politely. Privately, however, almost everyone in the French government considered the American demand for repayment a moral outrage, no matter how favorable the terms.

Frenchmen had altered their views not at all since the war, when the government-inspired press had focused its entire attention on the immense debt of gratitude that the United States owed France for its aid in the Revolutionary War and for bestowing on the world the principles of the French Revolution, while it scarcely mentioned the real debt that France was running up daily in America.[109] The eminently serious civil servant, Jean Parmentier, once gave the sentiment prevailing within French officialdom its classic formulation: France had already made a contribution to the common cause in blood that outweighed to a "shocking" degree the financial efforts of its allies. It was therefore "impossible to justify any English or American claim against France, which furnished the battlefield and bore all the sacrifices entailed by this circumstance." The French government, confident that history would ratify its stand, was entitled to maintain that in all fairness France "owed nothing, in any form or on any account, to any of the allied governments."[110] Publicly, of course, French statesmen never put it quite this way. Instead, they generally hewed to the official line, as expressed by Seydoux in December 1923, that France could begin payment on its debts only after receiving full compensation for its reconstruction expenses, which would place it on "a footing of equality with other powers regarding capacity to pay."[111] By this time Seydoux and his colleagues had virtually given up hope of collecting from Germany in full; hence this formula promised very little to the American ambassador.

Actually Herrick did his best, whatever his private reservations, to nudge the French toward a settlement.[112] Nevertheless, a widespread

108. For the American account of these negotiations, see U.S. 800.51W89 Fr/26, 71; also Herrick to Hughes, 21 December 1923, Box 25, Hughes Papers; and Herrick to Hughes, 8 February 1924, Box 59, Hughes Papers.

109. E.g., *L'Echo de Paris*, 2 July 1917; *Le Matin*, 25 March, 4 April 1917; 2 July, 14 November 1918, brilliantly summarized in Charles William Brooks, "America in France's Hopes and Fears, 1890–1920" (Ph.D. diss., Harvard University, 1974), pp. 348–52, 373–75, 417–25.

110. Minister of Finance to President of the Council, 22 October 1921, F^{30}/782. Finance Minister Paul Doumer toned down Parmentier's draft memorandum before forwarding it over his own signature.

111. Note Seydoux, "Dettes de la France vis-à-vis des Etats-Unis," 7 December 1923, copy in Millerand Papers.

112. Herrick to General Henry G. Sharpe, 5 December 1923, Folder 5, Container 13, Herrick Papers.

belief permeated Congress that Herrick, owing to his sympathy for the French predicament, failed to convey the depth of American feeling respecting the war debt. Chairman Stephen G. Porter of the House Foreign Affairs Committee went so far as to urge Secretary Hughes to "speak confidentially to the French ambassador and explain the mental condition of Mr. Herrick."[113] In early December 1923 anti-French forces in Congress cranked up for a new campaign on the debt issue. Isolationist Senator William Borah prepared an open letter to the secretary of the treasury inquiring about the state of negotiations, which he followed after a suitable interval with a vigorous denunciation of France on the Senate floor. President Coolidge hurriedly interpolated a reference to the problem in his State of the Union address on 5 December in order to head off further criticism of administration inaction. French Ambassador Jules Jusserand assured the Quai d'Orsay that, as Coolidge and Secretary Mellon had reaffirmed, the United States would not "knock at our door and badger us for prompt repayment." Still, Jusserand prompted, France's best friends in Washington felt that some gesture, preferably the dispatch of a new debt mission, was indispensable to quell growing public apprehension over ultimate French intentions.[114]

French officials continued to disdain appeals from the United States to honor their nation's contractual obligations on ethical grounds. Growing recognition of France's financial weakness, however, prompted a remarkable change in sentiment within the Paris ministries in early 1924. Both politicians and bureaucrats realized that they might be obliged to turn to the United States for some sort of financial assistance. They accordingly gave evidence of a new circumspection in regard to war debts.

At the Foreign Ministry, Political Director Emmanuel de Peretti de la Rocca* still championed the traditional view that France should not even

*Emmanuel Marie Joseph de Peretti de la Rocca (1870–1958), of Corsican background, entered diplomatic service, 1893; after a number of junior assignments in South America and at the Quai d'Orsay was detailed as first secretary in Washington, 1909–14, where he developed a lifelong admiration for America; returned to Foreign Ministry as deputy director for Africa, 1914; appointed as director of political and commercial affairs, 1920–24, became the principal permanent official upon suspension of Secretary-General Philippe Berthelot, December 1921. Banished to the field by the Cartel, Peretti served creditably as ambassador to Madrid, 1924–29, and to Brussels, 1929–31, but in 1940 he compromised his reputation by acting as president of Vichy's Council of Political Justice, a kangaroo court that passed politically inspired sentences on Third Republic leaders. A short, bespectacled man of unimpressive appearance, Peretti struck fellow diplomats in the 1920s (in U.S. Assistant Secretary of State Leland Harrison's formulation) as "straightforward, frank, unusually approachable, a pleasure to deal with."

113. Porter to Hughes, 21 February 1923, U.S. 800.51W89 Fr/105.

114. Jusserand to Poincaré, "Notre dette américaine," 9 December 1923, F^{30}/783a. For the French view of the Borah campaign as it developed in subsequent weeks, see especially President of the Council to Minister of Finance, no. 279, 22 January 1924, and Jean Boyer [financial attaché in New York] to Minister of Finance, 25 January 1924, also in F^{30}/783a.

consider repayment until it had collected enough from Germany to cover rebuilding the devastated districts. Even an agreement along the lines suggested by Herrick, extending a complete moratorium for several years, appeared to him a trap. While not carrying an immediate monetary cost, he maintained, it would detract from the "special character" of the debt as a purely political obligation. On the other hand, Deputy Political Director Jules Laroche argued with equal spirit that it would be incautious to turn down in a "peremptory manner" an American offer promising some years' respite. Jacques Seydoux won Poincaré's strong endorsement of the latter view in late January 1924 by showing—well before the acute exchange crisis which obliged France to turn to Morgan's—that the nation would eventually require a big American loan both to support the franc and for more general purposes of financial reconstruction. And such assistance presupposed at least an acknowledgment of the debt to keep American goodwill.[115]

Even as the Expert Committees began their work, Seydoux foresaw that no matter how advantageous their recommendations might be for France, several years would elapse before Germany resumed reparations payments substantial enough to cover French reconstruction expenses. Only payments in capital would fully meet French needs. Germany could not raise large capital sums on international markets until its credit was sufficiently restored so that it could plausibly offer the resources of the Reich as security. But, Seydoux realized, the Experts' work would actually place German public finances on a sound footing immediately. France would be left with "a depreciated currency, open to easy attack," while the German mark, "painstakingly stabilized" on a gold basis, would be "sheltered from exchange fluctuations." To protect itself, France would have to tap the financial resources of London or New York. Seydoux and Poincaré ruled out London as "particularly badly disposed" to France in the foreseeable future. They were hardly less fearful of the guarantees of a political nature that the New York market might seek to impose if France sought help before a reparations settlement came to fruition. In directing Finance Ministry officials to examine the debt question anew and to prepare for conversations with the United States, then, Poincaré sought to propitiate American opinion and keep financial markets there accessible while yielding as little of substance as possible.[116]

Less pragmatic than Poincaré, Finance Minister Charles de Lasteyrie allowed his distaste for the prospect of debt negotiations to dictate the pace of his investigation. The French financial attaché in New York did explore the range of possible plans for partial forgiveness of the debt

115. President of the Council [written by Seydoux] to Minister of Finance, "Baisse du franc et dettes de la France," 29 January 1924, F^{30}/783a.

116. Ibid.

with J. P. Morgan & Co. However, since Pierre de Mouÿ, director of the *Mouvement général des fonds*, advised that nothing constructive could be accomplished before the Dawes Committee submitted its report, the matter was allowed to drift.[117] The delay, as it turned out, proved not unwelcome to the United States. Secretary Hughes decided that public opinion would more likely sanction a generous debt settlement with France once the Dawes Committee had successfully completed its work. He left the French in no doubt, however, that the debts would become the next order of business.[118]

American staff members attached to the Expert Committees, meanwhile, reached the conclusion that acceptance of the Dawes Plan would inevitably entail a fresh look by the United States at the whole problem of continental war debts. The Dawes Plan established a precedent. The general principles brought to bear in the German case—limitation of payment to economic capacity and concession of a moratorium for fiscal and monetary reform before resumption of large international transfers—could be applied with equal justice to Allied debtor nations.[119] After the Dawes Plan was framed, the most farsighted American monetary authorities proposed an even bolder reevaluation of national policy. Governor Benjamin Strong of the New York Federal Reserve Bank insisted to Secretary Mellon that "the financial advantage of collecting the debts is a consideration of minor importance to the country and its welfare compared to the major consideration of a sound monetary situation."[120] The administration should direct its efforts, argued Strong, toward international monetary reform rather than focus on such narrow issues as collection of war debts and the costs of the postwar occupation army in Germany.

Just back from weeks of meetings with Montagu Norman of the Bank of England and other European central bankers, Strong feared that a failure to adjust interallied debts realistically might prejudice his already well-developed plans for a return to the international gold standard.[121] He considered the British debt settlement reasonable and probably not in excess of British capacity to pay. But he remained concerned lest

117. Lamont to Harjes, 31 December 1923; Harjes to Lamont, 31 January 1924; both in TWL 113/2.

118. President of the Council to Minister of Finance, 29 January 1924, F30/783a.

119. [State Department Economic Adviser] Arthur N. Young, "The Question of Debts Due to the United States with Particular Reference to Experts' Reports," May 1924, Box 6, Arthur N. Young Papers.

120. Benjamin Strong to Andrew W. Mellon, 27 May 1924, copies in Box 86, Record Group 56, Department of the Treasury General Records, U.S. National Archives, Washington, D.C., and in Correspondence file 790, Strong Papers. Chandler, *Benjamin Strong*, pp. 266–67, 273–77, 282–85, reproduces selected portions of Strong's letter.

121. For consideration of strategy in the return to gold, see Clarke, *Central Bank Cooperation*, pp. 71–96; and for the British point of view, D. E. Moggridge, *The Return to Gold, 1925* (Cambridge, 1969), and *British Monetary Policy, 1924–1931* (Cambridge, 1972), pp. 37–112.

France and Italy be pressed into agreements which, cumulating the sum that Great Britain had already contracted to pay and German remittances for back occupation costs, might exceed the capacity of the world as a whole to pay the United States without heavy gold shipments. If the French stabilized at the current rate of exchange and then attempted to fund the full debt contracted at the old parity, monetary reform in France would break down. Strong drew the conclusion that "the permanence . . . of monetary reform by a return to the gold standard depends not only upon the tolerance and safeguards which characterize the settlement with Germany, but upon equal tolerance and like safeguards in settlements between the European nations themselves and especially in their settlements with us."[122]

Strong further contended that international exchange stability and augmented American lending abroad would hasten the recovery of incomes and purchasing power in Europe, thus spurring demand for American exports, especially from the lagging agricultural sector of the economy.[123] Actually, this argument did not do justice to the complexity of world trade patterns. As prosperity returned, the European population would increase its consumption of domestically raised meat, cut down on bread, and possibly buy even less of the gigantic American wheat surplus.[124] On more general grounds, however, Strong—like most monetary experts—viewed a return to the gold exchange standard as the most direct road back to normal world economic conditions. In this era before successful experimentation with managed currencies, most bankers considered flexible exchange rates largely responsible for international monetary instability. Among the major industrial powers, only the United States remained on the gold exchange standard uninterruptedly after the war. From late 1920 through 1924 gold shipments increased the stock of this precious metal in the United States by 70 percent. America already held half the world's monetary gold. It did not make sense to let additional gold accumulate unproductively in New York, to a point exceeding what was needed to support the volume of credit and projected international capital movements, while American trade suffered because European nations lacked the reserves requisite to stabilize their own currencies.

Continued gold imports, moreover, posed the more immediate menace of unwanted inflation in the United States. The excess gold resulted in an increase of commercial bank reserves. It also created a temptation for

122. Strong to Mellon, 27 May 1924, Box 86, Treasury General Records.

123. Ibid.

124. Professor Alonzo E. Taylor [of Stanford Food Research Institute] to Herbert Hoover, 1 August 1923 and 5 January 1924, Box 84, Hoover Papers–Commerce Personal files; also Commerce Department internal memorandum, "Europe's Bread Ration and Prospective Demand for Imported Wheat" [fall 1923], Box 118, and Julius Klein [Bureau of Foreign and Domestic Commerce] to Hoover, 13 April 1925, Box 5, Hoover Papers–Commerce Official files.

the Reserve banks, whose reserve ratios far surpassed the legal minimum, to yield to political pressures for easy money. Between 1920 and 1924, the Federal Reserve System pursued a policy usually described by laymen (though the term is not really accurate) as gold "sterilization." This policy minimized the direct impact of incoming gold on the banking system. In the immediate postwar years, 1920–22, gold imports served to preserve the credit base (commercial bank deposits and reserves) during a period of declining prices. Then in 1922–24, years witnessing a permanent jump in the nation's currency requirements, the Reserve System offset the additional gold stock by replacing federal reserve notes in hand-to-hand circulation with gold certificates.

By 1924, however, Federal Reserve authorities doubted if they would remain in a position to counteract the potential inflationary effects of future gold imports in similar fashion. The gold already employed by the banking system had indirectly prompted an increase of commercial bank reserves and deposits to record levels without giving rise to a normal volume of corresponding indebtedness to the Reserve banks. At the same time, a number of other economic developments weakened the Federal Reserve's control over the American credit structure.[125] Strong kept this technical picture well in mind as he warned: "Our own interests demand that no effort be spared to secure a return to the gold standard, and so arrest the flood of gold which threatens in time to plunge us into inflation."[126]

Top officials at the Treasury Department in Washington were not unsympathetic to Strong's general approach to European stabilization problems. In fact, the groundwork for a return to gold had been laid concomitantly with elaboration of the Dawes Plan. On the war debt issue, however, Strong did not make much headway. When he suggested at the Federal Reserve Board meeting on 22 May that the French debt should be adjusted, as the Dawes Plan had adjusted the German debt, on an "ability to pay" basis, he encountered immediate opposition. Dr. Adolph C. Miller strongly defended the popular view that the "business debt" should be paid in full to protect the "sacredness of an international obligation."[127] Miller, though negative in temperament, ranked as the most intellectually gifted member of the Reserve Board, and he served as a close adviser to Secretary of Commerce Hoover.

125. Chandler, *Benjamin Strong*, pp. 188–246; William Adams Brown, Jr., *England and the New Gold Standard, 1919–1926* (New Haven, 1929), pp. 143–54, 196–208; Brown, *The International Gold Standard Reinterpreted*, 1:239–82; Milton Friedman and Anna Jacobson Schwartz, *A Monetary History of the United States* (Princeton, 1963), pp. 244–49, 279–87; *Interpretations of Federal Reserve Policy in the Speeches and Writings of Benjamin Strong*, ed. W. Randolph Burgess (New York, 1930), pp. 231–33, 299–304; Elmus R. Wicker, *Federal Reserve Monetary Policy, 1917–1933* (New York, 1967), pp. 77–94.

126. Strong to Mellon, 27 May 1924, Box 86, Treasury General Records.

127. Charles Hamlin Diary, 22 May 1924, vol. 8, pp. 151–55, Charles Hamlin Papers, Library of Congress, Washington, D.C.

Indeed, Hoover drew the conclusion from debates like this one that Strong was "a mental annex to Europe."[128]

At any rate, no high administration official thought the time propitious to take a bold public stand in favor of a new look at the war debts problem. A presidential campaign was about to get under way. President Coolidge would under no circumstances give his blessing to fundamental reconsideration so long as public opinion remained hostile. The president's infrequent, laconic, and platitudinous statements on the subject of war debts betrayed no personal study or technical expertise on the level necessary to formulate policy. Moreover, Coolidge did not dissent from the general public attitude on the matter. It is not clear whether he ever said: "They hired the money, didn't they?" But as his wife later confirmed, this statement did not distort the sense of his personal feelings.[129] Hence the summer of 1924 passed without any response to Strong's appeal for cooperation between administration representatives and banking experts to coordinate a new approach to the problem. At the London Conference, American negotiators continued to require treatment of German reparations in isolation and deferred formal discussion of the related issue of the French debt.

Officially, the United States government tenaciously held to the legal position that no connection existed between reparations and war debts. In private discussions, American diplomats did concede that de facto reduction of the German debt according to the Dawes agreement would eventually have to lead to a corresponding diminution of American claims on the European Allies. In the year and a half that had elapsed since the British had funded their debt, American opinion had shifted considerably. Back in early 1923, the terms of the British settlement seemed singularly generous to most Americans, who compared the 3 to 3.5 percent interest rate required by that agreement with the commercial rate on international loans of 7 to 8 percent. Now the illusion of easy repayment faded. It became clear to informed American opinion that the other Allies could not be induced to refund at anything approaching the British interest rate. Still, those who, like Governor Strong, were willing to approach the debt problem in a wholly new way remained in a minority.

A plan drawn up during the summer of 1924 by Edward N. Hurley, former chairman of the War Shipping Board and a recent appointee to the World War Foreign Debt Commission, typified moderates' rethink-

128. Herbert Hoover, *The Memoirs of Herbert Hoover*, 3 vols. (New York, 1952), 3:9.

129. *The Talkative President: The Off-the-Record Press Conferences of Calvin Coolidge*, ed. Howard H. Quint and Robert Ferrell (Amherst, Mass., 1964), p. 176, quoting Grace Coolidge. A number of people wrote President Coolidge in late 1923 and early 1924 urging him to consider cancellation of war debts as a way to break the diplomatic deadlock in Europe. His pithy reply to William Jennings Bryan was typical: "It has not seemed moral to me to cancel obligations" (Case file 513A, Box 196, Calvin Coolidge Papers, Library of Congress, Washington, D.C.).

ing of the issue. Hurley started from the premise that the American public would insist on repayment of the principal of the French debt. The British settlement, after all, had set a precedent. And Congress would never hear of a cancellation plan that resulted in an increased domestic tax burden. But with the 1924 elections past, Hurley was convinced, Congress would accept a "fair proposition" respecting the interest rate. His scheme called for funding over a sixty-three-year period with an average interest rate of 2.5 percent. That figure was at the upper end of the range discussed by Ambassador Herrick with the French some months earlier. Hurley, however, added elaborate safeguards against "transfer" difficulties similar to those in the Dawes Plan. He also ingeniously proposed reinvestment within France of half the amount collected; this sum would spur French industrial development, particularly through electrification of railways and expansion of hydroelectric capacity to generate power and light.[130]

Hurley ardently commended the scheme to Mellon and Hoover, his colleagues on the debt commission. He also promoted it on a European trip in discussion with Clémentel and other figures at the London Conference, including Pirelli and Francqui of the Dawes Committee. By traditional standards the Hurley plan was generous enough. However, it did not take into account the precarious balance of French public finance in 1924. Nor did it give full consideration to the strength of French sentiment against a substantial settlement—even one that would in effect amount to forgiveness of well over half the debt. Clémentel did not voice a direct challenge to Hurley's insistence that France repay the principal of the debt. Instead, he raised the question whether Germany would actually continue to pay France under the Dawes Plan. Hurley responded that the United States wished to see Germany continue to pay France so that France would be in a better position to reimburse the United States. But he confirmed that America would offer no guarantee linking the debt with reparations.[131]

Hurley's démarche made Clémentel aware of the serious dialogue on war debts proceeding within the administration, and it put him on notice that the United States could not be put off indefinitely with sweet words. Actually, the State Department, more liberal than the debt commission as a whole, was inclined to offer France better terms than those adumbrated in the Hurley plan. Economic Adviser Arthur N. Young agreed in thinking it desirable to push for a rapid settlement with France. The other continental debtors, he pointed out to Secretary

130. Edward N. Hurley, "Suggested Plans for the Adjustment and Settlement of the War Debt Due by France to the United States," 10 September 1924, in Hurley to Mellon, U.S. 800.51W89 Fr/36, and in Box 371, Hoover Papers–Commerce Official files; see also Hurley to Hoover, 25 August 1924, Box 162, Hoover Papers–Commerce Official files.

131. Economic Adviser Arthur N. Young, "Memorandum: Mr. Hurley's Plan for Dealing with European Indebtedness to the U.S.," 12 September 1924, U.S. 800.51W89 Fr/90.

Hughes, would hold back until an arrangement on this "key debt" set a pattern. However, he considered it against the national interest to "make an agreement which would clearly be too onerous for France to carry out." The Hurley plan, cautioned Young, would place an excessive strain on France. A slight pecuniary advantage for the United States was "not worth the risk of 62 years of injured relations." Arguing from a more restricted set of assumptions than did Benjamin Strong, Young reached a similar conclusion, namely, that it would be "shortsighted" to jeopardize French financial recovery by pressing prematurely for debt payment. From the Allies' experience of trying to collect reparations from Germany he drew the conclusion that it was "unsound to try to obtain large international payments except when derived from current tax revenue of a country having a reasonably sound currency." Accordingly, he advised giving France a reasonable period to balance its budget and work out currency reform. For this purpose he explicitly recognized that "further foreign loans may be necessary."[132]

Secretary Hughes accepted this economic analysis, though he remained "greatly troubled" by its political implications. As a lawyer, Hughes was accustomed to analyzing issues on the most narrow possible grounds. This enabled him to avoid what he considered idle speculation and to work efficiently on the practical problems within his jurisdiction. At the same time, such an approach disinclined him to take on moral leadership of a campaign to change public opinion in a matter where the rights and wrongs were so unclear. As he saw it, Congress had legislated, against administration advice, that the World War Foreign Debt Commission should take charge of the debts. The State Department, consequently, could only act as a "vehicle of communication," bearing in mind that the matter did not lie within the scope of conventional diplomacy. Hughes envisioned only one way to advance matters: the French government should appoint a delegation to meet with the debt commission and "put all the cards on the table." The United States, he felt, would have to face economic realities. France, on the other hand, would have to relinquish its hope to avoid paying the debt and give up the notion that it ought not to be paid. Hughes expected that a candid exchange, following the procedure mandated by Congress, would be most likely to affect opinion in that body favorably. In short, Hughes determined to proceed with utmost caution, particularly before the November 1924 American elections, and to keep a weather eye cocked to the political winds.[133]

Negotiations for the French loan on which Clémentel set his hopes

132. Arthur N. Young memorandum, "The French Debt," 20 September 1924, U.S. 800.51W89 Fr/91; also another version dated 19 September 1924 in Box 6, Arthur N. Young Papers.

133. The best exposition of Hughes's view is found in his letter to Ambassador Myron Herrick, 6 February 1925, U.S. 800.51W89 Fr/65.

proceeded at the same time as the election campaign. The State Department could have issued an ultimatum to France making debt refunding a condition precedent to approval of the loan. Such a course would have been politically popular. But Hughes did not wish to press the French in a crude way. Instead, he concentrated during this crucial period on a subsidiary goal, namely, lining up French support for the American formula allocating German payments under the Dawes schedule. The United States insisted that a portion of the annuities be earmarked to pay back the costs of the postwar American occupation army in the Rhineland. The British opposed, although the Treaty of Versailles clearly entitled the United States to compensation. During the London Conference and afterward, Clémentel signified his general intention to work "in close accord" with the American government on this issue. But the State Department, fully supported by President Coolidge, held up approval of the Morgan loan until Clémentel gave a more formal commitment of support.[134] After creation of a common front over this relatively minor issue, the State Department authorized Morgan's to proceed with the loan. These negotiations, however, provided luminous confirmation of the reserves of power that the department could have brought to bear on France.

In fact, other members of the cabinet faulted the State Department for excessive lenience. Secretary of Commerce Hoover expressed open dissatisfaction with the whole drift of State Department policy. The time had come, he insisted, to take a "very strong stand" not only against France but against Belgium and Italy as well, by making clear to the bankers that Washington would not countenance further private lending to these nations unless they declared themselves prepared to settle their war debts. Hoover reiterated the view, which he had expressed with mounting irritation since 1922, that the "financing operations of these governments were merely covert schemes of finding money for unproductive purposes, largely for military purposes." The French loan sought by Clémentel, he maintained, was no exception. The United States government's duty, he added ominously, might lead it to insist that foreign governments pay their war debts to relieve the American taxpayer before repaying private individuals who lent money abroad through the bond market.[135] Fundamentally, Hoover considered the French de-

134. U.S. 851.51/497, 500, 506–7; U.S. 462.00R 296/694a.

135. Memorandum of conversation with Mr. Herbert Hoover by Assistant Secretary Leland Harrison, 20 November 1924, U.S. 851.51/506; Hoover to Hughes, 20 November 1924, U.S. 800.51/499; same document and the Commerce Department background memorandum, Financial and Investment Division to Stokes, "Proposed Loan to French Government," 14 November 1924, Box 375, Hoover Papers–Commerce Official files. For Hoover's continued and ultimately successful campaign to call the French to account, see Boxes 132, 371, 376–77, Hoover Papers–Commerce Official files, and especially Box 20, Hoover Papers–Commerce Personal files. Hoover later offered a watered-down public version of his views in *The Memoirs of Herbert Hoover*, 2:85–91.

ceitful and deserving of no better final terms than had been accorded the British.[136]

The secretary of commerce did not speak simply as an uncommonly sophisticated exponent of provincial economic nationalism. He too believed in an integrated world order in which America would play a directing and constructive role, if not an altruistic one by the standards of Benjamin Strong. However, his views struck a responsive chord among segments of public opinion that did not share the subtlety of his thought. His ideas were also more closely attuned to those governing the debt commission's hard-nosed congressional members than were the attitudes of Hughes and Mellon. Finally even Hoover, while maintaining his stand that the French loan served "unsound" purposes, grudgingly conceded the political desirability of letting it go through. The crackdown on what he called "recalcitrant European governments" was postponed, though only until the second Coolidge administration took office in March 1925. Then the Belgians found themselves the first target: American financial markets were closed to them pending their agreement to dispatch a mission empowered to negotiate a debt settlement.[137] This potent sanction eventually brought the Belgian, the French, and other defaulting European governments around.

In 1924 the relatively liberal position of the State Department temporarily prevailed. The French war debt did not emerge as a focus of major public controversy until the complex of problems surrounding the Ruhr occupation and the adoption of the Dawes Plan was cleared away. At the London Conference, the subject of the later part of this narrative, the connections between war debts and French domestic finance were not placed in the forefront of discussion. Still, the French delegation at London could hardly ignore the limitations imposed upon its freedom of action by the unresolved problem of the debt.

In 1924 American war debts policy stood at a crossroads. There existed a wide divergence of views within the Coolidge administration on how to deal with the problem. Financial authorities in France were perfectly well aware of the contending views in Washington. They knew that if they wished American capital markets to remain accessible to them, they would have to go some way to convince moderates in the American government that they were not maintaining a high level of "unproductive" military expenditure with funds which might otherwise be employed to repay their debts.

136. When the French finally sent over a debt mission in 1925, Hoover denounced delegation leader Joseph Caillaux to the secretary of state as a "roulette table croupier" and expressed the conviction that "no agreement with France would be a real agreement" (Hoover memorandum, 23 September 1925, Box 20, Hoover Papers–Commerce Personal files).

137. Thomas Lamont, "Proposed Belgian Government Loan," 22 May 1925, a comprehensive memorandum tracing the evolution of U.S. government policy, in TWL 84/4.

Supposing that the French at the London Conference had dragged their feet on evacuation of the Ruhr, or had offered stronger resistance regarding the numerous technical details that together determined the spirit in which the Dawes Plan was applied, would the United States government have shown less magnanimity? Specifically, would officials in Washington favoring an easy policy on loans and debts have lost influence to less broad-minded colleagues? Herriot, evincing a noteworthy measure of candor, confirmed the attention paid to these questions when he was overthrown a year later. The foreign debt of France, he then stated explicitly, "constricts our action in foreign policy: there are moments when one wonders indeed if France retains all her independence. Yesterday a creditor everywhere, France has become today often a debtor state. And a debtor state, you know, does not have entire freedom of maneuver with regard to other nations."[138] Admittedly, this was a dramatic formulation. But financial weakness undoubtedly narrowed the range of options open to the Cartel government, both at the London Conference and thereafter.

138. *J.O.S. Déb.*, 10 April 1925, pp. 843–44.

Part II

The Adoption of the Dawes Plan

Chapter 6

The Dawes Plan, the Great Powers, and the Strategy of Poincaré

The Experts' Inquiry in Historical Perspective

When Germany abandoned passive resistance in the Ruhr in September 1923, many in French political circles saw immense opportunities opening before them. It was "Armistice once again," exclaimed Marshal Foch. "Von Hoesch at the Quai d'Orsay is like Erzberger coming to my railway car in the Rethondes station."[1] Foch, President Millerand, and others both in and outside the cabinet now thought it possible to end the cycle of German subterfuge, postponement, and default that had heretofore stymied the collection of reparations. They hoped not merely to enforce payment at last, but to remedy other defects in the Versailles settlement. Might not direct negotiations with the German government or with German industrialists lead to interpenetration of the two countries' heavy industries, to French participation in key German enterprises as a form of reparations compensation, and to creation of a continental economic bloc—a sort of precursor of the Common Market—under French hegemony? Alternatively, might not France, without excessive risk, find a way to depart from the protective framework of the Versailles treaty and to ensure its future security by revision of the Rhineland's political status?

Premier Poincaré was doubtful on both counts. He did not wish to risk a definitive break with England, since that nation, however different in

1. Charles Reibel, "Une Grande Occasion manquée: Le Premier Drame de la Ruhr," *Ecrits de Paris*, May 1949, p. 29. See also the more candid unpublished version by Reibel, "Après la capitulation de l'Allemagne," Annex 11 to Alexandre Millerand, "Mes souvenirs–Contribution à l'histoire de la Troisième République," MS in Millerand Papers; and the earliest complete public version of the story, *Le Journal des débats*, 5 January 1930. On the broader policy alternatives in September 1923, see Jacques Chastenet, *Raymond Poincaré* (Paris, 1948), pp. 248–55, and "Une Occasion manquée: L'Affaire de la Ruhr," *Revue de Paris*, July 1959, pp. 5–19; Raoul Persil, *Alexandre Millerand* (Paris, 1949), pp. 150–54; and Jules Laroche, *Au Quai d'Orsay avec Briand et Poincaré, 1913–1926* (Paris, 1957), pp. 179–81.

outlook, remained France's only prospective ally of military significance. And he was determined to seek a permanent solution to the reparations problem (in accord with pledges made when France occupied the Ruhr) within an interallied framework and following procedures stipulated by the treaty. From the first, consequently, he intended to return jurisdiction over the payments issue to the legally responsible body: the Reparation Commission.[2]

The principal issue facing European diplomats in the autumn of 1923 was not so much whether a new investigation of reparations would take place, or even whether a committee of experts set up along lines suggested by Secretary of State Hughes in December 1922 would conduct this investigation—all parties were willing to make that much accommodation to secure American participation. Controversy focused rather on the purposes and powers of the investigative committees that the Reparation Commission proposed to establish. Once the United States declined to participate in a severely circumscribed inquiry and Poincaré, however reluctantly, consented to an investigation of practically unlimited scope, the die was cast. Events led ineluctably to the effective discard of the London Schedule of Payments, the downward revision of Germany's reparations obligation, and to a new system substituting internationally approved but more tenuous guarantees of German payment for the tangible productive pledges held and operated by Franco-Belgian forces in the Ruhr.[3]

Public finance, as we have seen, constituted the weakest link in France's diplomatic armor. Financial penury had largely motivated France's occupation of the Ruhr to enforce the reparations settlement in the first place. Finance paradoxically became a major determinant of the nation's failure to profit more from the temporary success of that occupation. The franc's precarious balance and its dependence on the confidence of Anglo-American financial markets provided reason enough for France to eschew any adventurous or unilateral policy after the end of German passive resistance. Indeed, from the day French troops entered the Ruhr, the harried officials of the Finance Ministry had vigorously fought against all schemes requiring increased circulation of the franc in the occupied areas; the several proposals advanced by the French high commissioner in the Rhineland for taking advantage of the German monetary debacle to foster separatist movements there foundered largely owing to opposition at the rue de Rivoli.[4] Similarly, Poincaré could not

2. For the premier's most explicit subsequent defense of his strategy, see Raymond Poincaré, "La Ruhr et le Plan Dawes," *Revue de Paris*, 1 January 1930, pp. 5–6.

3. Dieter Bruno Gescher, *Die Vereinigten Staaten von Nordamerika und die Reparationen, 1920–1924* (Bonn, 1956), pp. 193–205; Etienne Weill-Raynal, *Les Réparations allemandes et la France*, 3 vols. (Paris, 1947), 2:493–520; Rufus C. Dawes, *The Dawes Plan in the Making* (Indianapolis, 1925), pp. 285–96; *Papers Relating to the Foreign Relations of the United States, 1923* (Washington, D.C., 1938), 2:68–110.

4. See "Dossier Tannery: Monnaie rhénane," F^{30}/1276; also Otto Jung, "Reparation,

overlook the impoverishment of the nation's treasury when in December 1923 he reluctantly acquiesced in the proposal by England and the United States for a broadly conceived Experts' inquiry.[5]

Certain limitations on France's freedom of action had thus become apparent to Paris policymakers even before financial troubles assumed crisis dimensions in the public consciousness during the first months of 1924. The international speculators' attack on the franc and the extended tax controversy in France coincided with the reparations investigation carried out by the Expert Committees. France, we have noted earlier, met the immediate threat to the franc after a fashion, but without solving the fundamental problems of public finance. The danger of another speculative attack still menaced the franc; the contradiction between French fiscal and monetary policies remained unresolved; and the electoral commitments of the Cartel exacerbated the chronic budgetary disequilibrium bequeathed by war and reconstruction. Dependent on further help from abroad over a wide spectrum of financial problems, France needed to reach a reparations settlement establishing the conditions for continued access to American capital markets. In response to the Dawes Report, furthermore, it was obliged to pursue a policy that would encourage the United States and Great Britain to offer generous terms regarding its war debt. In short, by the summer of 1924 France was entering upon a period of fiscal and monetary turmoil. Political priorities would rule out any foreign policy course that might place additional financial burdens on the nation.

The first part of this study underscored the pivotal role played by the financial crisis in determining the outcome of the May 1924 French elections. Ideologically committed to peace and inexperienced in the subtle ways of diplomacy, the leaders of the new-minted Cartel government subscribed to the belief then gaining popular currency that a strenuous demonstration of goodwill, irrespective of substantive issues, could dissipate the enmity between France and Germany. A Sorbonne student newspaper mirrored the emerging public mood exactly. Was the Rhine, it wondered, "more difficult to cross than the Pont St.-Michel?"[6]

Diplomatic negotiations for adoption of the Experts' Report took place against this unpromising backdrop. France found itself caught in a morass of internal political, financial, and economic difficulties. It will become clear that these difficulties not only reduced France's bargaining power in dealing with the Experts' Report, but also decreased its ability

Währung, und französische Rheinlandpolitik, 1920–1923," 2 vols., 1:122–56, 170–84, 190–95; 2:204–19, MS in Sammlung Otto Jung, no. 1, ZSg 105, Bundesarchiv, Koblenz.

5. Laroche, *Au Quai d'Orsay*, p. 185; Gescher, *Die Vereinigten Staaten und die Reparationen*, p. 199.

6. *Le Bulletin du Comité d'Action Universitaire* [June 1924], copy in Paul Painlevé Papers, Archives Nationales, Paris.

to maintain the European security structure established by the Treaty of Versailles.

Charles G. Dawes, chairman of the more important of the two Expert Committees, described its investigation of the reparations problem in retrospect as a device to secure "the proper balancing of economic and political considerations." The Dawes Plan represented "a compromise between economic principles and political necessities," he declared, "but it was a compromise whose findings were dominated by economic experts."[7] Within the Dawes Committee, sharp disagreements arose concerning the amount of the German reparations annuity, the nature of guarantees, and numerous other issues. The English generally took one side, the French, Belgians, and Italians the other, while the Americans mediated between the two groups.[8] Notwithstanding disputes so serious that they more than once led the committee close to the breaking point, the Experts agreed unanimously in the end that the plan presented to the Reparation Commission on 9 April 1924 provided the most workable arrangement under the circumstances. It represented "the irreducible maximum of concessions of the various powers," reported American member Owen D. Young. Any changes would have meant a "split report," he pointed out, and the committee completed its task with the recognition that the alternative to unanimity was "economic chaos and the further embittering of Franco-German and Franco-British relations."[9]

Not surprisingly, then, the carefully worded Dawes Report left many delicate issues unresolved. Much would depend on the responses of the principal European powers. The interests of these powers diverged as greatly as did the views of their respective Experts. Not least because of their budgetary requirements, the French still fought to secure a durable reparations settlement as large in magnitude as possible. The English attached greater importance to liquidating the economic and political aftermath of the war. The relatively small sums that would accrue to the British Treasury on reparations account, they believed, could not adequately compensate for the related decrease in German demand for British goods, the increased German competition for British exports in third markets, and the disruption of world trade generally. The Belgians, perceiving in a conflict between France and Great Britain a menace to their own security, attempted as ever to mediate between their two powerful protectors. The Italians, true to their own historical tradition, sought to sell their support to the highest bidder, and whereas in 1923 French control of Ruhr coal had been trump, by the next year Italy saw

7. Essay originally intended as preface for *A Journal of Reparations* (London, 1939) but finally omitted, in "Reparations, 1924–29" file, Dawes Papers.

8. For a frank contemporary description of these difficulties see Sir Josiah Stamp's letters, cited in J. Harry Jones, *Josiah Stamp, Public Servant* (London, 1964), pp. 215–30.

9. Quoted in James A. Logan to State Department, 14 April 1924, U.S. 462.00R 296/268.

greater potential profit in an agreement with Great Britain on war debts. The Germans wished to make the minimum reparations payments that circumstances permitted and to extrude foreign occupation troops from their territory as fast as possible. Since their domestic financial resources had proved unequal to the task of sustaining passive resistance in the Ruhr, they shifted to the tactic of mobilizing international pressure on France by cooperation with the Experts' inquiry. While France found itself mired in ever greater financial difficulty, moreover, Germany had started up the road to recovery. The danger that centrifugal forces might reverse Bismarck's achievement was overcome, and the new currency introduced in November 1923 held up at least so long as hope endured that a permanent solution to the problems of German finance might issue from the Experts' work.

The reemergence of the United States as a limited participant in European affairs occasioned the greatest alteration of the diplomatic balance in 1924. Every west European nation had regretted the withdrawal of the United States into political isolation after the Senate's rejection of the Versailles treaty.[10] France, of course, lost the security umbrella that the Anglo-American pact of guarantee had been expected to provide, and England missed the moderating influence of the United States in interallied councils, but Germany felt the absence of active American representation equally keenly. To be sure, much resentment lingered in the Reich among those who remained convinced—quite contrary to fact—that President Wilson had tricked them into signing a compromise armistice on the basis of the Fourteen Points and then had betrayed them at the peace conference. Most Germans, nevertheless, recognized the relative disinterestedness of the United States. They regarded an American presence as a bulwark against France's possible manipulation of reparations claims to achieve territorial objectives or security aims thwarted at Versailles.[11]

All European nations therefore welcomed American participation in the work of the Expert Committees. They sought to lay the groundwork for a continued American diplomatic role. But what European nations wanted most from the United States was financial aid. Owing to a particular confluence of the business cycle and monetary conditions, the United States was entering a five-year period with ample resources available for foreign lending. Europe, meanwhile, was starved for investment capital.

The problem of attracting American capital to Europe had changed but little during the eventful years from 1919 to 1924. There existed remarkable continuity even among the men who handled the problems, though

10. See the perceptive account by journalist Frank H. Simonds, *How Europe Made Peace without America* (New York, 1927).

11. Robert Gottwald, *Die deutsch-amerikanischen Beziehungen in der Ära Stresemann* (Berlin, 1965), pp. 12–22, 104–18.

in 1919 the protagonists acted in an official capacity, while five years later they held private positions in Wall Street firms. During the Paris Peace Conference, Thomas Lamont and Norman H. Davis, President Wilson's financial advisers on the scene, engaged in a protracted exchange on the strategy of economic reconstruction with the Treasury Department's chief architect of European policy, Assistant Secretary Russell Leffingwell. American financial specialists were well aware of Europe's multitudinous credit needs in 1919. The war-ravaged continent required funds to purchase raw materials, transport equipment, and agricultural machinery; to reconstruct and restock factories in France, Belgium, and Italy; to establish sound currencies in the newly constituted countries of eastern Europe; and to provide working capital for defeated Germany. Political circumstances in the United States, however, made it impossible for government officials to contemplate massive aid programs like those which were to spur European recovery after World War II.[12]

At the Paris Peace Conference, Lloyd George put forward a bold European recovery scheme originated by John Maynard Keynes of the British Treasury. In effect, this scheme would have funneled the resources of the American taxpayer to Europe by means of an American "guarantee" of German reparations payments to the Allies.[13] Given a realistic assessment of the American public mood and the limitations of the banking and currency system at the time, the Keynes plan—as Assistant Secretary Leffingwell described it—was simply "preposterous," and it served largely to confirm the author's reputation in top banking circles as a man with more imagination than good sense.[14]

Keynes's proposition is nevertheless worthy of remark because it was the precursor of innumerable schemes for "commercializing" Germany's reparations obligation. The European Allies never gave up hope of securing the participation in one way or another either of the American government or of American private investors in funding the reparations debt. The variants on the Keynes plan hatched by European treasuries throughout the 1920s all followed a common principle: the United States should extend massive public or private credits to Germany so that when that country finally defaulted on reparations, America would be

12. See the extensive correspondence of Lamont and Davis in Paris with Leffingwell, Strauss, and Rathbone at the Treasury Department in Washington, in Folder 3, Box 16A, Norman H. Davis Papers, Library of Congress, Washington, D.C.

13. J. M. Keynes Scheme for Rehabilitation of European Credit (1919), P.R.O., T 172/988, Chancellor of the Exchequer, Miscellaneous Papers.

14. Edward C. Grenfell, head of Morgan's London branch, later remarked of Keynes: "He always thinks and writes clearly, but there is a want of practical knowledge which shows up at times and makes one fearful of his judgment" (Grenfell to Lamont, 25 October 1924, TWL 111/16). At the time of the peace conference, the bankers were even less charitable (Lamont to Grenfell, 23 December 1919; Grenfell to Lamont, 8 January 1920, TWL 111/12). Sir William Tyrrell of the Foreign Office similarly dismissed Keynes as "an economist gone mad—who would prefer to see Europe ruined sooner than see an economic dogma impaired" (Tyrrell minute, 4 September 1924, F.O. 371/9864: C 13931/11642/18).

left holding the bag. In drafting the president's rejection of the Keynes plan, Lamont touched on the objection that would be made repeatedly in succeeding years to proposals for American loans to rehabilitate German finance: "How can anyone expect America to turn over to Germany in any considerable measure new working capital to take the place of that which the European nations have determined to take from her?"[15]

Lamont and Davis made no headway within the American government, even with carefully limited proposals for assistance to meet the most pressing needs of European economic reconstruction.[16] President Wilson sympathized in principle. But particularly after returning home from the peace conference, he became so involved in the struggle for ratification of the Versailles treaty that he failed to give top priority consideration to the more prosaic problems of rebuilding European industrial and commercial life. No doubt also, Leffingwell and his associates in the Treasury Department had correctly gauged the temper of Congress and the American people. Americans thought of themselves as having "performed heroic deeds and borne great sacrifices" to save Europe from "annihilation by the Hun"; they would interpret a call for the United States government to supply additional financial assistance as an overweening attempt by Europe to take advantage of their generosity.[17]

The practical problem as it appeared to men in Washington and on Wall Street, from 1919 on, was thus how to harness the initiative of private American capital and of American export interests to meet Europe's needs. The question, as Leffingwell put it, was not "whether America will help," but whether the Europeans possessed "adaptability enough and vigor enough to work out some business transactions and [to] interest American businessmen in their financial and economic restoration."[18] In the years immediately following the war, as it turned out, substantial American investment abroad did not take place; in fact, the capital flow went so strongly the other way that excess gold imports created a serious inflationary danger for the United States. Central and east European countries particularly faced an intractable circular difficulty in trying to attract capital. A capital influx was a prerequisite for economic recovery, which in turn would promote greater social and political stability. Paradoxically, since such stability constituted the most reliable guarantee that investment would remain safe, foreign lenders would not offer their capital until it had already been achieved.

15. Woodrow Wilson to David Lloyd George [drafted by Lamont], 5 April 1919, Folder 3, Box 16A, Davis Papers.

16. Lamont and Davis to Leffingwell, 27 May 1919, Folder 3, Box 16A, Davis Papers.

17. Leffingwell to Davis [for the President], 7 May 1919, Folder 3, Box 16A, Davis Papers.

18. Ibid.

Repeated attempts to arrange a foreign loan for rehabilitation of German finances broke down over this issue. Few Allied financial experts accepted at face value the claim, put forward with virtual unanimity by the Germans, that reparations demands produced the deficit in the Reich's balance of payments and that this deficit provided the motor force for runaway inflation. Leading American bankers, however, consistently took the position that they could not float a loan for Germany until reparations payments were scaled down to a level which investors believed safely within Germany's capacity to pay. Otherwise the risk of social upheaval and economic disorganization that might infringe on the loan's security would be too great. There existed no hope of interesting American investors in lending money, consequently, before modification of Germany's final reparations liability under the London Schedule of Payments. A Bankers' Committee (prominently including J. P. Morgan), established in May 1922 to investigate the possibility of a German loan, dispelled any lingering illusions on this score.[19] Morgan's partner Dwight Morrow defined the problem as the bankers saw it: finding "a method of enabling France to recede . . . from an indefensible position with reference to reparations . . . compatible with the dignity of a great nation which contributed so much to the winning of the war and which bore so much of the suffering of the war."[20]

Probably no French government in mid-1922 could have agreed to reduce reparations further and yet hope to survive. Certainly Poincaré, who had made enforcement of reparations the raison d'être of his ministry, could hardly acquiesce in the bankers' demands. The German government's failure to halt the inflation and to take measures for the rehabilitation of Reich finances might be attributed to weakness or intentional policy. The documentary evidence now available points to a measure of truth in both explanations,[21] but at the time the French felt strongly that the Germans were deliberately ruining their own currency to give a fraudulent impression of national bankruptcy. It appeared

19. "Report of the Bankers' Committee to the Reparation Commission on the Question of a German Loan, 10 June 1922," London *Times*, 12 June 1922, French version in Ministère des Affaires Etrangères, *Documents relatifs aux réparations*, 2 vols. (Paris, 1922), 1:243–50. See also J. P. Morgan's statement of 9 June 1922 in Dawes Report file, DWM; Logan to Leland Harrison, 2 and 9 June 1922, U.S. 462.00R 29/1773, 1790; Weill-Raynal, *Les Réparations allemandes*, 2:166–82; Carl Bergmann, *The History of Reparations* (Boston and New York, 1927), pp. 130–38; and Sir Henry Clay, *Lord Norman* (London, 1957), pp. 196–205.

20. Morrow to Lamont, 1 May 1922, Lamont file, DWM.

21. Reich Chancellery, Foreign Ministry, and Finance Ministry files confirm the contemporary impressions of Costantino Bresciani-Turroni, *The Economics of Inflation* (London, 1937). At the time, Bresciani-Turroni served as head of the export control section of the Committee of Guarantees (the Reparation Commission's permanent delegation in Berlin). See also Karl Hardach, "Zur zeitgenössischen Debatte der Nationalökonomen über die Ursachen der deutschen Nachkriegsinflation," and Peter-Christian Witt, "Finanzpolitik und sozialer Wandel in Krieg und Inflation, 1918–1924," in *Industrielles System und politische Entwicklung in der Weimarer Republik*, ed. Hans Mommsen, Dietmar Petzina, and Bernd Weisbrod (Düsseldorf, 1974).

virtually incontrovertible to official Paris that, even allowing for domestic political difficulties, Germany had made no more than a perfunctory effort to fulfill the London Schedule.[22]

The French occupation of the Ruhr represented a desperate attempt to break the pattern of German resistance. Poincaré undertook this hazardous operation only when every alternative method for compelling payment appeared to have failed and when efforts to secure the international banking community's assistance to Germany without revising the reparations schedule had also broken down. The Committee of Experts in 1924 predicated its work on the assumption that it could arrange the long-sought mobilization of private foreign capital for German financial rehabilitation. Wall Street and the London City would have to float a loan for the German government to start the operation of the Dawes Plan. The Experts anticipated that additional capital would be forthcoming to satisfy German business needs and to promote the prosperity on which the smooth payment of reparations depended. To assure the Dawes Plan's success, France found itself obliged at the London Conference of July and August 1924 to make the accommodation that Poincaré had so long resisted to the investment markets' requirements.

In the preliminary negotiations for implementation of the Experts' Report and at the London Conference—the most significant since the Paris Peace Conference five years earlier—a new political configuration began to emerge in Europe. Adoption of the Dawes Plan assured the depoliticization, at least for some years, of the main issue that had poisoned relations between France and Germany. By its very nature the reparations imbroglio carried with it overtones of the bitter dispute over responsibility for the cataclysm that had engulfed Europe. By transforming the controversy into what henceforth could be presented to the public of the various countries as a problem of technical economics, the Dawes Plan defused remaining wartime passions and prepared the way for the development of normal diplomatic relations.

The London Conference marked the beginning of a new era of rapid European industrial development, based in large part on access to American capital markets and leading for a time to a level of prosperity which, though unequally distributed, exceeded that attained in the *belle époque*. But France's acceptance of a minimum—and obviously impermanent—reparations settlement without any compensation regarding war debts,

22. See particularly the notes written with mounting pessimism by Jean Tannery, head of the German affairs section at the French Finance Ministry: "La Faillite de l'Allemagne," 7 November 1921, F30/1360 (26 September 1921 version of similar note, inspired by Louis Loucheur, in Folder 3, Box 5, Loucheur Papers); "Le Problème des réparations au début de 1922," 30 January 1922, F30/1277; "La Position actuelle du problème des réparations et la situation financière," 17 June 1922, F30/1304; and especially the analysis signed by Finance Minister Charles de Lasteyrie, "Note sur la demande de moratorium de l'Allemagne," 15 July 1922, F30/1360.

trade, or most important, security, marked a diplomatic turning point as well. At the London Conference the Germans were accorded equal status for the first time since the war. The Locarno Pact, concluded hardly more than a year later, symbolized a new political relationship among the European nations. Having already attained a large measure of equality—*Gleichberechtigung*—the Germans could now make the nature and direction of territorial revision a serious issue for the future. The trade agreements and industrial arrangements concluded in the years after the London Conference to replace the expiring economic provisions of the Versailles treaty also rested on a recognition of Germany's industrial preeminence and technological superiority. For France this period was one of recurring crisis in public finance. Stabilization of the franc finally resolved the nation's financial difficulties in 1928. But the political hegemony that France seemed to hold for a few brief years following the Treaty of Versailles was lost forever.

Anatomy of the Dawes Plan

Fundamental economic and political weakness would in any event have undermined France's position in the Ruhr during the spring of 1924. But the work of two committees of Experts largely determined the shape of the reparations settlement which ultimately replaced direct Franco-Belgian exploitation of that region. The Reparation Commission charged the first and most important of these committees with the specific task of considering means to balance the German budget and to stabilize the German currency. As a result of Anglo-American pressure, however, the scope of the First Committee's investigation was sufficiently broadened so that it could propose a comprehensive new plan for reparations payments. Associated in the public mind with the name of its chairman, Chicago banker and later vice-president Charles G. Dawes, the First Committee actually was most influenced by three other men. Owen D. Young of the General Electric Company, the second American delegate, provided the leadership that pacified the several factions and made possible a unanimous report. British tax expert and industrialist Sir Josiah Stamp composed the technical memoranda on which the committee largely based its recommendations. Finally, Sir Arthur Salter, a British civil servant attached to the League of Nations secretariat—whose participation had to be kept secret because of the latter connection—lent his considerable drafting skill to obfuscate unresolved issues and to package the product in a form designed to win the plaudits of world public opinion.[23]

23. The texts of the Experts' Reports have been reprinted in many forms. This study cites the official bilingual edition, Commission des Réparations, *Report of the First Committee of Experts*, Annexe 2075; *Report of the Second Committee of Experts*, Annexe 2076 (Paris, 1924).

Little need be said of the Second Committee, headed by London banker Reginald McKenna. The Reparation Commission assigned to it the mission of estimating the amount of exported German capital and of considering ways to ensure the return of this capital to the Reich for productive use. But in view of the technical limitations governing exchange controls at that time, the experts all agreed that only restoration of confidence in the German currency could effectively discourage the flight of additional capital and induce the repatriation of capital already abroad. The Second Committee, therefore, was little more than a sop to public opinion. The technical specialists' estimates of German capital exports diverged so greatly, in fact, that the Second Committee despaired of making an accurate estimate and, to hide its embarrassment, simply settled on a plausible compromise figure.[24]

In its final report, the Dawes Committee candidly observed that "political considerations necessarily set certain limits" on a reparations solution if it were to stand "any chance of acceptance." The committee insisted, nevertheless, that "business and not politics" had governed its deliberations. The Dawes Report carefully avoided assigning responsibility for the collapse of German finances and currency. The Experts sought to design a plan that all parties would find expedient to carry out in good faith. The "business" character of the plan, they hoped, would itself serve as the primary guarantee of its execution.[25]

The Dawes Committee specifically disclaimed any intention to offer definitive solutions. It proposed instead an arrangement that would last "for a sufficient time to restore confidence, . . . [and] so framed as to facilitate a final and comprehensive agreement . . . as soon as circumstances make this possible."[26] Sidestepping the issue of Germany's total liability, the committee put forward only a schedule of annual payments. The committee's mandate did not authorize it to reopen the question of the total sum owed by the Reich. It was evident, moreover, that no practical means existed of reaching agreement to reduce Germany's theoretical debt of 132 milliard gold marks ($33 billion).

This figure, it will be recalled, had never formed the basis of an actual

---

The reports of both committees were subjected to exhaustive contemporary analysis. See, for example, the particularly fine reparations supplement in the *Economist*, 27 May 1924; Harold G. Moulton, *The Reparation Plan* (New York and London, 1924); Roland W. Boyden, "The Dawes Report," *Foreign Affairs* 1 (June 1924): 583–97; and the subsequent studies, Rufus C. Dawes, *The Dawes Plan in the Making* (Indianapolis, 1925); George P. Auld [accountant-general of the Reparation Commission], *The Dawes Plan and the New Economics* (Garden City, N.Y., 1927); Max Sering, *Germany under the Dawes Plan*, trans. S. Milton Hart (London, 1929).

24. Reparation Commission, "Minutes of the Second Committee of Experts," especially 31 January; 1, 5 February; 16, 17, 21, 22 March 1924, MS in Hoover Institution, Stanford University, Stanford, Calif.

25. Commission des Réparations, *Report of the First Committee of Experts*, p. 3.

26. Ibid., p. 35.

collection plan. Nor did it correspond to an evaluation of the damage actually caused by Germany. The nations entitled to reparation had filed claims amounting to 266 milliard gold marks in 1921, and in initial deliberations the Reparation Commission was inclined to validate claims amounting to approximately 226 milliard gold marks.[27] Through a process of political bargaining, the representatives of the Allied powers finally reduced the stated German juridical liability to 132 milliards—a sum which, the French persistently contended, reflected in some sense German "capacity to pay" rather than a statistical determination of the destruction for which Germany was responsible.[28]

Because of vengeful public demands for enormous payments, statesmen in France and other Allied countries found it expedient not to emphasize the extent to which they had scaled down the German debt. Actually, however, the London Schedule of Payments of May 1921 saddled Germany with an immediate liability of only 50 milliard marks. In theory, Germany could be asked to begin payment on the balance—82 milliards of so-called C bonds—either when its export trade justified an additional levy, or after it completed payment on the first 50 milliards, in thirty-six years. But on the wholly improbable assumption that Germany would consent to assume this additional obligation two generations hence, the 1921 current or "present value" of the London Schedule still amounted to no more than 64 milliard gold marks.[29] This sum did not much exceed what conservative American financial experts at the Paris Peace Conference had calculated Germany could pay. And it represented a burden well below that which moderate Germans had been prepared to inflict on the Allies if the Reich had won the war.[30] The political wisdom of imposing the London Schedule and thereby perpetuating the German people's resentment remains open to question. But hindsight suggests that, from a purely economic point of view,

27. The claims against Germany are itemized in Department of State, *The Treaty of Versailles and After: Annotations of the Text of the Treaty*, Conference Series no. 92 (Washington, D.C., 1947), pp. 470–75. For the Reparation Commission deliberations, see Weill-Raynal, *Les Réparations allemandes*, 1:287–367.

28. See Seydoux's classic statement of the case in President of the Council no. 1285 to French delegate to the Reparation Commission, 29 October 1923, F^{30}/1360.

29. Weill-Raynal, *Les Réparations allemandes*, 1:640–59.

30. When the war broke out in 1914, the German government requested the advice of five leading bankers regarding the size of the indemnity to be levied on the enemy after victory. The most moderate of the bankers, Max M. Warburg of Hamburg—who after the war advised the Reich how to minimize reparations—thought in 1914 that 50 milliard gold marks could be collected without raising transfer difficulties; his sophisticated recommendations for effecting transfer would have proved instructive to the Allies. Warburg emphasized that his figure did not include territorial seizures to compensate for human losses and that it should be increased if the war lasted longer than four months. Adjusted for the change in world price levels, Warburg's figure corresponded to a levy of about 80 milliard g.m. in 1921. See Warburg to Reich Chancellor, 26 November 1914, Anlage 4 to Jahresbericht 1914, vol. 155, Max M. Warburg Papers, Brinckmann, Wirtz & Co., Hamburg.

Germany could almost surely have made the required payments.[31]

In practice the Dawes Plan marked another sharp reduction of the German debt. Its 1924 value was roughly equivalent to a capital sum of 39 to 40 milliard gold marks—assuming that it continued in operation without emendation for the maximum period of sixty-four years.[32] No one knew how long the Dawes Plan would actually last, of course. But after the experience of the first five postwar years, even optimistic Allied financial experts no longer expected that Germany would continue to accept the drain of reparations as a normal item in the balance of payments for many decades after Allied troops had withdrawn from the Rhineland and the perpetrators of wartime destruction had passed from the scene. According to any realistic assessment, therefore, the Dawes Plan offered a mere interim arrangement. It might endure for a few years or for a generation, but in any event it had a real capital value far less than 40 milliard marks.

The Dawes Plan called for German payments beginning with 1 milliard marks in 1924–25 and rising gradually to a standard annuity of 2.5 milliards, a rate to be reached in 1928–29. Thereafter Germany's obligations might be adjusted upward according to an "index of prosperity" that measured the Reich's economic growth.[33] This annual sum represented the total amount for which Germany would be held liable. It would cover all costs arising from the war, including the expense of maintaining occupation armies and commissions of control and supervision, interest on the foreign loan to Germany which would launch operation of the plan, and private clearinghouse payments, in addition to reparations.[34]

Only half the standard annual payment would come from the German budget. The rest would derive from interest on first mortgage bonds issued on the assets of German industry and the German railway system. The German government had many times itself proposed a direct contribution from heavy industry, which the inflation had freed from

31. Etienne Mantoux, *The Carthaginian Peace or the Economic Consequences of Mr. Keynes* (London, New York, and Toronto, 1946); also Philip Mason Burnett, *Reparation at the Paris Peace Conference from the Standpoint of the American Delegation*, 2 vols. (New York, 1940). There exists a vast specialized economics literature dealing with unilateral capital flows in general and the transfer problem in particular, beginning with Bertil Ohlin's pioneering work, *The Reparation Problem* (Stockholm, 1928). For a guide to this literature see American Economic Association, *Readings in the Theory of International Trade* (Philadelphia, 1949). Recent studies of the problem include James Edward Meade, *The Theory of International Economic Policy*, vol. 1, *The Balance of Payments* (London, 1962); and Fritz Machlup, *International Payments, Debts, and Gold: Collected Essays* (New York, 1964).

32. See the calculations based on various contingencies and alternatives in Weill-Raynal, *Les Réparations allemandes*, 2:627–49.

33. Commission des Réparations, *Report of the First Committee of Experts*, pp. 12–13, 23–24, 73–74.

34. Ibid., pp. 24–25.

most of its commercial debt.[35] The railway experts' investigation had shown that transport and railway debentures could easily supply a standard annual contribution of 950 million marks if the German railways were reorganized as a joint stock company to maximize net revenue. German railways were probably the best in the world. Under government ownership they had failed to show a profit, but for reasons unrelated to their business potential. The government had kept passenger and freight rates low to spur economic development; it had enormously overstaffed the railways to prevent unemployment; and it had permitted extravagant capital expenditures that the Dawes Committee's experts attributed to the "megalomania" of German railway officials.[36] Anticipating controversy regarding the Franco-Belgian railway *Régie*'s bid to retain some control over the Rhineland lines for security purposes, the experts framed their recommendations so that in the proposed reorganization the German railways might conceivably be divided into several systems with the same general rates and regulations.[37]

Critics of reparations had sharply distinguished between the German taxpayers' capacity to pay in marks and the capacity of Germany as a whole to transfer reparations to the Allies without endangering currency stability. According to the classical theory of international trade, the amount of real values transferred could not in the long run exceed Germany's export surplus. Only subsequently did economists recognize how a money transfer causes changes in the purchasing power of both exporting and recipient countries that facilitate the real transfer of goods through operation of the foreign trade multiplier. A money transfer, increasing the Allies' ability to buy German goods, would in this case have worked to increase the German export surplus. Because the Dawes Committee pretty much accepted the classical analysis of the transfer problem, it set German reparations liabilities well below the Versailles treaty's stipulation that the German people should shoulder a tax burden at least commensurate with that borne by the Allied peoples.[38]

Even Sir Josiah Stamp, who within the Dawes Committee consistently argued in favor of reducing German obligations, conceded that the Reich could raise 4.5 milliard gold marks annually for reparations if it levied taxes as heavy as England's.[39] The Dawes Committee finally set the standard German annuity at scarcely more than half that figure for two essential reasons. First, as Owen D. Young later emphasized, it realized

35. Ibid., pp. 22–23, 104–5.
36. Ibid., pp. 19–22, 77–94.
37. Ibid., pp. 20, 82.
38. Ibid., pp. 11, 39–42.
39. Sir Josiah Stamp Note no. 2, "The Equivalent Burden of Debt Charge," 4 February 1924, Box R-5, Owen D. Young Papers, in family possession, Van Hornesville, N.Y.

that there were "no statistics that were reliable."[40] In addition, it concluded that Germany could probably transfer abroad only a fraction of what it could raise through taxation at home. Faced with conflicting prognostications by economists, the Dawes Committee took the position that "experience, and experience alone, can show what transfer into foreign currencies can in practice be made."[41] It therefore limited Germany's responsibility to raising the specified sums internally and depositing them to the account of the agent for reparation payments in a newly created Bank of Issue in Berlin. The agent would bear chief responsibility for administration and coordination of the Dawes Plan. Together with a Transfer Committee composed of five financial specialists he would determine how much Germany could safely transfer to the Allies without occasioning foreign exchange difficulties. If the Transfer Committee considered the delivery of the full amount due in cash and in kind ill-advised, it could authorize long-term investments in the German economy instead of deposits between 2 and 5 milliard gold marks.[42]

The Experts viewed the Transfer Committee as the best mechanism for reconciling divergent estimates of the economic possibilities of transfer. Their scheme, however, lay open to criticism from both sides. The French could justifiably argue that the judgment whether any particular sum could safely be transferred was ultimately political; this fact assumed added importance because the Transfer Committee as proposed would have an Anglo-Saxon coloration. The Germans welcomed a forum in which they could attempt to demonstrate that a substantial transfer was impossible. But they desired the alternative to be cessation of payment rather than—as under the Transfer Committee scheme—investment of nontransferable reparations proceeds in German industrial undertakings, since such investment might limit their own control over the domestic economy.

The Dawes Committee believed that taken together, a partial moratorium lasting four years, delimitation of specific sources of reparations revenue, and the transfer mechanism afforded Germany sufficient protection against foreign interference to inspire renewed domestic confidence. This confidence would in turn lead to the development of a proper climate for durable reform of the German fiscal system and establishment of a new Bank of Issue and stable currency. The committee deemed an external loan to Germany of 800 million gold marks "an essential condition" for beginning the plan. This loan would serve partly to provide a foreign currency reserve for the new Bank of Issue, partly to finance deliveries in kind during the preliminary period of economic

40. Young speech at Stone & Webster dinner, 25 June 1925, Box 15, Owen D. Young Papers.

41. Commission des Réparations, *Report of the First Committee of Experts*, p. 14.

42. Ibid., pp. 27–28, 107–9.

recovery, and more generally "to create the confidence upon which the whole success of the scheme depends."[43] Compared with credits suggested in earlier schemes for German financial rehabilitation, the proposed loan was of modest size. But whereas no genuine prospect had existed that the international financial world would actually commit its money in previous years, the Dawes Committee expected its plan to provide enough assurance of tranquillity and safety to offer appeal to investors.

Finally, the plan assumed restoration of the fiscal and economic unity of the Reich. France and Belgium, the Dawes Report clearly implied, would have to terminate direct exploitation of productive pledges in the Ruhr. The report specified that existing measures, insofar as they hampered free economic activity, would have to be "withdrawn or sufficiently modified" as soon as Germany put the recommended plan into execution. These measures were not to be reimposed "except in cases of flagrant failure to fulfill the conditions accepted." What would happen if Germany defaulted again was left vague. The committee set forth a conspicuously elusive formula: "In case of such failure it is plainly for the creditor governments, acting with the consciousness of joint trusteeship for the financial interests of themselves and of others who will have advanced money upon the lines of the plan, then to determine the nature of sanctions to be applied and the method of their rapid and effective application." The Dawes Report left the door open, however, for maintaining a purely military occupation in the Ruhr. It noted circumspectly that questions of military occupation, or of political guarantees and penalties if these were considered desirable to ensure execution of the plan, lay outside the committee's jurisdiction.[44]

The Dawes Plan, in short, mixed concrete and well-conceived proposals for German financial rehabilitation with purposeful obscurity on issues where opposing positions appeared irreconcilable. It offered both a hope and a challenge—a hope of ending the stalemate in the Ruhr and in the chancelleries of Europe, and a challenge to each nation concerned to negotiate, within the general framework of the plan, a reparations settlement most advantageous to its political and economic interests. Weakened by internal financial crisis, France found itself compelled in these negotiations to liquidate the Ruhr occupation on terms relatively less favorable than might otherwise have been the case.

The Immediate Response of the Powers

The Expert Committee's work, heralded for months in the world press, aroused public hopes and expectations for an equitable repara-

43. Ibid., pp. 10, 15, 30–32.
44. Ibid., p. 4.

tions arrangement in all the Allied countries, and even in Germany. Skillful publicity pictured the Experts as a relatively disinterested and independent group of practical men of affairs who could accomplish what "politicians" could not. All the governments assumed, therefore, that the Experts' Report would represent the starting point for further discussion. But it remained uncertain whether the powers would resume the pattern of acrimonious diplomatic jockeying that had led to repeated deadlock in the past, or if somehow they could carry forward the momentum of good fellowship and interallied cooperation that the Experts had taken care to project in public appearances.

On the whole, the Experts believed that they had struck the best practicable compromise. They explicitly discouraged the powers from picking and choosing the parts of the plan most agreeable to each: "We regard our report as an indivisible whole. It is not possible, in our opinion, to achieve any success by selecting certain of our recommendations for adoption and rejecting others."[45] The latter procedure, they were convinced, would simply reopen the Pandora's box that they had closed with such difficulty.

Because of limitations on its terms of reference, however, the Expert Committee left numerous issues unresolved. Not least among these were the arrangements necessary to effect a transition from the system of productive pledges in the Ruhr to the new régime of interallied control. The committee had not dealt at all with French security or interallied debts, and though these problems related only indirectly to Germany's capacity to pay reparations, the respective governments could hardly ignore them in any general European settlement. The French president of the Reparation Commission, Louis Barthou, emphasized as he formally accepted the Experts' Report on 9 April 1924 that their plan could mark merely the beginning of a long negotiating process. "Of course one cannot expect your conclusions, even though unanimous, to meet with unanimous approval in the face of a public opinion shaken by so many passionate controversies and conflicting interests," Barthou reminded the Experts. "But no one can dispute the technical value and moral authority of such important studies." The Reparation Commission, he stated pointedly, now needed to resume the deliberative mission assigned to it by the Treaty of Versailles, conscious of its own "difficulties and responsibilities."[46]

Only in the United States did official circles hail the Dawes Plan unreservedly as a new charter of European stability. Given the American people's isolationist temper, the Coolidge administration had taken a political risk in an election year by allowing American representatives,

45. Ibid., p. 34.

46. *Le Temps*, 11 April 1924. A free translation is found in Charles G. Dawes, *A Journal of Reparations*, pp. 220–22.

however ostensibly private their mandate, to involve themselves deeply in a "European" problem. Washington now felt jubilation that the venture had turned out so well. Dawes had completed the work of Pershing, the press proclaimed; the New World's ingenuity had once again shown the way to end the chaos of the Old. The *Literary Digest* summarized the tenor of editorial opinion: "In the darkest days of the war the Yankee troops on the battle-line brought the Allies assurance of final victory; five years after the war an actual solution of the interminable reparation problem is reached through the advice and aid of three Americans."[47]

If the Coolidge administration decided to restrain its public exultation and to let the Dawes Report speak for itself initially, it acted solely for reasons of political prudence. Otherwise, Republican strategists feared, they would find "the Democrats on [their] backs at once, damning the report from top to bottom, only because of the situation on [Capitol] Hill."[48] The State Department took particular pride in the outcome, since Secretary Hughes had first proposed the idea of a reparations investigation by independent businessmen and economic specialists, and the Dawes Committee had so neatly accomplished the purposes he had outlined in December 1922. Under Secretary William Phillips went into Hughes's office when the report was released and told him he ought to be one of the "happiest men in the world"; the secretary responded that he was "so much delighted that he hardly dared show it."[49] Two weeks later, after the electorate's favorable reaction had become unmistakable, President Coolidge allowed himself publicly to express the hope that a final adjustment of reparations would mark "the beginning of a new era of peace and good will" and pave the way for further limitation of armaments, codification of international law, and a larger market for American agricultural products in Europe.[50]

At the Reparation Commission's Paris headquarters in the Hotel Astoria—in later years the famous building would house General Eisenhower's command and then host the French capital's gilded youth as *Le Drugstore*—the professional staff and most of the delegates shared a mood of similar satisfaction. "Theorists can pick holes in any plan," cabled James A. Logan, America's unofficial observer, "but all seem to agree and I am also convinced that this is the most intelligent and businesslike step yet taken toward a practicable settlement." Those who had followed the many twists and turns of reparations negotiations since the war felt that even if the Dawes Plan failed to work permanently, it represented such a successful effort to conciliate diverse points of view

47. "Dawes Completing the Work of Pershing," *Literary Digest*, 26 April 1924, pp. 10–12; see also ibid., 19 April 1924, pp. 5–8.

48. Under Secretary William Phillips to James A. Logan, 10 April 1924, U.S. 462.00R 296/275a.

49. William Phillips Diary, 10 April 1924, Phillips Papers.

50. *Papers Relating to the Foreign Relations of the United States, 1924* (Washington, D.C., 1939), 2:13–15.

that it would "assure economic peace for the present" and thus provide a respite for the development of "better cooperation and adjustment."[51]

The European powers, however, were too suspicious of each other's intentions and felt that too much was at stake to take this sanguine attitude. Each of the principal European nations concerned prepared a maneuver to turn the report to its own advantage. In the ensuing months the role of mediator among conflicting national views fell largely to Belgium. Dangerously exposed both by its financial and its geographical position, Belgium resolved not to let negotiations over implementation of the Dawes Plan break down and bent every effort to compromise the differences which arose. Prime Minister Georges Theunis at once indicated that he would press for integral acceptance of the plan.[52] Belgium considered it imperative to find some basis for agreement that would permit liquidation of its own part in the Ruhr occupation and restoration of the solid Anglo-French entente essential to its security. Only with great reluctance had the Belgians joined the French in the Ruhr venture originally. They had never entertained the illusion that direct exploitation of the Ruhr would be particularly profitable, but England, by proposing in January 1923 to end the Belgian priority in regard to reparations receipts, had driven Belgium into the arms of France.[53] Besides, as the Belgian ambassador in Washington had confidentially informed the State Department, Belgium was "a very small ally . . . as much afraid of France as it is of Germany," and apprehensive that if it held aloof from the Ruhr occupation it would find itself permanently "encircled" by France, economically if not indeed militarily.[54]

Participation in that occupation, however, had placed Belgium in a predicament from which there appeared no easy escape. By acting as France's partner, Belgium had thoroughly alienated England, notwithstanding its continuing efforts to serve as a bridge between its two great allies. "No Belgian government will ever play any role other than the jackal of France," concluded Miles W. Lampson of the Foreign Office Central Department in January 1924. "They are a contemptible crew, when all is said and done."[55] Other British diplomats heartily agreed. Sir William Tyrrell characterized Belgian Foreign Minister Henri Jaspar as "a slippery eel" and his successor Paul Hymans as a windbag "who never ceases to blow," while Ambassador Sir George Grahame in Brussels

51. Logan to State Department, 14 April 1924, U.S. 462.00R 296/268.

52. Daniels [Brussels] to State Department, 10 April 1924, U.S. 462.00R 296/257; Paul Hymans, *Mémoires*, 2 vols. (Brussels, 1958), 2:575; Jane Kathryn Miller, *Belgian Foreign Policy between Two Wars, 1919–1940* (New York, 1951), p. 133; Dawes, *A Journal of Reparations*, p. 223.

53. Theunis's statement to MacDonald at Chequers on 2 May 1924, F.O. 371/9743: C 7427/70/18; reported also to American diplomats, U.S. 462.00R 296/352.

54. Memorandum by William R. Castle [chief, West European Division] of conversation with Baron de Cartier de Marchienne, 10 December 1923, U.S. 462.00R 296/127.

55. Lampson minute, 17 January 1924, F.O. 371/9810: C 1135/1043/18.

dismissed Theunis as "the instrument for carrying out the particular form of legal tyranny to which M. Poincaré was addicted, viz. majority decisions in interallied missions."[56] Even to outsiders, Foreign Office officials made no attempt to hide their irritation. The Belgians had "always shown great timidity, never making . . . clear upon which side of the fence they were, even when asked for an explicit definition of their views," fulminated Lampson's deputy, Harold Nicolson, to the American ambassador.[57] In short, by the early spring of 1924 the British government was quite prepared to write off Belgium as an independent force in determining "the real issues on the continent."[58] The Belgian government therefore set for itself a delicate diplomatic task: to reestablish its credentials as a mediator between France and England, and to implement the Dawes Plan in such a way as to maximize Belgian reparations receipts, permit a graceful disentanglement from commitments in the Ruhr, and encourage renewed American participation in the quest for European security. As Belgian leaders clearly understood, their small kingdom's ultimate safety depended above all on the creation of a stable and peaceful Europe.[59]

For several months the German government had sought to avoid bilateral talks with France on significant issues. German policy rested on the premise that reestablishment of an international framework for discussion of reparations offered the most promising avenue to ridding the Ruhr of foreign occupation.[60] The Wilhelmstrasse planned to respond to the Experts' Report as positively as political circumstances allowed. A Reichstag election, the first since 1920, was scheduled for the first week in May, however, and political analysts forecast victory for both extremes at the expense of the middle parties. In campaign speeches during March, Gustav Stresemann, foreign minister and leader of the German People's party, foreshadowed the government's response to the Experts' labors. By skillfully evoking the "Bismarckian conception of *Realpolitik*," he provided a nationalist justification for a policy of diplomatic cooperation as leading "through sacrifice and work to freedom."[61]

56. Assistant Permanent Under Secretary Sir William Tyrrell's minute on Jaspar, 25 December 1924, F.O. 371/10531: W 11182/9992/4; on Hymans, 31 December 1924, F.O. 371/10531: W 11329/9992/4; Grahame to Sir Eyre Crowe, 15 January 1924, F.O. 371/9810: C 1135/1043/18.

57. Frank B. Kellogg to State Department, 18 February 1924, U.S. 462.00R 296/200.

58. Ibid.

59. Sir George Grahame, "Brief Survey of the Foreign Policy of Belgium," 28 January 1924, F.O. 371/9810: C 1680/1043/18; Charles Wingfield [Brussels] no. 53 to Foreign Office, 11 April 1924, F.O. 371/9740: C 6071/70/18; Sir George Grahame to prime minister, 24 April 1924, F.O. 800/218/22–30, MacDonald Correspondence.

60. Gustav Stresemann, *Vermächtnis*, vol. 1, *Vom Ruhrkrieg bis London*, ed. Henry Bernhard (Berlin, 1932), pp. 367–68.

61. See particularly his speech in Hanover, 30 March 1924, in *Vermächtnis*, 1:373–79. On Stresemann's political difficulties in his own party and elsewhere, see Henry Ashby Turner, Jr., *Stresemann and the Politics of the Weimar Republic* (Princeton, 1963), pp. 159–63.

Stresemann was "really delighted" by the Dawes Report, he told intimates. It constituted the first major, tangible recompense for his patient diplomatic efforts, and he hoped that it might halt the drift away from the moderate parties at the polls.[62] The plan, he explained to the ministers-president of the German states, offered "a respectable peace which, after the lost battle in the Ruhr, brought renewed control over the economy and railways in the occupied areas." Since the war, the virulence of world opinion against Germany had gradually diminished: "the figures cited from time to time for the German debt had become continually smaller." As a provisional solution the report thus represented "significant improvement." For the future Stresemann foresaw two possibilities. Either Germany would pay as stipulated, and other nations would begin to oppose payment as their fears of promoting German export competition grew, or Germany would find itself "not in a position to pay," so that the possibility of transfer would not arise. In either case a new settlement would become necessary within a measurable period of time. Meanwhile, renewed participation in European affairs by the United States, "perhaps the only power that still had some influence on France," augured favorably for the future.[63]

Stresemann and his leading colleagues—Chancellor Wilhelm Marx and Finance Minister Hans Luther—therefore resolved to accept the report as a "practical basis" for a reparations settlement. Buttressing their determination to do so was a suspicion that Poincaré really wished them to turn the report down. Such a rejection would diminish foreign support for the Reich and might give France a free hand again.[64] To the sympathetic British ambassador, Lord D'Abernon, Stresemann denounced the "idiots" in Berlin political circles who pounced on the high

---

For a more general account of the German election campaign, consult Michael Stürmer, *Koalition und Opposition in der Weimarer Republik, 1924–1928* (Düsseldorf, 1967), and Roland Thimme, *Stresemann und die deutsche Volkspartei, 1923–1925* (Lübeck and Hamburg, 1961).

62. So he told, among others, the Austrian minister in Berlin: see Alanson B. Houghton to State Department, 13 and 15 April 1924, U.S. 462.00R 296/266, 269; see also Turner, *Stresemann*, pp. 163–64.

63. "Niederschrift über die Sitzung der Reichsregierung mit den Staats- und Ministerpräsidenten der Länder," 14 April 1924, BA, Alte Reichskanzlei, R 43 I/41/149–156.

64. Ibid.; also "Ministerbesprechung," 9 April 1924, and "Besprechung mit den Parteiführern," 15 April 1924, BA, R 43 I/41/103–105, 136. The official reply by the Deutsche Kriegslastenkommission on 16 April 1924 is reproduced in Reparation Commission, *Official Documents*, vol. 14, *The Experts' Plan for Reparation Payments* (London, 1927), p. 129. Hans Luther states in his memoirs (*Politiker ohne Partei: Erinnerungen* [Stuttgart, 1960], pp. 270–71) that the German cabinet intended, even after sending an affirmative reply to the Reparation Commission on 16 April, to seek emendations and to convert the Dawes Plan into a "mere basis for negotiation." Only the unexpected endorsement of the plan by the Reichsverband der Deutschen Industrie on 24 April, he suggests, forced the cabinet to abandon this tactic and to defend integral acceptance in the election campaign. German cabinet protocols, however, do not provide evidence to substantiate Luther's claim that his government's basic decision remained in doubt until late April.

annuities and "unjustified" infringement of German sovereignty and failed to grasp the overriding importance of the report's provisions for reestablishing German economic unity.[65]

At the outset, nevertheless, Stresemann proceeded circumspectly. The political balance in Berlin remained delicate. On the domestic front, Stresemann had to win over the three leading ministers who had directed the occupied regions' affairs—Karl Jarres, Rudolf Oeser, and Heinrich Brauns—all of whom initially favored postponing action on the Dawes Plan until after the election of a new Reichstag. In foreign affairs, he feared most immediately that the French might force the Ruhr industrialists to renew the M.I.C.U.M. agreements (stipulating delivery of coal, coke, and other products) for an indefinite period before all parties had acted on the report.[66] Fearing interpenetration of French and German heavy industry on unfavorable terms, the government of the Reich had for many weeks strongly advised its own industrialists not to renew these accords. Stresemann worried lest the industrialists in the occupied areas make an agreement at the last minute providing benefits for themselves but undermining his general policy. The German cabinet finally agreed to extension of the M.I.C.U.M. agreements only after their clear delimitation as a temporary expedient, scheduled to disappear when the Experts' Report became operative.[67]

Stresemann's public caution derived also from a desire to preserve the greatest possible flexibility for driving a hard bargain. Poincaré had repeatedly told Leopold von Hoesch, the German ambassador in Paris, that he would insist on maintaining productive pledges in the Ruhr until other guarantees of equal value had been firmly established.[68] Alongside its political benefits for Germany, the Dawes Plan contained many features of control or supervision, as well as a maximum annuity figure, that evoked unrelenting criticism not only from the nationalists but across the whole German political spectrum. The cabinet had determined, as Stresemann emphasized in his election speeches, to accept the report only if every vestige of limitation on the economic, fiscal, and administrative sovereignty of the Reich in the occupied areas were swept away.[69]

As for the purely military presence of the French and Belgians in the Ruhr, Stresemann believed that a sharp reduction in the number of occupation troops would follow "automatically" upon termination of the

65. Lord D'Abernon tel. no. 127, 6 April 1924, F.O. 371/9739: C 5701/70/18.

66. Houghton to State Department, 9 April 1924, U.S. 462.00R 296/251; also Stresemann, *Vermächtnis*, 1:381–84.

67. "Sonderverhandlungen der Rhein-Ruhr Industriellen mit den Besatzungsmächten," BA, R 43 I/454/35–204.

68. Hoesch dispatch, 4 April 1924, cited in Stresemann, *Vermächtnis*, 1:380–81.

69. See Stresemann's speech on 12 April 1924, cited in *Vermächtnis*, 1:389–90; and the discussions in the cabinet and with the ministers-president of the German states in BA, R 43 I/41/103–105, 149–156.

economic arrangements for exploiting the productive pledges.[70] His cabinet colleagues, however, objected to any delay in eliminating the Franco-Belgian military encampments that would continue to symbolize German humiliation, even when they ceased to serve an immediate functional purpose. These ministers hoped to impress on the Americans and the English that unconditional military evacuation would persuade the German people to accept the Dawes Plan "in spirit"—in turn a necessary condition for inspiring confidence in those who would float the international loan.[71]

While the response of several nations would determine the course of negotiations to some degree, in the first instance the Dawes Plan's success depended on its reception in Great Britain and France. Most of the difficulties of the previous two years derived from the two preponderant European powers' failure to agree on the vital questions of central Europe. When Britain and France formed a common front, Germany had always judged it expedient to bow to superior force; when they divided, as they had over reparations and the seizure of productive pledges in the Ruhr, Germany had exploited this division. Did the Dawes Plan provide a suitable basis for the reestablishment of harmonious cooperation?

British officials had followed the work of the Dawes Committee with steadily mounting dissatisfaction. Before agreeing to represent Great Britain on the committee, Sir Josiah Stamp had plainly warned Sir Otto Niemeyer, the controller of finance, that it would be impossible "to get a unanimous decision and one in accordance with the extreme views of the British Treasury."[72] The French financial debacle of early 1924, however, had briefly raised Whitehall's hopes for decisive French concessions to its point of view. Shortly after arrangement of the Morgan loan, British reparations delegate Sir John Bradbury reported that because of financial desperation, France would have "to swallow anything on which the Americans choose to insist, and will find it difficult to resist us wherever we obtain American support." Unfortunately, Bradbury warned, both Dawes himself and Owen D. Young were "according to our ideas very unsound."[73] As the Dawes Committee moved toward completion of its work, Stamp and the second British member, Sir Robert Kindersley, continued to complain that Young in particular possessed "an entirely exaggerated notion of Germany's recuperative powers and her capacity to pay."[74] The American Experts' effort to stake out a

70. BA, R 43 I/41/149–156.

71. Note particularly the formula proposed by Reichsbank President Hjalmar Schacht, "Sitzung des Reichsministeriums," 3 May 1924, BA, R 43 I/41/188–189.

72. "Memorandum Recording a Private Interview between H. M. Minister at Paris and Sir Josiah Stamp," 20 March 1924, F.O. 371/9825: C 4769/G.

73. Sir John Bradbury to Chancellor of the Exchequer Philip Snowden, 12 March 1924, F.O. 371/9739: C 4525/70/18.

74. Eric Phipps to Sir Eyre Crowe, 20 March 1924, F.O. 371/9825: C 4769/G.

middle ground between the French and British made them seem "impossible" to the latter, and at the Foreign Office Sir Eyre Crowe minuted in a fit of pique: "The less we allow the Americans to meddle the better. They do nothing but complicate and spoil matters."[75]

Up to the last week in March, Stamp repeatedly threatened to file a minority report if his colleagues on the Dawes Committee refused to give Germany a longer moratorium and to reduce the maximum reparations annuity. He found his political isolation all the more galling because the other members of the committee, while rejecting his conclusions, relied almost totally on his technical expertise regarding the German budget and tax system. The British Experts also toyed for tactical reasons with the idea of demanding a postponement of the report until after the German and French elections. Over the weekend of 22–24 March, however, they came home to consult in London and ultimately decided to press ahead with the report on the most satisfactory basis obtainable.[76]

Stamp's threat to bolt the committee resulted in substantial last-minute accommodations to his views. He would have preferred to limit the maximum German annuity to 2.25 or even 2.0 milliard gold marks, but he had secretly targeted 2.5 milliards as an acceptable compromise figure several weeks before—and this turned out to be the committee's final recommendation.[77] Treasury and Foreign Office analysts in London, nevertheless, remained unenthusiastic about the end product of the Dawes Committee's labors. They considered the payments too burdensome, the transfer provisions unworkable, and the prospect of penalties in the event of German default ominous.

Bradbury thought that the British government should accept only the report's "general principles" and reserve its opinion on details, and Prime Minister MacDonald initially was tempted to agree. With assistance from the Foreign Office, however, Governor Montagu Norman of the Bank of England convinced an interdepartmental committee to endorse the report as it stood. "Mere matters of detail," argued Norman and his Foreign Office colleagues, should not deflect British policy from the main objective: to restore Germany's economic and fiscal unity and pry loose the French stranglehold on the productive pledges in the Ruhr.[78] The British cabinet thereupon decided to accept the plan in its

75. Minute on the Expert Committee by Sir Eyre Crowe, 25 March 1924, F.O. 371/9813: C 5110/1288/18.

76. Leonard P. Ayres Journal, 21–28 March 1924, Leonard P. Ayres Papers, Library of Congress, Washington, D.C.; F. W. Leith-Ross to Sir Otto Niemeyer, 27 March 1924, F.O. 371/9739: C 5218/70/18; Jones, *Josiah Stamp*, pp. 225–28; George Glasgow, *MacDonald as Diplomatist: The Foreign Policy of the First Labour Government* (London, 1924), pp. 59–60.

77. For Stamp's defense of the 2.0 milliard figure within the Dawes Committee, see his Note no. 7, "The Index of Prosperity," [revised version] 11 March 1924, Box R-1, Owen D. Young Papers; for his intention to settle for 2.5 milliards, see his statement to Eric Phipps, British minister at Paris, 20 March 1924, in F.O. 371/9825: C 4769/G.

78. Miles W. Lampson "Rough Notes on the Experts' Report," and Sir Eyre Crowe's minute, 9 April 1924, F.O. 371/9740: C 6080/70/18; Sir Otto Niemeyer, "The Reparation Ex-

entirety provided that all the other parties concerned proved willing to take the same course, "agreeing to give the experiment a real chance" and, as they put it delicately, "waiting to make any modifications which may appear necessary after experience and by common agreement."[79] Niemeyer of the Treasury took heart from the reflection that the scheme was "probably to a large extent a façade" which would eventually crumble—according to Foreign Office calculations, within six years.[80]

Having set aside his reservations, MacDonald moved energetically on the diplomatic front to obtain "absolute unanimity for unconditional acceptance" of the Dawes Plan. He worried that the French might condition their own acceptance on the promise of British participation in joint sanctions in the event of a new German default, on an agreement to provide security for France against German aggression, or on a downward adjustment of the French war debt to Great Britain. He was determined to avoid concessions on any issue not strictly germane to the Dawes Plan. But if the Germans made a "clumsy" reply, he realized, the French might find a pretext to open the bargaining process.[81]

To counter this threat MacDonald designed a two-pronged attack. He quickly alerted Stresemann to the danger that a point-by-point discussion of the Experts' proposals would give France the opportunity "to eliminate the provisions . . . favorable to Germany," and he convinced the German statesman to follow the British tactical lead.[82] At the same time he deployed the attractive though elusive rhetoric of international conciliation that had become almost second nature to experienced Labour politicians, in the hope of inducing the French to "play up." "We are tired of squabbling," he assured the Quai d'Orsay; "we want to get things on a new basis of friendship and cooperation."[83] Still, the smokescreen of propitiatory diction camouflaged MacDonald's real intentions only imperfectly. Great Britain could not commit itself to take part in sanctions if Germany defaulted under the Dawes Plan, he informed the British ambassador in Paris; to prepare ahead of time for a replay of the

---

perts' Report," 14 April 1924, F.O. 371/9740: C 6331/70/18; Minutes of a meeting at the Treasury, 10 April 1924, F.O. 371/9744: C 7637/70/18.

79. P.R.O., CAB 23/48, Cabinet Conclusions: 26(24), 10 April 1924.

80. Niemeyer memorandum, 14 April 1924, F.O. 371/9740: C 6331/70/18; Lampson "Rough Notes," 9 April 1924, F.O. 371/9740: C 6080/70/18.

81. Frank B. Kellogg to State Department [reporting MacDonald's tactics], 16 and 17 April 1924, U.S. 462.00R 296/271, 273.

82. See Carl von Schubert's memorandum on the British ambassador's démarche, 12 April 1924, G.F.M. L1491/5352/L436697–699, and Stresemann's explanations of MacDonald's aims to a conference of ministers in Berlin, 17 April 1924, BA, R 43 I/41/103–105. On British tactics, and particularly for evidence of the Foreign Office's fear between 11–16 April that Germany would play into France's hands and, in Lampson's words, "make a mess of it by some absurd quibble," see F.O. 371/9740: C 6062, 6104, 6317, 6320/70/18.

83. MacDonald to Lord Crewe [British ambassador in Paris], 17 April 1924, F.O. 800/218/228a–230, MacDonald Correspondence.

dolorous events that had led to the Ruhr occupation would be "sheer stupidity." MacDonald hoped instead to "transfer pledges from paper to the affections of people." "Can we ever settle anything," he asked somewhat disingenuously, "by continuing to assure Germany that we assume its dishonesty and, whilst *forcing* it to sign something, we inform it that we have our programme of action ready to put into operation when it defaults?"[84]

Although not privy to the calculations that shaped policy in London and Berlin, Poincaré naturally sought to protect French interests by withholding definite endorsement of the Dawes Report until he had probed the limits of the British position and obtained tangible assurances of German goodwill. The last-minute reduction of the German annuity figure at British behest had disappointed him grievously.[85] By temperament cautious and suspicious, the French premier offered an easy target for satire. Literati of his era delighted in portraying him as a narrow and rigid legalist, so attached to the minutiae of precedent and to the diplomatic documents heaped upon his desk as to render him incapable of sensing the broader aspirations of his fellow men, of hearing the "still, sad music of humanity."[86] From another vantage point, however, this deficiency figured as one of Poincaré's greatest strengths. The premier's comprehensive grasp of intricate detail did much to reinforce his cool-headed conviction that broad formulae and improvements in the international atmosphere did not suffice to solve intractable problems. He never forgot France's demographic and industrial weakness and the consequent fragility of its long-term diplomatic position. France's most effective defense, as he saw it, lay in its unassailable legal standing under the Treaty of Versailles. He understood the defects of this treaty well, but he prized it as "our law" and was fond of reminding his countrymen, "we must respect it and make all respect it."[87] Poincaré had shown himself unwilling to carry through policies exceeding the bounds of the Versailles treaty in September 1923, when France held a dominant position; he remained no less firmly determined to head off ill-considered changes in the institutional machinery set up by the treaty during the process of implementing the Dawes Report.

The domestic financial crisis of 1924, as we have noted earlier, severely restricted France's freedom of action. Although international assistance to support the franc entailed no specific political commitments, France's financial duress rendered direct exploitation of the Ruhr increasingly

84. MacDonald to Lord Crewe, 23 April 1924, F.O. 800/218/231–233, MacDonald Correspondence.

85. See his subsequent statement in *J.O.S. Déb.*, 10 July 1924, pp. 1022–23.

86. See the unfair characterization of Poincaré, thinly disguised as Rebendart, in Jean Giraudoux, *Bella* (Paris, 1926); and the somewhat more subtle characterization by Albert Thibaudet, *Les Princes lorrains* (Paris, 1924).

87. *J.O.S. Déb.*, 10 July 1924, p. 1023.

impractical if that would interfere with access to international capital markets. Though his chief assistants at the Quai d'Orsay exuded gloom and he himself could not escape a measure of demoralization, Poincaré nevertheless doggedly exploited those legal and diplomatic weapons remaining within his grasp. A survey of Anglo-French relations after the MacDonald government's access to power suggests why, in the face of existing limitations, Poincaré moved with such prudence and seemingly petty reliance on the letter of treaty texts.

Anglo-French Relations: Mirage and Reality

The Labour plurality in the British general election of December 1923 might have been expected to arouse considerable apprehension in France. Prime Minister-designate J. Ramsay MacDonald and many of his leading colleagues described themselves as "pacifists" of long standing. They had opposed the prewar military arrangements with France, the British war effort, and the Treaty of Versailles—not least the reparations clauses of that document.[88] The French government nevertheless looked forward with relief to Lord Curzon's departure from the Foreign Office. Prime Minister Stanley Baldwin's fumbling but well-intentioned efforts to restore good relations with France in the last months of 1923 had repeatedly foundered on his foreign secretary's opposition.

By every criterion of intellect and professional competence, Curzon surpassed Baldwin (as well as his presumptive successor MacDonald). Yet his increasingly unpleasant personal manner offended subordinates, colleagues, and foreign diplomats alike and seriously undermined his effectiveness. Wracked by constant pain from back trouble, distracted by the cruel indifference of a wife to whom he unaccountably remained very much attached, and still smarting from the humiliation of losing the prime minister's post to a lesser man, Curzon should have commanded more sympathy as he bravely though numbly soldiered on with his daily duties. Instead his peevish temperament and haughty demeanor exacerbated the grave substantive differences separating France and Great Britain.[89] In October 1923 Curzon had learned through a wiretap on the French Embassy of the ambassador's involvement in a plot to contrive

88. For discussion of ideological views within the Labour party and copious quotations from party conference and periodical literature, see Gerda Richards Crosby, *Disarmament and Peace in British Politics, 1914–1919* (Cambridge, Mass., 1957); William P. Maddox, *Foreign Relations in British Labour Policies* (Cambridge, 1934); William Rayburn Tucker, *The Attitude of the British Labour Party towards European and Collective Security Problems* (Geneva, 1950), especially pp. 13–35, 54–93; and Henry R. Winkler, "The Emergence of a Labour Foreign Policy in Great Britain, 1918–1929," *Journal of Modern History* 28 (1956): 247–58.

89. Harold Nicolson, *Curzon: The Last Phase, 1919–1925* (Boston and New York, 1934), pp. 351–78; Marchioness of Curzon, *Reminiscences* (New York, 1955), pp. 180–222; Richard W. Lyman, *The First Labour Government, 1924* (London, 1957), pp. 157–59; Glasgow, *MacDonald as Diplomatist*, pp. 13–30.

his dismissal as foreign secretary; this discovery sent him into a paroxysm of rage against things Gallic from which he never quite recovered, and he afterward cut off all but formal relations with the French.[90] The arch-conservative French ambassador, the Count de Saint-Aulaire,* though so snobbish that he normally restricted his social intercourse to the most pedigreed members of the English aristocracy, came to believe that even MacDonald would be an improvement. Notwithstanding its "dogmatism or charlatanism," he cabled the Quai d'Orsay, "the Labour party's attitude will be governed by the empiricism which is the fundamental rule of all British government. We can therefore count on the facts to bring it back, if we aid it, on to our road."[91]

Once he became prime minister and foreign secretary, MacDonald rapidly and forcefully moved to assure England's allies that a socialist government's assumption of power would mean no fundamental change in basic policies. Parliamentary opponents and even some of his Labour colleagues considered MacDonald rather muddled in thought and confused in speech. When in office, however, he relied for advice almost exclusively on the professional diplomats at the Foreign Office, led by the razor-sharp permanent under secretary, Sir Eyre Crowe.[92] MacDonald's efforts, both official and private, to woo Americans by personal cordiality and by touching appeals for the assistance of "a good wise schoolmaster" proved extraordinarily effective. Within weeks even the normally unemotive President Coolidge expressed the ardent hope that

*Auguste Félix de Saint-Aulaire (1866–1954), scion of a distinguished church-oriented noble family; educated at the Ecole des Sciences Politiques; member of the diplomatic service, 1892–1924; minister to Austria, 1909–12, to Morocco, 1912–16, where he served with Lyautey; minister to Romania, 1916–20, ambassador to Spain, 1920; chosen by Millerand to succeed Paul Cambon as ambassador to Great Britain, 1920; dismissed from the diplomatic service by Herriot, December 1924; subsequently made a career as a man of letters and diplomatic historian; described by fellow ambassador George Harvey as "a high-spirited representative of the old Régime, and very sensitive."

90. For details of the plot, including the intercepts of the French telegrams and the foreign secretary's furious, accusatory letters to Baldwin, see the dossier personally compiled by Curzon, F/1/4, F/1/5, and Green Folder F/1/7, Box Z, Lord [George Nathaniel] Curzon Papers, MS Eur. F. 111, India Office Library, London. For Curzon's subsequent refusal to meet the "arch intriguer" Saint-Aulaire, and for his prediction that Poincaré would rue the "sinister attempt" to hound him out of office once he had experienced MacDonald's "much stiffer and more throttling embraces," see Curzon to Lord Crewe, 11 and 12 December 1923, F/7/3 and F/8/1, Box 22, Curzon Papers.

91. Saint-Aulaire to Poincaré, 21 December 1923, quoted in Comte de Saint-Aulaire, *Confession d'un vieux diplomate* (Paris, 1953), p. 689.

92. See the clear evidence on this point which emerges from the Foreign Office political correspondence files and MacDonald's own correspondence, F.O. 800/218–219. Both sources offer confirmation for Jacques Bardoux's early interpretation, *L'Expérience de 1924* (Paris, 1930), pp. 66–82. For critical views of MacDonald's abilities by his colleagues, consult "Personal and Semiofficial Papers . . . Confidential Notes on Political and Fiscal Conditions in Great Britain, France, and Italy, 1918–26," Box 11, Norman H. Davis Papers; for an adverse judgment on MacDonald's subsequent career, note Robert Skidelsky, *Politicians and the Slump: The Labour Government of 1929–31* (London, 1967).

the "reasonable liberality of a Labor regime in Britain may point the way to a gradual adjustment of all the difficult European problems, both international and social."[93]

MacDonald demonstrated similar apparent cordiality in his relations with the French. In two agreeably phrased exchanges of letters with Poincaré, he invoked joint sacrifices for the "common cause" and underlined his "personal respect" for the French premier. These communications, carefully crafted by the Foreign Office staff with a view to later publication, were calculated to illustrate British goodwill in solving mutual problems. In his second letter, dispatched on 21 February, MacDonald even intimated that under a common policy to remedy European ills, Great Britain would not remain indifferent to French desiderata concerning security and war debts. He saw no reason why, if the interested parties examined the "broader aspect" of the reparations problem "conjointly with the related question of interallied debts," they could not reach a settlement at an early date after the Experts had completed their work. And while noting that the British people sought security in the "wider significance" of the term—security against war rather than merely security against Germany—MacDonald declared that he remained open-minded about the most effective way to allay international suspicions. He offered careful consideration of the methods for achieving security—implicitly, in the Rhineland—by "local demilitarization and neutralization, by the creation between certain states of bands of neutralized territory under mutual or even collective guarantee and supervision."[94]

In public statements to the House of Commons and in private talks with the French ambassador, MacDonald consistently demonstrated circumspection regarding substantive issues as well as earnest, almost evangelical goodwill. Saint-Aulaire still felt intuitively that MacDonald was "too cordial to be honest, and especially too conciliatory to be sincere."[95] Diplomatic rumor hinted at the influence of French Socialists advising MacDonald not to take a public position that might rally the French voting public behind Poincaré before the elections; could this provide an explanation for the prime minister's obliging manner?[96] For some time, particularly in February 1924, Saint-Aulaire half-discounted

93. J. Ramsay MacDonald to Norman H. Davis, 1 January 1924, Container 40 (MacDonald file), Davis Papers; Calvin Coolidge to Ambassador Frank B. Kellogg, 18 February 1924, Case file 712, Box 203, Coolidge Papers.

94. MacDonald to Poincaré, 26 January 1924, and Poincaré to MacDonald, 28 January 1924, in *L'Europe nouvelle*, 9 February 1924, p. 185; MacDonald to Poincaré, 21 February 1924, and Poincaré to MacDonald, 25 February 1924, in *L'Europe nouvelle*, 14 June 1924, pp. 771–73; English versions in London *Times*, 4 February and 3 March 1924; original letters in F.O. 800/218/191–194, 207–213, MacDonald Correspondence, and in vol. 16008, pp. 14–23, Poincaré Papers. See also Poincaré's remarks in his "Récit historique," annex to Georges Suarez, *Herriot, 1924–1932: Nouvelle Edition de "Une Nuit chez Cromwell"* (Paris, 1932), pp. 266–75.

95. Saint-Aulaire, *Confession d'un vieux diplomate*, p. 690.

96. Though Saint-Aulaire never found proof, the rumor was true. See H. N. Brailsford

his own suspicions. The Labour party would garner substantial political advantage, after all, if it could boast of reaching agreement with France where its Conservative predecessors had failed. And MacDonald's team at the Foreign Office let pass no opportunity to oil the waters. Parliamentary Under Secretary Arthur Ponsonby wrote typically: "The policy of pinpricks and quarrels all along the line leads nowhere and I hope that [it] will be abandoned; we must get down to fundamentals, and before doing that we must create a good and friendly atmosphere."[97] Though not devoid of skepticism, the French ambassador reflected that "in the land of fair play, one is often duped by fear of being duped."[98]

The Quai d'Orsay, moreover, eagerly wished to reciprocate MacDonald's overtures. Even at the zenith of French power the previous autumn, Poincaré had at no time evinced readiness to carry direct action in Germany so far—through more intense exploitation of productive pledges, agreements with German industrialists, or support for the Rhineland separatist movement—as to bring about permanent estrangement from England. He remained true to what, before embarking on the Ruhr occupation, he had described as "the dream of his life": to reach a comprehensive understanding with England along lines of the 1904 Entente, provided it could be achieved on "equitable" terms.[99] The French financial crisis and the consequent deterioration of the nation's position in the Ruhr impelled Poincaré to reevaluate what would constitute equitable terms. In mid-February 1924, he sent a private emissary to London to assure Whitehall that "the situation in France, and in fact in Europe, makes it more than ever imperative that France and England should come to a definite understanding."[100]

Significantly, those French government officials, like President Millerand, who took an economic rather than a purely juridical approach to the reparations problem and therefore had led the proponents of direct understanding with German industry, also strongly advocated rapprochement with England. During early February 1924, Jacques Seydoux, the chief reparations expert at the Quai d'Orsay, circulated to top government officials a position paper calling for a fresh look at the whole European situation in the light of French financial needs. Seydoux had

---

to MacDonald, 3 February 1924, reporting Blum's advice, F.O. 800/218/189–190, MacDonald Correspondence; and Eric Phipps to Sir Eyre Crowe, 9 February 1924, passing on similar counsel from Joseph Paul-Boncour, F.O. 371/9812: C 2279/1288/18.

97. Arthur Ponsonby to Professor L. Bretano, 6 February 1924, F.O. 800/227, Arthur Ponsonby Correspondence, Public Record Office, London.

98. Saint-Aulaire, *Confession d'un vieux diplomate,* pp. 691–92.

99. Phipps to Crowe, 10 January 1923, reporting Poincaré's statement to Georges Robineau of the Bank of France and to former ambassador Maurice Paléologue, in F.O. 800/243/218–221, Sir Eyre Crowe Correspondence, Public Record Office, London.

100. Sir Eyre Crowe memoranda, 19 and 22 February 1924, reviewing interviews with Poincaré's emissary, former president de la Barra of Mexico, F.O. 371/9825: C 2900/G, 3414/G.

consistently favored agreements linking French and German industry and, as will be suggested subsequently, he labored vigorously outside official diplomatic channels through March 1924 to further contacts between the Comité des Forges and the Stinnes interests.[101] But at the same time he saw an Anglo-French entente as the irreplaceable cornerstone of a political structure facilitating European economic rehabilitation, which France now needed almost as much as did Germany. The time was propitious, Seydoux argued, for greater cooperation on European economic problems:

> Both England and we ourselves are more ready for it than we were two years ago. England has abandoned the chimeras of the Lloyd George plan for the reconstruction of Europe with the help of financial committees; it needs Europe and can not act alone there; on the other hand, we have become conscious of the fact that our financial situation and the debts which we have contracted abroad make us dependent on the Anglo-American financial market and we know that the key to Wall Street lies in the City.[102]

During February and the first half of March, at the height of the financial emergency, this reasoning received wide approbation in Paris.[103] Time had in any case disposed of several substantive disagreements that had stymied earlier accord between Great Britain and France. An ingenious formula had bridged the differences over terms of reference for the Expert Committees. The French had backed down after initially demanding sanctions when the former crown prince's unauthorized return to the Reich spotlighted Germany's evasion of its disarmament obligations. And the M.I.C.U.M. agreements, which British industrialists at first had feared as the harbinger of a continental economic bloc directed against them, had proved far less consequential than expected.

In January 1924, the French gradually terminated their discreet support for the separatists, and the massacre of the remaining separatist forces in the Palatinate put an effective though sanguinary end to an issue that had greatly disturbed Anglo-French relations. Then, a compromise resolved the long-standing dispute over the railway *Régie*'s transit rights through the British occupation zone in the Rhineland, the French accepting the Cologne railway's offer to transport their goods through the British zone. Finally, on 5 March in the permanent Conference of Ambassadors, the French and British reached agreement respect-

101. Abbreviated reference in Stresemann, *Vermächtnis*, 1:368–69; Karl Ritter memorandum, 17 March 1924, Handakten Ritter, G.F.M. L177/4079/L051727; see also reports on meetings of Stinnes's representatives with Seydoux and French metallurgists, January-March 1924, in G.F.M. L1491/5352/L436757–778.

102. Seydoux memorandum, 4 February 1924, excerpted in Weill-Raynal, *Les Réparations allemandes*, 3:16–17; also reported and interpreted in Sir Charles Mendl to Sir William Tyrrell, 3 March 1924, F.O. 371/9812: C 3956/1288/18.

103. *Le Temps*, 4 and 6 March 1924; also commented on in Mendl to Tyrrell, 11 March 1924, F.O. 800/220/14–23, Correspondence between Assistant Under Secretary Sir William Tyrrell and Sir Charles Mendl [News Department representative in France], Public Record Office, London.

ing future military control of Germany. The occupation of the Ruhr had led—as a result of German resistance—to effective suspension of the Interallied Military Control Commission's investigatory work. The Allied powers now decided to restrict further supervision by the control commission to the five key disarmament requirements that Germany had violated most flagrantly.[104] The professional staff at the Quai d'Orsay and even in Whitehall experienced a brief swell of optimism: the way seemed clear for concerted action on the major problems of central Europe. "The atmosphere between France and Great Britain had not been so favorable for years for a settlement of the vital questions," Assistant Permanent Under Secretary Sir William Tyrrell of the Foreign Office told the American ambassador in London.[105]

By the last part of March, however, mutual suspicions again hovered as dark as ever. The British Experts' continued pressure within the Dawes Committee to reduce the size of the reparations annuities fanned Poincaré's instinctive skepticism about the worth of a détente limited to improving the international atmosphere. From discussion with Foreign Office officials, Saint-Aulaire gradually confirmed two impressions: that MacDonald aimed to get the French out of the Ruhr without any substantive commitments by England, and that his vague promise of future cooperation in regard to security and interallied debts was a simple "injection of morphine for French public opinion."[106] Presumably some intimation of the English double game on the M.I.C.U.M. agreements had reached Paris, for while MacDonald publicly affected a prudent hands-off attitude concerning the renewal of these agreements, chairman Reginald McKenna of the Second Committee of Experts was privately warning the Germans that continued coal deliveries to France would create a bad impression in English financial and industrial circles.[107] The defeat of the speculative attack against the franc also strengthened France's confidence in its ability to take a hard line as its interests required.

Poincaré instructed Saint-Aulaire to reiterate that France would with-

104. For a brief summary, see Bardoux, *L'Expérience de 1924*, pp. 165–73; Glasgow, *MacDonald as Diplomatist*, pp. 46–48; "Récit historique de R. Poincaré," in Suarez, *Herriot*, pp. 266–75; and Arnold J. Toynbee, *Survey of International Affairs, 1920–1923* (London, 1925). Each of these issues has also received monographic attention: separatism in Karl Dietrich Erdmann, *Adenauer in der Rheinlandpolitik nach dem Ersten Weltkrieg* (Stuttgart, 1966), J. A. Dorten, *La Tragédie rhénane* (Paris, 1945), and Erwin Bischof, *Rheinischer Separatismus, 1918–1924* (Bern, 1969); the *Régie*'s problems in a study by its director, Henri Bréaud, *La Régie des chemins de fer des territoires occupés, 1923–1924* (Paris, 1938); and German disarmament in Michael Salewski, *Entwaffnung und Militärkontrolle in Deutschland, 1919–1927* (Bonn, 1966).

105. Kellogg to State Department, 16 and 18 February 1924, U.S. 462.00R 296/175, 200.

106. Saint-Aulaire, *Confession d'un vieux diplomate*, pp. 692–94.

107. MacDonald's speech in House of Commons *Debates*, 5th Series, 27 March 1924, col. 1596–99; McKenna's views reported by Dufour-Feronce to Schubert, 27 March 1924, G.F.M. L1491/5352/L436716–719; see also Weill-Raynal, *Les Réparations allemandes*, 3:22.

draw its military—as distinguished from its "economic"—occupation of the Ruhr only in proportion to tangible reparations receipts. Thus France insisted on maintaining the fundamental policy promulgated jointly with Belgium in March 1923.[108] Poincaré would exchange the direct exploitation of the Ruhr by Franco-Belgian forces for other, more productive financial pledges if the Experts recommended them. But a skeleton military occupation would have to continue, so that sanctions could be easily reapplied in the event of renewed German default. England's promise to "associate itself with sanctions should the occasion arise" would constitute the best guarantee against such a relapse.[109]

When Saint-Aulaire delivered this message formally on 24 March, MacDonald simply listened in silence. The ambassador discerned enough irritation underneath the reserved English exterior to merit his warning the Quai d'Orsay not to "take this silence for acquiescence."[110] But momentarily he failed to gauge the full measure of the prime minister's displeasure. Actually MacDonald and his staff had been gripped by unbridled fury ever since, some days before, they had learned informally of Poincaré's intentions. They had earlier taken encouragement from the intimation by Poincaré's private emissary to London that the French would prove ready to "evacuate the Ruhr altogether" if the Experts' scheme offered real guarantees of payment.[111] The British minister in Paris had cautioned them not to believe it; it was "impossible to keep up with all the lies" turned out by the Quai d'Orsay, he wrote, and Poincaré, while "perfectly honest from the financial point of view," should not be trusted otherwise.[112] Notwithstanding this exhortation, Whitehall seethed with outrage when, within days after the Morgan loan had successfully buoyed the franc, Poincaré's pronouncements began to imply a reversion to his previous position regarding the Ruhr. "M. Poincaré is again revealing the slipping character which infects all his proceedings and professions," minuted Sir Eyre Crowe in disgust. ". . . Now we know that [he] will in no case give up the military occupation, and will only abandon the 'economic' occupation on receiving a British guarantee that Great Britain will join France in occupying further German territory . . . if Germany, egged on by French continued aggressive policy, should show further opposition. These are impossible conditions." MacDonald wondered if Poincaré had composed his earlier let-

108. Joint declaration of 14 March 1923, in France, Ministère des Affaires Etrangères, *Documents diplomatiques: Documents relatifs aux notes allemandes des 2 mai et 7 juin sur les réparations, 2 mai–3 août 1923* (Paris, 1923), no. 37; and in Belgium, Ministère des Affaires Etrangères, *Documents diplomatiques relatifs aux réparations du 26 décembre 1922 au 27 août 1923*, nos. 16 and 18.

109. Saint-Aulaire, *Confession d'un vieux diplomate*, p. 694, reproduces Poincaré's instructions in part.

110. Saint-Aulaire, *Confession d'un vieux diplomate*, p. 694.

111. Memorandum by Sir Eyre Crowe, 19 February 1924, F.O. 371/9825: C 2900/G.

112. Eric Phipps to Crowe, 28 February 1924, F.O. 371/9825: C 3421/G.

ters of goodwill "similarly crookedly."[113] By the end of March, in short, British diplomats no longer were prepared to place any reliance on Poincaré's assurances. He would "turn and twist his statements," reported Eric Phipps from Paris, "to mean anything that he may happen to wish at the moment, or that may suit his electoral book."[114]

Shortly thereafter, Saint-Aulaire came upon evidence seeming to prove that MacDonald was simply postponing decisions until after the French elections and that the British Intelligence Service was doing its best in the meantime to subsidize the opposition in France. Sir William Tyrrell, an Anglo-Irish aristocrat hostile to the Labour government with whom Saint-Aulaire enjoyed a certain intimacy grounded in their common class background, hinted that "an exceptional effort is being made here to get Poincaré's hide." In itself this was not an extraordinary revelation: Labour political figures had explained their calculations with such frankness to German and American Embassy personnel that it would have been surprising if Saint-Aulaire had not picked up some wind of them on the London diplomatic circuit. But in the ambassador's eyes Tyrrell's intimation assumed added importance in the light of other reports. These reports suggested that British Intelligence had provided the funds with which Republican-Socialist deputy and cognac heir Jean Hennessy had bankrolled *Le Quotidien* and that the British Labour party had subsidized the French Socialist weekly, *Le Populaire*. On 4 April the ambassador rushed over to Paris to apprise Poincaré of the danger.[115]

Poincaré Digs In

The French premier appeared unruffled. He suspected that the reports of MacDonald's black designs had been blown out of proportion by Saint-Aulaire's English informants, who like the ambassador himself came from a rarefied upper stratum of society willing to believe the worst of any socialist. Besides, virtually all French newspapers received hidden subsidies from one source or another. Poincaré doubted whether such subsidies decisively affected politics. The pressure of public opinion and the logic of events, he told the ambassador, would oblige any French government to follow much the same policy.

Still, the news brought by Saint-Aulaire could hardly fail to reinforce Poincaré's hard-nosed inclinations and to strengthen his resolve to avoid substantive concessions. On 2 April, in typical juridical fashion, he had

113. Poincaré speech to French Senate, *J.O.S. Déb.*, 13 March 1924, pp. 281–86; Phipps to Crowe, 18 March 1924, relaying Peretti's exegesis of this speech, Crowe and MacDonald minutes, 19 March 1924, F.O. 371/9825: C 4760/G.

114. Phipps to Crowe, 3 April 1924, F.O. 371/9825: C 5850/G; similar sentiment expressed in Crowe to Phipps, 20 March 1924, F.O. 371/9825: C 4760/G; and in Miles W. Lampson's minute, 19 March 1924, F.O. 371/9813: C 4546/1288/18.

115. Comte de Saint-Aulaire, "L'Angleterre et les élections de 1924," *Ecrits de Paris*, May 1953, pp. 9–19; *Confession d'un vieux diplomate*, pp. 694–99.

reminded Louis Barthou,* president of the Reparation Commission, that sanctions lay outside the commission's competence according to the Versailles treaty and were reserved for direct consideration by the Allied governments. Therefore, the commission could not recommend "certain opinions expressed by the Experts . . . the interpretation of which could lead in particular either to abandoning the pledges that we hold at the present time, or to returning the railways operated by the Franco-Belgian *Régie* to the disposition of the Reich, without the guarantees indispensable for our security."[116]

Barthou was flexible and realistic. Thirty years earlier he and Poincaré had served as young ministers together, and his political and personal standing made him one of the few men in French public life who could argue successfully with the premier. When negotiations over formation of the Expert Committees had threatened to collapse during the preceding autumn, Barthou had played an instrumental role in convincing Poincaré to adopt a less rigid attitude.[117] He had worked closely with the Experts throughout the course of their deliberations. And he was prepared to throw his own prestige into the balance—so he assured colleagues on the Reparation Commission—to ensure that the French government eschewed legal haggling and responded to the broad spirit of the Dawes Report. His cooperativeness notwithstanding, Barthou remained "outspokenly suspicious of the whole British attitude"[118]—but not suspicious enough to suit Poincaré's taste. The premier feared that after long immersion in the atmosphere of interallied fellowship at the Hotel Astoria, Barthou would not defend the French position with sufficient vigor.

On 11 April the two men held a long and somewhat strained discussion concerning France's tactical options. A note presented by the British

*Louis Barthou (1866–1934), son of a hardware dealer, earned a doctorate in law, then returned to his native Basses-Pyrénées to open a legal practice and edit a local newspaper; elected to the Chamber as a moderate republican against heavy odds in a still-monarchist district, served as deputy, 1889–1922, senator, 1922–34; rapidly won notice for his forensic talent; appointed as minister of public works, 1894, a frequent participant in ministerial combinations for forty years thereafter; president of the council, 1913, put through three-year military service law and incurred permanent enmity of the Radical-Socialists; minister of war, 1921–22, of justice, 1922, 1926–29, president of the Reparation Commission, 1922–26; minister of foreign affairs, 1934, assassinated by Croatian terrorist. A man of high culture, bibliophile, patron of the arts, author of many works on poetry and music, Barthou himself joked about his unabashed hunger for office and his reputation for deserting political colleagues who came under attack: "I have never conspired against a ministry to which I did not belong."

116. The following account draws largely on Poincaré to Barthou, 12 April 1924, and Barthou to Poincaré, 14 April 1924, Folder 6, Box 7, Louis Loucheur Papers. These letters cite and summarize previous correspondence and conversations.

117. Leon Fraser, "The Evolution of the Terms of Reference for the Committee of Experts," in Rufus C. Dawes, *The Dawes Plan in the Making* (Indianapolis, 1925), pp. 290–96.

118. Logan to State Department, 24 April 1924, U.S. 462.00R 296/285.

ambassador had already made clear that Great Britain sought to bind France to all the Experts' conclusions before the Reparation Commission had considered them in detail. Compounding Poincaré's anxiety, the Belgians seemed ready to endorse any procedure conducive to an early withdrawal from the Ruhr. "It is evident," the premier told Barthou, ". . . that the British government, in agreement with the German government, seeks to make us abandon our pledges without conditions, even before the Experts' Plan has been implemented. We will not allow this claim and we will not give up our pledges until the Experts' program is entirely operational and can be automatically substituted, with all desirable guarantees, for the system of pledges currently in force." In any event, he continued, France sought the right to determine "the precise extent" to which the Experts' program would be applied and to set the "conditions and guarantees" necessary before specific pledges—the coal tax, the customs barrier around the occupied area, the railway *Régie*, and so forth—were handed back to Germany.

To reserve maximum scope for maneuver, then, Poincaré intended to employ every legal stratagem available to him under the Versailles treaty. The Reparation Commission, he urged, should first accord the Germans a hearing and invite them to express approbation of the Experts' Reports. Only after the Reich had demonstrated its willingness to cooperate, he insisted, should the Reparation Commission take formal action. At that point, the commission should not extend blanket approval to the Experts' Reports, but should rather proceed under the powers delegated by the treaty to make a complete and detailed decision. For this purpose it could "draw the data" from the reports, but would need to fill certain lacunae to create a comprehensive plan.[119]

Barthou conceded that this was the "most juridical" way to proceed. But in view of world opinion's overwhelmingly favorable reaction to the Dawes Plan, France would find itself "isolated" if it asked the Reparation Commission to postpone a vote. And quite apart from this tactical consideration, he thought the time had come to "show France's true countenance, and to profit from the Experts' conclusions, clearly accepted as a basis for discussion, to demonstrate that despite widely spread calumnies the Ruhr occupation was a means, not an end, and that it did not dissemble annexationist intentions." Barthou claimed to agree with Poincaré on fundamental policy. He believed, however, that if France accepted "inevitable adjustments," it could protect its interests satisfactorily and secure the guarantees which it considered indispensable within the context of the Experts' recommendations.

In the course of discussion with Poincaré, Barthou acceded to the premier's wish to summon the Germans for a preliminary hearing, although he declined to accept "rigorous instructions" on this issue.

119. Poincaré to Barthou, 12 April 1924, Folder 6, Box 7, Loucheur Papers.

When he returned to Reparation Commission headquarters, however, he found the English delegate, Sir John Bradbury, ready with a proposal for immediate and definitive acceptance of the Experts' Reports. Barthou thereupon decided to throw his support to a more restricted compromise resolution.[120] The commission agreed to "approve the conclusions and to adopt the methods" of the Experts' Reports insofar as these fell within its jurisdiction, but only to "recommend" those conclusions relating to matters under the direct authority of the Allied governments.[121]

The commission's decision placed Poincaré in a delicate position. The French election campaign was entering its final weeks. For Poincaré to admit publicly that France had suffered a diplomatic setback would hardly be politic: success in foreign affairs alone could provide a plausible justification in the eyes of the hard-pressed Bloc National for the premier's neutrality on domestic issues. On the other hand, he could not permit the situation to drift without voicing French reservations about the Experts' work.

Poincaré attempted to resolve this dilemma, first in a subtle speech on 15 April to an electoral banquet of the *Parti républicain démocratique et social* at Luna Park in Paris,[122] and then in a formal reply to the Reparation Commission along similar lines ten days later.[123] The Experts' Reports, he claimed, provided "the most brilliant justification" of the Ruhr occupation. Productive in itself, that occupation had also demonstrated to the Allies that reparations were collectible. The Experts, he said, had carried out their investigation within the appropriate predetermined limits. They had demonstrated that Germany could pay and had proposed a schedule of annuities superior to those stipulated by the Bonar Law Plan.[124] Moreover, they had not reduced Germany's theoretical total liability as established in the London Schedule of Payments. They had thus left France in a strong position to bargain for a reduction of its own war debts in a subsequent comprehensive settlement. Conveniently forgetting his earlier hesitations, Poincaré now boasted of his satisfaction that he had "taken the initiative" in proposing the convocation of the Expert Committees.

120. Barthou to Poincaré, 14 April 1924, ibid.

121. Decision of 11 April 1924, reproduced in Reparation Commission, *Official Documents*, vol. 14, *The Experts' Plan for Reparation Payments* (London, 1927), p. 128.

122. *Le Temps*, 17 April 1924.

123. The text of the French reply, as well as of other responses to the Reparation Commission, is reproduced in *L'Europe nouvelle*, 3 May 1924, pp. 582–83.

124. Weill-Raynal, *Les Réparations allemandes*, 2:627–65, concludes after extensive mathematical computations that although the Bonar Law Plan stipulated somewhat smaller payments from Germany, it provided for an intra-European debt settlement which on balance made it more advantageous to France than the Dawes Plan. All such calculations rest on so many contingent variables that they are hypothetical at best. The Bonar Law Plan, drawn up by the British Treasury for the Paris conference of January 1923 preceding the Ruhr occupation, proposed a four-year unsecured moratorium for Germany. If this plan had been adopted, it is most unlikely—for obvious political reasons—that reparations payments would ever have been resumed.

But the premier juxtaposed praise of the Experts' work with a reaffirmation that France would not give up the system of direct economic exploitation then in operation until the Reparation Commission had developed and actually put into effect a wholly acceptable alternative. At Luna Park Poincaré attempted to justify this position by reference to the text of the Dawes Report:

> This plan in its entirety will no doubt imply reestablishment of the Reich's economic and fiscal unity. But it is not after a declaration in principle, not after a forced and artificial acceptance, it is only—as the Experts themselves have clearly written—after fulfillment by Germany, that we can be asked to exchange our pledges for others, more ample and remunerative. There can, of course, be no question of our withdrawal from the Ruhr before payment of what is due; nor can there be any question of loosening our hold, without retaining the means to reestablish it surely and swiftly in case of need.

Writing to the Reparation Commission, Poincaré went further, contending that once the German government put the plan into operation, the Allied governments should exercise their prerogative to examine which of the pledges presently held could be made "the object of a fusion or exchange."[125]

Poincaré appeared to be trying not only to ensure the continued military occupation of the Ruhr—a subject that the Experts had passed over in discreet silence—but also to save as much as possible of the productive pledge system. Were his statements to be strictly interpreted, or was he merely attempting to stake out a bargaining position? Undoubtedly, Poincaré was emotionally reluctant to evacuate the Ruhr, even if as a responsible public official he recognized that events might well require it.[126] Privately, however, Peretti de la Rocca, the top career official at the Quai d'Orsay, indicated that France would prove flexible.

By late April French career diplomats had more or less abandoned hope of making progress either on war debts or security problems in connection with the Dawes Report. Feelers to Great Britain for an intra-European debt adjustment had produced no result. Believing, in Niemeyer's phrase, that debts remained their "only weapon if the Allies seek to disturb the settlement unduly,"[127] the British had made it known that they would take a "stiff" position. Since the funding offer made in the Bonar Law Plan the previous year no longer seemed open, the French decided not to make debts a matter of first priority. Peretti acknowledged, moreover, that France lacked compelling grounds to advance security demands at this particular juncture. The Ruhr occupation, after all, had been designed to make the Germans pay. Whatever

125. Poincaré to Reparation Commission, 25 April 1924, *L'Europe nouvelle*, 3 May 1924, pp. 582–83, also F.O. 371/9742: C 6809/70/18; advance explanation of French position in Poincaré to the Marquess of Crewe, 20 April 1924, F.O. 371/9741: C 6614/70/18.

126. See Belgian Foreign Minister Paul Hymans's testimony, *Mémoires*, 2:576.

127. Sir Otto E. Niemeyer memorandum, "The Reparation Experts' Report," 14 April 1924, F.O. 371/9740: C 6331/70/18.

suspicions foreigners held, it had not originated from security needs—the French General Staff considered that purely as a military operation the Ruhr occupation actually weakened the French front by siphoning off troops from the Rhineland.[128]

What then could France hope to achieve? Peretti frankly expressed his lack of confidence in German good faith. Germany would continue to carry out the Dawes Plan only if the Allies united to enforce it. France therefore sought some assurance that in the event of flagrant default, Great Britain would join in reoccupying the Ruhr. Failing this, France hoped for an understanding that Britain would at least acquiesce in a French and Belgian reoccupation.[129]

The French deeply feared the ultimate intentions of the Germans—and for good reason. Diplomats at the Wilhelmstrasse might find it expedient to protest their good faith. Industrialists and bankers in the occupied areas, however, openly proclaimed that though the German government might well accept the Dawes Plan and even carry it out for a few years in order to obtain the desired initial loan, it would certainly repudiate the agreement later when the exactions were found too heavy to bear.[130] Foreign observers perceived a radical change of mood in the occupied areas during the early spring of 1924. Berlin's triumph over Rhineland separatism and over centrifugal forces in other parts of Germany had prompted a recovery of public confidence and a buoyancy of spirit unknown since the 1918 defeat. The collapse of passive resistance now appeared in retrospect as a mere temporary setback. At the outset passive resistance had fired a general hope of ending reparations once and for all through confrontation. In their newly optimistic mood, many Germans took the view that they had simply misjudged the length of time that France could hold out. As they saw it, the French financial crisis confirmed their enemy's ultimate vulnerability. The assistance of American bankers had given the French a temporary reprieve, financial authorities in the Rhineland conceded, but they calculated that "the franc would collapse again immediately in case the financial world should conclude that the endeavors to settle the reparations problem had failed." The broad consensus of opinion in Germany, moreover, continued to reject the idea that reparations constituted a moral obligation. As the American consul in Cologne summarized the situation, the

128. See Peretti's several statements to British, Belgian, and American diplomats: Hughe Knatchbull-Hugessen to Miles W. Lampson, 22 April 1924, F.O. 371/9741: C 6672/70/18; Myron T. Herrick to State Department, 25 April 1924, U.S. 462.00R 296/288; James A. Logan to State Department, 30 April 1924, U.S. 462.00R 296/305; Frank B. Kellogg to State Department, 3 May 1924, U.S. 462.00R 296/312.

129. Herrick to State Department, 25 April 1924, U.S. 462.00R 296/288.

130. Memorandum by Under Secretary Joseph Grew of conversation with André de Laboulaye, counselor of the French Embassy, who presented substantiating evidence, 16 June 1924, U.S. 462.00R 296/372. Peretti had voiced similar suspicions earlier: see Phipps to Crowe, 15 April 1924, F.O. 371/9741: C 6514/70/18.

Germans would "not pay reparations unless compelled to do so" or until they concluded that obstruction would bring more disadvantageous consequences than would payment.[131]

In the press and in private conversations alike in the western part of Germany, one argument for accepting the Dawes Report appeared decisive: it offered the only way to recover administrative and fiscal control of the occupied areas and to overcome the economic problems attendant on a dearth of liquid capital.[132] Nationalists from Pomerania and the protected regions east of the Elbe or Communists from Thuringia might call boldly for further resistance, but hardly anyone in the Ruhr and Rhineland wished to renew the grim test of brute strength with the French. Moderates confidently hoped to achieve their ends by means of negotiations. "When we once have the French where they are ready to negotiate with us," said one Cologne banker, "we have them beaten to a frazzle." The Dawes Plan, after all, offered many possibilities for quiet evasion. It might require considerable ingenuity to repudiate the railroad and industrial debentures provided for in the plan if these were publicly marketed in neutral countries. To arrange a demonstration that payments could not be made from the Reich budget would prove easier. The stipulation that a Transfer Committee decide to what extent marks could safely be converted into foreign currency opened a further field for inventiveness. Numerous ways existed to show that imports of raw materials and even luxury goods could not be curtailed. Already some German financial authorities were predicting the impossibility of any reparations transfer without adversely affecting the foreign exchanges.[133]

Private citizens in Germany could speak their minds more freely than those holding public office, of course. But as the German election campaign drew to a close, even so calculating a politician as Foreign Minister Stresemann came close to uncovering his true intentions. "If I have not got power, I must take what I can get to achieve freedom," he explained frankly to a nationalist audience on 29 April, adding that the government considered acceptance of the Dawes Plan a sound policy because it gave Germany the chance "to become a land again capable of political action by another method."[134] Significantly, Chancellor Marx continued to echo similar sentiments after the elections were over. When Lord Mayor

131. Emil Sauer [American consul-general in Cologne], "Reception Given in Western Germany to the Reports of the Committee of Experts," 7 June 1924 (actually drafted several weeks earlier), U.S. 462.00R 296/376.

132. See the daily newspaper survey in Haut Commissariat de la République française dans les pays rhénans, presse et information, "Analyse de presse," April-June 1924, copy in Bibliothèque de Documentation Internationale Contemporaine, Nanterre.

133. Emil Sauer, "Reception Given . . . to the Reports," 7 June 1924, U.S. 462.00R 296/376.

134. *Vossische Zeitung*, 30 April 1924, quoted in D'Abernon no. 330 to MacDonald, 1 May 1924, F.O. 371/9743: C 7378/70/18.

Konrad Adenauer opened the Cologne Fair on 11 May with a warm endorsement of the Dawes Plan and a ringing call for establishment of a "true and lasting peace" among the countries of western Europe, Marx pointedly replied that his government had accepted the Experts' Report as a "temporary solution" because Germany needed a "breathing spell" and because there appeared no other way of attaining the liberation of the Ruhr. Even those who did not wish to hear could hardly fail to draw the obvious conclusion. "The Chancellor's speech," minuted the German desk officer at the Foreign Office in London, "does not increase one's confidence that Germany will play straight."[135]

In the face of all these discouraging signs the French could easily predict what might happen in a few years. It was not as simple to design practical steps to guard against the future peril. Belgium held the key in the immediately forthcoming negotiations. Italy would presumably align itself with Great Britain in the hope of receiving preferential treatment on its own war debt.[136] If Belgium too lined up on the British side, France could be outvoted on the Reparation Commission and, in view of world opinion, could not afford to maintain an isolated position.[137]

The Diplomatic Kaleidoscope

Belgian Prime Minister Georges Theunis and his new foreign minister, Paul Hymans, made a tour of Allied capitals in order to mediate among the powers and attempt to create some sort of consensus. The Belgians asserted that such a good opportunity to settle the reparations question would not recur. The Ruhr occupation could not be prolonged without grave political, economic, and financial risks. No doubt the Experts' conclusions meant a reduction of what had been hoped for, said Theunis, but in politics one must be "content with what is possible."[138]

135. Marx speech in *Frankfurter Zeitung*, 12 May 1924; comment by German desk officer J. C. Sterndale Bennett, 20 May 1924, F.O. 371/9745: C 7967/70/18; contrast with Adenauer views emphasized by Lord Kilmarnock no. 852 to MacDonald, 17 May 1924, F.O. 371/9745: C 8062/70/18.

136. During May and June the Italians made several approaches to the British, offering a general alignment of Italian reparations policy with that of Great Britain in return for generous treatment regarding the Italian war debt and territorial concessions in the Mediterranean and East Africa. Some Treasury officials showed interest, but MacDonald and the Foreign Office finally vetoed the idea. MacDonald in particular came to despise the blackmailing tactics of Italian diplomacy. Although he claimed to be accustomed to Italy's negotiating style through his "experience in an Oriental bazaar," he declined to enter into "pettifogging bargains." He preferred to postpone settlement of interallied debts, correctly calculating that Italy would play along merely on the hope of favorable consideration later (F.O. 800/219/60–105; F.O. 371/9743: C 7148/70/18; also explanations to the Americans, U.S. 462.00R 296/348, 365).

137. Logan to State Department, 24 April 1924, U.S. 462.00R 296/285.

138. In accordance with their policy of trying to draw the United States into European affairs, the Belgians furnished transcripts of their conferences to American diplomats. Otherwise unidentified quotations in the account that follows come from the transcripts in State Department files: enclosures in Kellogg to State Department, 2 June 1924, U.S.

When the Belgians presented this line of argument to Poincaré, Finance Minister François-Marsal, and Marshal Foch at the Quai d'Orsay on 28 April, the discussion became "somewhat acrimonious."[139] Poincaré began elaborating on his Luna Park position: only gradually could France relinquish control of the Ruhr on a schedule corresponding to Germany's performance after the Dawes Plan became operative. Theunis pointed out that a gradual release was incompatible with the Experts' Report and that no foreign loan could be floated on such a basis. Despite the inconclusive debate on this point, Theunis remained confident that ultimately, perhaps after the elections, the French would give up economic control. Poincaré had made so many speeches against yielding control before receiving payment that the Belgian premier thought he needed "some time to readjust himself and find some basis on which he could retreat."

The Belgians felt equally optimistic that Poincaré and François-Marsal would eventually drop their objections to the Transfer Committee. The French contended that this organ would facilitate German obstruction of payment. They also protested that the Transfer Committee, on which France was to have but one vote in six, would usurp some of the Reparation Commission's authority (on the latter body France had one vote in four but in practice enjoyed a preponderant voice). Let the Reparation Commission exercise the Transfer Committee's functions for the first two years, proposed the French. During this period no substantial amount of cash would accumulate on reparations account; thereafter the Allies might review the question again. The Belgians countered with the pertinent observation that world finance lacked confidence in the Reparation Commission because of the political coloration ascribed, however unjustly, to its past decisions; unless the Transfer Committee were created forthwith, the chances of floating a loan for Germany would be remote. On this issue too the Belgians and French remained at loggerheads, though Theunis inferred that the French might soften their resistance if they were pleased with the personnel appointed to administer the Dawes Plan.

Poincaré indicated that he would give priority to two other claims. As expected, he placed paramount importance on a binding agreement that if Germany defaulted in the future, certain sanctions defined in advance would become automatically operative. As his second desideratum, he called for retention of Allied control over the Rhineland railway network. The Franco-Belgian *Régie*, he insisted, was operating satisfactorily. It

---

462.00R 296/368. The Belgians also filled in the English on their negotiations in Paris (see Sir George Grahame tel. no. 67, 29 April 1924, F.O. 371/9742: C 7066/70/18).

139. Logan to State Department, 30 April 1924 [based on report by Belgian delegate to the Reparation Commission Léon Delacroix], U.S. 462.00R 296/305; additional comment by Theunis in Kellogg to State Department, 3 May 1924, U.S. 462.00R 296/312.

guaranteed the communication lines and safety of Allied occupation troops as well as military security generally. If the *Régie* maintained its regional administrative control, it could still assure the economic unity of the German railways as required under the Experts' Plan by adopting the same rates and regulations as the other German lines.

In a possible future war between France and Germany, control of the Rhineland railways might conceivably tip the balance. Because German transport officials had long suspected the French of plotting to gain permanent control of the Rhineland rail network, they had organized passive resistance of railway personnel with meticulous care in 1923.[140] General Payot had in fact prepared some detailed studies of the Rhineland railways for the French General Staff in 1922 and 1923, and French officials on the Rhineland High Commission undoubtedly favored retaining maximum control.[141] However, by April 1924 the French War Ministry had defined more modest goals. Marshal Foch told the Belgians that a guarantee of free movement for military supply trains represented the only indispensable military requirement. At General Weygand's behest Foch had worked out a plan for a separate Rhineland railway administration which circulated for months at the rue St.-Dominique.[142] But the Marshal really doubted whether such a narrowly conceived proposal—"more or less justified," as he later put it—could have any decisive significance in the absence of a bold and comprehensive general policy in the occupied areas.[143]

Foch expressed as much skepticism about the viability of a transport system dependent on cooperation with the Germans as he did about industrial cooperation with them. Since 1922 he had repeatedly advocated division of the Ruhr and Rhineland into two areas. His numerous plans called for "absorption" of a restricted region, including parts of the Rhineland, the Saar, and the Düsseldorf-Essen section of the Ruhr, as a sort of reparations province either permanently or for a fifty- or sixty-year period. The French would run the coal mines, chemical industry, and transport system directly in the reparations province. The remainder of the Ruhr might be returned to German control in exchange for a fixed annual payment.[144] But Foch had never made any headway in political circles with his scheme for an integrated occupation. The diplomatic obstacles were overwhelming, and the French financial crisis

140. "Reisetagebuch" of Reich Transport Minister Wilhelm Groener, 24 February, 2 June 1923, General Wilhelm Groener Papers, H08–46/140, Bundesarchiv-Militärarchiv, Freiburg-im-Breisgau.

141. Otto Jung, "Reparation, Währung, und französische Rheinlandpolitik, 1920–1923," 1:77–82, 2:52–78, MS in Sammlung Otto Jung, no. 1, ZSg 105, Bundesarchiv. [Jung cites French records used when Paris fell under German occupation in 1940.]

142. Bardoux, *L'Expérience de 1924*, p. 211.

143. Ferdinand Foch Cahiers, 28 July 1924, Dossier G, p. 176, photocopy, Bibliothèque Nationale, Paris.

144. Foch Cahiers, 22, 28 December 1923, 8–9 January 1924, Dossier G, pp. 163–66.

made the plan impracticable. In any case, Poincaré conceived of the Ruhr occupation primarily as an economic, not a military enterprise, and like most Third Republic statesmen, he paid little heed to the advice of military men on political questions.[145] Future events would bear out the Belgian foreign minister's shrewd surmise: Poincaré's insistence on continued railway control after the Dawes Plan became operative was less a deeply grounded security requirement of the War Ministry than a tangible claim on which the premier had fastened in his desire to maintain some visible symbol of the existing occupation regime.[146]

The Belgians maintained that the operation of the German railway system as a unit constituted an essential feature of the Dawes Plan. They conceded only that the railway experts who had served as consultants to the Dawes Committee should be directed to work out a program for safeguarding the future movement of supply trains, under the assumption that exclusive control of railway operations would rest for the time being with the German authorities. Creation of a divisional railway administration at Cologne, for example, would make it technically easier for the Allies to detach the Rhineland railways from the integrated German system in the event that renewed military sanctions proved necessary.[147] The intricate problem of the Rhineland rail network—interwoven with the questions of the Ruhr and then the Cologne zone evacuations, with preparations for the contingency of reimposing sanctions, and with the quest for broader security arrangements—remained one of the most thorny for the London Conference to settle.[148]

Continuing their travels, the Belgian ministers met with MacDonald and Sir Eyre Crowe on 2–3 May at the British prime minister's country residence, Chequers.[149] When the hapless Belgians elaborated on French views with some degree of sympathy, they met with a frosty reception. Sanctions to be applied in the event of future German default provided the main focus of the discussion. Theunis pleaded for something to "save Poincaré's face." He recognized that the British government could not commit itself in advance to send a military force across the Channel. He had gotten Poincaré to agree that in case of deliberate default, it would be sufficient for England to undertake economic or naval measures, for example, a boycott of German imports or a blockade of German exports. But MacDonald remained immovable; he declared it "out of the question" for Britain to do more than "consult" with its allies. Schemes could not be manufactured "like automatic chocolate

145. Foch Cahiers, 9 February, 23 March 1924, Dossier G, pp. 166–67.

146. Hymans, *Mémoires*, 2:576.

147. U.S. 462.00R 296/305, 312.

148. See Poincaré's further remarks in *J.O.S. Déb.*, 10 July 1924, pp. 1018–38.

149. "Notes on Conversations Held at Chequers," 2–3 May 1924, F.O. 371/9743: C 7427/70/18, and U.S. 462.00R 296/352; additional comment by the British prime minister in MacDonald to Crewe, no. 135, 6 May 1924, F.O. 371/9743: C 7339/70/18, and in Kellogg to State Department, 6 May 1924, U.S. 462.00R 296/318.

machines which delivered the goods when anyone put a penny into the slot." The British prime minister saw neither the necessity nor the practicability of arrangements providing for automatic application of sanctions "on the occurrence possibly many years hence, of events the exact significance of which could hardly be measured, and still less effectively countered so long in advance." Nor, he added, would marshaling threats regarding the procedure to be followed if Germany defaulted again promote a "spirit of ready cooperation." The specific financial provisions of the Experts' Plan should prove guarantee enough, suggested MacDonald vaguely, though he would also be "glad to bring in the moral authority of the League [of Nations], which should not be undervalued."

When it came to describing what would happen if "owing to the unreasonable attitude of M. Poincaré," the Experts' Plan should fail of adoption, the British prime minister became more definite. Great Britain would begin by challenging the legality of the Ruhr occupation, the railway *Régie*, and the M.I.C.U.M. agreements. It would be, he said, "a most deplorable situation." Then MacDonald turned briskly to a suggested agenda for adopting the new system. Since the plan imposed obligations on Germany that went beyond those stipulated in the Treaty of Versailles, a "protocol" would be needed to specify precise dates for economic evacuation of the Ruhr and for withdrawal of the various measures used to enforce the policy of productive pledges. This protocol had to be negotiated directly with the Germans. The international bankers, MacDonald hinted, might decline to float a loan without military evacuation of the Ruhr also.[150]

Finally, the prime minister addressed himself to Belgium's position, a matter "of the utmost practical importance, but of a delicate character." If for some reason Belgium felt compelled to continue its support of Poincaré's policy, a deadlock might ensue at the forthcoming conference—an eventuality that could not be contemplated without dismay. Sir Eyre Crowe pressed the point home. If the French premier, contrary to his experience at previous conferences, found himself confronted by Belgium and Italy, joined with Great Britain in united opposition, would he not "see the wisdom of bowing to the moral forces arrayed against him"?

150. Even before the Dawes Committee submitted its report, Governor Montagu Norman of the Bank of England had declared flatly that British financiers would advance no money "until the French are out of the Ruhr bag and baggage" (F.O. 371/9825: C 4769/G). By early May, Norman professed to know quite definitely that bankers in New York as well as London would insist on military evacuation to improve security for the proposed loan. Although the American market was likely to take guidance from the City when the question arose, in fact neither J. P. Morgan nor other New York bankers had demanded military evacuation at this time (Kellogg to State Department, 6 May 1924, U.S. 462.00R 296/318). The British Treasury, on the other hand, had strongly endorsed Norman's call for immediate withdrawal of the troops (Niemeyer memorandum, 14 April 1924, F.O. 371/9740: C 6331/70/18).

These encounters emphasized Great Britain's firm resolve to regain the diplomatic initiative in European affairs which it had not possessed since France's march into the Ruhr fifteen months before, and its determination to liquidate that operation on its own terms.[151] To this end, MacDonald next arranged a personal meeting with Poincaré. The French premier accepted an invitation to visit Chequers immediately after the elections of 11 May.[152]

To what extent would he have been able to hold firm in the difficult negotiations that lay ahead? It is not possible to answer precisely, since after the defeat of the Bloc National at the polls, Poincaré gave notice of his intention to resign and felt obliged to cancel his trip to England.[153] Instead, he sent MacDonald a formal statement of his position. Cordial in form, his missive represented in substance a vigorous reiteration of minimum French demands on five key points: productive pledges, military occupation, future sanctions, the railway *Régie*, and French security.[154]

On economic evacuation Poincaré retreated somewhat, now conceding that the economic hold on the Ruhr should cease on the very day that Germany "carried out the suggestions of the Experts in their entirety and obeyed their directions." But he still insisted on maintaining some form of inconspicuous military occupation for an indefinite period. The attempt to get Germany's "free consent" had always led to disappointment in the past, and Poincaré refused to place reliance on that nation's signature of a protocol. "We think it prudent to preserve guarantees," he stated, and to remain "in a position to take back pledges in the event, which unfortunately is not impossible, of Germany's defaulting again on its obligation to make reparation." In a later public elucidation, he explained that he did not expect French troops to remain in the Ruhr twenty-five years or more. Their continued presence for the time being, however, might spur Germany to commercialize the railway and industrial bonds issued under the Experts' Plan—in other words, to pay France in capital rather than annuities in order to get rid of the troops.[155]

If England declined to commit itself regarding future sanctions, Poincaré made clear, his own nation had to reserve the right to act unilaterally. He demanded that some method be found to continue the railway *Régie*. Finally, he raised the question of security, though in-

151. Central Department memorandum [by J. C. Sterndale Bennett], "The Objects of His Majesty's Government," 23 April 1924, F.O. 371/9741: C 6671/70/18.

152. R. Poincaré, "Récit historique," in Suarez, *Herriot*, p. 275; also Lord Crewe to MacDonald, 9 May 1924, F.O. 371/9744: C 7592/70/18.

153. Saint-Aulaire to MacDonald, 13 May 1924, F.O. 371/9744: C 7852/70/18.

154. See Poincaré to MacDonald, 14 May 1924; also later letters of 15 and 25 May 1924, and MacDonald's letters to Poincaré, 11 and 23 May 1924, complete correspondence published in London *Times*, 29 May; *Le Temps*, 30 May 1924; and in *L'Europe nouvelle*, 14 June 1924, pp. 773–74.

155. See Poincaré's later explanation in *J.O.S. Déb.*, 10 July 1924, pp. 1018–38.

directly, by calling attention to reports from the Interallied Military Control Commission which proved that Germany was "deliberately violating" the military stipulations of the treaty. Recalling once more the failure of Britain and America to make good the security guarantees promised France at Versailles, he called for further discussion to remedy a deficiency that "might be fatal to the peace of the world when the Allied armies came to evacuate the Rhineland."[156]

Poincaré was not appealing obliquely here for consideration of the kind of Anglo-French security pact that had aborted in 1922, for he thought it tactically unwise to confound the questions of reparations and security at this point.[157] Nor did he appear to be bidding primarily for full-scale resumption of armaments control. Although General Nollet, president of the Control Commission, had recently prepared a graphic report outlining the scope of German rearmament, those in close touch with the commission's work understood that "the era of great material results had passed" and that even the most strenuous diplomatic efforts would not now impede Germany's slow recovery of its military capabilities.[158] In all likelihood, Poincaré aimed essentially to lay the groundwork for summoning Great Britain to continue occupation of the Cologne bridgehead in the Rhineland past 10 January 1925, the date scheduled for evacuation if Germany fulfilled its various obligations under the Versailles treaty.

At first glance, it appears that Poincaré defended his legal dossier with habitual tenacity and attention to detail, and with undiminished vigor, up to the very end of his tenure at the Quai d'Orsay. The tenor of diplomatic conversations in April and May insufficiently mirrors the extent to which French policymakers, pressed by the imperfectly resolved domestic financial crisis, felt compelled to make concessions in order to reach a settlement. Some students of the period have concluded, in fact, that because the franc had recovered and because direct exploitation of the Ruhr remained temporarily profitable, France held "all the trumps in its hand" in the forthcoming negotiations.[159] This conclusion obscures the true situation.

The contemporary French press interpreted the Herriot government's accession to power in June as marking a fundamental departure from previous foreign policy, and it saw in ideology the motivating force behind the change. The press of the left and of the right each had compelling political reasons for portraying developments in this fashion. The leading Cartel press organs, *L'Oeuvre* and *Le Quotidien*, continued unabated their campaign for a new spirit in foreign affairs, based on the

156. Poincaré to MacDonald, 14 May 1924, *Le Temps*, 30 May 1924.

157. *J.O.S. Déb.*, 10 July 1924, pp. 1018–38.

158. General [Charles] Nollet, *Une Expérience de désarmement: Cinq ans de contrôle militaire en Allemagne* (Paris, 1932), pp. 155–56.

159. For example Bardoux, *L'Expérience de 1924*, pp. 180–81.

longing to which Herriot had given such dramatic and eloquent expression during the election campaign, for "peace, real peace, the good peace, peace with all."[160] They considered Herriot's concessions a relatively unimportant price to pay for an improvement in international understanding and even morally desirable in themselves.[161] On the right, informed journalists such as Pertinax of *L'Echo de Paris* stood ready with chapter and verse from Poincaré's public statements, and with his declared position of 14 May as a yardstick, to ascribe successive French concessions to Herriot's incompetence as a diplomat and to the Cartel's naively pacifist principles.[162]

To be sure, foreign officials correctly expected that it would prove somewhat easier to deal with Herriot than with his predecessor. MacDonald, at first inclined to pursue discussions during the interregnum in France with a view to bending Poincaré to a more moderate course before the latter went into opposition, decided after receipt of the 14 May letter to await a more pliable successor; he broke off correspondence, pleading the "great pressure of work."[163] In any case, however, financial and economic exigency would have severely limited the policy options of any French government. The failure of high-quality news media in France to address such problems in a serious way reflected a deficient appreciation and inadequate understanding of economic issues even by the more sophisticated social strata in the population.

Though Poincaré took a hard line in preliminary negotiations, it does not follow that if he had remained in power, he would ultimately have escaped the conditions imposed on Herriot. Belying his reputation abroad for inflexibility, Poincaré invariably proceeded with prudence bordering on timidity and tried to avoid taking diplomatic stands disproportionate to his country's resources. Even in conference with the wily Lloyd George over the Near East and over reparations during the first year of his ministry, he had often cited legal precedents with the greatest vigor just when preparing a tactical retreat on substantive issues. The circumspection of his speeches regarding Herriot's diplomatic efforts at the London Conference suggests that there too he would have made drastic concessions rather than allow negotiations to break down.[164]

Additional evidence supports this interpretation. At the very moment when Poincaré was assertively maintaining his position vis-à-vis MacDonald, the chief French reparations specialist, Jacques Seydoux, was confidentially reminding his colleagues in the Paris ministries that they

160. *Le Quotidien*, 10 May 1924.

161. *Le Quotidien* and *L'Oeuvre*, 17 June–31 August 1924.

162. See his daily articles in *L'Echo de Paris* from 22 June to 31 August 1924.

163. MacDonald minute, 17 May 1924, F.O. 371/9745: C 7989/70/18; also his explanations to the American ambassador, Kellogg to State Department, 16 May 1924, U.S. 462.00R 296/338; and MacDonald to Poincaré, 23 May 1924, London *Times*, 29 May 1924.

164. *J.O.S. Déb.*, 10 July 1924, pp. 1018–38; *J.O.S. Déb.*, 26 August 1924, pp. 1295–1314.

had yet to hear from the international bankers who would have to float the Dawes loan. The bankers, Seydoux warned on 10 May, would probably "set forth a series of conditions to which we shall have to yield, for all resistance will be met by the answer: the lenders will not come forward." With uncommon prescience he expressed concern that the bankers might prove even "more demanding than the British government concerning the political and economic liberation of the occupied territories." By the end of May, Seydoux had become still more pessimistic. He now predicted that British bankers would settle for nothing less than complete military evacuation of the Ruhr.[165]

Commercial Constraints on French Policy

For commercial reasons alone France needed almost desperately to reach a satisfactory settlement with Germany. The Treaty of Versailles had compelled the Reich to grant duty-free entry to goods from Alsace-Lorraine (and also from the Saar) and most-favored-nation treatment to all French imports for a period of five years. These measures were designed to give France time to reorient markets in the areas reannexed or placed under French administration and to coordinate the economy of these areas with that of France as a whole. The treaty stipulated that Germany would regain unrestricted freedom to determine its tariff policy on 10 January 1925, unless the League of Nations Council unanimously agreed a year earlier to extend France's privileges.

The five-year grace period, however, had not proved long enough to reintegrate Alsace-Lorraine's industry into the French economy. Metallurgical products, textiles, machine tools, automotive products, wine, agricultural commodities, and a host of other goods from these provinces continued to find their principal markets in Germany. If the Reich effectively closed its borders by erecting a prohibitive tariff, severe economic distress would grip the whole area. The reimposition of French administration—with all its bureaucratic peculiarities—following half a century of German rule had already stirred nascent impulses toward autonomy in Alsace. A regional economic depression could not fail to exacerbate local resentment, and the French government, which before the war had long portrayed the region as groaning under the Teutonic yoke, feared potential embarrassment. France faced even greater difficulty in the Saar. There a plebiscite scheduled after fifteen years' administration by the League of Nations would almost certainly return sovereignty to Germany, unless the area could in the interim be bound economically to France.[166]

165. Seydoux memoranda quoted by Weill-Raynal, *Les Réparations allemandes*, 3:63.

166. For a comparatively frank discussion of the political side of these problems, see speeches by former commerce minister Lucien Dior and Finance Minister Etienne Clémentel, *J.O.C. Déb.*, 29 December 1924, pp. 4892–4900, and *J.O.C. Déb.*, 12 November 1925,

Since 1920 the French Commerce Ministry and the Quai d'Orsay had kept up a running feud over what should be done to ensure Alsace-Lorraine's industrial future. The Commerce Ministry had ritually insisted that France petition the League of Nations Council for extension of free entry rights, or at least for a duty-free quota applying to specified quantities of distress goods. The Foreign Ministry had taken the view that if France appealed to the League and received an altogether likely rebuff, the exposure of weakness would put the nation in a poor position to begin direct negotiations with Germany. Some Foreign Ministry officials, Jacques Seydoux in particular, had also advanced a broader consideration. The temporary advantages accorded France under the treaty were inflexible; by stirring German resentment, they led to a partial boycott and the effective stifling of private trade. Seydoux believed that France's long-run advantage lay in seeking a trade agreement with Germany on an equitable and mutually acceptable basis, covering a large range of products though stopping short of unrestricted most-favored-nation treatment for the Reich. If France modified its nearly prohibitive tariff against German goods and held out the prospect of substantial markets, he had hoped, the German government and industrialists might cease to place obstacles in the way of reparations in kind.

To be sure, protectionist sentiment in France remained strong. Small-scale French industries feared competition from more efficient German firms. In the face of organized domestic pressure, French negotiators might not have obtained a mandate permitting them sufficient flexibility to make an agreement possible. But as it turned out, the German industrialists were the ones who backed out of the negotiations arranged by Seydoux for July 1920. Then in the fall of 1921, when the French government once again put forth a serious bid for commercial talks, the Germans, acting on the assumption that the French would make inadequate concessions, handled the overture in a "dilatory way."[167]

---

pp. 3678–79. This account draws also on the files of the head of the economic section at the German Foreign Ministry, Handakten Karl Ritter–Frankreich (June 1922–October 1925), G.F.M. L177/4079–4080. For the ambivalent attitudes of some Alsatians, see Jean-Claude Delbreil, *Les Catholiques français et les tentatives de rapprochement franco-allemand, 1920–1933* (Metz, 1972). On the Saar, see Sarah Wambaugh, *The Saar Plebiscite* (Cambridge, Mass., 1940), pp. 77–103; Laing Gray Cowan, *France and the Saar, 1680–1948* (New York, 1950), pp. 121–70; and Michael T. Florinsky, *The Saar Struggle* (New York, 1934), pp. 1–85.

167. See the extensive correspondence between the Foreign and Commerce ministries, 1920–24, in the dossier "Négociations franco-allemandes," F¹²/8860, Ministère du Commerce et de l'Industrie, Archives Nationales, Paris. For an angry summary of the Commerce Ministry view, see Director of Trade Agreements Daniel Serruys's "Note pour le ministre" [May 1924], F¹²/8864. Seydoux outlined his position in an anonymous article, "L'Accord commercial avec l'Allemagne," *L'Europe nouvelle*, 23 August 1924, pp. 1080–82; reprinted in his posthumous collection, *De Versailles au plan Young* (Paris, 1932), pp. 148–57; and in statements to German Embassy officials, e.g., Hoesch tel., 21 May 1924, BA, R 43 I/41/481–483. On French efforts to negotiate in 1920 see Ambassador Wilhelm Mayer's

Once Poincaré became premier, these efforts at direct negotiations had ended. Yet even Lucien Dior, who had served as Briand's commerce minister and continued in office under Poincaré, ultimately recognized how dim were the prospects for his preferred alternative, an appeal to the League Council. If Great Britain withstood heavy pressure from domestic textile interests and refrained from imposing a veto, the several neutral countries on the Council would nonetheless remain ill-disposed to according France advantages at the expense of their own export industries.

Dior's director of trade agreements, Daniel Serruys, made a searching review of the whole problem in 1923. Seydoux and Serruys had long been bureaucratic rivals and were loath to admit agreement on anything. Without entirely adopting Seydoux's broader perspective, however, Serruys and his chief finally came around to the conclusion that only one policy offered any chance of success—"to talk directly with Germany, since we were protected by the mortgage of the Ruhr." Between October and December 1923, Dior implored Poincaré at least four times to take advantage of France's temporary dominance to impose upon Germany a minimum three-year extension of the status quo. Such an interim arrangement would have allowed time to redirect Alsace-Lorraine's economy toward the French and colonial markets, thereby putting France in a better position for subsequent general trade negotiations.[168] But Poincaré had turned a deaf ear to these appeals. The premier judged—no doubt correctly—that to put such economic pressure on Germany, even if it succeeded, would complicate his diplomatic relations with England.[169] It would surely have weakened his legal argument that France had undertaken and maintained the Ruhr occupation as a sanction solely because of Germany's default on its reparations obligations.

Still, France had let pass the most favorable moment for taking the initiative in negotiations for a trade treaty. An interministerial committee formed in Berlin in March 1924 under Economics Minister Eduard Hamm concluded that Germany would now enter trade negotiations with France in "a relatively strong position." Germany felt sufficiently reinvigorated to insist, prerequisite to beginning negotiations, on settlement of the "Rhine-Ruhr question," and also—notwithstanding France's traditional

memorandum of 18 May 1921, G.F.M. L1492/5352/L436835–853; on the similar French endeavor in 1921, see Ritter's "Aufzeichnung betr. deutsch-französische Wirtschaftsverhandlungen," 28 April 1924, G.F.M. L177/4079/L051724–726.

168. Minister of Commerce to President of the Council, 25 October, 13 and 26 November, 15 December 1923, F12/8860; quoted in part and interpreted by Dior in *J.O.C. Déb.*, 29 December 1924, pp. 4898–99.

169. See President of the Council [written by Seydoux] to Minister of Commerce, 5 December 1923, 16 January 1924, F12/8860; and Serruys's rejoinder in his May 1924 "Note pour le ministre," F12/8864.

protectionist tariff policy—on French agreement in principle to accord Germany most-favored-nation treatment on all products.[170]

Competition in Steel and Its Political Implications

In the light of technology available in the 1920s, steel production provided the single most important determinant of an industrial nation's economic strength and in the long run of its military power. The French iron and steel industry found itself in an especially vulnerable position.[171] Its commercial survival largely depended on an agreement with German heavy industry. By recovering Lorraine as a result of the war, France had doubled its iron ore reserves and plant capacity for pig iron production. But the coking coal necessary for smelting the ore, as well as the rolling mills and mechanical engineering industries that transformed the semifinished materials (billets, blooms, and bars) into finished products (wire rods, reinforcement bars, sheet metal, rails, etc.), remained in Germany. France possessed neither the "head" nor the "tail" of the industry, as the strong-willed, brilliant Robert Pinot, secretary-general of the Comité des Forges (the steel industry trade association), put it picturesquely.[172]

Most of the coal produced in France and the Saar was unsuitable for coking. Because France lacked a sophisticated chemical industry to utilize the by-products of the coking process, furthermore, prohibitively high costs deterred development even of such domestic coking coal resources as existed. Since domestic demand for metallurgical products was relatively inelastic, French manufacturers had no choice but to seek outlets for their increased steel production abroad. World steel output

170. "Handelsvertragsverhandlungen mit Frankreich," April 1924, G.F.M. L177/4079/L051721–723.

171. The literature on metallurgical problems is vast though not entirely satisfactory. Important monographs include Ferdinand Friedensburg, *Kohle und Eisen im Weltkriege und in den Friedensschlüssen* (Munich and Berlin, 1934); M. Brelet, *La Crise de la métallurgie: La Politique économique et sociale du Comité des Forges* (Paris, 1923); Henri Flu, *Les Comptoirs métallurgiques d'après-guerre, 1919–1922* (Lyon, 1924); J. Levainville, *L'Industrie de fer en France* (Paris, 1922); Paul Berkenkopf, *Die Entwicklung und die Lage der lothringisch-luxemburgischen Grosseisenindustrie seit dem Weltkriege* (Jena, 1925); Hans J. Schneider, *Der Wiederaufbau der Grosseisenindustrie an Rhein und Ruhr* (Berlin, n.d. [1931?]); C. Nattan-Larrier, *La Production sidérurgique de l'Europe continentale et l'entente internationale de l'acier* (Paris, 1929); Paul Ufermann, *Der deutsche Stahltrust* (Berlin, 1927); Guy Greer, *The Ruhr-Lorraine Industrial Problem* (New York, 1925); W. F. Ogburn and William Jaffé, *The Economic Development of Post-War France* (New York, 1929).

This account also rests heavily on the Archives de Pont-à-Mousson, particularly Camille Cavallier's notes on Comité des Forges meetings in PAM/7245–46; and on Robert Pinot's manuscript, "La Métallurgie lorraine et le charbon allemand," originally a lecture at the Ecole de Guerre, 5 April 1924, copies in PAM/7360 and in the Robert Pinot Papers, in family possession, Paris. Jacques Pinot of Lorraine-Escaut & Cie added details for the period during which he served as an aide to his father in a personal interview on 26 February 1965. For the German point of view, see Handakten Karl Ritter, Sachgebiet Industrie, G.F.M. L1491/5352/L436757–820, L1494/5352/L436881–890, L1495/5352/L436898–953.

172. Interview with Jacques Pinot, 26 February 1965.

had expanded so rapidly during the war, however, that overcapacity now plagued the industry in nearly every country. France could compete successfully on foreign markets only if it could procure reliable coke supplies at a cost low enough to allow the sale of French pig iron and crude steel at the depressed world price level. This problem affected metallurgy throughout France, not only in reannexed Lorraine. In fact, the older mills in the center of France and on the northern littoral—the traditional consumers of domestic coke—labored under the highest production costs of all. If the coke shortage worsened, these firms faced the gravest risk of ruin, and their bankruptcy would leave the country completely dependent on an exposed metallurgical industry uncomfortably close to the German border. The marketing of semiproducts presented a problem even more acute than that of assuring coke supplies. Excellent rail and canal transport facilities and the duty-free quota created a natural market for Lorraine "semis" in the transformation industry of the Rhineland and south Germany. But the Reich would possess the power to cut this whole market off when it recovered tariff sovereignty in 1925.

Fully cognizant of their precarious position, Pinot and his steel industry colleagues had long considered broad agreement among the principal countries producing metallurgical products the "most essential" element of a viable reparations settlement—in turn a prerequisite for the reestablishment of stable economic conditions in Europe. To make Germany live up to the letter of its treaty obligations was certainly desirable, the leadership of the Comité des Forges conceded, yet to make the pragmatic arrangement most advantageous for the French economy as a whole was still more important, even if this required a certain flexibility with regard to legal formulae. Among themselves, steel men grumbled continually about the muddling French bureaucracy's failure to address itself realistically to their industry's problems and about Poincaré's narrowly focused accountant's approach to reparations.[173] The premier had conspicuously failed to consult with anyone from the steel industry before deciding on the Ruhr occupation. Members of the Comité des Forges directorate knew "absolutely nothing" more about Poincaré's objectives in the Ruhr than what they read in the newspapers, and many of them remained distinctly skeptical, as steel-pipe manufacturer Camille Cavallier put it, whether an occupation designed to "conquer the people of the Ruhr with smiles, becoming manners, . . . potatoes, and sausages" would do much to solve France's coal and coke problems.[174]

Poincaré did not deny the desirability of accords among industrialists,

173. Comité des Forges–Commission de Direction, comptes rendus sommaires, 20 July, 16 November 1922, PAM/7246.

174. Camille Cavallier to Robert Pinot, 13 January 1923, PAM/7246.

but he preferred to postpone them until a general reparations settlement had been achieved. Private accords negotiated outside such a framework, he feared, might enrich "special interests" at the expense of the French public whose reparations equity he was pledged to defend.[175] Like most republican statesmen of his generation, Poincaré lacked training in economics. His background and outlook did not dispose him to pay close attention to industry's special needs, and he tended to hold unreasonable suspicions of big business. In this case, however, rational considerations of state fueled his mistrust of private agreements among metallurgists. Before and even during the Ruhr occupation, representatives of the Comité des Forges had approached their counterparts in the Verein Deutscher Eisen- und Stahlindustrieller on numerous occasions. The Germans had declined to negotiate seriously on a commercial basis unless the Comité des Forges could first induce the French government to make political concessions, such as termination of the Rhineland occupation, return of the Saar, and a radical reduction of the reparations bill.[176] German industrialists excercised such enormous power over both foreign and domestic policy in their own country that for a long time they failed to realize how limited was the influence wielded by the Comité des Forges in France.[177]

No French government—especially not that of Poincaré—could have acceded voluntarily to the demands posed by German industry. Once the French army obtained a firm foothold in the Ruhr, the Comité des Forges began to discuss alternative schemes for unilaterally imposing satisfactory terms on the Germans. But the metallurgists divided amongst themselves. Squabbling constantly over differential freight rates, an equitable price structure for their national cartel, and over division of the scarce coke resources extracted from the Ruhr, the steel magnates could scarcely ever agree on anything except the rapacity of

175. For a précis of Poincaré's views, see Hoesch to Schubert, 1 March 1924, G.F.M. L1491/5352/L436764–768.

176. For details of these negotiations, see "Förderung internationaler Wirtschaftsbeziehungen, Industrielle Verständigung mit Frankreich, 1922–31," and "Bestrebungen zur Bildung eines internationalen Eisenkartells, 1921–26," respectively vols. 255, 261–62 of BA, R 13 I, Verein Deutscher Eisen- und Stahlindustrieller. For the government perspective, see "Industrielle Beziehungen Frankreichs zu Deutschland," G.F. M. L1495/5352; and for the French side, PAM/19062.

177. See BA, R 13 I/261 for favorable comment by German steel magnates in 1922 on allegations by French socialist and communist journalists purporting to identify the secret "real government" of France at the rue de Madrid headquarters of the Comité des Forges. Only much later did the Germans correct this impression. When negotiations for a steel cartel began in earnest in 1925, German metallurgists were startled to learn that the Comité des Forges, in Fritz Thyssen's words, was "completely dependent" on the French government and possessed little power. See Thyssen's report on his Paris negotiations, 2 April 1925, vol. 400101222/2, Historisches Archiv, Gutehoffnungshütte, Oberhausen (hereafter cited as GHH, volume number). See also a similar reaction by Bruno Bruhn, "Entstehung und Bedeutung der westeuropäischen Eisenverträge," *Kölnische Zeitung*, 24 October 1926, copy in BA, R 13 I/270.

French coal mine owners. In April 1923 the representatives of Schneider-Creusot, the largest firm in the center of France, actually withdrew from the Comité des Forges in protest against its alleged domination by the Wendel interests of Lorraine, and the dissatisfaction did not stop there: two large firms in eastern France considered following Schneider's example.[178]

Throughout the spring and summer of 1923, the remaining members of the steelmakers' group hotly debated possible means for forcing Germany to transfer control over coal and coke resources to France. Robert Pinot's earlier moderate proposal of a 25 percent "participation" in the stock of selected German coal firms now appeared inadequate to many French steel executives; at the other extreme, Camille Cavallier favored "castrating" the Germans, "not physically, but economically, by taking away from them their two vital centers, Silesia and Westphalia."[179] By October most of the steelmakers had gravitated toward two competing positions. François de Wendel, president of the Comité des Forges, advocated erection of a permanent customs barrier on the Rhine, including a thirty-kilometer bridgehead around Duisburg on the right bank. German coal producers within this area, forbidden to ship coke to unoccupied Germany but left with full title to their mines, would find themselves obliged by natural economic forces to seek markets in France. Two vice-presidents of the steelmakers' association, Léon-Lévy of the Hauts-Fourneaux de Rouen and Théodore Laurent of the Aciéries de Rombas, proposed an alternative that won the adherence of a majority of their colleagues. This alternate plan called for total surrender to the French state of enough Ruhr mines to meet French needs—roughly an additional 6.5 million tons of coke annually. The Germans would receive compensation for the transfer of ownership in the form of a credit on their reparations account. The French government would lease the mines to a syndicate of French steel firms on advantageous terms. If the latter could obtain bargain-price coke and thereby drastically lower production costs, they could begin to sell their surplus steel abroad, thus solving the overcapacity problem that had plagued their mills.[180]

In view of Poincaré's distrust of the steel interests and his determination not to alienate England, how could the Comité des Forges hope to win their government's support for either of its proposals? Deploring Pinot's penchant for "clever" maneuvering and for trying "to get things without getting them, or without seeming to do so," Camille Cavallier demanded bold action. Since the government would need their coopera-

178. Comité des Forges–Commission de Direction, compte rendu sommaire, 19 April 1923; also "Note de service" for Camille Cavallier, 23 May 1923, PAM/7246.

179. Robert Pinot, "La Sidérurgie française et la question du règlement des réparations" [February 1923], Cavallier to Pinot, 14 February 1923, both in PAM/7246; Cavallier to Maurice Schwob, 6 April 1923, PAM/7361.

180. Comité des Forges–Commission de Direction, compte rendu sommaire, 29 October 1923, PAM/7246.

tion to run the mines profitably in order to make the Ruhr occupation pay, he contended, the steelmakers could for once negotiate with official Paris "as an equal, and not as a child."[181] But this call for militancy lacked realism. France remained, after all, a semi-industrialized country in mentality if not in fact. Many ministers so feared association in the public mind with reputedly predatory business interests that they hesitated before yielding even a hearing to the views of heavy industry.

Pinot prepared, therefore, a characteristically urbane, low-key appeal for government intervention. Noting that "only conditions imposed by a diplomatic act" could secure France's coke supplies, he evenhandedly set forth the advantages and disadvantages of the contending positions within the Comité des Forges.[182] But neither by cajolery nor by a show of business muscle was Poincaré to be deflected from his intended diplomatic course. The premier paid little heed to the demands of the Comité des Forges. And by the end of 1923, the leaders of that body had moderated their appetites. Reasonably priced German coke became available on an interim basis as a result of the M.I.C.U.M. agreements; at the same time the hard-pressed French metallurgists profited from the temporary shutdown of their competitors' blast furnaces in the Ruhr.[183] Once again the steelmakers began to explore the two possible business routes for solving their problems: direct negotiation on a commercial basis with German industrialists and restriction of world metallurgical output through revival of the prewar international steel cartel.[184]

German industrialists meanwhile bided their time despite their own difficulties during the dark weeks of autumn 1923 when the Reich itself seemed on the brink of dissolution. In the face of France's temporary political dominance, they maintained the faith that economic superiority would prove decisive eventually. Notwithstanding what one German steel executive was to call "all the foolish twaddle about the marriage of German coal and French iron ore,"[185] Germany actually had no pressing need for France's metallurgical products. Ruhr steelmakers had not concealed their bitterness at the loss of their Lorraine minette ore properties. With the compensation paid by the German government they had rationalized and adapted their smelters for the use of scrap steel and of higher grade iron ore from Sweden, Canada, and Spain. "We don't need

181. Compte rendu of 29 October 1923, ibid.; see also Cavallier's earlier objection to Pinot's "Parisian" tactics, Cavallier to Pinot, 29 April 1923, PAM/7246.

182. Robert Pinot note [for the President of the Council], 13 November 1923, PAM/7245; discussion and adoption at meeting of Comité des Forges, compte rendu sommaire, 15 November 1923, PAM/7246.

183. See Pinot's explanation as summarized in Hoesch to Schubert, 1 March 1924, G.F.M. L1491/5352/L436764–768.

184. Comité des Forges–Commission de Direction, compte rendu sommaire, 20 December 1923, 17 January 1924, PAM/7245.

185. Bruno Bruhn, "Entstehung und Bedeutung der westeuropäischen Eisenverträge," *Kölnische Zeitung*, 24 October 1926, copy in BA, R 13 I/270.

any minette ore now," German industrialist Peter Klöckner exulted to fellow steel magnates as early as 1922; "let [the French] choke on it."[186] The German inflation, moreover, enabled the great *Konzerne* to pursue a program of heavy capital investment in the mills for producing semiproducts, and they used the period of enforced plant idleness during the Ruhr occupation to complete this investment program.[187] By the spring of 1924, consequently, German heavy industry could boast that it stood ready to supply all the requirements of south and west Germany's finishing and mechanical engineering industries with its own domestic semiproduct production. J. Wilhelm Reichert, chief executive officer of the German steelmakers' association, thereupon proposed that when Germany recovered its tariff sovereignty, it should at once enact a prohibitive tariff to keep out pig iron and semiproducts coming from France.[188]

Clearly, if French metallurgy could not reach some agreement with German heavy industry while France held the upper hand in the Ruhr, it would face even greater difficulty in obtaining satisfactory terms later on. The limited scope of the Dawes Committee's work deeply distressed Robert Pinot. The very terms of reference governing the Experts' appointment foreordained that their investigation would focus on the banking and financial aspect of reparations, to the complete exclusion of related business and industrial problems.[189] In February and March 1924 the Comité des Forges made a last-ditch attempt to remedy this deficiency by opening negotiations with representatives of Ruhr coal magnate Hugo Stinnes. Grudgingly Poincaré permitted Jacques Seydoux to monitor and encourage these exploratory discussions. The premier remained as reluctant as ever to sanction private negotiations that might infringe on the government's exclusive responsibility to determine public policy; hence, his tolerance of Seydoux's initiative marked the endeavor with a new seriousness.

The Comité des Forges hammered out a proposal tempered to meet the most obvious objections of the German and British governments. This proposal amalgamated certain features of Léon-Lévy's earlier plan—couched in suitably attenuated form—with elements designed to regulate European steel production as a whole. The steelmakers set forth four desiderata. The French government should acquire on reparations ac-

186. "Aufzeichnung vom 27. April 1922 betreffend Internationales Eisenkartell," BA, R 13 I/261.

187. Bruno Bruhn, "Eisen und Stahl in den deutsch-französischen Wirtschaftsverhandlungen," *Deutsche Allgemeine Zeitung*, 4 February 1925, copy in BA, R 13 I/270; also interview given by Robert Pinot to Sanford Griffith of the *Wall Street Journal* on 29 July 1924, transcript in Pinot Papers.

188. See Reichert's official proposal of 26 May 1924, prepared after oral representations to Reich Economics Minister Eduard Hamm, in G.F.M. L177/4079/L051714–719.

189. Robert Pinot, "La Métallurgie lorraine et le charbon allemand," pp. 42–50, Pinot Papers.

count either full ownership or participatory shares in German coal mines capable of supplying annually the 4.5 million tons of coke that Lorraine had customarily obtained from the Ruhr before the war. A private long-term contract should provide for exchange of an additional 2.5 million tons of coke annually for an equivalent tonnage of Lorraine iron ore. Another long-term contract should guarantee the purchase of French semiproducts by the finishing industries on the right bank of the Rhine and ensure the exemption of these "semis" from German customs duty. Finally, the European steel-producing nations should conclude an agreement dividing up the market for rails as a first step toward formation of an international steel cartel. This final provision underscored the French metallurgists' willingness to take account of British steel interests, and in early March the Comité des Forges initiated preparatory talks with metallurgists from England, Belgium, and Luxembourg to seek their approval for the scheme.[190]

Some of the German coal magnates were willing to talk further. They rejected out of hand any thought of a one-sided transfer of shares in coal properties on reparations account. But a profitable private contract for coke delivery represented a more interesting proposition, since the German coal mine owners foresaw an eventual surplus of that commodity.[191] Their government, however, declined to authorize the coal industry leaders to continue the negotiations. Stresemann wished to put pressure on the French government to expedite the Experts' Report; he also objected on the ground that a special arrangement with French industry would offend English banking groups on whose support he counted to sustain the new German gold note bank.[192] Most of the German industrialists, in any case, were quite prepared to wait. Stinnes felt pressed to arrange a deal because his overextended conglomerate was experiencing a liquidity crisis, but he fell mortally ill. His colleagues in heavy industry calculated that their position would improve after conclusion of a reparations settlement and the now predictable collapse of the M.I.C.U.M. accords. Before entering into serious conference with

190. President of the Council to French delegate to the Reparation Commission, 13 March 1924, enclosing memoranda by Robert Pinot, 5 and 7 March 1924, recounting negotiations with the Germans, F[30]/1277; also Comité des Forges–Commission de Direction, compte rendu sommaire, 20 March 1924, PAM/7245; and from the German side, "Sonderverhandlungen der Rhein-Ruhr Industriellen mit den Besatzungsmächten," BA, R 43 I/454/52–126; also G.F.M. L1491/5352/L436757–820. Erdmann, *Adenauer in der Rheinlandpolitik*, pp. 372–81, prints a few relevant documents, though his own narrative, pp. 179–84, is misleading. On the broader issues, see J. C. Carr and W. Taplin, *History of the British Steel Industry* (Cambridge, Mass., 1962), pp. 366–428, and Ervin Hexner, *The International Steel Cartel* (Chapel Hill, N.C., 1943).

191. Dr. Woltmann to Paul Reusch, 14 March 1924; also minutes of German coal mine owners' meeting, "Besprechung am 17. März in Essen," GHH 4001012008/0.

192. Hugo Stinnes to Vice Chancellor Karl Jarres, 12 March 1924, Peter Klöckner to Stresemann, 15 and 17 March 1924, G.F.M. L1491/5352/L436770–772, L436781–787; Alte Reichskanzlei, Kabinettsprotokolle, U.S. National Archives Microfilms T-120, Washington, D.C., 3491/1752/D759696–697.

the French, furthermore, they wanted time to consolidate their hold over the domestic transformation and finishing industries. And they correctly prognosticated that once Germany recovered its tariff sovereignty, they would have the upper hand in negotiations.[193] In return for satisfying some of the French industry's needs they might then well regain the unrivaled preeminence among European steel industries that they had enjoyed before the war.

In vain Robert Pinot continued to argue that the Comité des Forges plan, "far from being opposed to the Experts' system . . . constitutes a propitious complement to it."[194] After April 1924 French metallurgists were obliged to come to terms with dolorous realities. Until the powers had settled the purely financial component of the reparations imbroglio along the lines set forth by the Experts, no further progress could be made toward solving the problems of their own sector of the economy. Since German heavy industry refused to talk until after the economic evacuation of the Ruhr, French industry soon recognized that to retard the necessary accommodation would be counterproductive.[195] While Poincaré remained notably resistant to pressure from business interests, many of the groups on which he traditionally relied for parliamentary support were more responsive to the views of the business community. The discussions among steelmakers in 1924 prefigure future developments: they begin to explain why such broadly based support evolved in France for a policy of accommodation with Germany later in the decade. Pragmatists in business circles who—seeking to protect noncompetitive French industry—pursued economic understanding with Germany in order to lay the groundwork for international cartels offered prescriptions for foreign policy problems that more closely resembled those proposed by idealists of the left than either group would have been pleased to acknowledge.

Prospects at the End of the Poincaré Ministry

Various economic and financial forces thus effectively crippled French foreign policy at the end of the Poincaré ministry. The treasury's

193. See Kommerzienrat Paul Reusch's explanations to the Stahlwerksverband, 26 March 1924, GHH 400101222/0, and to the Verein Deutscher Eisen- und Stahlindustrieller, 28 March 1924, BA, R 13 I/255; also Reusch to Chancellor Marx, 29 March 1924, Reusch to Director Konrad Spies, 6 April 1924, and "Protokoll über die Besprechung mit Herrn Piérard," 26 June 1924, all in GHH 400101222/2.

194. Pinot, "La Métallurgie lorraine et le charbon allemand," p. 43, Pinot Papers.

195. On the evolution of French industry's attitudes in the spring and summer of 1924, see the correspondence and minutes of Comité des Forges meetings in PAM/7224, 7230, 7245. For confirmation that German industry understood the general nature of French steelmakers' views, see *Westeuropäische Wirtschaftskorrespondenz*, April-October 1924, copies in BA, R 13 I/261. Note also Seydoux's observations on the steel industry's problems, President of the Council [written by Seydoux] to French delegate to the Reparation Commission, 14 April 1924, F^{30}/582; and Seydoux's comments to the German ambassador, Hoesch tel., 21 May 1924, BA, R 43 I/41/481–483.

continuing difficulties and the precarious nature of the franc's recovery impelled reliance on international financial markets, thus forging the most binding fetters on the country's independence. Mounting domestic pressure for strict limitation on military expenditures also played a not inconsiderable role. By the end of 1923 the Ruhr occupation had become a paying proposition from the strictly bookkeeping point of view, but to garrison large numbers of troops there indefinitely grew politically impracticable. Financial necessity obliged the War Ministry to reduce French forces on the line in the Ruhr during the spring of 1924. The reduction was quiet but drastic: no more than one-fifth the number of troops which had occupied that region a year before still remained.[196] This corporal's guard, comparatively speaking, would not be able to control the Ruhr if German resistance revived. Finally, with the approach of the date—justly anticipated with trepidation—when Germany would recover its tariff sovereignty, the advantages of maintaining constraints had to be carefully balanced against the risks of retarding vital trade negotiations.

The decision to accept an "international solution" to the reparations problem thus emerged as the inescapable consequence of the Expert Committee's appointment in December 1923. Poincaré reserved his freedom of action upon a number of issues, but they were of relatively secondary import and often merely technical in nature. Foreign policy specialists in the ministries might deem it important to maintain residual military occupation of the Ruhr or the vestiges of the railway *Régie* as bargaining points. They might argue for preserving the prerogatives of the Reparation Commission and the right of France to take independent sanctions under contingent circumstances in the future. But it would be far from easy to persuade world opinion, not concerned with fine details, that upon such points depended the future of French civilization.

Privately, moreover, Poincaré and his professional staff expressed little optimism that the Ruhr could be effectively employed as a bargaining counter to gain substantial last-minute concessions from Great Britain on war debts or, even more essential, on French security. A realist could hardly expect meaningful progress on security matters, however polite the diplomatic exchanges, when Labour backbenchers and the MacDonald government's Liberal supporters regularly proclaimed in their weeklies that France represented the real menace to European peace, and when the British prime minister himself stated in an unguarded moment that he considered military security "a stupid idea."[197] Some hope remained for exploiting the Ruhr position to extract a temporary

196. François-André Paoli, *L'Armée française de 1919 à 1939*, vol. 2, *La Phase de fermeté* (Paris, 1972), p. 256a, annex 4.

197. MacDonald's speech at York, 19 April 1924, differing versions in the London *Times* and the *Daily Telegraph*, 21 April 1924; phrase also quoted by Lyman, *First Labour Government*, p. 170.

extension of the duty-free quota for certain products shipped from Alsace-Lorraine to Germany. Yet any attempt to link the Dawes Plan with far-reaching commercial concessions would in all likelihood have aroused such opposition from German industrialists as to diminish the prospects for steering the necessary enabling laws through the Reichstag.

Although circumstances thus severely circumscribed France's room for maneuver, whoever held the reins of responsibility at the Quai d'Orsay could still influence the course of events. Options in diplomacy are often narrow. Poincaré could have drawn on his experience and energy to present the best possible case for France at the London Conference. His departure from office on 1 June 1924 precluded that effort. At the time, indeed, his resignation was widely interpreted abroad as marking symbolically the end of France's unilateral determination to enforce Germany's strict conformity to obligations under the Treaty of Versailles.[198]

Poincaré did not look back with regret on any of his major foreign policy decisions. If anything, he reproached himself for having paid insufficient attention to the home front.[199] But the transition he perceived in the nation's mood preoccupied his thoughts. "Decidedly," he told his staff on the day after his electoral defeat, "the French are too tired to follow me."[200] Although resentment of higher taxes rather than disappointment with the fruits of the Ruhr occupation had tipped the election results, the outcome nonetheless called attention to the populace's growing desire for an end to militancy, struggle, and sacrifice without visible recompense. Jules Romains captured the prevailing spirit in a popular poem of the period:[201]

> We have strength barely enough
> For each day's task—
> That's all. We've got no more to give.
>
> So don't put yourself out
> To invent heroic burdens for us.
> I tell you plain that peace
> Is not that hard to find.

198. Saint-Aulaire, *Confession d'un vieux diplomate*, pp. 702–4.

199. Phipps to MacDonald, no. 1893, 30 August 1924, reporting Poincaré's private comments to political associates the previous May, F.O. 371/9820: C 13819/1288/18.

200. Jacques Chastenet, *Raymond Poincaré* (Paris, 1948), p. 260.

201. "Haine à la guerre," *Nouvelle revue française*, 1 May 1924, quoted also by *Le Progrès civique*, 5 July 1924. The original reads: "Nous avons assez de courage/Pour le travail de chaque jour . . . /Mais c'est tout. Nous n'en donnons plus.// . . . Ne prenez donc pas tant de peine/A forger des malheurs sublimes/Je vous assure que la paix/Est plus façile qu'on ne dit."

Chapter 7

Herriot Embattled: The British, the Germans, and the American Bankers

The Untried Pilot

In diplomacy as in finance, Edouard Herriot was an "untried pilot."[1] The new French premier was well-traveled, but he had not passed through the sobering school of long ministerial responsibility that had led his predecessor to understand the intractability of foreign policy problems. Herriot found it almost irresistibly tempting to believe that the flatulent rhetoric which evoked such enthusiastic applause at Sunday afternoon gatherings of Radical-Socialist militants could be translated readily into national policy. Dreaming nobly of "progress through reason," he aimed "little by little to orient politics toward science and ethics."[2] He considered the problem of reparations "one of morality even more than one of economics and finance." With regard to the wartime foe, he professed "no hostility—quite the contrary—for the immortal spirits of Beethoven and Goethe," and sought only to "dispel the shadow of Bismarck."[3]

Where Poincaré was sometimes accused of a failure to enlist world sympathies because of his punctilious insistence on the outdated written procedures of the old diplomacy, Herriot by contrast entertained exaggerated hopes of what might be achieved by frank discussion among statesmen at the highest level. A man of generous impulses, convivial and sentimental, Herriot loved even as president of the council to dazzle his staff with discursive literary talk over a bottle of good wine or with a

1. See the American ambassador's appraisal, Herrick to State Department, 7 June 1924, U.S. 851.002/109.

2. Edouard Herriot, "Les Traits essentiels de la doctrine du parti radical," *Le Progrès civique*, 26 April 1924.

3. Edouard Herriot, "The Program of Liberal France," *Foreign Affairs* 1 (June 1924): 559–60.

virtuoso performance of Mozart on the piano.[4] But he completely lacked the tough-minded combativeness and instinctive wiliness that render a statesman effective in international negotiations. Foreign diplomats were not slow to take the new premier's measure. "Herriot is the exact opposite of Poincaré," reported British Minister Eric Phipps. "Not only, as he himself said, has he nothing up his sleeve, but he has no sleeve. His whole attitude conveys the impression of . . . a man laying all his cards on the table. He has, of course, the defects of his qualities, for he fails to pick up the cards when the press come into the room."[5]

Herriot found no time to study the reparations problem closely in the weeks between the elections and his assumption of office. Throughout his ministerial tenure, he continued to exert active leadership in the Radical party, the largest in the Chamber. Driven by a constant need for approval and flattery, he derived considerable gratification from the easy camaraderie that accompanied his party duties. Accordingly, he gladly interrupted his work at the Quai d'Orsay to receive party and parliamentary delegations. He declined, moreover, to surrender official responsibility in his beloved Lyons, where he had served as mayor for close to twenty years. Despite the exigencies of national concerns he traveled down on the train almost every weekend to attend to the municipality's affairs. These multiple burdens would have overwhelmed even a disciplined man, and this unfortunately Herriot was not. Indeed, his proverbial lack of organization became a source of malicious amusement in Paris political circles: everyone knew that the cabinet would usually have to meet without a prepared agenda and that sessions would linger far into the night.[6]

A strong ministerial team might have compensated for some of these deficiencies. But Herriot chose his colleagues predominantly from the younger group in the Radical-Socialist party. Many of his appointees would carve out distinguished careers in the future, but few could boast substantial administrative experience at that time. Aside from Clémentel, only one minister enjoyed a national reputation. This was the nonpolitical General Charles Nollet,* president of the Interallied Military Con-

*Charles Marie Edouard Nollet, born 1865 in Marseille, graduate of the Ecole Polytechnique, became a career officer in the army; assistant professor of military history and tactics at the Ecole Supérieure de la Guerre, 1903; named military commandant of the Senate, where he established many political connections, 1914; served on the western front, in latter part of the war as commander of the Twelfth Army Corps; president of the Interallied Military Control Commission, 1919–24. Acclaimed as an officer of great distinction, Nollet was a firm republican, but—contrary to a widely held belief—not a pacifist. Having observed German secret rearmament at close hand, he aimed as war minister to "apply to the reorganization of the French army . . . the results of the experience" thus acquired.

4. See the testimony of Jules Laroche, who served as director of political affairs at the Foreign Ministry under Herriot, in *Au Quai d'Orsay avec Briand et Poincaré* (Paris, 1957), pp. 202–3; also Jacques Bardoux, *L'Expérience de 1924* (Paris, 1930), pp. 190–94.

5. Phipps to Sir Eyre Crowe, 15 June 1924, F.O. 371/10534: W 5043/115/17.

6. Louis Lévy, *Les Nuits du Cartel* (Paris, 1929). This account draws also upon Michel Soulié, *La Vie politique d'Edouard Herriot* (Paris, 1962); Edouard Herriot, *Jadis*, vol. 2, *D'une*

trol Commission, whom Herriot appointed to the rue St.-Dominique.

The initial reluctance of the Cartel government to rely on the judgment of the *hauts fonctionnaires* at the Quai d'Orsay also hobbled its effective operation. The Cartel press frequently charged that among the key diplomatic personnel many were lukewarm toward the republic. There existed little foundation for this allegation, but the diplomatic service had in fact long been the preserve of the rich and well born, of those claiming aristocratic or clerical backgrounds. With considerable plausibility, Cartel publicists could reproach the leading career officials for hostility to the "new diplomacy," deficient "democratic spirit," and for rather tepid enthusiasm in regard to the League of Nations and international channels of arbitration and mediation.[7] Under these circumstances, Herriot's personal entourage exercised unusual influence. Notable among them was the premier's *chef de cabinet*, Gaston Bergery.* A slim and pallid young man with darting eyes and intense ambitions whose icy reserve and staccato speech contrasted strikingly with the style of his chief, Bergery soon became known—in a misleading reference to Richelieu's gray eminence—as the "Père Joseph of Cartel diplomacy."[8]

*Gaston Bergery (1892–1974), trained as a specialist in international law; wounded at the battle of Champagne, wangled a post as interpreter with the British army for the balance of the war; translated for Loucheur at the Paris Peace Conference and with his backing then secured assignment as deputy secretary-general on the permanent staff of the Reparation Commission, 1919–24; rose rapidly in the Radical-Socialist hierarchy owing to Herriot's support, but later broke with him violently; Radical-Socialist deputy, 1928–34, defeated when he scandalized suburban housewives by campaigning with a provocatively dressed Schiaparelli model (accompanied everywhere by her pet monkey) and introducing the lady as his wife; founded Popular Front weekly, *La Flèche*; reelected to Chamber in 1936 and headed left-oriented *Front sociale* splinter party; strongly advocated collaboration with the Communists in 1936, accommodation with the Germans in 1940; appropriately named by Vichy as ambassador to Moscow, 1941, to Ankara, 1942–44; indicted after the liberation but won acquittal and resumed the practice of law, 1949. A pseudonymous writer of fiction as well as a brilliant journalist, Bergery demonstrated many talents but few moral commitments; he showed consistent loyalty only to his own personal advancement.

guerre à l'autre, 1914–1936 (Paris, 1952); Francis de Tarr, *The French Radical Party from Herriot to Mendès-France* (London, 1961); and particularly on Peter J. Larmour, *The French Radical Party in the 1930's* (Stanford, 1964).

7. See for example the revealing article by George Scelle, professor of international law at the University of Dijon and a leading Cartel academic, "Les Erreurs de notre politique extérieure," *Le Progrès civique*, 21 May 1924; also comments by Senator François-Albert, who served as minister of education under Herriot, "Vous devriez bien, ô Marianne, rafraîchir un peu l'air du Quai d'Orsay," *Le Progrès civique*, 21 April 1923; his "Bonneteau politique," ibid., 1 November 1924; and Victor Vivier, "De la suppression de la diplomatie secrète," ibid., 2 August 1924.

8. Bardoux, *L'Expérience de 1924*, pp. 201–12; Georges Suarez, *Herriot, 1924–1932* (Paris, 1932), p. 95; see also the file later compiled by the Ministry of the Interior on Bergery, F^7/13961, Ministère de l'Intérieur, Archives Nationales, Paris; and J. Theodore Marriner to J. Pierrepont Moffat, 1 May 1934, vol. 6, J. Pierrepont Moffat Papers, Houghton Library, Harvard University, Cambridge, Mass.

Although certain Cartel press organs predicted a radical reorientation of French foreign policy, Herriot actually intended to proceed with caution. His first ministerial statements reflected what the acerbic columnist Pertinax of *L'Echo de Paris* called "prudent indecision."[9] To be sure, Herriot made the required obeisance to Cartel doctrine with the ringing declaration: "We are hostile to the policy of isolation and force which leads to occupations and the seizure of territorial pledges."[10] Yet in subsequent interpellations he implied that he too would attempt to secure the guarantees of payment and security which Poincaré had demanded in his 14 May letter to MacDonald.[11]

Instead of preparing his case diligently before plunging into foreign consultations, however, Herriot planned to leave for talks with MacDonald at Chequers immediately after his government won confirmation. The British prime minister had offered to come to Paris, but Herriot considered it useful to make the gesture of going to England to "redress . . . at a single stroke . . . the stupid campaigns of ignorance that have been conducted in France against our allies."[12]

A statesman better versed in diplomacy would have conferred first with his own professional staff and then taken pains to create a common front with the Belgians, who had become restive and eager to show independence. Herriot did neither. He met only casually with Belgian Foreign Minister Hymans when the latter made a brief stopover between trains on the way from Geneva to Brussels.[13] He paid even less attention to the views of French diplomats. From London, Ambassador de Saint-Aulaire filed an urgent dispatch recommending that any concessions on the Ruhr occupation be conditioned on a British dispensation of equal value regarding the French war debt.[14] But several weeks earlier, the ambassador had warned too forcefully against the impending presidential crisis, which he said would harm French prestige abroad by conveying the impression that domestic affairs took precedence over foreign policy. Actually, Saint-Aulaire's premonitions came close to the mark: the German Foreign Ministry did follow the campaign to compel Millerand's resignation closely and—since the president of the republic had been the chief proponent of the Ruhr occupation—considered his ouster a signal that the new French government was "in earnest" about liquidating the Ruhr conflict.[15] Nevertheless, by his insistence the ambas-

9. *L'Echo de Paris*, 18 June 1924.

10. *J.O.C. Déb.*, 17 June 1924, pp. 2305–7.

11. Ibid., 19 June 1924, pp. 2340–44.

12. Herriot to Saint-Aulaire, 29 May 1924, quoted by Saint-Aulaire in *Confession d'un vieux diplomate* (Paris, 1953), p. 709; also Lord Crewe to MacDonald, 25 May, and MacDonald to Crewe, 26 May 1924, F.O. 371/9843: C 8508/8509/8510/G, and F.O. 800/218/276–280, MacDonald Correspondence.

13. Bardoux, *L'Expérience de 1924*, p. 199; Saint-Aulaire, *Confession d'un vieux diplomate*, p. 712; *L'Europe nouvelle*, 28 June 1924, pp. 820–21.

14. See partial text in Saint-Aulaire, *Confession d'un vieux diplomate*, pp. 730–32.

15. Gustav Stresemann, *Vermächtnis*, 3 vols. (Berlin, 1932), 1:436–37.

sador had irretrievably compromised himself in the eyes of the Cartel; his further advice was unwelcome. Indeed, throughout subsequent negotiations in London, Herriot's entourage virtually boycotted the French Embassy at the Albert Gate.[16]

In the hectic days before the Chequers interviews not even top career officials at the Quai d'Orsay were granted sufficient access to Herriot to brief him fully. Peretti de la Rocca, political director at the Foreign Ministry, met with Herriot, Bergery, and General Nollet on the evening before departure, but the suave Bergery did most of the talking. Weaving an elaborate gossamer of schemes for Franco-British collaboration, Bergery treated the general, who argued in somewhat simplistic terms against abandoning the military occupation of the Ruhr, as a comic figure.[17]

Originally, Herriot planned to go to England without the encumbering assistance of any member of the bureaucracy. Ingenuously expecting an informal discussion, he had instead tentatively invited two journalists to accompany him.[18] The British had been the ones to suggest that Herriot bring with him an official of standing. Whitehall sought to walk a fine tactical line. For an entire month a political crisis had absorbed the energies of the French. Officials in London, meanwhile, had worked intensively on a draft protocol embodying British views for making the Dawes Plan operational. They hoped to win Herriot's endorsement of their approach before the Poincarist bureaucracy at the Quai d'Orsay could take him in hand. But if Herriot came to Chequers alone, they feared, he might not feel confident enough to make firm commitments.[19] British Minister Eric Phipps therefore intimated that Seydoux (who had recently shown an accommodating spirit) would make a suitable second; failing Seydoux, who as a cripple had difficulty traveling, Bergery would make a satisfactory substitute. Phipps took "every possible step" to prevent assignment of the hard-liner Peretti, whose presence at Chequers, he warned, "would not make for agreement." And the French premier's personal staff promised cooperation.[20]

Thus when Herriot's train pulled out from the Gare du Nord on the morning of 21 June, with a euphoric crowd on the platform shouting "Vive la Paix!" and tossing flowers, Bergery alone had been designated to accompany his chief to England. Peretti, who still awaited his chance to discuss the subjects that would arise at Chequers, finally was scheduled to give the premier the requisite briefing in the train. Having brought neither his toothbrush nor his dinner jacket, Peretti maneuvered

16. Saint-Aulaire, *Confession d'un vieux diplomate*, pp. 707–14.
17. Suarez, *Herriot*, pp. 37–40.
18. Lord Crewe tel. no. 343 to MacDonald, 1 June 1924, F.O. 371/9843: C 8888/G.
19. Walford Selby to S. de Montille, 18 June 1924, also minute by Sir Eyre Crowe, 19 June 1924, F.O. 371/9747: C 9700/9716/70/18.
20. Phipps to Sir Eyre Crowe, 17, 19, 22 June 1924, F.O. 371/9748: C 9793/9862/9957/70/18.

a last-minute invitation to come along across the Channel only by accident: Herriot's appointments, as usual, ran late, and the train reached Calais before the premier could interrogate the principal permanent official of the Quai d'Orsay.[21]

Herriot had made preparations of his own, after a fashion. Late the previous evening, he had set down a few general principles ("show oneself liberal but never exposed") and had vaguely sketched out French desiderata in regard to sanctions and guarantees for the Dawes Plan, security, and debts.[22] On the boat across the Channel, he even went so far as to flutter this penciled document in the breeze at a discreet distance from some journalists.[23] But once the white cliffs of Dover came in sight nothing more was to be heard of it. With guileless optimism Herriot put his faith in man-to-man talk with MacDonald.

The Conversations at Chequers

Cartel newspapers of the period conjured up a lyrical idyll around the Chequers meetings, the essence of which has been preserved in a book written by the journalist Georges Suarez with Herriot's "friendly assistance."[24] The elegant evangelical Scotch socialist MacDonald differed profoundly in temperament from the professorial Herriot, but they were said to share "a social and humane mystique" that favored the immediate flowering of intimacy. Herriot believed that he had won MacDonald over to the "French cause." Even in later years he recalled their friendship with emotion; if it failed to bear fruit at subsequent conferences, the "trickeries of expert appraisals and the ambushes of diplomats" were largely to blame.[25] Suarez recalls the human details of the visit with a certain bathos. During a lull in the conversation on the evening of arrival, Herriot reputedly took the English classics from Chaucer to Milton down from their places on the Chequers library bookshelves and examined them with "an expert hand." Unable to sleep in the early morning hours, he awakened Bergery to share his anxieties, and expressed fatherly concern over the thermal qualities of his young friend's pajamas; then still insomniac, he greeted the dawn in the garden with an appropriate quotation from Shakespeare: "It was the lark, the herald of the morn."[26]

The transcripts of the business meetings convey a quite different impression. MacDonald and Permanent Under Secretary Sir Eyre Crowe

21. Phipps to Crowe, 22 June 1924, F.O. 371/9748: C 9957/70/18; relatively accurate accounts also in *L'Echo de Paris*, 21 June 1924, and in *L'Europe nouvelle*, 28 June 1924, p. 816.
22. "Plan Herriot," 21 June 1924 (evening), Herriot Papers.
23. *L'Europe nouvelle*, 12 July 1924, p. 879.
24. Suarez, *Herriot*, pp. 9–15, explains the circumstances of this collaboration.
25. Suarez, *Herriot*, pp. 18–19, 54.
26. Ibid., pp. 76–78, 87–99; also *L'Europe nouvelle*, 28 June 1924, p. 816. The Shakespeare passage comes from *Romeo and Juliet*, 3. 5. 6.

of the Foreign Office had prepared their case meticulously and operated as a brilliant team. MacDonald exerted his inimitable powers of obfuscation to avoid making any embarrassing commitments, while Crowe, with his mastery of detail and disciplined intelligence, pinned down the hapless French premier on point after point.[27]

The British opened the discussion by suggesting that a specific date be set for economic evacuation of the Ruhr. With studied casualness, Crowe developed an idea that the Foreign Office legal staff had cleverly worked out as a tactic to undermine the prerogatives exercised by France by virtue of the Versailles treaty.[28] The Allies should not simply decide amongst themselves on terms for putting the Dawes Plan into operation, Crowe maintained; rather, they would have to conclude a "reciprocal arrangement" with Germany in the form of a mutually binding protocol, linking economic evacuation with adoption of enabling legislation by the Reich. Disposed to treat this merely as a technical question, Herriot accepted without cavil. He agreed that economic evacuation could begin as soon as the Reparation Commission certified the new organs of control as ready to function, and he reserved only the delicate matter of the Rhineland railways.

MacDonald then turned to what he called the "central point"—adequate guarantees for the bankers who would float the loan to Germany. Prospects for a loan would become uncertain, he warned, in the absence of satisfactory agreement on evacuation "economic and otherwise" and the restoration to the Reich of control over all railways within German boundaries. Actually, the American bankers had not yet disclosed their position on military evacuation. Herriot, nevertheless, imprudently conceded that the questions of military evacuation and the loan were connected. Retreating from what he called Poincaré's "extreme" position, he expressed willingness to withdraw militarily in proportion to com-

27. For minutes of the Chequers meetings, see the English translation of Camerlynk's original stenographic notes in F.O. 371/9749: C 10427/70/18. Herriot later became embarrassed and demanded certain changes, "quelques legères retouches" (Massigli to R. Wigram, 24 July 1924), in order to protect his political position in case the transcripts became public. The final approved version is found in F.O. 371/9751: C 11976/70/18 and in the Herriot Papers. As Herriot had feared, hostile career diplomats at the Quai d'Orsay did eventually leak substantial excerpts from the revised version of the minutes to the newspapers (see *L'Eclair*, 26 December 1924, and the amused British reaction, F.O. 371/9755: C 19310/70/18). Suarez, *Herriot*, pp. 55–87, 99–148, reprints *L'Eclair*'s version. This account draws also on Jacques Bardoux's brilliant satirical commentary in *L'Expérience de 1924*, pp. 205–17; Herriot's account in *Jadis*, 2:138–45; and Etienne Weill-Raynal, *Les Réparations allemandes et la France*, 3 vols. (Paris, 1947), 3:31–47.

28. For Foreign Office and Treasury background planning regarding an overhead agreement to supersede sections of the Versailles treaty, see Bradbury's memorandum, "Measures for Restoring Economic and Fiscal Unity throughout German Territory," 1 May 1924, F.O. 371/9743: C 7168/70/18; Minutes of a meeting at the Treasury, evidencing Foreign Office–Treasury tactical differences, 20 May 1924, F.O. 371/9745: C 8187/70/18; and the Central Department's final planning document for Chequers, "Memorandum on the Immediate Steps to Be Taken to Apply the Dawes Scheme," 19 June 1924, F.O. 371/9748: C 10073/70/18.

mercialization of the railway and industrial bonds for which Germany would become responsible under the Dawes Plan.

There existed little likelihood, of course, that the international financial community would ever gain sufficient confidence in German good faith to warrant offering these bonds for public purchase. But the French premier's intimation of flexibility afforded the British an opening to claim that if tangible assets such as real property, railways, and industry secured the revenues earmarked for reparations, paper pledges of actual payment should prove guarantee enough. "I don't see what difference it would make whether the securities are in the hands of Germans or of foreigners," Crowe said blandly. And MacDonald went on to suggest that if the Germans resolved not to pay under any circumstances, no recourse short of war could compel them to do so; a military occupation, if maintained, would only "enlarge the difficulty." The British prime minister apparently sensed the weakness of this argument, however, for he finally admitted that there existed "no objection to an invisible occupation"—retention by the French military of a few key points—provided that the "aggressive occupation" were eliminated. Herriot missed the chance to secure a precise engagement on this subject. "I have proposed a system," he responded, "but I do not claim to have found a definitive formula. I ask only for the adoption of a satisfactory system and, in any case, to continue the conversation."

The French premier showed himself similarly reluctant to press his case concerning sanctions to be applied in the event of renewed German default. "We are opposed to laying down precise sanctions in advance," Crowe asserted flatly. MacDonald followed with a disquisition explaining why a definite plan would simply serve the interests of the German debtors. Herriot expressed "confidence in the word of Great Britain." He asked only for a "joint declaration, in writing and of general import"—an undertaking so vague that his interlocutors could give untroubled consent.

But who would establish in the future whether a willful default had actually occurred? On this subject the British admitted no imprecision. The Treaty of Versailles had given the Reparation Commission the right to determine default by majority vote. The French had taken advantage of their dominant position on that body to establish the legal basis for occupying the Ruhr in January 1923, at a time when the British deemed it politically inexpedient to recognize that flagrant default had occurred. The British now sought to ensure that France could never again resort to sanctions without their approval. Crowe therefore advanced the view that the Dawes Plan represented a "new treaty" requiring the voluntary signature of Germany. Since the Reparation Commission was entitled to decide only on those matters falling "within the four walls of the Treaty of Versailles," Crowe contended, it possessed no legal mandate to determine default under the new system. In the future, he preferred to delegate this task to the innocuous Financial Committee of the League of Nations; the latter body's finding of default would become final only after unanimous approval by the powers entitled to reparations and the United States.

Herriot reacted mildly, even when prompted by Peretti. This was a "period of transition," he observed. Could they not work out some system whereby the Reparation Commission "established" default and the Financial Committee of the League "appraised" it before the governments met to consider sanctions? He did not insist on any specific procedure, but found it "difficult to admit" that a single power's veto could "impede everything." In the end, no formal agreement resulted. Herriot fell in ambiguously with MacDonald's proposal for some form of international arbitration in case the powers differed about the flagrancy of a default. "The important thing," he told the British prime minister with touching sincerity, "for you as for me is to succeed in establishing peace."

On 22 June, the second day of discussion, attention focused on technical questions, first of all on the railway *Régie*. Crowe maintained that the Dawes Report required "absolute" restoration of German economic unity. Hence Foreign Office and Treasury experts could not assent to preservation of the Franco-Belgian *Régie* "in any form whatsoever." Taking a more active role than on the previous evening, Peretti explained why the French thought it essential to secure their military communications by keeping control over certain key lines, for example in the Trier district. The army of occupation in the Rhineland would otherwise find itself dependent on the goodwill of the German railway administration: if the railwaymen's strike called by Berlin at the start of the Ruhr occupation had become effective one week earlier, the French would not have been able to reinforce their soldiers on the Rhine. For once Herriot stood firm. "I cannot deal with the security of the troops without Marshal Foch and the General Staff," he said. On this issue a temporary deadlock ensued. MacDonald finally conceded that the railway experts who had advised the Dawes Committee might explore the matter further, but significantly, he did not promise to follow their recommendations.

The British then set forth a procedure to govern the forthcoming conference and outlined the protocol that Germany and the Allies should sign in order to give effect to the Dawes Report. For the most part Herriot went along again. Once he and MacDonald had agreed on "principles," the French premier cheerily observed, the "details" would follow. Herriot did balk at a few secondary points. Where Crowe suggested referring disputes over future interpretation of the protocol to the International Court at The Hague, Herriot would only agree to study the idea. And whereas the British diplomat insisted on inviting Germany to the conference from the start in order to create the conscious impression of negotiating "on a footing of equality," Herriot held out for delay until the Allies had reached a measure of understanding among themselves. But these were not matters of great import. On every essential issue—economic evacuation, maintenance of an invisible military presence, restrictions on future sanctions, limitations on the Reparation Commission's powers—Herriot had made substantial concessions, either explicit or implied, without receiving any compensation from Great Britain.

Only when the main issues directly connected to the Dawes Report had been disposed of did Herriot gingerly broach the problems of war debts and security. In the case of debts he adopted a supplicatory tone: "My predecessors are going to say that in their time the questions of [reparations] credits and debts were treated together. A democratic government comes to power; shall I be the first without general ideas on the subject of debts? I don't ask for promises, but to know on what I can count."

Adding some precision, Peretti produced a copy of Britain's last formal statement on the debts—contained in a note sent by Curzon in August 1923[29]—which MacDonald claimed to have "forgotten." At that time, the British government had intimated a willingness to offer the continental allies, under certain circumstances, terms more favorable than those set forth in the 1922 Balfour note. The Balfour note had laid down the principle that Britain would not seek to collect from Germany and the continental allies together more than the amount necessary to cover its debt to the United States. Admittedly, the British cabinet had originally conceived of the Balfour note as a stratagem to embarrass the United States into forgiving the British debt rather than as a serious attempt to squeeze the continental states.[30] Nevertheless, the note implied that, if America refused to cancel and Germany continued to default, Britain reserved the right to ask France and the smaller allies to shoulder part of the British obligation to the United States.[31]

In 1923, however, Great Britain had gone beyond the Balfour note, twice suggesting that in the event of a satisfactory reparations settlement, it might accept an increased share of reparations receipts—a generous offer in view of the precariousness of German remittances—in lieu of direct debt payments by the continental allies. MacDonald's February 1924 letter to Poincaré, expressing a cautious willingness to examine reparations and interallied debts conjointly, appeared to indicate that Britain remained flexible on the issue.

29. Lord Curzon to the French ambassador, 11 August 1923, Cmd. 1943, *Correspondence with the Allied Governments respecting Reparation Payments by Germany* (London, 1923), pp. 61–63.

30. For cabinet debate on the subject see P.R.O., CAB 23/30, Cabinet Conclusions: 29(22), 23 May 1922; 35(22), 16 June 1922; 36(22), 30 June 1922; 38(22), 7 July 1922; 42(22), 25 July 1922.

31. For the text of the Balfour note (1 August 1922), see Cmd. 1737, *Despatch to the Representatives of France, Italy, Croat-Slovene State, Roumania, Portugal and Greece at London respecting War Debts* (London, 1922).

But now at Chequers, Crowe abruptly declared that the 1923 offer was "dead." MacDonald simply declined to discuss war debts, claiming that he "didn't know that the question would arise." He refused even to designate a Treasury specialist to begin exploratory discussions with the French, at least until the reparations settlement was safely out of the way.

In the face of this resistance, Herriot did not belabor the matter. He turned immediately to the subject dearest to his heart, negotiation of a nonaggression pact to assure French security. At this time, journals of the French left had already begun to declare with surprising frequency that only "moral" or "juridical" means could lead to the achievement of true security.[32] To his credit, Herriot did not fully endorse this view either during his diplomatic debut in 1924 or later in the decade, when it became a virtual article of faith for many of his compatriots. Despite his equally strong revulsion against war, he realized throughout that the organization of collective security would offer the best guarantee of peace. At Chequers, Herriot expressed the hope that revivification of the Entente would permit reconsideration of the sort of security arrangement with which Lloyd George had tantalized Briand in January 1922 at Cannes. Peretti promptly furnished the details. The Quai d'Orsay proposed, first, a Franco-British pact modeled after the treaty discussed at Cannes, but with a "new text" providing for a serious military agreement along the lines arranged by France with its east European allies. After that, France and Britain together might conclude a nonaggression pact with Germany. Both pacts could be tailored to fit within the wider framework of the Draft Treaty of Mutual Assistance prepared under the auspices of the League of Nations.[33] Simultaneously, Peretti suggested,

32. See Georges Scelle, "Les Erreurs de notre politique extérieure," *Le Progrès civique*, 31 May 1924, and many articles of similar import in *Le Quotidien*, *L'Oeuvre*, and *L'Ere nouvelle*, May-September 1924.

33. For the text of the Draft Treaty, see Cmd. 2200, *Correspondence between His Majesty's Government and the League of Nations respecting the Proposed Treaty of Mutual Assistance* (London, 1924), pp. 4–9. The Draft Treaty had emerged in 1923 from a committee appointed directly by the League Assembly. Lord Robert Cecil of Great Britain and Lieutenant-Colonel Edouard Réquin of France provided the treaty's main inspiration, but they served as independent experts, not as government representatives. Although conscious of the treaty's limited value, the Quai d'Orsay had adopted a positive attitude once the provisions concerning limitation of armaments were rendered innocuous. No responsible organ of the British government, on the other hand, had ever taken the treaty seriously. The fighting services, Foreign Office, Cabinet Secretariat, and Committee of Imperial Defence vied in denouncing it as "impracticable," "undesirable," "rotten and unworkable," and "absurd." The Foreign Office particularly resented Cecil as an impractical visionary who unwittingly encouraged foreign statesmen into thinking that Whitehall might endorse his purely personal schemes. For development of the treaty see "Documents concerning the Treaty of Mutual Assistance and the Projects of Lord Robert Cecil and Lt.-Colonel Réquin," 1923–24, Edouard Réquin Papers, Hoover Institution, Stanford University, Stanford, Calif.; and for the British attitude, F.O. 371/10568–569; also P.R.O., Minutes of the Committee of Imperial Defence, CAB 2/4, meetings 171, 176, 183, 187; and CAB 4/10, C.I.D. Papers 431–B, 459–B, 464–B, 465–B, 484–B.

the League Council could create a permanent technical committee, on which the Allies would retain a dominant influence, to take over responsibility for enforcing the Versailles treaty disarmament clauses and to carry out on-site inspection to ensure permanent demilitarization of the Rhineland.

When MacDonald began to elaborate objections to the French scheme, Herriot launched an impassioned oration. In the Palais Bourbon such a speech might have evoked a clamor for *affichage*, but delivered in these international negotiations, it bordered on the ingenuous:

> My country has a dagger directed at its breast, a centimeter from the heart. Common efforts, sacrifices, the war dead—all that will have been in vain if Germany can resort to violence again. . . . I should prefer that France not be paid, if it must renounce security. If there is a new war, France will be erased from the map of the world. . . . Can't we try to find a formula of guarantee to avoid the danger of an eventuality that would render the Experts' Report useless?

MacDonald declared that he was "touched," indeed "not indifferent to the perilous position of France." But speaking frankly, he could not offer a military guarantee of security. The British public would not support a pact; the Dominions would not accept obligations; the professionals at the War Office and Foreign Office opposed the Draft Treaty of Mutual Assistance because it might require an increase in British armaments.[34] Falling back on the empty phraseology developed through years of practice in Labour party journalism, the prime minister declared himself ready immediately to "take all measures necessary to begin study of the question," and to "bring the League of Nations into play." He looked forward to inaugurating a "new method" of settling ques-

34. The British government did not dispatch its formal rejection of the Draft Treaty to the League of Nations until 5 July, and it released the text publicly only on 19 July 1924. Actually, however, the cabinet had definitively turned down the treaty on 30 May, several weeks before MacDonald met with Herriot. Cabinet discussion revealed that the Labour government did not frown merely on this particular arrangement, but that it stood "definitely opposed in principle" to the whole idea of seeking mutual security through the League. The cabinet's strictures would apply to the Geneva Protocol, framed in the fall of 1924, just as much as they did to the Draft Treaty. The cabinet softened the text of its rejection in order to emphasize the "constructive side" of its attitude. A close reading of MacDonald's final dispatch, however, should have made it clear that a Labour government would never participate in any meaningful arrangement for collective security under League auspices. MacDonald contended that the League Council was an "inappropriate body" to entrust with control of military operations and that the Draft Treaty involved an "undesirable extension" of its functions. He opposed the regional security arrangements permitted by the treaty on the ground that they might lead to the reappearance of the system of alliances and counter-alliances which in the past had proved "such a serious menace to the peace of the world." Finally, he noted that the Draft Treaty afforded a guarantee "so precarious that no responsible government will feel justified in consenting to any material reduction of armaments in return." This last objection was crucial in view of Labour's emphasis on general disarmament as the best way to achieve security. See CAB 23/48, Cabinet Conclusions: 35(24), 30 May 1924; Foreign Office minutes in F.O. 371/10568: W 4633/4799/134/98; and the final reply to the League, in Cmd. 2200, *Correspondence . . . respecting the Proposed Treaty of Mutual Assistance*, pp. 10–14.

tions, that of "friendship and constant collaboration" in order to assure the well-being of their respective countries and to resolve "the great moral problems of world peace." This, MacDonald added, was "perhaps a very vast conception of broad policy and continuous collaboration, but one which should be pleasing to the French mind."

Herriot grasped at the proffered straw: "In short, the most important conclusion of our interview is a sort of moral pact of continuous collaboration between us, for the good of our two countries and in the general interest of the whole world." The meeting drew to a close; from the detritus of the French position Herriot salvaged only a last-minute commitment by MacDonald to sign a "vigorous" joint telegram to the German government appealing for its cooperation with a terminal inspection by the Interallied Military Control Commission.[35] Even the final communiqués for the press reflected the underlying divergence in view. The French version spoke of "complete agreement" and the conclusion of "a moral pact of continuous collaboration," while the English version referred only to "general agreement" and omitted the reference to a pact.[36]

So persistent was Herriot's optimism that he nevertheless left for Brussels (where he intended to brief Belgian leaders) believing that his diplomatic debut had proved eminently successful. The cordial tone of the discussions and the parting embrace in the French manner on the Chequers doorstep led him to feel that he had managed to reestablish the Entente on a solid footing.[37] On the train from Ostend to the Belgian capital he assured a sympathetic reporter from *L'Indépendence Belge* that MacDonald had not asked him for "any sacrifice." On the contrary, he boasted: "Already I have the assurance, in case of Germany's premeditated aggression, of a defensive pact which would bind France, England, and Belgium. . . . I have Mr. MacDonald's most explicit promise that today as in 1914 a German attack would find England at the side of France and Belgium."[38] This euphoric mood continued even after Herriot returned home. His bearing conveyed the impression, in the words of British Ambassador Lord Crewe, that he had "settled in three days matters which baffled other statesmen for five years."[39]

35. For texts of the notes exchanged, see *L'Europe nouvelle*, 5 July 1924, pp. 865–70. For Stresemann's ingenious explanation of the German reply to the press, to the effect that an end to military control following a last *pro forma* inspection was imperative to sustain the recent improvement in international relations, see *Vermächtnis*, 1:441–48. For the Reich's subsequent preparations to minimize the general inspection, see Michael Salewski, *Entwaffnung und Militärkontrolle in Deutschland, 1919–1927* (Munich, 1966), pp. 249–64.

36. On the drafting of the communiqués, see George Glasgow, *MacDonald as Diplomatist* (London, 1924), p. 134.

37. Soulié, *La Vie politique d'Edouard Herriot*, p. 162; Suarez, *Herriot*, pp. 18–19.

38. *L'Indépendence Belge*, 24 June 1924, amplified in Charles Wingfield [Brussels] to Foreign Office, 26 June 1924, F.O. 371/9730: C 10298/32/18; and in Crewe to Foreign Office, 24 June 1924, F.O. 371/9818: C 10078/2048/18.

39. Crewe tel. no. 410 to Foreign Office, 25 June 1924, F.O. 371/9748: C 10147/70/18.

The French premier soon began to acquire wisdom in a sharp school. The British Foreign Office lost no time in denying that it had made the sort of commitment claimed by Herriot. In two appearances in the House of Commons, MacDonald emphasized that he did not intend "to make any exclusive arrangements between any two powers" and that the agenda for the forthcoming conference would specifically exclude security as well as interallied debts.[40] Meanwhile, Herriot's discussions in Brussels had not gone well. Theunis and Hymans had resigned themselves to making virtually any sacrifice necessary to give the Dawes Plan practical effect in order to clear the way for reopening the security question, but they did not think that Herriot had handled matters properly. "He is a child," Theunis muttered privately.[41]

Yet even the most sophisticated and hard-bitten among French political analysts would have registered shock had they seen the evidence revealing Whitehall's real calculations regarding war debts and security at this time. At Chequers, MacDonald had lifted no more than a corner of the veil masking British intentions on these two issues, which—once the powers had disposed of the immediate problems connected to the Dawes Report—would become the most critical confronting Europe.

British Views on War Debts and Security

Although not quite ready to announce its stand publicly, the British Treasury was swiftly moving toward the view that France should pay the war debt to the uttermost farthing. Earlier, it will be recalled, permanent Treasury officials had taken the opposite position. In 1920, when the United States declined to be drawn into a scheme for general cancellation of debts, Controller of Finance Basil P. Blackett had tried to interest the cabinet in unilateral forgiveness of debts owed to Great Britain. He had confronted his political superiors with hard facts: while their country could well afford to reimburse the United States, substantial repayment by the continental allies of the sums borrowed from Britain was "out of the question."[42] Again in 1922, the Treasury had called for generous treatment of European debts and fought against the Balfour note. While Lloyd George, Churchill, and their political allies had maneuvered to throw the burden of economic adjustment on the

40. *Daily Telegraph*, 26 June 1924; London *Times*, 27 June 1924; House of Commons *Debates*, 5th Series, 23 June 1924, col. 2143, 26 June 1924, col. 2310.

41. William Phillips [Brussels] to State Department, 20 June 1924, U.S. 462.00R 296/375; *Le Temps*, 25–26 June 1924; *L'Europe nouvelle*, 28 June 1924, pp. 820–21; Louis Marcellin, *Voyage autour de la Chambre du 11 mai* (Paris, 1925), p. 126.

42. Basil P. Blackett memorandum for Sir Warren Fisher, "Interallied Indebtedness," 2 February 1920, CAB 24/97: C.P. 584; see also Lord Curzon's able supporting memorandum, "Foreign Policy and Inter-Allied Debts," 17 April 1920, CAB 24/104: C.P. 1093; Churchill's hostile critique of 23 April 1920, CAB 24/104: C.P. 1156; and the cabinet's final negative judgment, CAB 23/21, Cabinet Conclusions: 30(20), 21 May 1920.

United States—"shamming bankrupt in order to put [America] in the dock, demeaning ourselves in order to blacken her and defraud her of her debt," as Lloyd George's private secretary wrote in disillusionment—Blackett and his Treasury colleagues had insisted vainly that Britain settle with America without reference to what Europe owed. Britain's ability to pay depended on restoration of a peaceful world with which to trade, Blackett contended; the country would profit more by exporting to a prosperous continent than by siphoning off funds that France, Belgium, Italy, and other debtors might otherwise direct into economic reconstruction.[43]

The Bonar Law Plan of January 1923 bore the stamp of this broader Treasury view regarding war debts. By expressing willingness to accept German reparations bonds in payment of interallied debts at the same time as it proposed to reduce German obligations substantially, the British government was in effect offering to forgive most of the French debt in return for a satisfactory general settlement. The total package held no attraction for France. It included a stipulation granting Germany a four-year moratorium that would have led inevitably to the end of reparations; rather than accept this, the French had occupied the Ruhr. But the specific British offer on war debts continued to intrigue them. It corresponded closely to the idea long promoted by the French bureaucracy for liquidating war debts through an exchange of rights to the near-valueless German "C" bonds.

The British Treasury's enthusiasm for taking the long view, however, did not survive the bitterness engendered by the Ruhr occupation. On 28 April 1924 the Treasury informed the Foreign Office that Bonar Law's offer had lapsed. Treasury officials felt under no obligation to repeat it in connection with the Dawes Plan, which was not of British origin and in their view increased the chances of default by setting German payments too high. Only after the "real value" of the reparations asset represented by the new plan had become clear, stated the Treasury, would it contemplate a reexamination of war debts in the light of each debtor's financial circumstances and the obligations that Great Britain had to bear.[44]

The British government did not wish to disclose its change of front abruptly to the French, because there existed "no convenient peg to hang it on."[45] For a number of reasons, moreover, Whitehall believed that to adjourn discussion of debts until the Dawes Plan had been put

43. Sir Edward Grigg to the prime minister, "Our Debt to the U.S.A. and the European Position," 6 July 1922; Sir Basil Blackett memorandum for the prime minister, Chamberlain, and Baldwin, 24 July 1922; both in Box 19 (Foreign Affairs Subject File III), Edward W. M. Grigg [1st Lord Altrincham] Papers, in family possession, London. For the official statement of the Treasury case, see Chancellor of the Exchequer Robert S. Horne, "British Debt to the United States Government," 8 June 1922, CAB 24/137: C.P. 4020.

44. See the review of these events in Miles W. Lampson to Sir O. E. Niemeyer of the Treasury, 30 June 1924, F.O. 371/9749: C 10426/70/18.

45. Ibid.

into force would strengthen its position. The Treasury had not yet abandoned hope—despite many contrary indications—that after the 1924 presidential election took place, the administration in Washington would participate in a conference to discuss reduction or cancellation of debts. At such a conference Great Britain might conceivably find a dignified way to reopen consideration of its own settlement with the United States by confounding its case with that of less solvent debtors. In view of American fears that the continental nations would evade their obligations, the Treasury thought it wise in any event to avoid examination of the issue until the United States had subscribed to the Dawes loan. Meanwhile, British negotiators could make use of the unfunded French debt as a particularly potent "weapon" to ensure that the French demonstrated the proper spirit in facilitating operation of the control mechanisms set up under the Dawes Plan.[46]

When at length the Treasury invited the French to begin the bargaining process, it intended to impose stiff terms. Permanent Treasury officials now wished to return strictly to the policy of the Balfour note—requiring enough from Germany and Allied debtors together to meet America's demands—and Chancellor of the Exchequer Philip Snowden wondered whether the facts warranted even this much generosity.[47] The Treasury's detailed calculations showed the potential implications for France. Assuming that Germany made full payment according to the Dawes schedule of $625 million (2.5 milliard gold marks) in a standard year, the British Empire's share would amount to $137.5 million. The principle of the Balfour note implied that France, as Britain's only partially solvent debtor, would have to make up the difference between this sum and the $184 million standard annual payment due the United States. Since the United States held a far more solidly grounded claim on France than did Great Britain, it could hardly consent to ask less of France than Britain did. It followed from these considerations that France could not expect to keep much over two-thirds of the $325 million maximum it would receive from Germany annually. And most of this sum would go to support the occupation army, the various control commissions, and to pay for coal, timber, and other deliveries in kind. Under the best of circumstances, France would thus find the mirage of cash reparations vanishing and would have to pay off from its own resources the short-term debt that had financed reconstruction of the devastated areas.[48]

Actually British Treasury officials expected the transfer mechanism to limit German payments under the Dawes Plan to far less than 2.5

46. Niemeyer to Foreign Office, 4 July 1924, F.O. 371/9749: C 10720/70/18.

47. On Snowden's views, see Niemeyer to Harold Nicolson, 23 August 1924, F.O. 371/9683: C 13570/11/62.

48. Ibid.; also see Niemeyer to Foreign Office, 14 August 1924, F.O. 371/9683: C 13040/11/62.

milliard gold marks a year. MacDonald had maintained at the Chequers meetings that the Dawes Plan did not require the additional guarantee which residual military occupation would provide because the railway bonds, industrial debentures, and assigned revenues from customs and taxes specified in the plan itself offered ample security for integral payment. At the same time Controller of Finance Sir Otto E. Niemeyer based his projections on the assumption that German remittances would average only 1 milliard gold marks a year. Niemeyer estimated the true capital worth of the remaining German reparations liability at no more than 16 milliard gold marks. Armies of occupation and other peace treaty charges would consume 6 milliards. The British share of the balance would amount to 2.2 milliard gold marks (£110 million)—a relatively trivial sum compared to the capital value of the British war debt settlement with the United States of £710 million (the equivalent of 14.2 milliard gold marks). According to the logic of the Balfour note, Britain would demand not less, but proportionately more from its continental allies as the probability of significant reparations payments from Germany receded.[49]

The British government had not yet decided in the summer of 1924 how far it would push the logic of the Balfour note, but the direction of the shove was clear. As Whitehall's interest in maximizing reparations payments diminished, its eagerness to collect war debts increased. In 1922 Winston Churchill had exhorted his cabinet colleagues not to let their nation remain "a sort of spongy, squeezable mass" caught between the "obstinately expressed" will of the United States to exact payment from Great Britain and the equally clear resolve of France to "pay nobody."[50] Two years later, Treasury professionals had come to agree with Churchill's conviction that Britain should not put up with "being fleeced." First under Snowden, and then under Churchill himself as chancellor of the exchequer, they readied a policy of "debt reclamation" and prepared to send the bailiff to the rue de Rivoli.[51]

Few Frenchmen either in or out of the Herriot government recognized clearly what the future portended in regard to the British debt. From Paris, British Ambassador Lord Crewe cautioned MacDonald on 29 June that "a great many people here, including some by no means intellectually deficient, have been living in a fool's paradise on this particular matter, and their awakening will have to be conducted with delicacy and caution."[52] Taking the warning to heart, MacDonald remained studiously vague about British debt policy throughout the London Con-

49. Niemeyer to Foreign Office, 4 July 1924, F.O. 371/9749: C 10720/70/18.

50. Memorandum by the Secretary of State for the Colonies (W. S. C.), "Interallied Debts," 3 August 1922, CAB 24/138: C.P. 4149.

51. Churchill (Chancellor of the Exchequer) to Austen Chamberlain (Foreign Secretary), 1 December 1924, F.O. 371/9683: C 18178/11/62.

52. Lord Crewe to J. Ramsay MacDonald, 29 June 1924, F.O. 800/218/307–308, MacDonald Correspondence.

ference. He replied to private entreaties from French Socialists who presumed that they enjoyed some special relationship with a Labour prime minister, as he answered repeated importunities from Herriot and other French officials, with the bland assurance that the British government would consider war debts further at the proper time.[53] The French would find out soon enough what lay in store for them.

Had Herriot possessed the power at Chequers to read the British prime minister's thoughts regarding security, his disillusionment would have been complete. "Nothing will induce this government to give any sort of military guarantee to France," Cabinet Secretary Sir Maurice Hankey had reassured Prime Minister J. C. Smuts of South Africa on 22 May.[54] In fact, Hankey had written earlier, MacDonald disliked "all schemes" for a British guarantee of France, just as he abhorred the various proposals for achieving mutual guarantee through the League of Nations. The Labour leader put his faith instead in the League's moral force, which he hoped to strengthen by the inclusion of Germany and Soviet Russia, and also in universal disarmament. Like Smuts, MacDonald perceived "the imperialistic tendencies of France" as the chief danger to European peace. And at least so long as Poincaré remained in power, Downing Street feared that the French would offer no more than "lip service" to the idea of disarmament unless the unstable position of the franc eventually forced their hand.[55]

Members of the Labour government who counted on disarmament to prevent international conflict did not stand alone in opposing British commitments on the continent of Europe. Hankey, who in the Cabinet Office and the Committee of Imperial Defence had long advocated such retrenchment, rejoiced to find a new mood favoring disengagement sweeping through the Liberal party and the left wing of the Conservative party in the spring of 1924, even among those who had formerly expressed willingness to contemplate some type of limited security arrangement with France. "People are beginning to see," Hankey informed Smuts, "that though we cannot disinterest ourselves in European affairs, our best attitude is one of aloofness, rather on the lines of the United States, though for geographical, commercial and other reasons we cannot segregate ourselves as completely as they."[56]

Curiously, quite accurate knowledge of illegal German rearmament did not affect the revulsion against French "imperialism" in Whitehall, nor did it moderate the growing sentiment there in favor of isolationism. During the spring of 1924, British military intelligence furnished numer-

53. See the cabinet secretary's review of this pressure, Sir M. P. A. Hankey to Miles W. Lampson, 16 August 1924, F.O. 371/9683: C 13266/11/62.

54. Hankey to Smuts, 22 May 1924, 1st Baron Hankey Papers, Churchill College, Cambridge University, Cambridge.

55. Hankey to Smuts, 1 April 1924, ibid.

56. Hankey to Smuts, 22 May 1924, ibid.

ous detailed reports on the upsurge of nationalistic fervor in Germany. Intelligence sources chronicled the increase in paramilitary activity, much of it government-subsidized, ranging from simple propaganda to the operation of assassination squads. They charted the rapid progress of the Reichswehr's program to create, through various intermediaries, a system for basic training of short-term volunteers.[57] But mounting evidence of German military preparation did not perturb the Foreign Office. Miles W. Lampson of the Central Department concluded philosophically that "treaty or no treaty, the German is instinctively inclined to form himself into patriotic societies etc., and . . . nothing which we may do or say has the ghost of a chance of eradicating that instinct from his nature."[58] In Lampson's view, the French had only themselves to blame for the intensification of nationalism in Germany. Throughout, he labored to restrain Paris from embarking on a "fatuous struggle" to suppress the patriotic societies, an effort that he thought would only generate additional friction.[59] MacDonald wholeheartedly agreed with the judgment of his staff. "What can we expect?" he minuted. "Would we not do the same thing here if we had been defeated and . . . used with the same treatment? Nationalism is inflamed not suppressed by suppression. This danger will continue till we get a new policy at work."[60]

What MacDonald meant by a "new policy" never became entirely clear. On the whole, the prime minister presided over the bureaucratic machinery of the Foreign Office with professional aplomb. He followed the work of his diplomatic advisers closely, and his final decisions usually reflected the convictions of Foreign Office career personnel regarding Britain's permanent interests. Occasionally, however, on matters touching his old ideological commitments, he would drift off into woolly abstractions.

General disarmament, MacDonald consistently maintained, offered the best solution for European security problems. But what specific policies would promote this goal? Theoretically, the Versailles treaty had provided for disarmament of Germany. England, in order to effect budgetary savings, had already reduced its armed forces to the lowest point compatible with Imperial safety, indeed in many respects below that point. Might not a call for "general" disarmament accordingly represent in practice a demand for dismantling the defensive forces of France and its east European client states? If MacDonald's policy did not

57. See the weekly reports of the Military Control Commission in Berlin to M.I. 3, in F.O. 371/9839–41: C 7070/18; and the reports from the British Army of the Rhine's separate intelligence staff, in F.O. 371/9825: C 2977/18.

58. Lampson minute, 19 May 1924, F.O. 371/9825: C 7715/2977/18.

59. Lampson minute, 14 May 1924, and approving minute by MacDonald deploring the tone of French reports on secret German military preparations, 15 May 1924, F.O. 371/9825: C 7742/2977/18.

60. MacDonald minute, 18 April 1924, F.O. 371/9825: C 6157/2977/18.

point consistently in this single direction, one reason lay in his penchant for vagueness in general formulations—a vagueness that contrasted strikingly with the orderly precision of his directives concerning day-to-day matters requiring immediate action. A wide-ranging though desultory exchange between the War Office and Foreign Office about the employment of League of Nations authority in relation to a possible German threat to France, for example, fizzled out with a typically confused homily by MacDonald on 3 July 1924 about considering League problems from the point of view of "psychology." Exhorting his subordinates not to draw "false distinctions between idealism and practicalism [*sic*]," the prime minister contended with portentous obscurity that since "sage materialists and self-styled idealists" would never produce anything but wars, efforts to avoid an arms race should center on "changing the qualities of our minds."[61]

Although discussion on this level of generality persisted throughout Labour's tenure in office, bureaucrats at several ministries in Whitehall concomitantly devoted serious thought to more concrete problems of European security. Few experts outside the General Staff shared French perceptions of the menace posed by a resurgent Germany or exhibited much patience with French proposals for parrying the potential military danger. In the long run this fundamental lack of sympathy among British career officials who would remain to advise successor governments was quite as ominous for France as the hostility of Labour politicians.

In the winter and spring of 1924, the Foreign Office focused its primary attention not on France's security requirements, but rather on the threat to British interests created by putative French designs on the Rhineland. Slow to recognize the collapse of French schemes to promote separatism in that area, the Central Department still ritually sounded the tocsin in February 1924: Poincaré's "unremitting" efforts to dominate the Rhineland, following in a tradition a thousand years old, appeared to British diplomats uncomfortably close to realization. A febrile imagination informed their speculations on the potential strategic consequences of his success. French forces, warned the Central Department, might subsequently use the Rhineland as a "jumping-off point for an incursion into Central Europe." Even worse, they would virtually encircle Belgium and take up a position allowing them to drive a wedge through the center of Holland, posing "a direct menace to the Scheldt and Zuider Zee, and therefore an indirect menace to this country."[62]

61. MacDonald minute, 3 July 1924, on a General Staff "Memorandum on the Question of so Strengthening the Authority of the League of Nations that the European Nations, with Special Reference to France, Will Be Content to Rely Largely upon that Body for Their Future Security," 24 June 1924, F.O. 371/9818: C 10067/2048/18.

62. Central Department memorandum [by J. C. Sterndale Bennett], "British Policy regarding Occupied Territories of Germany," 5 February 1924; endorsed by MacDonald as "admirable," 18 February 1924, F.O. 371/9813: C 2028/1346/18.

Foreign Office professionals cast about for a workable scheme that might induce France to renounce present efforts to control the Rhineland by increasing its psychological sense of security against German aggression in the future. They ruled out any plan involving a British military commitment or requiring unilateral sacrifices by Germany. The Reich, they held, bore no responsibility for the failure of the United States and Great Britain to ratify the treaty of guarantee promised to France in 1919. It could not be called upon to accept a further infringement on its sovereignty without some compensating advantage. Their thoughts thus logically turned to conceivable "mutual guarantees against aggression" in which Germany could freely join. They discerned two promising approaches: a revival in some form of Chancellor Wilhelm Cuno's 1922 proposal for a moral pledge by Germany, France, Great Britain, and Italy not to go to war, or alternatively, demilitarization of Alsace-Lorraine to balance that of the Rhineland, with supervision of both areas by an enlarged League of Nations offering Germany an important role.[63]

German officials, as might be expected, mulled continually over schemes that might later justify a demand for early termination of the Rhineland occupation. The idea of mutually guaranteeing Germany's western frontiers constituted a staple dish on the Wilhelmstrasse's diplomatic menu, from the day that Cuno first served it up until the French finally swallowed it at Locarno. With just the slightest prompting from Lord D'Abernon, the German Foreign Office dispatched a timely memorandum reiterating its willingness to explore either of the alternatives that appealed to London in February 1924.[64] Whitehall felt no real urgency. Sir Eyre Crowe deemed it tactically wise to aim first for a reparations settlement and complete evacuation of the Ruhr, leaving the question of security "to be discussed afterwards."[65] Yet some sort of Rhineland pact, the consensus among British career diplomats held, offered the best eventual prospect for diminishing tensions in the area.

From Paris Eric Phipps objected that the French were unlikely to consider paper guarantees sufficient, "however stout the paper."[66] But the Central Department retorted impatiently that Great Britain strove for a solution "which would prevent future war and not merely give France a free hand to do as she likes in Europe."[67] Significantly, the British

63. Central Department memorandum, ibid., also supporting minutes by Harold Nicolson, Miles W. Lampson, Sir Eyre Crowe, and Lord Parmoor over the period 5–25 February 1924, in F.O. 371/9813: C 2028/1346/18, and in F.O. 371/9818: C 2048/2048/18.

64. Memorandum communicated by the German Embassy, 11 February 1924, F.O. 371/9818: C 2048/2048/18; also British ambassador in Berlin Lord D'Abernon to MacDonald, 19 February 1924, F.O. 371/9818: C 2842/2048/18.

65. Crowe minute, 25 February 1924, F.O. 371/9818: C 2842/2048/18.

66. British Minister Eric Phipps to MacDonald, 14 March 1924, F.O. 371/9818: C 4393/2048/18.

67. J. C. Sterndale Bennett minute, 18 March 1924, F.O. 371/9818: C 4411/2048/18; cf. similar negative comments by Lampson and Crowe on Phipps's dispatch opposing de-

diplomatic establishment took no stock in naive assertions by self-styled experts in the Labour party that French demands for security and military alliance were largely "imaginary" and that nonpolitical Frenchmen didn't "care a damn about the 'next war.'"[68] Nor was it ill informed about Germany's general intentions. Its policies reflected, on the contrary, a coherent set of basic assumptions. Foreign Office professionals believed that Joseph Addison, counselor of embassy in Berlin, had hit the nail on the head: "What we must aim at," Addison wrote, "is to get the French out of the Rhineland, placate German national feeling and invent some formula which, whether efficacious or not, would at least give time for mutual passions to simmer down and for the conviction to gain ground that war is foolish as well as inhuman." Coupled with a "window-dressing device" for reparations, he thought, some sort of nonaggression pact—if not regarded as an end in itself—might provide this necessary "breathing space for opinion to become sensible on both sides."[69]

In the short run, meanwhile, MacDonald remained overwhelmingly preoccupied with the danger of France's upsetting the European security balance. French policy responded to a "historical craving," he asserted shortly after assuming office; "it is a mistake to assume that events forced by France are in consequence of feeling insecure."[70] At the prime minister's behest, the three service departments in March 1924 examined the implications of indefinite French military control over the Ruhr and Rhineland for British security.

Since 1921 Air Marshal Sir H. M. Trenchard and his political boosters had repeatedly drawn a lurid picture of the threat posed by French superiority in the air. If the prospect of a bombing raid on London was presently remote, they contended, unscrupulous French statesmen might nonetheless not hesitate to employ their air power as a diplomatic weapon.[71] The Air Staff did not let slip their latest opportunity. France's permanent possession of the Rhineland and consequent domination of the Low Countries, they emphasized, would in the event of war facili-

---

militarization of Alsace-Lorraine, 25 and 26 February 1924, F.O. 371/9813: C 2028/1346/18.

68. C. Delisle Burns [foreign policy expert of the Labour Party and Trades Union Congress "Joint Research and Information Department"] to Under Secretary Arthur Ponsonby, 23 April 1924, F.O. 371/9818: C 6790/2048/18.

69. Joseph Addison to Harold Nicolson, 1 March 1924; endorsed by Miles W. Lampson as "very helpful," 12 March, and by Sir Eyre Crowe as "good and sensible," 13 March 1924, F.O. 371/9813: C 3814/1346/18. Addison also contended that the Allies should frankly face the necessity for territorial adjustments, at least in eastern Europe. Crowe differed on this one point. He considered a fresh examination of the question of Danzig, Memel, and Germany's eastern frontiers impracticable, since that would raise "the whole problem of the possibility of a Polish state."

70. MacDonald minute, 18 February 1924, F.O. 371/9813: C 2028/1346/18.

71. See Minutes of the Committee of Imperial Defence, CAB 2/3: Meetings 145–47, 157–58, 162–63; and the memoranda by the Air Staff and the C.I.D. Subcommittee on the Continental Air Menace, CAB 3/3: C.I.D. Papers 102–A, 105–109A, 111–112A, 114–116A; CAB 3/4: 118–A and 145–A.

tate air attack on industrial centers in the Midlands by enabling French bombers to bypass the heavily defended zone southeast of London.[72] The Admiralty sounded a similar note of alarm: control of Dutch and Belgian ports would allow French warships to operate behind the "Dover block" against trade entering the Thames and North Sea, completely undermining the Royal Navy's contingency plan for war against France.[73] Only the War Office refused to tack with the prevailing wind. "Not only is France, however extravagant a search for security she might indulge, no danger to us," the General Staff insisted, "but . . . her security is ours."[74]

The military men interpreted the portents with a prescience all the more remarkable given the curious judgments of those around them. In time, they advised, Germany would "inevitably" clash with Great Britain again under circumstances marking "simply a repetition of the conditions which brought us into the late war." The General Staff foresaw Germany reconditioned, redisciplined, and thirsting for revenge by the time the last Allied troops left the Rhineland in 1935. France's manpower reserves, according to predictable demographic trends, would then measure less than half of Germany's and stand on the verge of further precipitous decline. The restraints imposed by the Versailles treaty would retain "no value at all" once Germany felt strong enough to override them. The Reich could rearm in nine months when supervision of disarmament ended. It could easily sweep away all schemes for demilitarization, neutralization, League of Nations observation, and railway control at the moment hostilities began. The Rhineland occupation offered genuine protection so long as it endured (though evacuation of the Cologne bridgehead would substantially diminish its strategic importance), but even if France discovered a suitable legal pretext, it could afford neither the men nor the money to prolong the occupation indefinitely. France's eastern alliances, finally, possessed no real military worth. In short, concluded the General Staff, the French were right to see themselves as "practically helpless" unless they obtained efficient guarantees in the ten years remaining before the danger became acute.

War Office strategists understood that there existed only one such guarantee in practice: a "military alliance of first-class powers" sufficiently powerful to coerce Germany. They contended, furthermore, that Britain could not disinterest itself in the fate of France; it needed that country as a military "buffer" against Germany almost as much as France needed Britain. Yet, heedful of the low esteem in which civilians

72. Air Staff Memorandum on the Status of the Rhineland from the Aspect of the Developments of Air Warfare, 18 March 1924, F.O. 371/9813: C 4640/1346/18.

73. British Policy in the Rhineland with Special Reference to French Security, Admiralty memorandum, 22 March 1924, F.O. 371/9813: C 4893/1346/18.

74. General Staff Memorandum on the Military Aspect of the Future Status of the Rhineland, 28 March 1924, F.O. 371/9813: C 5185/1346/18; printed also in CAB 4/11: C.I.D. Paper 516–B.

held the military mind, the generals did not dare draw the explicit logical conclusion—that Whitehall should reverse policy and conclude a serious defensive pact. They accepted as self-evident that Great Britain desired "no permanent military commitments on the Continent." They also realized that neither the political leadership nor the British public would tolerate an open-ended obligation to maintain the nation's armed forces at a standard dictated by "growing French weakness or growing German strength." So after all their analysis they suggested mere half-measures: limited naval and air assistance to France for a fifteen-year period, and efforts to strengthen the League of Nations in order to improve opportunities for "creating alliances *ad hoc* in such situations as . . . Germany running amok."[75]

Whatever the military men might have hoped to accomplish by displaying tactical caution, the diplomats gave short shrift to their views. The Central Department declined to accept the premise that war with France was impossible or war with Germany inevitable, and found the General Staff study leading "nowhere constructive."[76] On the day after Herriot departed from Chequers in a happy frame of mind, Miles W. Lampson wrote Lord D'Abernon to describe the trend of thought at the Foreign Office: the General Staff was probably "quite right" that only through permanent occupation of the Rhineland or a mutual defense pact with Great Britain could France hope to achieve real security. But neither solution lay within the bounds of practical politics. The first was contrary to treaty and impossible on grounds of finance and manpower. The second required something that no British government could give—an ability to impose conscription in order to meet a claim for help in advance. "My own view," concluded Lampson, "is that *real* security, in the sense the French use the word, is almost unattainable. You cannot keep a people of seventy millions permanently in subjection."[77]

The various reasons adduced within the British government for avoiding a military pact with France were not all strictly consistent. Some, indeed, logically contradicted one another. MacDonald particularly exhibited a talent for altering justifications as easily as actors change clothes. On one level the prime minister could argue in an ideological mode that, notwithstanding the views of the General Staff, a definite military agreement constituted "the very worst possible security."[78] On another level, he could advance the hard-headed calculation that "if we

75. Ibid.

76. Miles W. Lampson minute, 16 April 1924, F.O. 371/9813: C 5185/1346/18; see also the Foreign Office's formal rejection of the General Staff's conclusions as "too speculative" for adoption, in C. Howard Smith to War Office, 21 July 1924, F.O. 371/9818: C 11164/2048/18.

77. Lampson [writing at behest of Sir Eyre Crowe] to Lord D'Abernon, 23 June 1924, F.O. 371/9820: C 9313/2072/18.

78. MacDonald minute, 17 July 1924, commenting on War Office memorandum of 24 June 1924, F.O. 371/9818: C 11164/2048/18.

made France secure, thereby we would give her a free hand to work out her own political and economic policy in Europe and relieve her of all military implications which might result from her policy."[79]

In the end, the reasons hardly mattered. France would obtain nothing but words and, as a final reward for arduous lobbying, possibly some formal scrap of paper from Great Britain. In the meantime, though, British diplomats did not completely disdain the chance to dangle the lure of potential assistance before the French for ulterior purposes. In a survey prepared on 8 July for British Empire delegates at the London Conference, the Central Department underscored the advantage which the Foreign Office might draw from the French security quest: "That France knows her danger is only too apparent, and it is a shrewd surmise that her knowledge of it will finally stop her ever breaking from this country once she knows that we mean business. In all our controversies where we have held firm France has always given way. She knows that our support is indispensable."[80]

Crowe's Miscalculation and the Paris Rescue Operation

Our glance behind the scenes of British policymaking gives us a perspective denied to Herriot and his counselors at the Quai d'Orsay. It casts a rather altered light on the diplomatic exchanges of June and July 1924. The narrowly circumscribed immediate issue remained, of course, to complete preparations for launching the Dawes Plan. On this matter too the British determined to make the most of opportunity.

MacDonald and Crowe recognized that Herriot had acted "too impulsively and without enough knowledge of statecraft" in accepting their formulae at Chequers. But since Peretti had attended throughout, they thought that the understandings reached there would hold.[81] Long and rather disagreeable experience had led the British Foreign Office to confirm all agreements with the Quai d'Orsay as soon as possible in writing. In order to "tie the French down" in this case, the Foreign Office sent a memorandum to the principal governments concerned, inviting them to the forthcoming London Conference and setting forth an agenda along the lines sketched out at Chequers.[82]

79. Minutes of the Committee of Imperial Defence, CAB 2/4: 188th Meeting, 2 October 1924.

80. Central Department "Memorandum on French Security" [by John M. Troutbeck], 8 July 1924, F.O. 371/9818: C 11164/2048/18; printed also as CAB 4/11: C.I.D. Paper 513–B.

81. See MacDonald's explanation to Lamont, Thomas Lamont to Dwight Morrow, 11 July 1924, T. W. Lamont file, DWM; also Crowe's comments to the German ambassador, Sthamer tel., 17 July 1924, G.F.M. 3398/1736/D740001–007.

82. Cmd. 2184, *Correspondence concerning the Conference Which It Is Proposed to Hold in London on July 16, 1924 to Consider the Measures Necessary to Bring the Dawes Plan into Operation* (London, 1924). The invitation to the United States, not included in this collection, is found in *Papers Relating to the Foreign Relations of the United States, 1924* (Washington, D.C., 1939), 2:28–30.

This strategy might well have worked except that Crowe overreached himself. Instead of sending the same invitation to the several powers in straightforward fashion, he inserted slight but crucial differences into each communication.[83] The Foreign Office therein unveiled the protocol by which it proposed to give effect to the Dawes Report. The text followed the draft prepared in Whitehall several weeks before and did not take account even of the feeble objections made by the French at Chequers. In the note framed for the Quai d'Orsay, the Foreign Office described its suggestions merely as "the principal heads of subjects which . . . ought to be dealt with" and cautiously claimed that "on most of the points there was no serious disagreement." But its communications to the other powers gave no hint of remaining differences, and it informed the United States that the French and Belgians had "generally agreed" to "exact measures."

Crowe was not content to register the many specific points on which Herriot had given way; his categorical formulations conveyed the impression that everything was settled, even on matters where at Chequers Herriot had hesitantly demurred. Crowe denied that he sought to give the planned protocol "the appearance of a treaty explicitly modifying the Treaty of Versailles," but the tone of his dispatches fairly breathed the intention to alter key provisions of the Versailles settlement in practice. To no point had Crowe's drafting team devoted greater care than to eliminating loopholes through which the Reparation Commission might retain its prerogatives. The British communications elaborated the thesis that the Treaty of Versailles had "strictly determined" the commission's functions. Hence that body could not "properly be entrusted" with determining default under the Dawes scheme, which, according to the British theory, to a large extent lay "outside the scope" of the treaty.

In addition to its conscious maneuvers on questions of substance, the Foreign Office also committed a breach of etiquette by failing to include a formal "invitation" to the conference in the note sent to France. This latter oversight was quite inadvertent, but those in France intent on upsetting the Chequers agreement could seize upon it as a symbol of British duplicity.

Almost from the moment of Herriot's return home, meanwhile, a gnawing anxiety about what had occurred at Chequers took hold in Paris political circles. Herriot's vague and elusive explanations to parliament on 26–27 June did nothing to calm apprehensions.[84] Even some members of his own party joined the critics in the lobbies. Herriot, one moderate Radical complained, had "spoken to Ramsay MacDonald as he

83. For proof that the differences in wording were deliberate and not the result of carelessness, see successive drafts for the invitations by Harold Nicolson and Crowe in F.O. 371/9748: C 10070/70/18.

84. *J.O.S. Déb.*, 26 June 1924, pp. 928–29; *J.O.C. Déb.*, 27 June 1924, pp. 2369–73; reactions chronicled in *Le Matin* and *L'Echo de Paris*, 27 June, *Le Temps*, 28 June 1924.

speaks to Léon Blum."[85] Day after day Pertinax pounded away at the ministry in *L'Echo de Paris*, exposing the contradictions between Herriot's public explanations and those furnished by MacDonald in the House of Commons. French career diplomats largely shared these misgivings. Finally Saint-Aulaire, possibly with tacit encouragement from colleagues at the Quai d'Orsay, leaked the text of the British memorandum—and the news that France had not received a formal invitation to the conference—to *L'Echo de Paris*.[86] These revelations set off a tremendous storm in the press. The proposed protocol, Pertinax thundered, constituted nothing less than a "veritable treaty of insurance against independent action by France, bestowed upon the German Reich." He saw looming on the horizon a "new Sedan."[87] Unable to find any appropriate way to defend the government, the Cartel newspapers seemed disoriented.[88]

Herriot too was shaken. At a joint session of the Chamber Finance and Foreign Affairs Commissions on 4 July, he asserted that the ideas embodied in the British memorandum did not bind the French government, and he blamed the difficulties on "misrepresentations" in the press. But his hesitant and self-contradictory testimony did little to improve the atmosphere. The premier emerged visibly wilted after precise and hostile questioning by Louis Dubois, former president of the Reparation Commission, and by former premier Aristide Briand, whose adroitly posed queries carried the unmistakable implication that he remained available if his colleagues decided that the times required a more sophisticated statesman at the helm.[89]

In the next days Herriot appeared a forlorn and pathetic figure, hardly knowing which way to turn, overwhelmed by the treasury's financial difficulties as well as by a belated recognition of the complexities of diplomacy. To foreign visitors he repeated compulsively that though the "fate of Europe" hung in the balance, he could not foresee the outcome and did not know if his government would survive the coming Senate debate. The American ambassador offered an uncharitable but not unjust evaluation: "While the situation is undoubtedly grave . . . I cannot

85. "Bonneteau politique," *Le Progrès civique*, 12 July 1924.

86. *L'Echo de Paris*, 3–4 July 1924. On the source of the leak, see extensive correspondence by British diplomats in F.O. 371/9846: C 10657/10193/18; F.O. 371/9847: C 10912/10193/18; and F.O. 371/9849: C 10831/10831/18; also Crowe's explanation to Sthamer, 17 July 1924, G.F.M. 3398/1736/D740001–007. (Herriot was slow to catch on. He complained to the German ambassador on 8 July that Pertinax must have obtained his information through a leak in the Wilhelmstrasse: see G.F.M. 3398/1736/D739898–901.)

87. *L'Echo de Paris*, 4 July 1924; also *Le Matin*, 4 July 1924.

88. Hoesch tel., 5 July 1924, G.F.M. 3398/1736/D739881–883; Herrick to State Department, 5 July 1924, U.S. 462.00R 296/399; Crewe no. 432 to MacDonald, 4 July 1924, F.O. 371/9846: C 10719/10193/18.

89. Crewe no. 437 to MacDonald, 6 July 1924, F.O. 371/9846: C 10788/10193/18; Hoesch tel., 6 July 1924, G.F.M. 3398/1736/D739885–886; *L'Echo de Paris*, 5 July 1924; "Bonneteau politique," *Le Progrès civique*, 12 July 1924.

help feeling that Herriot's pessimism is largely due to the fact that, vulgarly speaking, he finds he is not a big enough man for the job."[90]

Desperately seeking a way to calm public opinion, Herriot finally begged MacDonald to come to Paris on a rescue mission.[91] This appeal found the professional staff at Whitehall still seething with fury over disclosure of the British memorandum to the press. And Peretti, they felt, had added offense to injury, by first calling in their ambassador and denying that the French government had ever accepted the British program for the London Conference and then charging (quite illogically) that the British Foreign Office had itself leaked the embarrassing documents to *L'Echo de Paris*.[92] Peretti's claim to have learned this from a tap on Pertinax's telephone was obviously a bluff—British intelligence carried out similar surveillance of Pertinax's London contact, Maurice Gerothwohl of the *Daily Telegraph*, and knew perfectly well from whence disclosure had come. But the British Embassy in Paris had long suffered inconvenience because of the Surêté's annoying habit of listening in on its phones (British intelligence operatives worked with far greater subtlety). The Quai's open admission that it practiced undercover arts offered the Foreign Office its long-awaited opportunity to protest. Sir Eyre Crowe noted the "great indignation" felt in the Office at the "slanderous habits and practices of the Quai d'Orsay." It had hitherto proved difficult to "nail them down and expose their lies," he told the prime minister, but here was "a flagrant case where we can do so definitely."[93]

MacDonald entirely agreed that Peretti's "behaviour in making trouble was abominable." Publicly, he sought to slither out of responsibility for the terms of the invitation to the conference. He had not looked at the documents before their dispatch, the prime minister told newspaper friends, because "not knowing French it was useless for him to see the originals and if he had seen a translation he could not have checked its accuracy"—a singular defense in view of the fact that the notes were sent out in English.[94] Within the confines of the Foreign Office, however, MacDonald kept his attention focused on the main problem of saving the Herriot government from the consequences of the gaffe, even

90. Herrick to State Department, 7 July 1924, U.S. 462.00R 296/403. See also Hoesch tel., 8 July 1924, G.F.M. 3398/1736/D739898–901; and the British press attaché's report that professionals in parliament considered Herriot "not of a caliber to defend the interests of France," Sir Charles Mendl to Sir William Tyrrell, 2 July 1924, F.O. 800/220/155–159, Mendl–Tyrrell Correspondence.

91. M. de Montille to Foreign Office, 6 July 1924, F.O. 371/9849: C 10908/10794/18; Crewe no. 439 to MacDonald, 7 July 1924, F.O. 371/9849: C 10794/10794/18.

92. Crewe no. 427 to MacDonald, 3 July 1924, F.O. 371/9846: C 10658/10193/18; Hughe Knatchbull-Hugessen to Miles W. Lampson, 4 July 1924, F.O. 371/9849: C 10831/10831/18.

93. Sir Eyre Crowe minute for the prime minister, 5 July 1924, F.O. 371/9849: C 10831/10831/18.

94. MacDonald comments to C. P. Scott and J. A. Hobson, 15 July 1924, in *The Political Diaries of C. P. Scott, 1911–1928*, ed. Trevor Wilson (Ithaca, N.Y., 1970), pp. 459–60.

while his more experienced career advisers seemed tempted to pursue a vendetta on a subsidiary issue with their French counterparts. "We perhaps did not show our best judgment in issuing the invitations in the form which we did," MacDonald told his staff on 5 July. "The situation must not be handled in a stilted and formal way. No stone must be left unturned to settle this trouble. Otherwise it may be the end of the conference."[95]

From Paris, meanwhile, Eric Phipps advised "some spectacular action" to show public opinion that Herriot had succeeded where "his sinister predecessor failed." Agitation in the French capital had spread far beyond the usual circles of "nationalist malevolence" to engulf many moderates, Phipps informed the prime minister, and even their closest socialist friends, including Léon Blum, had appeared at the Embassy to express concern. Drawing on his special expertise, Phipps added a tip on Gallic psychology to clinch the argument for dramatic intervention: "It is difficult for us to realize that the most sound and level-headed Frenchman is, in certain respects where his dignity and amour-propre are at stake, or supposed to be, more unreasonable than a hysterical Englishman (if such a person exist)."[96]

Fearing that if he failed to respond and Herriot fell, the potential advantages to be gained from the Dawes Report and Chequers "would go for naught," MacDonald made ready to visit Paris for a new round of meetings.[97] The first task at hand was to cast a veil of obscurity over the events of the preceding weeks. MacDonald's explanation of the Chequers agreement and the British memorandum to the House of Commons on 7 July set up such an impenetrable thicket of confusion that Liberal leader Herbert Asquith paid a high if inadvertent compliment to the effect achieved: "I am in a state of absolute bewilderment—unilluminated, complete bewilderment, as to what has happened or what is going to happen."[98]

Accompanied by Sir Eyre Crowe, MacDonald arrived in Paris the next afternoon. On this occasion Herriot was flanked by Seydoux and Parmentier as well as Peretti, and the Quai d'Orsay had prepared a stiff working paper expressing its own ideas on the best procedure for implementing the Experts' Plan.[99] The hectic schedule of meetings al-

95. MacDonald minute, 5 July 1924, F.O. 371/9846: C 10657/10193/18.

96. Eric Phipps to the prime minister, 6 July 1924, F.O. 371/9849: C 10907/10794/18.

97. See MacDonald's explanation to Thomas Lamont in Lamont to Dwight W. Morrow, 11 July 1924, Lamont file, DWM. Crowe, who was still angry at Peretti and Saint-Aulaire, reconciled himself to the necessary shift in tactics reluctantly. Initially he told the French chargé d'affaires that the prime minister could not take time out to visit Paris because of the press of parliamentary business and the claims made on his attention by an urgent crisis in Abyssinia (memorandum by Sir Eyre Crowe, 6 July 1924, F.O. 371/9849: C 10964/10794/18).

98. House of Commons *Debates*, 5th Series, 7 July 1924, col. 1753–54, 1801–13.

99. For the French procès-verbaux of these meetings, see copies in the Herriot Papers and in F.O. 371/9849: C 12828/10794/18. The English texts, including corrections in the British delegates' statements, are in F.O. 371/9849: C 11468/11469/12031/10794/18.

lowed the two sides insufficient time to review the manifold technical issues before them in any depth, however, and the delicate problem of handling French public opinion remained the primary focus of concern. MacDonald came resolved to "get up a new and temporary formula that would give Herriot something to stand upon in the Chamber even if both of them knew it was not workable." He told the French premier frankly, though, that when the London Conference began, they would have to "get back once more to a common basis of working out the Dawes Report sensibly and without such regard for French susceptibilities as was required . . . in preparation of a French ministerial crisis."[100]

The Englishman held his ground adamantly in the face of French attempts to reopen discussion on interallied debts and security. Herriot once more marshaled his battalion of tired adjectives to describe the danger he foresaw in ten years, when France, owing to the disastrous decline in its birthrate during the world war, would have an alarmingly small number of men under arms. He insisted on no particular formula for a pact; he expressed willingness to explore every alternative, even a treaty including Germany; and he offered the enticement that British cooperation would enable him to reduce the length of French military service to a year and to scale down his nation's military organization notwithstanding probable nationalist opposition. But such puny bait as a 10 percent diminution in French forces could hardly tempt MacDonald. The primer minister merely cranked up the gramophone and played the usual record when the course of the conversation seemed to require it: he was well disposed toward "continued moral collaboration" and would "so much like to be able to conclude the closest of alliances, that which is not written on a sheet of paper." Eventually he wearied of Herriot's badgering, and once he so far forgot his affectation of sympathy as to let slip the observation that "a respectable number of Englishmen perceived in French military preparations a possible threat to British security."[101]

MacDonald did accede to a number of French suggestions for revising the London Conference agenda, more indeed than Crowe believed wise.[102] Herriot deemed it crucial that the powers do nothing incompatible with the terms of the Versailles treaty when implementing the Experts' Report. To discuss the treaty and "call everything into question," he fretted, "could only lead us to a new war." He no longer wished to sign a protocol with the Germans. Now he only wanted to notify them that economic evacuation would take place after they had satis-

100. MacDonald's account to Lamont, reported in Lamont to Morrow, 11 July 1924, Lamont file, DWM; confirmed by Crowe's explanations to the German ambassador, Sthamer tels., 12 and 17 July 1924, G.F.M. 3398/1736/D739955–958, D740001–007.

101. Notes taken during a meeting at the British Embassy, 8 July 1924, 10 P.M., F.O. 371/9849: C 11468/10794/18.

102. See Kellogg to State Department, 10 July 1924, U.S. 462.00R 296/418.

fied the Reparation Commission. He insisted above all on guarding the Reparation Commission's undiminished power to declare default, though in deference to the bankers who would make the loan to Germany, he proposed that an American citizen vote with the commission hereafter whenever it considered the question.

At length, MacDonald reluctantly assented to this formula. The groggy negotiators, who had stayed up half the night, could not reach definite conclusions on other matters. No meeting of minds emerged on the details and timing of economic evacuation, on when to invite the Germans to the forthcoming conference (and in what capacity), on whether sanctions would depend on a unanimous vote in the event of future default, on who would interpret the Dawes Report in case of disagreement, and on a host of other issues. The memorandum drawn up to serve as the new agenda for the London Conference simply failed to mention these important matters or referred to them in high-flown language designed to paper over the continuing differences of opinion.[103] Once back in England, Sir Eyre Crowe hastened to reassure the German ambassador that "the new note could only have been drafted as ambiguous if it were to serve its purpose, to calm down the French," but that "one need hardly attribute particular importance to it."[104]

The Paris meetings therefore obscured rather than clarified the true status of negotiations. All that had been achieved was to make the conference possible and to give Herriot a new lease on office. The subsequent debate in the French Senate proved anticlimactic. Poincaré gave a five-hour encyclopedic review of all political, historical, and legal subjects under consideration, but his performance was oddly muted. Obviously, he sought not to create difficulties but merely to stiffen Herriot's back for the coming London negotiations.[105] When Herriot fumbled in reply, Poincaré intervened repeatedly to correct him regarding technical intricacies, but conspicuously abstained from comment on his successor's pessimistic general assessment of the prospect. "Henceforth for France," admitted Herriot, "the best solution of the reparations problem is simply the lesser evil."

If Herriot evinced little candor about the real import of the Paris communiqué, he was frank about the nation's fundamental position. He saw no alternative to holding the conference and putting the Dawes Plan into operation as soon as possible. The M.I.C.U.M. accords that provided France with reparations in kind could not last. The government could not contemplate resuming a full blockade of the Ruhr with all its

103. Cmd. 2191, *Franco-British Memorandum of July 9, 1924 concerning the Application of the Dawes Scheme* (London, 1924); also *Foreign Relations of the United States, 1924,* 2:46–49.

104. Sthamer tel., 12 July 1924, G.F.M. 3398/1736/D739955–958. MacDonald gave parliament a slightly more discreet explanation: House of Commons *Debates*, 5th Series, 10 July 1924, col. 2464–67.

105. *J.O.S. Déb.*, 10 July 1924, pp. 1018–38.

attendant difficulties should the Germans recommence resistance. In order to obtain the loan for Germany required to launch the Dawes Plan, it was imperative to satisfy the moneylenders somehow. And above everything came French security. Herriot put it bluntly, "Before knowing if we will live rich or poor, we must find out whether we will live at all." So the government had to give first priority to what it considered indispensable for peace: restoration of a real entente with England.[106] Stripped of grandiloquent rhetoric, this assessment offered little ground for serious contest. To achieve a reparations settlement and to create an atmosphere in Europe conducive to the search for security, France would have to pay a price. In the next few days Herriot met with increasing pressure from two directions—first from the Germans, then from the international bankers in coordination with the English. This pressure confirmed the French opposition's worst premonitions of how high that price might be.

German Objectives

At this juncture the performance of German leaders could hardly fail to command admiration, even from those opposed to their substantive goals. These leaders, demonstrating a rare combination of skill and judgment in assessing the tactical options, took into account both their domestic constraints and the quality and mentality of the foreign statesmen with whom they would have to reckon. Though possessed of mediocre intellectual gifts, Chancellor Wilhelm Marx radiated such integrity and evident Christian selflessness that he created an atmosphere in which the most recalcitrant of his political associates could come to grips with inescapable realities. Finance Minister Hans Luther seemed the archetype of the stolid, rather rigid Prussian bureaucrat. But his bullheaded toughness and prodigious capacity for work had brought precarious order out of chaos in Reich finances, and he proved uncompromising in holding to priorities necessary to consolidate the progress already made. Foreign Minister Gustav Stresemann towered above the others. Stresemann projected a dual image in these years. Abroad he appeared the good European working for détente, at home a man sharing at many points the Nationalists' outlook and ultimate goals. But he showed himself always—in the Bismarckian tradition to which he often quite consciously appealed—rigorously pragmatic and careful in the tactics pursued toward achievement of those goals.[107]

106. Ibid., 11 July 1924, pp. 1050–60.

107. No biography of Chancellor Marx exists. See, however, the careful edition of his papers: *Der Nachlass des Reichskanzlers Wilhelm Marx*, ed. Hugo Stehkämper, Mitteilungen aus dem Stadtarchiv von Köln, vols. 52–55 (Cologne, 1968); the introductory essay in *Akten der Reichskanzlei, Weimarer Republik, Die Kabinette Marx I und II*, ed. Günter Abramowski, 2 vols. (Boppard am Rhein, 1973), 1:vii–xlix; the descriptions scattered through Rudolf Morsey, *Die Deutsche Zentrumspartei, 1917–1923* (Düsseldorf, 1966); and the memoirs of

On 3 July 1924 the Reich cabinet and the ministers-president of the German states conducted an all-day review of prospects for the London Conference. The meeting bore witness to the remarkable abilities of all three men.[108] With virtual unanimity the assemblage recognized that Germany's need for long-term American capital had to determine policy. "Sad as it is," said Marx, "we must nevertheless follow the only path which can lead to our obtaining the absolutely essential foreign credits."[109] Luther offered striking proof that no viable alternative existed to bringing the Dawes Plan into operation by October at the latest. The war and inflation had entirely dissipated investment and working capital. After stabilization of the currency in autumn 1923, taxation had drained out of the private sector what liquid capital remained. Now tax receipts too had dropped alarmingly, government resources approached depletion, and business credit from German banks was unavailable on any terms. Agriculture faced a particularly desperate situation. As things stood, the fall harvest could not be financed. The structure and seasonal marketing pattern of the crucial artificial fertilizer industry rendered it peculiarly vulnerable to the credit shortage. An all too predictable upsurge of urban unemployment also threatened to magnify the danger of social instability.

In two ways only could the Reich generate sufficient capital to avoid these difficulties: through foreign borrowing or a new inflation. The latter alternative was not to be contemplated. The 1923 hyperinflation had left no practicable way to prime the economy by means of moderate and carefully controlled monetary expansion. The general public did not have confidence in the permanence of monetary stabilization. Statistics showing a relatively high volume of cash and demand deposits in contrast to the dearth of funds available for investment furnished evidence of popular skepticism. At the first sign of renewed inflation, Luther pointed out, the public would become so alarmed that the velocity of money would increase radically. Prices could rise sixfold with the currency presently in circulation. The situation might rapidly deteriorate to the point where the populace would no longer accept any fiduciary means of payment, and this would immobilize the whole economy.

Center party politician Heinrich Köhler, *Lebenserinnerungen des Politikers und Staatsmannes* (Stuttgart, 1964). Luther wrote *Politiker ohne Partei: Erinnerungen* (Stuttgart, 1960); his sometime research assistants Karl Bernhard Netzband and Hans Peter Widmaier elaborated on his technical contribution to Reich finance in *Währungs- und Finanzpolitik der Ära Luther, 1923–1925* (Basel, 1964). Studies of Stresemann include Hans W. Gatzke, *Stresemann and the Rearmament of Germany* (Baltimore, 1954); Annelise Thimme, *Gustav Stresemann* (Hanover and Frankfurt am Main, 1957); Roland Thimme, *Stresemann und die deutsche Volkspartei, 1923–1925* (Lübeck and Hamburg, 1961); Henry Ashby Turner, Jr., *Stresemann and the Politics of the Weimar Republic* (Princeton, 1963); and Robert Gottwald, *Die deutsch-amerikanischen Beziehungen in der Ära Stresemann* (Berlin, 1965).

108. "Niederschrift über die Sitzung der Reichsregierung mit den Staats- und Ministerpräsidenten," 3 July 1924, BA, R 43 I/42/244–431.

109. BA, R 43 I/42/345–346.

Luther enlarged on the grim prospect of starving and half-crazed city residents roaming the countryside, farmers burning the harvests, in short, general social breakdown. Without long-term foreign credits he saw "no possibility at all of further existence for the German people."[110] Did this constitute rhetorical exaggeration, belying Luther's habitual sobriety? At a minimum, Stresemann pointed out, to reject the Dawes Plan and thus condemn the occupied areas to remain a "reparations province" would be gambling with the unity of the Reich.[111]

But if economic circumstances dictated German acceptance of the Dawes Plan for the moment, the ministers in Berlin confidently expected to profit from the fact that France labored under a similar compulsion. American enthusiasm for the Experts' work provided the essential cue for German diplomacy. England alone, Stresemann observed, was too weak to stand against France: "If the United States, on the other hand, were only to push the button and summon France to pay the back interest on its war debt, then the franc would fall into the abyss, and the whole French economy and French investors would face the chaos to which the collapse of our currency exposed us." Hence the French cabinet, he reasoned, would not dare take a stand in opposition to America.[112]

Stresemann believed that the German interest lay in encouraging investment of American capital in the Reich over the long as well as the short term. Some people might not approve capitalism's decisive role in world affairs, he reflected, but "if American capitalism had not been against us, then we certainly would not have lost the war." Once international capital acquired a material interest in German prosperity, he held, the major financial powers would take quite a different view of things.[113]

Thus the standard annual reparations payment of 2.5 milliard gold marks stipulated by the Dawes Plan did not worry Stresemann unduly. He endorsed Luther's judgment concerning the "overwhelming probability" that Germany could never make a payment of such magnitude. But his conversations with Reginald McKenna, chairman of the Second Committee of Experts, had left him with the intuition that the English and Americans had "arranged things in such a way as to prove to the world that the whole reparations business wouldn't go as it has up to now, when Germany was simply told, 'You must pay so and so much.'" Here Stresemann perceived the political significance of the Transfer Committee. He felt sure that the Anglo-Saxon powers would not wish Germany to develop its trade hegemony up to the point where it could actually transfer the specified standard payment.[114]

110. BA, R 43 I/42/267–285.
111. BA, R 43 I/42/261.
112. BA, R 43 I/42/262.
113. BA, R 43 I/42/354–359.
114. BA, R 43 I/42/263–264.

In any event, according to the Treaty of Versailles, Germany could request a fresh examination of its capacity to pay after three years had elapsed, and the Reich would not neglect this opportunity. Of course, Stresemann noted, he could not admit this publicly. "Otherwise there would be an immediate outcry: 'Aha! They haven't even signed, yet there they go again, already thinking about how to avoid fulfillment!' " But he deemed another review of German capacity essential by 1928—the first year in which the Dawes schedule obligated the Reich to make substantial cash payments in addition to deliveries in kind and support for the occupation armies in the Rhineland. Stresemann explained why he felt confident that this investigation would lead to further reduction of the German debt: "Let a few years go by in which France receives no reparations, because they are to be paid only out of a surplus in the German economy, and final capacity to pay will be conceived differently than it has been up to now."[115]

The explicit tone of this discussion in the privacy of the Reich Chancellery would no doubt have dismayed certain optimists on the French left. Still, even the most fervent partisans of the Cartel des Gauches could hardly fail to comprehend the general nature of German calculations. Pertinax, for one, reminded them daily. Without a complete reversal in policy, he prophesied on 11 July, France was "fated to record the definitive victory of the Germans in the affair of reparations."[116] In point of fact, no one segment of the French political spectrum held a monopoly on pessimism in this regard. Herriot, as we have seen, avowed his own uneasiness about the prospects for collecting reparations in the future, and experts at the Finance Ministry furnished concrete facts and figures to reinforce his feeling of gloom.[117] To what extent did a basis exist for Herriot's hope that accepting the inevitable gracefully in this area might open the way for progress toward a more secure Europe?

Stresemann's ultimate objectives during the six crowded years when he directed German foreign policy cannot be divined by focusing single-mindedly on his views at one particular time, but much of what he said at the 3 July planning session prefigured future developments. With characteristic clarity he explained the tangible political advantages that would accrue to the Reich as a result of the reparations settlement. He defined the goal as a change in the world's "whole attitude" toward Germany. He sought to foster an international climate in which the Germans would not have to appear "with bowed heads" and which would lead other nations to recognize that even if political means existed

115. BA, R 43 I/42/263–264, 266, 347–348.

116. *L'Echo de Paris*, 11 July 1924.

117. See the note by Henri Clerc, Finance Ministry bureau chief in charge of technical preparation for the forthcoming conference, "Comment se posera la triple question des réparations, des dettes interalliées et du budget français après la mise en application du plan des experts," 10 June 1924; cf. also Clerc's even more negative "Note pour le président du conseil," 26 July 1924; both documents in Herriot Papers.

"to carry through a scandalous treaty, that did not make it moral truth."[118] Stresemann deprecated the domestic pressure (to which he nonetheless capitulated some weeks later) to denounce the so-called war guilt lie publicly. That sort of gesture, he maintained, would not alter actual power relationships in Europe. Endeavoring by contrast to create a sense of trust, he aimed to set forces in motion that would produce military evacuation of the occupied areas. He already discerned one hopeful sign: distinguished figures on the left in England were criticizing the military preparations of the east European nations and asserting that in contrast Germany had fully disarmed.[119]

What of the more distant future? State President Wilhelm Bazille of Württemberg expressed the Nationalist position: In the face of a united front by the three great Western democracies Germany might have to acquiesce for the moment, but "one day the problems of Europe could only be resolved by the sword." There existed, in his view, "not the slightest hope for a peaceful solution."[120] To this Stresemann made a revealingly pragmatic response:

> I fervently hope that if it comes to that—and I believe that in the final analysis these great questions will always be decided by the sword—the moment may be put off as long as possible. I can only foresee the downfall of our people so long as we do not have the sword—that much is certain. If we look forward to a time when the German people will again be strong enough to play a more significant role, then we must first give the German people the necessary foundation. . . . To create this foundation is the most urgent challenge facing us.[121]

In short, Stresemann and his principal colleagues in the German government seemed inclined to strike a bargain on the Dawes Plan—whatever the terms they could obtain for the moment. They counted on future opportunities to redress such defects as remained in the settlement. But their shrewd calculations had also to take the domestic parliamentary opposition into account. The outcome of the May 1924 German elections placed them in a delicate political position. The balloting had witnessed a sharp swing to both political extremes. Subsequently, extended negotiations had taken place with the aim of facilitating participation by the Nationalist party (DNVP) in the cabinet. These negotiations led to no positive result largely because Nationalist leaders, though eager for inclusion, showed themselves unwilling to abandon their outright opposition to the Dawes Plan publicly so soon after they had vaunted that opposition as the major plank in their campaign platform. The Marx-Stresemann ministry had therefore continued in office without major personnel changes. However, one legislative enactment essential to implement the Dawes Plan—that involving reorganization of the

118. BA, R 43 I/42/256–258.
119. BA, R 43 I/42/254–255, 352–353.
120. BA, R 43 I/42/286–289.
121. BA, R 43 I/42/360.

German Railway Company—necessitated certain amendments to the Weimar Constitution. These amendments required approval of two-thirds of the Reichstag. Neither the Communists nor the German Racialists Freedom party (as the National Socialists then called themselves) could be won for any constructive endeavor. Together these two anti-parliamentary groups comprised one-fifth of the new Reichstag. The two-thirds majority for the railway law could be achieved only through cooperation of at least a fraction of the Nationalist delegation.[122]

The *Kreuzzeitung* continued to hurl imprecations at the Dawes Plan with undiminished partisan fervor, but actually the more moderate Nationalist leaders, such as Professor Otto Hoetzsch, eagerly sought to find some method of accommodation that would permit ratification of the Dawes Plan and enable their party to resume negotiations for joining the cabinet. They realized full well that if they torpedoed the plan, the government's only recourse would be to dissolve the Reichstag and hold new elections—in all likelihood under conditions disadvantageous to the DNVP.[123] The industrial wing of the party was acutely aware of the need for foreign capital to relieve the credit shortage and to bolster the precariously balanced rentenmark. The Reichswehr too advanced a number of compelling reasons in favor of acceptance. General von Seeckt held that the benefits of French withdrawal from the Ruhr would far outweigh the new obligations imposed on the Reich, which in the long run would "come to an end by themselves because of their inherent impracticability." For those who assigned first priority to rebuilding the German army, the choice seemed clear. In another election following rejection of the plan, the pendulum might swing back toward the Social Democrats, and this could endanger smooth progress in the secret rearmament program. Rejection might also delay abolition of the Interallied Military Control Commission.[124]

Hence, rational calculations of self-interest should have dictated endorsement of the Dawes Plan even by those sharing the Nationalist weltanschauung. Yet some segments of the party opposed reparations

122. Erich Eyck, *A History of the Weimar Republic*, trans. Harlan P. Hanson and Robert G. L. Waite, 2 vols. (Cambridge, Mass., 1962), 1:299–300, 306–7, 314–15; Stresemann, *Vermächtnis*, 1:408–14; Turner, *Stresemann*, pp. 167–71. For the crucial 15 and 24 May 1924 cabinet meetings on the question of Nationalist participation in the government, see BA, R 43 I/41/415–421, 518–520.

123. See Ambassador Alanson B. Houghton's reports on his discussions with Hoetzsch and other Nationalist leaders, U.S. 462.00R 296/322, 334, 532; U.S. 862.00/1491, 1516, 1526, 1539. For general discussion of the Nationalists' dilemma, see Werner Liebe, *Die Deutschnationale Volkspartei, 1918–1924* (Düsseldorf, 1956), pp. 76–86; and Lewis Hertzmann, *DNVP: Right-Wing Opposition in the Weimar Republic, 1918–1924* (Lincoln, Neb., 1963), pp. 204–39.

124. Major-General Otto Hasse [chief of the *Truppenamt*], "Tagebuch," May–June 1924, Stück 281, Roll 26, General Hans von Seeckt Papers, microfilm copy, Harvard College Library, Cambridge, Mass.; General Marcks to Friedrich von Rabenau, 1 August 1939, Stück 290, Roll 26, and Seeckt's letters to his wife, May–August 1924, Roll 28, Seeckt Papers.

payments and détente within the framework of the hated Versailles treaty with such blind passion that they disdained judicious cerebrations. The DNVP was beset by factional disputes, and ever since Karl Helfferich's accidental death in April it had lacked firm leadership. Up to the last minute, therefore, it remained doubtful whether enough Nationalists would vote for the enabling laws to implement the Dawes Plan. Throughout the summer Stresemann skillfully turned this domestic political difficulty to diplomatic advantage by repeatedly impressing upon the Allies that substantial concessions alone could ensure the requisite Reichstag majority.

In telegrams of mounting urgency to Ambassador von Hoesch in Paris, Stresemann called military evacuation the "cardinal point of the whole situation" from the parliamentary perspective. He sought an assurance that French troops would leave not only the Ruhr proper but also all other areas occupied since 1920 to force compliance with the treaty, particularly the three cities controlling Ruhr communications and transport—Düsseldorf, Duisburg, and Ruhrort—which had been seized as a sanction in March 1921. Without satisfactory guarantees on this matter, the foreign minister indicated, the Nationalists would not abandon their opposition, and he might not possess the power to hold his own party, the German People's party (DVP), in line.[125]

Stresemann and his advisers at the Wilhelmstrasse did not insist that French troops withdraw immediately. "Provided that I have a fixed date for evacuation I can afford to agree to a date within fairly wide limits," the foreign minister told Lord D'Abernon on 2 July. Evacuation within the second year of the Dawes Plan, Stresemann had earlier calculated, would give him sufficient leverage to overcome the doubts of waverers in the Reichstag. The one requirement of overriding importance, in his view, was to secure a binding commitment that on some specific date the last foreign soldier would leave the Ruhr.[126] Though the Experts' Report had passed over the matter with conspicuous silence, he anticipated no better opportunity than this moment, when the Allies sought Germany's voluntary signature, to mobilize world opinion in favor of military evacuation. Unless a terminal date were fixed irrevocably, he feared that the status quo might "simply be accepted" with the passage of time and fading recollections of the original issues in dispute. As Herriot's parliamentary weakness became increasingly apparent, Stresemann perceived an additional reason to settle as many questions as possible quickly, for once Herriot were overthrown, the future seemed "at least

125. See Stresemann's exchanges with Hoesch, 28 June–15 July 1924, G.F.M. 3398/1736/D739845–740007; also Stresemann, *Vermächtnis*, 1:457–59.

126. Carl von Schubert memorandum for Lord D'Abernon, 1 July 1924, F.O. 371/9749: C 10638/70/18; D'Abernon tel. no. 292 to Foreign Office, 2 July 1924, F.O. 371/9749: C 10650/70/18; cf. also a Central Department review of Stresemann's earlier confidential statements, 3 June 1924, F.O. 371/9747: C 8966/70/18.

doubtful," even if Briand or Loucheur took his place at the Quai d'Orsay.[127]

When Hoesch first broached the question of military evacuation after Herriot's return from Chequers, the French premier sought to avoid commitment. Military evacuation, he observed, was "a delicate subject." He intimated that the London Conference would concentrate on the economic settlement; military withdrawal would have to "emerge of itself from the development of events" afterward.[128] Through the first days of July, nevertheless, Stresemann remained relatively optimistic that if he calmly persisted, Herriot would eventually yield. Assurances made by British financial officials that the international bankers charged with floating the loan would probably "take care of" the matter buoyed his confidence.[129]

The public outcry in France that followed publication of the British memorandum and agenda for the London Conference undermined these sanguine calculations. German diplomats followed events in Paris with growing apprehension. On 7 July Bergery told Hoesch that surrender of "the only tangible guarantee"—namely, the military occupation—would begin to appear possible only when commercialization of some of the railway and industrial bonds had created a "world interest in German fulfillment."[130] Herriot offered even less precision when he saw the German ambassador the next day. Referring plaintively to his "good will" and "honest endeavor to produce peace," he nevertheless declared that the state of public opinion made any commitment on military evacuation "absolutely impossible." Hoesch added his own evaluation to guide Berlin: if Herriot now set a definite date for military withdrawal, it would undeniably cause his "immediate fall."[131]

Stresemann did not underestimate the precariousness of Herriot's parliamentary position, and he did not wish to add to the latter's difficulties by untoward stridency of tone. But to achieve his own substantive objectives he would willingly demonstrate that two could play at the game of falling ministries. He declined to consider any connection between military evacuation and commercialization of the railway and industrial obligations since that, he charged, would in effect leave the timing of withdrawal up to the Allies. He insisted also that detailed planning for economic evacuation could not be left to the Reparation Commission and the Allied powers alone. Aside from the French, only the Germans possessed intimate administrative knowledge of the occu-

127. Stresemann's exchanges with Hoesch, 28 June–15 July 1924, G.F.M. 3398/1736/D739845–740007; Stresemann's analysis of 3 July 1924, BA, R 43 I/42/245–252.

128. Hoesch tel., 28 June 1924, G.F.M. 3398/1736/D739845–848.

129. Julius Ruppel tel., 3 July 1924, reporting views expressed at Reparation Commission headquarters by British delegate Sir John Bradbury, G.F.M. 3398/1736/D739864–865.

130. Hoesch tel., 7 July 1924, G.F.M. 3398/1736/D739887–888.

131. Hoesch tel., 8 July 1924, G.F.M. 3398/1736/D739898–901.

pied areas. Thus Stresemann considered it imperative for German representatives to participate in the final planning for evacuation. In view of the sensitivity of public opinion in the Reich to matters of prestige, moreover, the German government could not simply accept a protocol that the Allies had agreed upon ahead of time, for such a document whatever its actual content would appear to the Reichstag as a de facto ultimatum. In consequence, the German delegation solicited an invitation to participate in the London Conference on a footing of equality and, if not at the beginning, at least in time to play a meaningful part in the proceedings. If Herriot held to ideas hitherto prevailing on these matters, Stresemann warned, a fall of the German government seemed "inevitable." This would endanger the fate of the Experts' Report and the position of Herriot's ministry as well.[132]

The German cabinet endorsed this stiffer posture. It resolved to serve notice on the Allies that unless they gave Germany firm assurances respecting military evacuation, it would decline to cooperate in carrying the Dawes Plan legislation through the Reichstag.[133] The English could offer no immediate satisfaction. They succeeded in persuading German diplomats that MacDonald had not irredeemably compromised their case during his emergency visit to Paris. Nonetheless, the Germans felt stymied. They could see no tangible signs of progress toward their principal objective.[134]

When Hoesch finally got to see Herriot again on the evening of 14 July, he found the French premier "extraordinarily depressed and pessimistic." Shaken and disillusioned, Herriot poured out his heart: he had erred in thinking that "good will and sincerity alone" could solve Europe's problems. He had thrown himself boldly into a difficult undertaking, but had clearly "gone too quickly." Demands that no one would have made to Poincaré pressed in upon him from all sides. Preparation for the London Conference had been insufficient, and he did not know if the French and English could reach agreement there. At any rate, his guiding rule would be to allow no alterations in the Versailles treaty, even if this meant leaving the conference. No doubt such an action would gravely disappoint his electoral supporters who had hoped for a policy of reconciliation, but by nipping in the bud "a danger of war inextricably linked with curtailment of the peace treaty" he would perform a service for future generations. In sum, he refused for the moment to make any further promises, with respect to conditions for military

132. Stresemann to Hoesch, 7, 8, and 13 July 1924, G.F.M. 3398/1736/D739889–892, D739902–907, D739959–968.

133. "Ministerbesprechung," 9 July 1924, BA, R 43 I/42/621–626; excerpted in Stresemann, *Vermächtnis*, 1:451–54.

134. Stresemann conversation with Lord D'Abernon, 10 July 1924, G.F.M. 3398/1736/D739938–940; Hoesch tel., 11 July, Sthamer tel., 12 July 1924, G.F.M. 3398/1736/D739948–951, D739955–958.

evacuation, or the date on which the Germans might expect an invitation to the conference, the procedure to govern cases of default, or indeed anything else.[135]

The French premier's new caution disappointed the Wilhelmstrasse. State Secretary Ago von Maltzan, the leading German career diplomat, regretted that Herriot had allowed "the old crowd of technical officials" in the French government departments to dampen his "idealistic ardor" with their traditional misgivings and prejudices.[136] Yet the German cabinet did not give way to undue pessimism. Its diplomatic campaign of the preceding weeks had at least succeeded in making clear to the French that they could not take political stability in the Reich for granted. The ministers in Berlin foresaw various means—enlisting the support of the other Allied nations, enlarging on the "spirit" of the Dawes Report, above all soliciting the bankers' opinion regarding the necessary prerequisites for a loan—by which they might still obtain military evacuation of the Ruhr.[137] The initiative, in Stresemann's view, now rested with the Allies until clarification of the basic issue: "whether at London the Anglo-American thesis of negotiation and understanding or the French thesis of unilateral decision and dictation prevails."[138]

J. P. Morgan & Co. and the Dawes Plan

The international bankers exerted the second and, as it turned out, decisive influence on Herriot. They would have to float the 800 million mark loan to Germany that the Dawes Committee considered essential to its plan. They would have to be satisfied that the reparations settlement concluded at the London Conference gave such promise of stability that they could recommend the loan to investors with confidence.

Chief among the bankers stood J. P. Morgan & Co., the same firm whose line of credit had saved the franc in March. French financial authorities, as we have seen, considered Morgan's continued support indispensable to help their nation cope with a broad range of problems in public finance. France therefore needed to retain the bankers' goodwill. Morgan's too was sincerely committed to promoting restoration of sound French finance not simply as a business proposition but out of the same genuine sympathy that had motivated its wartime efforts on behalf of the Allies. How paradoxical, therefore, that these same bankers should find themselves obliged by circumstances to play a central role in forcing France to yield to its opponents in the reparations dispute! The reasons

135. Hoesch tel., 15 July 1924, G.F.M. 3398/1736/D739972–977.

136. Maltzan to Otto Wiedfeldt [Washington, D.C.], 15 July 1924, G.F.M. 3398/1736/D739982–983.

137. "Ministerbesprechung," 15 July 1924, BA, R 43 I/42/631–635.

138. Stresemann to Hjalmar Schacht, 15 July 1924, G.F.M. 3398/1736/D739978.

for this development can be traced to the conditions under which the Dawes Plan originated.

As the dominant firm in the New York securities market, Morgan's had handled most major government financing in America since the war—not only for the former European allies, but also for Japan and for rehabilitation of Austria. Along with the Bank of England, Morgan's had customarily been consulted about the possibility of reparations loans; a scheme for German financial reform that did not bear the Morgan stamp of approval would scarcely inspire the confidence of the banking community and the investment public requisite to success.

Some competitive firms resented Morgan's imperturbable assumption of preeminence in international securities markets. Morgan's was "busy everywhere in Europe" and "exceedingly active and pushing," Otto Kahn of Kuhn, Loeb had complained in 1923 (ironically reversing the common Wall Street ethnic stereotype).[139] Undoubtedly Morgan's acted arbitrarily on occasion. J. P. Morgan, for example, harbored a burning hatred of one prominent German-American banking house that had shown sympathy for the Central powers during the war; when he determined to exclude this firm from a role in the Dawes loan on the ground that its appearance in the underwriting syndicate would "degrade" Morgan's in the eyes of "every decent man," no practical arguments advanced by his partners or by associated banking houses could sway his mind.[140] The style of Morgan leadership also provoked disgruntlement elsewhere on Wall Street. After Morgan's had already decided exactly how to proceed with the Austrian rehabilitation loan of 1923, for instance, partners Dwight Morrow and Thomas Cochran came over to Kuhn, Loeb and other firms and pretended to "confer." The furious Otto Kahn was not appeased by the fact that "all of this high-handedness is clothed in admirable manners and high-bred demeanor."[141]

Still, when all was said and done, even the most acerbic of Morgan's critics was bound to concede that the firm earned its leadership role by willingness—uncharacteristic of other Wall Street firms—to risk immediate financial loss for a broader purpose. During the war Morgan's had repeatedly wagered the prosperity of its own balance sheet to float loans for the Allies in a precarious financial environment. In the postwar era it assumed a similar posture. Charles E. Mitchell of the National City Bank—the one firm rivaling Morgan's in volume of international

139. Otto H. Kahn to Mortimer Schiff, 20 September 1923, Box 211, Otto H. Kahn Papers, Princeton University Library, Princeton, N.J. On the background to the conflict between Morgan's and Kuhn, Loeb, see John Brooks, *Once in Golconda: A True Drama of Wall Street, 1920–1938* (New York, 1969), pp. 50–56.

140. J. P. Morgan to J. P. Morgan & Co., 3 October 1924, TWL 177/21; also related correspondence in TWL 177/19.

141. Kahn to Mortimer Schiff, 4 June 1923, Box 211, Kahn Papers.

business—evaluated foreign investment purely from the standpoint of profitability. In the case of the Austrian loan, Mitchell had refused to contemplate absorption by his bank of those bonds that could not be sold to the public. J. P. Morgan, by contrast, had exhorted the underwriting syndicate that "it was the plain duty of American financial leaders to participate in a transaction which was of great and auspicious significance" in helping Europe regain its financial footing; his firm would "even be willing to incur a temporary financial lockup of reasonable proportions rather than have America fail to do its proper share."[142]

Thus most members of the financial community took it for granted that a major loan to Germany required Morgan sponsorship. Shortly before the Dawes Committee issued its report, Thomas Lamont reminded the Experts of the need for a strong underwriting group, implicitly under the aegis of his firm, to put over a loan in America: "Leadership in any German operation cannot be divided and cannot be entrusted to a town meeting. Those in authority on the other side must make up their minds . . . just who is to lead and direct the operation and then must rely fully upon that leadership."[143]

Strangely, the American Experts had made no special effort during the period of the report's gestation to consult with Morgan's more than with other firms. Owen D. Young, its principal author, later explained that he "did not want, if investigation came, to have the report called a Morgan Report."[144] Gerard Swope, Young's associate at the General Electric Corporation, had sounded out a representative sample of leading New York bankers regarding the conditions that would make flotation of a loan feasible. On behalf of Morgan's, Dwight Morrow gave advice consistent with that of other Wall Street spokesmen. New York financial leaders optimistically believed that the American market might absorb half of the $200 million loan under consideration in Paris, especially if the Experts carefully presented it as a banking and currency support operation rather than as a flotation for the direct payment of reparations. On the crucial issue of continued occupation of the Ruhr by French troops, the New York banking community did not show itself particularly exigent. If keeping French troops in the Ruhr produced a recrudescence of passive resistance in Germany or seriously dampened Britain's enthusiasm for the rehabilitation plan, the New York bankers advised, it would interfere with placing the loan. But if the soldiers remained as part of a general scheme to which all parties assented and their presence did not interfere with the region's economic life, Morrow in particular held that the occupation "would not affect, in any way, the marketing of the bonds in this country."[145]

142. Kahn to Schiff, 1 May 1923, Box 211, Kahn Papers.
143. Lamont to Morgan, Harjes et Cie, 25 March 1924, TWL 176/8.
144. Dwight Morrow to Lamont, 24 July 1924, Lamont file, DWM.
145. Owen D. Young to Gerard Swope, 27 February, 19 March 1924; Swope to Young, 28

As the Dawes Committee neared the end of its assigned task in April 1924, however, Morgan analysts at 23 Wall Street became steadily more apprehensive about other features of its work, which they had followed through the newspapers. The partners voiced concern that under political pressure the Dawes Committee might set the total schedule for German payments too high. "There is no one here who would not like to see the German reparations payments made just as large and just as soon as possible and who does not realize the great importance to France that this should be so," Lamont and Leffingwell cabled to their Paris office. "Our sympathies are all for making Germany pay to the last drop." Yet they fretted lest emotional considerations again prevent, as in earlier reparations diplomacy, a sober evaluation of what the international balance of payments would permit.[146] The actual release of the Dawes Report on 9 April, far from allaying this uneasiness, confirmed the worst fears at Morgan corner. "Now that Dawes and Owen [Young] have discovered the simple formula of making bread without flour, the wonder is that no one thought of it before," commented Russell Leffingwell with heavy sarcasm. "I hope our cables have left no impression in Paris that we could sell this gold brick."[147]

Detailed analysis of the Dawes Plan at Morgan offices over the next months served only to deepen this original pessimism. The Morgan partners' unfavorable assessment of the plan is one of the great ironies of the period, for their political predilections and human sympathies should naturally have led them to approve of it. For years Dwight Morrow had preached that any policy "which would bring the United States in some way on to the same side of the table with France and England in discussion with Germany about the reparation payment would be the first step toward economic recovery."[148] Morrow, and undoubtedly his partners too, had clearly understood that America could provide assistance most effectively by mediating among the European countries to help them work out an essentially political settlement. Morgan analysts had recognized that the economic component of the reparations problem—evaluation of German capacity to pay—played a distinctly secondary role. "In the first place no living man can tell how much they can pay," Morrow had advised his Amherst classmate Calvin Coolidge when the latter assumed the presidency, "and in the second place the question how much they can pay is and has been for the last three years a very minor question in the larger political one."[149]

February, 21 March 1924; copies in Folder 1/67, Box 7, Owen D. Young Papers; and in TWL 176/8.

146. Lamont and Leffingwell to Morgan, Harjes et Cie, 1 April 1924, TWL 176/8.

147. Leffingwell to Lamont, 9 April 1924, TWL 103/10.

148. See, e.g., Morrow to Charles J. Bullock, 22 April 1921, Reparations 1920–26 file, DWM.

149. Morrow to F. W. Stearns [Coolidge adviser and campaign manager], Calvin

Morrow had taken a quite optimistic view, furthermore, about the amount Germany could pay once postwar difficulties had been resolved and normal economic conditions restored. He flatly dismissed the neo-mercantilist arguments so dear to the liberal journals of that period. American liberal weeklies often contended that there existed only a limited amount of trade in the world and that an increase for Germany meant a decrease for other nations; hence, if the Allies insisted on extracting reparations, they would ineluctably disadvantage their own export industries. Morrow reached the conviction from his reading in economic history that, quite to the contrary, productivity and the standard of living were "constantly rising" so that the potential amount of world trade was "unlimited." Ultimately, he concluded, it was feasible for Germany to pay and advantageous for the Allies to accept reparations. The essential problem lay in the political sphere: to set an amount that "the German people are willing to believe that they can pay and will honestly set about paying" and thereby to encourage a fundamental "change in the German point of view" that would provide genuine security for France.[150]

Having been absent from the Experts' deliberations in Paris, Morrow and the other Morgan partners could not fully appreciate how delicate the Dawes Committee had found the task of reconciling so many different political influences. Yet indisputably that committee had achieved some political objectives which Morgan's had long favored. The United States had resumed its informal participation in European affairs, and the Experts had produced a report which, whatever its economic weaknesses, provided an appealing political basis for restoring Allied unity and settling with the Germans. There existed every reason to believe that as a matter of public policy the Morgan partners would show themselves well disposed and even enthusiastic.

However, J. P. Morgan & Co. was not a public institution. A grave weakness of the international monetary system of that era lay in the failure of governments and central banks to command regular instrumentalities of their own through which they could channel foreign lending when the national interest or international comity required it. In the absence of governmental institutions to facilitate international credit operations, private bankers had to assume certain quasi-governmental functions by default. This condition obtained nowhere more completely than in the United States, where Federal Reserve authorities in Washington concerned themselves primarily with regulating the domestic money

Coolidge/F. W. Stearns file, DWM. On Morrow's relationship with Coolidge, see also Harold Nicolson, *Dwight Morrow* (New York, 1935), pp. 33–34, 229–34, 267–72.

150. See Morrow's 1922 memorandum, "Reparations and Security," Reparations 1920–26 file, DWM. To justify his optimism regarding the long-term growth potential of the German economy, Morrow relied heavily on J. H. Clapham, *The Economic Development of France and Germany, 1815–1914* (Cambridge, 1921).

supply, while foreign lending remained almost exclusively the province of a small number of investment bankers in New York.

The Morgan partners worried seriously about the problem of public accountability and control. "The Morgan firm is an anachronism," Dwight Morrow once admitted; "it is accountable to nobody but its own sense of responsibility."[151] Private bankers attempting to pursue public purposes inevitably found themselves in difficulty, for however public-spirited they might be, they always had to reconcile and balance wider aims against specific business obligations. Whatever theoretical views Morgan partners held on world politics and the importance of European economic recovery for their own country, their business was to sell bonds. Though they considered a settlement of the reparations problem highly desirable, their primary responsibility remained quite narrowly to ensure the safety of securities underwritten by their firm.

A statistical analysis would probably demonstrate that institutional investors and wealthy private individuals comprised the major part of the New York market for foreign securities in the 1920s. More often than not, such investors possessed sufficient information and judgment to make their own rational assessment of the risks and benefits of placing funds overseas. But the Morgan bankers subscribed with apparent sincerity to what today's skeptics would consider a peculiarly ingenuous notion of their function. Thomas Lamont spoke of a "trust" for the "American widow and orphan who may have a few pennies to invest." The American investing public, in his view, consisted of "small investors" who distrusted Germany because that country had "a very bad record as to paying reparations as promised and fulfilling her other treaty obligations." These people did not much want to buy German bonds, but they would do so if assured that the investment was safe and if they felt that they "would be helping France somewhat."[152] The essential question facing the Morgan bankers, therefore, was whether the Dawes Plan offered a real guarantee of the rehabilitation of Germany—not of Germany's currency and economy alone, but also of its social stability and its credit in the broadest sense as a member of the community of nations. This would enable the bankers confidently to recommend a loan as "the obligation of a solvent government and a solvent country."[153]

As a consequence of this approach to the problem, the Morgan partners gradually came to formulate desiderata for emendations and changes in the Dawes Plan as prerequisites for a loan. Several of the partners felt uncomfortable about posing political demands—particularly on France—as the price of their cooperation; perhaps not surprisingly, they proved

151. Recollection by Sir Esmond Ovey, 1933, Biography–Reminiscences file, DWM.

152. See several memoranda that Lamont prepared for his own use, justifying the firm's position at the London Conference, in TWL 176/4; also Lamont to J. L. Garvin [of the *Observer*], 27 July 1924, TWL 176/20.

153. Lamont and Leffingwell to Morgan, Harjes et Cie, 1 April 1924, TWL 176/8.

notably reluctant to recognize that this was effectively what they were doing. A month after publication of the Experts' Plan, Dwight Morrow complained plaintively to his Paris partners about the enthusiasm for it in American government circles and in the press: "There is the natural pride in the fact that America has made a real contribution toward world peace, and there is not much detailed analysis of the loan."[154] The optimistic public assessment made by financial houses that would not have to share direct responsibility for floating the loan added to Morrow's distress.[155]

Outside the confines of Morgan corner at Broad and Wall streets, the partners nevertheless displayed reluctance to admit the full measure of their disappointment. The Experts' work had received such "thoughtless approval" and acclaim, cabled Lamont, "that we don't want to be the targets . . . responsible for declaring that changes in the Dawes Plan are necessary as precedent to any loan."[156] Hence even in late May when Jean Parmentier, a French member of the Dawes Committee, inquired whether Morgan's had "any questions to ask," Morrow drew up a discreet response tailored to mask the firm's uncertainty: banking opinion had "not crystallized very much," but there existed "a disposition on all sides to do everything that can be done" and a "hope that all the political difficulties can be gotten out of the way in time to save the rentenmark."[157]

Meanwhile the Morgan partners' private estimations waxed more and more pessimistic. Russell Leffingwell, who possessed the most incisive mind in the firm, conducted the technical analysis of the Experts' Report. Leffingwell's memoranda characteristically penetrated to the heart of a specific situation with the precision of a laser. It was his strength, yet also his weakness, that unlike his colleagues Morrow, Lamont, and J. P. Morgan he rarely allowed sentiment or a sense of the imponderables of human behavior to influence his business judgments. From April through July, Leffingwell subjected the report to line-by-line scrutiny and produced four major studies, each more negative than the previous.[158]

"Ultimately," Leffingwell recognized, "we must deal with the Dawes Report as an historic event and see what can be done about it." But his otherwise comprehensive analysis placed little emphasis on the larger

154. Morrow to N. Dean Jay, 20 May 1924, Dawes Plan file, DWM.

155. See, for example, the unqualified endorsement by Chase National Bank economist Benjamin M. Anderson, "The Report of the Dawes Committee," *Chase Economic Bulletin* 4, no. 1 (28 April 1924); and an analysis similar in tone by Vice-President George E. Roberts of the National City Bank, "The Reparations Report," 18 June 1924; also a series of articles in the *Journal of Commerce*, 29 April 1924 et seq.; all in Dawes Report 1922–24 file, DWM.

156. Lamont to J. P. Morgan, 21 April 1924, TWL 176/9.

157. Morrow to Jean Parmentier, 20 May 1924; also Parmentier to Morrow, 7 June 1924, Dawes Plan file, DWM.

158. Russell C. Leffingwell, "The Dawes Report," I. 18 April 1924, II. 5 May 1924, III. 1 July 1924, IV. 22 July 1924; copies in Dawes Report 1922–24 file, DWM; first three memoranda also in TWL 176/8, 176/9, 176/11.

meaning of that historical event, namely, that the report represented a delicate political compromise offering the only practical alternative to political and economic chaos in Europe. Leffingwell looked at things from one angle only, that of prospective bondholders. He consequently regarded as major weaknesses many of the provisions that made the plan an effective political document. As he saw it, the Experts had tried too hard to please everybody:

> The report is consistently two-faced. It is a skillful performance in carrying water on both shoulders. Germany must have the Ruhr; but France need not get out of it. Germany must pay reparations; but she need not if it would disturb her foreign exchange and currency system. Germany must have a loan of $200,000,000 to furnish a gold reserve for her currency; but the proceeds of the loan can perfectly well serve that purpose and at the same time be spent in Germany to pay reparations in kind. The Allies can ultimately obtain 2,500,000,000 gold marks a year from Germany without German taxpayers having to pay more than 1,250,000,000 gold marks a year. Germany's budget must be balanced; but it won't do any harm if it isn't balanced right away; probably it won't be.[159]

For our purposes it is sufficient to indicate only a few of the many problems delineated in what Leffingwell called his jeremiad.[160] He feared first that the proposed loan was expected to accomplish too much; it could not serve as a gold reserve for the new German currency and at the same time remain available to finance payment of reparations in kind. The new bank of issue would begin operation with an insufficient gold reserve in any event; if it could not dispose freely of the international loan as monetary conditions required, its position would be "imperiled at the outset."

The Experts, Leffingwell argued further, had not provided a "margin" to allow for the possibility that removal of the inflation stimulant might cause a temporary depression and consequently reduce government revenue. Given the uncertainty surrounding all budgetary forecasts in Germany, he questioned the wisdom of counting on the Reich to pay any reparations within the framework of a balanced budget during the next two or three years.

In general, Leffingwell thought that the schedule of payments under the Dawes Plan began too soon, increased too quickly, and mounted too high. The Experts' failure to grant Germany an effective moratorium on reparations in kind during the first year especially disturbed him. He noted that the mandated deliveries of coal, coke, and other products which the Allies would otherwise have to purchase commercially during this period would place a drain on Germany's balance of payments not really distinguishable from that imposed by a cash remittance. Leffingwell also considered the maximum standard annuity excessive. He be-

159. Leffingwell, "The Dawes Report," I. 18 April 1924, Dawes Report 1922–24 file, DWM.

160. Leffingwell to Lamont, 5 July 1924, TWL 176/11.

lieved that the Reich's impressive physical assets, industrial plant, and equipment had led the Experts to overestimate the country's recuperative powers. They had not paid sufficient attention, in his view, to the difficulties involved in generating enough working capital to allow its economic machinery to function smoothly.

Undoubtedly, Leffingwell underrated the advantages, in terms of capital investment and full employment, which had accrued to Germany as a result of inflation.[161] Taking instead a static view of the economy, he derided as a "wholly topsy-turvy notion" the idea that elimination of the German domestic debt through inflation might have increased that nation's ability to pay reparations. "How could robbing German Peter to pay German Paul increase the ability of the German firm of Peter, Paul & Co. to pay outside creditors?" he wondered. Yet Leffingwell based his prediction that Germany would face a continuing liquidity crisis as well as serious problems in maintaining a favorable balance of payments not on an evaluation of economic prospects alone, but also on his assessment of German capitalists' intentions:

> Is there any reason to suppose that the acceptance of the Dawes Plan and the making of an external loan of 800,000,000 marks will so completely reassure timid or cautious German capital, will so completely erase from the minds of Germans all thought of further difficulties with France, of further political and social disturbances at home in Germany, and of the possibility of a renewed currency breakdown, that they will rush to convert their dollar, sterling, and franc balances into marks? I think not. On the contrary, it seems not at all impossible that Germans, as soon as they are provided again with a mark that can be sold, will sell it.[162]

Leffingwell's analysis led to the conclusion that if Germany sought to achieve a position from which it could eventually amortize the foreign loan and pay reparations out of current income, it would be best advised actually to increase its disposable liquid assets for the next few years. This could be accomplished both by encouraging repatriation of the capital that German nationals held abroad and by attracting additional foreign investment. But if Germany were required from the outset to hand over its surplus whenever it generated a momentarily favorable balance of payments, Leffingwell predicted, "confidence will not be restored, foreign capital will not flow in, the flight from the mark will be resumed." Institutional machinery designed to halt a reparations transfer whenever there appeared a risk of currency depreciation did not fully meet his objections. Subjective judgment would always be involved, and

161. For evidence supporting the view that, notwithstanding sectoral dislocations, the German economy as a whole benefited from the inflation, see Karsten Laursen and Jørgen Pedersen, *The German Inflation, 1918–1923* (Amsterdam, 1964); and Jörgen Pedersen, "Einige Bemerkungen zur deutschen Inflation von 1919–1923," *Zeitschrift für die gesamte Staatswissenschaft* 122 (July 1966): 418–30.

162. Leffingwell, "The Dawes Report," II. 5 May 1924, Dawes Report 1922–24 file, DWM.

events might place the Transfer Committee in an "unenviable political position."

Finally, Leffingwell advanced numerous technical criticisms of the Dawes Plan. The American business environment had shaped his outlook, and it led him to conclusions diverging from those which the Experts had drawn from examination of peculiarly European conditions. The Experts, for example, had placed specific obligations on German railways and industry. They had also worked out a schedule, based on studies elaborated the previous year by the Belgians, for specific levies on the customs, and on sales of alcohol, tobacco, beer, and sugar. They had resorted to these expedients because long practical experience had demonstrated the political difficulty of obtaining an all-inclusive payment directly from the German state budget. Not having wrestled with this political problem, Leffingwell clung to the theoretically unimpeachable view that general taxes of the broadest scope were more productive and economically sound.

Leffingwell's sobering experience with the railways as assistant secretary of the treasury, moreover, had affected his judgments significantly. An increase in American railroad rates in 1920, following hard upon a rise in the Federal Reserve discount rate, had in that year deepened a severe recession that the Treasury Department had not fully anticipated.[163] Leffingwell feared that a similar sequence of events might occur in Germany. He did not question the Dawes Committee's conclusion that the railroads there could be run at a profit if the German government raised freight and passenger rates to cover costs, discharged superfluous employees, and eliminated the hidden subsidy to business. But he believed that a sharp increase in transport rates might well cause the sort of recession which had afflicted the United States when he served in the Treasury. The decrease in the Reich's income from general taxation and the added cost of paying unemployment compensation would in that case more than outweigh increased state revenue deriving from the railroads.

In summary, therefore, Leffingwell felt that the Dawes Plan did not offer sufficient certainty of German economic rehabilitation to commend itself to investors. Neither a balanced budget, nor equilibrium in the balance of payments, nor stability of the German currency was assured beyond question. Under these circumstances no specific guarantees could offer real security, for however complete the "ostensible priority"

163. The federal government took over American railroads in March 1918, but returned them to private enterprise under the Esch-Cummins Transportation Act of February 1920. Transportation experts had predicted more economical operation of the railroads as a result of wartime consolidation of the lines. When the expected savings failed to develop, the railroads sharply raised freight and passenger rates in the summer of 1920. See Rogers MacVeagh, *The Transportation Act, 1920: Its Sources, History and Text* (New York, 1923); D. Philip Locklin, *Railroad Regulation since 1920* (New York and London, 1928); and Aaron Austin Godfrey, *Government Operation of the Railroads, 1918–1920* (Austin, Tex., 1974).

conferred upon a foreign loan, in practice the domestic obligations of the German government remained "a prior charge." Even if airtight priority for the loan could somehow be arranged, it would remain in France's power to decide whether to take action when the "inevitable default" occurred. The conclusion emerged inescapably: "Without modification in the plan in the interest of the investors in the proposed loan, the bonds are not a good risk."[164]

Notwithstanding this pessimistic theoretical analysis, the Morgan partners realized from the start that the firm's dominant position in investment markets and the configuration of political pressures left them little practical choice. If they declined to assume leadership of the underwriting syndicate, the chance of a satisfactory European settlement would be much diminished. And the French were particularly eager to bring the firm in because they feared that the political sympathies of Montagu Norman, governor of the Bank of England, might lead him to impose yet harsher conditions than Morgan's.[165]

J. P. Morgan met informally with Louis Barthou and Sir John Bradbury at Reparation Commission headquarters in Paris on 26 April, before he had fully reflected on the implications of the negative assessment made by his partner in New York. Somewhat imprudently, Morgan volunteered the judgment that he saw no "insurmountable difficulties" from the bankers' side in arranging a German loan once the governments concerned had reached agreement.[166] At the time he gave this surprising assurance, the New York bond market was still extremely bearish on European government securities. The League of Nations project for Hungarian financial reconstruction, in fact, was soon to be postponed because the necessary financing could not be arranged.[167] Later in the spring, however, the Federal Reserve System adopted an easy-money policy, partially to combat domestic recession but also in large part deliberately to promote foreign borrowing in the New York market. By reducing interest rates in the United States to a level below that prevailing in Great Britain, the Federal Reserve sought to shift demand for international loans from London to New York. It hoped thereby to ease the drain on the British balance of payments and to facilitate an appreciation of sterling. This would constitute one important step toward return to the gold exchange standard.[168] As a result of

164. Leffingwell, "The Dawes Report," II. 5 May 1924, Dawes Report 1922–24 file, DWM.

165. James A. Logan to State Department, 24 and 26 April 1924, U.S. 462.00R 296/285, 289.

166. J. P. Morgan to J. P. Morgan & Co., 26 April 1924, TWL 176/9.

167. Lamont to Morgan, Grenfell & Co., 22 May 1924, TWL 176/10. On the general question of Hungarian financial reconstruction, see Ozer Carmi, *La Grande-Bretagne et la Petite Entente* (Geneva, 1972), pp. 88–115.

168. Stephen V. O. Clarke, *Central Bank Cooperation, 1924–31* (New York, 1967), pp. 74–78; Lester Chandler, *Benjamin Strong, Central Banker* (Washington, D.C., 1958), pp. 241–46, 271–72, 305–8.

easier general monetary conditions, the mood at Morgan offices also became more expansive. By the beginning of July even the more cautious partners were quite confident that they could successfully market a German loan—provided that terms for the security and protection of the bondholders proved satisfactory.[169]

Within the firm a certain difference of opinion obtained as to how to achieve this security. J. P. Morgan had always maintained that bankers should restrict themselves to the limited function of interpreting the sentiment of investment markets. The entire history of the reparations question made him reluctant to take any step that could be construed as an attempt by bankers to impose their private political views. He therefore objected to "putting J. P. Morgan & Co. into the breach between England and France and Germany, before they agree among themselves concerning fundamental political questions." However, in early July Owen D. Young, who was supervising technical preparations for adoption of the Dawes Plan, and James A. Logan, American unofficial delegate to the Reparation Commission, solicited the bankers' suggestions regarding requirements for the prospective bondholders' security and protection. Leffingwell argued that if the firm delayed further in making its views known, it ran "the risk of permitting the situation to become so crystallized . . . that we may be obliged to choose between refusing to do the business altogether and doing it without adequate safeguards." After deliberation, the partners finally decided to advise Governor Norman and Young of their desires in an informal manner.[170]

But while Morgan staff members prepared a suitable memorandum on the subject, a controversy erupted over selection of the agent for reparations payments who would assume chief responsibility for overseeing the administration of the Dawes Plan. The difficulty centered on personalities rather than policy. Its roots lay buried in the shifting sands of American domestic politics. The dispute was inconsequential in itself, but no substantive reparations issue took anywhere near a comparable amount of the time and energy of American officials and financiers in the summer of 1924. The imbroglio had far-reaching consequences. It eroded the bankers' earlier circumspection and engendered such bitterness and suspicion as to imperil cooperation among Americans at the London Conference.[171]

169. J. P. Morgan & Co. to Morgan, Grenfell & Co., 2 July 1924, TWL 176/11.

170. Leffingwell to Lamont, 5 July 1924, TWL 176/11.

171. This account draws upon the papers of James A. Logan, Dwight Morrow, Thomas Lamont, Charles G. Dawes, Owen D. Young, Calvin Coolidge, Charles Evans Hughes, Joseph Grew, Leland Harrison, and Alanson B. Houghton, as well as on State Department records, and British Foreign Office and Treasury files. Previously published references to the question are incomplete: see, e.g., Nicolson, *Morrow*, pp. 273–76; and Charles G. Dawes, *A Journal of Reparations* (London, 1939), pp. 230–34.

The Selection of the Agent-General and American Domestic Politics

Owen Young had demonstrated such ability as a conciliator within the Dawes Committee that many of those who had followed the Experts' work closely originally hoped that he would consent to become the agent. But Young did not wish to leave the General Electric Corporation, though he offered his services for an interim period to get the Dawes Plan started. Meanwhile, James A. Logan* had begun a quiet but intensive campaign for his own appointment. In the State Department's socially cohesive upper echelon Logan had long been considered America's "unofficial ambassador to Europe," an appellation amply justified by the quality of his dispatches and the range of his connections, which radiated outward from Reparation Commission headquarters at the Hotel Astoria to chancelleries all over the continent. Forthright, lively, and knowledgeable despite gaps in his formal education, he enlisted the support of General Dawes, Ambassador Houghton, and others influential on the American political scene and secured the endorsement of his continental colleagues on the Reparation Commission.

Early in the selection process, the British Treasury had fastened on the strategy of demanding appointment of an American agent as the best way to ward off French claims to the post.[172] But the Treasury and the London City did not favor Logan. They considered him deficient in economic training and of low stature in the financial world. They also suspected him, as a former protégé of Herbert Hoover, of holding anti-British attitudes, even though British observers could point to "no clear signs of this" in several years of contact at the Hotel Astoria. More to the point, Logan had probably displayed his puckish wit once too often at the expense of the self-important Sir John Bradbury, who accused him of a "very strong taste for devious diplomacy."[173]

*James Addison Logan, Jr. (1879–1931), scion of a Philadelphia Main Line family, dropped out of Haverford College to join the army in the Spanish-American War; rose from private to lieutenant colonel, 1899–1922; chief of American military mission with French army, 1914–17; assistant chief of staff, G.H.Q., American Expeditionary Force, 1917–18; principal assistant to Herbert Hoover in the American Relief Administration, 1918–19; assistant unofficial U.S. delegate to the Reparation Commission, 1919–23; unofficial delegate, July 1923–May 1925; banker with Dillon, Read, 1925–31. Overweight, a bon vivant, he entertained so widely that Voisin's noted three-star restaurant became known to the initiated as "Logie's." Logan could draw on strong personal friendships in the American diplomatic establishment. His bachelor flat on the rue Monsieur served as Paris pied-à-terre for innumerable American diplomats in Europe; his former housemates in a Washington establishment called "The Family" included officials who in 1924 occupied the positions of assistant secretary of state, ambassadors to Belgium and Italy (both former under secretaries), assistant secretary of the treasury, and governor of the Federal Reserve Bank of New York.

172. Sir O. E. Niemeyer memorandum for the chancellor of the exchequer, 12 May 1924, P.R.O., Treasury Finance files, T160/178/F6970/01/2; also minutes of a meeting at the chancellor of the exchequer's room at the House of Commons, 6 June 1924, F.O. 371/9747: C 9213/70/18.

173. Bradbury to Sir Eyre Crowe, 3 June 1924, F.O. 371/9747: C 8963/70/18.

Seeking evidence to show the French that Wall Street opposed Logan too, Montagu Norman cabled J. P. Morgan, soliciting the latter's views and asking him to name an alternative candidate who would generate more enthusiasm among prospective American lenders. Morgan agreed that Logan, "while admirable in many ways, is not quite sufficiently a first-class man for this particular job."[174] At first Morgan did not seek to dictate a choice of his own. His fundamental concern was to ensure the selection of an agent possessing the ability to make economic decisions without relying on others and whose experience and reputation would justify the confidence of investors. He would not have objected to the appointment of an Englishman or Frenchman who filled the bill. To oblige Norman, however, Morgan scouted around for a suitable American nomination. Canvassing the field under the pressure of time in the middle of June, Morgan's choice fell on his own partner, Dwight Morrow. Morrow agreed to undertake the task provided that the American government gave its "hearty approval."[175]

The nomination of Morrow, ostensibly made by Montagu Norman, initially met with general acclaim. Secretary Hughes, who had earlier shown an inclination to support Logan, felt pleased that the British had taken the initiative. The United States government could therefore avoid appearing to have determined the choice of the reparations agent. The French expressed enthusiasm too. For many years Morrow had served as the chief Morgan expert on French financial problems. He had taken charge of France's financing in America and was known for his warm sympathies for that country. Naturally, his appointment would aid in flotation of the loan to Germany and indeed would virtually commit the Morgan firm to carry the project through.[176] The disconsolate Logan at first advised that appointing a banker would provoke criticism that the Experts' Plan represented capitalist dictation. He argued that regardless of Morrow's personal merits, the latter's selection would be a mistake in the context of "the present political psychology of Europe with its strong socialist and anticapitalist trend." But once he recognized the strength of Morrow's support among the nations represented on the Reparation Commission, he resigned himself to accepting the personal setback with an outward show of good grace.[177]

The path thus seemed clear for Morrow's designation as reparations agent. On 1 July Morrow met at the White House with President Coolidge, Secretary Hughes, General Dawes (who had just been nominated

174. J. P. Morgan to E. C. Grenfell (for Norman), 10 June 1924, TWL 176/10; quoted with satisfaction in Bradbury to Crowe, 13 June 1924, F.O. 371/9747: C 9495/70/18.

175. J. P. Morgan to Grenfell, 19 June 1924; Dwight W. Morrow to Grenfell, 21 June 1924, both in TWL 176/10.

176. Grenfell to Morrow, 30 June 1924, TWL 176/10; Robert M. Kindersley to Owen D. Young, 1 July 1924, Box R-3, Owen D. Young Papers.

177. Logan to Owen D. Young, 27 June 1924, Box R-13, Owen D. Young Papers; Logan to State Department, 25 June and 2 July 1924, U.S. 462.00R 296/384, 393.

for vice-president on the Republican ticket), and Owen Young. Young voiced some hesitancy because he wondered whether Morrow really believed in the Experts' Plan. He also stressed the importance of obtaining approval for the nomination from all important groups in Germany.[178] The upshot of the meeting, however, appeared to be unanimous endorsement of Morrow, provided that the principal German interests approved.

The very next day Ambassador Houghton arrived on a short visit from Germany. Houghton (who was really still partial to Logan) suggested that the German electorate might show displeasure if an international banker, particularly a member of the firm which had helped finance the Allied war effort, were "put in charge of the country." The German government itself, he intimated, privately regarded the Morrow appointment as a potential liability. The appointment could provide those Nationalists who remained on the fence with another plausible excuse to vote against the Dawes Plan enabling legislation. Houghton recommended that Young serve as agent temporarily, and that Logan succeed him eventually. Coolidge and Hughes took advantage of this opportunity to reverse themselves. They dispatched Dawes to New York to persuade Young to take the job and to straighten out matters with the Morgan interests.[179]

Morrow no longer found his lucrative life on Wall Street much of a professional challenge, and the prospect of serving as agent had stirred his imagination. He tried, nevertheless, to accept the disappointment philosophically. He told friends that "he did not mind being abused as an international banker" and would lean over backward to avoid doing anything that might impede the successful launching of the Dawes Plan. J. P. Morgan actually experienced a sense of relief, because now Morrow would stay with the firm. Morgan declared that he was fully prepared to work with Young as agent.[180]

But Montagu Norman could not believe that the Germans were "quite damn fools enough not to know an experienced banker is going to be the most conservative in the imposition of German obligations." He checked back through Berlin and discovered that the German government had not expressed the slightest opposition to Morrow's nomination.[181] The German ambassador in Washington, in fact, shortly thereafter informed the State Department that Berlin "would be delighted to have Mr. Mor-

178. Morrow to Lamont, 2 July 1924; Morrow to Grenfell, 2 July 1924; both in TWL 176/11; also Owen D. Young to J. P. Morgan, 4 August 1924, J. P. Morgan & Co., Partners file, DWM.

179. Morrow to Lamont, 24 July 1924, Lamont file, DWM; Dawes, *A Journal of Reparations*, pp. 232–33.

180. J. P. Morgan to J. S. Morgan, 3 July 1924; J. P. Morgan to Grenfell, 3 July 1924; both in TWL 176/11.

181. Lamont to Morrow, 8 July 1924, Lamont file, DWM; Grenfell and Lamont to J. P. Morgan, 8 July 1924, TWL 176/11.

row."[182] In light of this development, J. P. Morgan felt deeply humiliated. As he saw it, he had been drawn into offering the services of a trusted partner as a public service. His recommendation had then been rejected on the flimsiest of pretexts.[183] As outrage mounted at 23 Wall Street, Lamont jumped to the conclusion that Young had secretly decided he wanted the post after all and had "hornswoggled" Morrow out of it by planting the idea of German opposition in the mind of the suggestible "puddingface" Houghton.[184]

Actually Young had behaved fairly and in an entirely aboveboard manner. He had acted with only one purpose—to create the most favorable conditions possible for implementing the Dawes Plan. He harbored no wish to be drafted as agent. Though he continued to exercise the agent's preliminary functions on an interim basis, he also pushed steadily for appointment of a successor until after two months of uncertainty S. Parker Gilbert, Leffingwell's close associate first in law practice and then in the Treasury Department, won designation for the position. In the final analysis, President Coolidge had made the decision to drop his college classmate and supposed friend Morrow. And what really had determined Coolidge's change of heart, and possibly Houghton's judgment too, was concern not so much about opinion in Berlin as about the sentiment of ethnic Germans in America.

During these first days of July, while the decision on Morrow hung fire, the Progressive party convention was meeting to nominate Senator Robert M. La Follette for president. Liberal intellectuals who found the smug self-satisfaction of Coolidge's America repugnant and sought to restore the impetus for progressive reform set the tone for La Follette's campaign. But contrary to the self-indulgent hopes of the liberal elite, the La Follette program actually held little appeal for farmers or workers as economic groups. The mass basis of the senator's support—as the quantitative data now decisively confirm—came from German- and Irish-Americans, either foreign born themselves or of foreign parentage. In these ethnic groups many were attracted to La Follette precisely because of his record of opposition to the war effort and to the Treaty of Versailles.[185]

In the Middle and Far West particularly, there existed a potential for coalescence of pro-German sentiment with traditional isolationism and agrarian hatred of the ill-understood Eastern "money interest." La Follette could derive a fair amount of political mileage in these areas with

182. Memorandum of conversation between German ambassador and William R. Castle, 14 July 1924, U.S. 462.00R 296/481.

183. Lamont to Morrow, 12 and 13 September 1924, Lamont file, DWM.

184. Lamont to Morrow, 8 July 1924, ibid.

185. Samuel Lubell, *The Future of American Politics* (New York, 1956), pp. 135–42; brilliantly confirmed by Keith Ellison, "The 1924 Presidential Election in the Middle West: A Quantitative Analysis" (B.A. thesis, Harvard University, 1972). Kenneth Campbell MacKay, *The Progressive Movement of 1924* (New York, 1947), misses the point.

his stock explanation that America had gone to war to protect the Morgan bank. In his statement of principles the senator denounced the Coolidge administration for perpetuating Woodrow Wilson's degradation of the State Department to the level of a "trading post" for "financial imperialists" and "international bankers . . . engaged in the exploitation of weaker nations . . . contrary to the will of the American people, destructive of domestic development and provocative of war."[186]

The German-American vote had gone overwhelmingly to Harding in 1920. But anguished party workers in the field were now warning the Republican National Committee of probable mass defections to La Follette unless President Coolidge could demonstrate his sympathy for this important segment of the electorate in a tangible way.[187] The main purpose for Houghton's visit, in fact, was to lay plans for a carefully orchestrated autumn campaign in those areas of the country with heavy German ethnic concentrations.[188] In the meeting in Washington, Coolidge had apparently misled Morrow by saying that to consider the domestic political effect of the latter's appointment would only be "confusing." But after reflection the president decided that selection of a "representative of the 'predatory interests'" would constitute an unacceptable political liability.[189] Indeed, as the summer wore on and La Follette perfected his campaign strategy, Coolidge became ever more adamant on the subject. When in August the British sought briefly to revive the Morrow candidacy, the president completely lost his fabled equanimity: he became, as Under Secretary of State Grew described it (in diction characteristic of the era), "about the maddest white man" that Grew had ever seen.[190]

The first inkling of what had really doomed the Morrow candidacy did not reach the Morgan bank until almost the end of the London Conference.[191] In the meantime the partners—with the single exception of Morrow himself, who suspended judgment—blamed Owen Young for the fiasco. Strained personal relations undoubtedly contributed to the

186. "Statement and Platform of Robert M. La Follette, presented on July 4, 1924 to the Progressive Conference at Cleveland, Ohio" (Chicago, 1924), copy in Case file 1996, Box 237, Coolidge Papers. For evidence suggesting that La Follette's fears concerning Morgan domination of the United States (and of the world at large) exceeded rational bounds, see the senator's handwritten ruminations in J. P. Morgan folder, Box B-194, Robert M. La Follette, Sr., Papers, Library of Congress, Washington, D.C.

187. See the voluminous correspondence between the president's office, the Republican National Committee, and the Republican Congressional Committee in Case file 198A, Box 136, Coolidge Papers.

188. Joseph Grew Diary, 18 June 1924, Joseph Grew Papers, Houghton Library, Harvard University, Cambridge, Mass.

189. Morrow to Lamont, 2 July 1924, TWL 176/11. For evidence that the political liability was genuine, see the White House staff study, "The Dawes Report in the German-American Press," Case file 295, Box 166, Coolidge Papers; also Case file 513, Box 196, Coolidge Papers.

190. Grew Diary, 2–9 August 1924, Grew Papers.

191. J. P. Morgan to Morrow, 8 August 1924, TWL 176/23.

growing feeling in Morgan offices that Young, like Logan, was excessively committed to the Dawes Report as an "absolutely complete and definite document" and would prove reluctant to sanction changes if its provisions failed to work in practice.[192] The evolution of sentiment among the bankers can be dated precisely. On 3 July, J. P. Morgan cabled concerning appointment of the agent: "We all believe Young will do it very well"; on 9 July, "Now we know more, we think differently." By 16 July, Morgan explicitly advised Lamont: "With Owen D. Young appointed to the place of power we feel that we must be extremely careful to get from the nations now everything that we are going to require in the way of safety of the bond, as he could not be relied upon to help us later on, if it seemed to make the carrying out of the Dawes Plan less probable."[193]

The Bankers Move to Center Stage

Above all else, the Morgan partners wanted the Allied powers to sign a protocol in which they promised to respect "the political independence, the territorial integrity, and the sovereignty" of Germany and agreed not to interfere with German economic life in such a way as to impair the security or service of the prospective loan. In other words, Morgan's sought to ensure that France would never again seize productive pledges unilaterally and that, if the Allied governments together deemed such action essential, they would jointly and severally assume responsibility for the loan. Such a protocol figured as a "fundamental and indispensable condition" precedent to their offering German bonds on world markets.[194] There existed various ways, of course, to secure the requisite assurances. The several principal partners formulated specific demands slowly, and in accord with their respective temperaments. Not surprisingly, shades of difference persisted among them. Although deeply affected by the controversy over naming an agent, Morgan remained the least eager to throw the firm into the political fray; the tough economic analyst Leffingwell stood for the most rigorous guarantees; of the three, Morrow showed most sensitivity to the nuances of European politics.

Morrow, on whose political judgment the others tended to rely, did not feel strongly opposed at first to France's retaining a vestigial military presence in the areas occupied since 1923. He thought that it would not be hard to "dress up a face-saving proposition" conceding France's right

192. Morrow to Lamont, 24 July 1924, Lamont file, DWM.

193. J. P. Morgan to Grenfell, 3 July 1924, TWL 176/11; Morgan and Morrow to Grenfell and Lamont, 9 July 1924, TWL 176/12; Morgan to Lamont, 16 July 1924, TWL 176/15.

194. Morgan and Morrow to Grenfell and Lamont, 9 July 1924, TWL 176/12. Morrow enlarged further on Morgan desiderata in a conference with Secretary of State Hughes: see Morrow to Hughes, 12 July 1924, copies in TWL 176/13 and in Reparations file, DWM.

to "have troops under certain conditions in the Ruhr, or accessible to the Ruhr, merely on the basis of French security." The French could herald this as a great victory and, having obtained security, could then make "substantial concessions on the whole reparations question." As Morrow saw things, the ultimate fate of the Dawes Plan depended on France's accepting the view that reparations and security were compatible rather than contradictory goals, and that real security—that is, reduction of the likelihood of future war—could best be achieved by treating Germany in a way that enabled it to pay as smoothly as possible for the damage it had done. Did Morrow and his colleagues, accustomed to the sober world of high finance where men much like themselves made decisions through rational calculations of self-interest, underestimate the strength of irrational forces in German society? They never questioned the assumption, at any rate, that normalization of economic and business conditions offered the best hope for restoring German political stability.[195]

The Dawes Report's great virtue, Morrow told Secretary Hughes, was "the spirit" in which it was conceived. The detailed provisions, on the other hand, had to be considered "problematical until tried." Morrow expressed particular concern whether Germany could without undue strain maintain the specified schedule of deliveries in kind during the first two years of the plan. He feared that if the Reich defaulted on its promise to supply these reparations in kind and the Allies reimposed sanctions, thereby throwing the German economy into confusion, the investor of new money might find his first lien on German resources jeopardized. Morrow would have preferred to take the burden off Germany entirely by offering independent loans to France and other countries entitled to deliveries with which they could pay for the needed coal, coke, and dyestuffs. But at a minimum, he held, the Transfer Committee should be empowered to suspend reparations in kind if that proved expedient.[196]

Aside from this suggestion on handling the short-term problem, Morrow and his colleagues at Morgan corner began with no precise idea of what might happen if Germany were to refuse payment again. Morrow kept returning to the theme of voluntary compliance. He doubted whether a supervisory body with a large administrative apparatus could operate effectively in a "highly industrialized, extremely nationalistic Empire like Germany." Would it not best preserve the fundamental spirit of the Dawes Plan, he wondered, to call its chief executive officer a "reparations mediator" rather than "agent general," and to make his

195. Morrow to Hughes, 12 July 1924, TWL 176/13; Morrow to Lamont, 24 July 1924, Lamont file, DWM.

196. Morrow to Hughes, 12 July 1924, TWL 176/13. For a more extensive discussion of the problem, see also Morrow's "Memorandum for T. W. L." [ca. 1 July 1924], Lamont file, DWM.

duties "mainly fact-finding" and his powers "largely moral"? Similarly, Morrow saw no great objection to keeping the Reparation Commission in existence—provided it became a simple "fact-finding body." In the future, he held, only a conference of prime ministers should rule upon a charge of default. If the prime ministers could not settle the question or agree to refer it for adjudication to the Hague Court or to the League of Nations, then "a breakdown" would result.[197] In contemporary terms, this was the equivalent of thinking about the unthinkable—except that the dreaded eventuality was almost sure to occur.

In summary, the Morgan partners in New York would show some flexibility regarding tactics, but on essential matters of substance they would prove unbending. Before undertaking to float the loan, they would seek to hedge it round with multiple guarantees—enough to assure its security whatever the circumstances of a future reparations crisis.

On 7 July, meanwhile, Thomas Lamont arrived in London to handle the European end of negotiations, and Montagu Norman immediately took him in tow.[198] Though Governor of the Bank of England for close to a quarter century and much in the public eye, Norman remained an enigma even to those who knew him well. He had never completed his formal university education. Instead he had spent two happy years studying in central Europe (mostly in Dresden); the experience deeply affected his outlook. Just as his loathing for the French persisted even when their countries made common cause, so his sympathy for the Germans survived the diplomatic vagaries of the years. In personal relations too, Norman nourished passionate loyalties and enduring dislikes. The bond of friendship that he formed with Reichsbank President Hjalmar Schacht in 1924 lasted as long as he lived: in 1938–39 he volunteered to serve as go-between for Schacht's ingenious plan to improve the Reich's balance of payments by ransoming off its remaining Jews, and during the Second World War he continued to send Schacht food packages through the Swiss Red Cross. A man of uncertain political judgments and unusual habits, a neurasthenic who traveled the world's ocean liners in disguises, Norman also demonstrated prodigious energy, immense capacity for work, and great financial acumen. Few men proved immune to his extraordinary personal magnetism. Lamont, who first met Norman during the war, called him "the wisest man" he had ever known, and conceived for the British banker an admiration bordering on veneration.[199]

197. Ibid.; also Morrow's memorandum for Lamont, 21 July 1924, and Morrow to Lamont, 24 July 1924, tracing the evolution of opinion at the firm, in Lamont file, DWM.

198. Edward C. Grenfell, Conservative M.P. and head of Morgan's London branch, felt constrained from taking an active part in negotiations because he feared that if things went badly the Labour party might turn on him and say that the Bank of England and Morgan's constituted a "money trust" (see Grenfell to Lamont, 25 October 1924, TWL 111/16).

199. Sir Henry Clay, *Lord Norman* (London, 1957); Andrew Boyle, *Montagu Norman*

When Prime Minister MacDonald returned from Paris on 9 July, he promptly began to explore ways to retreat from the agreement he had made to save Herriot and the conference. He had found his experience in the French capital distasteful. To intimates he denounced "the whole crew of French politicians—underhand, grasping, dishonourable." At a state dinner he had met about seventy of the breed and discovered not "a good face among them."[200] MacDonald's legal advisers, moreover, discerned a major substantive difficulty lurking in the very form of the Paris understanding. No doubt the plan to give an American citizen voting rights on the Reparation Commission when it considered a charge of default offered some protection against precipitous action by that body. But, Sir John Bradbury cautioned, the Dawes Plan really constituted a complete replacement—not a modification—of the Versailles treaty's reparations provisions. If one kept the shell of the existing treaty as a "show-window dummy," there was always the danger that some future French government would "reach it down and try to make it work."[201]

MacDonald immediately grasped the point. In order to strengthen his hand, he turned to Montagu Norman, and on the latter's recommendation also called in Lamont to inquire what effect the formulae reached in Paris would have upon the bond offering in England and America. The prime minister prompted the bankers: he "took no stock" in any notion that investors would subscribe to the loan if the Reparation Commission retained any power to determine default. But he desired an opinion from financial interests in order to "emphasize" this view. Lamont could foresee a whole variety of contingencies that might furnish the Allies with grounds to take action against Germany under the treaty. He considered it unlikely that they would give a blanket pledge not to resort to territorial sanctions regardless of circumstances. And MacDonald ruled out a direct guarantee of the bonds by the Allied governments as politically impracticable. Lamont therefore found it expedient to take a stand on the issue suggested by MacDonald, namely, who would have power to declare default. He proposed that the Transfer Committee, which the English and Americans could together control, should assume this responsibility. The Reparation Commission, Lamont stated frankly, had "become anathema to the American investment public." If any possibility remained for that commission to "poke its fingers in and

---

(London, 1967); Henry L. Feingold, *The Politics of Rescue: The Roosevelt Administration and the Holocaust* (New Brunswick, N.J., 1970), p. 53; Malcolm Muggeridge, *Chronicles of Wasted Time*, vol. 2, *The Infernal Grove* (New York, 1974), p. 220; Lamont to Norman, 4 December 1946, TWL 122/2.

200. Remarks to C. P. Scott and J. A. Hobson, 15 July 1924, in Scott, *Political Diaries*, p. 460.

201. Bradbury to Sir Eyre Crowe, 8 July 1924, enclosing memorandum by Sir J. Fischer-Williams, legal adviser to the British delegation at the Reparation Commission, "Manquements and Sanctions"; also Crowe and MacDonald minutes, 15 July 1924, F.O. 371/9750: C 11050/70/18.

declare default, or otherwise mess up the situation," the American public would not take the bonds.

This was exactly what MacDonald wanted to hear. He pleaded for confirmation in writing. The situation was desperate, and such a statement might "have great effect on Herriot and his henchmen in bringing them to the London Conference in the proper attitude." After some urging, Lamont finally agreed to prepare a letter including those points that MacDonald thought would appeal most effectively to "the Herriot psychology."[202]

Thus the American bankers were suddenly thrust into the forefront of negotiations. Still reluctant to recognize how central a role he would have to play, Lamont wrote Morrow that he intended henceforth to "keep strictly out of the mess unless somebody high in authority again asks us to express an opinion on some more or less technical point."[203] On 15 July, however, Governor Norman drew up a memorandum for Lamont and his London partner, E. C. Grenfell, setting forth conditions for a German loan on which they might jointly insist. This proposal went far beyond the "technical" points to which Lamont had referred only a few days earlier. In fact, it amounted to nothing less than a complete political program.

The Norman memorandum demanded immediate military evacuation of the Ruhr, a timetable for gradual evacuation of the Rhineland, abolition forthwith of the Rhineland Commission and of railway control throughout the occupied territories, and assurance that the Transfer Committee would become the sole body competent to declare default "under any conditions under the treaty or Dawes Report." Without fully reflecting, apparently, on the gravity of these demands for the European balance of power, Lamont handed them on to Young and Logan (who had recently arrived in London to represent the United States government) as a "possible platform upon which both American and British investors could fairly stand."[204]

Within two weeks J. P. Morgan & Co. had moved from a position of prudent reserve to virtual endorsement of far-reaching political demands on France. What accounted for the change? In the first place, Montagu Norman, firmly resolved to play a strong hand, kept reminding the Morgan partners that "the conference must rely upon himself and American bankers" and that if together they advocated a common policy, "all the Allies must follow their advice."[205] Secondly, Lamont's

202. Lamont and Grenfell to Morgan and Morrow, 10 July 1924, and Lamont to Morrow, 11 July 1924, TWL 176/12; Lamont to MacDonald, 12 July 1924, TWL 176/13. Lamont also furnished the American ambassador in London with a copy of his letter to the prime minister: see Box 8, Frank B. Kellogg Papers, Minnesota Historical Society, St. Paul, Minn.

203. Lamont to Morrow, 11 July 1924, TWL 176/12.

204. Norman memorandum, 15 July 1924, also Lamont to J. P. Morgan & Co., 15 July 1924, TWL 176/14.

205. Grenfell to J. P. Morgan, 16 July 1924, TWL 176/15.

poor opinion of Herriot and MacDonald reinforced his inclination to follow Norman's lead. Both prime ministers struck him as weak reeds compared to other European statesmen he had known. Herriot, he observed privately, "does not know the game and does not deserve to win it until he has gained more experience." MacDonald he considered "a very nice man, wanting to do the right thing," but unskilled and "too sketchy" in his grasp of details, in short, not really "up to his job." From the investor's point of view, moreover, the conference would start "on the wrong footing entirely" for, having obtained a presumed commitment from MacDonald in Paris, the French would not readily agree to "throw the Reparation Commission overboard" once they reached London.

Finally, Lamont endorsed Norman's formulation of maximum demands for tactical reasons. The bankers might be obliged to compromise as the conference proceeded, he realized, but unless they took a strong stand at the beginning, the governments might never agree on an acceptable formula for floating the loan.[206] "I am not at all sure," he wired home, "that J. P. Morgan is not correct in his theory that bankers should not be within gunshot until governments settle their differences. The only answer to that, however, is that in the present case they would never settle them, and I doubt very much whether they will anyway."[207]

Lamont's reasoning met with full approval in New York. The partners at Broad and Wall streets continued to view the flawed understanding between France and Britain with trepidation and to fear that Owen Young, Logan, and others might promote a compromise at their expense. "We must be very sure," cabled J. P. Morgan, "not to let our desire to help the politicians straighten out the tangled affairs of Europe lead us away from the [banking] fundamentals."[208] Acting on the assumption that they were not posing demands of their own but merely interpreting sentiment in the financial markets, the bankers sought to demonstrate that the American investor was "not an eager lender and must be convinced that the security is adequate."[209]

The French would find cold consolation in the fact that the American bankers advanced their requirements without animus and in the guise of confirming impersonal economic forces. The bankers' demands, Herriot expostulated to the German ambassador, constituted "one of the most intolerable pressures" exerted on him.[210] But in the context of the financial constraints on France, it was pressure from which there appeared no escape.

206. Lamont to Morrow, 11 July 1924, TWL 176/12; Lamont to J. P. Morgan & Co., 15 July 1924, TWL 176/14.

207. Lamont to J. P. Morgan & Co., 18 July 1924, TWL 176/15.

208. J. P. Morgan to Grenfell, 16 July 1924, also Morgan and Leffingwell to Lamont, 16 July 1924, TWL 176/15.

209. J. P. Morgan to Lamont, 16 July 1924, TWL 176/15.

210. Hoesch tel., 15 July 1924, G.F.M. 3398/1736/D739972–977.

Chapter 8

The London Conference

Opening Moves

The London Reparations Conference opened on 16 July 1924 with a round of anodyne speeches voicing hope for the economic restoration of Europe and the beginning of an era of peace and stability.[1] But similar incantations had proved to be a prelude to deadlock and breakdown at many such gatherings since the war. On this occasion too, the assembled statesmen and officials expressed far less confidence privately that they could reach satisfactory agreement. Secretary Hughes caught the prevailing mood precisely: when on the eve of his departure for London an aide remarked that he would arrive to find the conference "in full swing," Hughes observed that the comment lay "open to two interpretations—the Southern idea of 'in full swing' generally conveyed a somewhat lugubrious meaning."[2]

In deference to domestic isolationists, the Coolidge administration had resolved to abstain from official participation in the conference. But before it could quietly make this decision known, the British Foreign Office boldly announced to the press that it had extended an invitation to Washington. Rather than suffer the embarrassment of appearing to hold back at the last minute after having claimed much of the credit for originating the Dawes Plan, the United States agreed, for the first time since Versailles, to take a formal place in European diplomatic councils.[3]

At London, American diplomats were destined to play a central mediating role. The elderly, white-haired ambassador to the Court of

1. The most complete documentary source is *Proceedings of the London Reparation Conference*, vol. 1, *The Interallied Conference*, vol. 2, *The International Conference*, printed by the British government for limited distribution (n.p., n.d.), copies in P.R.O., CAB 29/103–104, and in Harvard College Library, Cambridge, Mass. The principal European powers published more restricted documentary selections: Great Britain, Cmd. 2270, *Proceedings of the London Reparation Conference, July and August 1924* (London, 1924); France, Ministère des Affaires Etrangères, *Documents diplomatiques. Conférence de Londres, 16 juillet–16 août 1924* (Paris, 1925); Belgium, Ministère des Affaires Etrangères, *Documents diplomatiques relatifs aux réparations. Conférence de Londres du 16 juillet au 16 août 1924* (Brussels, 1924); Germany, Auswärtiges Amt, *Die Londoner Konferenz, Juli–August 1924* (Berlin, 1925).

This account focuses on political developments at the conference. For technical detail bearing on adoption of the Dawes Report, see Etienne Weill-Raynal, *Les Réparations allemandes et la France*, 3 vols. (Paris, 1947), 3:66–123.

2. Joseph Grew Diary, 14 July 1924, Grew Papers.

3. *Papers Relating to the Foreign Relations of the United States, 1924*, 2 vols. (Washington, D.C., 1939), 2:24–32.

St. James, Frank B. Kellogg, known to newspaper reporters as "nervous Nellie" and valued more for his sincerity and amiability than for mastery of European problems, served as chief of the official American delegation. James A. Logan, whose technical expertise somewhat compensated for the shortcomings of his senior colleague, acted as Kellogg's deputy. Other American leaders, in accordance with traditional policy, arrived informally and studiously maintained a low profile. Secretary Hughes possessed a legitimate cover: the American Bar Association, which he headed, was holding its annual convention in London, and he had long been scheduled to deliver the keynote address. The remaining American officials came as tourists, ostensibly to shoot grouse or to consult their tailors in Savile Row. Their "coincidental" convergence on the British capital was not without its comic aspect. Nevertheless, they performed useful functions on the sidelines. Secretary of the Treasury Andrew Mellon served as a buffer in the frequent disputes between the bankers and official delegates. Ambassador Houghton conveyed reassurance to the Germans, who at the start had only a couple of technical-level observers on the scene and were anxiously waiting in Berlin for an official invitation to join the proceedings. Owen Young assumed nominal status as a representative of the Dawes Committee, but in practice his position could hardly be distinguished from that of the American government delegates.[4]

For Great Britain the chief figure next to MacDonald was Chancellor of the Exchequer Philip Snowden. Crippled in a childhood accident, Snowden had by fierce determination overcome every disadvantage of background and earned recognition as one of the most capable minds in the Labour party. But he had paid a severe personal price; his thin-lipped, hard, and wizened face revealed the inner man. Unfailing in opposition to the work of Versailles, Snowden lost no opportunity to castigate what he called "a treaty of blood and iron which betrayed every principle for which our soldiers thought they were fighting." He held the whole concept of reparations to be morally abhorrent as well as practically injurious to debtor and creditor alike, and he was bent on promoting revision as fast as possible. Impatient with the fine distinctions and subtle equivocations characteristic of traditional diplomacy, Snowden prided himself on holding firmly to principles and tended to view issues in terms of black and white. From the beginning of the reparations controversy, he noted in his memoirs, the British government had taken "a very reasonable attitude, which was in striking contrast to that of

4. Beerits memoranda, "The European Trip of 1924" and "The Dawes Plan," respectively in Containers 173/54 and 172/27, Hughes Papers; also Merlo J. Pusey, *Charles Evans Hughes*, 2 vols. (New York, 1951), 2:587–93; and David Bryn-Jones, *Frank B. Kellogg: A Biography* (New York, 1937), pp. 144–55.

France."[5] At London, Snowden assumed a posture of such consistent support for the German position, and delivered his opinion in a tone so acerbic, that he placed himself tactically at odds with his own prime minister. The Germans themselves came to fear that he might harm their cause by excess. His relations with the French and Belgians threatened several times to break down altogether, and once when he began, "My chief point is," the Belgian foreign minister continued in a stage whisper, "to stand always on the side of the German delegation."[6] Still, not until the latter part of the conference did Snowden, in concert with Montagu Norman, present an open challenge to MacDonald.[7]

Notwithstanding incipient conflict at the top, the British delegation operated with a degree of precision and coordination far superior to that of the other Allied powers. In order to maximize the tactical advantage afforded by location, the British Foreign Office had discouraged other nations from designating a large number of technical experts to assist their respective plenipotentiaries in London. Variously pleading the need to save the deliberations from unwieldiness and the lack of suitable hotel accommodations in the English capital, the Foreign Office managed to induce the continental countries to limit the size of their deputations. Whitehall counted it a particular success when the French government abandoned its original plan to bring over Marshal Foch and General Degoutte (commander of French troops in the occupied territories), whose presence in London might have led to speculation that the conference would deal with security questions after all.[8]

The British Foreign Office, Treasury, and War Office, by contrast, could call upon the services of scores of second- and third-rank specialists to furnish expertise on the myriad technical matters that would define and shape the political options discussed at a higher level. Well before the other delegations arrived in London, teams headed by Miles W. Lampson of the Foreign Office and Sir Otto E. Niemeyer of the Treasury had worked out a detailed brief on every economic, political, and legal question likely to arise, and throughout the proceedings Whitehall bureaucrats continued to turn out flawlessly crafted background papers

5. Philip Viscount Snowden, *An Autobiography*, 2 vols. (London, 1934), 2:528, 664, 778–79; also Colin Cross, *Philip Snowden* (London, 1966).

6. Stresemann tel., 12 August 1924, BA, R 43 I/266/157–161, watered-down version in Gustav Stresemann, *Vermächtnis*, 3 vols. (Berlin, 1932), 1:488; Hans Luther, *Politiker ohne Partei: Erinnerungen* (Stuttgart, 1960), p. 286; Paul Hymans, *Mémoires*, 2 vols. (Brussels, 1958), 2:577.

7. On the growing conflict between Snowden and MacDonald, see Cabinet Secretary Sir M. P. A. Hankey's letters to his wife, Lady Adeline Hankey, 1–14 August 1924; also Hankey Diary, 11 October 1924, Hankey Papers; and "London Conference: Notes of Meetings of the British Empire Delegation, 11 July–15 August 1924," P.R.O., CAB 29/105.

8. See Foreign Office pressure on the Belgians, F.O. 371/9845: C 10423/10448/10193/18; on the Italians, F.O. 371/9846: C 10596/10193/18; on the French, F.O. 371/9847: C 10884/11181/10193/18.

that gave their political superiors the edge in negotiating with continental statesmen.[9]

Cabinet Secretary Sir Maurice Hankey, a stickler for efficient administration, awarded MacDonald high marks for resourceful personal diplomacy, but complained that the prime minister was "dreadfully unsystematic in his methods" and thus did not fully capitalize on the civil servants' careful preparation. Yet Hankey himself remedied this deficiency, arranging schedules, supervising the paper flow, and serving as MacDonald's factotum and alter ego in the delicate late-night and early-morning private meetings at which crucial political compromises were arranged.[10] Hankey defined the objective as the British delegation perceived it at the beginning of negotiations. France, he noted, might not "really be in the mind to do business until the franc has gone." And if Herriot failed to make concessions, agreement would be impossible. On the other hand, if the opposition in Paris could prove that Herriot had given way, the French premier would fall and the work of the conference would be undone. "So the problem on which we are all at work," the cabinet secretary explained to Smuts of South Africa, "is to get a real concession but [also] to save Herriot's face."[11]

The French brought a talented group of some forty experts to London, but within their delegation uncertainty and confusion reigned supreme. Should France seek to trade on its position in the Ruhr in order to enlist British cooperation for steps against German illegal rearmament? Should it attempt instead to link evacuation with extension of the Alsace-Lorraine duty-free quota or negotiation of a Franco-German tariff agreement to replace the soon-to-expire economic stipulations of the Versailles treaty? Alternatively, should France insist on commercialization of the newly created railroad and industrial bonds as a prerequisite to military evacuation of the Ruhr, on the assumption that commercialization would create a world interest in upholding the Dawes Plan and thus make it harder for the Reich to default? How vital was it to maintain the powers of the Reparation Commission and to preserve France's right to enforce sanctions independently, and what domestic financial sacrifices were feasible should the international bankers decline to cooperate on a politically acceptable basis? Though French officials had given thought to all these issues, they had established no clear priorities, and they had developed

9. On background planning, see Miles W. Lampson's memorandum, 9 July 1924, F.O. 371/9847: C 11033/10193/18; the judgment on the quality of British staff work during the conference finds support in Foreign Office records, especially F.O. 371/9850–62, also F.O. 371/9751–55, 9807, 9828, 9832–34, and in supplementary Treasury files, notably P.R.O., T160/178/F6970/01/5.

10. Hankey Diary, 11 October 1924, Hankey Papers; expurgated version in Stephen Roskill, *Hankey: Man of Secrets*, vol. 2, *1919–1931* (London, 1972), pp. 368–69.

11. Hankey to J. C. Smuts, 17 July 1924, Hankey Papers.

no procedures to facilitate communication among those charged with responsibility for specific problems.[12]

Herriot himself proved incapable of inspiring confidence or exerting leadership in the delegation. He appeared to have a weaker grasp of precise objectives to be sought than of changes in the international atmosphere that he wished to foster. After observing the French premier's performance for some weeks, Hankey described him as "a poor creature . . . very deficient in political courage," who more than once cried in the presence of MacDonald and Crowe.[13] Secretly, Herriot's professional advisers could hardly fail to make a similar evaluation. As negotiations progressed and the constraints on French action became increasingly manifest, Herriot's confidence in his own ability as a diplomat also faltered badly. Two weeks into the conference, he began to compare himself with those who had carried the responsibility of settling with Bismarck after the disastrous defeat of 1870, and to one sympathetic parliamentary associate he lamented in a moment of dejection: "I have the impression that I am about to sign a Treaty of Frankfurt."[14]

Moreover, Herriot became embroiled in increasingly serious disputes with his fellow delegates and cabinet colleagues, War Minister Nollet and Finance Minister Clémentel. General Nollet, greatly alarmed by German rearmament, was soon disillusioned by the drift of the premier's policy and challenged him openly even in the company of foreign statesmen. Clémentel, when impelled to complain, took to dropping in on Thomas Lamont for confidential chats.[15] Yet another handicap for the French delegation derived from the presence of a large number of Socialist deputies, presidents of provincial Radical committees, and other Cartel dignitaries. Thinking that the epoch of open diplomacy preached during the election campaign had begun, these worthies descended on London to offer advice. Their appearance shocked the sensibilities of conservative diplomatists; Saint-Aulaire wrote of a "swarming, gesticulating, vociferous horde" turning the lobby of the French Embassy into "a public meeting hall without a chairman to arbitrate disputes and without police to throw out the disorderly."[16] At best, these amateur counselors required pampering and devoured time that Herriot and his staff could better have spent on planning their strategy. In short, the French delegation found itself unable to compensate for an inherently

12. Jacques Bardoux, *L'Expérience de 1924* (Paris, 1930), pp. 236–43.

13. Hankey Diary, 11 October 1924, Hankey Papers.

14. Phipps tel. no. 494 to Foreign Office, 31 July 1924, F.O. 371/9863: C 12256/11642/18; cf. Herriot's emphasis on the objective difficulties of the French position in his subsequent evaluation: *Jadis*, vol. 2, *D'une guerre à l'autre, 1914–1936* (Paris, 1952), p. 154.

15. On personal relations at the conference, see particularly Thomas Lamont to Dwight Morrow, 12 September 1924, Lamont file, DWM; and Logan's memorandum, "The London Conference," 5 September 1924, "Secret Dawes Report: The Reparation Question," vol. 2A, pp. 233–35, James A. Logan Papers, Hoover Institution, Stanford University, Stanford, Calif.

16. Comte de Saint-Aulaire, *Confession d'un vieux diplomate* (Paris, 1953), p. 718.

weak substantive position with diplomatic skill and coordination.

The cumbersome plenary sessions of the conference, in which Japan and the minor European nations with a claim to reparations took part, served a largely ceremonial function. The real work devolved upon three technical committees and on a council composed of five heads of delegation—MacDonald, Herriot, Kellogg, Prime Minister Theunis of Belgium, and Finance Minister De Stefani of Italy—which met every morning in the cabinet room at No. 10 Downing Street. The First Committee's function was to determine procedure in the event of German default. The Second Committee undertook to elaborate, in conjunction with the Reparation Commission, a concrete plan for economic evacuation of the Ruhr and the reestablishment of economic and fiscal unity in Germany; the question of control over the Rhineland railways thus fell under its aegis. The Third Committee assumed responsibility for examining the prospective use of reparations payments, the modalities of transfer, and arrangements for deliveries in kind.[17]

The Controversy over Default and Sanctions

During the early part of the conference attention focused on the First Committee. In this arena the bankers set forth proposals designed to prevent a repetition of the Ruhr occupation if—or rather when—the Germans defaulted again. The French made no more than a perfunctory effort to uphold the agreement reached during MacDonald's emergency preconference visit to Paris. That understanding, which would have left the essential powers of the Reparation Commission unimpaired, offered but one major safeguard against precipitate action in the future—that an American citizen would vote with the commission when it ruled upon a charge of default. French representatives on the First Committee yielded to the logic of Snowden's argument that to secure a foreign loan their country would have to make a substantial effort to satisfy the bankers' principal demands concerning both the procedure for declaring default and guarantees necessary to protect the bondholders in case sanctions had to be applied. The search began for a formula that would enable the French to save face yet meet the requirements of investment markets.[18]

Consulting privately with Clémentel and his staff, Thomas Lamont discovered with agreeable surprise that the Frenchmen "had a clear view of the situation and were not trying to stick their heads in the sand." Coached by his confidential adviser, Jean Monnet, Clémentel assured the American banker that his government recognized the "disastrous" character of Poincaré's policies and had resolved to do its utmost to

17. For the evolution of these committees' terms of reference, see *Proceedings of the London Reparation Conference,* 1:7–11, 70, 251, 302, 319–20.

18. Minutes of Meetings of the First Committee, 16–18 July 1924, *Proceedings of the London Reparation Conference*, 1:252–67.

appease Germany and to restore that nation's economic freedom. His government realized that the Dawes Plan might fail and France receive very little, but it would nonetheless "refrain from action and would go along quietly" unless Germany defaulted so flagrantly as to arouse public attention everywhere or made an open attempt to rearm. He pleaded for preservation of the Reparation Commission's prerogatives solely on grounds of political necessity: Poincaré had created a domestic climate of opinion such that no French government could agree to "scrap" the commission or to deprive it completely of power. On the other hand, Clémentel insisted, the French government would go "to the limit" in order to protect the bondholders in the unlikely event that it proved impossible to avoid having recourse to sanctions. The French finance minister went so far as to suggest that any government obliged to enforce sanctions unilaterally against Germany undertake automatically to guarantee the bonds. But Lamont remained adamant. The securities markets "could not analyze all these fine points," he observed, and if the Reparation Commission continued to retain the power to declare default, investors simply would not buy the bonds.[19] Lamont dismissed the addition of an American voting member to the Reparation Commission as "unimportant." It would do no harm, but it would not eliminate the possibility that "something" might happen—i.e., that the three continental members might outvote the Anglo-Saxons.[20]

Owen Young, meanwhile, sought desperately to find some compromise that would bridge divergent views and ward off a sudden breakdown of the proceedings. Young's skills as a negotiator had helped the Dawes Committee over many tight spots. Resuming his accustomed role, he shuttled back and forth among the several delegations, drafting and redrafting. He developed a strategy of trying to separate the "political question" of declaring default from the "financial question" of providing affirmative protection for the security and service of the loan. The Dawes Report had clearly contemplated that the Reparation Commission would retain the power to declare default. Once the political issue came into the open, Young felt that he could not possibly support the bankers in a demand "contrary to the fair inference of the plan."[21] Instead, Young, with Logan's collaboration, sought to piece together a formula that would enable the delegates to surmount the immediate deadlock on the narrow question of declaring default. Later, if necessary, the conference could appoint a special committee to investigate modifications required for successful flotation of a German loan in investment

19. Lamont to J. P. Morgan & Co., 17 July 1924, TWL 176/15; Lamont to J. P. Morgan & Co., 20 July 1924 [reporting conversations with Clémentel on 18 and 19 July], TWL 176/17.

20. Ibid.; see also Lamont's undated notes for his own use in TWL 176/4.

21. Owen D. Young to J. P. Morgan, 4 August 1924, J. P. Morgan & Co., Partners file, DWM; see also Young's unsent letter of 24 July 1924, composed for members of the official American delegation and framed in terms much less sympathetic to the bankers, in Box R-16, Owen D. Young Papers.

markets. French public opinion, Young and Logan calculated, would accept an unpleasant decision with better grace if it emerged from the deliberations of financial experts than if it appeared clearly as a political setback for Herriot and Clémentel.[22]

But the bankers, not least the Morgan partners in New York who were obliged to follow developments by cable, suspected that this strategy might result in an arrangement which conceded the outward aspect but denied the substance of investors' demands. "It is not so much the form of the protocol or agreement that concerns us, or the machinery which is adopted to carry it out," they wired, "as it is the real intention of the Allied governments with reference to the future of Germany." As a prerequisite for cooperation, the House of Morgan asked for genuine agreement between England and France to further German economic restoration, not merely "some happy formula by American representatives, official and unofficial, to glide their differences over."[23]

Thus the outlook for finding a solution that satisfied everyone was dim from the outset. Young's initial proposal would have required the Allied governments to pledge that if they applied sanctions, they would regard the service of the loan as a first charge upon all German revenues coming into their possession. Otherwise, it imposed no significant restrictions on their freedom of action in dealing with future default beyond those embodied in the Paris agreement.[24] This formulation convinced the French that they could count on Young's sympathy, and thereby served the purpose for which that psychologically sensitive negotiator had probably designed it. It won no plaudits from the bankers or from the English, however, and examination of several conflicting schemes left the First Committee still far from agreement.

Early on 19 July the French representatives came to Young and reported that they had exhausted every possibility for settlement: unless he could "tone down" Norman and Lamont, the conference would collapse. Young then confronted the two bankers personally, but to no avail. Norman, taking the lead, would "not budge an inch." The governor demanded the exclusion of the Reparation Commission from any role in default proceedings. He insisted on a complex procedure, requiring unanimous agreement by the agent for reparations payments and the five-man Transfer Committee, to sustain a charge of default. He asked the Allied powers to commit themselves further not to undertake sanctions except by unanimous consent even after a finding of flagrant default, notwithstanding any other guarantees provided to protect the bondholders. In brief, as Lamont put it, "Norman did not offer a single loophole for the French to work through."[25]

22. Lamont to J. P. Morgan & Co., 18 July 1924, TWL 176/16.
23. Morgan, Morrow, and Leffingwell to Lamont, 18 July and 19 July 1924, TWL 176/16.
24. "Note Young" [initialed also by Kellogg], 17 July 1924, Herriot Papers.
25. Lamont to J. P. Morgan & Co., 20 July 1924, TWL 176/17.

Though very much discouraged, Young saw no alternative under the circumstances but to push ahead within the formal structure of the First Committee. Finally even Snowden tentatively agreed to meet the French halfway. Prime Minister MacDonald had directed British representatives to aim for concrete results, and Niemeyer and other Treasury career officials reasoned that if they could secure strong enough "moral guarantees" of the "reasonableness" of the Reparation Commission's future policy, they could afford to take a chance with a legally binding arrangement falling short of the ideal.[26] On the afternoon of 19 July, therefore, the First Committee adopted a compromise draft amalgamating various features of the schemes put forward by the British Treasury, Peretti de la Rocca and Bergery on behalf of France, and by Owen Young.[27] The American delegate Logan, however, took care to sound a warning: even though the approved draft ran along "satisfactory lines," only further consultation with the bankers could prevent "a collapse of the present favorable American sentiment." Snowden also reminded the committee that the financiers had not spoken their final word.[28]

At no time did the negotiators lose sight of the critical political issue—whether and under what conditions France, as a practical matter, could enforce sanctions if Germany defaulted again. Occasionally the delegates appeared to be splitting hairs over wording, but as Thomas Lamont reminded his partners at Morgan corner, the outcome of a clearly substantive political struggle necessarily found expression in circuitous legal formulations that, to the impatient, might seem "a good deal technical and sometimes damnfoolery."[29]

The First Committee's report stipulated that when default was to be considered, an American citizen would vote with the Reparation Commission. If that body found Germany in default, then the interested governments would "confer at once on the nature of the sanctions to be applied and on the method of their rapid and effective application."[30] What would happen if the governments did not agree at this stage was left conspicuously unspecified. Two provisions addressed the needs of potential investors. The Allied powers declared that if sanctions proved necessary they would "safeguard any specific securities" pledged to the service of the German loan and that they considered the loan entitled to

26. Sir Otto Niemeyer's statement to Owen Young, reported in Lamont to J. P. Morgan & Co., 20 July 1924, TWL 176/17; also MacDonald's explanation of strategy to the British Empire Delegation, 84th Conference, 18 July 1924, CAB 29/105.

27. Minutes of the First Committee, 19 July 1924, *Proceedings of the London Reparation Conference*, 1:268–73. Some of the intermediate proposals are given in ibid., 1:290–96.

28. Logan comments in ibid., 1:272–73; Snowden report to the British Empire Delegation, 86th Conference, 21 July 1924, CAB 29/105.

29. Lamont to J. P. Morgan & Co., 20 July 1924, TWL 176/17.

30. Report of the First Committee, *Proceedings of the London Reparation Conference*, 1:66–69. The French text of this statement—"se concerteront immédiatement en vue de déterminer la nature des sanctions à appliquer et de les organiser de façon qu'elles soient promptes et efficaces"—conveyed a subtly different meaning.

"absolute priority" in respect to German resources subject to a general lien or arising from the application of sanctions. The Allied powers also agreed that, for the duration of the loan, they would not resort to sanctions unless the Reparation Commission declared a default to be flagrant "by a reasoned decision after taking the opinion of the agent-general for reparation payments and of a representative of the foreign bondholders."

This text pleased the French. It imposed moral restraints on their freedom to act in case of German refusal to pay, but left them with the right to reimpose sanctions, even alone, should political circumstances warrant a bold response. Though apprehensive about sentiment within the British and American delegations, Herriot at first sought to whistle down the wind. He maintained some hope that the full conference might endorse the First Committee's formulation without drastic change; to President of the Republic Gaston Doumergue he wrote with muted optimism that though the game was "far from won," France had nevertheless "constantly gained ground."[31]

Faced with a fait accompli, the bankers did not quite know how to proceed. Norman remained wholly immovable. Lamont put on an equally tough front and denounced the weakness of Owen Young to Secretary Hughes in no uncertain terms. Actually he was prepared to show some flexibility. He believed that Herriot really would be overthrown if obliged to return to Paris having completely "scrapped" the Reparation Commission. Personally he took the view that if the bankers could secure entirely satisfactory protection for the loan, they need not maintain quite so rigid a stance concerning the procedure for determining default. Despite admiration for Norman and an inclination to defer to the governor's experience, he thought that his British colleague was "sticking out too far" in insisting that each individual member of the Transfer Committee hold veto power over a declaration of default. The issue did not impress him as important enough to justify the bankers' taking responsibility for breaking up the conference, an event that might lead to the fall of the French government and possibly of the British government as well.[32]

In his quandary Lamont appealed to New York for advice. His partners also wished to help save the French position "especially in view of the fine attitude of Clémentel." Nevertheless, as they pursued their discussion at J. P. Morgan's Locust Valley estate, where the manicured gardens and the yachts calmly bobbing at anchor off Matinecock Point conduced to dispassionate financial analysis, they could scarcely appreciate the political forces buffeting Lamont in London. As isolated psy-

31. Herriot notation, 19 July 1924, Herriot Papers; Herriot to Doumergue, 20 July 1924, Herriot Papers, quoted also in part in Herriot, *Jadis*, 2:153–54, and in Michel Soulié, *La Vie politique d'Edouard Herriot* (Paris, 1962), pp. 168–69.

32. Lamont to J. P. Morgan & Co., 20 July 1924, TWL 176/17.

chologically from the hurly-burly of the conference as they were far removed physically, they inevitably saw things exclusively from the prospective investor's point of view. They were chary of permitting Lamont to embark on a bargaining process that might result in a political compromise furnishing no satisfactory grounds for proceeding with the loan. Could not the conference adjourn for a few weeks, they wondered, in order to allow time for a committee of finance ministers including Secretary Mellon to consult banking opinion in the various countries and to work out a sound basis for the bond issue? Lamont attempted to enlarge his partners' perspective. "It may sound paradoxical to you," he wired, "but the governments do not consider that they have come together primarily for the purpose of 'getting the new money essential et cetera' . . . but rather to arrive at many important [political] undertakings."[33]

Forced to make a quick decision, the New York partners came down on the side of Montagu Norman. They did not share the governor of the Bank of England's political animus toward France. Indeed, they pitied Herriot, who they thought had been "treated very badly." They regretted that the American and British governments had rushed the Dawes Plan through "the stages of apparent confirmation" without more detailed analysis. They were sorry that Young, Logan, or MacDonald had not earlier explained frankly to the French premier the nature of the difficulties he would have to face.[34] Nevertheless, as J. P. Morgan, Morrow, and especially Leffingwell reflected further on the problem during the decisive week of 20–26 July, their conviction solidified that the procedure governing future determination of default was vital: they could not in good conscience recommend a loan to investors so long as any serious possibility existed that Germany might again be held in default.

The crux of the matter was that the bankers were being asked to arrange a loan for twenty-five years, while every sign pointed to the breakdown of the Dawes Plan long before that. Leffingwell considered a breakdown virtually inevitable because the plan rested on a fundamental ambiguity: it renewed French hopes of large reparations while offering to Germany the assurance that "these payments would not be exacted if inconvenient."[35] How long the arrangement might endure remained a matter for conjecture, but the Morgan partners picked up rumors about German intentions similar to those current on the diplomatic circuit. An Equitable Trust Company official just back from the Ruhr, for example, reported to Morrow on 21 July that the chief difference among leading

33. J. P. Morgan, William H. Porter, D. W. Morrow, Edward R. Stettinius, and R. C. Leffingwell to E. C. Grenfell and T. W. Lamont, 20 July 1924; Morgan to Lamont, 20 July 1924; and Grenfell and Lamont to J. P. Morgan & Co., 21 July 1924, TWL 176/17.

34. Morrow to Lamont, 24 July 1924, Lamont file, DWM.

35. Leffingwell memorandum, "First Principles," 26 July 1924, copy in J. P. Morgan & Co., Partners–Leffingwell file, DWM.

industrialists there lay between those favoring an open admission that Germany could never make the mandated payments and those who counted on England and the United States to bring about another revision of the reparations schedule once the Reich had "tried and failed."[36]

Significantly, even Wall Street observers not privy to confidential information expressed skepticism about the safety of a German bond offering. The Federal Reserve's easy-money policy had sparked a sudden boom in securities markets, yet the investment public seemed "curiously indifferent" to the progress of the London Conference and to the prospective loan.[37] "The average investor is disinclined to 'buy into a quarrel,'" wrote the *Wall Street News*, "and if there is no assurance that the French will not reenter the Ruhr at some future date with the avowed purpose of compelling Germany to live up to the letter of the law in connection with its reparation payments, . . . a German loan offering in this country will fall flat."[38]

Thus the Morgan firm's real objection, as Leffingwell phrased it, was "not to the Reparation Commission as such, but to it as the ready instrument of French governmental policy," and not to the First Committee's formula in itself, but to the French attitude toward Germany to which it bore witness. Despite Clémentel's assurance that his nation would "go along quietly," France's ultimate intentions remained open to question so long as it sought indirect budgetary relief through the mechanism of a reparations loan by Americans and Englishmen to Germany, while it attempted to reserve the right to obtain a declaration of default and even to apply sanctions independently in the future. Bondholders could find no security in any "mere form of words" devised to conceal a divergence in policy on this score. Leffingwell's conclusion left no room for equivocation: "Germany cannot sell bonds secured by the proceeds of the next military invasion of the Ruhr. She cannot sell bonds except on the basis of Allied unity."[39]

Did the Morgan partners desire, then, to create circumstances that sooner or later would permit Germany to default without fear of retaliation, merely in order to provide security for a bond issue of $200 million? The proposed loan, after all, represented a relatively modest sum in comparison with the total value of international indebtedness. It would require a maximum annual payment of no more than $20 million for interest and amortization. The bankers realized that the Allies could indubitably find a way to give an unimpeachable guarantee of this amount if the very future of Europe depended on it.

36. Morrow to Lamont, 24 July 1924, Lamont file, DWM.

37. See Leffingwell to Lamont, 22 July 1924, TWL 176/18.

38. *Wall Street News*, no. 97, 24 July 1924, copy in Germany–miscellaneous file, DWM.

39. Leffingwell memorandum, "First Principles," 26 July 1924, J. P. Morgan & Co., Partners–Leffingwell file, DWM.

But as the bankers intimated privately, their concern extended beyond the initial flotation. The issue was not so much security for the Dawes loan as security for subsequent foreign investment in Germany and elsewhere on the Continent. Successful launching of the Dawes loan would give a green light to numerous other European financing proposals already in the planning stage. Hence the bankers deemed it particularly important that conditions for the first loan command the complete confidence of investors. If at some future date France menaced Germany with a declaration of default on reparations, the mark and then the franc would plummet, and European financial operations might be thrown into disorder—undermining the market value of all foreign investments on the Continent—irrespective of the ultimate disposition of the charge.[40]

Beyond such comparatively parochial business concerns, however, the House of Morgan hoped that a settlement along the lines it advocated might pay high dividends in terms of European peace. The New York partners commended to Lamont as a "first class analysis" an editorial appearing in the *New York World*, long a stalwart of Wilsonian internationalism:

> What people with a true sense of international politics are really working for today, once all pretenses and facesavers are laid aside, is an arrangement by which France and Germany can live for ten years or so. Such an arrangement involves lending money to both of them in the hope that time and the development of common sense will take care of the rest.[41]

Meanwhile, in London the conference delayed final consideration of the First Committee's formula while consultations with the bankers continued. On 21 July Lamont and Norman met with the finance ministers, Clémentel, Snowden, and Theunis. Theunis advanced several successive versions of a scheme requiring the Reparation Commission to seek an affirmative vote from the Dawes Committee, which would be constituted as a permanent body, before it declared default or recommended sanctions.[42] Owen Young and his Dawes Committee colleague, Sir Robert Kindersley of Lazard's, London, also kept busy devising various formulae.[43] Lamont, uncomfortable in his role as the obdurate financier, went unhappily from one meeting to another. Herriot made an impassioned plea for help to France, in which he evoked "ancient friendships" and dramatically threw himself upon the "mercy" of the

40. See MacDonald's report to Dominion representatives on the essential issue as the bankers had explained it to him, British Empire Delegation, 88th Conference, 28 July 1924, CAB 29/105.

41. *New York World*, 23 July 1924; quoted and commented on in Morrow, Thomas Cochran, and Leffingwell to Lamont, 23 July 1924, TWL 176/18.

42. Grenfell and Lamont to J. P. Morgan & Co., 22 July 1924, TWL 176/18. For the final version of the Theunis plan, see *Proceedings of the London Reparation Conference*, 1: 296.

43. Owen Young to Lamont, 22 July 1924, TWL 176/18; Grenfell and Lamont to J. P. Morgan & Co., 26 July 1924, TWL 176/20.

Morgan firm—the spectacle moved and embarrassed Lamont though it did not cause him to modify his position. MacDonald, torn by conflicting motives, appealed to the representatives of the investment markets to meet the situation somehow, even by accepting the Theunis scheme, to avoid the tragic consequences of the conference's failure. Secretaries Hughes and Mellon, with whom Lamont conferred repeatedly, seemed to endorse the bankers' substantive demands up to a point, but expressed themselves as "exceedingly anxious" to see some adjustment reached.[44]

All this diplomatic activity merely laid bare the fundamental differences separating the conferees. Garbled press accounts purporting to reveal the details of discussions caused further confusion. Morgan partners on both sides of the ocean exploded in outrage at intimations by leading newspapers in Paris and New York that they were "using financial pressure to help England's game." *L'Oeuvre*, for example, suggested darkly that Lamont had "yielded to the influence of certain persons in the British Treasury." *Le Petit Journal* regretted the absence of Otto Kahn of Kuhn, Loeb (Morgan's chief Wall Street competitors in the investment banking field) and pointedly described him as "so alive to the needs of France." And the *New York Times* commented tartly: "The fact is sometimes overlooked that the real purpose of the Dawes Plan is to secure and facilitate the payment of reparations rather than to offer attractive new investments to the public."[45]

These criticisms strengthened the feeling of the Morgan partners in New York that to allow debate to drag out further over the same barren ground would merely heighten the risk of their being cast before world public opinion as the villains of the piece. Late on 23 July, J. P. Morgan wired Lamont: "We are all very sure that the time has come for you to make our position quite clear and definite and then to refrain from listening to all these various suggestions."[46] Morgan also drew up a press communiqué clarifying the firm's position. The bankers were not trying to "make any political suggestions," much less attempting to "enforce any political views," he asserted; they were simply informing the politicians about investment conditions at the latter's request.[47]

Almost simultaneously, Lamont concluded that he should stop dickering. He and Norman had acquired a reputation for being "very stiff," but he attributed this largely to the fact that MacDonald, in his eagerness to find some means of accommodation, had left the bankers with the task of

44. Grenfell and Lamont to J. P. Morgan & Co., 23 July 1924, TWL 176/18.

45. Grenfell and Lamont to J. P. Morgan & Co., 22 July 1924, quoting *L'Oeuvre*, *Le Petit Journal*, and other newspapers of that date; Morrow, Cochran, and Leffingwell to Lamont, 23 July 1924, quoting that day's *New York Times*, both cables in TWL 176/18.

46. J. P. Morgan to Lamont, 23 July 1924, TWL 176/18.

47. See successive drafts for this communiqué in TWL 176/19 and in Germany–miscellaneous file, DWM.

explaining the harsh realities of economic life to the French. Lamont saw no evidence that opinion at the principal banks in the London City differed substantially with that of the Bank of England. Kindersley of Lazard's had been "nibbling away at Norman's defenses" and would rest content with lesser safeguards regarding default and sanctions, and probably so would Reginald McKenna of the Joint City and Midland—but only provided, Lamont observed cynically, that they "did not have the responsibilities of fathering the bonds."

Nor did Lamont take seriously the feeble counterpressure mounted by the French. Clémentel invited a number of French bankers over to London and leaked a story to the press that an independent group headed by Kuhn, Loeb and the Banque de Paris et des Pays-Bas stood ready to underwrite a loan on easier terms. Lamont claimed that this would represent a "happy solution," but he had explored the matter with Paul Warburg in New York the previous month and come away with the impression that it did not figure as a live possibility.[48] Actually, Kuhn, Loeb partners Otto Kahn and Mortimer Schiff would have loved to call Lamont's bluff and to take over leadership of the underwriting syndicate; far less pessimistic than Morgan's, they considered Germany on the road to recovery, the loan intrinsically sound, and investment demand in America strong enough so that they could carry off the flotation themselves. Kahn, letting professional jealousy get the better of him, had done some loose talking in Paris along these lines, and thereby provoked Lamont to anger. But the sober judgment of Kuhn, Loeb partners compelled them to recognize that supplanting Morgan's entirely would not be "wise policy," since the latter's nonparticipation in the loan would suggest that the House of Morgan did not regard it as a good risk.[49] It was perfectly clear, moreover, from what François-Marsal had told Herman Harjes as far back as April, that the Paris bankers could not conceivably float a loan to Germany by themselves; only with extreme difficulty, in fact, could they hope to induce the French public to subscribe the token amount upon which an Anglo-American syndicate would insist.[50] Thus no real alternative existed to handling matters through Morgan's and the Bank of England. Clémentel, noted Lamont, retained his "affection," but had been "acting quite stupidly."[51]

In order to clarify the Morgan position, Lamont composed another letter, which he cleared with Hughes and then delivered to MacDonald on 25 July. "My firm has been somewhat embarrassed by the continued

48. Grenfell and Lamont to J. P. Morgan & Co., 24 July 1924, TWL 176/19; J. P. Morgan to Grenfell and Lamont, 24 July 1924, TWL 176/19; Grenfell and Lamont to J. P. Morgan, 26 July, and Lamont to Morrow, 28 July 1924, TWL 176/20.

49. Otto Kahn to Mortimer Schiff, 16 July, 5 and 21 August 1924, Box 237, Kahn Papers; see also Kahn–Kuhn, Loeb cables, 1 July–20 August 1924, Box 227, Kahn Papers.

50. François-Marsal's analysis of Paris banking opinion is found in Morgan, Harjes et Cie to J. P. Morgan & Co., 23 April 1924, TWL 176/9.

51. Grenfell and Lamont to J. P. Morgan, 26 July 1924, TWL 176/20.

assumptions in the public press that the representatives of the investment markets have brought forth new and unforeseen conditions," Lamont observed. "This you will doubtless agree is not the case. On the contrary the conditions are the same as they have always been." The bankers would make a loan available only if the Allied governments showed a willingness to "cover the position both of the loan and of the debtor. Nothing more than this will be needed: nothing less than this can be considered."[52]

This unwelcome missive simply compounded the frustrations of MacDonald's advisers at the Foreign Office. The point, they held, was to secure an efficient practical safeguard against independent action by France in the event of flagrant German default. The formula proposed by the First Committee provided reasonable certainty that another Ruhr occupation would never take place. Thus Lamont seemed to them needlessly obtuse. They saw no reason to jeopardize the success of the conference by overkill.[53]

After all, reports from Paris confirmed Clémentel's intimation that the French delegation sought to save appearances rather than to lay the legal groundwork for applying sanctions again. Senator Henry de Jouvenel, the moving spirit behind *Le Matin* and an influential moderate who had served in Poincaré's last cabinet, assured British Minister Eric Phipps that Poincarism was "dead and buried." His colleagues at the Palais Luxembourg, Jouvenel declared, wanted to maintain the powers of the Reparation Commission less because they expected to exercise those powers in the old way than because they considered it vital to preserve the Versailles treaty framework for the sake of French security. Léon Blum embroidered on the same theme: independent French action to enforce the reparations settlement was henceforth "unthinkable" even if Poincaré returned to power; nevertheless, it was essential to find some way of "saving M. Herriot's face." After completing soundings in French political circles, Phipps advised MacDonald to try to round the corners of the financiers' demands somewhat: "The danger appears to be not that you should get too little out of M. Herriot, but rather that you should get too much, thereby causing his fall and an inevitable reaction in French public opinion."[54]

Foreign Office professionals did not worry unduly about an adverse reaction in Paris to a "reasonable settlement." Responsible French statesmen understood that a breakdown in London would likely result in the

52. Lamont to MacDonald, 25 July 1924, copies in TWL 176/19 and in Box 9, Kellogg Papers.

53. Miles W. Lampson to Sir O. E. Niemeyer, 19 July 1924, F.O. 371/9851: C 11781/11495/18; Lampson memorandum for Sir Eyre Crowe, 24 July 1924, F.O. 371/9751: C 11924/70/18. See also MacDonald's remarks: "Note of an Informal Meeting Held at 10 Downing Street," 24 July 1924, F.O. 371/9855: C 12820/G.

54. Phipps tel. no. 480 to MacDonald, 24 July 1924, F.O. 371/9863: C 11925/11642/18.

rapid depreciation of the franc, wrote a Central Department analyst, so Herriot's domestic opponents, however loudly they might talk, would "think more than twice before actually throwing him out."[55] On the other hand, Whitehall diplomats did not want to undermine Gallic prestige needlessly or to require the French openly to abjure their "sacrosanct Treaty of Versailles." As the drama unfolded, Miles Lampson began to suspect that the bankers aimed to achieve something beyond security for the loan. Montagu Norman, he noted on 22 July, was "certainly not over-inclined to take the French point of view into consideration—to judge from our experience of him during recent months," and Lamont appeared "very much in the pockets of the governor of the Bank." The bankers' continuing refusal to bend reinforced Lampson's skepticism whether it was "bona fide fear about the market so much as their personal political views" that motivated their demands.[56]

With some irritation, therefore, the Foreign Office began to explore ways to give the bankers "yet one more safeguard against independent action by France." The most promising suggestion emerged from the legal staff. Sir John Fischer-Williams, lawyer for the British delegation at the Reparation Commission, emphasized the advantages of providing for arbitration in the event of future disputes over interpretation of the reparations sections of the Versailles treaty. The original treaty contained no provision for breaking a deadlock over interpretation; hence in 1923 the British had found themselves without a legal forum in which to press their contention that the Ruhr occupation was not a legally authorized sanction. Fischer-Williams proposed to fill this gap in the treaty by providing that, failing unanimity on a point of interpretation, the powers submit the question to the World Court at The Hague. Herriot had previously endorsed the general principles of arbitration recommended in the League Covenant; he could hardly turn down this scheme for implementation without embarrassment.[57]

The idea intrigued Prime Minister MacDonald. Obviously, if Britain could appeal a French decision to bring specific sanctions to bear, it would hold what amounted to a veto power over their application. The World Court conducted business at a leisurely pace. It was not immune to political pressure. And like every international organization, it had particularist concerns of its own: it would almost inevitably seek to preserve a reputation for "impartiality" by evading an unpopular politi-

55. Miles W. Lampson and J. C. Sterndale Bennett minutes, 28 July 1924, on Phipps tel. no. 482, 25 July 1924, F.O. 371/9863: C 11962/11642/18.

56. Lampson memorandum, 22 July 1924, F.O. 371/9751: C 11973/70/18; Lampson memorandum for Crowe, 24 July, and attached note, 25 July 1924, F.O. 371/9751: C 11924/70/18.

57. Fischer-Williams memorandum, "Interpretation of the Dawes Agreement and of the Treaty of Versailles," 21 July 1924, F.O. 371/9752: C 12395/70/18; elaboration by Miles W. Lampson, 24 July 1924, F.O. 371/9751: C 11924/70/18.

cal decision. The French would hesitate a long time before risking an endless legal snarl at The Hague. By comparison, even an unsatisfactory compromise within the confines of the Reparation Commission would appear the more attractive course. The French could not possibly overlook the practical consequences of an undertaking to adopt arbitration. Yet surprisingly, when Foreign Office legal adviser Sir Cecil Hurst broached the subject to Henri Fromageot, his counterpart at the Quai d'Orsay, the latter expressed keen interest. His political superiors, Fromageot indicated, would examine favorably any arbitration proposal that did not infringe on the present powers of the Reparation Commission.[58]

As it turned out, it took some days for the plan to mature. But eventually the French were to embrace the principle of arbitration wholeheartedly and agree to extend it to almost every form of dispute under the Dawes Plan and the Versailles treaty. Herriot would boast that arbitration constituted his own unique contribution to the success of the conference. Thereby, the French forged the legal chains that would bind them to months of litigation and preclude a vigorous immediate response if Germany violated its commitments.[59]

Before the British strategy could take effect, however, Secretary Hughes decided that the moment had come to throw the weight of the United States government into the balance. In characteristic fashion, Hughes proceeded on two levels. At lunch with the French premier, he talked in general terms about the importance of reaching agreement. In view of his unofficial status in London and the uncertainties of American public opinion, he found it expedient to direct Herriot's attention to the specific requirements of the situation through intermediaries.[60] The secretary of state told Lamont to inform Belgian Premier Theunis that only he could "persuade Herriot that his best chance of handling his parliament was to grasp the nettle, make his adjustments with the British and then go to Paris and tell them to take it or leave it." Lamont explained to Theunis that no simple formula would meet the situation: "Herriot must give way or else the conference will end." Lamont enlarged on what might

58. MacDonald minute, 24 July, Sir Cecil J. B. Hurst minute, 26 July 1924, F.O. 371/9751: C 11924/70/18.

59. See Herriot's claim to have "spontaneously" proposed arbitration as the basis for the London agreement and his prediction that the arbitral principle would henceforth "dominate all diplomatic arrangements," *Daily Telegraph*, 4 August 1924; further evidence of careful manipulation by British officials, F.O. 371/9854: C 12569/11495/18 and F.O. 371/9862: C 15624/11495/18; finally the Central Department's review memorandum, "Arrangements Made in the London Reparation Settlement of August 1924 for the Submission to Arbitration of Disputes Arising out of the Application of the Dawes Plan," 10 December 1924, F.O. 371/9755: C 18597/70/18.

60. On Hughes's personal meeting with Herriot, see Frank B. Kellogg to Robert E. Olds, 5 August 1924, Box 8, Kellogg Papers; also Beerits memorandum, "The Dawes Plan," p. 27, Container 172/27, Hughes Papers. For the message passed on by Hughes through New York lawyer Frederic R. Coudert, see Herriot notation, 23 July 1924, Herriot Papers.

then happen to the franc, and also to the Belgian franc. "Sovereignty was dear to the heart of the French people," he bluntly observed, "but the franc was much dearer, as Herriot would find out—too late—to his cost." Somewhat gratuitously, the American financier added that Herriot, who at the moment was "a bit suspicious of all bankers," might interpret any direct talk from him about the fall of the franc as a threat to pull it down. Theunis, however, as a banker and businessman himself, could "appreciate" the situation and put it to Herriot with appropriate delicacy. The Belgian premier declared himself "flattered" by Hughes's message and promised to do his best.[61] And while the statesmen debated further how to work their way around the impasse, Lamont departed on a motor trip to contemplate the natural splendors of Devon and Cornwall.

The French could hardly expect to stand up indefinitely against the multiple pressures converging upon them. The head of the French financial mission in the Ruhr suggested that the German economy was recovering so fast that possibly the Reich might not need the loan after all, but Herriot and Clémentel did not dare to act on this information.[62] Herriot's memoirs, despite their inaccuracy and vagueness, reveal the French premier's fatalism in striking fashion:

> The reparations question entered into its financial phase after its mystical phase and its procedural phase. The fall of the franc had led us to accept American intervention. . . . The granting of the Morgan credit entailed the acceptance of the Dawes Plan as a consequence. Now this plan linked in indivisible fashion the four parts of the German financial payment. . . . Understandably, therefore, [the bankers] were justified in asking for certain political and military guarantees.[63]

If Herriot failed to comprehend fully the magnitude of the domestic financial difficulties that breakdown of the conference would entail, a deputation of bankers arriving from Paris took care to complete his enlightenment.[64] The French delegation, nevertheless, held its ground until 28 July, when a verbal duel between Snowden and Clémentel in the First Committee brought matters to the verge of collapse. Catastrophe was averted only because Logan, affecting the manner of a magician pulling a rabbit out of a hat, dramatically set forth a new proposal and then promptly called for adjournment.[65] The search for a satisfactory formula intensified. Even President Coolidge in Washington recognized the gravity of the crisis. Recalling that one of his predecessors had

61. Lamont to Morrow, 28 July 1924, copies in TWL 176/20, and in Lamont file, DWM.

62. Inspector of Finances Etienne Moeneclaey to Finance Minister Clémentel, 27 July 1924, copy in Herriot Papers.

63. Herriot, *Jadis*, 2:155–56.

64. Kellogg to State Department, 30 July 1924, U.S. 462.00R 296/463.

65. Minutes of the First Committee, 28 July 1924, *Proceedings of the London Reparation Conference*, 1:274–82; additional details in Kellogg to State Department, 29 July 1924, U.S. 462.00R 296/458, 461; and in F.O. 371/9852: C 12020/12021/12192/11495/18.

dispatched the chief justice of the Supreme Court to arbitrate a boundary dispute between Costa Rica and Nicaragua, Coolidge considered offering similar assistance should the London Conference find no other way to compose its differences.[66]

The European powers finally were spared this indignity. On 30 July the French proposed a variant of the Fischer-Williams arbitration scheme that served to break the deadlock. They suggested that if the Reparation Commission did not make a unanimous ruling on a charge of flagrant default, the minority might appeal the decision to a panel composed of three members headed by an American for final, binding arbitration.[67] This procedure, billed as Herriot's "last word," met with approval from MacDonald and American government representatives after minor emendations, and on 2 August a plenary session of the conference endorsed it.[68] A spirited debate took place over the question whether the Allied powers could act individually to apply sanctions if Germany were somehow adjudged in default under the agreed scheme. In the end, the negotiators passed over this issue in discreet silence. They decided to follow the Belgian foreign minister's dictum that the conference "could not provide . . . for every contingency which might arise."[69]

As a practical matter, it became evident, the contingency would not arise. For all intents and purposes the French had surrendered the right to obtain a judgment of default except in extraordinary circumstances. Even Montagu Norman admitted privately that though the "name" of the Reparation Commission remained, its actual powers had been "scrapped." Neither the French nor the British government could easily give a formal commitment not to apply sanctions under any circumstances, Norman recognized, for such a promise would leave the Allies virtually without recourse in case Germany rearmed flagrantly or restored the monarchy under extreme nationalist auspices. But the likelihood of sanctions to enforce the reparations settlement, even if the Reparation Commission acted *in extremis* to certify a German default, had greatly diminished. The British Treasury had managed to secure yet an additional safeguard at the last minute. It obtained approval for an amendment to the agreed scheme that entitled the Reparation Commission, after declaring default, to recommend what action it considered necessary. Norman conceded that the British and American members of the commission could "hardly be deaf" to representations made by the agent general or by the Transfer Committee. Given the configuration of

66. Joseph Grew Diary, 27–30 July 1924, Grew Papers; also U.S. 462.00R 296/460a–d, correspondence covering the period 28–30 July 1924.

67. *Proceedings of the London Reparation Conference*, 1:298–301; background in Sir J. Fischer-Williams to Crowe, and Fischer-Williams memorandum for the prime minister, 29 July 1924, F.O. 371/9852: C 12168/11495/18.

68. *Proceedings of the London Reparation Conference*, 1: 283–90, 33–34, 92–95.

69. Ibid., 1:286.

political forces, one might reasonably hope that even in the event of a serious default, the Reparation Commission would declare no action "necessary."[70]

The governor of the Bank continued nevertheless to express keen dissatisfaction. He reminded MacDonald that the formula adopted did not begin to meet the conditions which the bankers had twice set down in writing explicitly for his benefit. Lamont, summoned back to London, again consented to follow the tactical lead of his Bank of England colleague.[71] And Norman, now drawing increasingly open support from Snowden and other Treasury officials, raised such a multitude of objections that the American delegates started to suspect that he was "really inclined to upset the whole plan."[72] Kellogg and Logan wondered whether Norman and his Treasury allies, by deliberately creating difficulties, might be seeking to oblige those forces within the trades unions and British industry that wanted the conference to fail.[73] In fact, though several important economic groups—notable among them textile manufacturers and coal miners—fretted openly about the effect of rapid German recovery under the Dawes Plan on British export opportunities, neither Norman nor Snowden appears to have acted in direct response to domestic pressures.[74]

When pushed to the wall by MacDonald, Norman took refuge in the argument that though an arbitration court might indeed overturn a politically motivated declaration of default by the Reparation Commission, in the interim period (say, a month) before the arbitration court reported, the credit of Germany would suffer, and grave losses would result on other loans. But this, MacDonald noted, was a "hair-spun objection"; the formula adopted hedged the Reparation Commission round with enough conditions and obstacles so that "when either the Reparation Commission or any government found that so much difficulty was involved in declaring and bringing home a default to Germany, they would hesitate before taking any action in this direction."[75]

In the final analysis, general antipathy to reparations and sympathy

70. J. P. Morgan, Charles Steele, Grenfell, and Lamont to J. P. Morgan & Co. [reporting Norman's views], 6 August 1924, TWL 176/22.

71. Grenfell and Lamont to J. P. Morgan & Co., 4 August 1924, TWL 176/21; Montagu Norman memorandum, 5 August 1924, copy in TWL 176/22.

72. Kellogg to Hughes, 1 August 1924, copies in U.S. 462.00R 296/510 and in Box 8, Kellogg Papers.

73. Kellogg and Logan to State Department, 30 July 1924, U.S. 462.00R 296/463.

74. For postconference apprehensions expressed by Lancashire cotton mill owners, see F.O. 371/9867: C 14280/15040/14053/18; for representations made by the Miners' Federation of Great Britain, see P.R.O., PREMIER 1/37. The union leaders claimed that the Dawes Plan would ruin the British coal industry and favored its outright rejection. The prime minister, significantly, put off seeing the Miners' Federation representatives from 25 July to 1 October 1924, and then challenged the economic basis for their claims.

75. See MacDonald's withering remarks to the British Empire Delegation, 89th Conference, 31 July 1924, CAB 29/105.

for Germany's plight appear to have motivated both Norman and Snowden. Each morning as he entered the Bank of England, Norman passed the famous bronze of Wellington astride his horse and seeming to stare with all the imperious confidence of Victorian statuary across the roundabout toward Lombard Street. How often did the thought cross Norman's mind that he might check the overweening ambition of France in the financial sphere, as Wellington had done by force of arms a century before? In the case at hand Norman, like Snowden, calculated that Herriot would yield when pressed hard enough and thought that MacDonald erred in not exploiting French weakness to the full.[76]

The American government representatives, who had earlier shown some willingness to accommodate the bankers' demands for additional guarantees, now deplored continued foot-dragging by the House of Morgan. They became impatient with Lamont's failure to agree that security for the loan was now demonstrably adequate. "Norman and Snowden were constantly taking the general position 'that the American bankers will not agree to this or that,' and making a general sucker out of Lamont," Logan complained in retrospect.[77]

This characterization was less than fair. Nevertheless, the extent and consistency of cooperation between Lamont and Norman does call for explanation, particularly since the two men differed fundamentally in their political sympathies. Undoubtedly, Lamont and other Morgan partners operated on the general assumption that their firm and the Bank of England constituted the two great forces for stability in the financial world and therefore ought to stick together.[78] Lamont did not inquire too closely into Norman's political biases; his tendency to defer to the governor's judgment stemmed largely from the conviction that the English banker kept in closer touch with European conditions and therefore would better understand the requirements of the situation than he, a recent arrival from the United States. Both Lamont and his partners at home, however, also developed their own rationale for declining to float the loan without additional guarantees.

Lamont put it thus on 2 August: The American investor expected the Dawes Plan "to mark a new order—a tranquillized and hard-working Germany, Allies working in harmony, no more Ruhr invasions, no more sanctions, Germany paying reparations at last upon a scale steady and fairly adequate." The French, however, did not appear ready to burn their bridges behind them and to embrace the Dawes Plan as a "new

76. This interpretation finds support in Snowden, *Autobiography*, 2:664–79, and in Sir Henry Clay's authorized biography, *Lord Norman* (London, 1957), pp. 212–17.

77. Logan memorandum, "The London Conference," 5 September 1924, "Secret Dawes Report: The Reparation Question," vol. 2A, p. 233, Logan Papers.

78. For a relatively unsympathetic appraisal of the Morgan policy of collaboration with the Bank of England in various parts of the world, as contrasted with the more competitive principles followed by the National City Bank, see Carl Parrini, *Heir to Empire: United States Economic Diplomacy, 1916–1923* (Pittsburgh, 1969), pp. 55–65, 112–37, 265–66.

charter of European liberties"; as the controversy over default and sanctions confirmed, they continued to hold reservations, expressed or implied. Lamont thought this quite understandable in view of Germany's "very bad record as to paying reparations as promised and fulfilling her other treaty obligations." Yet without the inauguration of a "new order," the American investor had no reason to buy a German bond. Of course, if France acquired security against German aggression, that nation might give way on other points; but to guarantee security did not lie within the bankers' province. Doubting that the conference would find a way out of the dilemma, Lamont gave way to momentary despair.[79]

At Morgan offices in New York, Leffingwell's preoccupations ran along similar lines. It would prove difficult to determine objectively whether Germany's "not improbable" future default was willful. Hence France's insistence on reserving the right to apply sanctions independently aroused Leffingwell's suspicions. Important groups in France, he feared, were "really less concerned about reparations than 'security,'" which they conceived of as keeping Germany weak. "That may be good policy for France," he concluded, "—indeed, many Americans think it is—but it is not very alluring to the American who is asked to put money into a German bond."[80]

When Lamont, in company with Norman, met with MacDonald again on 3 August, each of the financiers emphasized the problem troubling him most. The American stressed the need for a "complete and favorable change of atmosphere" at the conference in order to induce investment markets to overlook "certain technical weaknesses" in the settlement. Norman outlined the bankers' specific political demands. They wished to secure further assurances concerning default procedures and the right of each ally to impose sanctions separately. They asked also to be "informed" regarding the military evacuation of the Ruhr, withdrawal of French and Belgian railwaymen from the German lines, the timetable set for evacuating the Rhineland, the Rhineland Commission's future policies, and procedures for interpreting the Versailles treaty. Norman stated flatly that until the bankers obtained satisfaction on these points, negotiations for a loan could not begin. MacDonald replied on a conciliatory note: he wanted to make an optimistic report to the House of Commons on the morrow and hoped to denounce "unwarranted criticism of bankers who had been most cooperative." However, he could not hold out the prospect of rapid and satisfactory agreement with the French on the points that Norman had raised.[81]

This inconclusive interview marked the end of the bankers' interven-

79. Lamont memorandum for his own use, 2 August 1924, TWL 176/4.
80. Leffingwell to Grenfell and Lamont, 5 August 1924, TWL 176/22.
81. Grenfell and Lamont to J. P. Morgan & Co., 4 August 1924, TWL 176/21; Norman memorandum, 5 August 1924, TWL 176/22.

tion in the first part of the conference. They had sharply limited the possibility of any future declaration of default, but had failed to establish their other prerequisites for a loan. Norman determined to keep up the pressure. Exhibiting perfect timing, Hjalmar Schacht, head of the Reichsbank, cabled him on 4 August announcing his plans to leave for London and warning in a friendly way, as one central banker to another, that the Reichstag would not agree to accept the Dawes charges unless it obtained "freedom" for the Ruhr and Rhine and various other compensations.[82] After consulting with Snowden, Norman suggested that Lamont and J. P. Morgan, who had also just arrived in England, join him in conveying their position with all details to Schacht. The American bankers declined, saying that until the Allied governments ironed out their own differences, they would not "discuss any question with any German." But Norman took Schacht into his confidence anyway, and with satisfaction the Reichsbank president described the Anglo-American bankers' conditions to his own delegation as so severe that they "almost go beyond the German claims."[83]

As Schacht correctly sensed, Morgan, traditional financial agent of the Entente, was distressed to find himself the champion of France's foes, even at one remove. Having made their conditions clear, the bankers could do little more, Morgan felt. "I am distinctly impressed," he wrote privately a few days later, "with the idea that if governments settle the pending questions and still do not give us the necessary political conditions to issue a loan, they can find a way out which does not involve issue of a German loan in the U.S.A. for the present and we shall get away from the responsibility without preventing a settlement. This would be a great comfort to me personally."[84] But Morgan's expression of sentiment found no reflection in the public position of his firm. In practice, the bankers' requirements would weigh heavily in the balance in the next phase of negotiations, that between the Allies and the Germans.

The Rhineland Railways Dispute

While the wrangle over default and sanctions dominated the political arena, the first part of the conference witnessed substantial progress on technical matters. By 2 August, when an invitation was dispatched to the Germans, the delegation staffs had, with a minimum of friction, completed most of the background work necessary for launch-

82. Schacht to Norman, 4 August 1924, Norman Papers.

83. Norman memorandum, 5 August 1924, TWL 176/22; Stresemann tel., 6 August 1924, G.F.M. 3398/1736/D740230–232. For Schacht's meetings with other Allied financiers in London see also BA, R 43 I/266/323–331.

84. J. P. Morgan to Morrow and Leffingwell, 6 August 1924, TWL 176/22; Grenfell and Lamont to J. P. Morgan & Co., 6 August 1924, TWL 176/22; Morgan, Grenfell, and Lamont to J. P. Morgan & Co., 11 August 1924, TWL 176/24.

ing the Dawes Plan. They had drawn up a comprehensive program for restoring German economic and financial unity.[85] Despite the complexity of the commercial interests involved, they had developed procedures to govern the delivery of reparations in kind. A committee of jurists had determined what agreements the Allies would have to sign with the Reich. The Germans submitted informal observations concerning these issues on 30 July, and then on 6 August, after the arrival of their delegation in London, delivered a more detailed statement of their views.[86] To meet their objections or to assuage their fears about hidden meanings of obscure clauses, the Allies consented to make numerous changes.

Previous postwar conferences had taken place in an atmosphere so fraught with tension that differences over small technical points had often ballooned into major controversies. Hence the expeditious settlement of these intricate problems represented no slight accomplishment. But where vital national interests conflicted, there were obvious limits to what goodwill could achieve. Two further political disputes overshadowed the diligent labors of the specialists on the conference committees. One concerned the future status of the Rhineland railway system. The other, though it appeared nowhere on the agenda, lay at the very center of all these negotiations: it pertained to the military evacuation of the Ruhr.

In the opening days of the conference, French military experts working under the leadership of General Nollet set forth a plan for separate regional management of all railways in the Ruhr and Rhineland. They proposed amalgamation of the key railway district offices in the occupied areas—the most important located at Koblenz, Cologne, Aachen, and Düsseldorf—into one large administrative unit. Though they preferred that Allied personnel actually manage the railways in these areas, subject only to general direction by the Railway Board in Berlin, they expressed willingness to let the Germans handle day-to-day administration, provided that the latter operate in coordination with an Allied supervisory body empowered to take all measures necessary to safeguard the security of the occupying forces.[87]

85. For details see Weill-Raynal, *Les Réparations allemandes et la France*, 3:68–70, 86–97. The formal minutes and documents reproduced in *Proceedings of the London Reparation Conference* give a more accurate picture of technical discussions than they do of political disputes, where the decisive negotiations took place outside the official framework.

86. German Foreign Office memorandum, 30 July 1924, copies in G.F.M. 3398/1736/D740126–142, and in F.O. 371/9853: C 12319G/11495/18; "Observations of the German Delegation," 6 August 1924, *Proceedings of the London Reparation Conference*, 2:40–53.

87. "Railway Securing Measures Considered Necessary by the French Government in the Event of the Disappearance of the Franco-Belgian Régie for the Rhineland Railways," 18 July 1924, *Proceedings of the London Reparation Conference*, 1:308–9; French version in F.O. 371/9851: C 11639/11495/18. For a general description of the German railway system and the effects of the Dawes Plan on it, see Sir William Acworth, "Railways in Pledge," London *Times*, 19 September 1924; for an overall review of railway negotiations at the

The French couched their plan in language so obscure that it lay open to a variety of interpretations, and indeed the French experts themselves divided about what they hoped to achieve. Their proposal, however, bore enough resemblance to earlier schemes promoted by Henri Bréaud, director of the Franco-Belgian railway *Régie*, so that the British War Office immediately construed it as an attempt to perpetuate the *Régie* in camouflaged form.[88]

At any rate, when General Godley, British military representative on the Second Committee, flatly rejected the idea of a separate railway administration, the French retreated to a second line of defense. Belatedly coordinating their position with the Belgians, they now asked for retention of thirty-five hundred to four thousand civilian railway personnel in the Trier district, on the lines running toward Koblenz, Gerolstein, and Mainz. These men would actually operate the trains and signals and furnish the senior staff for stations on the affected lines, but they would follow German regulations and remain subordinate to the German railway system's district manager in Trier. The French workers would not come into contact with the traveling public. The Belgians similarly proposed to employ seven hundred to one thousand men to run a certain number of trains each day on the line leading from the Belgian frontier through Aachen to Krefeld. French representatives contended that deployment of operating personnel in this way would enable the Allied armies to maintain communication and logistic lines without a hiatus if the Germans, attempting to exert pressure for premature evacuation of the Rhineland or for other purposes, interrupted rail service or resorted to harassment and sabotage as they had in 1923.[89]

But the French delegation never decided exactly what it wanted. From day to day it juggled the figures for the total number of men required. The French army, supported by Bréaud, sought an arrangement that would endure to the end of the Rhineland occupation. Other French railway specialists hinted that they would rest content with an interim agreement lasting until evacuation of the Ruhr.[90] The Belgians stood ready to abandon their claim entirely if British resistance became too strong. General Desticker, chief of staff to Marshal Foch, reported home in a discouraged tone: "The absence of method and of order creates a distressing atmosphere here."[91]

London Conference, see MacDonald no. 820 to Lord Kilmarnock, 25 August 1924, F.O. 371/9858: C 13173/11495/18.

88. On the Bréaud plan, see H. C. F. Finlayson memorandum for Miles Lampson, 14 August 1924, F.O. 371/9857: C 13023/G.

89. *Proceedings of the London Reparation Conference*, 1:303–18, 326–29; Sir Alexander Godley, *Life of an Irish Soldier* (New York, 1939), pp. 294–95; also Bardoux, *L'Expérience de 1924*, pp. 245–47 [based on reports by General Desticker, Marshal Foch's chief of staff].

90. See reports of State Secretary Johannes Vogt, German railroad expert assigned to liaison duty, G.F.M. 3398/1736/D740162, D740174, D740185–186.

91. Bardoux, *L'Expérience de 1924*, p. 246.

The British military resisted the imposition of any Allied personnel on the German railways. The existing Rhineland agreement, they asserted, afforded the occupation authorities sufficient opportunity to gain practical working knowledge of the railways so that they could take them over in the event of trouble. They claimed further that a few thousand civilian railwaymen could not prevent a strike or sabotage if the Germans determined on those measures and that, with proper planning and stockpiling of supplies, the armies could meet their immediate needs through motor transport in case the lines became temporarily paralyzed.[92]

The actual logistic problems loomed somewhat larger than British military transport specialists were prepared to concede. The War Office analysis appeared to rest on the assumption that the Allied occupation armies and the Germans would not clash openly in the Rhineland again. In western Germany the British maintained only a small detachment numbering less than ten thousand men, all located within a tight defense perimeter drawn around the city of Cologne proper. These troops performed useful intelligence functions and served a variety of symbolic purposes (keeping watch upon the French as well as the Germans). But at least since 1920, when the General Staff conceded that the British Army of the Rhine "bore no relation to the possible requirements of any situation in which it may become involved," they had not constituted an effective fighting force.[93] The British cabinet would withdraw the troops rather than cope with a serious menace to their safety; hence the War Office did not need to concern itself with emergency contingency plans for keeping communication lines open.

The French looked at matters in an entirely different light. The 100,000 French soldiers on the Rhine represented the main bulwark of national security. The French army's ability to dominate the communications network in the event that hostilities resumed would figure as an important measure of its capacity to fulfill its primary mission. In short, the Anglo-French dispute over railway control reflected a more profound divergence in view about the nature and ultimate aims of the Rhineland occupation.

The French military had no desire to advertise their crippling transport problems—though Herriot later unguardedly revealed the difficulty to Stresemann—but in fact the entire French army contained but two understrength regiments of railway engineers. This small force could barely hope to maintain the rolling stock, trackage, and bridges within France at a proper level of efficiency in case of war; to siphon off any portion of it for emergency service in the Rhineland, military planners felt, would "irredeemably compromise" mobilization at home. Given

92. Note by the British Military Experts, 21 July 1924, F.O. 371/9851: C 11888/11495/18; also *Proceedings of the London Reparation Conference*, 1:310–12.

93. General Staff memorandum, "Military Liabilities of the Empire," 27 July 1920, P.R.O., CAB 4/7: C.I.D. Paper 255–B.

the climate of financial constraint, the army despaired of convincing parliament to appropriate funds for a third railway engineer regiment; indeed, the cost-conscious deputies had already slashed the military budget to such an extent that none of the army technical services could afford to keep the requisite number of experienced noncommissioned officers on the rolls. Officials familiar with the Alsace-Lorraine railways, meanwhile, cautioned against imposing a heterogeneous reserve force of civilian workers on the rail network there; such a plan, they held, would "gravely offend" already sensitive regional feelings.[94] These arguments might seem self-serving to foreigners; nevertheless, French military men believed that without a detachment stationed directly on the Rhineland railways, their troops would find themselves at the mercy of the Germans if a confrontation recurred.

Unable to resolve their differences, the military specialists on the Second Committee appealed for a judgment to the two independent railway consultants who had advised the Dawes Committee and were now engaged in preparing an official plan for German railway reorganization. Much to Whitehall's chagrin, the consultants, Sir William Acworth and Gaston Leverve, prepared two successive reports sympathetic to the French position. They affirmed that a single Allied-dominated railway administration for the occupied territories such as the French had originally demanded might not be compatible with the economic unity of the Reich mandated by the Dawes Plan. But they found no such objection to the scaled-down French proposal. The employment of a few thousand foreign railway workers carrying out their duties under German regulations and management, the consultants held, would not in itself "seriously affect the operations of the [German Railway] Company as a whole or prevent it from earning a net revenue sufficient to meet the reparations payments provided for in the Dawes Plan." After vigorous prodding by Sir Eyre Crowe, Acworth agreed to add a postscript to his second report calling attention to the risk of "friction between the foreign and German personnel leading to unfortunate consequences." This small caveat, however, did not change the thrust of his opinion.[95]

British Foreign Office and Treasury representatives, having earlier welcomed the appeal to the consultants, now angrily refused to accept their advice. Crowe roundly denounced Acworth's "curious mental attitude," and Lampson added that "the only language in which to speak

94. "Note sur l'organisation des troupes techniques d'exploitation: Sécurité ferroviaire de l'Armée du Rhin," 2 August 1924, Herriot Papers; Herriot revelation to the German foreign minister in Stresemann tel., 13 August 1924, G.F.M. 3398/1737/D740380–384.

95. Sir William Acworth and M. Leverve to Sir Warren Fisher, 24 July 1924, F.O. 371/9851: C 11928/11495/18; "Second Joint Report as to the Retention of French and Belgian Personnel on the Rhineland Railways," F.O. 371/9852: C 12204/11495/18; also *Proceedings of the London Reparation Conference*, 1:304, 316–18, 326–29.

of Sir W. Acworth is not suitable for an official minute." Hankey had plainly instructed the British consultant not to compromise the government's position. But Acworth, a crusty septuagenarian, who after long service as a director of the London subways had won renown as an adviser on transport economics to countries all over the world, did not consider himself a government official and declined to accept dictation. Privately, Acworth agreed with Crowe that the French probably sought to "keep a hand on . . . the most important strategic railways in the Rhineland" and that their purported aim of safeguarding the troops was a "transparent absurdity." He insisted, nevertheless, that his role as a railway expert obliged him simply to evaluate the technical merits of the Franco-Belgian plan, and not to impose his political opinions or to voice his personal suspicions about French motives.[96]

But even where fortune played into their hands, the French proved incapable of taking advantage of the situation. MacDonald, feeling that Acworth had "sold the pass," told the British cabinet on 30 July that he might make some concession regarding the railwaymen in order to reach agreement on other points.[97] Almost simultaneously, the German ambassador expressed the foreboding that the French would prevail, since the issue did not really interest the Americans, and the English would hesitate to provoke a crisis over it.[98] Herriot, however, vacillated. General Nollet urged him to push for a definitive settlement, but Alfred Margaine, the premier's Radical-Socialist party comrade, counseled prudence. Beset by greater worries, Herriot decided to await the views of the German government before pressing the point.[99] Foreign Office bureaucrats, meanwhile, argued that to give in would produce "a most lamentable effect upon British prestige," and convinced MacDonald to stick to his guns.[100] Even Acworth found that his principles permitted him to inform the Germans that other members of the French delegation did not attach the "particular importance" to the railwaymen that the military did. He advised the Germans to hold out, and predicted that the French would yield.[101]

In the end, events confirmed Acworth's prognostication. On 11 August Herriot revealed to Stresemann that he would give way at the last minute in regard to the railwaymen. He cautioned the German foreign minister not to make untimely use of this knowledge. Certain generals were "still always thinking about war," he observed, and it would

96. Assistant secretary of cabinet to Acworth, 26 July 1924, F.O. 371/9852: C 12064/11495/18; Crowe to prime minister, 30 July 1924, F.O. 371/9852: C 12204/11495/18; Miles W. Lampson to Crowe, 5 August 1924, F.O. 371/9854: C 12547/11495/18.

97. P.R.O., CAB 23/48, Cabinet Conclusions: 44(24), 30 July 1924.

98. Sthamer tel., 30 July 1924, G.F.M. 3398/1736/D740152–156.

99. Bardoux, *L'Expérience de 1924*, p. 254.

100. Lampson, Crowe, and MacDonald minutes, 5 August 1924, F.O. 371/9854: C 12547/11495/18.

101. Sthamer tels., 2 and 3 August 1924, G.F.M. 3398/1736/D740194–196.

obviate difficulties if his French delegation colleagues did not know of his decision beforehand.[102] Actually, the French premier told Stresemann a half-truth: he had won authorization from his cabinet to drop the question against open and determined opposition on the part of Nollet and Clémentel.[103] In the waning days of the conference, both dissident ministers tried to revive the issue in separate approaches to the British, Clémentel promoting the old Bréaud scheme for a regional railway administration under Allied control, Nollet advocating extension of the Rhineland Commission's jurisdiction to railways in the Ruhr. MacDonald turned a deaf ear to these entreaties, however, and they failed to influence the course of affairs.[104]

Within the narrow context of negotiations at London, Herriot's concession regarding the railwaymen took on symbolic importance. The premier's flaccid defense of his country's claim exposed the bureaucratic incoherence, the contradictory policy objectives, and the incapacity to seize available opportunities that characterized French diplomacy throughout the conference. Yet the intrinsic strategic significance of the watered-down scheme on which the French delegation finally took its stand should not be overestimated. The *Régie*'s ambition to perpetuate its control over the rail network on the left bank of the Rhine had at least conformed to consistent logic in autumn 1923, when Germany's internal crisis appeared to open the way for changing the Rhineland's political status (making it autonomous or even independent of the Reich). To hold the Rhineland railways under those circumstances would have conferred a marked advantage of logistics and mobility on France in any new armed conflict or action in defense of treaty rights. Merely to station a few thousand men on three small lines as an isolated vestige of the *Régie*, by contrast, would ultimately serve little purpose. Such a plan, as Ambassador Kellogg remarked, would not provide enough men to take over the Rhineland railways in the event of trouble, but would involve just enough to create friction in the meantime.[105]

In summary, the controversy over the railwaymen calls attention to a fundamental alteration in France's political stance. By entering into an arrangement sharply limiting its chances of obtaining a judgment of default under the Dawes Plan, France had taken a major step toward accepting the logical corollary: territorial sanctions would probably not prove feasible, no matter how flagrantly the Reich violated its treaty obligations in the future. Recognition of this fact would almost inevitably lead to changes in attitudes and expectations both by the occupying

102. Stresemann tel., 13 August 1924, G.F.M. 3398/1737/D740380–384.

103. Clémentel's report to Hankey, in M. P. A. Hankey to prime minister, 11 August 1924, F.O. 371/9856: C 12940/11495/18.

104. H. C. F. Finlayson memorandum for Lampson, 14 August 1924, F.O. 371/9857: C 13023/G; MacDonald memorandum, 16 August 1924, F.O. 371/9858: C 13173/11495/18.

105. Kellogg to Hughes, 1 August 1924, Box 8, Kellogg Papers.

forces and by the Rhineland's population. Radical modification of the administrative régime in the occupied territories might not follow immediately. But a confrontation so serious that France would attempt by itself to take over and run the Rhineland railways became an increasingly remote possibility.

Military Evacuation: The French Delegation Considers Its Options

Herriot had managed to ward off any definite commitment to military evacuation of the Ruhr in the preconference negotiations. But he could scarcely expect to evade the question indefinitely. In official and unofficial discussions in London, the German ambassador and other representatives of the Reich underscored the "decisive importance" of military evacuation.[106] As previously noted, the American bankers, who earlier in the spring had placed no special emphasis on this point, subsequently endorsed Norman's demand that the French withdraw militarily from the Ruhr. And had Prime Minister MacDonald not felt strongly on the matter, important elements in his own party would have balked at a settlement that failed to provide for the retirement of French and Belgian troops.[107] Accordingly, it occasioned no great surprise when MacDonald broached the subject in the meeting of delegation heads on 24 July and then presented Herriot and Theunis with a formal letter asking them to produce an evacuation plan.[108]

Personally, Herriot had always wished to withdraw the troops as soon as possible. In his capacity as a public official, he felt obliged to resist demands for precipitate evacuation. He feared for the solidity of his parliamentary majority, and he recognized that even members of his own party were reluctant to relinquish the one tangible guarantee of German fulfillment in return for another mere "scrap of paper." Yet his inner convictions led him in the opposite direction.

Herriot saw an important moral issue at stake. French troops had originally entered the Ruhr not to carry out a military operation, but rather to protect a mission of engineers sent to manage the "productive guarantees." It seemed to Herriot that when direct economic exploitation terminated, the justification for military occupation ended as well. The premier did not accord equal moral status to the policy developed as a consequence of German resistance and formally promulgated in March

106. See particularly Ambassador Sthamer's memorandum for MacDonald, 16 July 1924, F.O. 371/9751: C 11379/70/18; and Stresemann's further instructions to Sthamer, 21 July 1924, G.F.M. 3398/1736/D740045–052.

107. Snowden, *Autobiography*, 2:673–77.

108. MacDonald to Herriot and Theunis, 24 July 1924, F.O. 371/9752: C 11930/70/18; quoted in part by Bardoux, *L'Expérience de 1924*, p. 248; see also Herriot's explanations in *J.O.C. Déb.*, 21 August 1924, p. 2958, and in *Jadis*, 2:156–57. On MacDonald's tactics, see his comments to Snowden, J. H. Thomas, Crowe, and Hankey in "Notes of an Informal Meeting Held at 10 Downing Street," 24 July 1924, F.O. 371/9855: C 12820/G.

1923, to the effect that the troops would depart only in proportion to payments made. To maintain the military occupation, he believed, would leave France open to an accusation of bad faith and increase its political isolation at a time when he assigned high priority to reestablishing cordial working relations with Great Britain and the United States. The dictates of logic, Herriot thought, required France to make a fundamental choice between two systems, one that left it with the onerous responsibility of securing payment by force, the other that in effect "placed the whole Dawes Plan under the control of the United States." Finally, Herriot found it comforting that French security, conceived in a narrowly defined immediate sense, did not require continued military occupation of the Ruhr.[109]

Herriot's method of analyzing the problem reveals a great deal about his approach to diplomacy. He focused upon a single decision: whether to evacuate or not. Once assured that withdrawal of the troops would not endanger national security, he dealt with the issue as one of ethics as much as one of practical politics. But the actual problem facing French negotiators could be viewed in a quite different way. Realistic insiders no longer cherished the hope that France could maintain troops indefinitely in the Ruhr, where they would have no clearly defined purpose beyond exerting general pressure on Germany to fulfill the Dawes Plan and serving as an advance guard primed to reimpose sanctions in the event of default. According to the Dawes Plan, the stipulated annuities would cover Germany's entire financial liability arising from the Versailles treaty. The French War Ministry, consequently, would have to meet all future costs of quartering troops in the Ruhr directly from its own budget: henceforth it could not pass on these expenses to the local population or to the government of the Reich. Financial considerations alone would thus compel withdrawal of the troops at no too distant date. Nevertheless, a fundamental issue remained—not whether, but rather when, and under what conditions, French soldiers would leave the Ruhr.

In other words, what compensation could France exact as the price of withdrawal? Herriot's advisers mapped out three possible strategies. Paul Tirard, French high commissioner in the Rhineland, spoke for a group of military and civilian officials on the spot who proposed attempting to trade a Ruhr evacuation for a British commitment to prolong occupation of the Cologne zone for an additional five years. Tirard favored keeping control as well over Düsseldorf, Duisburg, and Ruhrort—the three cities dominating rail and river routes leading from the Ruhr—which had been seized as a sanction in 1921. He and his fellow commissioner, Baron Edouard Rolin-Jaequemyns of Belgium, argued that if the Allies maintained the Rhineland occupation intact until 1930, they would

109. See Herriot's retrospective summary of his convictions in *Jadis*, 2:161–66.

win the time and political leverage necessary to develop a system of permanent security guarantees, including some type of recognized international status for the Rhineland.[110]

General Nollet also saw the security problem as paramount. He advocated linking evacuation of the Ruhr in some fashion with the unresolved question of German disarmament, though he thought that the Reich's disarmament violations would serve in addition to justify postponement of the Cologne zone evacuation. Finally, Jacques Seydoux of the Foreign Ministry and Daniel Serruys, chief civil servant at the Ministry of Commerce, both stressed the prime importance of achieving economic understanding with Germany before France's position of political advantage deteriorated further. As usual, however, these two bureaucratic rivals failed to agree on the specific nature of the concessions to be sought.[111]

At times Herriot demonstrated an evanescent interest in one or another of the proposals that issued from his entourage, but he could not sustain genuine enthusiasm for any of them. The process of bargaining was not congenial to him, nor was it readily compatible with his aspiration to foster a new spirit in Europe through the magnanimous conduct of diplomacy. Almost inevitably, therefore, France emerged with empty hands. Yet it is by no means a foregone conclusion that Herriot would have achieved much beyond minor successes of outward form had he acted more audaciously. The bolder approaches suggested by Tirard and Nollet, at least, took little account of the financial weapons that France's opponents could bring to bear. Even a close review of the dramatic diplomatic exchanges that marked the second half of the conference provides no definitive answer to the question whether, through Herriot's failure to take a strong line, anything significant was lost.

Like most Radical-Socialists of his generation, Herriot had little tolerance for military men. Marshal Foch, with his stiff manner, vociferous expression of fixed ideas, and ultraclerical leanings, appealed to him even less than most. Some weeks before the conference began, the premier had savored an officer's report that Foch, a "representative of militarism," was as unpopular in England as Wellington had been in France after Waterloo.[112] Nevertheless, apprised of Nollet's reluctance to evacuate the Ruhr, Herriot sought to cover his flank by seeking an opinion from Foch, whose position as president of the Allied Military Committee at Versailles placed him outside the chain of command responsible to the minister of war.[113]

110. Tirard tel. no. 256, 1 July 1924, Herriot Papers.

111. See the excellent analysis by the German ambassador in Paris, particularly of Nollet's and Seydoux's views, in Hoesch tel., 11 August 1924, G.F.M. 3398/1736/D740329–331.

112. Herriot notation, 3 July 1924, Herriot Papers.

113. Herriot notations, 24 and 25 July 1924, ibid.

On 25 July Herriot called in General Desticker, the marshal's chief of staff, and explained his dilemma. Not only did he have grave moral qualms about remaining in the Ruhr, Herriot confessed, but material constraints would in any case oblige him to evacuate within "a few months." Moreover, as soon as MacDonald demanded military evacuation, Theunis had announced Belgium's willingness to withdraw. Though the British had made no explicit threats, Herriot believed that his refusal to discuss the matter would lead to a rupture that France for financial reasons could not afford. How could he alone insist on an evacuation by stages corresponding to payments, the premier wondered also, when France might find itself "compelled to evacuate totally" for logistic reasons once Great Britain withdrew from the Cologne zone of the Rhineland—as it might very well do on 10 January 1925? Desticker, though he kept his composure, was appalled. He had already tried to alert a number of sympathetic members of the delegation to the drawbacks of hasty evacuation. He discreetly invited the premier's attention to less drastic alternatives, and gave him the obvious advice: to survey all eventualities and then to strike the best possible bargain.[114]

Marshal Foch himself, reached after some delay at his country retreat in Brittany, took action immediately to prevent misrepresentation of his position. First, he sent Herriot a copy of a note originally prepared in July 1923, in which he had sketched an audacious plan for permanent occupation of an autonomous Rhineland and starkly warned that France and Belgium would find no security whatsoever once their troops had abandoned the Rhine bridges. Then, hastening back to Paris, he drew up instructions which, on 30 July, he phoned to Desticker and submitted also by way of precaution to President of the Republic Doumergue.

Germany had not carried out the terms of the Versailles treaty, Foch asserted categorically. Hence evacuation of the Cologne zone in January 1925 was simply out of the question. The British government should "recognize and declare it." As for the Ruhr, he maintained an equally firm stand. He did not endorse Nollet's proposal to link the Ruhr to the

114. Desticker's *compte rendu* for Foch, 25 July 1924, quoted by Bardoux, *L'Expérience de 1924*, pp. 247–52. Embarrassed that the military did not favor rapid evacuation, Herriot obliged Desticker to give misleading testimony in the Chamber debates on the London agreements (*J.O.C. Déb.*, 23 August 1924, pp. 3074–75). As the years went by, his recollection of Desticker's real views dimmed further (see, e.g., *J.O.C. Déb.*, 17 July 1929, p. 2598). Writing in 1952 (*Jadis*, 2:157), Herriot alleged that Desticker had told him: "It is unnecessary to bother the Marshal [Foch]. I know his point of view and will explain it to you. If you could see to it that the Ruhr were evacuated by tomorrow night, you would have performed a great service for France. . . . We have troops exposed there in the midst of the most complicated network of industries, mines, factories, and railroads. If the situation became so serious as to make us fear war, our first act would be to recall them." As Herriot recollected his response, he appreciated "the difference which separates a real military man from the strategists of newspaper offices, cafés, or the parliamentary lobbies." It is clear that Desticker never uttered the remarks attributed to him by Herriot, and that neither he nor Foch saw any military necessity to withdraw the troops from the Ruhr.

question of German disarmament violations—that was a matter to be handled separately. On the other hand, he saw no incompatibility between continuation of a purely military occupation of the Ruhr and implementation of the Dawes Plan. France, he insisted, should evacuate the Ruhr in stages corresponding to the effective materialization of payments. Since the extent to which Germany would actually fulfill the plan remained in doubt, he thought it only prudent for France to withhold commitment to any precise timetable for withdrawal. Affecting indifference to the political and financial constraints of which his compatriots in London had become painfully aware, he counseled Herriot to reserve the right to decide later on exactly how and when French troops would leave the Ruhr.[115]

But behind this firm front Foch concealed his true discouragement. Germany had paid almost no attention to the note regarding illegal rearmament sent to it after Chequers. The Interallied Military Control Commission encountered as much obstruction as ever as it sought to ferret out details of the mounting violations. Hardly a week went by when Foch's office at the Invalides did not receive a confidential report describing General von Seeckt or some other German army leader boasting of outwitting the control commission or gloating over plans for future revenge. Yet the Allied Military Committee found itself virtually powerless to take effective action. Preoccupied by these developments in his own sphere of responsibility, Foch considered the whole framework of the London negotiations far too narrow. He doubted whether the French delegation could withstand the assault of Anglo-American and "Jewish" finance if it agreed to limit the scope of discussion to implementation of the Dawes Plan alone and failed to address the wider question of maintaining the European order established in 1919. Disdaining fine distinctions, he gave way privately to utter despair about France's entire postwar civilian leadership. "Clemenceau, Millerand, Poincaré, Herriot have lost the peace in confrontation with England," he lamented; "they have abdicated or neglected to take carefully prepared and sustained action in opposition to hers. . . . When will we ever have a government confident that it has behind it a victorious people asking only to work and wishing to see its government work (and not just talk) for the good of the country?" He could only hope that France would avoid complete defeat and humiliation at the conference.[116]

Foch's martial imperatives, as he feared, fell on unreceptive ears. Indeed, before his message arrived in London, events had rendered it obsolete. Yielding to MacDonald's importunity, Herriot agreed in principle during the meeting of delegation heads on 28 July to evacuate

115. Foch instructions for Desticker, 30 July 1924, Herriot Papers, quoted also in Bardoux, *L'Expérience de 1924*, pp. 252–53.

116. Foch Cahiers, 21, 28, and 29 July 1924, Dossier G, p. 176.

the Ruhr within two years.[117] Herriot's floundering conveyed the impression to the British prime minister that his French counterpart did not really know what he wanted in return. At first Herriot (and also Theunis) hinted that they wished to link military evacuation with an intra-European debt settlement. When MacDonald stonily refused to confound these two questions, Herriot then voiced interest in considering the Ruhr evacuation in connection with the impending decision about Allied withdrawal from the Cologne zone. His tentative allusions to the matter led MacDonald to conclude that if the British offered to extend the Cologne occupation for an additional twelve months after January 1925, the French would agree to withdrawal of all Allied troops from the Ruhr and Cologne at the same time. Finally, Herriot expressed eagerness to learn of German suggestions for an evacuation timetable. Meanwhile he would prepare his own plan, and then, he intimated confidentially, he might "accept the arbitration of the British government as between the two."[118]

Torn by passionate internal disputes, the French delegation debated over the next two weeks what in fact it wanted. It never clearly posed the alternatives, and never satisfactorily resolved them. The successive proposals that issued from its midst with varying degrees of official standing neither possessed internal coherence nor followed a logical battle plan. To the world outside, the delegation betrayed enough of this confusion so that it finally lost whatever initiative it might otherwise have had.

In accordance with the pledge made to the British, Jacques Seydoux and Camille Gutt (secretary-general of the Belgian delegation to the Reparation Commission) undertook the task of developing a specific evacuation program. The Seydoux-Gutt plan readied on 30 July provided for departure of the troops in stages over a two-year period. French and Belgian forces would leave the Hagen area as soon as the bankers floated the Dawes loan. They would then withdraw successively from the Dortmund, Bochum, and Essen regions in return for the sale on private financial markets of 1.5 milliard gold marks of the railroad bonds created under the Dawes Plan. The troops would complete their withdrawal by August 1926, even if commercialization of the bonds did not prove feasible, but only on condition that Germany carried out its disarmament obligations.[119]

117. Kellogg to Hughes, 28 July 1924, U.S. 462.00R 296/513.

118. MacDonald's report to the British Empire Delegation, 88th Conference, 28 July 1924, CAB 29/105; and to the cabinet, CAB 23/48, Cabinet Conclusions: 44(24), 30 July 1924.

119. "Texte proposé pour l'évacuation," 30 July 1924, and Seydoux note, "Evacuation militaire de la Ruhr," 30 July 1924, Herriot Papers; further details in Bardoux, *L'Expérience de 1924*, pp. 254–56, and in Hoesch tels., 30 July and 1 August 1924, G.F.M. 3398/1736/D740158–159, D740170.

The essentials of the Seydoux-Gutt plan immediately leaked to the press, probably through a calculated indiscretion by military men in the French delegation who sought to rally support for it.[120] As a diplomatic stratagem, this leak failed to achieve its purpose. British diplomats cautioned the Germans not to risk forfeiting the world's sympathy by rejecting the Franco-Belgian proposal out of hand, and Ambassador Kellogg also thought that Berlin would make a bad impression by showing itself "too stiff."[121] Neither British nor American officials, however, could muster the slightest enthusiasm for the specific details of the plan. And the Germans themselves declined to beat about the bush. Carl Bergmann, their reparations expert on the spot, denounced the scheme as "blackmail of the worst sort."[122] A two-year delay before final evacuation was clearly far too long to suit German tastes, but the Wilhelmstrasse's ire focused particularly on the idea of commercializing the railroad bonds.

For foreign consumption, Stresemann set forth the argument that it would prove self-defeating to make early evacuation dependent on such commercialization; the American public, he held, would surely not purchase the railroad bonds so long as military occupation of the Ruhr heightened the risk of disorders there.[123] In the privacy of the Reich Chancellery, German politicians advanced a rather different consideration: they opposed transformation of any part of the reparations debt into an ordinary commercial obligation, for once so converted, that part of the debt would remain a permanent burden on the nation even were the Dawes Plan later revised.[124]

Before the extent of resistance to the 30 July proposal had become clear, however, Herriot disassociated himself from the project. He abruptly announced to the Belgian ministers that he did not wish to bind himself prematurely to any particular formula. Then on 1 August, he intimated to MacDonald and Kellogg that he might eventually consent to reduce the evacuation period to about a year provided that Germany carried out the Dawes Plan punctiliously.[125] Herriot had good reason to propitiate the British prime minister at this critical juncture: the dispute with the bankers had broken wide open, and he feared to jeopardize the French compromise proposal on default procedures, which MacDonald appeared on the brink of endorsing, by showing inflexibility on the issue of military evacuation. But actually, Herriot's sudden reversal stemmed

120. *Le Temps*, 31 July 1924.

121. Hoesch tel., 1 August 1924, G.F.M. 3398/1736/D740170; Kellogg to Hughes, 1 August 1924, Box 8, Kellogg Papers.

122. Bergmann tel., 31 July 1924, G.F.M. 3398/1736/D740163.

123. Chargé d'affaires René de St.-Quentin tel. nos. 5–12 to Herriot, 4 August 1924, Herriot Papers.

124. See Reich Chancellery basic analysis of the issue, "Zum Sachverständigengutachten," 1 June 1924, BA, R 43 I/266/258–262.

125. Kellogg to Hughes, 1 August 1924, Box 8, Kellogg Papers.

less from this calculation than from a last minute change of heart by Jacques Seydoux.[126]

Upon reflection, Seydoux had concluded that an attempt to make evacuation of the Ruhr dependent on completion of German disarmament would backfire. France had repeatedly proclaimed that it had occupied that region solely to enforce the reparations settlement and not for reasons of security. Seydoux, who had drafted many of Poincaré's pronouncements on the matter, knew this as well as anyone. If France sought at this late date to connect the Ruhr directly to security, a misunderstanding was inevitable. Great Britain could not possibly countenance such a claim. On the other hand, the Allies possessed a legal right to remain in the Cologne zone, the first of three slated for evacuation at five-year intervals, until Germany fulfilled all its treaty obligations. Sir Otto Niemeyer had suggested that French agreement to retire from the Ruhr on terms Whitehall deemed satisfactory might persuade Great Britain to keep its troops in Cologne after January 1925, pending settlement of the German disarmament imbroglio. At least as a means of appeasing French public opinion, Seydoux saw considerable advantage in an agreement linking withdrawal of troops from the Ruhr and from Cologne. France might do well to offer evacuation of the Ruhr in a year, he thought, in return for a British promise to stay in Cologne for two years—long enough, possibly, to resolve the outstanding disarmament controversy and also to perfect a scheme for permanent military supervision of the Rhineland under League of Nations auspices.

In the final analysis, nevertheless, Seydoux believed that France had far more to gain from an economic understanding with Germany than from a relatively brief extension of any purely military occupation. Betraying unmistakable alarm, he warned Herriot that unless the Lorraine iron mills could reestablish their prewar business arrangements with firms in the Ruhr and secure long-term contracts for coke, many French steel manufacturers would find themselves "delivered into the hands . . . of German industry" and "condemned to disappear."

Apparently seeking to persuade his chief that the exchange of "participations" in industrial enterprises would constitute a progressive innovation consonant with Cartel ideology, Seydoux offered a rather strange analysis of the reasons why Franco-German industrial negotiations had broken down the previous spring. The hard-headed Seydoux rarely fell victim to wishful thinking, yet on this occasion he somehow failed to recall that neither the majority of German industrialists nor their government had shown serious interest in the proposals put forward by the Comité des Forges. Instead he blamed Poincaré for having refused to pursue discussions officially at the most suitable moment. He urged

126. Herriot notation, 30 July 1924, also Note Seydoux, "Evacuation militaire de la Ruhr," 30 July 1924, Herriot Papers.

Herriot to reopen the question as soon as the German delegation arrived in London. This time France might sweeten the pot by giving the Germans participations in Normandy minette ore properties and in Saar coal deposits unsuitable for coking as compensation for shares in the coveted Ruhr mines that produced coking coal. As part of the bargain, France could also volunteer to evacuate the Ruhr forthwith. "The guarantee of our coke supply," Seydoux concluded, "is of infinitely greater interest to us than the military occupation of the Ruhr can be."[127]

Herriot marked this down as an "important" insight but did nothing to follow it up. As discussions within the French delegation became ever more vehement in the first days of August, he began to feel overwhelmed. From a perspective at variance with Seydoux's, General Nollet badgered the premier to employ the Ruhr and Cologne zone occupations unabashedly as bargaining counters in an effort to protect French security.

French troops had originally entered the Ruhr because of a reparations default, Nollet conceded. Yet their presence there provided a security safeguard that "partly filled the gap" left by the Allies' failure to ratify the 1919 treaty of guarantee. The occupation of the Cologne zone now served an analogous purpose. Though this "situation of fact" resulted from happenstance, Nollet argued, France could not ignore the advantage thereby conferred upon it. The war minister recommended a tough line: France should refuse even to discuss withdrawal from the Ruhr unless Britain concomitantly agreed to stay on in the Cologne zone pending completion of German disarmament. If Britain claimed that it was too early to judge whether the Reich had fulfilled the conditions precedent to evacuation of Cologne, France should serve notice that all three powers involved in the Rhineland occupation had to approve a decision to pull out of that zone and that it stood ready to replace British troops if the latter retired unilaterally. At the same time, France should summon Whitehall to open the general discussion on security which MacDonald had promised at the Paris meeting in July. Finally, it should demand British cooperation in development of an effective plan for permanent League of Nations supervision of Rhineland demilitarization.[128]

Herriot shrank instinctively from this sort of aggressive action. But at least as the military men interpreted his reaction, he had no clear alternative in mind. When cornered, he expatiated evasively on the value of the League of Nations and the importance of the arbitration principle.[129] Finally Seydoux, seeking to create common ground on which the entire

127. Note Seydoux, "Evacuation militaire de la Ruhr," 30 July 1924, Herriot Papers.

128. Nollet memoranda, "Sécurité" and "Evacuation de la zone de Cologne," 3 August 1924, Herriot Papers.

129. Desticker report to Foch, 3 August 1924, cited by Bardoux, *L'Expérience de 1924*, pp. 255–56.

delegation could firmly stand, pieced together various elements of the original 30 July Franco-Belgian plan, Nollet's ideas, and his own economic proposals into a not entirely congruent whole. Stripped of its purposeful equivocations, this compromise plan called for agreement with Britain to maintain the Cologne occupation indefinitely pending examination of disarmament and security matters, for a maximum two-year delay in evacuating the Ruhr, and for an intimation to Germany that it could secure early withdrawal of the troops in either of two ways: by commercializing some of the railroad bonds or by guaranteeing France's coke supply and thereby furnishing proof of its desire for "appeasement and conciliation."[130] But Herriot still hesitated. When the German delegation arrived in London on 5 August, the French had decided nothing.

The Cologne Zone and French Security

At least part of Herriot's perplexity stemmed from his preoccupation with British intentions in regard to the Cologne zone and from his anxiety lest MacDonald peremptorily decide to end British participation in the Rhineland occupation in January 1925. The French premier had stated to General Desticker in their awkward meeting on 25 July that France would have no choice but to withdraw from the Ruhr if the British pulled out of Cologne.[131] It is difficult to comprehend why Herriot persisted in this belief in the face of his military advisers' strongly expressed convictions to the contrary. For obvious geographical reasons, France and Belgium would have difficulty continuing the Ruhr occupation once sovereignty over the entire Cologne zone reverted to Germany. But a decision to terminate any portion of the Rhineland occupation required unanimous approval by the powers concerned. In this respect France held an impregnable legal position. As a practical matter too, French and Belgian troops had occupied well over four-fifths of the area in the Cologne zone ever since the peace treaty went into effect.[132] If the British withdrew unilaterally from the city of Cologne and its environs, therefore, the French and Belgians could march right in to replace them.

MacDonald understood this perfectly. He fervently wished to end the Cologne zone occupation as soon as possible. It seemed to him that the continued presence of foreign troops on German soil simply delayed the restoration of amicable relations in Europe. But he had no intention of pulling out the token British force until he had secured French and Belgian agreement to evacuate the entire zone. Foreign Office specialists held that for Britain to withdraw prematurely would increase the prospect of friction between France and Germany, would leave France free

130. Note Seydoux, "L'Evacuation de la Ruhr," 4 August 1924, Herriot Papers.
131. Bardoux, *L'Expérience de 1924*, p. 250.
132. See map in François-André Paoli, *L'Armée française de 1919 à 1939*, vol. 2, *La Phase de fermeté* (Paris, 1972), p. 380a.

"to pursue unchecked her separatist or other designs in the Rhineland," and might affect British trade interests adversely. MacDonald completely endorsed this view.[133] The Germans, moreover, looked on a British presence as a form of protection against the French. Not only did the German government want the British to stay in Cologne until the French withdrew, it also inspired a discreet press campaign calling for British troops to remain in the rest of the Rhineland after evacuation of the first zone.[134]

Thus Herriot's tactical position was stronger than he realized. According to the Versailles treaty, the Allies were supposed to withdraw from the Cologne zone "at the expiration of five years" provided Germany faithfully carried out the conditions stipulated in that document.[135] Up to 1924, however, Germany had failed to fulfill the treaty in at least three important respects—reparations, disarmament, and delivery of war criminals. The Reich might assert, after accepting the Dawes Plan, that it had belatedly made good on its financial obligations. As yet, it had made no effort to satisfy the demands of the Interallied Military Control Commission in regard to reorganization of the paramilitary police, surrender of unauthorized equipment, delivery of documents permitting an inventory of Reichswehr matériel, revision of military legislation, and transformation of factories for peacetime production. But if it allowed a terminal "general inspection" and reached a compromise with the now-disheartened control commission over these "five points"—which had been in dispute since 1922—it might then lay claim to have complied with the disarmament clauses of the treaty. Even so, in respect to war criminals, Germany had served notice that it would never fulfill the treaty. From a purely legal standpoint, therefore, the Allies were and would be under no obligation to evacuate the Cologne zone.[136]

Of course, the real issue concerned not the legal right, but rather the political advisability of prolonging the Rhineland occupation. At the Paris Peace Conference, Clemenceau had most reluctantly given up his demand for permanent occupation of the Rhineland. Defying severe domestic criticism, he had made this renunciation as a calculated gamble

133. Central Department memorandum, "Execution of the First Stage of the Progressive Evacuation of the Rhineland Contemplated in Article 429 of the Treaty of Versailles," 2 August 1924, pronounced "excellent" by MacDonald, 9 August 1924, F.O. 371/9832: C 12302/4736/18.

134. For confirmation of German views, see Chancellor Marx's comments to MacDonald on 12 August 1924, BA, R 43 I/268/80–89; also Vice Chancellor Jarres's remarks to German party leaders, 15 August 1924, R 43 I/265/320–330; for guidelines to the press, see Karl Spiecker to Presseabteilung, 10 August 1924, G.F.M. 3398/1736/D740308–309.

135. For development of the treaty text through successive drafts, see France, Ministère des Affaires Etrangères, *Documents diplomatiques: Documents relatifs aux négociations concernant les garanties de sécurité contre une agression de l'Allemagne* (Paris, 1924), pp. 38–42; note also exegesis by British legal adviser Sir Cecil Hurst in F.O. 371/9833: C 17469/4736/18.

136. See Stresemann's frank and illuminating discussion of this issue in a closed session of the Reichsrat Foreign Affairs Committee, 3 January 1925, BA, R 43 I/274/124–141.

on Allied solidarity and only in return for the promised treaty of guarantee. His strategy miscarried when the United States and Great Britain subsequently failed to ratify the treaty.[137] The supplementary agreement reached after arduous debate in the Council of Four, providing for a fifteen-year occupation of the Rhineland with evacuation of its three zones at five-year intervals, represented a makeshift political compromise. From a military point of view, it satisfied nobody. Marshal Foch stood by no means alone in his belief that the temporary occupation constituted a military guarantee of French security "equal to zero."[138] British military opinion concurred entirely with his. Lloyd George himself remarked that "there was something to be said for Marshal Foch's view that the Rhine should become the frontier of France, although personally he could not agree to it, but there was nothing to be said for the fifteen years' occupation."[139] A military presence of this brevity would only generate friction with the local population and create a heavy financial burden. It would terminate just at the moment when it might begin to serve a legitimate security need against a recrudescence of German might. Even André Tardieu, defending the peace treaty in the French Chamber, had not tried to justify the truncated occupation as an end in itself, but rather had stressed the interrelations among the various safeguards of French security.[140]

From 1920 to 1924 French policymakers faced a continuous dilemma: whether to foster circumstances that might provide a second opportunity to make the Rhineland occupation permanent, or whether to cling to the option chosen at Versailles and to rely on the alliance system as the ultimate bulwark against German attack, notwithstanding the absence of a formal Anglo-American guarantee. In point of fact, none of the successive governments of France had ever entertained much doubt that the latter alternative would prove safer. Demographic inferiority, relative technological backwardness, and the disequilibrium of public finance that epitomized the difficulty of restoring prewar stability—all these factors bespoke prudence. At no time, consequently, did the French government seriously contemplate embarking on a Rhineland

137. For details see Jere Clemens King, *Foch versus Clemenceau: France and German Dismemberment, 1918–1919* (Cambridge, Mass., 1960); Louis A. R. Yates, *The United States and French Security, 1917–1921* (New York, 1957); John Paul Selsam, *The Attempts to Form an Anglo-French Alliance, 1919–1924* (Philadelphia, 1936); and Arno J. Mayer, *Politics and Diplomacy of Peacemaking: Containment and Counterrevolution at Versailles, 1918–1919* (New York, 1967).

138. "Observations présentées par le Maréchal Foch," 6 May 1919, in Ministère des Affaires Etrangères, *Documents relatifs aux négociations concernant les garanties de sécurité*, pp. 52–55.

139. Notes of a meeting between Lloyd George, Wilson, and Clemenceau, 2 June 1919, in Cmd. 2169, *Papers respecting Negotiations for an Anglo-French Pact* (London, 1924), pp. 106–7.

140. *J.O.C. Déb.*, 2 September 1919, cited in Ministère des Affaires Etrangères, *Documents relatifs aux négociations concernant les garanties de sécurité*, pp. 61–89.

adventure that might lead to the end of the Entente or to a reversal of alliances. Even when a possible occasion arose during the fall of 1923 to detach the Rhineland from the Reich through bold support for the separatist movement, Poincaré remained circumspect. The broader diplomatic aims of Paris circumscribed the bounds within which local French officials were permitted to promote dissociative tendencies on the left bank of the Rhine. The Quai d'Orsay resolved not to let Whitehall catch it red-handedly transgressing the limitations imposed by the treaty on the occupation authorities' prerogatives in regard to German internal affairs.

Prolonging the Rhineland occupation on grounds for which sanction could be found in the Versailles treaty itself, however, was quite a different matter. The text of that document was ambiguous about the date from which the quinquennial period for occupation of the first Rhineland zone would be measured. The British, on the basis of peace conference drafting minutes, contended that the framers of the clause in question actually intended the period to begin on 10 January 1920, the date that the treaty entered into force. Only when five years had elapsed, the British argued, were the Allies entitled to examine whether Germany had "faithfully carried out" its obligations and qualified for evacuation. The French, on the contrary, had traditionally read the disputed clause to mean that the five-year period would not even begin until the Reich began to comply with the treaty. The Quai d'Orsay had always insisted that, in consequence of German violations, the stipulated delay before evacuation had not yet begun to run.[141]

Did this oft-repeated argument betray the French government's intention to find a legal pretext for remaining in the Rhineland indefinitely? Poincaré's announcement in March 1923 that French troops would withdraw from the Ruhr only in proportion to German payments had carried the clear implication that troops would remain in the Rhineland as well until full payment had been made. The latter intimation bore an obvious resemblance to an idea that Poincaré, then president of the republic, had promoted at the time of the peace conference, namely, holding the Rhineland as a reparations guarantee for a minimum thirty-year period.[142] Still, Poincaré invariably exhibited more flexibility in private discussion than in official pronouncements. As early as 1922, in fact, he had assured a representative of the French business community that he would not stand in the way of a Rhineland evacuation, even ahead of schedule, provided Germany abandoned its pattern of resistance to the

141. See Sir Cecil J. B. Hurst's retrospective legal review of the question, "French Desiderata regarding Cologne Zone," 24 November 1924, F.O. 371/9833: C 17469/4736/18; also Hurst's previous legal opinion on the delays, 10 July 1922, F.O. 371/9832: C 12302/4736/18.

142. Poincaré to Clemenceau, 28 April 1919, cited in Ministère des Affaires Etrangères, *Documents relatifs aux négociations concernant les garanties de sécurité*, pp. 45–47, and in Cmd. 2169, *Papers respecting Negotiations for an Anglo-French Pact*, pp. 97–104.

treaty and agreed to a reasonable modus vivendi.[143]

Nevertheless, these preliminary conditions clearly did not obtain by the summer of 1924. In the Senate debate that preceded the London Conference, Poincaré, defending traditional Rhineland policy, had sought a clarification of Herriot's intentions. The new premier gave him full satisfaction. "As for the left bank of the Rhine," Herriot said, "I take advantage of the first available opportunity to confirm the declarations of previous governments regarding the evacuation delays."[144] But as a result of events at the London Conference, Herriot changed his mind. In debate within his own delegation in early August, he took the view that the stipulated occupation period had indeed begun to run. From this legal determination it followed that the Allied governments were obligated to inform the Reich exactly what conditions it still had to fulfill before they would remove their troops from the Cologne zone.[145]

Once the French government accepted the principle of a Rhineland evacuation, only the most restricted policy alternatives would remain. Military men in the delegation found the tenor of discussion distasteful in the extreme. "The same arguments, endlessly repeated, are summarized and abandoned one after another," Desticker reported to Foch, "and it is impossible to establish anything at all except the complete absence of any fixed purpose."[146]

Finally, on 6 August, Herriot endorsed a scheme ostensibly designed to take into account Nollet's preoccupation with German rearmament, but only insofar as the restrictive legal conceptions embraced by the premier allowed. This proposal stipulated that France would evacuate the Ruhr after payment of the second Dawes annuity. As for the Cologne zone, the Allies would frankly recognize that Germany did not intend ever to discharge certain of its treaty obligations, such as those relating to war criminals. They would not renounce these demands formally until Germany agreed to cooperate with residual League of Nations supervision over Rhineland demilitarization. But as a practical matter they would evacuate the Cologne zone once the military control commission had carried out its general inspection and reported that the Reich had complied with its demands regarding the "five points." Moreover, if Germany satisfied the control commission before payment of the second annuity, France would agree to withdraw from the Ruhr at

143. See German industrialist Paul Reusch's August 1922 report of conversations between Poincaré and Senator Gaston Japy, who served as an intermediary between the Comité des Forges and the German steelmakers' association, in "Industrielle Verständigung mit Frankreich 1922–31," BA, R 13 I/255, Verein Deutscher Eisen- und Stahlindustrieller.

144. Poincaré in *J.O.S. Déb.*, 10 July 1924, p. 1036; Herriot's reply in ibid., 11 July 1924, p. 1059.

145. Desticker's reports to Foch, 1 and 3 August 1924, quoted in Bardoux, *L'Expérience de 1924*, p. 255.

146. Desticker to Foch, 6 August 1924, quoted in Bardoux, *L'Expérience de 1924*, p. 256.

the same time as the English left Cologne, on the theory that completion of disarmament created a presumption that the Reich would also fulfill its reparations obligations.[147]

French military men remained acutely distressed. Far from satisfying their demands for a linkage between the Ruhr and disarmament, this product of so many days of laborious calculation and drafting seemed, as General Desticker put it, simply to reveal "an ever-growing desire to pull out of the Ruhr under an honorable pretext."[148] Herriot, in any case, showed himself prepared to jettison the feeble safeguards embodied in the plan virtually as soon as the ink on it had dried. On 8 August the French premier asked MacDonald to join him and Theunis in an immediate declaration that the Allies would postpone evacuation of the Cologne zone if they found that the Reich had failed to meet the requisite preliminary conditions. Such a statement, he argued, would put Germany on notice to treat the military control commission's injunctions with appropriate seriousness and would also assist him in the delicate bilateral discussions concerning the Ruhr soon to begin with the Germans.

MacDonald, however, flatly refused and nonchalantly waved aside the elaborately drawn scheme for indirectly linking the issues of the Ruhr and Cologne that Herriot sought to press upon him. Herriot desisted forthwith. At length the two heads of government commissioned their respective legal advisers, Sir Cecil Hurst and Henri Fromageot, to draw up an innocuous announcement that the Allies would meet shortly before 10 January 1925 to ascertain whether Germany had faithfully carried out its obligations. MacDonald declined to promise anything more. The British had effectively severed the question of the Ruhr from that of disarmament and the Cologne zone. And withdrawal from the latter area, approved in principle, had become merely a matter of time. Hurst jubilantly celebrated "the final ending and abandonment of the Millerand-Poincaré thesis that the [Rhineland] evacuation periods have not yet begun to run."[149]

Herriot's concession on the Cologne zone marked the culmination of a remarkable and rather rapid shift in priorities among French leaders, military as well as civilian. Earlier, French strategic planners had insisted that the absence of an effective Allied military guarantee necessarily rendered their nation's security dependent on territorial safeguards. As the prospect of an extended Rhineland occupation vanished, however,

147. Formulation of 6 August 1924, as reported by Desticker to Foch, in Bardoux, *L'Expérience de 1924*, pp. 256–57; 8 August 1924 elaboration by French legal expert Henri Fromageot, "Mémoire sur l'article 429 du traité de Versailles (zone de Cologne)," in Herriot Papers.

148. Desticker to Foch, 6 August 1924, in Bardoux, *L'Expérience de 1924*, p. 257.

149. Hurst minute, 8 August, MacDonald minute, 14 August, MacDonald to Eric Phipps, 22 August 1924, F.O. 371/9833: C 12723/4736/18; Herriot notations, 7 and 8 August 1924, Herriot Papers.

they began to place increased emphasis, even in internal dialogue, on securing the completion of German disarmament. This new emphasis implied a measure of unacknowledged desperation, for the German disarmament problem, from the French point of view, was actually close to insoluble.[150]

The German government had grudgingly agreed, despite the Reichswehr's misgivings, to a terminal inspection by the military control commission before that body turned over its responsibilities to the League of Nations. But professional military men did not expect the inspection to yield lasting results.[151] Herriot apparently hoped to achieve a 50 percent reduction in the number of German troops under arms and to curtail the development of the so-called security police, who, though given regular army training and housed in barracks, allegedly provided a defense force against civil disorder.[152] During the preceding three years, General von Seeckt had succeeded in training half a million men through various subterfuges—denominating them civil guards, temporary volunteers, border guards, and so forth—and this effort symbolized German resolve to regain military power eventually.[153] But as Stresemann later remarked: "Whether we have a hundred thousand [effectives] more or less has no importance for our military position and strength."[154] Germany's military potential hinged on an ability to redevelop the heavy artillery, aircraft, mechanized equipment, and above all, the industrial capabilities that sustain modern warfare. Contemporary mobilization specialists estimated that the Reich could advance—provided it maintained the necessary economic base—from a state of near-total disarmament to one of complete readiness for offensive war within twelve months after the end of Allied military surveillance.[155]

150. For general treatment of the disarmament question, see Brigadier General J. H. Morgan, "The Disarmament of Germany and After," *Quarterly Review* 122 (October 1924): 415–57; the same author's *Assize of Arms: The Disarmament of Germany and Her Rearmament, 1919–1939* (New York, 1946); General [Charles] Nollet, *Une Expérience de désarmement: Cinq ans de contrôle militaire en Allemagne* (Paris, 1932); Hans Wilhelm Gatzke, *Stresemann and the Rearmament of Germany* (Baltimore, 1954); Michael Salewski, *Entwaffnung und Militärkontrolle in Deutschland, 1919–1927* (Bonn, 1966); John W. Wheeler-Bennett, *Nemesis of Power* (London, 1953); Friedrich von Rabenau, *Seeckt: Aus seinem Leben, 1918–1936* (Leipzig, 1940); Hans Meier-Welcker, *Seeckt* (Frankfurt am Main, 1967); and Francis Ludwig Carsten, *The Reichswehr and Politics, 1918 to 1933* (Oxford, 1966).

151. See Nollet's explicit statement in *Une Expérience de désarmement*, pp. 155–57.

152. Herriot notation, 8 August 1924, Herriot Papers.

153. See the information publicly revealed by the zealous J. H. Morgan, formerly professor of public law at the University of London and senior British officer on the control commission in charge of monitoring German effectives until his summary resignation at the end of 1923, in "The Disarmament of Germany and After," p. 446.

154. Stresemann testimony to the Reichsrat Foreign Affairs Committee, 3 January 1925, BA, R 43 I/274/135.

155. See the analysis made by the armaments subcommission of the Interallied Military Control Commission, endorsed also by the British General Staff, in Memorandum by the Secretary of State for War, "The Present and Future Military Situation in Germany," 29 January 1925, CAB 4/12: C.I.D. Paper 562–B.

No military control commission with a mandate due to expire shortly could do much, aside from temporary harassment, to inhibit the development of industrial potential to wage war. The war crimes trials that followed the Second World War featured a great deal of seemingly dramatic evidence showing how German industry had prepared from the start to "shake off the chains of Versailles."[156] Gustav Krupp von Bohlen und Halbach won notoriety with his boast: "Even the Allied spying commissions were duped. Padlocks, milk cans, cash registers, track repair machines, trash carts and similar small junk appeared really unsuspicious and even locomotives and automobiles made an entirely 'civilian' impression."[157] Actually the military control commission possessed a rather good intelligence network. It knew, for example, of the armaments research and design facility that the Krupp firm, with a subsidy arranged by Chancellor Wirth, had installed at its Essen works in 1922 and later moved to Spandau to avoid inquisitive visits by French occupation forces in the Ruhr.[158] However, the steel, heavy engineering, chemical, and dyestuffs industries that provided the foundation for military power also constituted the essential building blocks of German peacetime prosperity. Stresemann would later cogently argue that the Allies could not question Krupp's turning lathes, heavy presses, and Martin blast furnaces if they expected Germany to create the export surplus necessary to meet the Dawes schedule of payments.[159]

In the summer of 1924 the planning staff attached to the Conseil Supérieur de la Défense Nationale (National Defense Council) gave earnest consideration to the future of military control. Some months earlier, a League of Nations committee at Geneva had established general principles for military surveillance of ex-enemy states. Before proceeding to London, Herriot had instructed Joseph Paul-Boncour, the Socialist deputy and military expert who had recently won designation as president of the C.S.D.N. Study Committee, to initiate an examination of the League draft. The premier asked Paul-Boncour to produce a concrete proposal for permanently vesting the power to control German armaments in the League. Since the chief of staff, General Marie-Eugène Debeney, and his closest associates at the rue St.-Dominique had often voiced skepticism about the League's efficacy, Herriot and Navy Minis-

156. *Trials of War Criminals before the Nuernberg Military Tribunals,* vol. 9, *The Krupp Case* (Washington, D.C., 1950), pp. 66–79, 266–78, 322–23.

157. *Trials of War Criminals,* 9:263–64.

158. For J. H. Morgan's later testimony that the Allies knew of Krupp's activities, see *Trials of War Criminals,* 9:428–30; earlier references in his 1924 article, "The Disarmament of Germany and After," p. 453, and in Nollet's 1932 account, *Une Expérience de désarmement,* pp. 176–79. Georges Castellan, *Le Réarmement clandestin du Reich, 1930–1935* (Paris, 1954), suggests that French intelligence remained accurate even after withdrawal of the control commission.

159. Stresemann speech to Reichsrat Foreign Affairs Committee, 3 January 1925, BA, R 43 I/274/129; cf. Nollet's perceptive discussion in *Une Expérience de désarmement,* pp. 175–76, 183–88, 236–38.

ter Jacques-Louis Dumesnil took the precaution of passing the word that they would tolerate no foot-dragging from the uniformed services.[160]

Unlike those of his party comrades who professed antimilitary sentiments on principle, Paul-Boncour took his duties to provide for the national defense with deadly seriousness. In his anguished approach to the German disarmament problem, he bore a marked resemblance to Herriot: both men felt torn between an aspiration to assume leadership in promoting international reconciliation and a recognition of the harsh realities of France's vulnerable military position. "I no longer have any confidence in the feasibility of interallied control," Paul-Boncour wrote the premier on 25 July, "and I believe, more than ever, in the necessity of some control. There remains none other than that of the League of Nations." He therefore exhorted the military men to approve a scheme which, though admittedly "hurried" in preparation and rather vague in many of its details, might strengthen Herriot's hand in the London negotiations.[161]

The generals grumbled but acquiesced. On 29 July, at a full-dress meeting of the C.S.D.N. Study Committee, ranking army and navy commanders joined Jules Laroche, the somewhat muddle-headed deputy director of political affairs at the Quai d'Orsay, in endorsing the plan for investigation of German armaments through the League. The military men understood that League control could hardly be other than chimerical. But they also knew that they could not hope to influence fundamental policy. Accordingly, General Debeney concentrated his efforts on securing changes in detail that might make League control somewhat more strict. Paul-Boncour, conveying the results of the deliberations to the press, reported with satisfaction that the military had agreed that "if considerations of a political nature which could not be deemed within their competence should lead the French government to entrust the League of Nations with the task of watching over German armaments, the application of this plan offers France all desirable and necessary guarantees."[162]

Paul-Boncour apparently convinced himself that the League could devise a practical inspection system. At least so he claimed for public consumption.[163] Such a development might offer a way out of the dilemma besetting French policymakers: how to safeguard national se-

160. This account rests on Joseph Paul-Boncour to Herriot, 25 July 1924, Herriot Papers; "Déliberation du droit d'investigation de la Société des Nations," 29 July 1924, Commission d'Etudes, Conseil Supérieur de la Défense Nationale, meeting no. 662/DN1, Box 56, Archives du Service Historique de l'Armée, Château de Vincennes, Vincennes; also Paul-Boncour's public statement in *Le Matin*, 11 August 1924, and Ambassador Leopold von Hoesch's excellent survey, Hoesch tel., 11 August 1924, G.F.M. 3398/1736/D740332–335.

161. Paul-Boncour to Herriot, 25 July 1924, Herriot Papers.

162. *Le Matin*, 11 August 1924.

163. Ibid.

curity without offending the Allies or further alienating Germany. Safe in the knowledge that a properly constituted League agency would maintain active surveillance over Germany's chief armaments center, Herriot could then in good conscience evacuate the Ruhr without linking this step to security demands.

But the hope for effective League control was doomed to disappointment. It takes years of patient work to develop a functioning secret service. No League commission, on which various South Americans, Scandinavians, and eastern Europeans unskilled in the sophisticated arts of military intelligence would inevitably lay claim to pride of place, could possibly do the job. British military experts who had studied the matter said this privately.[164] Their French counterparts almost certainly came to the same conclusion. But it did not pay for the top brass at the rue St.-Dominique to risk their careers by challenging Paul-Boncour on a narrow basis. The military control commission's frustrating experience suggested that, ultimately, it made little difference which particular agency sought to carry out military control.

Among themselves, professional military men accepted as axiomatic what Brigadier-General J. H. Morgan, on the basis of his experience on the control commission staff, would shortly assert in public print: "The truth is that, as things are, the real security for the peace of Europe is not to be found in the results achieved, or likely to be achieved, by the control commission, or [by] any committee organized by the League of Nations, but in the occupation of the Rhineland and the Rhine bridgeheads."[165] When the London Conference came to an end, the British General Staff would also summon the courage to point out (though politicians and civilian bureaucrats in Whitehall did not pay much attention) that "the most effective means of preventing Germany from rearming, should she be detected doing so, would be by the reoccupation of the Ruhr."[166]

As a result of the settlement reached at the conference, however, neither an extended occupation of the Rhineland nor a reoccupation of the Ruhr would any longer appear to lie within the bounds of practical politics. In the future, France and the Allies collectively would have to resolve their differences with Germany without recourse to the more extreme sanctions authorized by the Versailles treaty. The conference itself marked a watershed in this respect. In the final stage of the London proceedings, Herriot would negotiate with the Germans on relatively restricted grounds. He had already agreed, in effect, to withdraw French

164. See the extensive discussion of the issue in the British General Staff survey, "The Present and Future Military Situation in Germany," 29 January 1925, CAB 4/12: C.I.D. Paper 562–B.

165. Morgan, "The Disarmament of Germany and After," p. 451.

166. "General Staff Memorandum on . . . French Security," 29 September 1924, CAB 4/11: C.I.D. Paper 516–B.

troops from the Ruhr within a year or two. He could still solicit economic compensation, appeal for cooperation with the military control commission, and bargain about the exact timing of withdrawal. But having conceded the essential point, he possessed little remaining leverage. His achievements would prove correspondingly modest.

Herriot under the Gun

Herriot's margin for maneuver diminished with each passing day. As the French premier prepared to open direct negotiations with the Germans, his Belgian counterpart Theunis disclosed an intention to seek a quick settlement. The Ruhr occupation had become highly unpopular in Belgium. Theunis knew that the opposition Socialists were watching him closely and would exploit his failure to arrange an early termination date in the parliamentary elections scheduled for the spring of 1925. Hence he could not promise to hold firm for any connection between the Ruhr and German disarmament or to postpone evacuation of Belgian troops very long.[167]

MacDonald, moreover, kept reminding both Herriot and Theunis that to avoid a breakdown they had to make an arrangement which the German representatives, who like themselves faced harsh criticism at home, also found "agreeable." Great Britain, he reiterated, considered the Ruhr occupation illegal. He would not countenance anything like the two-year evacuation delay that members of the French delegation had proposed.[168] MacDonald subtly applied and relaxed the pressure with keen sensitivity to Herriot's psychology, but his line of conduct did not reflect tactical calculations alone. Fundamentally, he considered the Ruhr occupation an offense against international morality; as the tenth anniversary marking the outbreak of the world conflagration went by, the prime minister told Hankey that in his opinion it was "really France and Russia who made the war, and that Germany blundered into it by sheer bungling."[169]

Such sentiments notwithstanding, MacDonald clearly ranked as the moderate within his own camp. Chancellor of the Exchequer Snowden upbraided him constantly for not having "driven the French far enough" to induce the bankers to undertake the Dawes loan.[170] When General Nollet dilated on the mortal terror which the prospect of a resurgent Germany inspired in his countrymen and expressed fears for his personal safety if he returned to France without having provided for the

167. For this and other constraints on Herriot, see Hoesch's reports, 10–11 August 1924, G.F.M. 3398/1736/D740314–315, D740329–331.

168. MacDonald's report to the cabinet, CAB 23/48, Cabinet Conclusions: 47(24), 5 August 1924; also MacDonald's account to the British Empire Delegation, 91st Conference, 7 August 1924, CAB 29/105.

169. M. P. A. Hankey to Lady Hankey, 5 August 1924, Hankey Papers.

170. M. P. A. Hankey to Lady Hankey, 7 August 1924, ibid.

nation's security, the chancellor snapped that the general should plan "to make his home in England."[171] Both French and Belgian ministers appealed privately to Hankey to do something about Snowden's flaunted obduracy, but the cabinet secretary considered it "not a bad thing as it throws into relief the impartiality and fairness of MacDonald."[172]

Between them the two chief figures in the British delegation produced a devastating effect on the French premier. MacDonald told British Empire representatives that Herriot appeared to him "only too willing to withdraw from the Ruhr provided he could get Marshal Foch or General Nollet to afford him any excuse for taking such action." The prime minister determined to furnish such an excuse. He had Crowe draw up another missive warning Herriot and Theunis that unless they rid themselves of their "not very honourable" military entanglement in the Ruhr, he would find himself under strong political pressure not to accept the Dawes Plan after all and compelled to announce to the world the reasons why.[173]

In short, Herriot had ample grounds for discouragement by the time he exchanged courtesy visits with Marx and Stresemann on 7 August. Conversation on these occasions turned awkwardly to Heine and the Lorelei, but the meetings nonetheless symbolized a remarkable evolution in international relations. For the first time since the war leading French and German statesmen conferred as equals, without the uncomfortable aura of confrontation between victor and vanquished. These informal contacts led to further direct discussion of crucial political issues.[174]

On the same day, Herriot and Clémentel explored possible terms for a settlement with Rudolf Breitscheid, the German Social Democrat. Breitscheid possessed many acquaintanceships of long standing on the French left and had served several times as an intermediary between the French government and his own. After an earlier talk with Herriot in June, Breitscheid had actually drawn up a secret report castigating the Dawes Plan as a scheme "completely permeated with the capitalist spirit" and replete with "anti-social" ideas. It would impose regressive taxation on the German working classes, he had charged, and facilitate unwonted

171. Snowden's subsequent account to the British Empire Delegation, 92nd Conference, 15 August 1924, CAB 29/105.

172. M. P. A. Hankey to Lady Hankey, 7 August 1924, Hankey Papers.

173. MacDonald's explanation to the British Empire Delegation, 91st Conference, 7 August 1924, CAB 29/105; MacDonald to Herriot and Theunis, 9 August 1924, F.O. 371/9807: C 12742/903/18.

174. For the clearest chronological account of negotiations between the two sides, see "Tagebuch über die Londoner Konferenz," BA, R 43 I/268/1–171, published with commentary in *Akten der Reichskanzlei, Weimarer Republik, Die Kabinette Marx I und II*, ed. Günter Abramowski, 2 vols. (Boppard am Rhein, 1973), 2:1283–1342. Excerpts from Stresemann's reports are found in *Vermächtnis*, 1:467–501. German interpreter Paul Schmidt provides colorful though not always reliable detail in *Statist auf diplomatischer Bühne, 1923–45* (Bonn, 1949), pp. 40–68.

interference by foreign business in the economy of the Reich.[175] But Herriot unknowingly assumed that because Breitscheid was a genuine democrat, he need not hesitate to address him virtually as a member of his own team.

Breitscheid formed the impression, which he immediately conveyed to his own compatriots, that the French premier had "completely collapsed under the burdens of the conference" and that the French delegation swarmed with "intrigue." Herriot inquired how the German government would react if he offered to pull French troops out of the Ruhr upon completion of the military control commission's inspection, with the understanding that the commission would finish its work within three or four months. If he alone could decide, Herriot said confidentially, he would evacuate the Ruhr immediately. He felt sure that Germany had a "clear conscience" in military matters. However, he needed an investigation in order to reassure his countrymen that evacuation would not endanger their security. Herriot added that he would be satisfied provided the inspection revealed no considerable number of machine guns or cannon. He also expressed keen interest in renewing consideration of a nonaggression pact between France and Germany, to be modeled on the proposal made by Chancellor Cuno shortly before the beginning of the Ruhr occupation. Clémentel, finally, asked whether the Germans would send a deputation to Paris to negotiate a new trade treaty. The finance minister voiced particular interest in securing a three-year extension, at least for specified products, of the exemption from German customs duty currently enjoyed by exports from Alsace-Lorraine.[176]

Herriot's rambling exposition contained much that seemed vague or self-contradictory. Marx and Stresemann, nevertheless, considered Breitscheid's report on the whole encouraging. The French premier's suggestion of synchronizing the Ruhr evacuation with termination of the general inspection did not tempt the German statesmen, for they knew what evidence of illegal rearmament the control commission was likely to find. They took heart, however, from the short time-frame in which Herriot was evidently thinking. If the terms proved satisfactory, they were quite willing to negotiate a trade treaty. And they positively welcomed a nonaggression pact—just so long as it did not apply to the Reich's eastern frontiers.[177] Stresemann, after all, had proposed a similar Rhineland pact (in which the outline of the Locarno agreements may be clearly discerned) twice in the past year alone. Even Nationalist party leader Otto Hoetzsch considered a security arrangement limited to the

175. "Report on Experts' Plan Written by Rudolf Breitscheid, M.d.R., Subsequent to Interview with Herriot," 18 June 1924, processed by British Intelligence, 5 July 1924, F.O. 371/9828: C 11024G/3314/18.

176. Stresemann tel., 8 August 1924, G.F.M. 3398/1736/D740256–269.

177. Ibid.

western borders "completely acceptable": it would establish a plausible basis for later claiming that the Rhineland occupation had become unnecessary, while it left Germany free eventually to pursue territorial revision in the east.[178]

In an effort to win a firm pledge from Herriot to evacuate the Ruhr with dispatch, Prime Minister MacDonald decided to proceed along two lines simultaneously. On the one hand he would work on the French premier directly and frame his appeal in terms of Allied solidarity. On the other, he would arrange for Herriot and Stresemann to pursue informal discussions, shielded from prying notice by journalists or antagonistic members of the French delegation. With the latter end in view he asked Ambassador Kellogg to sponsor an intimate dinner for the two statesmen at the American Embassy on the evening of 8 August. Herriot, no longer sure whom he could trust in his own entourage, insisted on coming unaccompanied; at his request, an American foreign service officer who knew both French and German undertook to perform the duties of translation.[179]

But before this carefully planned encounter could take place, the festering dispute within the French delegation burst into the open. On the night of 7 August, MacDonald invited Herriot, Theunis, and Belgian Foreign Minister Hymans to Downing Street for another chat about the Ruhr. General Nollet, who had not been asked to come along and who suspected his chief of preparing to sell out the French position, appeared unbidden and brushed his way past the messenger into the gathering. The general declaimed upon the vital importance of extending the military occupation for reasons of French security. The altercation between Herriot and Nollet became so violent that MacDonald finally adjourned the session, but the two Frenchmen continued to quarrel in the cabinet room below until long after midnight, when they went off into the street still arguing at the top of their lungs. The security-conscious Hankey was appalled by the behavior of "these foreigners" and, with the condescension proper to a superior civil servant, he noted, "luckily no one was about."[180]

The next day, as chronicled earlier, MacDonald declined to commit himself on conditions for withdrawal from the Cologne zone, and Herriot thereupon summarily abandoned the traditional French position on the Rhineland. The French premier also resolved to take the next logical step, namely, to renounce the whole idea, for which Nollet had served

178. See the accounts of subsequent discussions between French Ambassador Pierre de Margerie and State Secretary Ago von Maltzan of the German Foreign Office, reported in Maltzan to Stresemann, 12 August 1924, G.F.M. 3398/1737/D740360–361, D740365–366.

179. Hankey "very secret" memoranda nos. 2–3, 8 August 1924, F.O. 371/9833: C 12707/4736/G; Kellogg's retrospective memorandum in Bryn-Jones, *Kellogg*, pp. 148–50.

180. Hankey to Lady Hankey, 9 August 1924, Hankey Papers; Hankey memorandum for the prime minister, 8 August 1924, F.O. 371/9833: C 12821/4736/G; Thomas Jones, *Whitehall Diary*, ed. Keith Middlemas, vol. 1 (London, New York, and Toronto, 1969), p. 290.

as spokesman, of seeking to achieve a settlement of disarmament and security matters in connection with the Ruhr evacuation. Instead, he decided to return to Paris in order to face down Nollet before the Council of Ministers and to seek approval for unconditional evacuation of the Ruhr within a specified period of time.[181]

The private meeting between Herriot and Stresemann therefore proved anticlimactic. The German foreign minister presented the case for concessions to his country in the artful style which, later in the decade, won him renown as a master of diplomatic persuasion. Conjuring away the statistical evidence of the May 1924 elections, he asserted that extremist movements in Germany had "passed their peak." The National Socialists no longer received support from industry or agriculture; Ludendorff had lost his standing among the intellectuals; and a "great republican organization," the *Reichsbanner*, which bid fair to become the predominant voice among veterans because of the strong democratic and socialist orientation of the working classes, easily balanced the nationalist-minded groups that aroused such anxiety in France. Thus, Stresemann argued, all signs pointed to "peaceful evolution" in Germany after implementation of the Experts' Report, but everything hinged on the "psychological attitude" that would develop among his people. The Dawes Plan required Germany to accept great privations and infringements on its sovereignty. The Reich was entitled to demand certain compensations in return. The most important of these was evacuation of the Ruhr within a reasonable period of time, measured "by months, not by years."[182]

Herriot sought to propitiate his interlocutor. He warmly agreed with Stresemann's analysis and, without making a specific commitment, proposed to resume the discussion after his return from Paris, when he would be "more free to stand up for his point of view."[183] The hope—indeed the secular prayer—that generosity and trust might strengthen those elements in Germany inclined to peace and reconciliation provided Herriot's controlling motivation. Yet even those of his colleagues, like Nollet, who remained skeptical of German intentions, could not escape the harsh constraints imposed by financial circumstances. On the day of its departure, the French delegation received a forcible reminder of these constraints from a familiar source: the American bankers.

Montagu Norman had grown ever more concerned lest the conference lose sight of the bankers' requirements. He had assured Reichsbank President Schacht that the bankers would insist on further consultations before they put their imprimatur on a political settlement, but Owen Young, much to Norman's dismay, had given the Germans a different

181. Herriot notation, 8 August 1924, Herriot Papers; his later explanation in *J.O.C. Déb.*, 21 August 1924, p. 2958; Hoesch tels., 10–11 August 1924, G.F.M. 3398/1736/D740314–315, D740329–331.

182. Stresemann tel., 9 August 1924, G.F.M. 3398/1736/D740294–297.

183. Ibid.

impression.[184] When German Finance Minister Luther demanded at a plenary session on 7 August that negotiations for a loan become "an integral part" of the conference proceedings, the conflict within the Allied camp flared openly. Snowden, who, as Stresemann noted with satisfaction, let slip "no opportunity to deal the French a blow," vigorously supported Luther. But MacDonald retorted that the conference had to move ahead with its work and could not "go on bringing the bankers in at every moment."[185]

Norman and Snowden drew the conclusion from this contretemps that MacDonald would try to satisfy only so many of the bankers' desiderata as were compatible with making the conference a political success. The optimistic tenor of Clémentel's remarks confirmed the governor's impression that MacDonald had not explicitly passed on to the French and the Belgians the previous communications in which the bankers had set forth minimum market requirements for a loan. On 8 August Norman sought out J. P. Morgan and Thomas Lamont to alert them to the peril they faced: if the conference struck a political compromise that did not provide the necessary prerequisites for a loan, the bankers might find themselves blamed for the ultimate failure.[186]

Norman's sense of urgency reflected the special circumstances in which the British banking fraternity found itself. With the Bank of England's blessing, the London financial market had extended substantial short-term commercial credits to German traders in the preceding months. British bankers had taken an unusual risk because they hoped to corner the German banking business and to tie Germany to the use of sterling in its international transactions. They had proceeded on the assumption that the rentenmark would find wide support and that rapid economic recovery of the Reich would shortly begin. If political conditions made it feasible to float the long-term Dawes loan by October, then confidence in the German currency would be restored. The gamble would pay off for short-term lenders in the London City. Subsequently, private trade credits would become a matter of routine.

The Morgan firm was free from comparable pressures of time. The partners at headquarters in New York, in fact, were giving serious consideration to helping the French and Belgians meet their capital needs directly if the conference failed to provide a satisfactory basis for a German loan. They entertained the notion that the European nations

184. "Tagebuch über die Londoner Konferenz," 6–8 August 1924, BA, R 43 I/268/6–8; Hjalmar Schacht memoranda, 6 and 8 August 1924, R 43 I/266/323–326; Stresemann tel., 9 August 1924 [relating conversation with Reginald McKenna], G.F.M. 3398/1736/D740296–297.

185. Meeting of Heads of Delegations, 7 August 1924, *Proceedings of the London Reparation Conference*, 2:170–74; Stresemann to Maltzan, 8 August 1924, G.F.M. 3398/1736/ D740256–269.

186. Lamont undated memorandum, TWL 176/4; J. P. Morgan, Grenfell, and Lamont to J. P. Morgan & Co., 11 August 1924, TWL 176/24; also account of Snowden's views in Hankey to Lady Hankey, 7 August 1924, Hankey Papers.

might nonetheless find some way to put the Dawes Plan into effect for an interim period. Within a few months the plan might exert a stabilizing influence in central Europe and facilitate "important progress" toward withdrawal of troops from the Ruhr. Once everyone in Europe had become "committed to the charms of peace and reconstruction," New York would reconsider floating a German bond issue. For Montagu Norman, this order of things was out of the question. It was "all very fine for France," he observed, but meanwhile "Germany and the rentenmark . . . would go to pot"—and so, by implication, would the position of short-term lenders in the London City.[187]

J. P. Morgan and Lamont fully shared Norman's distress, however, at the impression which the newspapers had fostered and which some politicians were evidently trying to sustain, to the effect that the compromise formula adopted in respect to default and sanctions procedures had satisfied the bankers' most urgent demand. A widespread misconception appeared to exist that settlement of remaining questions prerequisite to a German loan would now be comparatively simple. Other prominent American financiers, meanwhile, had begun to drift into London with reports of a brilliant upturn in the New York bond market that made it possible to float a German loan without the rigorous safeguards required by Morgan's.[188] Mortimer Schiff of Kuhn, Loeb joined the firm's irrepressible Otto Kahn, who continued to trumpet his belief that, despite "considerable *shlemassel*" for German business, the Reich was "on the right road which leads out of the woods" for the first time since the Armistice.[189] Owen Young had asked his personal friend, Clarence Dillon of Dillon, Read, to serve as a "stalking horse" in order to put pressure on Morgan's, and Dillon obligingly spread the word that all the talk about needing assurances on default, sanctions, and the Ruhr evacuation was "poppycock."[190]

The Morgan partners had traditionally claimed simply to interpret investor sentiment. Yet surprisingly, this unmistakable evidence that American market conditions had eased failed to impress them. They concluded that the situation called primarily for an adjustment in rhetoric in order to take the ground out from under such "Sunny Jims" as Dillon and Schiff. Heretofore they had spoken of what the American investor would demand. In the future, Leffingwell advised, it might

187. J. P. Morgan & Co. to J. P. Morgan, Charles Steele, Grenfell, and Lamont, 9 August 1924, TWL 176/23; Lamont to J. P. Morgan & Co., 11 August 1924, TWL 176/24.

188. J. P. Morgan and Grenfell to J. P. Morgan & Co., 9 August 1924, TWL 176/23; Lamont to Paul M. Warburg, 11 August 1924, TWL 176/24; Lamont to J. P. Morgan & Co., 12 August 1924, TWL 176/25.

189. Kahn to Schiff, 16 July, 5 and 21 August 1924, Box 237; also Kahn to Paul Cravath, 5 August 1924, Box 220; Kuhn, Loeb & Co. to Kahn, and Kahn to Kuhn, Loeb & Co., 31 July 1924, Box 227; Kahn to M. Percy Peixotto, 5 August 1924, Box 234, Kahn Papers.

190. Lamont to J. P. Morgan & Co., 12 August 1924, TWL 176/25. For Young's dramatic recollection of Dillon's role, as told to his administrative assistant on 11 February 1929, see Stuart M. Crocker, "Personal Memoirs: Young Plan Days," pp. 1–5, MS in Box 2, Stuart M. Crocker Papers, Library of Congress, Washington, D.C.

prove expedient to refer to conditions which enabled the firm "to recommend the bonds to American investors rather than requirements which . . . investors themselves have formulated." But confident that Morgan's would continue to call the tune on Wall Street, Leffingwell professed to see little difference between the two ways of describing things. In practice, he noted, "American investors won't buy German bonds unless we recommend them, and of course, we won't recommend them unless we conscientiously can."[191]

Upon consideration, the Morgan partners thought it wise to furnish the French and Belgian governments with an explicit statement of their requirements. These governments figured also as the firm's financial clients. Duty, the partners convinced themselves, obligated them to inform their clients of banking conditions; they could not in fairness leave these governments under a misapprehension until it became too late to establish a suitable basis for a German financial operation. Accordingly, when Lamont met with Clémentel on 9 August to discuss French domestic finance and renewal of the Bank of France credit, he brought along a "clarifying memorandum" concerning the Dawes loan. Clémentel begged Lamont not to make any formal communication that Herriot might construe as an ultimatum at this delicate juncture. Lamont therefore took the document back and readdressed it to Belgian Premier Theunis, who had volunteered his good offices and who passed on a copy to Clémentel unofficially. This elaborate diplomatic ritual notwithstanding, the French delegation was left in no doubt about the Morgan position as it prepared to depart for the decisive convocation of the Council of Ministers in Paris.[192]

Lamont asserted that investors had "no precise formula to suggest" concerning military evacuation of the Ruhr, but that they insisted upon some arrangement for "prompt withdrawal" of foreign troops. They also required a "satisfactory announcement" of plans for evacuation of the Rhineland and of the Rhineland Commission's future policies, though on this issue American investment opinion was "less well informed than the British." Lamont carefully listed the many other points that he and Norman had earlier discussed with MacDonald. He disclaimed any intention to add to France's political difficulties. The American bankers submitted their requirements for the purpose of information and "in no sense as an ultimatum." The Morgan firm, Lamont stressed, did not seek to have dealings either with "the German government or German interests generally." It would contemplate a loan only with the hope of "rendering a service to the Allied governments and of assisting

191. Leffingwell to Lamont, 15 August 1924, TWL 176/27; see also the elaboration on this view in Leffingwell to Lamont, 19 August 1924, TWL 177/1.

192. Lamont to J. P. Morgan & Co., 9 August 1924, TWL 176/23; Lamont to Frank B. Kellogg, 10 August 1924, TWL 176/24; J. P. Morgan, Grenfell, and Lamont to J. P. Morgan & Co., 11 August 1924, TWL 176/24.

in the work of reconstruction of benefit to the European countries and secondarily to America."[193]

The attempt to coat the pill with sugared sentiments, though sincere, proved unsuccessful. Herriot denounced the bankers' behavior as "totally unheard of" and a few days later, his fury still unappeased, he remarked to Stresemann with bitter irony that perhaps he should offer two French provinces as security.[194] But the French premier's reaction simply confirmed the fact that Lamont's message had made its mark. On the verge of reopening serious negotiations for direct assistance from the Morgan bankers, the French could hardly afford to ignore their judgment on the question of the German loan.[195]

Thus the circumstances made it extremely difficult for the French Council of Ministers, meeting at the Elysée Palace on the evening of 9 August, to take a firm stand. No great public outcry demanded it. The press had earlier directed considerable criticism at Herriot's weakness as a negotiator, but now even newspapers of centrist orientation recognized the inevitability of major concessions.[196] Deputies and leading journalists, like most other well-to-do Parisians, had scattered for the traditional August holiday; the widespread grumbling over Herriot's intention to interrupt their vacations by calling parliament back into session as soon as the London Conference adjourned furnished striking evidence of the passivity and apparent indifference that ruled political circles.[197] Even the opposition leaders most dissatisfied by the trend of events clearly understood the limited range of alternatives. Secretary Hughes, on a tour of European capitals, had everywhere stressed in general terms the need for an accommodating spirit in order to bring the Dawes Plan to fruition. In Paris he had bluntly explained both to Poincaré and to ex-President Millerand: "Here is the American policy. If you turn this down, America is through."[198]

President of the Republic Gaston Doumergue tried nevertheless to rally resistance. For all his southern bonhomie, Doumergue had been a firm partisan of the Ruhr occupation, and he disliked Herriot intensely.[199] At Doumergue's behest Foch came in from Brittany to rehearse in person the arguments for remaining in the Ruhr that the marshal had

193. Lamont to Theunis, 10 August 1924, TWL 176/23, copy also in Box 9, Kellogg Papers.

194. Stresemann tel., 13 August 1924, BA, R 43 I/266/151–156.

195. For evidence of efforts by Clémentel and Theunis to mollify Lamont, see Lamont to J. P. Morgan & Co., 12 August 1924, TWL 176/25.

196. This characterization holds true for *Le Temps*, *Le Matin*, and *Le Journal des débats*, 16 July–11 August 1924, though not for *L'Echo de Paris* during the same period.

197. Hoesch tel., 9 August 1924, G.F.M. 3398/1736/D740275–277.

198. Beerits memoranda, "The European Trip of 1924," pp. 35–37, and "The Dawes Plan," p. 27, respectively in Containers 173/54 and 172/27, Hughes Papers; Hughes to Kellogg, 4 August 1924, U.S. 462.00R 296/503; Robert E. Olds to Kellogg, 2 August 1924, Box 8, Kellogg Papers.

199. On Doumergue's attitude to Herriot, see Adrien Dansette, *Histoire des présidents de la république* (Paris, 1953), pp. 222–25.

previously relayed through Desticker. But Foch, finding Herriot gloomy and preoccupied, succeeded only in antagonizing him.[200]

Acrimonious discussion followed in the Council of Ministers.[201] Nollet accused Herriot of having deceived him. To leave the Ruhr before imposing some effective curb on future war matériel production there seemed to him utter folly. Yet the war minister possessed no independent political base, and he realized that his resignation would serve no purpose other than to advertise the cabinet's disunity to the outside world. By stretching a point, moreover, Herriot could argue that MacDonald's implied agreement to review the results of the general inspection before withdrawing from the Cologne zone constituted a concession in the realm of security. And had not the highest military authorities acquiesced in Paul-Boncour's plan to turn over future control of German disarmament to the League of Nations?

Finally, Nollet, no less than Herriot himself, considered it essential to carry through the promised reduction of national military service from eighteen months to a year. Inspector-General Pétain had recently informed him that wretched salaries, blighted hopes for advancement, and uncertainty about the future had already corroded the spirit of army officers and career enlisted men to such an extent that he could not vouch unconditionally for the army's loyalty, let alone for its effective performance in the field.[202] Perhaps nothing could induce such a disenchanted officer corps to keep itself prepared over many years for valiant exertion, but the best chance of stemming the military "malaise" lay in concentrating the meagre financial resources available on the regular army. This in turn required the reduction of France's immediate military responsibilities—in the Ruhr and elsewhere—as rapidly as possible.

In short, however displeased with Herriot's style, neither Doumergue nor Nollet could formulate a coherent, dynamic counterproposal that would take into consideration both the nation's military and financial limitations and its spiritual lassitude. In the end, the Council of Ministers endorsed Herriot's position by a considerable margin and authorized him to evacuate the Ruhr unconditionally after a maximum delay of one year—a time schedule that some American representatives in London had hinted might prove acceptable.[203]

200. Foch Cahiers, 9 August 1924, Dossier G, pp. 177–79.

201. Hoesch tels., 10, 11, 12 August 1924, G.F.M. 3398/1736/D740314–315, D740329–331, 3398/1737/D740350–353; Adolf Müller tel. [Berne], 10 August 1924, G. F. M. 3398/1736/D740320; Phipps tel. nos. 512, 514, 10 August 1924, F.O. 371/9863: C 12743/12744/11642/18. See also the accounts given by Herriot to Stresemann, in Stresemann tel., 13 August 1924, BA, R 43 I/266/151–156; by Clémentel to Lamont, in Lamont to J. P. Morgan & Co., 12 August 1924, TWL 176/25; and by Clémentel to Hankey, in F.O. 371/9856: C 12940/11495/18.

202. Marshal [Henri-Philippe] Pétain to General Nollet, 18 July 1924, copy obtained by British Intelligence, 14 December 1924, F.O. 371/10550: W 10937/G.

203. For the suggestion by Logan and Houghton that a one-year delay might be a reasonable compromise, see Sthamer tel., 30 July 1924, G.F.M. 3398/1736/D740145–146.

Lingering French Illusions

Nothing better illustrates the contrasting approaches taken by the French and German governments to the diplomatic challenges confronting them at this moment than the way in which they respectively managed the domestic press. In Paris, the guidelines prepared for the heavily subsidized newspapers were designed to protect the reputation of Herriot and his associates and to prevent untimely revelation of the true state of affairs. In Berlin, the Wilhelmstrasse, sure of its purposes, manipulated press opinion so that the German delegation could plausibly appeal for concessions to appease an aroused public at home.

Following the decisive cabinet meeting at the Elysée, the official French news agency, Havas, announced that the ministers had agreed on a military evacuation plan which "obviously" would "take account of the security guarantees that France and Belgium have a right to demand."[204] According to the news release, Herriot and Nollet had together consulted Marshal Foch and the latter had "joined completely in their way of seeing things."[205] The premier also reportedly "confirmed" that a conference, at which American participation seemed assured, would meet the following November to settle interallied debts. Further negotiations for a mutual security pact with Great Britain were in the offing as well, though no "definite" engagements had yet been made.

While the French press was fed a misleading account of attainments close at hand, German newspapers were encouraged to stress how much remained to be accomplished. On 8 August State Secretary von Maltzan called in the leading journalists of Berlin and instructed them "not to put down success achieved up to now as such, but on the contrary to criticize vigorously."[206] Then, after the French delegation

204. See G.F.M. 3398/1736/D740314–315 for the Havas dispatch, and *L'Ere nouvelle*, 10–11 August 1924, for the "discreet" account specially prepared by Gaston Bergery. The author has not found a comprehensive list of newspapers that were in the pay of the government at this particular moment, but British Minister Eric Phipps's reports suggest that the Cartel had shown unusual largesse even by French standards (see, for example, Phipps no. 1893 to MacDonald, 29 August 1924, F.O. 371/9813: C 13819/1288/18). Receipts in the Painlevé Papers, 1924–25, indicate that both Herriot and Painlevé (who became the next president of the council) subsidized several mass-circulation dailies as well as Cartel newspapers and individual journalists.

205. Some historians have inaccurately accused Foch of a tendency to step beyond his proper military role (see, e.g., King, *Foch versus Clemenceau*). In this case it is particularly noteworthy that Foch took no steps to correct the grave distortion of his position. "So long as my government converses abroad," he noted, "I take care not to give the lie to it. . . . But for that, truth would be reestablished. When one thinks that France, which saved the world at the Marne, allows itself to be given conditions. . . . Above bankers, there are nations!" (Foch Cahiers, 13 August 1924, Dossier G, p. 179). Herriot acted with more selective discretion. To Stresemann he revealed that his conflict with Foch had been so violent that it might later lead to "a crisis," though to the French Chamber he continued to insist that he and the marshal saw eye to eye. (Cf. Stresemann tel., 13 August 1924, BA, R 43 I/266/151, with *J.O.C. Déb.*, 23 August 1924, pp. 3074–75, Herriot to René Coty in *Le Temps*, 30 August 1924, and *Jadis*, 2:165–66.)

206. Maltzan to Stresemann, 8 August 1924, G.F.M. 3398/1736/D740253.

returned to London, the German press was directed not to emphasize Herriot's triumph over Nollet, but instead to enlarge upon the nature of the French *Diktat* and "Germany's determination not to make the evacuation a subject for log-rolling."[207]

Management of the news did not just affect attitudes held by the general public. To some extent it reflected also the states of mind prevailing among leadership groups in Paris and Berlin. The German cabinet, in continual touch with its delegation in London, labored to resolve opposing views within the Reich and weighed with utmost care what inducement it might offer the French to evacuate the Ruhr more rapidly. In France, the several ministerial bureaucracies characteristically worked at cross purposes, and some of the Cartel's parliamentary spokesmen demonstrated a surprising degree of wishful thinking about the opportunities for advantageous security and war debt arrangements which, they thought, a resolute policy of international conciliation might yet create.

When Herriot returned to London, for example, he carried with him a fresh memorandum on the subject of security that the back-office staff at the Quai d'Orsay, following his instructions, had rushed to completion. This rambling document elaborated on the desiderata that Peretti de la Rocca had previously outlined to the British at Chequers in June and in the Paris meetings of early July. It spelled out the C.S.D.N. Study Committee's plan for League control of German armaments. It also reiterated the familiar French proposal for a series of related security pacts: first a defensive alliance between France and Great Britain, then analogous arrangements between the Allies bordering on Germany to the east, and finally a reciprocal nonaggression treaty with Germany under the aegis of the League of Nations. The note called also for reinforcement of the authority of the League by efficacious organization of "mutual assistance" against aggression—in other words for a revival under a different name of the Draft Treaty of Mutual Assistance that Britain had recently rejected.[208]

Lampson of the Foreign Office promptly informed Peretti that Whitehall could not respond to "so highly important a communication" without thorough study, and Peretti admitted that the Quai d'Orsay did not really expect action before the end of the London Conference.[209] But Herriot, and with him many luminaries of the French parliamentary left, continued to nurture the illusion that Britain might subsequently accede to at least part of what they had requested. In early September they would troop off to the League Assembly to fight for the first step in the

207. Spiecker to Presseabteilung, 10 and 14 August 1924, G.F.M. 3398/1736/D740308–309, 3398/1737/D740398–399.

208. Herriot to MacDonald, 11 August 1924, F.O. 371/9819: C 12870/2048/18.

209. Lampson minute, 13 August 1924, on conversation with Peretti the previous day, F.O. 371/9819: C 12870/2048/18.

program—adoption of the Protocol for the Pacific Settlement of International Disputes, lineal descendant of the old Draft Treaty. Not for many months would Herriot and his associates realize that there existed not the slightest chance of winning British approval either for the "Geneva Protocol" or for the rest of the French security program.[210]

Though British diplomats, in appreciation of Herriot's cooperative spirit, intended to be polite, their consideration of the French proposals would constitute little more than a charade. Harold Nicolson of the Central Department put the Foreign Office's objections to the French security note in a nutshell on 27 August: "It is not the details of this programme or that which will prove the difficulty, but the essential conflict of principle which underlies these programmes. Whatever the French may say, they wish, under the guise of the League, to forge iron chains which will encircle Germany and keep her captive: whatever we may say, we wish, while aiming at general pacification and disarmament, to avoid in any way committing ourselves to military intervention in Europe."[211] And MacDonald himself, returning from a much-heralded personal appearance at the League Assembly where he dramatically called for "a train service to peace," would instruct the Whitehall bureaucracy categorically: "On French views of security we must be rigid. We cannot accept them."[212]

Prominent Frenchmen close to the government proved similarly slow to abandon their hopes for lenient treatment on war debts. On 4 August Clémentel had made a half-hearted effort to raise the issue in London. In a note submitted to the British Foreign Office, he called for a "decision in principle" not to require war debt repayment until Germany had completed reimbursement for material damages.[213] In effect this policy would have postponed debt payments to the Greek calends. Sir Eyre Crowe could not suppress a flicker of anger at the French attempt to renege on the prior understanding to exclude debts from the conference agenda, but the proposal itself made almost no impression on him. It seemed an uninspired variant on countless earlier schemes by the French to award themselves a reparations priority. Crowe forwarded it to the Treasury for suitable interment and barely remembered it when Clémentel returned to the charge after coming back from Paris one week later.[214]

210. See the details of negotiations chronicled in F.O. 371/10568–572: W 134/98 and F.O. 371/10573: W 338/98.

211. Nicolson minute on the Central Department "Memorandum respecting French Security," 27 August 1924, F.O. 371/9819: C 13663/2048/18.

212. MacDonald speech to the League in London *Times*, 8 September 1924; MacDonald minute on French security, 10 September 1924, F.O. 371/9813: C 13819/1288/18.

213. "Note by the French Delegation on the Settlement of Interallied Debts, Submitted by M. Clémentel, Minister of Finance," 4 August 1924, F.O. 371/9683: C 12664/11/62; copy also in F[30]/1361, Ministère des Finances.

214. Crowe minute, 8 August 1924, F.O. 371/9683: C 12664/11/62; Crowe minute, 12 August 1924, F.O. 371/9863: C 12760/11642/18; see also the Treasury's routine dismissal of

In the meantime, however, French Socialists tackled the British prime minister directly on the debt issue. Vincent Auriol, president of the Chamber Finance Commission, who had rubbed elbows with MacDonald at many socialist gatherings, arrived in London to appeal to him as the "beloved head" of the Labour party and the "comrade so deservedly esteemed by the whole International." The Second International had passed many resolutions favoring cancellation of interallied debts and reduction of reparations to an amount equal to the cost of rebuilding the devastated areas. This formula would in practice largely exclude the British from any compensation. But, Auriol argued, French Socialists had suffered persecution as they fought the "mad policy" of the Ruhr; now that they had secured the repudiation of that policy by French democracy, could the Labour party possibly countenance a debt settlement "contrary to the wishes of the international proletariat"?[215]

MacDonald greeted Auriol with a fraternal welcome and gave him a tour of the House of Commons, but failed to answer his question.[216] On the day after Herriot's triumph over Nollet at the Elysée cabinet meeting, Léon Blum nevertheless appeared undaunted at the British Embassy in Paris to renew Auriol's appeal. Great Britain, he urged, should meet the more generous policy that France had chosen to follow on the Ruhr evacuation with a corresponding concession on debts, thus "lifting the whole issue out of the morass of legal technicalities into a higher realm of international good will." In particular, he suggested that Britain agree to divide the reparations kitty in proportion to material damages only (in other words to revise the "Spa percentages") and that it relieve France of the obligation to fund the war debt until the latter nation had collected five milliard marks from Germany.[217]

Treasury and Foreign Office officials laughed Blum's specific proposals out of court. But Lampson, at least, saw no objection to giving the French "a little pat on the back" in the form of a vague assurance that Britain remained prepared to examine the debts in a "friendly spirit," provided the French delegation continued to "play up for the rest of the conference."[218] And when Herriot and Clémentel returned to London, they really asked for little more than this. Clémentel had injudiciously

---

Clémentel's ideas as "out of the question," Sir O. E. Niemeyer to Foreign Office, 14 August 1924, F.O. 371/9683: C 13040/11/62.

215. Vincent Auriol to J. Ramsay MacDonald, 6 August 1924, F.O. 371/9761: C 12851/75/18.

216. The Treasury proposed to ignore Auriol completely, but the Foreign Office finally drafted an "anodyne and noncommital reply" (see Lampson minute, 4 September 1924, and MacDonald to Auriol, 15 September 1924, F.O. 371/9761: C 12851/75/18).

217. Phipps tel. no. 513, 10 August 1924, F.O. 371/9863: C 12760/11642/18; also Phipps to MacDonald, 10 August 1924, F.O. 371/9863: C 12946/11642/18.

218. Treasury reaction in Frederick Phillips memorandum for Niemeyer, 11 August 1924, F.O. 371/9863: C 12877/11642/18; Foreign Office response in J. C. Sterndale Bennett and Miles W. Lampson minutes, 11 August 1924, F.O. 371/9863: C 12760/11642/18.

told the French press that the connection between reparations and debts was now "completely established" and that he had reached an "absolute" understanding with MacDonald on this point.[219] He now pleaded with Crowe for confirmation of the 9 July Paris communiqué, in which the British prime minister had agreed to seek an "equitable solution" of the debt problem, "due regard being had to all the factors involved." A public reiteration of this formula, Clémentel stated, would be "of the utmost importance" in helping Herriot to handle the French parliament. But MacDonald, showing himself more adamant than his advisers, peremptorily refused. "I am tired of 'M. Herriot's parliamentary position,' " he minuted. "We must stand by what has been said and do not budge."[220]

Though the French delegates continued to badger MacDonald for some sort of statement on the debts until the final hours of the London Conference, they were obliged to go away empty-handed. The prime minister would go no further than to say that the Paris formula was "on record, and would remain there until it was withdrawn."[221] In fact, the British gave several hints that they intended to take a hardnosed approach and would indeed seek to maximize revenue from war debts in order to compensate for the anticipated diminution in reparations receipts.[222] But the French were reluctant to believe it. For many months Léon Blum continued to talk obliviously about modifying the Spa percentages in France's favor. And even professionals at the rue de Rivoli came to recognize only later that Britain would impose on them an onerous debt settlement whatever the ultimate fate of the Dawes Plan.[223]

The German delegation in London did not fall prey to comparable illusions. It made sober preparations for the bilateral talks with the French that would provide the great drama of the conference's final days. After the French ministers returned from Paris, discussion would focus primarily on two questions: economic relations between France and Germany, and the exact timing and conditions for military evacuation of the Ruhr. When the German delegates anticipated that the French might seek to connect evacuation with control of German armaments, they sent State Secretary Franz Bracht back to Berlin by airplane—no

219. *Le Matin*, 10 August 1924.

220. Sir Eyre Crowe minute, 12 August 1924, MacDonald minute, 13 August 1924, F.O. 371/9863: C 12760/11642/18.

221. Hankey to Lampson, note no. 10, 16 August 1924, summarizing conversation between the prime minister and the French delegation on interallied debts, F.O. 371/9683: C 13266/11/62.

222. Niemeyer to Crowe, 14 August 1924, F.O. 371/9683: C 13073/11/62.

223. See particularly Gabriel Dayras [head of the German affairs section], "Le Rendement effectif du plan Dawes et le problème des dettes interalliées," 1 December 1924, F30/1281; President of the Council to Minister of Finance no. 4017, 21 October 1924, Minister of Finance to President of the Council, 2 December 1924, also Rincquensen [French financial attaché in London] to Barnaud, "Dettes interalliées," 26 October and 5 December 1924, all in F30/1361.

routine mission in those days—to work out a tolerable scheme with General von Seeckt.[224] They gave no less careful consideration to the possibility that the French might pose economic prerequisites for evacuation. Contending interests within the Reich held sharply divergent views about the best approach to adopt. But the issues were thrashed out ahead of time in Berlin. By the time the French put forward their economic demands, the Germans had developed a coherent position and the London delegation could skillfully exploit the opportunities that presented themselves in negotiation.

Discussions on economic questions and on the timing of military evacuation proceeded simultaneously. It will promote clarity, however, to examine the two issues sequentially in this narrative. The dispute over the evacuation date captured the newspaper headlines. At times the opposing positions seemed irreconcilable, and more than once the entire conference appeared in peril of imminent collapse. But in the long run, the economic negotiations were of far greater moment.

At London, the French might have one last chance to talk with the Germans about trade relations at a time when they still held the upper hand politically. They might also pursue the elusive understanding between heavy industry in the two countries, without which French steelmakers despaired of finding a satisfactory fuel supply or an outlet for their excess production. After they had lost the leverage deriving from their presence in the Ruhr, the French would have to resign themselves to concluding an economic modus vivendi with the Germans on terms that faithfully reflected the disparity in industrial development on the two sides of the Rhine. When economic issues faded from active consideration in London, however, the broad public did not grasp the full significance of that development. World opinion riveted its attention instead on the timing of the Ruhr evacuation. For reasons of sentiment and prestige, this issue engaged passions. Yet the evacuation timetable, once effectively isolated from military control and economic questions, no longer played an important role in determining the shape of the new Europe as it would emerge in years to come.

The Stakes for European Heavy Industry

The special commercial advantages that the Versailles treaty conferred on France were scheduled to expire in January 1925. Thereafter the factors that had contributed to Germany's earlier rise to industrial preeminence in Europe—abundant natural resources, efficient business management, rapid technological innovation, a skilled and resourceful labor supply—would once again tend to give it the edge in international

224. "Tagebuch über die Londoner Konferenz," 8–9 August 1924, BA, R 43 I/268/8–11; Bracht tel., 10 August 1924, R 43 I/266/32–36.

trade. French engineers attached to M.I.C.U.M. who studied the German coal and steel industry came up with some alarming figures. Modernized Ruhr cokeries could now supply fuel to German steel mills at two-thirds of the world price. And the mills themselves had also rationalized their productive processes radically in the preceding two years; they currently operated with unit labor costs one-third less than those of their competitors in France, Belgium, and England. M.I.C.U.M. analysts predicted that when German firms overcame their temporary working capital shortage, they would find themselves in a position to "overwhelm" the European market for metallurgical products.[225]

Not every German industry, of course, had made such dramatic progress. Nevertheless, Reich Economics Minister Eduard Hamm could assure his cabinet colleagues after reviewing the data in preparation for talks in London: "Germany need fear nothing from a commercial connection to France. The closer this connection becomes, the more strongly will Germany's superiority make itself felt."[226] But though officials in Berlin perceived no danger in tariff negotiations that proceeded on the basis of mutual advantage, they remained apprehensive lest France demand perpetuation of most-favored-nation treatment without reciprocity or insist on a continued duty-free quota for iron goods, textiles, and farm products from Alsace-Lorraine.

German steel magnates worried particularly that the Comité des Forges might choose this delicate moment to revive its now familiar scheme to exchange French iron ore and semiproducts for Ruhr coke. They were haunted by the idea that French steelmakers might convince the Herriot government to couple the claims advanced by the Comité des Forges with the Ruhr evacuation question. French manufacturers obviously could not afford to wait: their iron and steel output capacity exceeded 12 million tons, while domestic demand fell well short of 5 million tons. Without formation of a European-wide cartel to regulate output, apportion markets, and set fixed prices to protect the less efficient producers, the French steel industry could not hope to operate at a profit. The mills in Lorraine faced an additional difficulty. They had traditionally depended on the finishing industries of south and west Germany to absorb some 1.75 million tons of semiproducts annually. Now Westphalian heavy industry was expanding its own semiproduct capacity with a view

225. Direction, Mission Interalliée de Contrôle des Usines et des Mines, "Réduction résultant du plan des Experts des charges imposées aux industriels allemands," no. 10133/S, 3 May 1924, F.O. 371/9746: C 8372/70/18; see also supporting material in other M.I.C.U.M. reports, Service Economique, "Les Travaux neufs dans les mines de la Ruhr depuis 1913," no. 8797/S, 11 April 1924, F.O. 371/9810: C 12172/990/18; and "Situation of German Industry at the Beginning of July 1924," F.O. 371/9810: C 15945/990/18. Cf., however, the challenge to M.I.C.U.M.'s specific calculations by British experts: Memorandum by Sir T. Urwick [British delegation, Reparation Commission], 10 June 1924, F.O. 371/9748: C 10162/70/18.

226. "Protokoll der Ministerbesprechung," 29 July 1924, BA, R 43 I/265/137–140.

to displacing the French, and failing prior agreement, the Reich could impose a prohibitive tariff that excluded Lorraine "semis" from the German market altogether beginning in 1925.[227]

Leaders of the German steel industry also fretted about the disproportion between world supply and demand for metallurgical products. They could foresee considerable advantage in formation of an international steel cartel eventually as a means to limit production. But they would only agree to join such an organization on terms that clearly recognized Germany's industrial predominance in Europe. For the moment they thought the idea premature. They had just begun work in June on the creation of a domestic *Rohstahlgemeinschaft* (a syndicate to restrict output and apportion market shares among ingot steel producers within the Reich). They did not wish to enter upon discussions with the Comité des Forges until they had attained internal union, first among basic steel producers in the Ruhr, and then between heavy industry and the finishing and mechanical engineering firms in south Germany. To complete these arrangements would take several months.[228] If German metallurgists could succeed in delaying negotiations with the French until they had formed a united front at home and secured evacuation of the Ruhr, they would subsequently have all the bargaining chips on their side.[229]

When the German steel industry had carried through its plans for horizontal and vertical integration on a national level, it proposed to begin talks with foreign metallurgists. But even then it would attach far greater importance to an understanding with British manufacturers than to the formation of a continental economic bloc that united French and German producers. France could offer little of economic value to the Reich except a market for surplus coke and for machine goods. German

227. See the review of metallurgical issues at the London Conference by C. J. Kavanagh, British commercial secretary at Cologne, 26 August 1924, F.O. 371/9865: C 14020/12698/18; Humbert de Wendel's article in *Le Matin*, 25 September 1924; and the reports of Sir William Larke, director of the National Federation of Iron and Steel Manufacturers, on his discussions with continental steel executives, October–November 1924, in F.O. 371/9868: C 16611/17220/17740/14053/18. The account here draws also on Archives de Pont-à-Mousson, especially PAM/7224, 7230, 7245, 7266; and on the Historisches Archiv, Gutehoffnungshütte, especially the "Stahlwerksverband" and "Verein Deutscher Eisen- und Stahlindustrieller" files, GHH 400101222/0, 2, 7.

228. See "Verhandlungen betr. Stahlwerksverband, 1924–25," GHH 400101222/0, especially Albert Vögler to Carl Gerwin, 2 May, Gerwin to Vögler, 12 May; Gerwin to Paul Reusch, 23 May 1924; Aufsichtsrat des Stahlwerksverbandes, "Besprechung in Essen," 26 June 1924; Vögler to Reusch, 15 September, Fritz Thyssen to Reusch, 2 October, Gerwin to Direktion der Gutehoffnungshütte, 7 October 1924; "Niederschrift über die Bildung einer Rohstahlgemeinschaft," 14 October 1924.

229. See the analysis by Georg Lübsen, key figure in the Rheinisch-Westfälisches Kohlensyndikat, Lübsen to Reusch, 9 September 1924, GHH 4001012003/9; also the reports of Commercial Secretary C. J. Kavanagh, British business specialist on the Rhineland High Commission, Kavanagh to John W. F. Thelwell, 26 August 1924, F.O. 371/9865: C 14020/12698/18; and Kavanagh to J. C. Sterndale Bennett, 11 December 1924, F.O. 371/9869: C 18829/14053/18.

steel mills could import water-borne iron ore from Sweden, Spain, and Canada more cheaply than they could obtain minette ore overland from Lorraine. The Ruhr magnates certainly did not need the rails, girders, tubes, plates, and rods that presently were choking the French market; these products would only compete with their own burgeoning transformation industry. England, by contrast, provided a substantial outlet for semifinished and specialty steels from Germany, and the economically booming white Dominions offered the fastest-growing market in the world outside the United States (where domestic producers were invincible) for metallurgical goods.

German steel executives believed, moreover, that while cartelization would provide a measure of relief, the long-range solution to the industry's world-wide overcapacity problem lay in increasing effective demand. American and British financiers would have to provide the capital necessary for public works projects and railway construction that utilized large quantities of steel and also for the general plant expansion that would augment personal income and thereby spur demand for automobiles, appliances, and similar consumer products in all industrial countries. In short, German metallurgists saw compelling economic reasons for maintaining good relations with Wall Street and the London City, as well as with leaders of the British steel industry. They were by no means unwilling to explore mutually advantageous arrangements with the French also, but this was a matter of lesser urgency for them. After recovering their tariff sovereignty, the Germans would be in a position to call upon the French to make political sacrifices—in regard to the Rhineland, the Saar, and military control—in return for economic concessions.[230]

Early in the spring of 1924 the principal figures in German heavy industry had declined to discuss the ambitious program of the Comité des Forges for acquiring shares in Ruhr mines and for exchanging coke and semiproducts. In May and June, therefore, French steelmakers concentrated on a more limited objective: interesting the Germans in reviving the prewar international railmakers' cartel (I.R.M.A.). The French had already completed preliminary arrangements with producers from Great Britain, Belgium, and Luxembourg. Robert Pinot commissioned M. Piérard, the Comité des Forges representative in Düsseldorf, to try to

230. See Kilmarnock to MacDonald, 28 October 1924, reporting Sir William Larke's discussions with German metallurgists and bankers, including Fritz Thyssen, Albert Vögler, Bruno Bruhn, Louis Hagen, and Baron Oppenheim, F.O. 371/9868: C 16611/14053/18; Alfred Dembitsch's article in *Rhein-und-Ruhr Korrespondenz*, 25 October 1924, confirmed also by Dr. Bruno Bruhn [general-director of Friedrich Krupp A. G.] to Larke, 4 November 1924, F.O. 371/9868: C 17740/14053/18; also "Aktenvermerk: Besprechung der Sechser-Kommission mit Staatssekretär Trendelenburg," 9 September 1924, and Lübsen to Reusch, 9 September 1924, in GHH 4001012003/9. For an explicit discussion of German steelmakers' political aims, see also Fritz Thyssen's retrospective report to the Stahlwerksverband on his Paris negotiations, 2 April 1925, GHH 400101222/2.

sell German metallurgists on the idea. The rails cartel would not only obviate "ruinous" competition, Pinot argued, but it would also assure "the restoration of economic peace in the world" on one particular point and thereby pave the way for broader agreement.[231]

Representatives of the Stahlwerksverband made it clear from the outset that they would refuse to connect the "economic" issue of the rails cartel with what they called the "the purely political" problem of coke and semiproduct exchanges, but they did grant Piérard a hearing on 26 June. Though they insisted on postponing serious consideration of the matter until after the end of the London Conference, German metallurgists revealed at this meeting the line that they proposed to adopt in subsequent negotiations. Paul Reusch, chairman of the Stahlwerksverband, asserted that because of a "desperate situation" in the domestic market, Germany could only meet the "heavy burdens" imposed by the Dawes Plan through a substantial increase in its exports. Notwithstanding the loss of the mills in Lorraine, therefore, German metallurgy would have to claim a much larger percentage share in a new rails cartel than it had enjoyed under the prewar marketing arrangement.[232]

The Ruhr magnates took an equally tough line in discussions with their own government. They thought it best to maintain an entirely free hand for the trade negotiations that would follow once Germany recovered its tariff sovereignty. They responded negatively when the Reich Economics Ministry began to explore, ever so tentatively, economic inducements which Germany might offer at London if necessary to get the French out of the Ruhr more quickly. Reusch, for example, stated that he had "no interest" whatsoever in business negotiations at the present time, for such talks could only result in an attempt by the French steel industry to force its iron ore and semiproducts on German metallurgy. "We need neither one nor the other," he wrote emphatically to the like-minded J. Wilhelm Reichert, chief executive of the Verein Deutscher Eisen- und Stahlindustrieller. "German bureaucrats must finally get out of their heads the old fairy tale that we are dependent on minette ore."[233]

Economics Ministry officials nevertheless continued to press heavy industry to indicate what it thought the German delegation might realistically propose should it find no way to avoid discussing economic questions in London. On 30 July, Hamm solicited Reichert's views on the feasibility of exchanging coke for iron ore, participating in the rails cartel, and extending the duty-free quota for goods from Alsace-Lorraine. In

231. Paul Reusch to Reich Chancellor Marx, 29 March 1924; Robert Pinot [secretary-general of the Comité des Forges] to M. Piérard, [7?] May 1924; Carl Gerwin to Paul Reusch, 10 May 1924, GHH 400101222/2.

232. "Protokoll über die Besprechung mit Herrn Piérard," 26 June 1924; also Reusch to Reich Economics Minister Eduard Hamm, 26 June 1924, GHH 400101222/2; also Comité des Forges–Commission de Direction, compte rendu sommaire, 24 July 1924, PAM/7245.

233. Reusch to Reichert, 15 June 1924, GHH 400101222/7.

hurried consultation on the telephone, Reichert and Reusch agreed that owing to an expected future coal surplus, German industry would probably find advantage in a long-term contract to meet French coke needs, just so long as the French paid high enough prices and committed themselves to continue their purchases in slack as in boom times. The metallurgists also considered prolongation of the duty-free quota for Lorraine steel products tolerable for a transition period, say a year, provided that German negotiators could "screw down" the amount to a fraction of the present figure and obtain a counterbalancing concession for the export of German machinery to France.[234]

But Reichert carefully avoided disclosing to the Economics Ministry that any such room for maneuver existed. Spurred on by the spokesmen for coal and steel, the trade policy committee of the Reichsverband der Deutschen Industrie (the umbrella organization for all German business) cabled the delegation in London on 6 August to demand that it reject any connection between reparations and trade treaty negotiations, "even if such concessions are required as compensation for evacuation of the Ruhr."[235] Peter Klöckner, who represented Ruhr heavy industry, contended that nothing would be gained by making important economic sacrifices to hasten the end of a military occupation which would in any case disappear in the course of time.[236]

To drive the point home, Klöckner and Reichert met with Hamm at the Reich Chancellery on 10 August. All of German industry faced bankruptcy, they averred—"only the hope of London kept it going." The two business leaders discerned the sole prospect for deliverance in "closing the borders to iron imports and rejecting any duty-free quota or tariff limitations, so that German market outlets are protected." Otherwise, Klöckner declared categorically, German industry would have to shut down. Reichert helpfully advised that if the French made a concerted effort to obtain economic concessions, the London delegation should appeal to the English and American bankers. These bankers, he reminded Hamm, had an important stake in restoration of orderly economic conditions in the Reich, but "no interest in having Ruhr iron thrown on the world market as a consequence of importing Lorraine iron into west and south Germany."[237] Following the model set by heavy industry, numerous other business concerns of lesser political impor-

234. Reichert to Reusch, 30 July 1924, ibid.

235. Gerhard Köpke to London delegation, 6 August 1924, G.F.M. L177/4079/L051711; copy of circular addressed to General-Director Eugen Köngeter of Gebr. Stumm, intercepted by French Intelligence, 16 August 1924, in Herriot Papers.

236. Hamm to State Secretary Ernst Trendelenburg, 9 August 1924, G.F.M. 3398/1736/D740302.

237. "Niederschrift über die Besprechung in der Reichskanzlei," 10 August 1924, BA, R 43 I/265/241–244; Reichert and Simon to Hermann Bücher, 11 August 1924, G.F.M. L177/4079/L051705–706.

tance hastened forward with similar warnings that their position had become "desperate" and "wholly unbearable."[238]

But Stresemann, as he had demonstrated in the perilous autumn of 1923, would not yield willingly to pressure from special interest groups, however powerful. No one knew how long Herriot would cling to power or who would succeed him. Therefore, Stresemann insisted, he could give precedence to no goal over securing an airtight evacuation agreement. German business would have to accept some temporary sacrifice if he found it impossible to avoid making carefully circumscribed economic concessions. "Political responsibility for the question rests with the government of the Reich," he reminded his colleagues sharply, "and not with the heavy industry of Rhineland-Westphalia." As for Klöckner's threat to close down the mills and factories, he plainly labeled it "nonsense," for France had enjoyed special trade privileges under the peace treaty for five years, and German industry had never yet closed down.[239]

Actually German industry was by no means in such desperate straits as its spokesmen publicly professed. A considerable amount of factory construction had already begun in the Ruhr, and industrialists were quietly making expansive plans in anticipation of a favorable outcome at London and a consequent business upturn.[240] Once Stresemann asserted leadership, the Economics Ministry confirmed his view that industry could afford a certain measure of flexibility. In short order, the cabinet endorsed a program elaborated in London by the Economics Ministry foreign trade expert, State Secretary Ernst Trendelenburg. Under this scheme, Germany would yield a six-month extension of most-favored-nation privileges to France, but only in return for some reciprocity, notably the concession of the French minimum tariff to key German exports. Keeping in mind the political clout of Ruhr industry, the delegation in London planned to make a show of resistance to prolonging the Alsace-Lorraine duty-free quota initially; it would then attempt to limit the extension to six months and to demonstrate that it had yielded under compulsion.[241]

The French, meanwhile, had found it difficult to reach agreement among themselves on an economic program. The bitter rivalry between Jacques Seydoux and Daniel Serruys made cooperation between the economics staffs at the Quai d'Orsay and the Commerce Ministry im-

238. BA, R 43 I/265/249–250; G.F.M. L177/4079/L051703–704.

239. Stresemann tel., 11 August 1924, G.F.M. 3398/1736/D740337–340.

240. See reports by Emil Sauer, American consul-general in Cologne, who maintained good connections in Ruhr industrial circles, 25 July and 2 August 1924, U.S. 462.00R 296/488, 525.

241. Trendelenburg tel., 12 August 1924, G.F.M. L177/4079/L051697–703; "Sitzung des Reichsministeriums," 12 August 1924, BA, R 43 I/265/288; Franz Kempner to Trendelenburg, 12 August 1924, R 43 I/266/113; Hamm to Trendelenburg, 12 August 1924, G.F.M. 3398/1737/D740372.

possible. The bureaucrats had wasted the critical weeks of June and July trading barbed formal notes in the names of their respective ministers without coming to a meeting of minds.[242] Both Seydoux and Serruys recognized that insufficient time remained to work out a definitive tariff agreement with Germany before the commercial provisions of the Versailles treaty expired. The French customs still operated on the basis of the prewar tariff, haphazardly increased by coefficients to adjust for price changes since 1914.[243] It would require at least a year to elaborate new levies that reflected the vast structural changes undergone by the French economy during the decade of war and inflation. The Commerce Ministry had just begun to consult trading interests and had not yet compiled the intricate schedules necessary to take account of various industries' often conflicting needs. Hence France was in no position to propose terms for a permanent trade settlement in London. The dispute between Seydoux and Serruys centered on a more limited issue, namely, the nature of the interim arrangement for which France should strive while it still held control of the Ruhr.

Serruys, who enjoyed the firm support of Eugène Raynaldy, Cartel minister of commerce, argued that France should bend every effort to secure an extension of its present trade privileges (most-favored-nation treatment and duty-free entry of goods from Alsace-Lorraine) in connection with the reparations settlement. He also favored the initiation of general conversations leading toward a permanent commercial treaty with Germany, but he warned against conclusion of a premature arrangement which, though provisional in form, might in practice bind France's hands in shaping future tariff legislation. Serruys did not object to offering limited modification of the current prohibitive tariff against German goods in a provisional accord. If this inducement proved insufficient to win voluntary cooperation from the Reich, however, he proposed to seek approval from the Allies for French objectives and to try to impose an interim extension of existing trade privileges in London. Finally, Serruys expressed trepidation about tying the delicate question of interpenetration of French and German heavy industry and the exchange of coke and iron ore to broader tariff negotiations. In view of French metallurgy's weak position, he thought it preferable to strike a

242. Minister of Commerce and Industry to President of the Council, 19 and 27 June, 10 July 1924; President of the Council to Minister of Commerce and Industry, 10 and 18 July 1924, F[12]/8864, Ministère du Commerce et de l'Industrie, Archives Nationales, Paris. See also Serruys's explanation of his position to M. Morin, Paris representative of Pont-à-Mousson, in Morin to Camille Cavallier and Marcel Paul, 13 August 1924, PAM/7230; cf. Serruys's later account to officials of the British Board of Trade, Sir Hubert Llewellyn Smith to Sir Sydney Chapman, 5 September 1924; F.O. 371/9868: C 14427/14053/18. Seydoux summarized his position in an anonymous article, "L'Accord commercial avec l'Allemagne," *L'Europe nouvelle*, 23 August 1924, pp. 1080–82.

243. On the complicated question of French tariff legislation during this period, see Frank Arnold Haight, *A History of French Commercial Policies* (New York, 1941), pp. 91–138.

bargain on political grounds by offering rapid evacuation of the Ruhr in return for a long-term contract guaranteeing France's coke supply.

Seydoux, to whom Herriot (insofar as he concerned himself with economic matters) and also Clémentel looked for advice, considered the Commerce Ministry approach far too narrow. Seydoux held that the time had come for a concerted effort to restore normal economic relations between France and Germany on a basis of mutual advantage. He thought it unlikely that the Allies would countenance an extension of privileges for Alsace-Lorraine, and he deemed it poor tactics, in any case, to connect this issue to the Dawes Plan and to threaten the Germans in London. In Seydoux's view, France had more to gain from low-key, bilateral negotiations for a far-reaching, albeit provisional, trade agreement. In such an arrangement, he was prepared to grant the Reich substantial access to the French market—though not fully reciprocal treatment—in return for the preservation of French trading privileges. Seydoux took encouragement from Stresemann's spontaneous affirmation to the French chargé in Berlin on 22 July that Germany was ready to negotiate and did not intend to break existing commercial links when it recovered tariff sovereignty in 1925.[244] During the next two weeks, however, Seydoux found himself busy trying to hold the fractious French delegation in London together, and in the meantime, his assistants in the commercial division of the Quai d'Orsay failed to agree with their confreres at the Commerce Ministry on a coherent response to Stresemann's initiative. Robert Pinot of the Comité des Forges concluded after a long talk with Serruys on 1 August that the government was still "rather at a loss" for an economic program.[245]

The French business press continued to complain that the delegation in London seemed preoccupied with political concerns to the exclusion of economic needs.[246] But in fact the fault lay partially with heavy industry itself. Unable to decide on priorities, business leaders did not furnish the government with much guidance. "We must put on a jaunty air and not act the crybaby in order to obtain continued free entry of goods into Germany," Camille Cavallier of Pont-à-Mousson declared at a meeting of the steelmakers' executive committee on 24 July.[247] But how could the French strike a pose of indifference that ran counter to well-established economic facts? Pinot was none too specific when he conveyed the metallurgists' views to Serruys one week later. If the French government admitted that the very existence of the nation's steel industry depended on duty-free rights for Lorraine and Saar products, he advised, it would simply tempt the Germans to cut off these privileges.

244. St.-Quentin tel. no. 599–600, 22 July 1924, copy in F^{12}/8864.

245. Robert Pinot to Camille Cavallier, 2 August 1924, PAM/7224.

246. *La Journée industrielle*, 1–15 August 1924.

247. Comité des Forges–Commission de Direction, compte rendu sommaire, 24 July 1924, PAM/7245.

If the negotiators in London, on the other hand, gave the impression that French mills could keep operating regardless, then the Germans would become "much easier to handle."[248]

Pinot's homilies on German psychology betrayed the absence of a concrete plan on which the Comité des Forges could unite. There was no getting around the fact that French metallurgy found itself caught in a vise. The Wendel interests and other mills in Lorraine desperately needed a duty-free quota in order to sell their semiproducts in the "natural" market for these goods in south Germany. The Germans possessed no economic incentive to grant this concession unless the French offered the "minimum tariff" on German specialty steels, machine tools, and appliances. But without the protection of a prohibitive tariff, the older, high-cost mills and manufacturing plants on the northern littoral and in the center of France could not compete with German enterprises even on the home market.[249] All French steelmakers operated so close to the margin, moreover, that their conflicting interests could not easily be reconciled; when Pinot, for example, explored the possibility of making Saar steel more competitive on German markets by artificially reducing railway freight rates from Saarbrücken to the ports of Antwerp, Dunkirk, or Strasbourg, he encountered fierce opposition from Lorraine smelters who evidently preferred to see the Saar escape from the French economic orbit entirely than to risk increased competition for their own production.[250]

Most metallurgists seemed to agree, however, that the essential question in the future would not be availability of coke, but its price. Though as eager as ever to obtain full or partial ownership of Ruhr mines, they thought it a macabre joke, as Cavallier put it, to "beg the Germans on bended knee" to enter into a long-term contract for the supply of a commodity that would soon be in surplus. To compete on world markets French steelmakers needed cheap coke. A commercial agreement stipulating delivery at a "domestic price" set by German official bodies would provide no guarantee of this. German coal and steel enterprises had largely integrated their operations. Hence the real cost of coke in the productive process might have nothing to do with the administratively determined "domestic price," which could be manipulated as needed with the flick of an accountant's pen. French steelmakers trusted nobody in this matter. They suspected the Germans of being such "cheats and rascals" that they might gang up with French coal producers to raise

248. Pinot to Cavallier, 2 August 1924, PAM/7224.

249. For clear evidence of the split in the steelmakers' ranks, see Comité des Forges–Commission de Direction, "Tarif franco-allemand," 3 September 1924; "Accords franco-allemands: Entrevue du Comité des Forges avec M. Serruys," 21 October 1924; A. Dreux to Camille Cavallier, 24 October, and Cavallier to Dreux, 29 October 1924, all in PAM/7230.

250. Pinot to Cavallier, 2 August 1924, PAM/7224; Cavallier to Pinot, 3 and 5 August 1924, PAM/7245; "Réunion du Comité des Forges," 15 September 1924, PAM/7245.

prices. Their own government, they feared, had ulterior motives in advocating a coke consumers' syndicate under its auspices; the bureaucrats in Paris might well fix prices in such a way as to sacrifice the interests of industry in order to maximize government revenue on reparations account. Finally, the steel companies—correctly—were suspicious of each other: the Wendel firm and others that owned coal properties across the Rhine were already scrambling to assure their own supplies without worrying about the needs of other French mills.[251]

Given the complex difficulties facing their industry, it is strange that French metallurgists made so little effort to explain the issues on a technical level and to suggest possible courses of action to the bureaucracy in Paris. Among themselves, the steelmakers flayed the Herriot government unmercifully for its "absolute incomprehension of all economic problems."[252] Yet they left that government virtually without guidance from the private sector at a time when negotiations in London would decisively affect the nation's industrial future. Serruys sharply reproached the Comité des Forges for refusing to give a lead. He pointed out that German businessmen, instead of "crying in their beer," had thronged the lobbies of London hotels since late July, their dossiers fully prepared. French industrialists, by contrast, had for political reasons "treated the Herriot ministry like a plague-bearer, giving it the cold shoulder, reviling it, abandoning it thus to contend with the English Labourites whom British banking and industry have known exactly how to surround and guide."[253] The steel executives replied, however, that they did not wish to offer advice which leaders of the Cartel des Gauches had not solicited. "Going to London," Cavallier shot back, "is not like taking a walk in the Bois de Boulogne."[254]

No doubt the metallurgists remained inactive partially because of an inability to surmount division within their own ranks. But their reticence can be traced back to a traumatic experience in 1919. Socialist critics had accused them of pulling strings to prevent wartime aerial bombardment of their mills when these properties fell under enemy occupation and thereby of sacrificing the nation's interests to private greed. Edouard Barthe and Fernand Engerand, the Socialist deputies who had led the attack, never adduced proof for these charges, but their claims found an echo nevertheless in the left-wing press for years thereafter.[255] The

251. On this involved question, see Camille Cavallier to Pinot, 16 September 1924, PAM/7224; earlier drafts with additional detail in PAM/7245; Marcel Paul to Camille Cavallier, 25 August 1924, PAM/7224; Camille Cavallier to Marcel Paul and Henri Cavallier, 15 September 1924, PAM/7245; and "Réunion du 25 septembre [1924] au Comité des Forges: Accords de Londres," PAM/7230.

252. See, e.g., Camille Cavallier to Emile Henry, 16 August 1924, PAM/7266.

253. Morin to Camille Cavallier and Marcel Paul, 13 August 1924, PAM/7230.

254. Camille Cavallier to Emile Henry, 16 August 1924, PAM/7266; see also Emile Henry to Morin, 16 August 1924, PAM/7230.

255. See, e.g., E. Beau de Loménie, *Les Responsabilités des dynasties bourgeoises sous la Troisième République*, 4 vols. (Paris, 1943–63), 3:69–72.

steelmakers were ever apprehensive lest the "spectre of Barthe" rise again, and this fear, as President Alexandre Dreux of the Aciéries de Longwy noted, so "intimidated" the members of the Comité des Forges that they hesitated to wield their influence even when to do so seemed quite legitimate.[256]

Whatever the reasons, French metallurgists, in contrast to their German counterparts, failed to play an active role in determining national economic policy. Indeed, the whole issue remained very much up in the air until the French delegation in London rushed home on 9 August for the Elysée cabinet meeting. Clémentel and Raynaldy then belatedly reached agreement on the outlines of an economic program, though they continued to haggle about the details by cable even while negotiations with the Germans went forward. Since the anticlerical Cartel des Gauches had already made itself unpopular in Alsace-Lorraine by announcing its intention to enforce rigid separation of church and state there, Clémentel thought it politically essential to mount a vigorous defense of the recovered provinces' economic interests.[257] He consequently embraced Serruys's suggestion of seeking to extend the duty-free quota. On the whole, however, the strategy chosen marked a clear victory for the views of Jacques Seydoux.[258]

Back in London on 11 August, Clémentel and Seydoux sketched out for Stresemann what they billed as a comprehensive plan for economic collaboration between the two nations. France sought nothing less, Seydoux asserted, than "the restoration of prewar relations of an industrial nature between France and Germany and in particular between Alsace-Lorraine and the Ruhr region." The French proposed that negotiations for a permanent trade treaty begin in Paris in October. They asked the Germans to extend most-favored-nation privileges, initially for six additional months, if the two sides had not reached final agreement when current arrangements expired in January 1925. As compensation, France would accord the Reich those trade advantages permitted by present legislation—a conspicuously obscure formulation that left unclear how far Paris would actually lower tariff barriers against German manufactures. For products from Alsace-Lorraine and the Saar, Clémentel requested prolongation of duty-free export privileges for three years, ostensibly on the ground that the German inflation had limited

256. Dreux to Camille Cavallier, 30 March 1925, PAM/7245. See also Cavallier's similar analysis: "We endeavor to be spoken of as if we were Caesar's wife," in Cavallier to Pinot, 16 December 1924, PAM/7245.

257. On the startling upsurge in regional feeling occasioned by the Cartel's decision to enforce the 1905 French religious and public school legislation in Alsace-Lorraine, see Crewe to MacDonald no. 2242, 13 October 1924, F.O. 371/10534: W 8907/115/17; brief discussion also in Edouard Bonnefous, *Histoire politique de la Troisième République*, vol. 4, *Cartel des gauches et union nationale, 1924–1929* (Paris, 1960), pp. 40–45, 322–29.

258. See Serruys's expression of dissatisfaction and imprecations against "this devilish Seydoux and his friends the Wendels" in Morin to Camille Cavallier and Marcel Paul, 13 August 1924, PAM/7230.

the recovered provinces' access to the German market during the earlier period for which provision had been made in the Versailles treaty. Finally, Seydoux trundled out a circumspect version of the program for interpenetration of French and German metallurgy in which he and the Comité des Forges had tried to interest the German steel industry some months earlier. The two governments, he proposed, should intervene directly to bring about the conclusion of long-term private contracts providing for the exchange of iron ore and semiproducts for coal and coke. The governments would also facilitate French industry's acquisition of shares in certain German coal mines.[259]

Clémentel and Seydoux did not go so far as to tie this program explicitly to the timetable for evacuation of the Ruhr. They alluded rather by indirection to the favorable effects that an economic settlement would produce on the negotiations over military withdrawal. But it was late in the game to begin considering economic and industrial issues of such scope and complexity in connection with the frenetic last-minute bargaining over an evacuation date. Louis Loucheur, leader of the Chamber "swing" group, on whose support Herriot had to rely to maintain his majority, had now arrived in London, and he advocated caution. Since Loucheur had long championed industrial collaboration with Germany, his tactical judgment could not be ignored. He advised the finance minister to concentrate his immediate efforts on one point only: extension of the duty-free quota for Alsace-Lorraine and the Saar.[260] From Paris, Raynaldy also expressed his misgivings in a steady stream of cables. The commerce minister worried lest the unwary Clémentel embark half-prepared on negotiations that would lead him to grant Germany the minimum duty on manufactured goods—thus breaching the tariff wall that protected less efficient French industries—in return for short-term and ultimately illusory benefits for Alsace-Lorraine.[261]

In the meantime, the Germans managed to alarm the other Allies over the French demands. MacDonald remarked with notable asperity that he could not see what legitimate connection a commercial agreement could have with the Dawes Plan. Snowden called the proposed terms for the trade treaty "outrageous" and sounded the tocsin for British industry.[262] Theunis protested discreetly to Stresemann against special

259. Stresemann-Clémentel meeting, 11 August 1924, G.F.M. L177/4079/L051707–710; see also written formulation of French demands, as passed on by German economics expert Karl Ritter to the British, in H. C. F. Finlayson memorandum, 14 August 1924, F.O. 371/9857: C 13023/G.

260. Loucheur notation on discussion with Clémentel, 11 August 1924, Folder 6, Box 7, Loucheur Papers.

261. Raynaldy to Clémentel tel. nos. 708–10, 711–15, 12 August 1924, F[12]/8864.

262. Meeting between MacDonald and German delegates, 12 August 1924, BA, R 43 I/268/88–89; Snowden comments to British Empire Delegation, 92nd Conference, 15 August 1924, CAB 29/105. See also Snowden's postconference warning to the textile and iron trades about the "danger from the proposed commercial treaty," in the London *Evening Standard*, 20 August 1924, cited in F.O. 371/9864: C 13423/11642/18.

advantages for France and expressed the wish that the Germans "not think too late about Belgium" when they recast their tariff structure.[263] Theunis and Hymans also confronted Herriot directly, telling him that France could not expect Belgian support in political matters while seeking economic concessions whose cost might fall indirectly on the Belgian textile and steel industries.[264]

Faced with doubts at home and disapproval from the Allies, Herriot and Clémentel abruptly changed tack. They decided not to press for economic compensation in direct exchange for military evacuation. At the first full-dress meeting between French and German trade specialists on the evening of 12 August, Clémentel seemed content to indicate the general direction of his thinking. He dwelt on the difficulties of Alsace-Lorraine's economy "as if he were talking to the presidents of the French Chambers of Commerce," but State Secretary Ernst Trendelenburg, the German spokesman, countered with a no less heartrending description of the dire predicament of business in his country. With justifiable confidence in the superior strength of Ruhr industry, the Germans insisted that any metallurgical agreement would have to be arranged "on a purely private economic basis with full reciprocal equality of rights."[265] To the German negotiators' astonishment and delight, the meeting ended on a note of amiable inconclusiveness. "Our men," the delegation reported to Berlin, "were able to keep our written formulation . . . of economically tolerable compromise suggestions in their pockets."[266]

Once the Germans realized that the French did not intend to make economic concessions a formal condition of military evacuation, they evaded further discussion of the issue. Up to the final day of the conference, Clémentel continued to hint that the French might examine the question of the evacuation date in a new light if the Germans spontaneously came forward with an offer in the commercial sphere. But the German delegates were not tempted. Though they knew that they could garner laurels in domestic politics by advancing the evacuation timetable, they became increasingly convinced that they should not pay "too dear a price."[267]

Thus economic questions imperceptibly faded out of the parleys in London. Both general trade negotiations and discussions among metal-

263. Stresemann tel., 12 August 1924, BA, R 43 I/266/157–161.

264. *Le Petit Parisien* and *La Journée industrielle*, 13 August 1924, cited in BA, R 43 I/498/172–177; Loucheur notation of 12 August 1924, Folder 6, Box 7, Loucheur Papers.

265. Trendelenburg memorandum, 12 August 1924, G.F.M. L177/4079/L051690–696. On Herriot's change in position, see also Carl von Schubert's report to the British: Hankey note no. 8 for Lampson, 13 August 1924, F.O. 371/9857: C 13130/11495/18.

266. Franz Bracht to Franz Kempner [ministerial director in the Reich Chancellery], 13 August 1924, BA, R 43 I/266/348–350.

267. Bracht to Kempner, 15 August 1924, BA, R 43 I/498/137–138; Minutes of Luther's meeting with Clémentel and Serruys, 16 August 1924, BA, R 43 I/268/18–19.

lurgists would begin in Paris in the autumn, but the road to agreement would prove long and tortuous. Since the French had failed to arrange a durable economic settlement while they still controlled the Ruhr, the Germans would be able to mark time in the commercial talks until after the establishment of a new political equilibrium in Europe.

The treaties initialed at Locarno in October 1925 possessed a symbolic importance that far transcended the specific provisions of the nonaggression and arbitration pacts relating to the Reich's frontiers. It is a commonplace to say that they marked Germany's restoration to political equality among the great powers and that they prepared the way for evacuation of Allied troops from Cologne and for Germany's admission to the League of Nations. No less important, however, was their function as a prelude to an economic understanding that accurately reflected the real balance of industrial power among the erstwhile wartime combatants. European rail producers (including the English) reached a preliminary compact in March 1926; continental metallurgists settled on terms for an international cartel to regulate steel production in September of the same year; and the French and Germans finally signed a definitive customs agreement in August 1927.[268] Taken together, these complex arrangements would assure the viability of French metallurgy and provide a sufficient measure of tariff protection for French business as a whole to operate profitably—at least until the depression upset all assumptions in the industrial world. But at the same time these accords would clearly confirm that Germany, surmounting the temporary restrictions that the Versailles treaty had imposed on its trade and the permanent loss of its Lorraine iron and Silesian coal, had succeeded in regaining industrial hegemony in Europe.

Closing the Ring

To those who followed events through the newspapers, the London Conference appeared in danger of breakdown throughout its final week over the exact date of military evacuation. Actually, the protagonists were never so far apart as the general public was led to believe. Officially, the Germans took the position that all foreign troops had to leave the Ruhr, as well as the Cologne zone, by January 1925 at the latest.[269] State Secretary von Maltzan told the French ambassador in

268. For the tariff negotiations, see Handakten Karl Ritter, G.F.M. L177/4079–4081, and Ministère du Commerce et de l'Industrie, F[12]/8862–8865; for documentation on the metallurgical agreements, see G.F.M. L1489/5352; GHH 400101222/0, 2, 7; GHH 40000090, GHH 40000092; BA, R 13 I/255, 261–62, 270; PAM/7230, 7245, 19061. The brief published accounts of the steel negotiations emphasize technical rather than political considerations: see, e.g., Ervin Hexner, *The International Steel Cartel* (Chapel Hill, N.C., 1943), pp. 65–79; and J. C. Carr and W. Taplin, *A History of the British Steel Industry* (Cambridge, Mass., 1962), pp. 406–28.

269. "Stand der Verhandlungen . . . bei Eintreffen der deutschen Delegation," 5 August 1924, G.F.M. 3398/1736/D740204–205.

Berlin, however, that it might be possible for France to keep some troops on the border until April 1925 in order to "save face"; among themselves the German ministers commonly talked in terms of an April deadline.[270]

When Herriot met with Stresemann again on 11 August, after returning from Paris, he offered evacuation within a year after the Dawes Plan became operative. Without reticence Herriot disclosed to the German foreign minister his troubles with Doumergue, Nollet, and Foch.[271] Personally he wished to pull out the troops as soon as possible, the French premier reiterated, but he could not oppose President Doumergue openly, and he had to take account of sentiment within his own party. Stresemann was emboldened to hope that Herriot might further reduce the delay. He emphasized how important it was to give some immediate satisfaction to German public opinion through a concrete step toward partial evacuation, and the French premier agreed to work out a plan for withdrawal by stages.[272]

German efforts to extract an additional concession proceeded simultaneously by direct discussion with the French and Belgians and through an attempt to secure British intercession. The direct approach did not prove fruitful. Herriot was disconcerted on the evening of 12 August by a conversation with Louis Loucheur, leader of the *Gauche radicale*. Loucheur sharply criticized a method of negotiation that resulted in settlement exclusively of those issues upon which France was obliged to make sacrifices, while all other questions—security, interallied debts, and commercial accords—were postponed for later consideration.[273] Contrary to what Herriot intimated to the Germans, Loucheur did not explicitly threaten to withdraw the support of his parliamentary group. But the premier was made to feel that he would find his position in jeopardy if he yielded anything more.

Marathon discussions among the French, Belgian, and German delegations on 13 August failed to resolve the dispute. Recalling that he had originally promised not to discuss the Ruhr evacuation at all in London, Herriot pointed out that he was already "in the position of a head of

270. Maltzan to Stresemann, 12 August 1924, G.F.M. 3398/1737/D740365–366; "Ministerrat," 14 August 1924, BA, R 43 I/265/305–311.

271. When the French translation of Stresemann's diaries appeared in 1932, Herriot was embarrassed by the revelation that he had denounced his colleagues. He composed an angry denial (see *L'Ere nouvelle*, 3 March 1932) and subsequently invented the story that he had not agreed to meet Stresemann, whose sincerity he distrusted, but only Chancellor Marx, who as a Rhinelander rated as a more sympathetic personality. Stresemann allegedly appeared unexpectedly at the rendezvous and cynically told Herriot that he was wasting his time trying to get along with the English and should ally himself with the Germans instead. At this point Herriot claims to have cut short the interview and gone to warn MacDonald. Despite its implausibility, some historians have accepted this account (see Herriot's lecture in *Les Annales conférencia*, 15 January 1950, pp. 7–9; *Jadis*, 2:166–67; and Soulié, *La Vie politique d'Edouard Herriot*, p. 176).

272. Stresemann tel., 13 August 1924, BA, R 43 I/266/151–156.

273. Loucheur notation in Folder 6, Box 7, Loucheur Papers; also Louis Loucheur, *Carnets secrets, 1908–1932*, ed. Jacques de Launay (Brussels and Paris, 1962), pp. 153–54.

government who had deceived his parliament." Thus, while two days earlier he had agreed to consider gradual evacuation, he now declared that he could "not go back a millimeter."[274] This sudden display of militance did not intimidate the Germans, but on the same day Ambassador Kellogg became convinced that Herriot was really bound to a one-year delay. A message from Secretary Hughes in Berlin had led Kellogg to believe that the Germans would probably also settle for the one-year limit if pushed to the wall. At the 13 August meeting of Allied heads of delegation, therefore, he endorsed this period for troop withdrawals as a realistic compromise.[275] Though MacDonald initially reacted with dismay, within the next twenty-four hours he too reluctantly came around to the view that this timetable probably represented the utmost concession that Herriot could make in light of his parliamentary circumstances.[276]

The Germans made no attempt to conceal their fury. "All this talk about securing the peace of Europe and the pacification of the world has become pure swindle," sputtered economics expert Karl Ritter to a British staff assistant.[277] Another German spokesman told the London *Evening Standard* that not only Kellogg, but MacDonald as well, had "gone into the French trenches." Kellogg, indignantly protesting that he had not taken sides and had in fact done his best to move the French to every feasible concession, acted to block transmission of the story by the American wire services. And MacDonald, who particularly prized his image as an impartial mediator, dispatched Hankey to remonstrate with Marx against this "outrageous travesty of the truth."[278]

At least in the case of MacDonald, it is clear that the charge fell wide of the mark. Throughout the final week of negotiations the British prime minister worked in coordination with the German delegates. He had assured them on 10 August that he could not take a public position on the evacuation date because he wished to preserve his option to "function as an arbitrator," but that he would do all he could to induce Herriot to shorten the delay.[279] Two days later, he also expressed his concern to settle the matter of the Cologne zone "in close understanding with the German government." Great Britain, he affirmed, stood by the "letter of

274. Record of German-French-Belgian discussions in "Tagebuch," BA, R 43 I/268/90–119; also Marx to Kempner, 13 and 14 August 1924, G.F.M. 3398/1737/D740388–393; Stresemann tel., 15 August 1924, G.F.M. 3398/1737/D740440–446.

275. Hughes to Kellogg, 4 August 1924, U.S. 462.00R 296/503; Bryn-Jones, *Kellogg*, p. 151; MacDonald's report to Stresemann, 13 August 1924, BA, R 43 I/268/120.

276. See the retrospective explanation in Hankey to Lampson, note no. 11, 16 August 1924, F.O. 371/9858: C 13256/11495/18.

277. Finlayson to Lampson, 14 August 1924, F.O. 371/9858: C 13170/11495/18.

278. London *Evening Standard*, 14 August 1924, quoted and commented on in Frank B. Kellogg to Alanson B. Houghton, 18 August 1924, copies in Box 8, Kellogg Papers and in Houghton Papers; British government response in Hankey to Lampson, 16 August 1924, F.O. 371/9858: C 13256/11495/18.

279. Marx-MacDonald meeting, 10 August 1924, BA, R 43 I/268/77–79.

the Versailles treaty" and would not occupy "a foot of German territory" any longer than necessary. He had to warn, however, that great difficulties over German disarmament lay ahead and that, unless things could be quietly arranged, he might find himself "in a hopeless fix" when the Allies met the following December to consider withdrawal from the Cologne zone.[280]

Largely by his own exercise of vigilance, MacDonald succeeded in preventing the untimely intrusion of the disarmament question in the final negotiations over the Ruhr. During the conference the German government had tried to forestall any untoward incident that might call attention to illegal rearmament. When Chancellor Marx, for example, was alerted to plans for a parade of Prussian military police on 10 August, he immediately directed that the men leave their rifles at home and that photographers be kept away from the line of march through the Berlin Lustgarten.[281] Similarly, before leaving for London, Marx and Stresemann had summoned Lieutenant-General Strempel, Reichswehr liaison officer with the military control commission, and given him strict orders to avoid controversy until the reparations settlement was complete.[282] But Strempel, a blunt-spoken officer of the old school, understood the details of his special assignment better than he did the exigencies of diplomacy. When the control commission's inspection of military installations in Stuttgart and Königsberg resulted in some minor disputes, Strempel wrote a letter to the commission president, the French general Walch, telling him exactly what the Reichswehr thought of the commission and all of its activities. *L'Echo de Paris*, always on the alert for evidence to support its view that Herriot's policy was leading to disaster, discovered that something was brewing. A major scandal might have broken had not the English representative on the control commission, General Arthur G. Wauchope—an officer carefully selected for his ability to deal with such emergencies—taken energetic steps to hush things up.[283]

MacDonald assured German leaders that Wauchope's mission was "to liquidate the control completely as soon as possible." Nevertheless, he could not very well avoid delivering a protest note to the German delegation in which he alluded to the bearing of the military control controversy on the reparations settlement. Privately, he appealed to Chancellor Marx to replace Strempel with a smoother diplomat. Otherwise, MacDonald observed, his hand might be forced when the time

280. MacDonald meeting with Marx, Stresemann, and Luther, 12 August 1924, BA, R 43 I/268/80–89.

281. See the Marx-Kempner exchange of cables in G.F.M. 3398/1736/D740270–284.

282. Marx to Reich President Friedrich Ebert, 13 August 1924, BA, R 43 I/266/209–212.

283. Account by Reich Chancellery officials in BA, R 43 I/498/81, 180–183; MacDonald's 13 August statement on the subject, R 43 I/268/83–87; *L'Echo de Paris*, 10 August 1924. On Wauchope's personal qualities see Alanson B. Houghton Diary, 19 May 1924, Houghton Papers.

came to consider withdrawal from the Cologne zone, and this, for reasons of geography, would also necessitate a reassessment of the Ruhr evacuation date.[284]

Reviewing the prospect on the evening of 13 August, the German delegation deemed Herriot's proposal for a one-year delay unacceptable in its present form. But it determined not to break off negotiations, nor to allow the conference to run aground because of the remaining differences over the timing of withdrawal.[285] After midnight, Stresemann conferred again with MacDonald, who counseled the Germans "to hold firm whatever happens" while he made one last attempt to obtain a further concession from Herriot.[286] Marx, meanwhile, cabled Reich President Ebert suggesting that the cabinet supersede General Strempel in order to furnish the British prime minister with "clear proof" of their desire to cooperate.[287]

The members of the German cabinet, roused from their beds for a predawn meeting on 14 August, found it difficult to decide on the best way to proceed. They quickly consented to sacrifice Strempel; this simple personnel change, they hoped, would head off any last-minute endeavor by France to connect military control with other pending issues. But the ministers in Berlin did not seem to grasp what had become clear to their colleagues in London: that the French had abandoned their attempt to extract specific economic advantages in return for evacuation.

One group, led by Vice Chancellor Jarres and Economics Minister Hamm, reasoned that continued occupation of the Ruhr "made no sense" unless the French intended somehow to employ their troops to exert pressure in the economic field. Though they could not divine what sinister scheme the French might have in mind, Jarres and Hamm thought it only prudent for the cabinet to forestall it by offering limited economic concessions immediately in exchange for earlier evacuation. Another group, which rallied behind Labor Minister Brauns, judged it preferable to accept the one-year delay after Marx and Stresemann had exhausted their efforts to secure British and American mediation. Yet ultimately both factions accepted President Ebert's view that they could not usefully make tactical suggestions from Berlin. Officials at the Wilhelmstrasse therefore prepared two telegrams. The first, designed to be shown to the Allies, categorically rejected Herriot's terms for settlement. The second cable, composed for the guidance of the delegation, called only for determination of some firm date for complete withdrawal of foreign troops, an alleviation of occupation methods, and for immediate evacuation of one part of the Ruhr if possible. In essence, it gave

284. "Tagebuch" for 12, 13, and 15 August 1924, BA, R 43 I/268/13–15, 83–87; Bracht to Kempner, 14 August 1924, G.F.M. 3398/1737/D740394.

285. Marx tel., 13 August 1924, BA, R 43 I/266/164.

286. Stresemann-MacDonald meeting, 13 August 1924, BA, R 43 I/268/120–121.

287. Marx to Ebert, 13 August 1924, BA, R 43 I/266/209–212.

representatives of the Reich in London authorization to do as they thought best.[288]

Playing their hand carefully, the German delegates at the conference gave no sign of their freedom to maneuver as the diplomatic poker game reached its climax on 14 August. At an early morning meeting, MacDonald and Kellogg finally persuaded Herriot to make a gesture of goodwill by secretly promising to withdraw from the Dortmund region after ratification of the London accords. Herriot also agreed to begin counting his "year" forthwith, so that the troops would actually withdraw ten months after the Dawes Plan began to function. Recognizing that Herriot could be pushed no farther, MacDonald now joined Kellogg in imploring the Germans to accept the bargain. "The present settlement doesn't please me either," he confided. "But this conference must be a success, if it is to usher in a new era."[289]

The German delegates waged fierce resistance. Speaking with deep emotion, they invoked the opposition of their nation's press and the problematic response of the Reichstag. At length, they resorted to an elaborate bluff—a plan to send Luther back to "consult" the cabinet in Berlin.[290] Their timing proved perfect: Luther's plane was ready to warm up at the aerodrome when his colleagues telephoned to say that he did not have to fly after all.[291] At a reception for delegates in the garden behind No. 10 Downing Street, the announcement of Luther's imminent departure had brought matters to a head. The French began to talk openly of withdrawal from Dortmund. MacDonald in a state of fury insisted that the interruption of negotiations would wreck the whole conference (as well as his vacation plans) and that a settlement must be reached somehow without further ado. The Germans, at last convinced that Herriot had made his "uttermost concession" and that the patience of other statesmen was reaching an end, agreed to send a cable putting the case for compromise to their colleagues in Berlin.[292]

Marx and Stresemann urged the cabinet to accept the bargain on grounds that reveal in striking fashion the true nature of German calculations. If the conference collapsed, negotiations would not resume for months, and the two leaders doubted whether the German populace, es-

288. "Niederschrift über den Ministerrat in der Reichskanzlei," 14 August 1924, BA, R 43 I/265/305–311; Maltzan and Köpke to Schubert, 14 August 1924, G.F.M. 3398/1737/D740412–414; Jarres to Marx, 14 August 1924, G.F.M. 3398/1737/D740401.

289. Meeting between MacDonald, Kellogg, and the German delegates, 14 August 1924, BA, R 43 I/268/123–128.

290. See the transcripts of various meetings in BA, R 43 I/268/129–133; also Stresemann's account composed on 15 August 1924, G.F.M. 3398/1737/D740440–446.

291. Luther, *Politiker ohne Partei*, p. 293.

292. Memorandum on the garden party discussions, 14 August 1924, BA, R 43 I/268/134–137; Stresemann tel., 15 August 1924, G.F.M. 3398/1737/D740440–446; also Hankey to Lampson, note no. 9, 14 August 1924, F.O. 371/9857: C 13131/11495/18. Published descriptions of this occasion include Stresemann, *Vermächtnis*, 1:495–96; Luther, *Politiker ohne Partei*, p. 293; Schmidt, *Statist auf diplomatischer Bühne*, p. 62.

pecially in the occupied areas, could bear the strain either economically or politically. They also feared that refusal would cause an uproar in the world press. Marx emphasized MacDonald's "barely disguised threats" to connect the question of the Cologne zone with illegal rearmament, and warned: "in this question world opinion can certainly be stirred up against us." Finally, evaluating the obligations entailed by acceptance, the Reich Chancellor noted "the possibility that remains open of putting an end to the essential consequences of the Dawes Report, if necessary through autonomous German action."[293]

The cabinet found these arguments compelling. The strongly nationalistic Jarres considered the outcome of the deliberations in London "favorable beyond expectation." Hamm termed the dissociation of trade and economic matters from the issue of evacuation "a vital alleviation."[294] Assembled Reichstag party leaders as well as the cabinet ministers recognized that once the French dropped their economic demands, the precise evacuation date became "solely . . . a question of prestige."[295] The Nationalist leader Hoetzsch still claimed to be dissatisfied, but privately even he distinguished between the railroad reorganization law, for which some of his party would have to vote to make up the two-thirds Reichstag majority, and the other agreements.[296] The cabinet drew up a long list of subsidiary demands, chief among them a request for assurances about the occupying forces' future administrative practices in the Ruhr and Rhineland, and in London Stresemann continued to press these claims assiduously. But the conference had surmounted its greatest crisis successfully.[297]

Ironically, the gravest threat on 14 August had come—unbeknown to many of the conferees—not from the Germans, upon whom all attention had focused, but from within MacDonald's own delegation. Montagu Norman had furnished Snowden with a copy of the letter setting forth the bankers' requirements for a loan that Lamont had drawn up some days earlier for Theunis and Clémentel. Both Norman and Snowden were furious that MacDonald, in pursuit of a political compromise that all could accept, had given the bankers such indifferent support.[298] Neither Snowden nor his acolytes in Treasury chambers had moderated their original antipathy to the general assumptions governing the Dawes Report; Niemeyer typically disparaged it behind closed doors as the

293. Marx tels., 14 August 1924, BA, R 43 I/266/175, 180.

294. "Niederschrift über den Ministerrat," 15 August 1924, BA, R 43 I/265/358–360.

295. "Niederschrift über die Besprechung mit den Parteiführern," 15 August 1924, BA, R 43 I/265/305–311.

296. Kempner to Stresemann, 14 and 15 August 1924, G.F.M. 3398/1737/D740424–430.

297. Stresemann-MacDonald meeting, 15 August 1924, BA, R 43 I/268/14–16; Stresemann tel., 16 August 1924, G.F.M. 3398/1737/D740463–467.

298. Montagu Norman memorandum, 13 August, Charles Whigham to Lamont, 13 August, and Norman to Lamont, 16 August 1924, all in TWL 177/1.

Americans' "beastly plan."[299] In addition to fundamental objections concerning the size of the reparations burden imposed on Germany, the chancellor of the exchequer considered many specific features of the settlement taking shape in London unfortunate. He thought that perpetuation of reparations in kind might have a detrimental effect on continental markets for the slumping British coal industry. He suspected that French industrialists, under cover of the continued military occupation, would pursue their designs on German business and thereby create a serious commercial threat to the British iron and textile trades. He claimed to believe that the French did not really accept the Dawes Plan and that they might well renege on their promise to withdraw their troops after a year had elapsed. He also, no doubt, felt personally aggrieved at his exclusion from the meetings where the heads of delegation had transacted the most important business of the conference. Above all else, Snowden exuded moral outrage at the very idea that his Labour party comrades could betray their principles by allowing the Ruhr occupation—"sign and symbol of the old and vicious policy," as he later described it to the *Manchester Guardian*—to persist for a single day after the Dawes Plan became operative.[300]

Through the small hours of the morning on 14 August Snowden argued bitterly with MacDonald. At 7 A.M., the prime minister, haggard from lack of sleep and very much frightened, summoned Kellogg and expressed the foreboding that "the whole conference was going to blow up." Snowden seemed so adamantly opposed to the one-year delay that MacDonald feared he would use Lamont's letter to Theunis as ammunition for a public speech against the settlement. There were but hours to spare before the decisive confrontation between the French and Germans would take place. Both Morgan and Lamont had left London by this time, so MacDonald and Kellogg had to carry on, feigning confidence that the bankers would float a loan if a political agreement were attained, while the American Embassy staff sought frantically to locate Lamont in Paris.[301]

The Morgan partners had not yet overcome their doubts whether enough security existed to float the loan—they ultimately agreed to undertake the task only after several weeks' further reflection[302]—but

299. Niemeyer to Basil Kemball Cook [assistant British delegate, Reparation Commission], 20 August 1924, F.O. 371/9753: C 13495/70/18.

300. See Snowden's remarks to the British Empire Delegation, 92nd Conference, 15 August 1924, CAB 29/105; also his postconference newspaper interviews: *Manchester Guardian*, 19 August, London *Evening Standard*, 20 August, *Daily Express*, 22 August 1924, cited respectively in F.O. 371/9753: C 13495/70/18; F.O. 371/9864: C 13423/11642/18; F.O. 371/9858: C 13493/11495/18.

301. See MacDonald's and Kellogg's assurances to the Germans on the morning of 14 August 1924, cited in BA, R 43 I/268/123–128; also Kellogg to Hughes, 18 August, and Kellogg to Donald S. Culver, 19 September 1924, Box 8, Kellogg Papers.

302. For the final negotiations concerning the loan, see Stephen V. O. Clarke, *Central Bank Cooperation, 1924–31* (New York, 1967), pp. 53–56, 67–71; Clay, *Lord Norman*, pp. 215–

they did not wish to be accused of blocking a political settlement, whatever the reasons. Lamont, after talking to Kellogg by phone, sent Norman a stiff cable. He reminded the English banker that his letter to Theunis was "not an ultimatum" but only a private statement to Morgan clients of "points to be considered." Snowden, he insisted, had "no possible right" to make use of it.[303]

What Snowden had actually planned to do never became clear. Norman denied that the chancellor of the exchequer intended to publicize the letter and suggested that this idea had originated in the "fertile and rather dangerous mind of Logan."[304] At any rate, Snowden was obliged to proceed more circumspectly. On the evening of the crucial day, while the cabinet in Berlin was weighing the final terms of settlement, the Treasury chief penned a letter to MacDonald charging that "to countenance the French claim in any shape or form" would be "deliberate suicide" and that "no sane person would lend a penny to a country whose chief industrial area was occupied by foreign troops." For good measure he added an insinuation of political reprisal to come: "I am sure that if the British government supports Poincaré [*sic*] in this matter, it will not only destroy all chances of a European settlement but will ruin your government."[305]

The next morning Snowden continued to rage at an *in camera* session of British Empire delegates. If the French did not become "more reasonable," he declared, Britain might threaten to withhold its contribution to the Dawes loan, with the consequence that the loan would fail and the franc would collapse. But by this time the Germans had virtually agreed to the one-year evacuation delay, and even the Commonwealth representatives perceived that Snowden was simply playing to the grandstand.[306] In the end, the chancellor of the exchequer refrained from creating further impediments, and contented himself with a harmless denunciation of the settlement in the newspapers after the termination of the conference.

At the final moment the Germans managed to extract two additional concessions from Herriot. The last meetings between the French and German delegations were not without an element of pathos. The two

---

17. From a strictly banking point of view, the financiers' hesitations were justified. In 1933, J. P. Morgan revealed to a congressional committee that only two foreign loans issued by his firm had ever gone into default. These were the Dawes loan and its successor, the Young loan, which was arranged at the behest of the Allied governments to help Germany meet its obligations during the 1930 reparations crisis.

303. Lamont to Norman, 14 August, and Lamont to Kellogg, 14 August 1924, TWL 176/25.

304. Norman to Lamont, 14 August 1924, TWL 176/25; Norman to Lamont, 16 August 1924, TWL 177/1.

305. Snowden to MacDonald, 14 August 1924, cited in Snowden, *Autobiography*, 2:675–76.

306. British Empire Delegation, 92nd Conference, 15 August 1924, CAB 29/105.

sides seemed to be operating at cross-purposes, with Herriot seeking to enlarge on his hopes for mutual reconciliation and the Germans working tenaciously to nail down the French to precise commitments. Stresemann found the sessions taxing, since, as he put it, Herriot "incessantly made big speeches in which he talked of peace among mankind and a new era, while he designated all pertinent matters as technical questions which he had not yet studied."[307] The French premier at length agreed to the immediate evacuation of Ruhrort, apparently without realizing that this inland harbor city served as the focal point of transport and logistics in the Belgian occupation zone and that he had no right to end the "interallied" occupation there unilaterally. When the Belgians pointed this out, he had to retract the concession in embarrassment. Instead he widened the area from which French troops would withdraw forthwith in the Dortmund region and elsewhere, and gave final approval to evacuation of the three "sanctions cities"—Düsseldorf, Duisburg, and Ruhrort—at the same time as the rest of the Ruhr.[308]

The foregoing arrangements, in any case, represented mere detail. A skeleton force of French troops kept the tricolor waving in the Ruhr for the appointed year. But even where they remained, these troops played no further role in events. The Ruhr occupation was effectively over, and with its disappearance, the era in which France could lay claim to great power status also effectively came to an end.

307. Stresemann tel., 16 August 1924, G.F.M. 3398/1737/D740463–467.

308. Ibid.; also Stresemann memorandum, 18 August 1924, G.F.M. 3398/1737/D740484–489; "Tagebuch" for 15–16 August 1924, BA, R 43 I/268/16–19, 140–148. For the conflict over Ruhrort with the Belgians, see Colonel Alphonse-Joseph Georges, "Note sur l'évacuation de Ruhrort," and Herriot notation, 16 August 1924, Herriot Papers.

Chapter 9
Epilogue

The London Conference of 1924 radically transformed relations among the nations of Europe. The political distinctions between the victors and the vanquished in the First World War did not disappear at once. But the London Conference marked a decisive turning point, and the participants themselves recognized this clearly. Prime Minister MacDonald called attention to the wider significance of the proceedings at the final plenary session. "We are now offering the first really negotiated agreement since the war," he observed. ". . . This agreement may be regarded as the first Peace Treaty, because we sign it with a feeling that we have turned our backs on the terrible years of war and war mentality."[1]

The Treaty of Versailles had rested on very different premises. The authors of that treaty, whatever their ideological disagreements and tactical disputes, had clearly aimed to construct a territorial, economic, and legal framework that would perpetuate Allied predominance in the postwar world. They sought to prevent the Reich from ever achieving those immoderate annexationist goals which a wide spectrum of German leaders from Bethmann Hollweg to Ludendorff had enthusiastically endorsed and which—to judge from the valor of German armies in the face of adversity and the sacrifices stoically borne by civilians at home—the majority of the German people appeared ready to support. To contain German ambition had been the central purpose of the war; for the French, it would continue to be the central issue of peacetime diplomacy.

The events of 1914 had made it painfully evident, however, that the vitality of treaties depended on maintaining the configuration of national interests which attended their formulation. When the balance of power changed, treaties could become mere "scraps of paper." The United States, Great Britain, and France had together possessed sufficient strength to overwhelm the German armies and to dictate a peace settlement representing a compromise between their various interests and conceptions of justice. Once the United States failed to ratify the Versailles treaty, withdrew its military forces, and declined to play an active role in enforcing the arrangements made at the peace conference, the distribution of power within Europe shifted substantially.

1. *Proceedings of the London Reparation Conference*, 2 vols. (n.p., n.d.), 2:7–8, copy in P.R.O., CAB 29/103–4.

Great Britain continued to pay lip service to the preservation of the Entente. Yet as wartime sentiment faded and the particular circumstances that had cemented the bonds of alliance between Britain and France lost their force, Whitehall also reverted to traditional policy—seeking to promote equilibrium among the continental nations, so that it could husband its energies to defend the far-flung interests of the British Empire. In the early 1920s, moreover, some British statesmen tended to exaggerate France's momentary political and military strength. They correspondingly underestimated the rapidity with which German industrial power and demographic superiority would again find reflection in the diplomatic arena. Thus they miscalculated the true balance of power on the Continent. With rather more justification, British politicians and bureaucrats considered a prosperous central Europe indispensable for a revival of British trade. Increasingly, therefore, they came to regard as inimical to their own nation's interests those features of the 1919 settlement that they thought retarded German economic recovery or fostered financial instability in the Reich.

Of the major victorious powers, France alone remained committed to an integral defense of the European political structure established at Versailles. Yet France was no match for a resurgent Germany. Without assistance from its partners in the wartime coalition, it possessed neither the population, the resources, nor the reserves of determination necessary to prevent the Reich from subverting the peace settlement. Within Germany, monarchists and republicans, industrialists and socialists alike held the essential territorial and economic provisions of the treaty to be unjust. No matter what political and social forces prevailed on the German domestic scene, the Reich would accept the inferior status that the treaty assigned to it only under duress.

Notwithstanding the obstacles, France made a strenuous effort to maintain its hegemony by force in the first half-decade following the Paris Peace Conference. The reparations question on which controversy focused during these years involved more than a dispute over payment for rebuilding the devastated districts. In a wider sense it represented also a contest for dominance in the European economy, or more precisely a struggle over access to scarce capital and energy resources in a period of increasing competition and shrinking markets, when all economically advanced countries could not expect to resume the growth rates that had earlier been the norm.

In the generation before the war, Germany had rapidly pulled ahead of other European nations in industrial capacity. Its iron and steel production—the key to military power—quadrupled in less than two decades and by 1913 virtually equaled the combined output of the United Kingdom, France, Italy, Belgium, and Luxembourg.[2] The fundamental

2. See figures in Ingvar Svennilson, *Growth and Stagnation in the European Economy* (Geneva, 1954), pp. 257–63.

issue that French statesmen might have explicitly addressed after the war (though in fact they did so only obliquely) was this: having recovered the iron fields of Lorraine, secured control of the Saar, and won entitlement to capital, coal, and coke on reparations account, could France somehow make a comparable leap forward and develop an industrial infrastructure that would enable it to maintain permanently the diplomatic position ensured for the moment by treaty texts?

The British approached postwar problems from an entirely different direction. Despite declining relative productivity, Britain sought to cling to its earlier position as "workshop of the world." Revenue from reparations could not possibly compensate for the economic turmoil and consequent impediments to British trade that the French attempt to compel payment and the German policy of resistance created in central Europe. Hence Great Britain desired a reparations settlement that facilitated Germany's return to prosperity, cleared the way for adoption of a stable monetary standard by the major industrial nations, and thereby spurred demand for British goods.[3]

After exhausting every alternative means to secure German compliance with the London Schedule of Payments, Poincaré reluctantly ordered the occupation of the Ruhr in 1923. We have seen how the inability of the French to decide on distribution of the fiscal burden at home and to cope with the difficult but not necessarily unmanageable problems of domestic public finance undermined the success of the Ruhr occupation and, at a critical moment, fatefully weakened the nation's power to impose a satisfactory reparations settlement. France's failure to maintain the financial equilibrium necessary for an independent policy of treaty enforcement can be traced to a number of causes: widespread misunderstanding of economic phenomena among the elites; internecine rivalry that often paralyzed the bureaucracy; and ossification of a parliamentary structure that, however well it reflected the appealing values and virtues of late nineteenth-century provincial society, proved ill-adapted to solve the problems of an industrializing nation in an interdependent world economy. Above all, this failure stemmed from a mood of profound fatigue that pervaded every aspect of French public life despite the persistence of a relatively stable social structure.

Paradoxically, the reluctance of the French people to accept further taxation eventually increased the burdens of reconstruction that they would have to meet with their own resources. France's continued dependence on support from the international financial community required accommodation to the bankers' conditions. Banking leaders in New York, in contrast with those in London, sympathized with France. But they would not channel substantial amounts of American capital to the other side of the Atlantic until the Europeans established a business

3. See the formulation by Joseph Addison, counselor of embassy in Berlin, 11 September 1924, F.O. 371/9753: C 14653/70/18.

climate that offered a promise of security for private investment. In practice, this meant that France would have to abandon its attempt to collect reparations by force.

Once Poincaré agreed to the Expert Committees' appointment, France would in any case have had to accept some sort of "international" solution to the reparations problem. But owing to the vulnerability of the French currency and Herriot's ingenuous conduct of diplomacy, the negotiations to implement the Dawes Plan resulted in an erosion of France's position in Europe that went far beyond the scaling down of German reparations obligations as stipulated in the plan itself. The London Conference of 1924 brought fundamental modification in the economic consequences of the peace; it also undercut the essential military and political supports that upheld the edifice created at Versailles.

When the Germans accepted the Dawes Plan, they fully intended to ask for another reduction in reparations within three or four years. The outcome at London, by tying France's hands in the event of default, made it virtually certain that the next German bid for downward revision would meet with success. Meanwhile, French troops were unconditionally bound to leave the Ruhr—as they did on schedule in August 1925. Germany remained free to take advantage of its industrial superiority in subsequent trade and metallurgical negotiations. In the following years German businessmen would often demonstrate greater willingness to work toward creation of what Seydoux described as a "West European Zollverein" than their protectionist-minded French counterparts. But this very fact bore eloquent witness to the Germans' confidence that the formidable economic organization of the Reich would enable them to dominate any such precursor of the Common Market.[4] The numerous visionary schemes for interpenetration of national industries mooted in European business circles in the late 1920s all foundered in the miasma of despair that accompanied the world depression. Nevertheless, events would ultimately bear out the faith of German industrialists in their own economy's progressive technology and high capacity for growth. By 1938, the figures would show that German heavy industry had actually increased its lead over the iron and steel industries of other European countries in comparison with their relative standings before the First World War.[5]

The London Conference marked an equally notable turning point with

4. Note Seydoux, "Les Perspectives d'accord économique entre les industries française et allemande," 18 January 1925, copy in F[12]/8864.

5. See iron and steel production figures for 1913 and 1938, cited in Svennilson, *Growth and Stagnation*, pp. 258–59, 262–63; also general discussion of the interwar steel industry in ibid., pp. 119–40. (Germany suffered more severely from the depression than other countries in 1930–34; hence comparative production figures for those years diverge from the long-term trend.)

respect to the Rhineland's status and the larger associated question of European security. Even before the conference began, Herriot had appointed a committee under Radical-Socialist deputy Lucien Lamoureux to investigate French military and civilian administration in the occupied areas and to make proposals for reducing the cost—and consequently the scope—of the Rhineland Commission's activities.[6] At London, MacDonald held out to German delegates the prospect that the character of the occupation would change after they agreed to a reparations settlement.[7] And gradually, the Rhineland Commission's administrative practices came to reflect unequivocally the postulate that the occupation represented a transitory instead of a permanent state of affairs.[8]

The dispute over German disarmament delayed evacuation of the Cologne zone until January 1926, one year past the scheduled date. But clearly, the French could not renege on the practical commitment that they had made in London to withdraw as soon as Germany complied with specific demands of the military control commission; henceforth they could fight for postponement of this step only on narrow grounds. The Allies finally pulled out their troops—as part of an informal understanding reached at Locarno—without having obtained satisfaction concerning the disarmament provisions of the Versailles treaty.[9]

The decision to leave Cologne required a reassessment of the fundamental assumptions that previously had governed French military planning. The rump occupation of the other two Rhineland zones no longer provided a solution to the problem of French security. French military men eventually recognized that it made no sense to expend scarce funds on barracks or other permanent installations in areas that their forces would in any case have to leave within a few years. Consequently, they came to favor hanging on in the Rhineland only long enough for the nation to devise alternative strategic plans and to begin work on the defensive fortifications that became known as the Maginot line.[10] In the late 1920s, French statesmen privately looked on their position in the Rhineland less as a shield against German revenge than as a pawn that they might deploy in economic battle against the United States. They continued to nurture the illusion that in a general settlement they could demand "commercialization" of the reparations bonds

6. Lucien Lamoureux, "Souvenirs politiques, 1919–1940," pp. 707–12, microfilm of MS at Bibliothèque de Documentation Internationale Contemporaine, Nanterre.

7. See MacDonald's assurance to Stresemann in "Tagebuch," 15 August 1924, BA, R 43 I/268/15.

8. "Rapport de la Commission Lamoureux–Boris sur l'occupation de la Rive gauche du Rhin et la Ruhr," 24 December 1924, Herriot Papers.

9. Jon Jacobson, *Locarno Diplomacy: Germany and the West, 1925–1929* (Princeton, 1972), pp. 47–66.

10. For the gradual shift from offensive to defensive planning, see General P. E. Tournoux, *Défense des frontières: Haut Commandement–Gouvernement, 1919–1939* (Paris, 1960), pp. 31–137, 332–36.

and forgiveness of the war debt as the price of a final Rhineland evacuation. Though Washington tried to disabuse them of this belief, the leading figures at the Quai d'Orsay and the rue de Rivoli never quite abandoned hope that the American investor and taxpayer might consent in this way to substantial sacrifice for the sake of European stability.

For security, however, the French would have to look elsewhere. After the London Conference ended, they would continue with mounting desperation to promote their familiar schemes for a series of defensive military treaties, but over the next months it became obvious that they would not achieve their goal. Most diplomatic observers expected the Germans to come forward with a counterproposal in the form of a Rhineland nonaggression pact as one element of their campaign to secure rapid evacuation of the Cologne zone. In fact, the particular model turned out by the legal assembly line at the Wilhelmstrasse in January 1925 differed only in refinements of styling from the prototypes that Stresemann had sought unsuccessfully to merchandise in 1923 and 1924. With the reparations issue out of the way, security figured as the next item on the diplomatic agenda of Europe, but neither the French nor the Germans offered anything particularly new. The British therefore held the key to the security arrangements that would emerge in 1925 and would continue to influence the course of affairs right down to the outbreak of the Second World War.

Some members of the Conservative government (which returned to office in November 1924) favored British participation in a loose quadripartite pact to guarantee the French frontier provided it required no military commitment; others doubted the advisability of any involvement. But both advocates and opponents of an active role largely agreed on the ultimate goals of British policy. Almost no one outside the General Staff took the French concern for their immediate security seriously. The French, contended Lord Balfour, now the Tory elder statesman, were "impossible people," "psychologically upset," and indeed "rather insane." They were "so dreadfully afraid of being swallowed up by the tiger," he complained to the Committee of Imperial Defence, "but yet they spend all their time poking it."[11] Even Foreign Secretary Austen Chamberlain, the cabinet member most sympathetic to France, did not believe that Germany would pose a real military threat before 1960 or 1970; he regarded a pact not as a means to provide for collective security but rather as a psychological instrument to relieve fears across the Channel and thereby to make French policy more "reasonable."[12]

Winston Churchill, mustering the arguments against involvement,

11. Minutes of the Committee of Imperial Defence, CAB 2/4: 195th and 196th Meetings, 13 and 19 February 1925.

12. Minutes of the Committee of Imperial Defence, CAB 2/4: 192nd and 195th Meetings, 16 December 1924 and 13 February 1925.

pointed out that, even together, Britain and France would probably not be able to defeat Germany on the Continent once the Reich had recovered its strength. With air and naval supremacy, however, Britain could maintain itself for an indefinite period even if the Channel ports and the Low Countries fell into the hands of a hostile power. Using the same rhetoric which he was to employ in 1940 in a very different context, Churchill insisted that his colleagues should never admit "that England cannot, if the worst comes to the worst, stand alone." Nevertheless, he conceded, in a second Armageddon, victory would bring ruin for the country scarcely less devastating than defeat. Hence Britain should encourage France to follow those policies that would prevent renewal of the Franco-German war. If Britain held aloof from Europe, Churchill reasoned, then France might be impelled to make "sweeping" concessions in order to obtain a "real peace" with Germany. A lasting settlement of a friendly character, he added, would require "a recasting of the arrangements of the Treaty of Versailles so far as the oriental frontiers of Germany are concerned."[13]

Chamberlain supported British participation in a Rhineland pact with remarkably similar objectives in mind. The foreign secretary sought to deter Germany from attempting to overrun Europe again. At the same time he wished to induce France to adopt a "more friendly" attitude toward the Reich. He considered it vital to take concrete steps to "make the position of Germany tolerable" so that that country's bitterness and sense of humiliation might diminish before it reconstituted its military power. Finally, he thought it important to draw Germany into the western camp to forestall a Russo-German understanding directed against the rest of Europe.[14] A quadripartite Rhineland pact would serve all these purposes at once. It would also actually reduce British liabilities on the Continent, Chamberlain insisted, for "by making it perfectly clear that we were prepared to make our maximum effort . . . in the case of one frontier, . . . it was implied that in the case of the other frontier we were not."[15] The Foreign Office legal adviser emphasized in his construction of the most likely scenario for the outbreak of hostilities that if Germany first attacked Poland, if France then chose to invade the Rhineland to assist its Polish ally, and if Germany, invoking the right of self-defense, sent its armies forward into France on a counterattack, Britain would have no obligation whatsoever to intervene under the proposed

13. Memorandum by the Chancellor of the Exchequer (W. S. C.), "French and Belgian Security," 24 February 1925, CAB 4/12: C.I.D. Paper 590-B; see also Churchill's remarks in Minutes of the Committee of Imperial Defence, CAB 2/4: 195th and 196th Meetings, 13 and 19 February 1925.

14. Minutes of the Committee of Imperial Defence, CAB 2/4: 196th and 200th Meetings, 19 February and 22 June 1925; see also the Foreign Office memorandum drawn up by Harold Nicolson on Chamberlain's instructions, "British Policy Considered in Relation to the European Situation," 20 February 1925, CAB 4/12: C.I.D. Paper 593-B.

15. Minutes of the Committee of Imperial Defence, CAB 2/4: 201st Meeting, 1 July 1925.

pact.[16] The French would soon draw the logical conclusion. As a result of the Rhineland guarantee, Chamberlain explained to the C.I.D., he expected that France would "gradually withdraw from or at least minimize her commitments to Poland," and that Czechoslovakia too, seeing the handwriting on the wall, would draw closer to the German economic orbit.[17]

Although not privy to these exchanges in Whitehall, the French could hardly fail to appreciate what lay at stake as negotiations for a security pact moved toward a conclusion in the summer of 1925. Aristide Briand, who succeeded Herriot at the Quai d'Orsay, may never have acquired the habit of reading the fine print of treaties to which he put his name, but his principal professional advisers certainly understood the dangers lurking in the Locarno agreements. French diplomats took the view, however, that something was better than nothing. The attempt to enforce the Versailles treaty had starkly exposed the constraints on French unilateral action. From the London Conference onward there seemed no alternative to the policy of appeasement that Herriot, Briand, and other French statesmen hoped might gradually reconcile the Germans at least to the general outlines of the 1919 territorial settlement.

The consequences of decisions made at London in the summer of 1924 would not become fully clear for some time to come. Yet the German Reichstag and French parliamentary debates that followed the London Conference prefigured future developments in striking fashion. For political effect German cabinet spokesmen claimed discontent with the outcome of negotiations (a practice they would repeat after future international meetings), but actually they realized perfectly well how much their delegation had achieved. The problem, as Labor Minister Brauns expressed it, was how to rally domestic public opinion in favor of the agreements while revealing "as little as possible about the advantages obtained" in order not to affect Herriot's position adversely.[18]

For some days a fierce controversy raged throughout Germany over ratification of the London accords. Sensational press accounts of the bitter confrontation in the Reichstag sustained the impression that the outcome remained in doubt until the final vote. In an effort to secure the requisite two-thirds majority, the cabinet mobilized lobbyists from industry and the Reichswehr to persuade those still on the fence, readied plans for an appeal to the public by plebiscite, and even contemplated

16. Sir Cecil J. B. Hurst, "The Proposed Rhineland Pact in Relation to France's Commitments to Poland," 17 June 1925, CAB 4/13: C.I.D. Paper 619-B.

17. Minutes of the Committee of Imperial Defence, CAB 2/4: 200th Meeting, 22 June 1925; see also Chamberlain's comments to the cabinet, CAB 23/50, Cabinet Conclusions: 45(25), 13 August 1925.

18. On discontent, see Frank B. Kellogg to Alanson B. Houghton, 18 August 1924, Box 8, Kellogg Papers; for the German cabinet's postconference analysis, see "Niederschrift über die Sitzung des Reichsministeriums," 18 August 1924, BA, R 43 I/273/8–10.

dissolution of the legislative body as a last resort. In fact, however, the cabinet had already resolved to sign the agreements and to find some way to put the Dawes Plan into operation whatever the Reichstag did.[19] Hence the drama on the Reichstag floor constituted political cabaret for the general public. Behind the scenes, party advantage figured as the real issue. The Nationalists, some of whose votes were required to pass the enabling legislation, sought to bargain their acquiescence in return for inclusion in the cabinet while they still expressed sufficiently vociferous opposition to dissuade their right-wing electoral supporters from defecting to the National Socialists. It was really no surprise, therefore, when at the last minute the Nationalists conveniently split their votes and the necessary legislation won approval by a comfortable margin.[20]

Yet if the result of the Reichstag deliberations was practically foreordained, the tone of these debates spoke volumes about the prospects for European peace and German democracy.[21] Even moderates referred to the Dawes Plan as a grievous burden that they would shoulder only to free the Rhine and Ruhr, and with no more enthusiasm than Prince Hardenberg had shown at Tilsit, when he agreed to pay a crushing indemnity in order to secure the retirement of Napoleon's armies from the provinces east of the Elbe. Few discerned a real opportunity for international reconciliation. The Nationalists condemned in extravagant terms the very agreement for which some of them were shortly to vote. And not for the last time under Weimar, Communists and National Socialists joined in a working coalition. Despite doctrinal differences, a mutual interest in obstructing the parliamentary process brought them together, and while the Nazis fashioned much of their revolutionary rhetoric on the Communist model, the Communists in turn did not hesitate to employ nationalist and anti-Semitic appeals when opportunity beckoned. The most eloquent of Communist *apparatchiki*, Professor Arthur Rosenberg (who later in exile would pose as a paladin of democracy), won gleeful approval from the National Socialists as well as from his party comrades by denouncing the Dawes Plan as a plot by American capitalists and international Jewry to seize control of the German economy. But Rosenberg also found cause to rejoice: at least the plan would "drive the last nails into the coffin of the German Republic." All too prophetically he promised that his party stood ready to give the republic the final shove, so that it would "meet the fate that it deserves."[22]

19. "Protokoll der Ministerbesprechung," 21 August 1924, BA, R 43 I/273/78–80.

20. Werner Liebe, *Die Deutschnationale Volkspartei, 1918–1924* (Düsseldorf, 1956), pp. 76–86; Lewis Hertzmann, *DNVP: Right-Wing Opposition in the Weimar Republic, 1918–1924* (Lincoln, Neb., 1963), pp. 216–39.

21. See *Verhandlungen des Reichstags, II. Wahlperiode, Stenographische Berichte*, vol. 381, 25–29 August 1924, pp. 771–1134.

22. *Verhandlungen des Reichstags*, 26 August 1924, 381:944–50. For Rosenberg's skillful exploitation of nationalist and anti-Semitic themes, see particularly his earlier attack on the Dawes Plan, in *Verhandlungen des Reichstags*, 25 July 1924, 381:680–89.

In France the London accords also encountered sharp criticism in parliament, but there the temper of discussion was far different.[23] The opposition faulted Herriot's skill as a negotiator and expressed heated objections to various details of the settlement. Yet significantly, even Poincaré, despite a long justification of past policies, did not set forth any positive alternative to the new course that French foreign policy seemed destined to pursue. Indeed, the former premier stressed the continuities in policy and attempted to show that his own conduct of affairs had prepared the way for the détente which those given to optimism now glimpsed shimmering on the horizon.[24]

These debates made clear that Frenchmen who varied widely in their political outlook had arrived at a common understanding. Theirs was a country with severely circumscribed resources, and its ability to make a powerful and recalcitrant adversary comply with the terms of an unpopular treaty was proportionately restricted. Perhaps comparative population statistics should have suggested this conclusion as early as 1919. But the failure of the Ruhr occupation to produce more tangible gains, in tandem with the financial crisis of 1924, provided a demonstration of the nation's limitations that had enormous psychological impact.

Herriot opened his defense of the London agreements on a panegyric note. French "idealism" dominated the results, he asserted, and though one could not expect to achieve permanent European equilibrium in a month, the conference had witnessed "the beginning of real peace."[25] As the debates proceeded, however, the harried premier disclosed more frankly the anguish and despair that had encroached upon his private thoughts in the course of his recent initiation into the realities of power. France, he explained, could not possibly return to a policy of force, nor could it have coped with the economic and monetary disorder that a rupture of the conference would have entailed.[26]

Who can doubt that here Herriot embodied the authentic voice of a generation which had lived through too much emotional suffering, physical decimation, and economic uncertainty:

> A country like ours cannot always be asked to stretch its will to the point where at certain hours it can break. . . . At this time, and to prepare for the future, permit this country to rest a bit. It needs the rest. We must think of all the problems facing us. We must reconstruct a solid financial framework for the country. Our finances must not be at the mercy, as we have seen these past days, of those interventions which we have felt and you have criticized. We must avoid being obliged to keep daily watch upon our exchange rate. . . . We must think of our population, we must give ourselves time to recover our losses of men, we must

23. For these debates, see *J.O.C. Déb.*, 21–23 August 1924, pp. 2953–3108, and *J.O.S. Déb.*, 26 August 1924, pp. 1285–1328.

24. *J.O.S. Déb.*, 26 August 1924, pp. 1295–1314.

25. *J.O.C. Déb.*, 21 August 1924, p. 2959.

26. Ibid., 23 August 1924, pp. 3076–84; *J.O.S. Déb.*, 26 August 1924, pp. 1314–23.

watch over the cradles of children with vigilant affection. Mothers must be reassured. That too is patriotism.[27]

So indeed it was. Necessarily, such a program of financial reconstruction and population recovery mandated a foreign policy of conciliation. But what if Germany would not agree to a reconciliation within the confines of Europe's existing political structure? "If I do not yet see the light of day," said Poincaré, "it is because the scaffolding of London still blocks my view of the rising sun. And what worries me the most is that this scaffolding rests upon quicksand: the good faith of Germany, the good faith, not only of the present government in Berlin, but of all those governments that will follow it."[28]

France, it was evident, could confidently expect neither to contain nor to appease Germany successfully. This posed a dilemma. A generation of French policymakers would struggle to solve it. They would find no solution, short of another war, another defeat, and another rescue by the United States.

27. *J.O.C. Déb.*, 23 August 1924, p. 3084.
28. *J.O.S. Déb.*, 26 August 1924, p. 1313.

Bibliography
Index

Bibliography

This bibliography is organized as follows:

1. Manuscript Sources.
2. Government Documents and Official Publications.
3. Newspapers.
4. Periodicals.
5. Books, Articles, and Dissertations:
   - A. General Works, Reparations and Diplomacy.
   - B. France, Financial and Economic.
   - C. France, Diplomatic and Political.
   - D. Germany.
   - E. Great Britain.
   - F. United States.
   - G. European Business.
   - H. Other.

1. *MANUSCRIPT SOURCES*

France

Official Archives

Bureau National des Charbons (sous-série AJ^{26}), Archives Nationales, Paris.

Conseil Supérieur de la Défense Nationale (procès-verbaux, and records of the Secrétariat Général, Commission d'Etudes), Service Historique de l'Armée, Château de Vincennes, Vincennes.

Délégation française à la Commission des Réparations (sous-série AJ^5), Archives Nationales, Paris.

Haute Commission interalliée des Territoires Rhénans; Haut Commissariat français dans les provinces du Rhin (sous-série AJ^9), Archives Nationales, Paris.

Ministère du Commerce et de l'Industrie (sous-série F^{12}), Archives Nationales, Paris.

Ministère des Finances, Administration centrale (sous-série F^{30}), formerly at Archives Nationales, now at Mission des Archives, Ministère de l'Economie et des Finances, Paris.

Ministère de l'Intérieur (sous-série F^7), Archives Nationales, Paris.

Personal Papers

Camille Barrère Papers, Ministère des Affaires Etrangères, Quai d'Orsay, Paris.

Emile Coste Papers, in family possession, Paris.

Hans Adam Dorten Papers, Hoover Institution, Stanford University, Stanford, Calif.

Jacques-Louis Dumesnil Papers, Archives Nationales, Paris.

Marshal Ferdinand Foch Cahiers, photocopy, Bibliothèque Nationale, Paris.

Frédéric François-Marsal Papers, in family possession, Paris.
Edouard Herriot Papers, Ministère des Affaires Etrangères, Quai d'Orsay, Paris.
Louis-Lucien Klotz Dossiers, Bibliothèque de Documentation Internationale Contemporaine, Nanterre.
Lucien Lamoureux, "Souvenirs politiques, 1919–1940," microfilm of MS at Bibliothèque de Documentation Internationale Contemporaine, Nanterre.
Louis Loucheur Papers, Hoover Institution, Stanford University, Stanford, Calif.
General Charles Mangin Papers, Archives Nationales, Paris.
Ernest Mercier Papers, Hoover Institution, Stanford University, Stanford, Calif.
Alexandre Millerand Papers, in family possession, Paris.
Paul Painlevé Papers, Archives Nationales, Paris.
Robert Pinot Papers, in family possession, Paris.
Raymond Poincaré Papers, Bibliothèque Nationale, Paris.
General Edouard Réquin Papers, Hoover Institution, Stanford University, Stanford, Calif.
Albert Thomas Papers, Archives Nationales, Paris.

Business Archives

Les Assemblées générales, rapports des conseils d'administration et des commissaires des comptes, 1919–25, collection available at Chambre Syndicale de la Sidérurgie Française, Paris.
Compagnie de Saint-Gobain-Pont-à-Mousson, Archives de Pont-à-Mousson, La Châtre (Indre).
Société de Commentry, Fourchambault, et Decazeville, Archives Nationales, Paris.
Société des Fours à Coke de Douai, Archives Nationales, Paris.

Germany

Official Archives

German Foreign Ministry Archives, U.S. National Archives Microfilms T–120, Washington, D.C.
For a complete directory to these records, see George O. Kent, ed., *A Catalogue of Files and Microfilms of the German Foreign Ministry Archives, 1920–1945*, 4 vols. (Stanford, Calif., 1962–72). For purposes of this study, the author surveyed the files in Büro des Reichsministers, Büro des Staatssekretärs, Politische Abteilung II, Abteilung II–Besetzte Gebiete, Geheimakten, Abteilung II–Wirtschaft, Sonderreferat Wirtschaft, Wirtschaftsreparationen, the Nachlässe (personal papers) or Handakten (personal files) of Gustav Stresemann, Ago von Maltzan, Carl von Schubert, and Karl Ritter, and the Kabinettsprotokolle in the Alte Reichskanzlei files. Footnote references identify documents with prefix "G.F.M." by serial/reel/frame number. The principal files cited in the footnotes of this study include:
3243/1642–54: Büro des Reichsministers, Reparationsfragen.
3398/1736–37: Büro des Reichsministers, Londoner Konferenz, 1924.
3491/1741–56: Alte Reichskanzlei, Kabinettsprotokolle, 1922–24.
4478/2214–16: Büro des Staatssekretärs, Politische Stimmungsberichte (Hauptakten).
K936/4505: Politische Abteilung II, Frankreich, Politische Beziehungen zu Deutschland.
L177/4079–81: Handakten Karl Ritter (handelspolitisch), Frankreich.
L1489–95/5352: Handakten Karl Ritter, Französische Eisenverhandlungen, Sachgebiet Industrie.

Official Archives: Bundesarchiv, Koblenz

Alte Reichskanzlei, 1919–33 (R 43 I). Footnote references identify documents with volume (Band)/page number. The principal files cited in the footnotes here include:

Bd. 20–42: Auswärtige Angelegenheiten, Ausführung des Friedensvertrags, 1921–24.

Bd. 203–30: Akten betreffend Besetzung des Ruhrgebietes, 1923.

Bd. 265–76: Ausführung des Friedensvertrags, Londoner Konferenz, 1924.

Bd. 453–54: Sonderverhandlungen der Rhein-Ruhr Industriellen mit den Besatzungsmächten, 1923–24.

Bd. 498: Handakten G. Ministerialrat Dr. Kempner, Londoner Konferenz, 1924.

Reichsfinanzministerium (R 2).

Reichsministerium für Wiederaufbau (R 38).

Personal Papers: Bundesarchiv, Koblenz

Nachlass Dr. Moritz Julius Bonn.

Nachlass Dr. Otto Gessler.

Nachlass Dr. Friedrich Grimm.

Nachlass Maximilian Harden.

Nachlass Dr. Karl Jarres.

Nachlass Dr. Erich Koch-Weser.

Nachlass Dr. Hans Luther.

Nachlass Paul Moldenhauer.

Nachlass Dr. Hermann Pünder.

Nachlassrest Dr. Walther Rathenau.

Nachlass Arnold Rechberg.

Nachlass Dr. Paul Silverberg.

Nachlass Max von Stockhausen.

Other Collections: Bundesarchiv, Koblenz

Sammlung Otto Jung betr. Rheinlandbesetzung und Separatismus (ZSg 105).

Wirtschaftsgruppe Eisenschaffende Industrie, Verein Deutscher Eisen- und Stahlindustrieller (R 13 I). Principal files cited in the footnotes here include:

Bd. 255: Förderung internationaler Wirtschaftsbeziehungen: Industrielle Verständigung mit Frankreich; Unterstützung der deutsch-französischen Wirtschaftsorganizationen, 1922–31.

Bd. 261–62: Bestrebungen zur Bildung eines internationalen Eisenkartells, 1921–26.

Bd. 270: Verhandlungen im Rahmen der Internationalen Rohstahlgemeinschaft über die Förderung des deutschen Exporthandels mit Eisen.

Personal Papers and Collections at Other Repositories

Akten des Büros des Oberbürgermeisters Dr. Konrad Adenauer, Stadtarchiv, Cologne.

Nachlass General Wilhelm Groener, Bundesarchiv-Militärarchiv, Freiburg-im-Breisgau.

Nachlass Wilhelm Marx, Stadtarchiv, Cologne.

NSDAP Hauptarchiv, Hoover Institution, Stanford University, Stanford, Calif.; microfilm copy, Harvard College Library, Cambridge, Mass.

Nachlass Dr. Hans Schäffer, Institut für Zeitgeschichte, Munich.

Nachlass General Kurt von Schleicher, Bundesarchiv-Militärarchiv, Freiburg-im-Breisgau.

Nachlass General Hans von Seeckt, microfilm copy, Harvard College Library, Cambridge, Mass.

Nachlass Dr. Gustav Stresemann, microfilm copy, U.S. National Archives, Washington, D.C.

Max M. Warburg Papers, formerly at Warburg Institute, London, now at Brinckmann, Wirtz & Co., Hamburg.

Business Archives

Historisches Archiv, August Thyssen-Hütte A.G., Duisburg-Hamborn.

Historisches Archiv, Gutehoffnungshütte, Oberhausen.

Werksarchiv, Friedrich Krupp A.G., Villa Hügel, Essen.

Great Britain

Official Archives: Public Record Office, London

Cabinet Office:

CAB 2: Committee of Imperial Defence, Minutes.

CAB 3: Committee of Imperial Defence, Memoranda on Home Defence, "A" Series.

CAB 4: Committee of Imperial Defence, Miscellaneous Memoranda, "B" Series.

CAB 21: Cabinet Registered Files.

CAB 23: Minutes of Cabinet Meetings; Conferences of Ministers.

CAB 24: Cabinet Memoranda.

CAB 27: Cabinet Committees, General Series.

CAB 29: International Conference Papers.

Foreign Office:

F.O. 408: Confidential Print, Germany.

F.O. 414: Confidential Print, North America.

F.O. 425: Confidential Print, Western Europe.

Foreign Office General Correspondence, Political:

F.O. 371: Footnote references identify documents as F.O. 371/volume number: document/file/country designator. The Foreign Office did not assign precise headings to subject files. The volumes most frequently cited in the footnotes are listed here with a rough description of contents: 4547–48, 5661–62, 7281–83, 8503–06, British war debt to the United States (1920–23); 8625–63, Reparations (1923); 8702–53, Occupation of the Ruhr (1923); 9394, French war debt (1923); 9682–84, Intra-European debts (1924); 9730–31, French policy toward Germany; 9738–55, Reparations and the Committee of Experts, main file; 9760–61, French conditions for a reparations settlement; 9769–70, Germany and European security; 9807, British policy toward Germany; 9809–10, Coal and steel; 9812–13, Anglo-French relations and British policy in the Rhineland; 9818–20, Security question; 9825 and 9828, Secret "green" papers; 9832–34, Evacuation of the Cologne zone; 9839–41, Interallied Military Control Commission; 9842–65, Chequers, Paris, and London Conferences; 9867–69, Franco-German commercial and steel negotiations; 10530–31, Belgian foreign policy; 10533–35, 10550, Reports of the British Embassy in Paris; 10538–40, Anglo-French rapprochement; 10568–73, Treaty of Mutual Guarantee and the Geneva Protocol (all of the above, 1924).

Foreign Office Private Collections, Ministers and Officials:

F.O. 800/147–158: Correspondence of George Nathaniel Curzon, 1st Marquess Curzon of Kedleston, 1919–24.

F.O. 800/218–219: Correspondence of James Ramsay MacDonald as prime minister and secretary of state, 1924.

F.O. 800/220: Correspondence between Assistant Under Secretary Sir William Tyrrell and Sir Charles Mendl, 1924.

F.O. 800/227: Correspondence of the under secretaries of state for foreign affairs, Ronald McNeill, 1922–24; Arthur Ponsonby, 1924.
F.O. 800/243: Correspondence of Sir Eyre Crowe.
F.O. 800/256–263: Correspondence of Sir Austen Chamberlain as foreign secretary, 1924–29.
Prime Minister's Office:
PREMIER 1: Correspondence and Papers.
Treasury:
T160: Treasury, Finance Files.
T172: Chancellor of the Exchequer's Office, Miscellaneous Papers.
T176: Sir Otto E. Niemeyer Papers.

Personal Papers
1st Lord Altrincham [Edward W. M. Grigg] Papers, in family possession, London.
1st Earl Baldwin [Stanley Baldwin] Papers, Cambridge University Library, Cambridge.
1st Earl Balfour [Arthur James Balfour] Papers, British Museum, London.
1st Viscount Cecil of Chelwood [Robert Cecil] Papers, British Museum, London.
Sir Austen Chamberlain Papers, Birmingham University Library, Birmingham.
Sir Winston Churchill Papers, in possession of Mr. Martin Gilbert, Oxford.
1st Marquess of Crewe [Robert Crewe-Milne] Papers, Cambridge University Library, Cambridge.
1st Marquess Curzon of Kedleston [George Nathaniel Curzon] Papers, India Office Library and India Office Records, London.
1st Viscount D'Abernon [Edgar D'Abernon] Papers, British Museum, London.
1st Lord Dalton [Hugh Dalton] Diary, British Library of Political and Economic Science, London School of Economics, London.
1st Viscount Davidson [J. C. C. Davidson] Papers, Beaverbrook Library, London.
17th Earl of Derby [Edward George Villiers Stanley] Papers, formerly in family possession, now in Liverpool City Library, Liverpool.
David Lloyd George Papers, Beaverbrook Library, London.
1st Baron Hankey [Maurice P. A. Hankey] Papers, Churchill College, Cambridge University, Cambridge.
Lord Hardinge of Penshurst [Charles Hardinge] Papers, Cambridge University Library, Cambridge.
Lord Keynes [John Maynard Keynes] Papers, Marshall Library of Economics, Cambridge University, Cambridge.
Andrew Bonar Law Papers, Beaverbrook Library, London.
James Ramsay MacDonald Papers, in possession of Mr. David Marquand, London.
Edmund D. Morel Papers, British Library of Political and Economic Science, London School of Economics, London.
Lord Norman of St. Clere [Montagu Norman] Papers, Bank of England, London.

United States

Official Archives: National Archives, Washington, D.C.
Record Group 39: Records of the Bureau of Accounts, Treasury [includes World War Foreign Debt Commission files].
Record Group 40: General Records of the Department of Commerce (Office of the Secretary).
Record Group 43: Records of United States Participation in International Con-

ferences, Commissions, and Expositions [includes Reparation Commission files].
Record Group 56: General Records of the Department of the Treasury.
Record Group 59: General Records of the Department of State, Decimal File, 1910–29. Footnote references identify documents with prefix, "U.S.," file/document number. The most useful files for purposes of this study include: 462.00R 29, Reparation from Germany in accordance with the Treaty of Versailles; 462.00R 296, Germany, Financial and Businessmen's Commission [Dawes Plan]; 611.629, Ruhr region; 763.72119, Political relations, termination of war; 800.51, Financial affairs, general [loans to foreign countries]; 800.51W89, World War Foreign Debt Commission, indebtedness growing out of the World War; 800.51W89 Fr, W.W.F.D.C., indebtedness of France; 800.51W89 GB, W.W.F.D.C., indebtedness of Great Britain; 841.00, Great Britain, internal political affairs; 841.002, Great Britain, cabinet; 841.51, Great Britain, financial conditions; 851.00, France, internal political affairs; 851.002, France, cabinet; 851.51, France, financial conditions; 851.5151, France, exchange; 851.6362, France, coal and coke; 862.00, Germany, internal political affairs; 862.01, Germany, government; 862t.01, Germany, Rhineland; 862.002, Germany, cabinet; 862.51, Germany, financial conditions.
Record Group 151: Records of the Bureau of Foreign and Domestic Commerce.

Personal Papers and Other Collections
Henry T. Allen Papers, Library of Congress, Washington, D.C.
Chandler P. Anderson Papers, Library of Congress, Washington, D.C.
Leonard P. Ayres Papers, Library of Congress, Washington, D.C.
William E. Borah Papers, Library of Congress, Washington, D.C.
Theodore H. Burton Papers, Western Reserve Historical Society, Cleveland, Ohio.
William R. Castle Papers, Herbert Hoover Presidential Library, West Branch, Iowa.
Calvin Coolidge Papers, Library of Congress, Washington, D.C.
Stuart M. Crocker Papers, Library of Congress, Washington, D.C.
William S. Culbertson Papers, Library of Congress, Washington, D.C.
Norman H. Davis Papers, Library of Congress, Washington, D.C.
Charles G. Dawes Papers, Northwestern University Library, Evanston, Ill.
Ellis Loring Dresel Papers, Houghton Library, Harvard University, Cambridge, Mass.
Henry P. Fletcher Papers, Library of Congress, Washington, D.C.
Joseph C. Grew Papers, Houghton Library, Harvard University, Cambridge, Mass.
Charles Hamlin Papers, Library of Congress, Washington, D.C.
Warren G. Harding Papers, Ohio Historical Society, Columbus, Ohio; microfilm copy, Harvard College Library, Cambridge, Mass.
George Leslie Harrison Papers, Butler Library, Columbia University, New York, N.Y.
Leland Harrison Papers, Library of Congress, Washington, D.C.
Myron T. Herrick Papers, Western Reserve Historical Society, Cleveland, Ohio.
Herbert C. Hoover Papers [Secretary of Commerce–Official and Secretary of Commerce–Personal files], Herbert Hoover Presidential Library, West Branch, Iowa.
Hoover Institution on War, Revolution, and Peace Collection: "Allied Powers, Reparation Commission" [Minutes, decisions, and communiqués of the Reparation Commission, 1920–24; Minutes of the First and Second Committees of Experts, 1923–24; Documents of the First Committee and of the U.S. group;

Memoranda of technical experts; Henry M. Robinson collection relating to the Dawes Committee], Stanford University, Stanford, Calif.
Alanson B. Houghton Papers, in family possession, Corning, N.Y.
Edward M. House Papers, Yale University Library, New Haven, Conn.
Charles Evans Hughes Papers, Library of Congress, Washington, D.C.
Otto H. Kahn Papers, Princeton University Library, Princeton, N.J.
Frank B. Kellogg Papers, Minnesota Historical Society, St. Paul, Minn.
Robert M. La Follette, Sr., Papers, Library of Congress, Washington, D.C.
Thomas W. Lamont Papers, Baker Library, Harvard Graduate School of Business Administration, Boston, Mass.
Walter Lichtenstein Papers, Baker Library, Harvard Graduate School of Business Administration, Boston, Mass.
Henry Cabot Lodge Papers, Massachusetts Historical Society, Boston, Mass.
James A. Logan Papers, Hoover Institution, Stanford University, Stanford, Calif.
Wesley C. Mitchell Papers, Butler Library, Columbia University, New York, N.Y.
Jay Pierrepont Moffat Papers, Houghton Library, Harvard University, Cambridge, Mass.
Dwight W. Morrow Papers, Amherst College Library, Amherst, Mass.
William Phillips Papers, Houghton Library, Harvard University, Cambridge, Mass.
Benjamin Strong Papers, Federal Reserve Bank of New York, New York, N.Y.
Paul M. Warburg Papers, Yale University Library, New Haven, Conn.
Arthur N. Young Papers, Hoover Institution, Stanford University, Stanford, Calif.
Owen D. Young Papers, in family possession, Van Hornesville, N.Y.

2. *GOVERNMENT DOCUMENTS AND OFFICIAL PUBLICATIONS*

France

Journal Officiel. Annexe. Documents administratifs. 1923–24.
Journal Officiel de la République Française. Débats parlementaires, Chambre des Députés. 1919–24.
Journal Officiel de la République Française. Débats parlementaires, Sénat. 1919–24.
Journal Officiel, Chambre des Députés. Documents parlementaires. Annexes aux procès-verbaux des séances. 1919–24.
Journal Officiel, Sénat. Documents parlementaires. Annexes aux procès-verbaux des séances. 1919–24.
Ministère des Affaires Etrangères. *Documents diplomatiques. Conférence de Washington, juillet 1921–février 1922*. Paris, 1923.
______. *Documents diplomatiques. Conférence économique internationale de Gênes, 9 avril–19 mai 1922*. Paris, 1922.
______. *Documents relatifs aux réparations*. 2 vols. Paris, 1922–24.
______. *Documents diplomatiques. Demande de moratorium du gouvernement allemand à la Commission des Réparations, 14 novembre 1922. Conférence de Londres, 9–11 décembre 1922. Conférence de Paris, 2–4 janvier 1923*. Paris, 1923.
______. *Documents diplomatiques. Documents relatifs aux notes allemandes des 2 mai et 7 juin sur les réparations, 2 mai–3 août 1923*. Paris, 1923.
______. *Diplomatic Correspondence. Reply of the French Government to the Note of the British Government of August 11, 1923 Relating to Reparations, August 20, 1923*. Paris, 1923.
______. *Documents diplomatiques. Documents relatifs aux négociations concernant les*

garanties de sécurité contre une agression de l'Allemagne, 10 janvier 1919–7 décembre 1923. Paris, 1924.

———. *Documents diplomatiques. Conférence de Londres, 16 juillet–16 août 1924*. Paris, 1925.

Ministère des Affaires Etrangères, Commission de publication des documents relatifs aux origines de la guerre 1939–1945. *Documents diplomatiques français, 1932–1939*. Series I, 6 vols., Series II, 7 vols. Paris, 1963–.

Ministère de l'Economie Nationale. *Annuaire statistique de la France, résumé retrospectif, 1946*. Paris, 1946.

Ministère du Travail, Statistique Générale de la France. *Annuaire statistique*, 1919–24. Paris, 1919–24.

Germany

Akten der Reichskanzlei, Weimarer Republik. Das Kabinett Cuno. 22. November 1922 bis 12. August 1923. Edited by Karl-Heinz Harbeck. Boppard am Rhein, 1968.

Akten der Reichskanzlei, Weimarer Republik. Die Kabinette Marx I und II. 30. November 1923 bis 3. Juni 1924. 3. Juni 1924 bis 14. Januar 1925. Edited by Günter Abramowski. 2 vols. Boppard am Rhein, 1973.

Auswärtiges Amt. *Die den Alliierten seit Waffenstillstand übermittelten deutschen Angebote und Vorschläge zur Lösung der Reparations- und Wiederaufbaufrage*. Berlin, 1923.

———. *Die Londoner Konferenz, Juli–August 1924*. Berlin, 1925.

Botschaft, France. *Die separatistischen Umtriebe in den besetzten Gebieten: Notenwechsel zwischen der deutschen und der französischen Regierung*. Berlin, 1924.

Verhandlungen des Reichstags. Stenographische Berichte. Vols. 351–61, 381. Berlin, 1921–24.

Great Britain

Accounts and Papers. State Papers (Command Papers):

Cmd. 1627: *Conference on Limitation of Armament. Washington, 1921–22*. London, 1922.

Cmd. 1737: *Despatch to the Representatives of France, Italy, Croat-Slovene State, Roumania, Portugal and Greece at London respecting War Debts*. London, 1922.

Cmd. 1742: *Correspondence between His Majesty's Government and the French Government respecting the Genoa Conference*. London, 1922.

Cmd. 1812: *Inter-Allied Conferences on Reparations and Inter-Allied Debts Held in London and Paris, December 1922 and January 1923*. London, 1923.

Cmd. 1943: *Correspondence with the Allied Governments respecting Reparation Payments by Germany*. London, 1923.

Cmd. 2169: *Papers respecting Negotiations for an Anglo-French Pact*. London, 1924.

Cmd. 2184: *Correspondence concerning the Conference Which It Is Proposed to Hold in London on July 16, 1924 to Consider the Measures Necessary to Bring the Dawes Plan into Operation*. London, 1924.

Cmd. 2191: *Franco-British Memorandum of July 9, 1924 concerning the Application of the Dawes Scheme*. London, 1924.

Cmd. 2200: *Correspondence between His Majesty's Government and the League of Nations respecting the Proposed Treaty of Mutual Assistance*. London, 1924.

Cmd. 2258: *Minutes of the London Conference on Reparations, August 1922*. London, 1924.

Cmd. 2270: *Proceedings of the London Reparation Conference, July and August 1924*. London, 1924.

Documents on British Foreign Policy, 1919–1939. Edited by E. L. Woodward, R. Butler, J. P. T. Bury, W. N. Medlicott et al. Series I, vols. 1–18, Series Ia, vols. 1–5. London, 1946–.

[Foreign Office]. *Proceedings of the London Reparation Conference*. Vol. 1. *The Interallied Conference*. Vol. 2. *The International Conference*. N.p., n.d.

Parliamentary Debates: Official Report. House of Commons. 1923–24. 5th Series, vols. 160–76.

Parliamentary Debates: Official Report. House of Lords. 1923–24. 5th Series, vols. 53–59.

United States

Conference on the Limitation of Armament. Washington, November 12, 1921–February 6, 1922. Washington, D.C., 1922.

Department of State. *Papers Relating to the Foreign Relations of the United States, 1920–24*. Washington, D.C., 1935–39.

Trials of War Criminals before the Nuernberg Military Tribunals under Control Council Law No. 10. Vol. 9, *The Krupp Case*. Washington, D.C., 1950.

Belgium

Académie royale de Belgique, Commission royale d'histoire. *Documents diplomatiques belges, 1920–1940. La Politique de sécurité extérieure*. Vol. 1. *Période 1920–1924*. Edited by Ch. de Visscher and F. Vanlangenhove. Brussels, 1964.

Ministère des Affaires Etrangères. *Documents diplomatiques relatifs aux réparations du 26 décembre 1922 au 27 août 1923*. Brussels, 1923.

———. *Documents diplomatiques relatifs aux réparations. Conférence de Londres du 16 juillet au 16 août 1924*. Brussels, 1924.

Other

Commission des Réparations. *Report of the First Committee of Experts*. Annexe 2075. *Report of the Second Committee of Experts*. Annexe 2076. Paris, 1924.

Reparation Commission. *Official Documents*. Vol. 14, *The Experts' Plan for Reparation Payments*. London, 1927.

3. *NEWSPAPERS*

France

L'Action française.

Bulletin quotidien de la société d'études et d'informations économiques.

L'Echo de Paris.

L'Ere nouvelle.

L'Information.

Le Journal des débats.

La Journée industrielle.

Le Matin.

L'Oeuvre.

Le Quotidien.

Le Temps.

Germany

Berliner Tageblatt.

Deutsche Allgemeine Zeitung.

Haut Commissariat de la République française dans les pays rhénans, presse et information, "Analyse de presse." A daily summary of the Rhineland press compiled by the French occupation authorities, copy in Bibliothèque de Documentation Internationale Contemporaine, Nanterre.

Great Britain

Daily Telegraph.
Manchester Guardian.
The Observer.
The Times.

United States

Journal of Commerce.
The New York Times.
Wall Street Journal.

4. PERIODICALS

France

Bulletin de la statistique générale de la France et du service d'observation des prix.
Les Documents politiques, diplomatiques, et financiers.
L'Europe nouvelle.
Le Progrès civique.
Revue des deux mondes.
Revue d'économie politique.
Revue militaire française.
Revue politique et parlementaire.

Great Britain

The Economist.
The Nation and the Athenaeum.

United States

Foreign Affairs.
The Literary Digest.
The Nation.
The New Republic.

5. BOOKS, ARTICLES, AND DISSERTATIONS

A. General Works, Reparations and Diplomacy

Albertini, Luigi. *The Origins of the War of 1914*. 3 vols. London, New York, and Toronto, 1952–57.
American Economic Association. *Readings in the Theory of International Trade*. Philadelphia, 1949.
Antonucci, Alceste. *Le Bilan des réparations et la crise mondiale*. Paris, 1935.
Auld, George P. *The Dawes Plan and the New Economics*. Garden City, New York, 1927.
Bardoux, Jacques. *Lloyd George et la France*. Paris, 1923.
———. *Le Socialisme au pouvoir: L'Expérience de 1924*. Paris, 1930.
Baruch, Bernard M. *The Making of the Reparation and Economic Sections of the Treaty*. New York and London, 1920.
Baumont, Maurice. *La Faillite de la paix, 1918–1939*. 2 vols. Paris, 1951.
Berg, Peter. *Deutschland und Amerika, 1918–1929: Ueber das deutsche Amerikabild der zwanziger Jahre*. Lübeck and Hamburg, 1963.
Bergmann, Carl. *The History of Reparations*. Boston and New York, 1927.
Birdsall, Paul. *Versailles Twenty Years After*. New York, 1941.
Bloch, Camille, and Renouvin, Pierre. "La Genèse et la signification de l'article 231 du traité de Versailles." *Revue d'histoire de la guerre mondiale* 10 (January 1932): 1–24.

Boyden, Roland W. "The Dawes Report." *Foreign Affairs* 2 (June 1924): 583–97.

Burnett, Philip Mason. *Reparation at the Paris Peace Conference from the Standpoint of the American Delegation*. 2 vols. New York, 1940.

Calmette, Germain. *Recueil des documents sur l'histoire des réparations, 1919–5 mai 1921*. Paris, 1924.

Castillon, Richard. *Les Réparations allemandes: Deux expériences, 1919–1932, 1945–1952*. Paris, 1953.

Chastenet, Jacques. *Vingt ans d'histoire diplomatique*. Geneva, 1946.

Craig, Gordon, and Gilbert, Felix, eds. *The Diplomats, 1919–1939*. Princeton, 1953.

Dawes, Charles G. *A Journal of Reparations*. London, 1939.

Dawes, Rufus C. *The Dawes Plan in the Making*. Indianapolis, 1925.

Dickmann, Fritz. *Die Kriegsschuldfrage auf der Friedenskonferenz von Paris, 1919*. Munich, 1964.

Documents regarding the European Economic Situation. International Conciliation. No. 182, January 1923.

Duroselle, J.-B. *Histoire diplomatique de 1919 à nos jours*. Paris, 1958.

Elcock, Howard. *Portrait of a Decision: The Council of Four and the Treaty of Versailles*. London, 1972.

Felix, David. *Walther Rathenau and the Weimar Republic: The Politics of Reparations*. Baltimore and London, 1971.

Fisk, Harvey E. *The Inter-Ally Debts: An Analysis of War and Post-war Public Finance, 1914–1923*. New York and Paris, 1924.

Fry, Michael G. *Illusions of Security: North Atlantic Diplomacy, 1918–22*. Toronto, 1972.

Furst, Gaston A. *De Versailles aux experts*. Paris, 1927.

George, David Lloyd. *The Truth about the Peace Treaties*. 2 vols. London, 1938.

———. *The Truth about Reparations and War-debts*. London, 1932.

Gescher, Dieter Bruno. *Die Vereinigten Staaten von Nordamerika und die Reparationen, 1920–1924*. Bonn, 1956.

Gottwald, Robert. *Die deutsch-amerikanischen Beziehungen in der Ära Stresemann*. Berlin, 1965.

House, Edward Mandell, and Seymour, Charles, eds. *What Really Happened at Paris: The Story of the Peace Conference by the American Delegates, 1918–1919*. New York, 1921.

Jacobson, Jon. *Locarno Diplomacy: Germany and the West, 1925–1929*. Princeton, 1972.

Jessop, T. E. *The Treaty of Versailles: Was It Just?* New York and London, 1942.

Jordan, William M. *Great Britain, France and the German Problem, 1918–1939*. London, 1943.

Jouvenel, Bertrand de. *D'une guerre à l'autre*. 2 vols. Paris, 1940.

Keynes, John Maynard. *The Economic Consequences of the Peace*. London, 1919.

———. *A Revision of the Treaty*. London, 1922.

Klotz, Louis-Lucien. *De la guerre à la paix: Souvenirs et documents*. Paris, 1924.

Kochan, Lionel. *The Struggle for Germany, 1914–1945*. Chicago, 1963.

Krüger, Peter. *Deutschland und die Reparationen, 1918/19: Die Genesis des Reparationsproblems in Deutschland zwischen Waffenstillstand und Versailler Friedensschluss*. Stuttgart, 1973.

Lenoir, Nancy Ruth. "The Ruhr in Anglo-French Diplomacy: From the Beginning of the Occupation until the End of Passive Resistance." Ph.D. dissertation, University of Oklahoma, 1972.

Lewis, William Arthur. *Economic Survey, 1919–1939*. London, 1950.

Loyrette, J. E. L. "The Foreign Policy of Poincaré: France and Great Britain in Relation with the German Problem, 1919–1924." B. Litt. dissertation, Oxford University, 1955.

McFadyean, Sir Andrew. *Reparation Reviewed*. London, 1930.
Machlup, Fritz. *International Payments, Debts and Gold: Collected Essays*. New York, 1964.
Mantoux, Etienne. *The Carthaginian Peace or the Economic Consequences of Mr. Keynes*. London, New York, and Toronto, 1946.
Mantoux, Paul, ed. *Les Délibérations du conseil des quatre, 24 mars–28 juin 1919*. 2 vols. Paris, 1955.
Mayer, Arno J. *Political Origins of the New Diplomacy, 1917–1918*. New Haven, 1959.
———. *Politics and Diplomacy of Peacemaking: Containment and Counterrevolution at Versailles, 1918–1919*. New York, 1967.
Meade, James Edward. *The Theory of International Economic Policy*. Vol. 1. *The Balance of Payments*. London, 1962.
Moulton, Harold G. *The Reparation Plan*. New York and London, 1924.
Moulton, Harold G., and Pasvolsky, Leo. *War Debts and World Prosperity*. New York, 1932.
Ohlin, Bertil. *The Reparation Problem*. Stockholm, 1928.
Poidevin, Raymond. *Les Relations économiques et financières entre la France et l'Allemagne de 1898 à 1914*. Paris, 1969.
Renouvin, Pierre. *Histoire des relations internationales*. Vol. 7, pt. 1. *Les Crises du XXe siècle*. Paris, 1957.
Rössler, Helmut, ed. *Die Folgen von Versailles, 1919–1924*. Göttingen, 1969.
Salin, Edgar, ed. *Das Reparationsproblem*. 2 vols. Berlin, 1929.
Schmidt, Royal J. *Versailles and the Ruhr: Seedbed of World War II*. The Hague, 1968.
Schultze, Ernst. *Ruhrbesetzung und Weltwirtschaft: Eine internationale Untersuchung der Einwirkungen der Ruhrbesetzung auf die Weltwirtschaft*. Leipzig, 1927.
Schwarzschild, Leopold. *World in Trance: From Versailles to Pearl Harbor*. New York, 1942.
Selsam, Jon Paul. *The Attempts to Form an Anglo-French Alliance, 1919–1924*. Philadelphia, 1936.
Sering, Max. *Germany under the Dawes Plan*. Translated by S. Milton Hart. London, 1929.
Simonds, Frank H. *How Europe Made Peace without America*. New York, 1927.
Tardieu, André. *La Paix*. Paris, 1921.
Taylor, A. J. P. *The Origins of the Second World War*. London, 1961.
Temperley, H. W. V., ed. *A History of the Peace Conference of Paris*. 6 vols. London, 1920–24.
Toynbee, Arnold J. *Survey of International Affairs, 1920–1923*. London, 1925.
———. *Survey of International Affairs, 1924*. London, 1926.
Wandycz, Piotr S. *France and Her Eastern Allies, 1919–1925*. Minneapolis, 1962.
Weill-Raynal, Etienne. *Les Réparations allemandes et la France*. 3 vols. Paris, 1947.
Wheeler-Bennett, John W., and Latimer, Hugh. *Information on the Reparation Settlement: Being the Background and History of the Young Plan and the Hague Agreements, 1929–1930*. London, 1930.
Wolfers, Arnold. *Britain and France between Two Wars: Conflicting Strategies of Peace since Versailles*. New York, 1940.
Wüest, Erich. *Der Vertrag von Versailles in Licht und Schatten der Kritik: Die Kontroverse um seine wirtschaftlichen Auswirkungen*. Zurich, 1962.

B. *France, Financial and Economic*

Allix, Edgard. *Traité élémentaire de science des finances et de législation financière française*. 4th–5th rev. eds. Paris, 1921–27.
Allix, Edgard, and Lecerclé, Marcel. *L'Impôt sur le revenu*. 2 vols. Paris, 1926.

Augé-Laribé, Michel. *La Politique agricole de la France de 1880 à 1940*. Paris, 1950.
Bettelheim, Charles. *Bilan de l'économie française, 1919–1946*. Paris, 1947.
Bouton, André. *La Fin des rentiers*. Paris, 1930.
Calmette, Germain. *Un des problèmes de la paix: Les Dettes interalliées*. Paris, 1926.
Casamajor, Jean. *Le Marché à terme des changes en France*. Paris, 1924.
Clémentel, Etienne. *Inventaire de la situation financière au début de la treizième législature*. Paris, 1924.
Dauphin-Meunier, Achille. *La Banque, 1919–1935*. Paris, 1936.
Decamps, Jules. *Problèmes financiers d'après-guerre*. Paris, 1922.
______. *La Situation monétaire et l'avenir du franc*. Paris, 1925.
Divisia, François; Dupin; and Roy. *A la recherche du franc perdu*. 3 vols. Paris, 1954–56.
Dubergé, Jean. *La Psychologie sociale de l'impôt dans la France d'aujourd'hui*. Paris, 1961.
Dulles, Eleanor Lansing. *The French Franc, 1914–1928*. New York, 1929.
Frayssinet, Pierre. *La Politique monétaire de la France, 1924–1928*. Paris, 1928.
Germain-Martin, Henry. *Les Finances publiques en France et la fortune privée, 1914–1925*. Paris, 1925.
Gide, Charles, ed. *Effects of the War upon French Economic Life*. Oxford, London, and New York, 1923.
Gide, Charles, and Oualid, William. *Le Bilan de la guerre pour la France*. Paris and New Haven, 1931.
Gignoux, Claude Joseph. *L'Après-guerre et la politique commerciale*. Paris, 1924.
______. *L'Economie française entre les deux guerres, 1919–1939*. Paris, 1942.
Goguel-Nyegaard, François. *Le Rôle financier du Sénat français*. Paris, 1937.
Goldey, David B. "The Disintegration of the Cartel des Gauches and the Politics of French Government Finance, 1924–1928." D. Phil. dissertation, Oxford University, 1961.
Gressent, Alfred Georges. *Le Mystère de la rue de Rivoli: Grandeur et décadence du franc sous le ministère de M. de Lasteyrie*. Paris, 1924.
Haig, Robert Murray. *The Public Finances of Post-War France*. New York, 1929.
Haight, Frank Arnold. *A History of French Commercial Policies*. New York, 1941.
Huber, Michel. *La Population de la France pendant la guerre*. Paris and New Haven, 1932.
Institut National de Statistiques et d'Etudes Economiques. *L'Intérêt du capital depuis 1857*. Paris, 1958.
Kemp, Tom. *The French Economy, 1913–39: The History of a Decline*. London, 1972.
Lachapelle, Georges. *Les Batailles du franc: La Trésorerie, le change et la monnaie depuis 1914*. Paris, 1928.
______. *Le Crédit public*. Vol. 2. *Emissions du trésor depuis 1914. Crises du change. Assainissement financier et monétaire. Amortissement de la dette*. Paris, 1932.
Lacour-Gayet, Robert. "Le Problème de la dette française envers les Etats-Unis après la première guerre mondiale, 1917–1932." *Revue d'histoire diplomatique* 75 (janvier–mai 1961): 10–24.
Landes, David S. "French Entrepreneurship and Industrial Growth in the Nineteenth Century." *Journal of Economic History* 9 (May 1949): 45–61.
Landry, Adolphe. *La Politique commerciale de la France*. Paris, 1934.
Laufenburger, Henry. *Enquête sur les changements de structure du crédit et de la banque, 1914–1938*. Vol. 1. *Les Banques françaises*. Paris, 1940.
Lauré, Maurice. *Traité de politique fiscale*. Paris, 1956.
Mermeix [Gabriel Terrail]. *Histoire du franc depuis le commencement de ses malheurs*. Paris, 1926.
Michel, Edmond. *Les Dommages de guerre de la France et leur réparation*. Paris, 1932.
Montigny, Jean, and Kayser, Jacques. *Le Drame financier: Les Responsables*. Paris, 1925.

Moreau, Emile. *Souvenirs d'un gouverneur de la Banque de France: Histoire de la stabilisation du franc, 1926–1928*. Paris, 1954.
Myers, Margaret. *Paris as a Financial Center*. New York, 1936.
Naudin, Jean. *Les Accords commerciaux de la France depuis la guerre*. Paris, 1928.
Ogburn, William F., and Jaffé, William. *The Economic Development of Post-War France*. New York, 1929.
Olphe-Gaillard, Gabriel. *Histoire économique et financière de la guerre, 1914–1918*. Paris, 1923.
Oualid, William, and Picquenard, Charles. *Salaires et tarifs*. Paris and New Haven, 1928.
Perrot, Marguerite. *La Monnaie et l'opinion publique en France et en Angleterre, 1924–1936*. Paris, 1955.
Petit, Lucien. *Histoire des finances extérieures de la France: Le Règlement des dettes interalliées, 1919–1929*. Paris, 1932.
———. *Histoire des finances extérieures de la France pendant la guerre, 1914–1919*. Paris, 1929.
Philippe, Raymond. *Le Drame financier de 1924–1928*. Paris, 1931.
Pietri, François. *Le Financier*. Paris, 1931.
Pirou, Gaëtan. *La Monnaie française depuis la guerre, 1914–1936: Inflation, stabilisation, dévaluation*. Paris, 1936.
Rist, Charles, and Pirou, Gaëtan, eds. *De la France d'avant-guerre à la France d'aujourd'hui: Vingt-cinq ans d'évolution de la structure économique et sociale française. Cinquantaire de la Revue d'économie politique*. Paris, 1939.
Rogers, James Harvey. *The Process of Inflation in France, 1914–1927*. New York, 1929.
Romanet du Caillaud, Jacques. *L'Indemnité de dommages de guerre: Son évaluation, son remploi, son paiement*. Paris, 1923.
Rosier, Camille. *Tous nos impôts*. Paris, 1926.
Sauvy, Alfred. *Histoire économique de la France entre les deux guerres*. 2 vols. Paris, 1965–67.
Sauvy, Alfred, and Depoid, Pierre. *Salaires et pouvoir d'achat des ouvriers et des fonctionnaires entre les deux guerres*. Paris, 1946.
Schneider, A. *La Banque de France depuis 1914*. Nancy, 1933.
Sédillot, René. *Du franc Bonaparte au franc de Gaulle*. Paris, 1959.
———. *Histoire du franc*. Paris, 1939.
Shoup, Carl S. *The Sales Tax in France*. New York, 1930.
Tabatoni, Pierre. "France." In *Foreign Tax Policies and Economic Growth*. Compiled by the National Bureau of Economic Research. New York, 1956.
Truchy, Henri. *Les Finances de guerre de la France*. Paris, 1926.
Vedel, Georges. "Le Rôle des croyances économiques dans la vie politique." *Revue française de science politique* 1 (January 1951): 40–50.
Wilson, J. S. G. *French Banking Structure and Credit Policy*. Cambridge, Mass., 1957.
Wolfe, Martin. *The French Franc between Two Wars, 1919–1939*. New York, 1951.
Wolff, Robert. *Economie et finances de la France*. New York, 1943.

C. France, Diplomatic and Political

Ackerman, Martin. "Quelques aspects de l'opinion publique en France sur le problème allemand, 1920–1940." Dissertation, Sorbonne, 1952.
Albrecht-Carrié, René. *France, Europe and the Two World Wars*. New York, 1961.
Allard, Paul. *Le Quai d'Orsay: Son personnel, ses rouages, ses dessous*. Paris, 1938.
Antériou, J.-L., and Baron, J. J. *Edouard Herriot au service de la république*. Paris, 1957.

Artaud, Denise. "A propos de l'occupation de la Ruhr." *Revue d'histoire moderne et contemporaine* 17 (1970): 2–21.
Aubert, Octave. *Louis Barthou*. Paris, 1935.
Baillou, Jean, and Pelletier, Pierre. *Les Affaires étrangères*. Paris, 1962.
Bainville, Jacques. *Journal, 1919–1926*. Paris, 1949.
Bankwitz, Philip C. F. "Weygand: A Biographical Study." Ph.D. dissertation, Harvard University, 1952.
Bariéty, Jacques. "Les Réparations allemandes après la première guerre mondiale: Objet ou prétexte à une politique rhénane de la France, 1919–1924." *Bulletin de la Société d'histoire moderne et contemporaine* 15 (1973): 21–33.
Barthou, Louis. *La Politique*. Paris, 1923.
Beau de Loménie, E. *Les Responsabilités des dynasties bourgeoises sous la Troisième République*. Vol. 3. *La Guerre et l'immédiat après-guerre, 1914–1924*. Paris, 1954.
———. *Les Responsabilités des dynasties bourgeoises sous la Troisième République*. Vol. 4. *Du Cartel à Hitler, 1924–1933*. Paris, 1963.
Benoist, Charles. *Souvenirs*. Vol. 3. *1902–1933*. Paris, 1934.
Berl, Emmanuel. *La Politique et les partis*. Paris, 1932.
Binion, Rudolf. *Defeated Leaders: The Political Fate of Caillaux, Jouvenel and Tardieu*. New York, 1960.
Bonnefous, Edouard. *Histoire politique de la Troisième République*. Vol. 3. *L'Après-guerre, 1919–1924*. Paris, 1959.
———. *Histoire politique de la Troisième République*. Vol. 4. *Cartel des gauches et union nationale, 1924–1929*. Paris, 1960.
———. *La Réforme administrative*. Paris, 1958.
Bonnet, Georges. *Le Quai d'Orsay sous trois républiques, 1870–1961*. Paris, 1961.
Bourgin, Georges; Carrère, Jean; and Guérin, André. *Manuel des partis politiques en France*. Paris, 1928.
Bréal, Auguste. *Philippe Berthelot*. Paris, 1947.
Bréaud, Henri. *La Régie des chemins de fer des territoires occupés, 1923–1924*. Paris, 1938.
Brogan, D. W. *France under the Republic: The Development of Modern France, 1870–1939*. New York and London, 1940.
Bugnet, Charles. *Mangin*. Paris, 1934.
Carrère, Jean, and Bourgin, Georges. *Manuel des partis politiques en France*. Paris, 1924.
Castellan, Georges. *Le Réarmement clandestin du Reich, 1930–1935, vu par le 2. Bureau de l'Etat-Major français*. Paris, 1954.
Chapman, Brian. *The Prefects and Provincial France*. London, 1955.
Charles-Roux, François. *Souvenirs diplomatiques: Une Grande Ambassade à Rome, 1919–1925*. Paris, 1961.
Chastenet, Jacques. *Histoire de la Troisième République*. Vol. 5. *Les Années d'illusions, 1918–1931*. Paris, 1960.
———. "Une Occasion manquée: L'Affaire de la Ruhr." *Revue de Paris*, July 1959, pp. 5–19.
———. *Raymond Poincaré*. Paris, 1948.
Colton, Joel. *Léon Blum: Humanist in Politics*. New York, 1966.
Cornilleau, Robert. *Du Bloc National au Front Populaire*. Vol. 1. *1919–1924*. Paris, 1939.
Cowan, Laing Gray. *France and the Saar, 1680–1948*. New York, 1950.
Cristiani, Chanoine L. *La Fin d'un régime: Tableau de la vie politique française de 1919 à 1939*. Lyon and Paris, 1946.
Dansette, Adrien. *Histoire des présidents de la république*. Paris, 1953.
Degoutte, General. *L'Occupation de la Ruhr*. Düsseldorf, 1924.
Dupont, Jacques. "La Campagne de presse du Cartel des Gauches." Dissertation, Institut d'Etudes Politiques, 1950.

Earle, Edward Mead, ed. *Modern France: Problems of the Third and Fourth Republics*. Princeton, 1951.
Echeman, Jacques. *Les Ministères en France de 1914 à 1932*. Paris, 1932.
Fabre-Luce, Alfred. *La Victoire*. Paris, 1924.
Fiérain, Jacques. "La Presse française et l'occupation de la Ruhr." Diplôme d'études supérieures, Sorbonne, 1950.
François-Poncet, André. *De Versailles à Potsdam*. Paris, 1948.
———. "Poincaré tel que je l'ai vu." *Le Figaro littéraire*, 16 June 1948.
Gedye, G. E. R. *The Revolver Republic: France's Bid for the Rhine*. London, 1930.
Giraudoux, Jean. *Bella*. Paris, 1926. Translated by J. F. Scanlan. New York and London, 1927.
Goguel, François. *Géographie des élections françaises de 1870 à 1951*. Paris, 1951.
———. *Histoire des institutions politiques de la France de 1870 à 1940*. Paris, 1951.
———. *La Politique des partis sous la IIIe République*. Paris, 1957.
Guitard, Louis. *Petite histoire de la IIIe République: Le Souvenir de Maurice Colrat*. Paris, 1959.
Halévy, Daniel. *La République des comités: Essai d'histoire contemporaine, 1895–1934*. Paris, 1934.
Hamon, Augustin, and X. Y. Z. *Les Maîtres de la France*. 3 vols. Paris, 1936–38.
Herriot, Edouard. *Etudes françaises*. Geneva, 1950.
———. *Jadis*. Vol. 2. *D'une guerre à l'autre, 1914–1936*. Paris, 1952.
———. "Souvenirs d'entre deux guerres." *Les Annales. Conférencia*. 15 January 1950, pp. 1–16.
Hoffmann, Stanley, ed. *In Search of France*. Cambridge, Mass., 1963.
Homberg, Octave. *Les Coulisses de l'histoire: Souvenirs, 1898–1928*. Paris, 1938.
Howard, John Edward. *Parliament and Foreign Policy in France: A Study of the Origins, Nature and Methods of the Parliamentary Control of Foreign Policy in France during the Third Republic with Special Reference to the Period from 1919 to 1939*. London, 1948.
Hughes, Judith M. *To the Maginot Line: The Politics of French Military Preparation in the 1920's*. Cambridge, Mass., 1971.
Jolly, Jean, ed. *Dictionnaire des parlementaires français, 1889–1940*. 7 vols. Paris, 1960–72.
Joseph-Maginot, Marguerite. *The Biography of André Maginot: He Might Have Saved France*. New York, 1941.
Jouvenel, Robert de. *La République des camarades*. Nouvelle édition précédé d'un avant-propos par P. Morand, vingt ans après. Paris, 1934.
Kessel, J., and Suarez, Georges. *Au camp des vainçus ou la critique du 11 mai*. Paris, 1924.
———. *Le 11 mai*. Paris, 1924.
King, Jere Clemens. *Foch versus Clemenceau: France and German Dismemberment, 1918–1919*. Cambridge, Mass., 1960.
Lachapelle, Georges. *Elections législatives du 11 mai 1924*. Paris, 1924.
Lafue, Pierre. *Gaston Doumergue: Sa vie et son destin*. Paris, 1933.
Larmour, Peter J. *The French Radical Party in the 1930's*. Stanford, 1964.
Laroche, Jules. *Au Quai d'Orsay avec Briand et Poincaré, 1913–1926*. Paris, 1957.
———. "La Grande Déception de Cannes (Souvenirs de 1922)." *Revue de Paris*, June 1957, pp. 39–51.
Lefranc, Georges. *Histoire du front populaire*. Paris, 1965.
Leonhardt, Fritz Hermann. *Aristide Briand und seine Deutschlandpolitik*. Heidelberg, 1951.
Lévis Mirepoix, Emmanuel de. *Le Ministère des Affaires Etrangères: Organisation de l'administration centrale et des services extérieurs, 1793–1933*. Angers, 1934.
Lévy, Louis. *Les Nuits du Cartel*. Paris, 1929.

Logue, William. *Léon Blum: The Formative Years, 1872–1914*. De Kalb, Illinois, 1973.

Loucheur, Louis. *Carnets secrets, 1908–1932*. Edited by Jacques de Launay. Brussels and Paris, 1962.

Manevy, Raymond. *Histoire de la presse, 1914 à 1939*. Paris, 1945.

Marcellin, Louis. *Politique et politiciens d'après-guerre*. Paris, 1923.

———. *Voyage autour de la Chambre du 11 mai*. Paris, 1925.

Mazedier, René. *Histoire de la presse parisienne de Théophraste Renaudot à la IVe République, 1631–1945*. Paris, 1945.

Miquel, Pierre. *La Paix de Versailles et l'opinion publique française*. Paris, 1971.

———. *Poincaré*. Paris, 1961.

Mordacq, General H. *La Mentalité allemande: Cinq ans de commandement sur le Rhin*. Paris, 1926.

Nobécourt, Jacques. *Une Histoire politique de l'armée: De Pétain à Pétain, 1919–1942*. Paris, 1967.

Nollet, General [Charles]. *Une Expérience de désarmement: Cinq ans de contrôle militaire en Allemagne*. Paris, 1932.

Paoli, François-André. *L'Armée française de 1919 à 1939*. Vol. 2. *La Phase de fermeté*. Paris, 1972.

Paul-Boncour, Joseph. *Entre deux guerres: Souvenirs sur la IIIe République*. 3 vols. Paris, 1945–46.

Peretti de la Rocca, Emmanuel de. "Briand et Poincaré: Souvenirs." *Revue de Paris*, 15 December 1936, pp. 775–88.

Persil, Raoul. *Alexandre Millerand*. Paris, 1949.

Pertinax [André Géraud]. *The Gravediggers of France*. Garden City, N.Y., 1944.

Pinon, René. *La Bataille de la Ruhr: Chroniques du ministère Poincaré*. Vol. 2. Paris, 1924.

———. *Le Redressement de la politique française, 1922: Chroniques du ministère Poincaré*. Vol. 1. Paris, 1923.

Prain, Roger. "Les Préoccupations démographiques de la défense nationale en France, 1870–1940." Dissertation, Institut d'Etudes Politiques, 1949–50.

Prévost, Jean. *Histoire de France depuis la guerre*. Paris, 1932.

Recouly, Raymond. *Le Mémorial de Foch: Mes entretiens avec le Maréchal*. Paris, 1929.

Reibel, Charles. "Une Grande Occasion manquée: Le Premier Drame de la Ruhr." *Ecrits de Paris*, May 1949, pp. 24–31.

Reynaud, Paul. *Mémoires*. Vol. 1. *Venu de ma montagne*. Paris, 1960.

———. *Mémoires*. Vol. 2. *Envers et contre tous*. Paris, 1963.

Saint-Aulaire, Comte Auguste Félix de. "L'Angleterre et les élections de 1924." *Ecrits de Paris*, May 1953, pp. 9–19.

———. *Confession d'un vieux diplomate*. Paris, 1953.

Seydoux, Jacques. *De Versailles au plan Young*. Paris, 1932.

Sherwood, John M. *Georges Mandel and the Third Republic*. Stanford, 1970.

Siegfried, André. *De la Troisième à la Quatrième République*. Paris, 1957.

———. *Tableau des partis en France*. Paris, 1930.

Soulié, Michel. *La Vie politique d'Edouard Herriot*. Paris, 1962.

Soulier, A. *L'Instabilité ministérielle sous la Troisième République*. Paris, 1939.

Suarez, Georges. *Briand, sa vie, son oeuvre*. Vols. 5 and 6. Paris, 1941–52.

———. *De Poincaré à Poincaré*. Paris, 1928.

———. *Herriot, 1924–1932: Nouvelle Edition de "Une Nuit chez Cromwell" suivie d'un récit historique de R. Poincaré*. Paris, 1932.

Talbott, John E. *The Politics of Educational Reform in France, 1918–1940*. Princeton, 1969.

Tarde, Alfred de, and Jouvenel, Robert de. *La Politique d'aujourd'hui*. Paris, 1924.

Tarr, Francis de. *The French Radical Party from Herriot to Mendès-France*. London, 1961.

Thibaudet, Albert. *Les Princes lorrains*. Paris, 1924.

______. *La République des professeurs*. Paris, 1927.

Thomson, David. *Democracy in France*. London, 1958.

Tirard, Paul. *La France sur le Rhin: Douze années d'occupation rhénane*. Paris, 1930.

Tournoux, P. E. *Défense des frontières: Haut Commandement–Gouvernement, 1919–1939*. Paris, 1960.

Varenne, Francisque. *Georges Mandel, mon patron*. Paris, 1947.

Weber, Eugen. *Action Française: Royalism and Reaction in Twentieth-Century France*. Stanford, 1962.

______. *Nationalist Revival in France, 1905–1914*. Berkeley, 1959.

Weygand, Maxime. *Foch*. Paris, 1947.

Williams, Philip M. *Crisis and Compromise: Politics in the Fourth Republic*. Hamden, Conn., 1964.

Wohl, Robert. *French Communism in the Making, 1914–1924*. Stanford, 1966.

Wormser, Georges. *Georges Mandel, l'homme politique*. Paris, 1967.

Ziebura, Gilbert. *Die deutsche Frage in der öffentlichen Meinung Frankreichs von 1911–1914*. Berlin, 1955.

______. *Léon Blum: Theorie und Praxis einer sozialistischen Politik*. Berlin, 1963.

Zimmermann, Ludwig. *Frankreichs Ruhrpolitik: Von Versailles bis zum Dawesplan*. Edited by Walther Peter Fuchs. Göttingen, Zurich, and Frankfurt am Main, 1971.

D. Germany

Angell, James W. *The Recovery of Germany*. 2d rev. ed. London, 1932.

Angress, Werner T. *Stillborn Revolution: The Communist Bid for Power in Germany, 1921–1923*. Princeton, 1963.

Beusch, Paul. *Währungszerfall und Währungsstabilisierung*. Edited by G. Briefs and C. A. Fischer. Berlin, 1928.

Bischof, Erwin. *Rheinischer Separatismus, 1918–1924: Hans Adam Dortens Rheinstaatbestrebungen*. Bern, 1969.

Böhme, Helmut. *Deutschlands Weg zur Grossmacht: Studien zum Verhältnis von Wirtschaft und Staat während der Reichsgründungszeit, 1848–1881*. Cologne, 1966.

Bonn, Moritz Julius. *Wandering Scholar*. New York, 1948.

Bracher, Karl Dietrich. *Die Auflösung der Weimarer Republik*. 2d rev. ed. Stuttgart and Düsseldorf, 1957.

Bratz, Maria. *Der deutsche Privatbankierstand in der Nachkriegszeit, 1918–1933*. Berlin, 1958.

Bresciani-Turroni, Costantino. *The Economics of Inflation: A Study of Currency Depreciation in Post-War Germany*. London, 1937.

Bretton, Henry L. *Stresemann and the Revision of Versailles: A Fight for Reason*. Stanford, 1953.

Bücher, Hermann. *Finanz- und Wirtschaftsentwicklung Deutschlands in den Jahren 1921 bis 1925. Reden*. Berlin, 1925.

Cagan, Philip. "The Monetary Dynamics of Hyperinflation." In *Studies in the Quantity Theory of Money*, edited by Milton Friedman. Chicago, 1956.

Carsten, Francis Ludwig. *The Reichswehr and Politics, 1918 to 1933*. Oxford, 1966.

Claussen, Peter Carsten, ed. *Neue Perspektiven aus Wirtschaft und Recht: Festschrift für Hans Schäffer zum 80. Geburtstag*. Berlin, 1966.

Cornebise, Alfred Emile. "Some Aspects of the German Response to the Ruhr Occupation, January–September 1923." Ph.D. dissertation, University of North Carolina, 1965.

Dorten, J. A. *La Tragédie rhénane*. Paris, 1945.

Ellis, Howard S. *German Monetary Theory, 1905–1933*. Cambridge, Mass., 1934.
Erdmann, Karl Dietrich. *Adenauer in der Rheinlandpolitik nach dem Ersten Weltkrieg*. Stuttgart, 1966.
———. "Deutschland, Rapallo, und der Westen." *Vierteljahrshefte für Zeitgeschichte* 11 (April 1963): 105–65.
Ersil, Wilhelm. *Aktionseinheit stürzt Cuno: Zur Geschichte des Massenkampfes gegen die Cuno-Regierung 1923 in Mitteldeutschland*. [East] Berlin, 1963.
Euler, Heinrich. *Die Aussenpolitik der Weimarer Republik, 1918/1923: Vom Waffenstillstand bis zum Ruhrkonflikt*. Aschaffenburg, 1957.
Eyck, Erich. *A History of the Weimar Republic*. Translated by Harlan P. Hanson and Robert G. L. Waite. 2 vols. Cambridge, Mass., 1962.
Favez, Jean-Claude. *Le Reich devant l'occupation franco-belge de la Ruhr en 1923*. Geneva, 1969.
Fischer, Fritz. *Griff nach der Weltmacht: Die Kriegszielpolitik des kaiserlichen Deutschland, 1914–18*. 3d rev. ed. Düsseldorf, 1964.
———. *Krieg der Illusionen: Die deutsche Politik von 1911 bis 1914*. Düsseldorf, 1969.
Florinsky, Michael T. *The Saar Struggle*. New York, 1934.
Friedensburg, Ferdinand. *Die Weimarer Republik*. Berlin, 1946.
Gatzke, Hans W. *Germany's Drive to the West: A Study of Western War Aims during the First World War*. Baltimore, 1950.
———. *Stresemann and the Rearmament of Germany*. Baltimore, 1954.
Gessler, Otto. *Reichswehrpolitik in der Weimarer Zeit*. Stuttgart, 1958.
Gordon, Harold J., Jr. *Hitler and the Beer Hall Putsch*. Princeton, 1972.
Graham, Frank D. *Exchange, Prices and Production in Hyper-Inflation: Germany, 1920–1923*. Princeton, 1930.
Grunewald, Jacques, and Scherer, André, eds. *L'Allemagne et les problèmes de la paix pendant la première guerre mondiale*. 2 vols. Paris, 1962.
Guske, Claus. *Das politische Denken des Generals von Seeckt*. Lübeck and Hamburg, 1971.
Hallgarten, George W. F. *Hitler, Reichswehr und Industrie: Zur Geschichte der Jahre 1918–1933*. Frankfurt am Main, 1955.
Helbig, Herbert. *Die Träger der Rapallo-Politik*. Göttingen, 1958.
Hermant, Max. *Les Paradoxes économiques de l'Allemagne moderne*. Paris, 1931.
Hertzmann, Lewis. *DNVP: Right-Wing Opposition in the Weimar Republic, 1918–1924*. Lincoln, Neb., 1963.
Hortzschansky, Günter. *Der nationale Verrat der deutschen Monopolherren während des Ruhrkampfes 1923*. [East] Berlin, 1961.
Kehr, Eckart. "Klassenkämpfe und Rüstungspolitik im kaiserlichen Deutschland." *Die Gesellschaft* 1 (1932): 391–414. Reprinted in *Der Primat der Innenpolitik*, by Eckart Kehr. Edited by Hans-Ulrich Wehler. Berlin, 1965.
———. *Schlachtflottenbau und Parteipolitik, 1894–1901*. Berlin, 1930.
Kessler, Harry. *Tagebücher, 1918–1937*. Frankfurt am Main, 1961.
———. *Walther Rathenau*. New York, 1930.
Köhler, Heinrich. *Lebenserinnerungen des Politikers und Staatsmannes*. Stuttgart, 1964.
Kohlhaus, Hans Helmut. "Die Hapag, Cuno und das deutsche Reich, 1920–1933." D. Phil. dissertation, University of Hamburg, 1952.
Laubach, Ernst. *Die Politik der Kabinette Wirth, 1921–22*. Lübeck and Hamburg, 1968.
Laursen, Karsten, and Pedersen, Jørgen. *The German Inflation, 1918–1923*. Amsterdam, 1964.
Liebe, Werner. *Die Deutschnationale Volkspartei, 1918–1924*. Düsseldorf, 1956.
Linke, Horst Günther. *Deutsch-sowjetische Beziehungen bis Rapallo*. Cologne, 1970.
Luther, Hans. *Politiker ohne Partei: Erinnerungen*. Stuttgart, 1960.

______. *Zusammenbruch und Jahre nach dem ersten Krieg in Essen*. Beiträge zur Geschichte von Stadt und Stift Essen, vol. 73. Essen, 1958.

Marx, Wilhelm. *Der Nachlass des Reichskanzlers Wilhelm Marx*. Mitteilungen aus dem Stadtarchiv von Köln. Vols. 52–55. Edited by Hugo Stehkämper. Cologne, 1968.

Maxelon, Michael-Olaf. *Stresemann und Frankreich, 1914–1929*. Düsseldorf, 1972.

Meier-Welcker, Hans. *Seeckt*. Frankfurt am Main, 1967.

Meissner, Otto. *Staatssekretär unter Ebert–Hindenburg–Hitler*. Hamburg, 1950.

Morgan, J. H. *Assize of Arms: The Disarmament of Germany and Her Rearmament, 1919–1939*. New York, 1946.

______. "The Disarmament of Germany and After." *Quarterly Review* 242 (October 1924): 415–57.

Morsey, Rudolf. *Die Deutsche Zentrumspartei, 1917–1923*. Düsseldorf, 1966.

Netzband, Karl Bernhard, and Widmaier, Hans Peter. *Währungs- und Finanzpolitik der Ära Luther, 1923–1925*. Basel, 1964.

Northrop, Mildred B. *Control Policies of the Reichsbank, 1924–1933*. New York, 1938.

Obermann, Karl. *Die Beziehungen des amerikanischen Imperialismus zum deutschen Imperialismus in der Zeit der Weimarer Republik, 1918–1925*. [East] Berlin, 1952.

Pedersen, Jörgen. "Einige Bemerkungen zur deutschen Inflation von 1919–1923." *Zeitschrift für die gesamte Staatswissenschaft* 122 (July 1966): 418–30.

Pinner, Felix [Frank Fassland]. *Deutsche Wirtschaftsführer*. Berlin-Charlottenburg, 1925.

Post, Gaines. *The Civil-Military Fabric of Weimar Foreign Policy*. Princeton, 1973.

Rabenau, Friedrich von. *Seeckt: Aus seinem Leben, 1918–1936*. Leipzig, 1940.

Rathenau, Walther. *Tagebuch, 1907–1922*. Edited by Hartmut Pogge-v. Strandmann. Düsseldorf, 1967.

Reichert, Jacob Wilhelm. *Rathenaus Reparationspolitik: Eine kritische Studie*. Berlin, 1922.

______. *Von Wilson bis Dawes: Vierzehn Kapitel Reparationspolitik*. Berlin, 1925.

Riekhoff, Harald von. *German-Polish Relations, 1918–1933*. Baltimore and London, 1971.

Respondek, Erwin. *Die Reichsfinanzen auf Grund der Reform von 1919–20*. Berlin and Leipzig, 1920.

______. *Wirtschaftliche Zusammenarbeit zwischen Deutschland und Frankreich*. Berlin, 1929.

Ritter, Gerhard. *Staatskunst und Kriegshandwerk: Das Problem des "Militarismus" in Deutschland*. Vols. 2–4. Munich, 1960–68.

Röpke, Wilhelm. *German Commercial Policy*. London, 1934.

Rosenberg, Arthur. *A History of the German Republic*. London, 1936.

Ruge, Wolfgang. *Die Stellungnahme der Sowjetunion gegen die Besetzung des Ruhrgebiets*. [East] Berlin, 1962.

Salewski, Michael. *Entwaffnung und Militärkontrolle in Deutschland, 1919–1927*. Bonn, 1966.

Schacht, Hjalmar. *Confessions of the Old Wizard: The Autobiography of Hjalmar Horace Greeley Schacht*. Boston, 1956.

______. *The Stabilization of the Mark*. London, 1927.

Schmidt, Paul. *Statist auf diplomatischer Bühne, 1923–45*. Bonn, 1949.

Schröder, Ernst. *Otto Wiedfeldt: Eine Biographie*. Beiträge zur Geschichte von Stadt und Stift Essen, vol. 80. Essen, 1964.

Sieveking, Kurt, ed. *Carl Melchior: Ein Buch des Gedenkens und der Freundschaft*. Tübingen, 1971.

Simpson, Amos E. *Hjalmar Schacht in Perspective*. The Hague and Paris, 1969.

Spethmann, Hans. *Der Ruhrkampf, 1923 bis 1925*. Berlin, 1933.

Stampfer, Friedrich. *Die vierzehn Jahre der ersten deutschen Republik*. Carlsbad, 1936.

Stegmann, Dirk. *Die Erben Bismarcks: Parteien und Verbände in der Spätphase des Wilhelminischen Deutschlands. Sammlungspolitik, 1897–1918*. Cologne and Berlin, 1970.

Steinberg, Jonathan. *Yesterday's Deterrent: Tirpitz and the Birth of the German Battle Fleet*. New York, 1965.

Stockhausen, Max von. *Sechs Jahre Reichskanzlei: Von Rapallo bis Locarno. Erinnerungen und Tagebuchnotizen, 1922–1927*. Edited by Walter Görlitz. Bonn, 1954.

Stolper, Gustav. *German Economy, 1870–1940*. New York, 1940.

Stresemann, Gustav. *Vermächtnis. Der Nachlass in drei Bänden*. Vol. 1. *Vom Ruhrkrieg bis London*. Edited by Henry Bernhard. Berlin, 1932.

Stucken, Rudolf. *Deutsche Geld- und Kreditpolitik 1914 bis 1963*. Tübingen, 1964.

Thimme, Annelise. *Gustav Stresemann*. Hanover and Frankfurt am Main, 1957.

Thimme, Roland. *Stresemann und die deutsche Volkspartei, 1923–1925*. Lübeck and Hamburg, 1961.

Turner, Henry Ashby, Jr. *Stresemann and the Politics of the Weimar Republic*. Princeton, 1963.

Vagts, Alfred. "M. M. Warburg & Co.: Ein Bankhaus in der deutschen Weltpolitik, 1905–1933." *Vierteljahrschrift für Sozial- und Wirtschaftsgeschichte* 45 (September 1958): 289–388.

Wambaugh, Sarah. *The Saar Plebiscite*. Cambridge, Mass., 1940.

Warburg, Max M. *Aus meinen Aufzeichnungen*. Glückstadt, 1952.

Weidenfeld, Werner. *Die Englandpolitik Gustav Stresemanns*. Mainz, 1972.

Wheeler-Bennett, John W. *The Nemesis of Power: The German Army in Politics, 1918–1945*. London, 1953.

White, David Glen. *Einige Kapitel aus der grossen Politik zur Zeit der Ruhrbesetzung*. Berlin, 1939.

Ziemer, Gerhard. *Inflation und Deflation zerstören die Demokratie: Lehren aus dem Schicksal der Weimarer Republik*. Stuttgart, 1971.

Zimmermann, Ludwig. *Deutsche Aussenpolitik in der Ära der Weimarer Republik*. Göttingen, Berlin, and Frankfurt am Main, 1958.

Zsigmond, László. *Zur deutschen Frage, 1918–1923*. Budapest, 1964.

E. Great Britain

Aldcroft, D. H. *The Inter-War Economy: Britain, 1919–1939*. New York, 1970.

Barnett, Correlli. *The Collapse of British Power*. London, 1972.

Beaverbrook, Lord. *The Decline and Fall of Lloyd George and Great Was the Fall Thereof*. London, 1963.

Beloff, Max. *Imperial Sunset*. Vol. 1. *Britain's Liberal Empire, 1897–1921*. New York, 1970.

Bertram-Libal, Gisela. *Aspekte der britischen Deutschlandpolitik, 1919–1922*. Göppingen, 1972.

Blake, Robert. *The Unknown Prime Minister: The Life and Times of Andrew Bonar Law, 1858–1923*. London, 1955.

Boyle, Andrew. *Montagu Norman*. London, 1967.

Brown, William Adams, Jr. *England and the New Gold Standard, 1919–1926*. New Haven, 1929.

Butler, James Ramsay Montagu. *Lord Lothian, Philip Kerr, 1882–1940*. London, 1960.

Cecil, Viscount Robert. *All the Way*. London, 1949.

Churchill, Randolph Spencer. *Lord Derby, King of Lancashire: The Official Life of Edward, Seventeenth Earl of Derby, 1865–1948*. London, 1959.
Clay, Sir Henry. *Lord Norman*. London, 1957.
Cole, G. D. H. *A History of the Labour Party from 1914*. London, 1948.
Connell, John [John Henry Robertson]. *The "Office": A Study of British Foreign Policy and Its Makers, 1919–1951*. London, 1958.
Cowling, Maurice. *The Impact of Labour, 1920–1924: The Beginning of Modern British Politics*. Cambridge, 1971.
Crosby, Gerda Richards. *Disarmament and Peace in British Politics, 1914–1919*. Cambridge, Mass., 1957.
Cross, Colin. *Philip Snowden*. London, 1966.
Curzon of Kedleston, Marchioness. *Reminiscences*. New York, 1955.
D'Abernon, Viscount Edgar. *An Ambassador of Peace*. 3 vols. London, 1929–30.
Elton, Baron Godfrey. *The Life of James Ramsay MacDonald, 1866–1919*. London, 1939.
Glasgow, George. *MacDonald as Diplomatist: The Foreign Policy of the First Labour Government*. London, 1924.
Hamilton, Mary Agnes. *Arthur Henderson: A Biography*. London, 1938.
Hardinge of Penshurst, Lord. *Old Diplomacy: Reminiscences*. London, 1949.
Harrod, R. F. *The Life of John Maynard Keynes*. London, 1951.
Hicks, Ursula K. *The Finances of British Government, 1920–1936*. London, 1938.
James, Robert Rhodes. *Memoirs of a Conservative: J. C. C. Davidson's Memoirs and Papers, 1910–37*. London, 1969.
Jones, J. Harry. *Josiah Stamp, Public Servant*. London, 1964.
Jones, Thomas. *Lloyd George*. London, 1951.
———. *Whitehall Diary*. Vol. 1. *1916–1925*. Edited by Keith Middlemas. London, New York, and Toronto, 1969.
Kahn, Alfred E. *Great Britain in the World Economy*. New York, 1946.
Kinnear, Michael. *The Fall of Lloyd George*. London, 1973.
Leith-Ross, Frederick. *Money Talks: Fifty Years of International Finance*. London, 1968.
Lloyd George, Frances. *The Years that Are Past*. London, 1967.
Lyman, Richard W. *The First Labour Government, 1924*. London, 1957.
McCallum, R. B. *Public Opinion and the Last Peace*. London and New York, 1944.
MacDonald, Malcolm. *Titans and Others*. London, 1972.
Maddox, William P. *Foreign Relations in British Labour Policies*. Cambridge, 1934.
Medlicott, William Norton. *British Foreign Policy since Versailles*. London, 1940.
Middlemas, Keith, and Barnes, John. *Baldwin: A Biography*. London, 1969.
Moggridge, D. E. *British Monetary Policy, 1924–1931: The Norman Conquest of $4.86*. Cambridge, 1972.
———. *The Return to Gold, 1925: The Formulation of Economic Policy and Its Critics*. Cambridge, 1969.
Morgan, E. Victor. *Studies in British Financial Policy, 1914–1925*. London, 1952.
Mosley, Leonard. *The Glorious Fault: The Life of Lord Curzon*. New York, 1960.
Mowat, Charles Loch. *Britain between the Wars, 1918–1940*. Chicago, 1955.
Nicolson, Harold. *Curzon: The Last Phase, 1919–1925*. Boston and New York, 1934.
Northedge, F. S. *The Troubled Giant: Britain among the Great Powers, 1916–1939*. London and New York, 1966.
Owen, Frank. *Tempestuous Journey: Lloyd George, His Life and Times*. London, 1954.
Petrie, Sir Charles. *The Life and Letters of the Right Hon. Sir Austen Chamberlain*. 2 vols. London, 1939–40.
Pigou, Arthur Cecil. *Aspects of British Economic History, 1918–1925*. London, 1947.

Pollard, Sidney. *The Development of the British Economy, 1914–1967*. 2d rev. ed. New York, 1969.

———, ed. *The Gold Standard and Employment Policies between the Wars*. London, 1970.

Reynolds, Philip A. *British Foreign Policy in the Inter-war Years*. London, 1954.

Riddell, Baron George Allardice. *Lord Riddell's Intimate Diary of the Peace Conference and After, 1918–1923*. London, 1923.

Ronaldshay, Earl of. *The Life of Lord Curzon*. 3 vols. London, 1928.

Roskill, Stephen. *Hankey: Man of Secrets*. Vol. 2. *1919–1931*. London, 1972.

Rothwell, V. H. *British War Aims and Peace Diplomacy, 1914–1918*. Oxford, 1971.

Sachs, Benjamin. *J. Ramsay MacDonald in Thought and Action: An Architect for a Better World*. Albuquerque, N.M., 1952.

Scott, C. P. *The Political Diaries of C. P. Scott, 1911–1928*. Edited by Trevor Wilson. Ithaca, N.Y., 1970.

Skidelsky, Robert. *Politicians and the Slump: The Labour Government of 1929–1931*. London and New York, 1967.

Snowden, Viscount Philip. *An Autobiography*. 2 vols. London, 1934.

Stevenson, Frances. *Lloyd George: A Diary*. Edited by A. J. P. Taylor. London, 1971.

Taylor, A. J. P. *Beaverbrook*. London, 1972.

———. *English History, 1914–1945*. New York and Oxford, 1965.

———, ed. *Lloyd George: Twelve Essays*. London, 1971.

Thomas, J. H. *My Story*. London, 1937.

Tucker, William Rayburn. *The Attitude of the British Labour Party towards European and Collective Security Problems*. Geneva, 1950.

Walder, David. *The Chanak Affair*. London, 1969.

Webb, Beatrice. *Beatrice Webb's Diaries, 1924–1932*. Edited by Margaret Cole. London, New York, and Toronto, 1956.

Weir, L. MacNeill. *The Tragedy of Ramsay MacDonald: A Political Biography*. London, 1938.

Young, George Malcolm. *Stanley Baldwin*. London, 1952.

Youngson, A. J. *The British Economy, 1920–1957*. Cambridge, Mass., 1960.

F. United States

Abbott, Charles Cortez. *The New York Bond Market, 1920–1930*. Cambridge, Mass., 1937.

Abrahams, Paul Philip. "The Foreign Expansion of American Finance and Its Relationship to the Foreign Economic Policies of the United States, 1907–1921." Ph.D. dissertation, University of Wisconsin, 1967.

Adler, Selig. *The Isolationist Impulse: Its Twentieth Century Reaction*. New York, 1957.

———. *The Uncertain Giant, 1921–1941: American Foreign Policy between the Wars*. New York, 1965.

Allen, Frederick Lewis. *The Lords of Creation*. New York and London, 1935.

Allen, Henry T. *My Rhineland Journal*. Boston, 1923.

Artaud, Denise. "Le Gouvernement américain et la question des dettes de guerre au lendemain de l'armistice de Rethondes." *Revue d'histoire moderne et contemporaine* 20 (1973): 202–29.

———. "Le Gouvernement des Etats-Unis et le contrôle des emprunts européens, 1921–1929." *Bulletin de la Société d'histoire moderne et contemporaine* 15 (1972): 17–26.

Brandes, Joseph. *Herbert Hoover and Economic Diplomacy: Department of Commerce Policy, 1921–1928*. Pittsburgh, 1962.

Brooks, John. *Once in Golconda: A True Drama of Wall Street, 1920–1938*. New York, 1969.

Bryn-Jones, David. *Frank B. Kellogg: A Biography*. New York, 1937.

Carosso, Vincent P. *Investment Banking in America: A History*. Cambridge, Mass., 1970.

Chandler, Lester. *Benjamin Strong, Central Banker*. Washington, D.C., 1958.

Coolidge, Calvin. *The Talkative President: The Off-the-Record Press Conferences of Calvin Coolidge*. Edited by Howard H. Quint and Robert Ferrell. Amherst, Mass., 1964.

Costigliola, Frank Charles. "The Politics of Financial Stabilization: American Reconstruction Policy in Europe, 1924–30." Ph.D. dissertation, Cornell University, 1973.

Crane, Katharine. *Mr. Carr of State*. New York, 1960.

Domhoff, G. William. *The Higher Circles: The Governing Class in America*. New York, 1970.

Dorfman, Joseph. *The Economic Mind in American Civilization*. Vols. 4–5. *1918–1933*. New York, 1959.

Duroselle, Jean-Baptiste. *From Wilson to Roosevelt: Foreign Policy of the United States, 1913–1945*. Cambridge, Mass., 1963.

Ellis, L. Ethan. *Frank B. Kellogg and American Foreign Relations, 1925–1929*. New Brunswick, N.J., 1961.

———. *Republican Foreign Policy, 1921–1933*. New Brunswick, N.J., 1968.

Feis, Herbert. *The Diplomacy of the Dollar: First Era, 1919–1932*. Baltimore, 1950.

Friedman, Milton, and Schwartz, Anna Jacobson. *A Monetary History of the United States*. Princeton, 1963.

Fuess, Claude M. *Calvin Coolidge: The Man from Vermont*. Hamden, Conn., 1965.

Gilbert, Charles. *American Financing and World War I*. Westport, Conn., 1970.

Glad, Betty. *Charles Evans Hughes and the Illusions of Innocence: A Study in American Diplomacy*. Urbana, Ill., 1966.

Grew, Joseph. *Turbulent Era: A Diplomatic Record of Forty Years, 1904–1945*. Edited by Walter Johnson. 2 vols. Boston, 1952.

Hicks, John D. *Republican Ascendancy, 1921–1933*. New York, 1960.

Hoover, Herbert. *The Memoirs of Herbert Hoover*. 3 vols. New York, 1951–52.

Hoyt, Edwin Palmer. *The House of Morgan*. New York, 1966.

Hughes, Brady Alexander. "Owen D. Young and American Foreign Policy, 1919–1929." Ph.D. dissertation, University of Wisconsin, 1969.

Hughes, Charles Evans. *The Autobiographical Notes of Charles Evans Hughes*. Edited by David J. Danelski and Joseph S. Tulchin. Cambridge, Mass., 1973.

———. *The Pathway of Peace: Representative Addresses Delivered during His Term as Secretary of State, 1921–1925*. New York and London, 1925.

La Follette, Belle Case, and La Follette, Fola. *Robert M. La Follette, June 14, 1855–June 18, 1925*. 2 vols. New York, 1953.

Lamont, Corliss, ed. *The Thomas Lamonts in America*. Cranbury, N.J., 1971.

Lamont, Thomas William. *Across World Frontiers*. New York, 1951.

Leffler, Melvyn P. "The Origins of Republican War Debt Policy, 1921–1923: A Case Study in the Applicability of the Open Door Interpretation." *Journal of American History* 59 (December 1972): 585–601.

———. "The Struggle for Stability: American Policy toward France, 1921–1933." Ph.D. dissertation, Ohio State University, 1972.

Link, Werner. *Die amerikanische Stabilisierungspolitik in Deutschland, 1921–32*. Düsseldorf, 1970.

Lochner, Louis P. *Herbert Hoover and Germany*. New York, 1960.

Locklin, D. Philip. *Railroad Regulation since 1920*. New York and London, 1928.

Lubell, Samuel. *The Future of American Politics*. New York, 1956.

McCoy, Donald R. *Calvin Coolidge: The Quiet President*. New York, 1967.
MacKay, Kenneth Campbell. *The Progressive Movement of 1924*. New York, 1947.
McKenna, Marian Cecilia. *Borah*. Ann Arbor, 1961.
MacVeagh, Rogers. *The Transportation Act, 1920: Its Sources, History and Text*. New York, 1923.
Maddox, Robert James. *William E. Borah and American Foreign Policy*. Baton Rouge, 1970.
Meyer, Richard H. *Bankers' Diplomacy: Monetary Stabilization in the Twenties*. New York, 1970.
Mott, T. Bentley. *Myron T. Herrick, Friend of France: An Autobiographical Biography*. New York, 1930.
Murray, Lawrence Leo, III. "Andrew W. Mellon, Secretary of the Treasury, 1921–1932: A Study in Policy." Ph.D. dissertation, Michigan State University, 1970.
Murray, Robert K. *The Harding Era: Warren G. Harding and His Administration*. Minneapolis, 1969.
———. *The Politics of Normalcy: Governmental Theory and Practice in the Harding-Coolidge Era*. New York, 1973.
Nicolson, Harold. *Dwight Morrow*. New York, 1935.
Parrini, Carl. *Heir to Empire: United States Economic Diplomacy, 1916–1923*. Pittsburgh, 1969.
Perkins, Dexter. *Charles Evans Hughes and American Democratic Statesmanship*. Boston, 1956.
Phillips, William. *Ventures in Diplomacy*. Boston, 1953.
Prothro, James W. *The Dollar Decade*. Baton Rouge, 1954.
Pullen, William George. "World War Debts and United States Foreign Policy." Ph.D. dissertation, University of Georgia, 1972.
Pusey, Merlo J. *Charles Evans Hughes*. 2 vols. New York, 1951.
Reed, Harold L. *Federal Reserve Policy, 1921–1930*. New York, 1930.
Rhodes, Benjamin Dagwell. "The United States and the War Debt Question, 1917–1934." Ph.D. dissertation, University of Colorado, 1965.
Russell, Francis. *The Shadow of Blooming Grove: Warren G. Harding in His Times*. New York, 1968.
Schlesinger, Arthur Meier. *The Age of Roosevelt*. Vol. 1. *The Crisis of the Old Order, 1919–1933*. Boston, 1957.
Schrecker, Ellen Wolf. "The French Debt to the United States, 1917–1929." Ph.D. dissertation, Harvard University, 1973.
Shideler, James H. *Farm Crisis, 1919–1923*. Berkeley, 1957.
Sinclair, Andrew. *The Available Man: The Life Behind the Masks of Warren Gamaliel Harding*. New York, 1965.
Soule, George H. *Prosperity Decade: From War to Depression, 1917–1929*. New York, 1947.
Stern, Siegfried. *The United States in International Banking*. New York, 1951.
Strong, Benjamin. *Interpretations of Federal Reserve Policy in the Speeches and Writings of Benjamin Strong*. Edited by W. Randolph Burgess. New York and London, 1930.
Tarbell, Ida M. *Owen D. Young: A New Type of Industrial Leader*. New York, 1932.
Timmons, Bascom N. *Portrait of an American: Charles G. Dawes*. New York, 1953.
Wandel, Eckhard. *Die Bedeutung der Vereinigten Staaten von Amerika für das deutsche Reparationsproblem, 1924–1929*. Tübingen, 1971.
White, William Allen. *A Puritan in Babylon: The Story of Calvin Coolidge*. New York, 1938.
Wicker, Elmus R. *Federal Reserve Monetary Policy, 1917–1933*. New York, 1967.
Williams, Benjamin H. *Economic Foreign Policy of the United States*. New York, 1929.

Wilson, Joan Hoff. *American Business and Foreign Policy, 1920–1933*. Lexington, Ky., 1971.
Winkler, John Kennedy. "Mighty Dealer in Dollars [J. Pierpont Morgan]." *New Yorker*, 2 February 1929, pp. 23–26; 9 February 1929, pp. 27–36.
Winters, Donald L. *Henry Cantwell Wallace as Secretary of Agriculture, 1921–1924*. Urbana, Ill., 1970.
Yates, Louis A. R. *The United States and French Security, 1917–1921: A Study in American Diplomatic History*. New York, 1957.

G. *European Business*

Baumont, Maurice. *La Grosse Industrie allemande et le charbon*. Paris, 1928.
Berkenkopf, Paul. *Die Entwicklung und die Lage der lothringisch-luxemburgischen Grosseisenindustrie seit dem Weltkriege*. Jena, 1925.
Brady, Robert A. *The Rationalization Movement in German Industry: A Study in the Evolution of Economic Planning*. Berkeley, 1933.
Brelet, M. *La Crise de la métallurgie: La Politique économique et sociale du Comité des Forges*. Paris, 1923.
Bühler, Rolf. *Die Roheisenkartelle in Frankreich: Ihre Entstehung, Entwicklung, und Bedeutung von 1876 bis 1934*. Zurich, 1934.
Burn, D. L. *The Economic History of Steelmaking, 1867–1939: A Study in Competition*. Cambridge, 1940.
Carr, J. C., and Taplin, Walter. *History of the British Steel Industry*. Cambridge, Mass., 1962.
Coston, Henri. *L'Europe des banquiers*. Paris, 1963.
Ehrmann, Henry Walter. *Organized Business in France*. Princeton, 1957.
Flu, Henri. *Les Comptoirs métallurgiques d'après-guerre, 1919–1922*. Lyons, 1924.
François-Poncet, André. *La Vie et l'oeuvre de Robert Pinot*. Paris, 1927.
Friedensburg, Ferdinand. *Kohle und Eisen im Weltkriege und in den Friedensschlüssen*. Munich and Berlin, 1934.
Greer, Guy. *The Ruhr-Lorraine Industrial Problem: A Study of the Economic Interdependence of the Two Regions and Their Relation to the Reparations Question*. New York, 1925.
Hexner, Ervin. *The International Steel Cartel*. Chapel Hill, N.C., 1943.
Klass, Gert von. *Albert Vögler: Einer der Grossen des Ruhrreviers*. Tübingen, 1957.
———. *Hugo Stinnes*. Tübingen, 1958.
La Bouillerie, Augustin de. "Le Creusot et la Société des forges et ateliers du Creusot." Dissertation, Institut d'Etudes Politiques, 1957.
La Bouillerie, Geoffrey de. "La Maison de Wendel: Evolution économique depuis 1918." Dissertation, Institut d'Etudes Politiques, 1953.
Laufenburger, Henry. *L'Industrie sidérurgique de la Lorraine désannexée et la France*. Strasbourg, 1924.
Ledermann, Ernst. *Die Organization des Ruhrbergbaus, unter Berücksichtigung der Beziehungen zur Eisenindustrie*. Berlin and Leipzig, 1927.
Levainville, J. *L'Industrie de fer en France*. Paris, 1922.
Lüthgen, Helmut. *Das Rheinisch-Westfälische Kohlensyndikat in der Vorkriegs-, Kriegs- und Nachkriegszeit und seine Hauptprobleme*. Würzburg, 1926.
Maschke, Erich. *Es entsteht ein Konzern: Paul Reusch und die GHH*. Tübingen, 1969.
Nattan-Larrier, C. *La Production sidérurgique de l'Europe continentale et l'entente internationale de l'acier*. Paris, 1929.
Pinot, Robert. *Le Comité des Forges de France au service de la nation, août 1914–novembre 1918*. Paris, 1919.

Pounds, Norman J. G. *The Ruhr: A Study in Historical and Economic Geography.* Bloomington, Ind., 1952.
Pounds, Norman J. G., and Parker, W. N. *Coal and Steel in Western Europe: The Influence of Resources and Techniques on Production*. Bloomington, Ind., 1957.
Raphaël, Gaston. *Krupp et Thyssen*. Paris, 1925.
———. *Le Roi de la Ruhr: Hugo Stinnes, l'homme–son oeuvre–son rôle*. Paris, 1924.
Schneider, Hans J. *Der Wiederaufbau der Grosseisenindustrie an Rhein und Ruhr.* Berlin, n.d.
Silverberg, Paul. *Reden und Schriften*. Edited by Franz Mariaux. Cologne, 1951.
Thyssen, Fritz. *I Paid Hitler.* New York and London, 1941.
Ufermann, Paul. *Der deutsche Stahltrust*. Berlin, 1927.

H. Other

Barros, James. *Betrayal from Within: Joseph Avenol, Secretary-General of the League of Nations*. New Haven, 1970.
———. *The Corfu Incident of 1923: Mussolini and the League of Nations*. Princeton, 1965.
Beyen, Johan Willem. *Money in a Maelstrom*. New York, 1949.
Beyens, Baron. *Quatre ans à Rome, 1921–1926*. Paris, 1934.
Brown, William Adams, Jr. *The International Gold Standard Reinterpreted, 1914–1934*. 2 vols. New York, 1940.
Clapham, J. H. *The Economic Development of France and Germany, 1815–1914*. Cambridge, 1921.
Clarke, Stephen V. O. *Central Bank Cooperation, 1924–1931*. New York, 1967.
Dexter, Byron. *The Years of Opportunity: The League of Nations, 1920–26*. New York, 1967.
Hymans, Paul. *Mémoires*. 2 vols. Brussels, 1958.
Isaacs, Asher. *International Trade, Tariff, and Commercial Policies*. Chicago, 1948.
Joll, James. *Intellectuals in Politics: Three Biographical Essays*. London, 1960.
Keynes, John Maynard. *Essays in Persuasion*. New York, 1931.
———. *The General Theory of Employment, Interest and Money.* London, 1936.
———. *A Tract on Monetary Reform*. London, 1923.
League of Nations [Ragnar Nurkse]. *International Currency Experience*. Princeton, 1944.
Miller, Jane Kathryn. *Belgian Foreign Policy between Two Wars, 1919–1940*. New York, 1951.
Shepherd, Henry L. *The Monetary Experience of Belgium, 1914–1936*. Princeton and London, 1936.
Sion, Georges. *Henri Jaspar: Portrait d'un homme d'état*. Brussels and Paris, 1964.
Zuylen, Pierre van. *Les Mains libres: Politique extérieure de la Belgique, 1914–1940*. Paris, 1950.

Index

C

Y